Android Application Development

ALL-IN-ONE

FOR DUMMIES

A Wiley Brand

2nd Edition

Android™ Application Development

ALL-IN-ONE

FOR DUMMIES®

A Wiley Brand

2nd Edition

by Barry Burd

Android™ Application Development All-in-One For Dummies®, 2nd Edition

Published by:
John Wiley & Sons, Inc.,
111 River Street,
Hoboken, NJ 07030-5774,
www.wiley.com

Copyright © 2015 by John Wiley & Sons, Inc., Hoboken, New Jersey

Published simultaneously in Canada

For general information on our other products and services, please contact our Customer Care Department within the U.S. at 877-762-2974, outside the U.S. at 317-572-3993, or fax 317-572-4002. For technical support, please visit www.wiley.com/techsupport.

Wiley publishes in a variety of print and electronic formats and by print-on-demand. Some material included with standard print versions of this book may not be included in e-books or in print-on-demand. If this book refers to media such as a CD or DVD that is not included in the version you purchased, you may download this material at http://booksupport.wiley.com. For more information about Wiley products, visit www.wiley.com.

Library of Congress Control Number: 2014958471

ISBN: 978-1-118-97380-6; 978-1-118-97385-1 (ebk); 978-1-118-97384-4 (ebk)

Manufactured in the United States of America

10 9 8 7 6 5 4 3 2 1

Contents at a Glance

Table of Contents

Introduction

Android is everywhere. In mid-2014, Android ran on 62 percent of all smartphones in the United States and on 84 percent of all smartphones worldwide.[1] In a study that spans the Americas, Europe, Asia, and the Middle East, Statista reports that Android tablet shipments outnumber iPad shipments by 23 million.[2] Over a million apps are available for download at the Google Play Store (more than double the number of apps that were available in June 2012).[3] And, in the year between June 2013 and June 2014, Google paid more than $5 billion in revenues to independent developers of Google Play apps.[4]

So if you read this book in a public place (on a commuter train, at the beach, on the dance floor at the Coyote Ugly saloon), you can read proudly, with a chip on your shoulder and with your chest held high. Android is hot stuff, and you're cool because you're reading about it.

How to Use This Book

You can attack this book in either of two ways. You can go cover to cover, or you can poke around from one chapter to another. You can even do both (start at the beginning and then jump to a section that particularly interests you). I designed this book so that the basic topics come first and the more involved topics follow the basics. But you may already be comfortable with some basics, or you may have specific goals that don't require you to know about certain topics.

In general, my advice is as follows:

✦ If you already know something, don't bother reading about it.

✦ If you're curious, don't be afraid to skip ahead. You can always sneak a peek at an earlier chapter if you really need to do so.

[1]See www.kantarworldpanel.com/global/smartphone-os-market-share/ and www.idc.com/getdoc.jsp?containerId=prUS25037214.

[2]See www.statista.com/statistics/273268/worldwide-tablet-sales-by-operating-system-since-2nd-quarter-2010/.

[3]See www.appbrain.com/stats/number-of-android-apps.

[4]See http://android-developers.blogspot.com/2014/06/google-io-design-develop-distribute.html.

Conventions Used in This Book

Almost every technical book starts with a little typeface legend, and this book is no exception. What follows is a brief explanation of the typefaces used in this book:

✦ New terms are set in *italics*.

✦ If you need to type something that's mixed in with the regular text, the characters you type appear in bold. For example: "Type **MyNewProject** in the text field."

✦ You also see this `computerese` font. I use computerese for Java code, filenames, web page addresses (URLs), onscreen messages, and other such things. Also, if something you need to type is really long, it appears in computerese font on its own line (or lines).

✦ You need to change certain things when you type them on your own computer keyboard. For instance, I may ask you to type

```
public void Anyname
```

which means that you type **public void** and then some name that you make up on your own. Words that you need to replace with your own words are set in *`italicized computerese`*.

What You Don't Have to Read

Pick the first chapter or section that has material you don't already know and start reading there. Of course, you may hate making decisions as much as I do. If so, here are some guidelines that you can follow:

✦ If you've already created a simple Android application, and you have all the right software installed on your computer, skip Book I and go straight to Book II. Believe me, I won't mind.

✦ If you have a modest amount of experience developing Android apps, and you're looking for material that puts things together and fills in gaps, start with Book II.

✦ If you're thinking about writing a special kind of app (a text-messaging app, a location-based app, a game, or something like that), work your way quickly and impatiently through Books I, II, and III, and dive in seriously when you reach Books IV and V.

✦ If your goal is to publish (and maybe sell) your apps, set Book VI as your ultimate goal. No one can tell you how to create the next great game sensation, but Book VI gets you thinking about the best ways to share your Android applications.

If you want to skip the sidebars and the Technical Stuff icons, please do. In fact, if you want to skip anything at all, feel free.

Foolish Assumptions

In this book, I make a few assumptions about you, the reader. If one of these assumptions is incorrect, you're probably okay. If all these assumptions are incorrect . . . well, buy the book anyway.

✦ **I assume that you can navigate through your computer's common menus and dialog boxes.** You don't have to be a Windows, Macintosh, or Linux power user, but you should be able to start a program, find a file, put a file into a certain directory . . . that sort of thing. Much of the time, when you practice the stuff in this book, you're typing code on your keyboard, not pointing and clicking your mouse.

On those occasions when you need to drag and drop, cut and paste, or plug and play, I guide you carefully through the steps. But your computer may be configured in any of several billion ways, and my instructions may not quite fit your special situation. So when you reach one of these platform-specific tasks, try following the steps in this book. If the steps don't quite fit, consult a book with instructions tailored to your system.

✦ **I assume that you can think logically.** That's all there is to application development — thinking logically. If you can think logically, you have it made. If you don't believe that you can think logically, read on. You may be pleasantly surprised.

✦ **I assume that you have some experience with Java.** In writing this book, I've tried to do the impossible. I've tried to make the book interesting for experienced programmers, yet accessible to people who don't write code for a living. If you're a Java guru, that's great. If you're a certified Linux geek, that's great, too. But I don't assume that you can recite the names of the Java's concurrency methods in your sleep, or that you can pipe together a chain of 14 Linux commands without reading the documentation or touching the Backspace key.

If you have a working knowledge of some Java-like language (C or C++, for example), all you need is a little Java overview. And if you have no experience with an object-oriented language, you can get some. Your favorite bookstore has a terrific book titled *Java For Dummies,* 6th Edition, by Barry Burd (John Wiley & Sons, Inc.). I recommend that book highly.

How This Book Is Organized

This book is divided into subsections, which are grouped into sections, which come together to make chapters, which are lumped finally into six books. (When you write a book, you get to know your book's structure pretty well. After months of writing, you find yourself dreaming in sections and chapters when you go to bed at night.) Each of the six books is listed here.

Book I: Getting Started with Android Application Development

This part is your complete, executive briefing on Android application development. It includes some "What is Android?" material, instructions for setting up your system, and a chapter in which you create your first Android app. In this minibook, you visit Android's major technical ideas and dissect a simple Android application.

Book II: Android Background Material

When you create Android apps, you write Java programs and work with XML documents. Book II provides a quick look at the Java programming language and at the XML document standard. In addition, Book II has a chapter on Android Studio — a tool that you will be using every minute of your Android-development day.

Book III: The Building Blocks

This minibook covers the big ideas in Android application programming. What is an activity? What is an intent? How do you handle button presses? How do you lay out the user's screen? The ideas in this minibook permeate all Android programming, from the simplest app on a cheapo phone to a killer app on an overpriced Android tablet.

Book IV: Programming Cool Phone Features

Some applications do very ordinary things, such as displaying lists or calculating sums. But other apps make use of a mobile device's unique capabilities. For example, apps can dial phone numbers, send text messages, surf the web, and track your travel direction. The Android platform has a rich set of built-in tools for programming each of these special capabilities. So in this minibook, you create apps that make the most of a device's vast feature set.

I did a quick count of the most popular apps on the Google Play Store. By far, the apps that people download the most are games. The Games category dominates in both paid installations and overall number of installations. Game development can be tricky because games have lots of moving parts — sprites that jump up and down, collisions between heroes and monsters, playing cards that snap into place, and other crazy things. Chapter 5 in Book IV covers some of these crazy things.

And what happens when you win a game? You share your score on Twitter so that other players are envious! To do this, you need some social networking tools. So Book IV shows you how to connect with social media sites.

Deep in the bowels of a place called "computer nerd city," some programmers shun the easygoing life of the Android Java programmer and strive toward a simpler, more primitive existence. These "wonks" (as they're known by clinicians and other professionals) prefer the rugged, macho lifestyle that programming in C or C++ provides. Along with this lifestyle, they get the ability to reach the corners of a mobile device that are hidden by Android's layer of abstraction. If any of these development alternatives tickle your fancy, please include Book IV, Chapter 6 in your travel plans.

Book V: Apps for Tablets, Watches, and TV Sets

Size matters! The first versions of Android were for smartphones and a typical smartphone has a four- or five-inch screen. (To discover a screen's size, measure along the diagonal.) Along came tablets, whose screens measure seven or ten inches. Apps that were designed for phones looked really ugly on the larger tablet screens, so later versions of Android had a new *fragments* feature. (On a tablet screen with sufficient space, a *fragment* is one of two window-like things. More on that in Chapter 1 of Book V.)

Next came Android Wear (for watches), and Android TV. A watch has a one-inch screen. And, in the parlance of user interface design, television is a "ten-foot experience." The user sits on a couch and controls the device with a remote control or a game controller.

Each kind of device has its own look and feel and its own app design strategies. So each kind of device has its own flavor of Android. Book V breaks away from Android's traditional attachment to smartphones, and covers some of the coding that you use in Android's expanding ecosystem.

Book VI: The Job Isn't Done Until . . .

Imagine earning a fortune selling the world's most popular Android app, being named *Time* magazine's Person of the Year, and having Tom Cruise or Julia Roberts buy the rights to star as you in a movie (giving you exclusive rights to the game for Android devices that's based on the movie, of course).

Okay, maybe your ambitions aren't quite that high, but when you develop a good Android app, you probably want to share that app with the rest of the world. Well, the good news is, sharing is fairly easy. And marketing your app isn't as difficult as you might imagine. Book VI provides the tips and pointers to help you spread the word about your fantastic application.

More on the Web!

You've read the *Android All-in-One* book, seen the *Android All-in-One* movie, worn the *Android All-in-One* T-shirt, and eaten the *Android All-in-One* candy. What more is there to do?

That's easy. Just visit this book's website — www.allmycode.com/ Android. (You can also get there by visiting www.dummies.com/go/ androidapplicationaio.) At the website, you can find updates, comments, additional information, and answers to commonly asked readers' questions. You can also find a small chat application for sending me quick questions when I'm online. When I'm not online (or if you have a complicated question), you can send me email. I read messages sent to android@ allmycode.com.

Icons Used in This Book

If you could watch me write this book, you'd see me sitting at my computer, talking to myself. I say each sentence in my head. Most of the sentences, I mutter several times. When I have an extra thought, a side comment, or something that doesn't belong in the regular stream, I twist my head a little bit. That way, whoever's listening to me (usually, nobody) knows that I'm off on a momentary tangent.

Of course, in print, you can't see me twisting my head. I need some other way of setting a side thought in a corner by itself. I do it with icons. When you see a Tip icon or a Remember icon, you know that I'm taking a quick detour.

Here's a list of icons that I use in this book.

A Tip is an extra piece of information — something helpful that the other books may forget to tell you.

Everyone makes mistakes. Heaven knows that I've made a few in my time. Anyway, when I think people are especially prone to make a mistake, I mark it with a Warning icon.

Question: What's stronger than a Tip, but not as strong as a Warning?

Answer: A Remember icon.

"If you don't remember what *such-and-such* means, see *blah-blah-blah,*" or "For more information, read *blahbity-blah-blah.*"

This icon calls attention to useful material that you can find online. (You don't have to wait long to see one of these icons. I use one at the end of this introduction!)

Occasionally, I run across a technical tidbit. The tidbit may help you understand what the people behind the scenes (the people who developed Java) were thinking. You don't have to read it, but you may find it useful. You may also find the tidbit helpful if you plan to read other (more geeky) books about Android app development.

Beyond the Book

I've written a lot of extra content that you won't find in this book. Go online to find the following:

+ **Cheat Sheet:** Check out www.dummies.com/cheatsheet/androidappdevelopmentaio.

+ **Online Articles:** On several of the pages that open each of this book's parts, you can find links to what the folks at *For Dummies* call Web Extras — short articles that expand on some concept I've discussed in that particular section. You can find them at www.dummies.com/extras/androidappdevelopmentaio.

Where to Go from Here

If you've gotten this far, you're ready to start reading about Android application development. Think of me (the author) as your guide, your host, your personal assistant. I do everything I can to keep things interesting and, most important, help you understand.

If you like what you read, send me an email, post on my Facebook wall, or tweet me a tweet. My email address, which I created just for comments and questions about this book, is android@allmycode.com. My Facebook page is /allmycode, and my Twitter handle is @allmycode. And don't forget — to get the latest information, visit one of this book's support web-sites. Mine is at `http://allmycode.com/android`, or you can visit `www.dummies.com/go/beginningprogrammingwithjavafd`.

Occasionally, we have updates to our technology books. If this book does have technical updates, they will be posted at `www.dummies.com/extras/androidappdevelopmentaio` and at `http://allmycode.com/android`.

Book I
Getting Started with Android Application Development

Contents at a Glance

Chapter 1: All about Android

Until the mid-2000s, the word "Android" stood for a mechanical human-like creature — a root'n toot'n officer of the law with built-in machine guns, or a hyperlogical space traveler who can do everything except speak using contractions. But in 2005, Google purchased Android, Inc. — a 22-month-old company creating software for mobile phones. That move changed everything.

In 2007, a group of 34 companies formed the Open Handset Alliance. The Alliance's task is "to accelerate innovation in mobile and offer consumers a richer, less expensive, and better mobile experience." The Alliance's primary project is *Android* — an open, free operating system based on the Linux operating system kernel.

HTC released the first commercially available Android phone near the end of 2008. But in the United States, the public's awareness of Android and its potential didn't surface until early 2010. Where I'm sitting in 2014, Canalys reports that, in the year's first quarter, 81 percent of all new smartphones in the world run Android.* (I know. You're sitting reading this book sometime after 2014. But that's okay.)

The Consumer Perspective

A consumer considers the mobile phone alternatives.

✦ **Possibility #1: No mobile phone.**

Advantages: Inexpensive, no interruptions from callers.

Disadvantages: No instant contact with friends and family. No calls to services in case of an emergency. No hand-held games, no tweeting, tooting, hooting, homing, roaming, or booping. And worst of all, to break up with your boyfriend or girlfriend, you can't simply send a text message.

*www.canalys.com/newsroom/third-smart-phones-shipped-q1-had-5-plus-displays

✦ **Possibility #2: A feature phone.**

I love the way the world makes up fancy names for less-than-desirable things. A *feature phone* is a mobile phone that's not a smartphone. There's no official rule defining the boundary between feature phones and smartphones. But generally, a feature phone is one with an inflexible menu of home-screen options. A feature phone's menu items relate mostly to traditional mobile phone functions, such as dialing, texting, and maybe some web surfing and gaming. In contrast, a smartphone's home screen provides access to the underlying file system, has icons, customizable skins, and many other features that used to be available only to general-purpose computer operating systems.

Advantages: Cheaper than a smartphone.

Disadvantages: Not as versatile as a smartphone. Not nearly as cool as a smartphone. Nowhere near as much fun as a smartphone.

✦ **Possibility #3: An iPhone.**

Advantages: Great graphics. More apps than any other phone platform.

Disadvantages: Little or no flexibility with the single-vendor iOS operating system. Only a handful of different models to choose from. No sanctioned "rooting," "modding," or "jailbreaking" the phone. No hesitation permitted when becoming a member of the Mystic Cult of Apple Devotees.

✦ **Possibility #4: A Windows phone, a BlackBerry, or some other non-Android, non-Apple smartphone.**

Advantages: Having a smartphone without belonging to a crowd.

Disadvantages: Other smartphones don't have nearly as many apps as Android phones and Apple phones.

✦ **Possibility #5: An Android phone.**

Advantages: Using an open platform. Using a popular platform with lots of industry support and with powerful market momentum. Writing your own software and installing the software on your own phone (without having to deal with Apple as an intermediary). Publishing software without facing a challenging approval process.

Disadvantages: Security concerns when using an open platform. Confusion about the variety of manufacturers, each with different hardware and with some changes to the Android platform. Dismay when iPhone users make fun of your phone.

For me, Android's advantages far outweigh the possible disadvantages. And you're reading a paragraph from *Android Application Development All-in-One For Dummies,* 2nd Edition, so you're likely to agree with me.

Having decided to go with an Android phone, the consumer asks, "Which phone?" And the salesperson says, "This phone comes with Android 4.4." (If you read between the lines, what the salesperson really means is "This phone comes with Android 3.2, which will eventually be upgraded to Android 4.0, or so claims the vendor.") So the consumer asks, "What are the differences among all the Android versions?"

Android comes with a few different notions of "version." Android has platform numbers, API levels, codenames, and probably some other versioning schemes. (The acronym *API* stands for *Application Programming Interface* — a library full of prewritten programs available for use by a bunch of programmers. In this case, the "bunch" consists of all Android developers.)

To complicate matters, the versioning schemes don't increase in lockstep. For example, from platform 1.5 to 1.6, the API level goes from 3 to 4. But platform 2.3 sports two API levels — level 9 for platform 2.3.1 and level 10 for platform 2.3.3. Versions that are skipped (such as API level 5 and platform 2.5) are lost in the annals of Android development history.

An Android version may have variations. For example, plain old Android 4.3 has an established set of features. To plain old Android 4.3, you can add the Google APIs (thus adding Google Maps functionality) and still use platform 4.3. You can also add a special set with features tailored for a particular device manufacturer or a particular mobile service provider.

Most consumers know Android's versions by their codenames. Unlike Apple (which named its operating systems after ferocious cats) or automakers (who name their SUVs after cowboys), Google names Android versions after desserts. (See Figure 1-1.)

A few notes on Figure 1-1 are in order:

✦ **The platform number is of interest to the consumer and to the company that sells the hardware.**

   If you're buying a phone with Android 4.3, for example, you might want to know whether the vendor will upgrade your phone to Android 5.0.

✦ **The API level (also known as the SDK version) is of interest to the Android app developer.**

   For example, the word MATCH_PARENT has a specific meaning in Android API levels 8 and higher. You might type MATCH_PARENT in code that uses API level 7. If you do (and if you expect MATCH_PARENT to have that specific meaning), you'll get a nasty-looking error message.

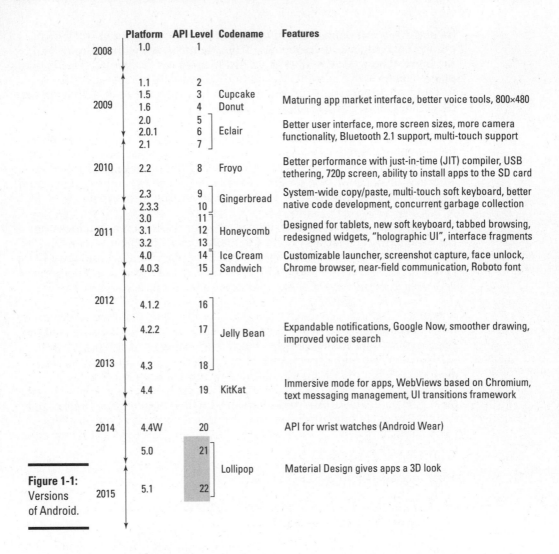

	Platform	API Level	Codename	Features
2008	1.0	1		
2009	1.1	2		
	1.5	3	Cupcake	Maturing app market interface, better voice tools, 800×480
	1.6	4	Donut	
	2.0	5		Better user interface, more screen sizes, more camera
	2.0.1	6	Eclair	functionality, Bluetooth 2.1 support, multi-touch support
	2.1	7		
2010	2.2	8	Froyo	Better performance with just-in-time (JIT) compiler, USB tethering, 720p screen, ability to install apps to the SD card
	2.3	9	Gingerbread	System-wide copy/paste, multi-touch soft keyboard, better
	2.3.3	10		native code development, concurrent garbage collection
	3.0	11		Designed for tablets, new soft keyboard, tabbed browsing,
2011	3.1	12	Honeycomb	redesigned widgets, "holographic UI", interface fragments
	3.2	13		
	4.0	14	Ice Cream	Customizable launcher, screenshot capture, face unlock,
	4.0.3	15	Sandwich	Chrome browser, near-field communication, Roboto font
2012	4.1.2	16		
	4.2.2	17	Jelly Bean	Expandable notifications, Google Now, smoother drawing, improved voice search
2013	4.3	18		
	4.4	19	KitKat	Immersive mode for apps, WebViews based on Chromium, text messaging management, UI transitions framework
2014	4.4W	20		API for wrist watches (Android Wear)
	5.0	21	Lollipop	Material Design gives apps a 3D look
2015	5.1	22		

Figure 1-1:
Versions
of Android.

+ **The code name is of interest to the creators of Android.**

A *code name* (also known as the *version code*) refers to the work done by the creators of Android to bring Android to the next level. Picture Google's engineers working for months behind closed doors on Project Jelly Bean, and you'll be on the right track.

For completeness, I should add that code names are interesting for consumers, too. My taste buds tingle when I reply to "Which Android version are you running?" with the name "KitKat."

As a rule, platform numbers change faster than API levels, and API levels change faster than codenames. For example, the Android platforms 4.1 and 4.1.1 both belong to API Level 16, and API Levels 16, 17, and 18 all have codename Jelly Bean.

New Android codename releases arrive every year or so. Codenames proceed alphabetically, starting with Cupcake, Donut and Éclair, and (if the trend continues) working their way to Zucchini Bread in this century's next decade. Depending on a device's manufacturer, model, and (if applicable) telephone service provider, a device may or may not get upgrades to newer Android releases.

Storks and fairies don't install updates on your Android devices. The updates come via Wi-Fi or phone service through your carrier or device manufacturer. But by downloading and installing an independently developed Android release, you can break free of the corporate giants. The most popular such release is called *CyanogenMod*. For more information, visit `www.cyanogenmod.org`. For information about some other independently developed releases, visit `http://forum.xda-developers.com/custom-roms`.

As a developer, your job is to balance portability with feature richness. When you create an app, you specify a minimum Android version. (You can read more about this in Chapter 4 of this minibook.) The higher the version, the more features your app can have. But the higher the version, the fewer the devices that can run your app. Fortunately, this book has lots of tips and tricks for striking a happy medium between whiz-bang features and universal use.

The Developer Perspective

Android is a multifaceted beast. When you develop for Android, you use many toolsets. This section has a brief rundown.

Java

James Gosling from Sun Microsystems created the Java programming language in the mid-1990s. (Sun Microsystems has since been bought out by Oracle.) Java's meteoric rise in use came from the elegance of the language and the well-conceived platform architecture. After a brief blaze of glory with applets and the web, Java settled into being a solid, general-purpose language with special strength in servers and middleware.

In the meantime, Java was quietly seeping into embedded processors. Sun Microsystems was developing Java ME (*Mobile Edition*) for creating *midlets* to run on mobile phones. Java became a major technology in Blu-ray disc players. So the decision to make Java the primary development language for Android apps is no big surprise.

An *embedded processor* is a computer chip that's hidden from the user as part of some special-purpose device. The chips in today's cars are embedded processors, and the silicon that powers your photocopier at work is an embedded processor. Pretty soon, the flowerpots on your windowsill will probably have embedded processors.

The trouble is, not everyone agrees about the fine points of Java's licensing terms. The Java language isn't quite the same animal as the Java software libraries, which in turn aren't the same as the *Java Virtual Machine* (the software that enables the running of Java programs). So in marrying Java to Android, the founders of Android added an extra puzzle piece — the Dalvik Virtual Machine. And instead of using the official Sun/Oracle Java libraries, Android uses *Harmony* — an open-source Java implementation from the Apache Software Foundation. Several years and many lawsuits later, companies are still at odds over the use of Java in Android phones.

For more information about the Dalvik Virtual Machine and its successor known as ART (the Android RunTime), see Book II, Chapter 2.

Fortunately for you, the soon-to-be Android developer, Java is deeply entrenched in the Android ecosystem. The time you invest in developing mobile Java-based apps will continue to pay off for a long, long time.

If you already have some Java programming experience, great! If not, you can find a fast-paced introduction to Java in Book II, Chapters 2, 3, and 4. For a more leisurely introduction to Java, buy *Java For Dummies,* 6th Edition or *Java Programming for Android Developers For Dummies*.

XML

If you find View Source among your web browser's options, you see a bunch of Hypertext Markup Language (HTML) tags. A *tag* is some text enclosed in angle brackets. The tag describes something about its neighboring content.

For example, to create boldface type on a web page, a web designer writes

```
<b>Look at this!</b>
```

The angle-bracketed b tags turn boldface type on and off.

The *M* in HTML stands for *Markup* — a general term describing any extra text that annotates a document's content. When you annotate a document's content, you embed information about the document's content into the document itself. So, for example, in the line of code in the previous paragraph, the content is Look at this! The markup (information about the content) consists of the tags <b> and </b>.

The HTML standard is an outgrowth of SGML (*S*tandard *G*eneralized *M*arkup *L*anguage). SGML is an all-things-to-all-people technology for marking up documents for use by all kinds of computers running all kinds of software, and sold by all kinds of vendors.

In the mid-1990s, a working group of the World Wide Web Consortium (W3C) began developing XML — the e*X*tensible *M*arkup *L*anguage. The working group's goal was to create a subset of SGML for use in transmitting data over the Internet. They succeeded. Today, XML is a well-established standard for encoding information of all kinds.

For a technical overview of XML, see Book II, Chapter 5.

Java is good for describing step-by-step instructions, and XML is good for describing the way things are (or the way they should be). A Java program says, "Do this and then do that." In contrast, an XML document says, "It's this way, and it's that way." So Android uses XML for two purposes:

✦ **To describe an app's data.**

An app's XML documents describe the look of the app's screens, the translations of the app into one or more languages, and other kinds of data.

✦ **To describe the app itself.**

Each Android app comes with an `AndroidManifest.xml` file. This XML document describes features of the app. The operating system uses the `AndroidManifest.xml` document's contents to manage the running of the app.

For example, an app's `AndroidManifest.xml` file contains the app's name and the name of the file containing the app's icon. The XML file also describes the app's screens and tells the system what kinds of work each screen can perform.

For more information about the `AndroidManifest.xml` file and about the use of XML to describe an app's data, see almost any chapter in this book.

Concerning XML, there's bad news and good news. The bad news is, XML isn't always easy to compose. The good news is, automated software tools compose most of the world's XML code. As an Android programmer, the software on your development computer composes much of your app's XML code. You often tweak the XML code, read part of the code for info from its source, make minor changes, and compose brief additions. But you hardly ever create XML documents from scratch.

When you create an Android app, you deal with at least two "computers." Your *development computer* is the computer that you use for creating Android code. (In most cases, your development computer is a desktop or laptop computer — a PC, a Mac, or a Linux computer.) The other computer is something that most people don't even call a "computer." It's the Android device that will eventually be running your app. This device is a smartphone, a tablet, a watch, or some other cool gadget.

Linux

An *operating system* is a big program that manages the overall running of a computer or a device. Most operating systems are built in layers. An operating system's outer layers are usually right up there in the user's face. For example, both Windows and Macintosh OS X have standard desktops. From the desktop, the user launches programs, manages windows, and so on.

An operating system's inner layers are (for the most part) invisible to the user. While the user plays Solitaire, the operating system juggles processes, manages files, keeps an eye on security, and generally does the kinds of things that the user shouldn't micromanage.

At the very deepest level of an operating system is the system's *kernel*. The kernel runs directly on the processor's hardware, and does the low-level work required to make the processor run. In a truly layered system, higher layers accomplish work by making calls to lower layers. So an app with a specific hardware request sends the request (directly or indirectly) through the kernel.

The best-known, best-loved general purpose operating systems are Windows, Macintosh OS X (which is built on top of UNIX), and Linux. Windows and Mac OS X are the properties of their respective companies. But Linux is open-source. That's one of the reasons why your TiVo runs Linux, and why the creators of Android based their platform on the Linux kernel.

Android's brand of Linux is an outlier among Linuxes (Linuces?). For a long time, Google wasn't merging Android's modifications of Linux back into the main Linux development tree. This seems to have been resolved in March 2012, but old wounds die hard. Blog posts by Linux and Android experts still waver on the question of Android's place within the Linux movement. So if you attend a Linux rally and you mention Android, be sure to do so with a wry look on your face. This protects you in case the person you're talking to doesn't think Android is "real" Linux.

Open-source software comes in many shapes and sizes. For example, there's the GNU General Public License (GPL), the Apache License, the GNU Lesser General Public License (LGPL), and others. When considering the use of other people's open-source software, be careful to check the software's licensing terms. "Open-source" doesn't necessarily mean "do anything at all for free with this software."

Figure 1-2 is a diagram of the Android operating system. At the bottom is the Linux kernel, managing various parts of a device's hardware. The kernel also includes a Binder, which handles all communication among running processes. (When your app asks, "Can any software on this phone tell me the current temperature in Cleveland, Ohio?" the request for information goes through the kernel's Binder.)

At the very top of Figure 1-2 are the applications — the web browser, the contacts list, the games, the dialer, and your own soon-to-be-developed apps. Both developers and users interact mostly with this layer. Developers write code to run on this layer, and users see the outer surface of the apps created by developers.

Applications

Home	Contacts	Phone	Browser	...

Android Application Framework

Activity Manager	Window Manager	Content Providers	View System	XMPP Service
Package Manager	Telephony Manager	Resource Manager	Fragment Manager	Location Manager	Notification Manager

Libraries

Surface Manager	Media Framework	SQLite
OpenGL | ES	FreeType	WebKit
SGL	SSL	libc

Android Runtime

Core Libraries
Dalvik Virtual Machine
ART Virtual Machine

Figure 1-2:
The Android system architecture.

Linux Kernel

Display Driver	Camera Driver	Flash Memory Driver	Binder (IPC) Driver
Keypad Driver	WiFi Driver	Audio Drivers	Power Management

As a developer, your most intimate contact with the Android operating system is through the command line, or the *Linux shell*. The shell uses commands, such as `cd` to change to a directory, `ls` to list a directory's files and subdirectories, `rm` to delete files, and many others.

The Google Play Store has plenty of free *terminal* apps. A terminal app's interface is a plain text screen in which you type Linux shell commands. And with one of Android's developer tools, the Android Debug Bridge, you can issue shell commands to an Android device through your development computer. If you like getting your virtual hands dirty, the Linux shell is for you.

For a look at the Android Debug Bridge, see Chapter 2 of this minibook.

The Business Perspective

I admit it. I'm not an entrepreneur. I'm a risk-averse person with a preference for storing money in mattresses. My closest brush with a startup business was a cab ride in Kuala Lumpur. The driver wanted me to help finance his new restaurant idea. "Not Kentucky Fried Chicken!" he yelled. "Kentucky Fried Duck!"

Anyway, the creation and selling of mobile phone apps is an enormous cottage industry. The Google Play Store had 1,000,000 apps in mid-2013. By the time you read this book, the number 1,000,000 will seem pathetically obsolete. Add the marketing potential of Amazon's Appstore for Android, and you have some very natural distribution channels for your apps.

Anyone can post an app on the Google Play Store and on Amazon's Appstore. You can post free apps, paid apps, and programs with in-app billing. You can test an app with a select group of users before making your app available to everyone. You make a small one-time payment to register as an Android developer. Then you design apps, develop apps, and post apps for the general public.

Book VI covers the business of posting apps on the Google Play Store and Amazon's Appstore for Android. I don't promise that you'll become a millionaire selling Android apps, but I promise that you'll have fun trying.

Chapter 2: Installing the Software Tools

In This Chapter

⮑ **Getting software tools for your development computer's operating system**

⮑ **Installing the tools on your computer**

⮑ **Running the tools**

There are two kinds of people — people who love tools, and people who don't have strong feelings about tools. (As far as I know, no one dislikes tools.) I'm a tool lover because I enjoy the leverage that tools give me. With the right tool, I can easily do things that would otherwise require monumental effort. And I can do these things over and over again, getting better with practice using the tools so that the tasks I'm dealing with become easier as time goes on.

Of course, my tool-o-philia isn't always a good thing. I'm not handy with skills like carpentry, car repair, or plumbing, but I can't resist buying greasy old screwdrivers and other such tools at garage sales. Among other things, I have what I think is the world's biggest monkey wrench, which I bought several years ago for only seven dollars. But I'd be useless (if not dangerous) using the wrench, so it sits in my attic waiting for my kids to deal with it when, years from now, they inherit my house full of junk.

But software tools are great. They're not greasy; many good tools are free; and if you lose a tool, you can usually find it by searching your computer's hard drive.

Anyway, this chapter is about Android development tools. Enjoy!

Installing Oracle's Java Development Kit

Java is the *lingua franca* of Android application development. To write Android apps, you normally use Java.

You can get your required dose of Java by visiting `www.oracle.com/technetwork/java/javase/downloads` and getting the JDK for the Java Platform, Standard Edition (Java SE). Figure 2-1 shows me clicking a Download JDK button (*circa* October 2014) at the Oracle website.

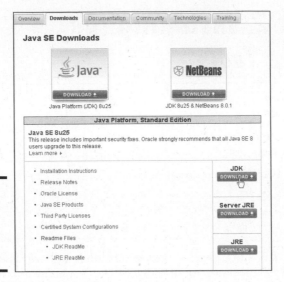

Figure 2-1:
Getting the
Java JDK
at Oracle's
website.

In Figure 2-1, you can see that I'm shunning the two JRE buttons in favor of
the JDK Download button.

I don't expect the URL www.oracle.com/technetwork/java/javase/
downloads to work forever and ever. But if you visit www.oracle.com and
poke around for Java, you'll certainly reach the Java Development Kit download page.

Figure 2-2 shows you what I see after clicking the JDK Download button

In Figure 2-2, I select the 64-bit Windows download. Oracle's website offers
many more download alternatives. (In the "Many Faces of Java" section, I
explain the reasons for these alternatives and help you make the right choice.).

Java SE Development Kit 8u25

You must accept the Oracle Binary Code License Agreement for Java SE to download this software.

Accept License Agreement   •   Decline License Agreement

Product / File Description	File Size	Download
Linux x86	135.24 MB	⬇ jdk-8u25-linux-i586.rpm
Linux x86	154.88 MB	⬇ jdk-8u25-linux-i586.tar.gz
Linux x64	135.6 MB	⬇ jdk-8u25-linux-x64.rpm
Linux x64	153.42 MB	⬇ jdk-8u25-linux-x64.tar.gz
Mac OS X x64	209.13 MB	⬇ jdk-8u25-macosx-x64.dmg
Solaris SPARC 64-bit (SVR4 package)	137.01 MB	⬇ jdk-8u25-solaris-sparcv9.tar.Z
Solaris SPARC 64-bit	97.14 MB	⬇ jdk-8u25-solaris-sparcv9.tar.gz
Solaris x64 (SVR4 package)	137.11 MB	⬇ jdk-8u25-solaris-x64.tar.Z
Solaris x64	94.24 MB	⬇ jdk-8u25-solaris-x64.tar.gz
Windows x86	157.26 MB	⬇ jdk-8u25-windows-i586.exe
Windows x64	169.62 MB	⬇ jdk-8u25-windows-x64.exe

Figure 2-2:
Selecting
a file to
download.

After downloading a big file from the Oracle website, you double-click the file's icon to start the installation. Here's what happens with each of the major operating systems:

✦ **Windows:** The downloaded file has the .exe filename extension. When you double-click the .exe file's icon, a wizard guides you through the installation.

✦ **Macintosh OS X:** The downloaded file has the .dmg filename extension. After double-clicking the .dmg file's icon, you see a .pkg file's icon. When you double-click the .pkg file's icon, a setup assistant guides you through the installation.

When you try to run software that's not from the Apple's App Store, you might get a "can't be opened" message because the app "is from an unidentified developer." To get past this stumbling block, Ctrl-click the app's icon. Then, in the resulting context menu, select Open. When you do, the "can't be opened" message turns into an "Are you sure you want to open it?" message. Click Open, and you're on your way.

✦ **Linux:**

What happens in Linux depends on your Linux distribution. Here's what works on many of my Linux machines:

• **For distributions with the RPM package manager:** I download the file whose name ends in .rpm. The .rpm file ends up in the Downloads directory — a subdirectory of my user home directory. So I open a Terminal window and type the following commands:

```
cd ~/Downloads
rpm -ivh name-of-the-downloaded-file.rpm
```

• **For distributions with no RPM package manager:** I download the archive file whose name ends in .tar.gz. The .tar.gz file ends up in the Downloads directory — a subdirectory of my user home directory. Then I extract the contents of the .tar.gz archive file to a convenient place on my computer's hard drive. If I'm feeling particularly geeky, I extract the contents by opening a Terminal window and typing the following commands:

```
cd
mkdir Development
cd ~/Downloads
tar zxvf name-of-the-downloaded-file.tar.gz \
--directory ~/Development
```

Notice the backslash (\) in the next-to-last command line. When I end a command line with a backslash, the computer displays its own little prompt at the start of the next line. That's okay. The little prompt means "You didn't finish typing the tar command, so finish typing the command on this last line."

TIP

If you're a Linux user, you can try skipping the visit to Oracle's website. Instead, issue the command `sudo apt-get install default-jdk` (or the equivalent `yum` command) in a Terminal window.

Make a note of the location on the hard drive where you've installed Java. I have a name for this place on my hard drive. I call it the *JAVA_HOME* directory. According to Figure 2-3, *JAVA_HOME* is `C:\Program Files\Java\JDK1.8.0` on my Windows computer. And, according to Figure 2-4, *JAVA_HOME* is `/Library/Java/JavaVirtualMachines/jdk1.8.0_05.jdk/Contents/Home` on my Mac.

Those pesky filename extensions

The filenames displayed in Windows File Explorer or in a Macintosh Finder window can be misleading. You may browse one of your directories and see the name `jdk-8-windows`. The file's real name might be `jdk-8-windows.exe`, `jdk-8-windows.zip`, `jdk-8-windows.`*somethingElse*, or plain old `jdk-8-windows`. Filename endings like `.zip`, `.exe`, and `.dmg` are called *filename extensions*.

The ugly truth is that, by default, Windows and Macs hide many filename extensions. This awful feature tends to confuse programmers. So, if you don't want to be confused, change your computer's system-wide settings. Here's how you do it:

- **In Windows XP:** Choose Start ⇨ Control Panel ⇨ Appearance and Themes ⇨ Folder Options. Then follow the instructions in the In All Versions of Windows bullet.

- **In Windows 7:** Choose Start ⇨ Control Panel ⇨ Appearance and Personalization ⇨ Folder Options. Then follow the instructions in the In All Versions of Windows bullet.

- **In Windows 8:** In the Start screen, hold down the Windows key while pressing Q. In the resulting search box, type **Folder Options** and then press Enter. Then

follow the instructions in the In All Versions of Windows bullet.

- **In Windows 10:** Choose Start. In the Start menu's Search box, type **Folder Options**. Then follow the instructions in the In All Versions of Windows bullet.

- **In all versions of Windows (XP and newer):** Follow the instructions in one of the preceding bullets. Then, in the Folder Options dialog box, click the View tab. Look for the Hide File Extensions for Known File Types option. Make sure that this check box is *not* selected.

- **In Mac OS X:** In the Finder application's menu, select Preferences. In the resulting dialog box, select the Advanced tab and look for the Show All File Extensions option. Make sure that this check box *is* selected.

- **In Linux:** Linux distributions tend not to hide filename extensions. So, if you use Linux, you probably don't have to worry about this. But I haven't checked all Linux distributions. So, if your files are named `jdk1.8.0-linux` instead of `jdk1.8.0-linux.rpm` or `jdk1.8.0-linux.tar.gz`, check the documentation specific to your Linux distribution.

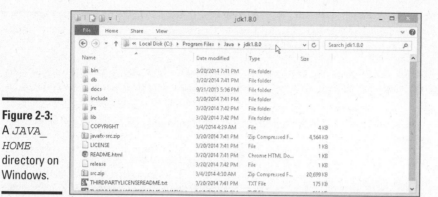

Figure 2-3:
A *JAVA_ HOME* directory on Windows.

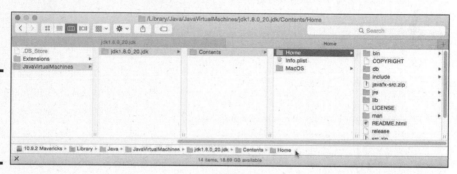

Figure 2-4:
A *JAVA_ HOME* directory on a Mac.

That's all you really need to know from this section. If you're a Windows user and you're happy with your Java installation, you can skip to the "Setting Up the Software." If you're a Mac user, go to the "Adding Apple's Java to the Stew" section and then to the "Setting Up the Software." But if you're any kind of user and if you want more details about installing Java, read on.

At the start of this section, I write that for Android apps, you *normally* use Java. I'm very careful not to imply that you always use Java. Android enjoys lots of different development modes. For example, with Android's *Native Development Kit* (NDK), you can write code that runs directly on a device's hardware in C or C++. You can also write HTML and JavaScript code to run on the device's browser. And companies create other specialized development environments all the time. Even so, Java is the language of choice in the Android community. Google creates new versions of Android with Java in mind. And in general, you get a good power-to-ease-of-use ratio when you develop Android apps in Java.

For a closer look at Android's Native Development Kit, see Book IV, Chapter 6.

Caring for the environment

Every operating system has *environment variables*. Here are some examples:

- In Windows, when I run `C:\Windows\System32\cmd.exe`, I type the following command:

    ```
    set PATH
    ```

- With this command, I'm telling the `cmd` window to show me the value of the computer's `PATH` environment variable.

- The `cmd` window responds with something like

    ```
    Path=C:\Windows\system32;C:\Windows;C:\
            Windows\System32\Wbem;
    C:\Windows\System32\
            WindowsPowerShell\v1.0\
    ```

- This response tells me that the computer's `PATH` environment variable has the value `C:\Windows\system32;C:\Windows; . . .` and so on. This "value" is actually a list of directories on my computer's hard drive.

- What purpose does this list of directories serve? When I type a program's name in the `cmd` window,

    ```
    Notepad
    ```

- the computer looks in several places to find a `notepad` program to run. These places include all the directories in the list (the `C:\Windows\system32` directory, the `C:\Windows` directory, and so on).

- (In Windows, the capitalization of `PATH` doesn't matter.)

- On a Mac and in Linux, when I run the Terminal app, I type the following command:

    ```
    echo $PATH
    ```

- With this command, I'm telling the Terminal app to show me the value of the computer's `PATH` environment variable.

- The Terminal app responds with something like

    ```
    /usr/local/sbin:/usr/local/bin:/usr/
            sbin:/usr/bin:/sbin:/bin
    ```

- This response tells me that the computer's `PATH` environment variable has the value `/usr/local/sbin:/usr/local/bin: . . .` and so on. This "value" is actually a list of directories on my computer's hard drive.

- What purpose does this list of directories serve? When I type a program's name in the Terminal app,

    ```
    Nano
    ```

- the computer looks in several places to find a `nano` program to run. These places include all the directories in the list (the `/usr/local/sbin` directory, the `/usr/local/bin` directory, and so on).

- (On a Mac and in Linux, the capitalization of `PATH` matters.)

Each operating system provides ways for you to create new environment variables and to change the values of existing environment variables. For example, on many Linux systems, you can add the following statements to the end of your `~/.bashrc` file:

```
export JAVA_HOME=~/Development/
    jdk1.8.0_25
export PATH=$PATH:$JAVA_HOME/bin
```

The first command creates a new environment variable named *JAVA_HOME*, and sets the variable's value to `~/Development/`

jdk1.8.0_25. The second command adds ~/Development/jdk1.8.0_25/bin to your PATH. With commands like these in your ~/.bashrc file (and with some other mojo whose exact nature depends on your computer's configuration) your PATH turns from

```
/usr/local/sbin:/usr/local/bin:/usr/
        sbin:/usr/bin:/sbin:/bin
```

to

```
/usr/local/sbin:/usr/local/bin:/usr/
        sbin:/usr/bin:/sbin:/bin:
  /home/your_user_name/Development/
          jdk1.8.0_25/bin
```

Creating a *JAVA_HOME* environment variable can make your life easier because some programs look for a *JAVA_HOME* variable to find out where you installed Java on your computer. Even if you don't actually create a *JAVA_HOME* variable, it's useful to think in terms of a *JAVA_HOME* directory. Throughout this book, the directory that I call *JAVA_HOME* always refers to whatever directory your JDK files live in.

✔ If you run Windows, your *JAVA_HOME* directory is probably named C:\ Program Files\Java\jdk1.8.0, C:\Program Files (x86)\Java\ jdk1.8.0, or something like that.

✔ If you have a Mac, your *JAVA_HOME* directory is probably named /Library/ Java/JavaVirtualMachines/ jdk1.8.0_05.jdk/Contents/ Home, or something like that.

✔ If you run Linux, your *JAVA_HOME* directory is probably named /home/ your_user_name/Development/ jdk1.8.0_25, /usr/lib/jvm/ default-java, or something like that.

There's no single way to create and set environment variables that works for every operating system (or even for every version of any one operating system). So I can't provide any one-size-fits-all instructions in this book. For a decent overview of the story on Linux distributions, visit unix.stackexchange. com/questions/88201/ whats-the-best-distro- shell-agnostic-way-to-set- environment-variables. To get a really nice tool for setting environment variables in Windows, visit www.rapidee.com and download the Rapid Environment Editor. If you have any doubts, consult the online documentation and forum discussions for your own operating system's procedures.

Adding Apple's Java to the Stew

To develop Android programs on a Mac, you need two flavors of Java — Oracle Java and Apple Java. You need OS X 10.5.8 or later, and your Mac must have an Intel processor. (The Android docs say that you can't develop Android apps on a PowerPC Mac or on a Mac with OS X 10.5.7. Of course, for every hardware or software requirement, someone tries to create a workaround, or *hack*. Anyway, apply hacks at your own risk.)

Fortunately, installing Apple Java is easy. Search the web for Apple Java 6, and look for a web page in the apple.com domain. As of October 2014, the best page seems to be support.apple.com/kb/dl1572. Click the Download button on that page.

The downloaded file has the .dmg filename extension. When you double-click the .dmg file's icon, you get a .pkg file's icon. When you double-click the .pkg file's icon, a setup assistant guides you through the installation.

The Many Faces of Java (for Inquiring Readers Only)

When you visit www.oracle.com/technetwork/java/javase/downloads, you find lots of options — too many options. Readers often send me email asking which options to select. Sad to say, the answer depends on your computer's configuration. One way or another, keep a few things in mind:

✦ **There's more than one kind of Java. The "official" Java comes from Oracle, but some organizations have created their own kinds of Java.**

Here are some examples:

- With Oracle's blessing, Apple developed its own Java to run on Macintosh computers. Apple stopped developing its own Java in 2011, but Apple continues to this day to issue updates as needed.

- Until 2011, the Apache Software Foundation developed another flavor of Java named *Apache Harmony*.

- When you create an Android app, you use Google's Android Java. Android Java comes originally from Apache Harmony, so Android Java isn't quite the same as Oracle Java.

  But here's the strange thing: When you create an Android app, you use both Android Java *and* Oracle's Java. You write your app's code in Android Java, but to create the code, you use software tools that were written using Oracle Java. If you're a Mac user, you also need Apple's Java on your computer. Believe it or not, this doesn't normally confuse people.

  By the way, Google's use of Android Java doesn't have Oracle's blessing. If you're curious, search the web for info about the never-ending series of Oracle versus Google lawsuits.

The rest of this section deals almost exclusively with Oracle Java — the flavor that you find on the www.oracle.com/technetwork/java/javase/downloads page.

✦ **Oracle Java comes in three separate editions.**

A bit of background here: A *programming language* is a bunch of rules describing the way you can write instructions for the computer to follow. An *application programming interface* (API) is a bunch of reusable code for performing common tasks in a particular language. (Another name for an API is a *library*.)

Oracle Java has three official APIs. When you download Java from
www.oracle.com, you download some Java language tools and one
of the three Java APIs. Taken together, the big bundle containing the
language tools and one of the three APIs is called an *edition* of the *Java
Software Development Kit* (SDK). The three available Java SDK editions are
as follows:

- *Java Platform, Standard Edition (Java SE)*

  The Standard Edition has code for anything you can imagine doing
  on a single desktop computer, and much more. This edition does
  text-handling, mathematical calculations, input/output, collections of
  objects, and much more.

  To develop Android apps, you want the Java Platform, Standard
  Edition.

- *Java Platform, Enterprise Edition (Java EE)*

  The Enterprise Edition has code for things you do on an industrial-
  strength server. This edition includes web server tools, sophisticated
  database tools, messaging between servers and clients, management
  of systems, and the entire kitchen sink.

- *Java Platform, Micro Edition (Java ME)*

  The Micro Edition has code for small devices, such as phones, TV
  set-top boxes, and Blu-ray players. This edition has limited capabilities that fit nicely into special-purpose devices that aren't as powerful
  as today's computers.

  At first glance, the Micro Edition seems perfect for Android app development. But the creators of Android decided to bypass Java ME and
  create their own micro edition of sorts. In a way, the Android SDK
  is an alternative to Java ME. To be more precise, the Android SDK is
  both an alternative to Java ME and a user of the Java SE. (That is, the
  Android SDK defers to Java SE to perform some important jobs.)

The stewards of Java flip-flop between the names *Java Software
Development Kit* and *Java Development Kit* (JDK). The two names are
synonymous.

As you plow through various pieces of documentation, you see several
uses of the acronym API. In this section, the Java API is a bunch of reusable code for performing common tasks with the Java programming
language. In later sections, the Android libraries form the *Android API* —
a bunch of reusable code for performing common tasks inside Android
apps. To create Android apps, you need both APIs — the Java API and the
Android API.

To develop Android apps, you want the Java Platform, Standard Edition. If you already have Java's Enterprise Edition and you don't want more stuff on your hard drive, the Enterprise Edition is okay. But the Enterprise Edition has much more than you need for developing Android apps, and the extra Enterprise features might confuse you. (I know this because the extra Enterprise features confuse me!)

✦ **For Windows and Linux, Oracle's site provides two different Java downloads — one for the 32-bit word length, and another for the 64-bit word length.**

You can spot the 64-bit downloads because they have the number *64* somewhere in their filenames or their descriptions. You can find the 32-bit downloads because they have *x86* or *i586* in their filenames or descriptions. (The characters *x86* and *i586* refer to model numbers for some older 32-bit processors.)

You can fuss all day deciding whether to download 32-bit Java or 64-bit Java. But instead of fussing, consider these guidelines:

• Most newer computers run 64-bit operating systems, so for you, the 64-bit download is probably okay.

• A 32-bit operating system cannot run 64-bit programs, but a 64-bit operating system can probably run 32-bit programs. So the 32-bit Java download is a very safe bet (or a "very safe bit!" Ha, ha!). In addition, any advantage that you gain from running the more powerful 64-bit Java is lost on the small examples that you run in this book.

✦ **Java comes in several different versions, with several updates to each version.**

Java's version numbering demonstrates what can happen when the marketing department disrupts the timeline in the space-time continuum. Java's earliest releases were numbered "1.0." Next came version "1.1," and then the strangely named "Java 2, version 1.2." The extraneous digit *2* hung around through "Java 2, version 1.3," "Java 2, version 1.4," and finally "Java 2, version 5.0." (The spontaneous jump from 1.4 to 5.0 was lots of fun.)

Next up was "Java 6" (with no extra 2 and no ".0"). After that came Java 7. Each version is updated often, so a visit to `www.oracle.com` may offer Java SE 8 Update 25 (Java SE 8u25) for download.

Any version of Java starting with Java 6 and onward is fine for Android development. Oracle's Java 7 is best for developing Android apps, but Java 8 will also work.

✦ **On Oracle's website, Java has two kinds of downloads.**

When you visit `www.oracle.com`, you see two acronyms floating around: *JRE* (Java Runtime Environment) and *JDK* (Java Development Kit). The JRE has everything you need in order to run existing Java programs. Whether you know it, your desktop computer probably has a version of the JRE.

The JDK has everything you need in order to run existing Java programs and everything you need in order to create new Java programs. The JDK has the entire JRE and more.

As an Android developer, you must create your own Java programs. So the download that you want is the JDK, which includes the JRE. You do *not* want the JRE alone.

Download and install the Java JDK, not the Java JRE.

✦ **On Oracle's website, Java might come with other tools.**

A glance at the Java download page shows several options — options to download Java with NetBeans, JavaFX, the Java source code, and some other stuff. In general, these extras (NetBeans, JavaFX, and the others) don't help with Android app development.

Setting Up the Software

The *Android Software Development Kit* (SDK) contains the libraries that you need for developing Android applications. The SDK has code for drawing forms on a device's screen, code for dialing phone numbers, code for taking pictures with the device's camera, and a lot more.

The kit also contains bare-bones tools for creating, running, and testing your Android applications. By *bare-bones tools,* I mean tools that you can run by typing instructions in your development computer's command window (in the Command Prompt on Windows, or in the Terminal application on Linux and on a Mac). These tools perform all the logic required to do full-fledged Android development, but the SDK has no friendly user interface for invoking these tools.

An *integrated development environment* (IDE) is a user interface for invoking software development tools. An IDE helps you create software easily and efficiently. You can develop software (including Android apps) without an IDE, but the time and effort you save using an IDE makes the IDE worthwhile. (Some hard-core developers disagree with me, but that's another matter.)

The official IDE for Android app development is called *Android Studio.* Android Studio is based on a more general-purpose product called IntelliJ IDEA.

For system requirements, Google's website lists the following:

✦ Windows 2003 or later to run Android Studio on a PC.

✦ OS X 10.8.5 or later to run Android Studio on a Mac.

✦ Linux with the GNOME or KDE desktop and GNU C Library (glibc) 2.15 or later.

All operating systems require at least 2GB RAM. For performance that isn't very, very slow, you want at least 4GB RAM.

If your computer doesn't meet the requirements, you might be able to find a workaround. Search the web and you might find what you're looking for.

Downloading the software

You can download Android's SDK and Android Studio in one big gulp. Here's how:

1. **Visit** `developer.android.com/sdk.`

Figure 2-5 shows you what this web page looks like in May of 2015 (commonly known as "the good old days") when I visit using my Windows computer.

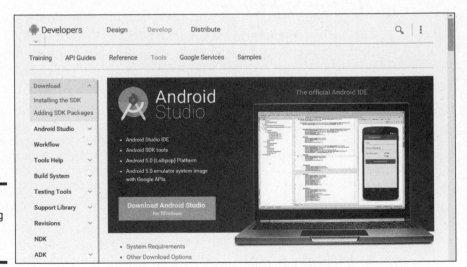

Figure 2-5: Downloading Android tools.

The page has a big button for downloading Android Studio. The Android Studio download includes the much-needed Android SDK.

By the time you read this book, the web page will probably have changed. But you'll still see an Android Studio download.

2. **Click the button to download Android Studio.**

3. **Agree to all the legal mumbo-jumbo.**

4. **Save the download to the local hard drive.**

The Android Studio download is either an `.exe` file (for Windows), a `.dmg` file (for a Mac), or a `.tgz` file (for Linux).

Installing the software

When you download Android Studio, you have either an `.exe` file (for Windows), a `.dmg` file (for a Mac), or a `.tgz` archive file (for Linux).

✦ **In Windows:** Double-click the `.exe` file's icon.

When you double-click the `.exe` file's icon, a wizard guides you through the installation.

✦ **On a Mac:** Double-click the `.dmg` file's icon.

When you double-click the `.dmg` file's icon, you see an `Android Studio` icon (also known as an `Android Studio.app` icon). Drag the `Android Studio` icon to your `Applications` folder.

✦ **In Linux:** Extract the contents of the `.tgz` or `.zip` archive file. (Where you put the extracted contents is up to you.) The steps for extracting the file's contents vary from one Linux distribution to another. Anyway, the following commands work for me:

For a `.tgz` file:

```
cd ~/Downloads
tar zxvf name-of-the-downloaded-file.tgz \
--directory ~/Development
```

For a `.zip` file:

```
cd ~/Downloads
unzip -d ~/Development name-of-the-downloaded-file.zip
```

In recommending these commands, I assume that your web browser placed the file in a `Downloads` directory (a subdirectory of your home directory). I also assume that your home directory has a `Development` subdirectory. (Refer to the earlier section "Installing Oracle's Java Development Kit".)

While you're still in the mood to follow my advice, note the location on the hard drive where the Android `sdk` lands. For example, in Figure 2-6, the `sdk` directory is `\Users\Barry\AppData\Local\Android\sdk`. I have a name for this `sdk` directory: the *ANDROID_HOME* directory.

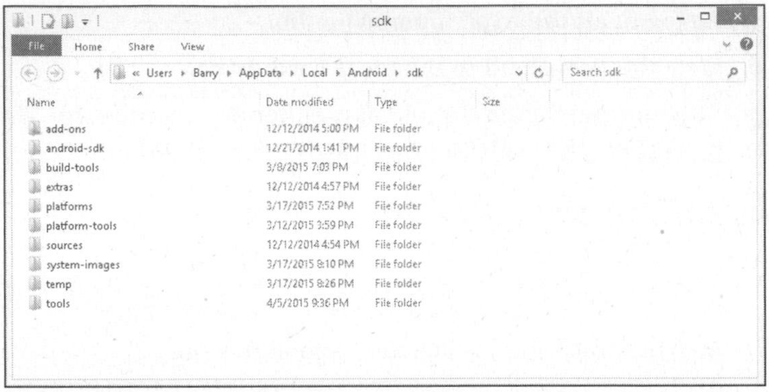

Figure 2-6:
The
*ANDROID_
HOME*
directory.

Take a few minutes to browse your *ANDROID_HOME* directory's contents. The directory has folders named docs, platform-tools, platforms, samples, tools, and others. The tools and platform-tools folders contain items that Android developers use all the time.

There's no place like home

This chapter is littered with things that have *home* in their names. If you've been reading every word (or, as I have, writing every word) you've seen references to the *JAVA_HOME* and *ANDROID_HOME* directories. In addition to these *_HOME* directories, your operating system maintains several *user home* directories — one such directory for each of the computer's users.

✔ To find your user home directory on a Windows computer, run the cmd program and type set HOMEPATH.

✔ To find your user home directory on a Mac, open the Finder and then press Cmd+Shift+H. Alternatively, you can use the Terminal windows and the same command that works in Linux.

✔ To find your user home directory on a Linux computer, run the Terminal app and type echo $HOME.

Unlike the *JAVA_HOME* and *ANDROID_HOME* directories, your user home directory is a starting point for subdirectories containing your own user files. On most computers, a user's home directory contains subdirectories named Documents, Downloads, and so on.

And here's one more thing to remember: To clearly distinguish this directory from the *JAVA_HOME* and *ANDROID_HOME* directories, I refer to this directory as the *user home* directory. But other authors simply write *home* directory (without the extra word *user*). And in fact, I probably become sloppy and write "home directory" here and there in this book. (Sorry about that!)

Launching the Android Studio IDE

In the previous sections, you downloaded and installed Android Studio. Your next task (should you decide to accept it) is to launch Android Studio. This section has the details.

In Windows

1. **In the File Explorer (also known as Windows Explorer), navigate to the directory where Android Studio is installed.**

Depending on your Windows version, this directory is probably `C:\Program Files (x86)\Android\android-studio` or `C:\Program Files\Android\android-studio`. The directory contains folders named `bin`, `lib`, `sdk`, and others.

2. **Still in the File Explorer, double-click the `bin` subdirectory of the Android Studio directory.**

3. **In the `bin` subdirectory, double-click the `studio.bat` file.**

On a Mac

1. **In a Finder window, visit the Applications folder.**

2. **In the Applications folder, double-click the Android Studio icon.**

If your Mac complains that Android Studio is from an unidentified developer, Ctrl-click the Android Studio icon and select Open. When another "unidentified developer" box appears, click the Open button.

In Linux

What you do to launch Android Studio depends on the steps you followed previously in this chapter. In particular, did you add your *JAVA_HOME* directory to your PATH environment variable? (For info about this, refer to the sidebar entitled "Caring for the environment.")

If you added your JAVA_HOME directory to the PATH:

In a Terminal window, type the following commands:

```
cd ~/Development/android-studio/bin
./studio.sh
```

(I assume that you extracted Android Studio to a `Development` subdirectory of your home directory. If that's not the case, change the first command appropriately.)

If you didn't add your `JAVA_HOME` *directory to the PATH:*

1. **In a Terminal window, navigate to the** `bin` **subdirectory of the directory in which you installed Android Studio.**

   To do this, you might type

   ```
   cd ~/Development/android-studio/bin
   ```

2. **Using your favorite text editor, create a new** `startStudio.sh` **file in this** `bin` **subdirectory.**

3. **In your new** `startStudio.sh` **file, put the following text:**

   ```
   export JAVA_HOME=~/Development/jdk1.8.0_25
   export PATH=$PATH:$JAVA_HOME/bin
   ./studio.sh
   ```

4. **In the Terminal window, give yourself permission to execute the** `startStudio.sh` **file's commands.**

   To do so, type

   ```
   chmod u+x startStudio.sh
   ```

5. **In the Terminal window, tell Linux to execute the** `startStudio.sh` **file's commands.**

   To do so, type

   ```
   ./startStudio.sh
   ```

In recommending these steps for Linux, I assume that your Java version is 1.8.0_25 (which is probably close, but not entirely correct). I also assume that you extracted both Java and Android Studio to a `Development` subdirectory of your user home directory. If any of these assumptions is inaccurate, change the commands appropriately.

Android Studio is running. Now the fun begins.

Fattening Up the Android SDK

In the earlier "Setting Up the Software," you install a small (but usable) portion of the Android SDK. At some point in your travels, you'll want to install more of the SDK. The following section tells you how.

The more things stay the same, the more they change

When you download the Android SDK, you get the code library (the API) for a particular release of Android. You also get several developer tools — tools for compiling, testing, and debugging Android code. For example, to test your code, you can run the code on an *emulator.* The emulator program runs on your development computer (your PC, your Mac, or your Linux computer). The emulator displays a picture of a mobile device (for example, a phone or a tablet device). The emulator shows you how your code will probably behave when you later run your code on a real phone or a real tablet device.

Another tool, the Android Debug Bridge (adb), connects your development computer to a device that's executing your new Android code. (The adb also "connects" your development computer to a running emulator, even though the emulator is running on your development computer.) The adb is an invaluable tool for testing Android applications.

Neither the basic emulator nor Android's adb tool change very much over time. But Android's user interface and the features available to Android developers change considerably from one version to another. One month developers work with Android 4.4, codenamed *Jelly Bean.* Later that year, developers use Android 5.0, codenamed *Lollipop.* Each version of Android represents a new *platform,* a new *API level,* or a new codename depending on the way you refer to the version.

For more information about Android API levels, visit `http://developer.android.com/guide/appendix/api-levels.html#level`.

To help you juggle the different Android versions, the people at Google have created two tools.

✦ The *Android SDK Manager* lists the versions of Android and helps you download and install the versions that you need on your development computer.

✦ The *Android Virtual Device Manager* helps you customize the basic emulator so you can imitate the device of your choice on your development computer.

The next few sections cover these stories in depth.

Installing new versions (and older versions) of Android

When you first install the Android SDK, you can probably skip this section's instructions. Follow this section's instructions when Google releases updated versions of Android, or when you work on a project that requires older versions of Android (versions that you haven't already installed).

To manage all the Android versions that are available to you (the developer), use the Android SDK Manager. Here's how:

1. **In Android Studio's main menu, choose Tools ➪ Android ➪ SDK Manager.**

After selecting this option, you see a new window, — namely, the Android SDK Manager window. (See Figure 2-7.)

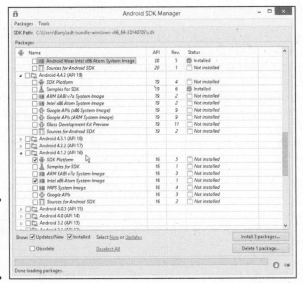

Figure 2-7:
The Android
SDK
Manager.

In the Android SDK Manager, you see a tree of Android versions and tools. For each item in the tree, the Status column tells you if you've already installed that item (and, if applicable, that an update is available for the item).

2. **Place check marks next to any items that you want to install, and next to any items that you want to update. (Refer to Figure 2-7.)**

You can expand parts of the tree in order to pick and choose from among the items in an Android version. For example, in Figure 2-7, I select only the SDK Platform and Intel x86 Atom System Image items in Android 4.1.2 (API 16). If you have lots of space on your hard drive, and you don't mind waiting a long time for the download to finish, you can select more items.

3. **In the lower-right corner of the Android SDK Manager window, click the Install Packages button.**

   After clicking this button, you see a Choose Packages to Install dialog box.

4. **Do any remaining license accepting and clicking to make the installations begin.**

Creating an Android virtual device

You might be itching to run some code, but first you must have something that can run an Android program. By "something," I mean either a real Android device (a phone, a tablet, an Android Wear watch, an Android-enabled refrigerator, whatever) or a virtual device. By a *virtual device,* I mean a program that runs on your development computer and creates a window that looks (and acts) like a real Android device. People call this device an *emulator,* but in truth, the virtual device has three parts:

✦ **A *system image* is a copy of one version of the Android operating system.**

   For example, in Figure 2-7, *Intel x86 Atom_64 System Image* refers to the software that runs Android 4.1.2 on a 64-bit Atom processor.

   You get a system image when you follow the steps in the section "Installing the software," earlier in this chapter. To get other system images, use the Android SDK Manager.

✦ **The *emulator* bridges the gap between the system image and the processor on your development computer.**

   You might have a system image for an Atom_64 processor, but your development computer runs a Core i5 processor. The emulator translates instructions for the Atom_64 processor into instructions that the Core i5 processor can execute.

   You get an emulator when you follow the steps in the section "Installing the software," earlier in this chapter.

✦ **An Android Virtual Device (AVD) is the representation of a real (physical) device's hardware.**

   The emulator translates Android code into code that your development computer can execute. But the emulator doesn't display a particular phone or tablet device on your screen. The emulator doesn't know what kind of device you want to display. Do you want a camera phone with 800-x-480-pixel resolution, or have you opted for a tablet device with its own built-in accelerometer and gyroscope? All these choices belong to a particular AVD. An AVD is actually a bunch of settings, telling the emulator all the details about the device to be emulated.

Steal this AVD!

You can copy an AVD from someone else's computer. That is, you don't really have to create an AVD. You can use an AVD that's already been created. On your development computer's hard drive, an AVD is an `.ini` file combined with a folder full of configuration information.

For example, my computer's `C:\Users\my-user-name\.android\avd\` folder has files named `Nexus5_4.4.2_API19.ini`, `Tablet_API17.ini`, and so on. When I open `Nexus5_4.4.2_API19.ini` in a text editor, I see this:

```
target=android-19
path=C:\Users\Barry\.android\avd\
        Nexus5_4.4.2_API19.avd
```

Don't let the dot in the name `Nexus5_4.4.2_API19.avd` fool you. The name

`Nexus5_4.4.2_API19.avd` refers to a folder. This folder contains files like `config.ini`, which in turn describes the virtual device's SD card size, RAM size, and so on. Here are a few lines from a `config.ini` file:

```
hw.lcd.density=480
sdcard.size=1000M
hw.ramSize=512
```

To copy an AVD from someone else's computer, copy the `.avd` folder to your development computer's hard drive. Then create an `.ini` file like my `Nexus5_4.4.2_API19.ini` file. (Don't forget to replace my `target` and `path` values with values that are appropriate for your computer.) Put all this stuff in your user home's `.android\avd` folder (or wherever fine AVD files are stored).

What kind of a processor does the device have? What's the screen resolution of the device? Does the device have a physical keyboard? Does it have a camera? How much memory does it have? Does it have an SD card? All these facts about a virtual device live in an AVD. An AVD runs on a particular system image which, in turn, runs on the emulator.

You create one or more AVDs before testing your code on a development computer. When you tell Android Studio to do a test run of your code, you can choose one of these AVDs.

So before you can run Android apps on your computer, you must first create at least one AVD. In fact, you normally create several AVDs and then use one of them to run a particular Android app.

To create an AVD, follow these steps:

1. **In Android Studio's main menu, choose Tools ⇨ Android ⇨ AVD Manager.**

    After selecting this option, you see a new window — namely, the Android AVD Manager window.

2. **In the Android AVD Manager window, click Create, as shown in Figure 2-8.**

   The Create New Android Virtual Device (AVD) window opens. That's nice!

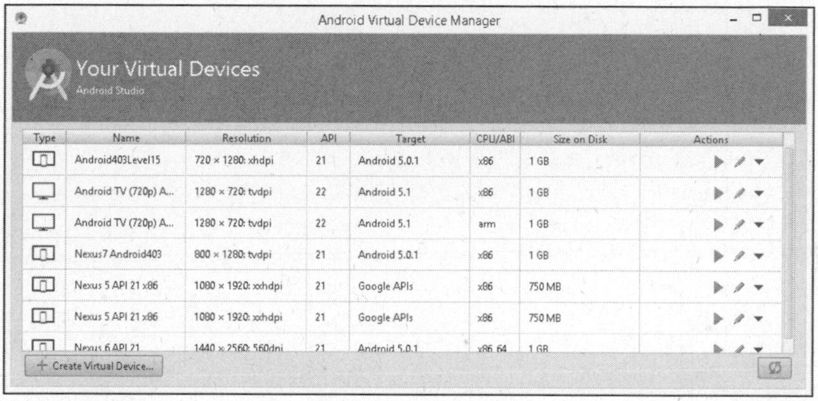

Figure 2-8: The Android AVD Manager.

3. **Create a name for your virtual device.**

   You can name your device My Sweet Petunia, but in Figure 2-9, I name my device Lollipop1. The name serves to remind me of this device's features.

4. **Select values in the drop-down lists.**

   In Figure 2-9, I select Nexus 5, Android 5.0, Intel Atom (x86_64), No skin, Webcam0, and Emulated back camera.

   Sometimes the choice you make in one drop-down list affects the options in other lists. For example, in the Target list, I might select *Android 4.4W*. (The *W* stands for *wear*. The target API applies to watches rather than phones or tablet devices.) As it happens, I haven't installed a system image for Android Wear devices, so when I make this Target selection, the CPU/API drop-down list is empty. It's time to install a system image for Android Wear, or to select a different target.

5. **Fill in the other entries in the Create New Android Virtual Device window.**

   For a novice developer, most of the defaults are okay. But a few of these options might make a big difference.

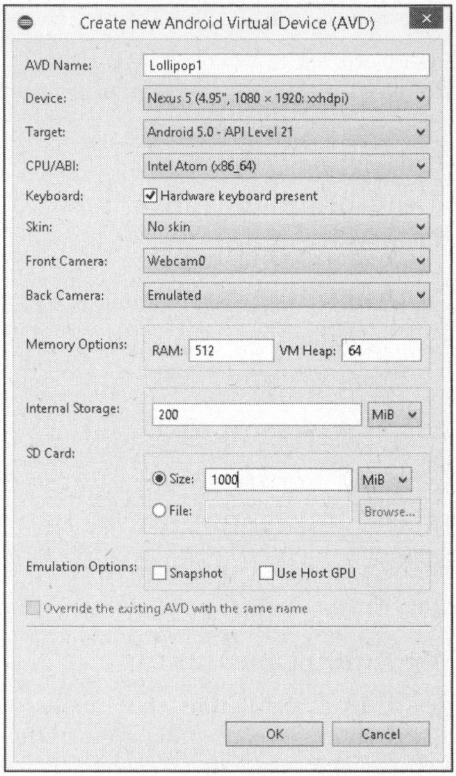

Figure 2-9: Creating a new Android virtual device.

- **If the emulator runs on a Windows computer, keep the RAM entry at or below 768.**

  With the value 768, the virtual device has 768MB of random access memory. A device with more RAM probably won't start if you try to run it on a Windows computer. To be safe, I always enter 512 or less in the RAM field.

- **If you select the Snapshot option, the emulator takes less time to start running.**

  An emulator snapshot is like a laptop computer's sleep option. The snapshot is a picture of the virtual device's state when you shut down the emulator. The next time you launch this AVD, the emulator picks up where it left off. This takes less time than restarting the Android operating system anew.

  The Android emulator can take a long time to start running. A normal startup can take minutes rather than seconds. Sometimes the startup takes so long that I wonder if the startup is making any progress at all. It's worth your while to try out any tricks that you find for speeding up the emulator's startup. (This includes my advice about enabling the Snapshot option.)

- **The Use Host GPU option can be a deal-breaker.**

   Not long ago, I had trouble launching the emulator. Every attempt to fire up the emulator failed with either an error message or a stalled startup. In a desperate attempt to get the emulator going, I found an online post advising me to put a check mark in the AVD's Use Host GPU option. It seemed to be good advice, but when I looked at the AVD's properties, I found that the Use Host GPU option was already checked. So I experimented by unchecking the Use Host GPU option. Oddly enough, that solved the problem.

Recently, my department hired a new person. We offered a salary of $50K, which (we thought) meant $50,000 per year. Little did we know that the new person expected to be paid $51,200 each year. Computer scientists use the letter *K* (or the prefix "Kilo") to mean 1,024 because 1,024 is a power of 2 (and powers of 2 are very handy in computer science). The trouble is, the formal meaning of "Kilo" in the metric system is 1,000, not 1,024. To help clear things up (and to have fun creating new words), a commission of engineers created the *Kibibyte* (KiB), meaning 1,024 bytes, the *Mebibyte* (MiB), which is 1,048,576 bytes, and the *Gibibyte* (GiB), meaning 1,073,741,824 bytes. Most people (computer scientists included) don't know about KiBs or MiBs, and don't worry about the difference between MiBs and ordinary megabytes. I'm surprised that the developers of Android's AVD Manager thought about this issue.

6. **Click the OK button.**

   After a somewhat uncomfortable delay, your computer returns you to the Android AVD Manager window, where you see a brand-new AVD in the list.

A third-party emulator

Android's standard emulator (the emulator that you download from Google's website) is notoriously messy. The startup is slow, and even after startup, the emulator's response can be painfully sluggish. In Chapter 3 of this minibook, I tell you how to test Android code on a real device connected via USB to your computer. The performance on a real device (even on an older Android device) is much snappier than on the standard emulator.

If you don't like the standard emulator, and you don't want to attach devices to your development computer, you have a third choice. At www.genymotion.com, you can download an alternative to the standard Android emulator. The alternative is available for Windows, Macintosh, and 64-bit Debian-based systems.

Genymotion's emulator is must faster and has more features than the standard emulator. If there's a downside to the Genymotion emulator, it's the cost. Genymotion's product is free for personal use, but costs from 100 to 300 Euros for commercial use.

Acting like a phone (when you're not a phone)

In computing, the words *emulator* and *simulator* have similar meanings. Some people use the words interchangeably, but if you're being picky, an *emulator* executes each program by doing what another kind of processor would do. In contrast, a *simulator* executes a program any way that's handy and ends up with the same result that an emulator would get. To be even pickier, an emulator mimics your processor's hardware, and a simulator mimics your application's software.

On your development computer's screen, a phone simulator would look like a picture of a phone and would carry out your mobile application's instructions for testing purposes. But on the inside, the simulator would be executing instructions the way your laptop or desktop executes instructions. The simulator would be translating instructions meant for a phone's processor into instructions meant for your laptop's processor. This juggling act (of instructions and processors) works fine on the whole. But in some subtle situations, a simulator doesn't precisely mimic a real phone's behavior.

The goal of precise, reliable mimicry is one reason why the Android crew decided on an emulator instead of a simulator. Android's emulator (the emulator that you download with the SDK starter package) is based on a very popular open-source program named QEMU. On its own, QEMU takes code written for a certain kind of processor (an Intel chip, for example), translates this code, and then runs the code on another kind of processor (an ARM or a PowerPC, for example). The emulator that comes with Android's SDK has add-ons and tweaks to accommodate Android mobile devices. For more information about QEMU, visit `http://qemu.org`.

If you develop apps only for personal use, or if you have money to spend on a commercial venture, then Genymotion's emulator is definitely worth considering.

And that does it! You're ready to run your first Android app. I don't know about you, but I'm excited. (Sure, I'm not watching you read this book, but I'm excited on your behalf.) Chapter 3 in this minibook guides you through the run of an Android application. Go for it!

Chapter 3: Creating an Android App

In a quiet neighborhood in south Philadelphia, there's a maternity shop named Hello World. I stumbled on to the store on my way to Pat's (to get a delicious Philly cheesesteak, of course), and I couldn't resist taking a picture of the store's sign.

Computer geek that I am, I'd never thought of Hello World as anything but an app. A *Hello World* app is the simplest program that can run in a particular programming language or on a particular platform.* Authors create Hello World apps to show people how to get started writing code for a particular system.

So, in this chapter, you make an Android Hello World app. The app doesn't do much. (In fact, you might argue that the app doesn't do anything!) But the example shows you how to create and run new Android projects.

*For an interesting discussion of the phrase *Hello World,* visit www.mzlabs.com/JMPubs/HelloWorld.pdf.

Creating Your First App

A typical gadget comes with a manual. The manual's first sentence is "Read all 37 safety warnings before attempting to install this product." Don't you love it? You can't get to the good stuff without wading through the preliminaries.

Well, nothing in this chapter can set your house on fire or even break your electronic device. But before you follow this chapter's instructions, you need a bunch of software on your development computer. To make sure that you have this software and that the software is properly configured, return to Chapter 2 of this minibook. (Do not pass Go; do not collect $200.)

When at last you have all the software you need, you're ready to launch Android Studio and create a real, live Android app.

Starting the IDE and creating your first app

To start the IDE and create your first app, you start, naturally, at the beginning:

1. **Launch Android Studio.**

   For details on launching Android Studio, see Chapter 2 of this minibook. To find out how to make the most of your Android Studio experience, see Book II, Chapter 1.

   When you launch Android Studio for the first time, you see the Welcome screen. (See Figure 3-1.) The Welcome screen lists any Android Studio projects that you've already created. (**Hint:** You haven't created any projects yet.)

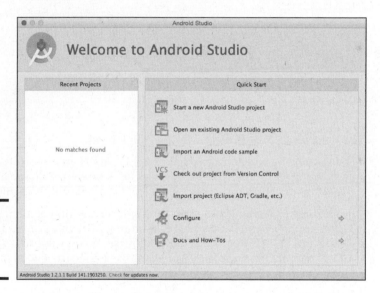

Figure 3-1:
Welcome
to Android
Studio.

The Welcome screen also offers you some Quick Start options, such as Start a New Android Studio Project, Open an Existing Android Studio Project, and so on.

2. **In the Welcome screen, select Start a New Android Studio Project.**

   As a result, the Create New Project dialog box appears, as shown in Figure 3-2. The Create New Project dialog box has fields for the Application Name, your Company Domain, and your Project Location. These fields contain some default values, such as My Application for the Application Name, and example.com for the Company Domain. You can change the values in these fields but, for now, I recommend accepting the defaults.

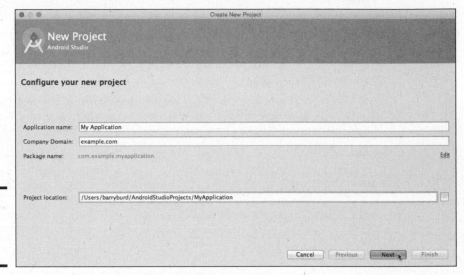

3. In the Create New Project window, click Next.

Doing so brings up another page of the Create New Project dialog box, as shown in Figure 3-3. This page has check boxes for Phone and Tablet, TV, Wear, and Glass. The page also has Minimum SDK drop-down lists.

In this first example, I guide you through the creation of a Phone and Tablet app, so you can accept the Minimum SDK value offered in the Phone and Tablet drop-down list. Of course, if you want to try creating a TV, Wear, or Glass app, or if you want to change the choice in the Minimum SDK drop-down list, feel free to do so.

For a Minimum SDK, you can select any API level that's available in the drop-down list. Just make sure that you have an Android Virtual Device (an AVD) that can run your chosen API level. For example, an AVD that runs Android 5.0 can handle projects whose Minimum SDK is Android 5.0, Android 4.4, Android 4.0.3, Android 3.2, and so on.

For an overview of Android versions, see Chapter 1 of this minibook. To find out more about the AVD that Android Studio creates when you first install it, see Chapter 2 of this minibook. (Chapter 2 also has information about creating additional AVDs.) To find out what kinds of promises you make when you choose a Minimum SDK, see Chapter 4 of this minibook.

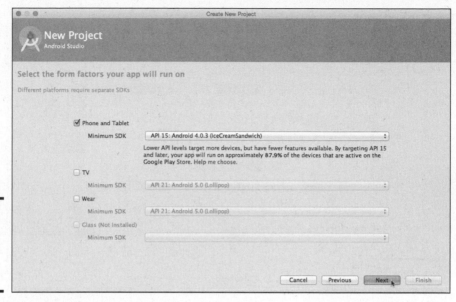

Figure 3-3:
Select form
factors and
minimum
SDKs.

4. **Click Next.**

   As a result, yet another page of the Create New Project window appears.
   (See Figure 3-4.) On this page, you tell Android Studio to create some
   Java code for you. The Java code describes an Android activity. For your
   first app, creating a blank activity (the default choice on this page) is a
   good idea.

   To start reading about Android activities, see Chapter 4 in this minibook.
   For more details about Android activities, see Book III, Chapter 1.

5. **Click Next yet again.**

   You get another Create New Project page. (What a surprise!) On this
   page, you make up the names of things associated with your activity.
   (See Figure 3-5.) Again, I recommend the path of least resistance (accepting the defaults).

   If you plan to publish your app, the names of things matter a lot. For tips
   on naming things, see Chapter 4 in this minibook.

6. **Click Finish.**

   The Create New Project page goes away. Android Studio displays its
   main window with the words *My Application* and *Hello world!,* as shown
   in Figure 3-6.

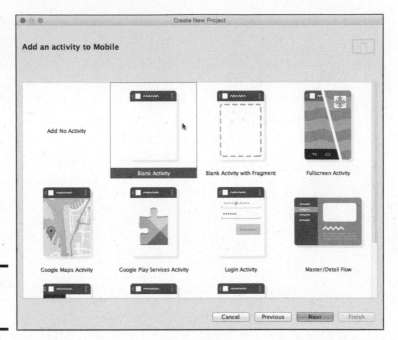

Figure 3-4:
Add an
activity.

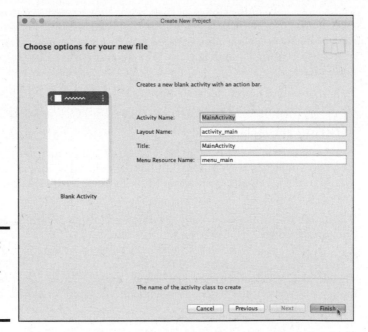

Figure 3-5:
Choose
options for
your new
activity.

Figure 3-6:
Android
Studio's
main
window.

The first time you create a project, you wait a *l-o-n-g* time for Android
Studio to build the Gradle project info (whatever that is). You see a pop-up
dialog box indicating that Android Studio is downloading something. The
pop-up contains one of those annoying "un-progress" bars — the kind that
doesn't show you what percentage of the work is completed. (On some
computers, the progress bar looks like a rotating, striped diagonal — the
kind you see on old barbershop poles. On other computers, a solid bar
simply moves back and forth, back and forth, back and forth. What were
they thinking when they designed this pop-up? They figured that I'll be
more willing to wait as long as this progress bar holds my cat's attention.)
Anyway, when Android Studio loads your first project, be prepared to wait
several minutes for any signs of life on your screen.

Launching your first app

You've started up Android Studio and created your first project. The project
doesn't do much except display *Hello world!* on the screen. Even so, you can
run the project and see it in action. Here's how you start:

1. **Take a look at Android Studio's main window.**

Refer to Figure 3-6. In Android Studio, your new app consumes the entire
main window. If, for some reason, more than one Android Studio is open,

make sure that the window you're looking at is the one containing your newly created Android app.

2. **In Android Studio's main menu, choose Run ➪ Run 'app'.**

The Choose Device dialog box appears, as shown in Figure 3-7.

If the Choose Device dialog box doesn't appear, your computer might be skipping the Choose Device dialog box and going straight to the Android emulator. If this happens, then (after a long wait) your app probably starts running in the Emulator window. That's okay, but if you don't like skipping the Choose Device dialog box, visit the section entitled "You don't like whatever AVD opens automatically," later in this chapter.

In the Choose Device dialog box, you see the option Choose a Running Device. But at this point, you probably haven't yet started any emulators running, so . . .

Figure 3-7:
The Choose Device dialog box.

3. **In the Choose Device dialog box, select Launch Emulator.**

4. **Choose an item in the Android Virtual Device drop-down list.**

If the drop-down list is empty, refer to the material in Chapter 2 in this minibook on creating an AVD.

5. **Click OK.**

A tool window named Android DDMS (or simply *Android*) appears along the bottom of Android Studio's main window, as shown in Figure 3-8.

If you don't see the Android DDMS tool window, look for an Android tool button in the lower-left corner of the Android Studio window. Click that tool button.

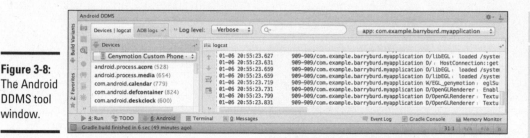

Figure 3-8:
The Android
DDMS tool
window.

You can get useful diagnostics about the progress of your app's launch. To do so, look for a Run tool button in the lower-left corner of the Android Studio window. If you click that button, the Run tool window appears. In this window, you might find the phrases Launching a New Emulator; Waiting for Device; and my personal favorite, Success. (See Figure 3-9.)

Figure 3-9:
The Run tool
window.

If your Run tool window doesn't display a bunch of text (such as Launching a New Emulator, Waiting for Device, and so on), try clicking the word *app* (preceded by a little Android icon) at the top of the tool window. (Refer to Figure 3-8.)

Running Your App

In this section, you kick your new app's tires and take your app around the block. Here's how:

1. **Launch your app by following the launch instructions in the "Creating Your First App" section.**

2. **Wait for the Android emulator to display a device locked screen, a home screen, or an app's screen.**

   First, you see the word *android* in shimmering, silvery letters. (See Figure 3-10.) Then, you see Android's device locked screen, a home screen, or an app's screen. (See Figures 3-11 and 3-12.)

5554:Nexus_6_API_21

android

Figure 3-10:
Android
starts
running
on the
emulator.

3. **I can't overemphasize this point: Wait for the Android emulator to display a device locked screen, a home screen, or an app's screen.**

   Android's emulator takes a long time to start. For example, on my 2.6GHz processor with 8GB of RAM, the emulator takes a few minutes to mimic a fully booted Android device. Some people blame the fact that it's an emulator instead of a simulator. (See Chapter 2 of this minibook for that argument.) Others claim that the translation of graphics hogs the emulator's time. For whatever reason, you need lots of patience when you deal with Android's emulator.

4. **Keep waiting.**

   While you're waiting, you might want to visit genymotion.com. For info on Genymotion's alternative to the standard Android emulator, see Chapter 2 in this minibook.

   Oh! I see that your emulator is finally displaying the device locked screen. It's time to proceed . . .

5. **If the emulator displays the device locked screen, do whatever you normally do to unlock an Android device.**

   Normally, you perform some sliding or swiping motion. With Android Version 5.0 (pictured in Figure 3-11), you swipe upward on the screen.

Figure 3-11:
The device
locked
screen for
Android 5.0
appears.

6. **See your app on the emulator's screen.**

Figure 3-12 shows the running of Android's Hello World app. (The screen even has Hello World! on it.) Android's development tools create this tiny app when you create a new Android project.

Android's Hello World app has no widgets for the user to push, and the app doesn't do anything interesting. But the appearance of an app on the Android screen is a very good start. Following the steps in this chapter you can start creating many exciting apps.

Don't close an Android emulator unless you know you won't be using it for a while. The emulator is fairly reliable after it gets going. (It's sluggish, but reliable.) While the emulator runs, you can modify your Android code and tell Android Studio to run the code again. When you do, Android Studio reinstalls your app on the running emulator. The process isn't speedy, but you don't have to wait for the emulator to start. (Actually, if you run a different app — an app whose minimum SDK version is higher than the running emulator can handle — Android fires up a second emulator. But, in many developer scenarios, jumping between emulators is the exception rather than the rule.)

Figure 3-12:
Your Hello
World app
in action.

You Can Download All the Code

Throughout this book I tell you how to create apps that illustrate Android development principles. "First, type this code; next type that code; *and so on*," says the book. You can follow the instructions in each and every chapter, but you can also bypass the instructions. You can scoop the book's examples from my website. Here's how:

1. **Visit www.allmycode.com/android.**

2. **Click the link to download this book's code.**

When the download completes, you have a .zip file (otherwise known as a *compressed archive file*).

3. **Unzip the downloaded file.**

"Unzipping" is the same as "uncompressing" or "expanding." On some computers, this unzipping happens automatically as soon as the download is finished. On other computers, you unzip the file by clicking (or double-clicking) the file's icon. On still other computers, you right-click or Ctrl-click the downloaded file's icon, and select an *unzip* (or *uncompress* or *expand*) option in the resulting context menu.

For more information about .zip files, see the sidebar "Compressed archive files."

After unzipping the file, you have a folder that contains several subfolders. These subfolders have names like 01-05-03. The folder with the name 01-05-03 contains the example whose code first appears in Book I, Chapter 5, Listing 3. (The correspondence between folder names and listing numbers isn't always perfect, but it's always pretty close.)

4. **Launch Android Studio.**

   For details, see Chapter 2 in this minibook.

   What you do next depends on what you see when you launch Android Studio.

5. **If you see Android Studio's Welcome screen, select Open an Existing Android Project.**

   The Open Project dialog box appears.

   If you see Android Studio's main window, choose File ⇨ Open in the main menu.

   The Open File or Project dialog box appears.

6. **In either dialog box, navigate to the folder containing the project that you want to open.**

   For example, to open the project containing the example that starts in Book I, Chapter 5, Listing 3, navigate to the 01-05-03 folder that's within the unzipped version of the stuff you downloaded.

7. **Whatever folder you select, look in that folder for a file named** build.gradle.

8. **Double-click the** build.gradle **file.**

   An Import Project from Gradle dialog box appears. The radio box labeled Use Default Gradle Wrapper should be checked.

9. **In the Import Project from Gradle dialog box, click OK.**

   As a result, you see a few churning progress bars.

   Android Studio has to download the default Gradle wrapper from the Internet. Make sure you have an Internet connection when you perform this step.

   You may or may not see a message asking if you want to reload because of a few language level changes (from Java 1.6 to Java 1.7, for example). Reload, or don't reload. Your choice.

   If you reload, you may or may not see a message warning you not to close the project because Gradle is running. Click Yes to close (and reload) the project.

   Eventually, you see Android Studio's main window. In the main window, you find a project containing one of this book's examples.

You can tell everyone that you created the project from scratch. I won't snitch.

Compressed archive files

When you visit this book's web site, you download a `.zip` file. You might also get a `.zip` file when you download Android development tools. A `.zip` file is a single file that encodes a bunch of smaller files and folders. So, for example, the `.zip` file from this book's web site encodes a folder named `01-05-03`, `01-06-01`, `03-01-01`, and so on. The `01-05-03` folder contains subfolders `app`, `build`, `gradle`, and others. These subfolders contain files and even more subfolders.

A `.zip` file is an example of a *compressed archive* file. Some other examples of compressed archives include `.tar.gz` files, `.tgz` files, and `.bin` files. *Uncompressing* or *extracting* means copying the files from inside the archive to a place on your hard drive. (For a `.zip` file, another word for "uncompressing" or "extracting" is "*unzipping*.") Uncompressing normally re-creates the folder structure encoded in the archive file. So, after uncompressing this book's examples, your hard drive has folders named `01-05-03`, `01-06-01`, and so on.

When you download a `.zip` file, your web browser may uncompress the file automatically for you. If not, you can see the `.zip` file's contents by double-clicking the file's icon. (In fact, you can copy the file's contents and perform some other file operations after double-clicking the file's icon.)

What If . . .

You try to run your first Android app. If your effort stalls, don't despair. This section has some troubleshooting tips.

Error message: Cannot resolve symbol 'R'

Every Android app has an `R.java` file. Android's development tools generate this file automatically. So normally, you don't have to worry about `R.java`. Occasionally, the file takes longer than average to be generated. In that case, Android Studio finds references to the `R` class in the rest of your project's code and complains that your project has no `R` class. My advice is, wait!

If one minute of waiting doesn't bring good results, choose Build ⇨ Clean Project in Android Studio's main menu.

Error message: Failed to find target

You've created a project with a certain target SDK or told the IDE to compile with a certain API level. But you haven't installed that API level. If Android Studio displays a link offering to Install Missing Platform(s) and Sync Project, then click the link. Otherwise, open the Android SDK manager and install that API level. For details, see Chapter 2 in this minibook.

If you don't want to install a new API level, you can tinker with the SDK version numbers in the project's `build.gradle` file. For details, see Chapter 4 in this minibook.

Error message: Android Virtual Device may be incompatible with your configuration

This message probably means that you haven't created an Android Virtual Device (AVD) capable of running your project. If Android Studio offers to help you create a new AVD, accept it. Otherwise, open the Android Virtual Device Manager to create a new AVD.

For information about Android Virtual Devices and the Android Virtual Device Manager, see Chapter 2 of this minibook.

You lose contact with the Android debug bridge (adb)

The Android Debug Bridge (adb) connects your development computer to a device that's executing your new Android code. (The adb also "connects" your development computer to a running emulator, even though the emulator is running on your development computer.)

If you see a message that hints of adb trouble, try restarting your development computer's Android debug bridge. Here's how:

1. **Click the Terminal tool button at the bottom of Android Studio's main window.**

Congratulations! You just opened Android Studio's Terminal tool window. If you're a Mac or Linux user, you see the shell prompt. If you're a Windows user, you see the Windows command prompt.

2. **In the Terminal tool window, go to your** *ANDROID_HOME*/platform-tools **directory.**

For help finding your *ANDROID_HOME* directory, see Chapter 2 of this minibook.

3. **In the** *ANDROID_HOME*/platform-tools **directory, type the following two commands:**

Windows:

```
adb kill-server
adb start-server
```

Macintosh and Linux:

```
./adb kill-server
./adb start-server
```

For more information about the Android debug bridge, refer to see Book I, Chapter 2.

You don't like whatever AVD opens automatically

In Chapter 2 of this minibook, you create an Android Virtual Device (an AVD). And, since the old Chapter 2 days, you may have created some additional AVDs. Now, when you launch an app, your computer fires up one of the many AVDs that you created. That's fine, but what if the computer fires up your least-favorite AVD? To get control over which AVD starts up, do the following:

1. **In Android Studio's main menu, choose Run ⇨ Edit Configurations.**

A Run/Debug Configurations dialog box appears.

2. **In this dialog box, choose Android Application ⇨ app.**

3. **On the right side of the dialog box, select the General tab.**

4. **Still on the right side of the dialog box, under the Target Device heading, select Show Chooser Dialog.**

5. **Uncheck the Use Same Device for Future Launches check box.**

6. **Click OK to close the dialog box.**

The next time you run this app, Android Studio prompts you with a Choose Device dialog box. In this box, a drop-down list shows you all the AVDs that you created. Pick an AVD, and then click OK.

If you accidentally pick an AVD that doesn't satisfy your app's minimum SDK requirement, Android Studio can't run your app. If the stars are aligned correctly, you see an INTALL_FAILED_OLDER_SDK message. If not, you simply have to try again with a newer AVD.

The emulator stalls during startup

After five minutes or so, you don't see Android's device locked screen or Android's home screen. Here are several things you can try:

✦ **Lather, rinse, repeat.**

Close the emulator and launch your application again. Sometimes, the second or third time's a charm. On rare occasions, my first three attempts fail, but my fourth attempt succeeds.

✦ **Restart the Android Debug Bridge (adb) server.**

Follow the instructions in the earlier section "You lose contact with the Android debug bridge (adb)." And while you're restarting things, it never hurts to restart Android Studio.

✦ **If you have a more powerful computer, try running your app on it.**

Horsepower matters.

✦ **Run your app on a real Android device.**

Testing a brand-new app on a real device makes me queasy. But Android's sandbox is fairly safe for apps to play in. Besides, apps load quickly and easily on real phones and tablets.

For instructions on installing apps to real Android devices, see the section "Testing Apps on a Real Device," later in this chapter.

✦ **Try the Genymotion emulator.**

For news about Genymotion, see Chapter 2 in this minibook.

✦ **Switch to an Android Virtual Device with a lower resolution and screen density.**

In my experience, older AVDs consume fewer resources on your development computer. So, if an AVD drags you down, follow the instructions in the earlier section "You don't like whatever AVD opens automatically." Then, when you run an app, Android Studio prompts you with a Choose Device dialog box. Pick an AVD with the lowest API level (one that satisfies your app's minimum SDK requirement), and you'll be on your way.

You can lower an app's target and minimum SDK version by editing the app's build.gradle file. But if your app requires features that aren't available in the lower target or SDK version, you won't be happy with the results. In the best case, Android Studio displays an error message as soon as you make the change. In the worst case, you see no error message until you try to run the app. When you try to run the app, it crashes.

Error message: The user data image is used by another emulator

If you see this message, some tangle involving the emulator keeps Android from doing its job. First try closing and restarting the emulator.

If a simple restart doesn't work, try the following steps:

1. **Close the emulator.**

2. **In Android Studio's main menu, choose Tools ➪ Android ➪ AVD Manager.**

3. **In the list of virtual devices, look for the AVD that's causing you trouble.**

4. **In the Actions column, click the tiny downward-pointing arrow associated with that AVD. (See Figure 3-13.)**

   A context menu appears.

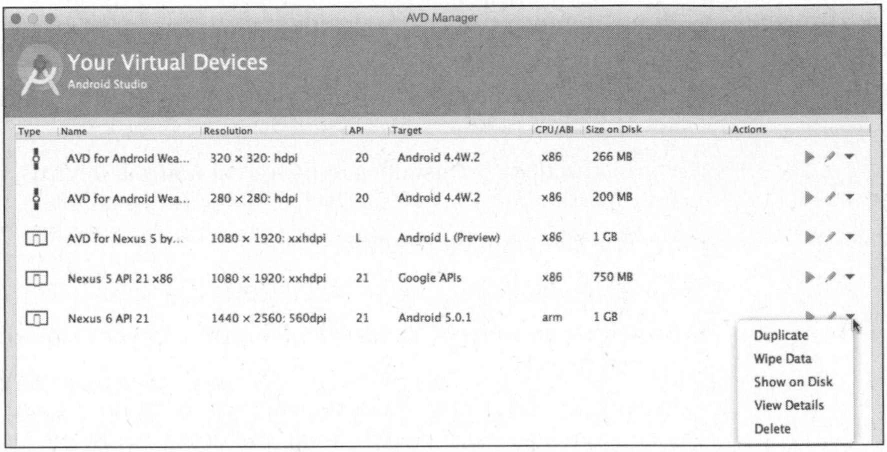

Figure 3-13: Using the Actions icons in the AVD Manager.

Type	Name	Resolution	API	Target	CPU/ABI	Size on Disk	Actions
	AVD for Android Wea...	320 × 320: hdpi	20	Android 4.4W.2	x86	266 MB	▶ ✎ ▼
	AVD for Android Wea...	280 × 280: hdpi	20	Android 4.4W.2	x86	200 MB	▶ ✎ ▼
	AVD for Nexus 5 by...	1080 × 1920: xxhdpi	L	Android L (Preview)	x86	1 GB	▶ ✎ ▼
	Nexus 5 API 21 x86	1080 × 1920: xxhdpi	21	Google APIs	x86	750 MB	▶ ✎ ▼
	Nexus 6 API 21	1440 × 2560: 560dpi	21	Android 5.0.1	arm	1 GB	▶ ✎ ▼

Duplicate
Wipe Data
Show on Disk
View Details
Delete

5. **In the context menu, select Wipe Data.**

   A pop-up dialog box appears. The dialog box asks you to confirm the wiping of the AVD's data.

6. **In the Confirm Data Wipe pop-up dialog box, click Yes.**

   The pop-up dialog box disappears (as you thought it would).

7. **In the Actions column, click the right-pointing arrow (the arrow that looks like a Play button).**

   As a result, Android Studio launches a new copy of the emulator, this time with a clean slate.

To read about the Android Virtual Device (AVD) Manager, see Chapter 2 in this minibook.

If the preceding set of steps doesn't work, take a firmer approach, as follows:

1. **Close the emulator.**

2. **Open whatever file explorer your computer uses to track down files.**

3. **In your user home directory, look for a folder named** .android **(starting with a dot).**

   For tips on finding your user home folder, see Chapter 2 in this mini-book.

4. **From the** .android **directory, drill down even deeper into the** avd **directory.**

   The avd directory contains a folder for each AVD that you've created.

5. **Drill down one more level to the directory for the AVD that's giving you trouble.**

   For example, if you were running an AVD named *Froyo1* when you saw the Data Image Is Used by Another Emulator message, navigate to your Froyo1.avd directory.

6. **Inside your AVD's directory, delete all the files whose names end with** .lock.

7. **Return to Android Studio and run your app again.**

Error message: Unknown virtual device name

Android looks for AVDs in your home directory's .android/avd subdirectory, and occasionally Android's search goes awry. For example, one of my Windows computers lists my home directory on an i drive. My AVDs are in i:\Users\bburd\.android\avd. But Android ignores the computer's home directory advice and instead looks in c:\Users\bburd. When Android doesn't find any AVDs, Android complains.

You can devise fancy solutions to this problem with *junctions* or *symbolic links*. But fancy solutions require special handling of their own. So I prefer to keep things simple. I copy my i:\Users\bburd\.android directory's contents to c:\Users\bburd\.android. That fixes the problem.

Error message: INSTALL_PARSE_FAILED_INCONSISTENT_CERTIFICATE

This error message indicates that an app that you previously installed conflicts with the app that you're trying to install. So, on the emulator screen, choose Settings ⇨ Apps. This brings up a list of apps installed on your AVD. In the list of applications, delete any apps that you installed previously.

If you have trouble finding your previously installed apps, you can uninstall apps using the adb tool in your development computer's command window. For example, the following exchange in the Windows command prompt deletes the app that I put in the com.allmycode.menus Java package.

(The stuff that I type is in boldface type. Other stuff is the computer's response.)

```
C:\>adb shell
# cd data
cd data
# cd app
cd app
# rm com.allmycode.menus.apk
rm com.allmycode.menus.apk
# exit
```

The emulator displays a "process isn't responding" dialog box

The formal name for this dialog box is the *Application Not Responding* (ANR) dialog box. Android displays the ANR dialog box when an app takes too long to do whatever it's supposed to do. When your app runs on a real device (a phone or a tablet device), the app shouldn't make Android display the ANR dialog box. (Other chapters in this minibook give you tips on how to avoid the dialog box.)

But on a slow emulator, a few ANR boxes are par for the course. When I see the ANR dialog box in an emulator, I usually select Wait. Within about ten seconds, the dialog box disappears, and the app continues to run.

Changes to your app don't appear in the emulator

Your app runs and you want to make a few improvements. So, with the emulator still running, you modify your app's code. But after choosing Run ➪ Run 'app', the app's behavior in the emulator remains unchanged.

When this happens, something is clogged up. Close and restart the emulator. If necessary, use the Wipe User Data trick that I describe in the section "Error message: The user data image is used by another emulator," earlier in this chapter.

The emulator's screen is too big

This happens when your development computer's screen resolution isn't high enough. (Maybe your eyesight isn't what it used to be.) This symptom isn't a deal breaker, but if you can't see the emulator's Home and Back buttons, you can't easily test your app. You can change the development computer's screen resolution, but adjusting the emulator window's size is less invasive.

Here's how you change the emulator window's size:

1. **In Android Studio's main menu, choose Tools ⇨ Android ⇨ AVD Manager.**

2. **In the list of virtual devices, look for the offending AVD (the AVD that takes up too much room on your development computer's screen).**

3. **In the Actions column, click the tiny pencil icon associated with your AVD. (Refer to Figure 3-13.)**

   The image of a pencil suggests that you're editing something. In particular, you're editing the properties of this AVD.

   In response to your icon click, a dialog box (labeled Virtual Device Configuration) appears.

4. **In the Virtual Device Configuration dialog box, look for the Startup Size and Orientation section.**

5. **In the Startup Size and Orientation section, look for the Scale drop-down list.**

6. **In the Scale drop-down list, select one of the ratios.**

   A ratio of *2dp on device = 1px on screen* means that two of the phone's pixels or tablet's pixels are squeezed into only one of your development computer screen's pixels. One way or another, you might have to try out a few of these ratios to figure out which ratio is best for you.

In your Android-related travels, you might see a fractional value (such as 0.75) for the emulator's scale. With a scale of 0.75, the emulator appears at three quarters of its normal size. The value for this scale option can be any number from 0.1 to 3.0. The scale 0.75 means that three computer screen pixels represent four Android device pixels. And the default scale of 1.0 means that each computer screen pixel represents exactly one Android device pixel.

In this section, my talk about *2dp = 1px* and an emulator's "normal size" isn't entirely accurate. For one thing, *2dp* doesn't really stand for two phone pixels or tablet pixels. Instead, it stands for two *device independent pixels*, (whatever they are). For another thing, a pixel on your computer screen doesn't take up the same amount of space as a pixel on your phone or tablet screen. So even with a *1dp = 1px* ratio or with a 1.0 scale, an emulator might be quite larger than the physical device that it's emulating.

To find out what a device-independent pixel is, see Book IV, Chapter 1.

In this section, I tell you how to troubleshoot the run of the Hello World app. But of course, there are always more things you can try. For more trouble-shooting advice, see my tidbits scattered throughout this book. Also visit `http://developer.android.com/resources/faq/troubleshooting.html`. And if you run into a problem that you can't overcome, shoot me an email, a Facebook post, or a tweet. My contact info is in the introduction to this book.

Testing Apps on a Real Device

You can bypass emulators and test your apps on a phone, a tablet device, or maybe an Android-enabled refrigerator. To do so, you have to prepare the device, prepare your development computer, and then hook together the two. This section describes the process.

Your device's Android version must be at least as high as your project's minimum SDK version.

The simplest way to test your app on a real device is to connect the device to your development computer using a USB cable. Not all USB cables are cre-ated equal. Some cables have wires and metal in places where other cables (with compatible fittings) have nothing except plastic. Try to use whatever USB cable came with your Android device. If, like me, you can't find the cable that came with your device or you don't know which cable came with your device, try more than one cable. When you find a cable that works, label that able cable. (If the cable *always* works, then label it stable, able cable.)

To test your app on a real device, follow these steps:

1. **On your Android device, find the USB Debugging option:**

   - If your Android device runs version 3.2 or older, choose Settings ⇨ Applications ⇨ Development.

   - If your Android device runs version 4.0, 4.0.3, or 4.1, choose Settings ⇨ Developer Options.

   - If your Android device runs version 4.2 or higher, choose Settings ⇨ About. In the About list, tap the Build Number item seven times. (Yes, seven times.) Then press the Back button to return to the Settings list. In the Settings list, tap Developer Options.

   Now your Android device displays the Development list (aka the Developer Options list).

2. **In the Development (or Developer Options) list, turn on USB debugging.**

Here's what my KitKat device displays when I mess with this setting:

```
USB debugging is intended for development purposes. Use it to copy data
between your computer and your device, install apps on your device without
notification, and read log data.
```

The stewards of Android are warning me that the USB Debugging option can expose my device to malware.

On my device, I keep USB Debugging on all the time. But if you're very nervous about security, turn off USB Debugging when you're not using the device to develop apps.

3. **Set up your development computer to communicate with the device.**

• *On Windows:* Visit `http://developer.android.com/sdk/ oem-usb.html` to download your device's Windows USB driver. Install the driver on your development computer.

• *On a Mac:* /* Do nothing. It just works. */

• *On Linux:* Visit `http://developer.android.com/guide/ developing/device.html` and follow the instructions that you find on that page. (Don't worry. To connect a device, you don't have to recompile the Linux kernel.)

4. **On your development computer, make sure that your IDE displays the Android Device Chooser or Choose Device dialog box when you run an app.**

To do this, follow the instructions in the earlier section "You don't like whatever AVD opens automatically."

5. **Make sure that your Android device's screen is illuminated.**

This particular step might not be necessary, but I've scrapped so many knuckles trying to get Android devices to connect with computers that I want every advantage I can possibly get.

While you follow the next step, keep an eye on your Android device's screen.

6. **With a USB cable, connect the device to the development computer.**

When you plug in the cable, you see a pop-up dialog box on the Android device's screen. The pop-up asks "Allow USB Debugging?"

7. **In response to the "Allow USB Debugging?" question, click OK.**

If you're not looking for it, you can miss the "Allow USB Debugging?" pop-up dialog box. Be sure to look for this pop-up when you plug in your device. If you definitely don't see the pop-up, you might be okay anyway. But if the message appears and you don't respond to it, you definitely won't be okay.

8. **Check the connection between your computer and your Android device.**

   To find out whether your device is connected to the computer, open a command window on the computer. (On Windows, run `cmd`. On a Mac, run the Terminal app.)

   In the command window, navigate to the computer's *ANDROID_HOME/*`platform-tools` directory and then type **adb devices**. (On a Mac or a Linux computer, type **./adb devices**.) If your computer's response includes a very long hexadecimal number, that number represents your connected device. For example, with my Galaxy Tab connected, my computer's response is

   ```
   emulator-5554   device
   emulator-5556   device
   2885046445FF097 device
   ```

   If you see the word *unauthorized* next to the long hexadecimal number, you probably didn't answer OK to the "Allow USB Debugging?" question in Step 7.

9. **In Android Studio, run your project.**

   Android Studio offers you a Choose Device dialog box or an Android Device Chooser dialog box. Select your connected device and (lickety-split) your app starts running on your Android device.

Eventually, you'll want to disconnect your device from the development computer. If you're a Windows user, you dread reading Windows Can't Stop Your Device Because a Program Is Still Using It. To disconnect your device, first issue the `adb kill-server` command as described in the earlier section "You lose contact with the Android debug bridge (`adb`)." After that, you get the friendly Safe to Remove Hardware message.

Chapter 4: Examining a Basic Android App

In This Chapter

✔ Finding your app's activities, layouts, menus, and other stuff

✔ Assigning names to things

✔ Choosing API levels

In Chapter 3 of this minibook, you run Android Studio to create a skeletal Android app. The skeletal app doesn't do much, but the app has all the elements you need for getting started with Android. You get a basic activity (a screen full of stuff for the user to look at). You get an elementary layout for your activity. You get an icon or two, and a little text thingy that says *Hello world!* You can even run the new app on an emulator or on a real Android device.

Unfortunately, this skeletal app contains many, many parts. The last time I checked, the skeletal app had 66 files and 119 different directories. All this just to display *Hello world!* on a mobile device's small screen!

So before you plunge headlong into Android development, you can pause to take a look at this skeletal app. Open Android Studio, make sure that the app from Chapter 3 is showing in the main window, and take this chapter's ten-cent tour of the app.

A Project's Files

Figure 4-1 shows a run of the skeletal app that Android Studio creates for you, and Figure 4-2 shows some of the files in this simple Android project. The tree in Figure 4-2 contains a manifests branch, a java branch, a res branch, and some other stuff.

Notice the word Android at the top of Figure 4-2. Under the word Android, you see a tree containing several branches. This tree with its Android title is called the Project tool window. Whenever you look at the Project tool window, you see one of its many views, including the Android view (which is showing in Figure 4-2), the Packages view, and the Project view. You might also see Project Files, Problems, Production, or Tests. (And while you're seeing things, see Figure 4-3.)

Figure 4-1:
A run of the app created by Android Studio.

Figure 4-2:
The structure of a new project in Android Studio.

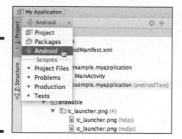

Figure 4-3:
Options
for the
Project tool
window.

On your own computer screen, look for the word Android at the top of the
Project tool window. If, instead of Android, you see the word Project, the
word Packages, or some other word, click that word. When you do, you
see a drop-down list, as shown in Figure 4-3. In that drop-down list, select
the Android option.

For more information about the Project tool window's views, see the sidebar
entitled "The many faces of Android Studio," later in this chapter.

The official Android Studio terminology can be confusing. The Project view
isn't the only view that belongs to the Project tool window.

The next several sections describe the files (and the branches of the tree) in
the Project tool window shown in Figure 4-2.

Trees, branches, files, and folders

The tree shown in Figure 4-2 can be misleading. Trees of this kind normally show up in your
operating system's File Explorer or Finder. In
the File Explorer and the Finder, branches
represent either files on your hard drive or
directories (also known as *folders*) containing
the files.

This story about files and folders is only partially true of the tree in Figure 4-2. For example,
when you create an Android app, your hard
drive contains a `res` folder, which in turn contains `layout`, `menu`, and `values` subfolders. That structure is very much like the tree in
Figure 4-2. But unlike the tree in Figure 4-2, your

hard drive's `res` folder might have subfolders
named `values-v21` and `values-
w820dp`. And instead of living directly inside
an `app` branch (as in Figure 4-2), the `res`
folder on your hard drive is inside a `main`
folder, which is inside a `src` folder, which is
(finally) inside an `app` folder.

The tree in the Android Project view presents
an abstracted picture of your app's files. You
don't see files and folders as you would in
Windows File Explorer or Macintosh Finder.
Instead, you see a hierarchy that helps
you understand the roles of the files in your
Android app.

The MainActivity.java file

Your app can have files named `MainActivity.java`, `MyService.java`, `DatabaseHelper.java`, `MoreStuff.java`, and so on. In fact, you can cram hundreds of Java files into a project. But when you create a new project, Android Studio typically creates one activity's `.java` file for you. In Chapter 3 of this minibook, when I create an Android project, I accept the default name `MainActivity`, so Android Studio creates a file named `MainActivity.java`. Listing 4-1 shows you the code in the `MainActivity.java` file.

Listing 4-1: Android Studio Creates This Skeletal Activity Class

```
package com.example.myapplication;

import android.app.Activity;
import android.os.Bundle;
import android.view.Menu;
import android.view.MenuItem;


public class MainActivity extends Activity {

  @Override
  protected void onCreate(Bundle savedInstanceState) {
    super.onCreate(savedInstanceState);
    setContentView(R.layout.activity_main);
  }


  @Override
  public boolean onCreateOptionsMenu(Menu menu) {
    getMenuInflater().inflate(R.menu.menu_main, menu);
    return true;
  }

  @Override
  public boolean onOptionsItemSelected(MenuItem item) {
    int id = item.getItemId();

    if (id == R.id.action_settings) {
     return true;
    }

    return super.onOptionsItemSelected(item);
  }
}
```

What you see in your editor might be different from the code in Listing 4-1. For example, you might see the line

```
import android.support.v7.app.ActionBarActivity;
```

You might also see

```
public class MainActivity extends ActionBarActivity
```

in place of the reference to Activity in Listing 4-1. Rest assured that, here in Chapter 4, the differences don't matter.

An Android *activity* is one "screenful" of components. Think of an activity as a form — perhaps a form for entering information to make a purchase on a website. Unlike most online forms, Android activities don't necessarily have text boxes — places for the user to type credit card numbers and such. But Android activities have a lot in common with online forms. When you extend the android.app.Activity class (or the similar ActionBarActivity class), you create a new Android activity.

For more information about Java, see Book II, Chapters 2, 3, and 4.

An Android application can contain many activities. For example, an app's initial activity might list the films playing in your area. When you click a film's title, Android then covers the entire list activity with another activity (perhaps an activity displaying a relevant film review).

Having one activity overlay another activity is typical of small phone screens. But on larger tablet screens, you can display a list of films and a particular film review side by side. Having side-by-side panels is a job for *fragments* rather than activities. To read about fragments, see Book V, Chapter 1.

Here's another (possibly surprising) thing to keep in mind: An Android app can invoke an activity belonging to a different app. For example, your app might display a Help button, and pressing Help might open a web page. With the web page housed somewhere on the Internet, your app's button fires up an activity belonging to Android's built-in web browser application. In the Android world, applications don't bogart their activities.

Every Android activity has a lifecycle — a set of stages that the activity undergoes from birth to death to rebirth, and so on. I describe the activity lifecycle in Book III, Chapter 1. But in this chapter, you get a peek at the activity lifecycle with the method onCreate in Listing 4-1.

The onCreate method

When Android creates an activity, Android calls the activity's onCreate method. This happens much more often than you'd think, because Android destroys and then re-creates activities while the user navigates from place to place. For example, if your phone runs low on memory, Android can kill some running activities. When you navigate back to a killed activity, Android re-creates the activity for you. The same thing happens when you turn the phone from portrait to landscape mode. If the developer doesn't override the default behavior, Android destroys an activity and re-creates the activity before displaying the activity in the other mode.

In Listing 4-1, the `onCreate` method has things named `savedInstanceState` and `R.layout.activity_main`.

✦ **The** `savedInstanceState` **variable stores information about some of the activity's values when the activity was previously destroyed.**

The statement `super.onCreate(savedInstanceState)` tells Android to restore those previous values. This way, the activity takes up where it last left off.

During what appears to the user to be a continuous run, Android might destroy and re-create an activity several times. An activity's `savedInstanceState` helps to maintain continuity between destructions and re-creations.

To be precise, the statement `super.onCreate(savedInstanceState)` calls the parent class's `onCreate` method. To read more about parent classes in Java, see Book II, Chapter 2.

✦ **The method parameter** `R.layout.activity_main` **is a roundabout way of coding the buttons, text fields, and the way they're all laid out.**

In Listing 4-1, the call to `setContentView` plops these buttons, text fields, images, and other stuff on the activity screen. For more about this, check the section "The R.java file", later in this chapter.

The onCreateOptionsMenu method

With a new Android activity comes a new menu. For older Android versions, a separate menu button is somewhere on (or near) the device's screen. But starting with Honeycomb, apps put a menu icon in an *action bar*. (In Figure 4-1, the activity's menu icon has three vertically-aligned dots. The icon appears in the screen's upper-right corner.)

✦ **In Listing 4-1, the call** `getMenuInflater().inflate(R.menu.menu_main, menu)` **does the same for the look of your menu items as a call to** `setContentView` **does for the overall look of your activity.**

The call puts items (and perhaps sub-items) in your app's menu.

✦ **The last statement inside the** `onCreateOptionsMenu` **method (the** `return true` **statement) tells Android to display your app's menu.**

If, for some reason, you don't want Android to display the menu, change this statement to `return false`.

In Listing 4-1, the `onCreateOptionsMenu` method creates your activity's menu. That's fine, but what happens when the user taps a menu item? When the user taps an item, Android calls your activity's `onOptionsItemSelected` method.

The onOptionsItemSelected method

In Listing 4-1, the `onOptionsItemSelected` method doesn't do too much.

✦ **The call to** `item.getItemId()` **grabs the code number of whatever item the user tapped.**

For some good reading about Android's use of code numbers, see the section "The R.java file," later in this chapter.

✦ **When your IDE creates a skeletal app, the app has one menu item named** `action_settings`. **The code in Listing 4-1 checks to find out if the user tapped this** `action_settings` **item.**

In a real-world app, the code would check to find out which of several menu items the user tapped.

✦ **Returning** `true` **tells Android that the tapping of this menu item has been handled. No further action is necessary.**

A return value of `false` would mean that some other code should do something in response to the user's tap.

✦ **Finally, the** `super.onOptionsItemSelected(item)` **call tells Android to do, with this menu item tap, whatever Android normally does by default for any old menu item tap.**

This is no big deal because, by default, Android does almost nothing.

To make use of the code in Listing 4-1, you have to know something about Java. For a big blast of Java, visit Book II, Chapters 2, 3, and 4.

The res branch

In this section, I'm plugging along and exploring the branches in the Project tool window's tree in Figure 4-2. The project's `res` branch (a branch within the `app` branch) contains resources for use by the project's Android application. The `res` branch has sub-branches named `drawable`, `layout`, `menu`, `mipmap`, and `values`.

The many faces of Android Studio

The res branch in the Project tool window displays the contents of a directory on your computer's hard drive. In fact, if you look for this directory in your operating system's File Explorer or Finder, you'll see a *MyApplication*/app/src/main/res directory. But if you look at the Project tool window, you may see only a res branch within an app branch. What's going on here?

The Project tool window has several views, including the Android view, the Project view, and the Packages view. Each view shows (basically) the same stuff, but each view organizes this stuff a bit differently.

✔ When the Project tool window displays its Android view, the res branch has sub-branches with simple names (such as drawable and values). But the directory on your hard drive has subdirectories named drawable, drawable-hdpi, drawable-xhdpi, values, values-v21, and others. In the Android view, the Project tool window presents an abstracted (or *developer-centric*) view of the files on your hard drive.

✔ When the Project tool window displays its Packages view, directories such as drawable, drawable-hdpi, values, and values-v21 appear immediately inside the app branch of the tree.

✔ When the Project tool window displays its Project view, you see (more or less) what you'd see in your operating system's File Explorer or Finder. That is, you see a res branch inside a main branch, which is inside a src branch, and so on. You also see sub-branches named drawable, drawable-hdpi, and so on.

To switch from one view to another, look for the button that appears atop the Project tool window. Click that button and select an option in the resulting drop-down list. (Refer to Figure 4-3.)

The res/drawable branch

The drawable branch contains images, shapes, and other such things. A single drawable item might come in several different sizes, each with its own dpi (dots per inch) level. The sizes include *mdpi* (a medium number of dots per inch), *hdpi* (a high number of dots per inch), *xhdpi* (extra high), and *xxhdpi* (extra-extra high). I wonder how many "*xs*" we'll need when Android starts powering digital displays on Times Square!

For more reading about drawables, visit, Book IV, Chapter 1.

The res/layout branch

The layout branch contains descriptions of your activities' screens.

A minimal app's layout branch contains an XML file describing an activity's screen. (See the activity_main.xml branch in Figure 4-2.) Listing 4-2 shows the code in the simple activity_main.xml file.

Listing 4-2:   A Small Layout File

```
<RelativeLayout xmlns:android=
        "http://schemas.android.com/apk/res/android"
    xmlns:tools="http://schemas.android.com/tools"
    android:layout_width="match_parent"
    android:layout_height="match_parent"
    android:paddingBottom="16dp"
    android:paddingLeft="16dp"
    android:paddingRight="16dp"
    android:paddingTop="16dp"
    tools:context=".MainActivity">

    <TextView
        android:layout_width="wrap_content"
        android:layout_height="wrap_content"
        android:text="Hello world!" />

</RelativeLayout>
```

An Android app consists of Java code, XML documents, and other stuff. The
XML code in Listing 4-2 describes a *relative layout.* (In a relative layout, each
element's position is relative to the positions of other elements. So buttons
and text fields appear to the right of one another, to the left of one another,
below one another, and so on.) Because of its `match_parent` attributes,
the layout is large enough to fill its surroundings. Its "surroundings" are the
entire screen (minus a few doodads on the edges of the screen).

In Listing 4-2, the only item inside the relative layout is an instance of
`TextView` — a place to display text on the screen. Because of the `wrap_
content` attributes, the text view is only wide enough and only tall enough
to enclose whatever characters it displays.

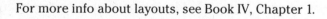

For more info about layouts, see Book IV, Chapter 1.

What you see isn't what you get

When you look at the `activity_main.xml` text in Android Studio's editor,
you see the stuff in Listing 4-2. But you can also visit the `activity_main.
xml` file using Windows File Explorer or Mac Finder. You can open this file
with Windows Notepad or Mac TextEdit. When you do, you see the text in
Listing 4-3.

Listing 4-3:   The Real activity_main.xml File

```
<RelativeLayout xmlns:android=
        "http://schemas.android.com/apk/res/android"
    xmlns:tools="http://schemas.android.com/tools"
    android:layout_width="match_parent"
    android:layout_height="match_parent"
```

```
      android:paddingBottom="@dimen/activity_vertical_margin"
      android:paddingLeft="@dimen/activity_horizontal_margin"
      android:paddingRight="@dimen/activity_horizontal_margin"
      android:paddingTop="@dimen/activity_vertical_margin"
      tools:context=".MainActivity">

    <TextView
        android:layout_width="wrap_content"
        android:layout_height="wrap_content"
        android:text="@string/hello_world" />

</RelativeLayout>
```

What you see in Listing 4-3 is the text that's really in the app's activity_ main.xml file. But what you typically see in Android Studio's editor isn't the same as the text in Listing 4-3. (In Listing 4-3, the text that I've set in bold is different from what you see in Android Studio's editor.)

Android Studio's editor doesn't show you all the text (and only the text) in a file such as activity_main.xml. Instead, the editor replaces some expressions with the values of those expressions. It's like displaying the number *42* when the actual file contains the text 20 + 22.

✦ **In the** activity_main.xml **file, the value of the expression** @dimen/ activity_vertical_margin **is 16.**

That's why you see @dimen/activity_vertical_margin in Listing 4-3, but you see 16 in Listing 4-2.

To be more precise, the expression @dimen/activity_vertical_ margin stands for *16 device independent pixels* (16dp). To find out what a device independent pixel is, see Book IV, Chapter 1.

✦ **In the** activity_main.xml **file, the value of the expression** @string/ hello_world **is** Hello world!

To find out why @dimen/activity_vertical_margin stands for 16dp and why @string/hello_world stands for Hello world, see the section "The res/values branch," later in this chapter.

In Android Studio's editor, things like "16dp" appear as light-gray characters. The light-gray shade indicates that the editor isn't showing you the text that's really in the activity_main.xml file (the text that you'd probably type if you were composing this code from scratch).

✦ If you hover over the light-gray text, a pop-up shows you the text that's really in the file.

✦ If you click on the light-gray text, Android Studio replaces it with the text that's really in the file. Instead of seeing Hello world! in light gray, you see @string/hello_world in an off shade of green.

✦ (Here's the thing that drove me crazy until I figured out what was going on.) You can select the text in the Android Studio editor, copy that stuff to the Clipboard, and then paste it into a regular editor (Windows Notepad, Mac TextEdit, or whatever). When you do, you don't necessarily see whatever you see in Android Studio's editor. You see `@dimen/activity_vertical_margin` instead of `16dp`, and you see `@string/hello_world` instead of `Hello world!` (As an author who regularly copies and pastes material into a Word document, this behavior sends me running and screaming!)

The res/menu branch

Each file in the `menu` branch describes a menu belonging to your app. The simple app that your IDE creates contains only one menu. The file to describe that menu is named `menu_main.xml`.

Listing 4-4 contains the bare-bones `menu_main.xml` file.

Listing 4-4:   The menu_main.xml Menu File

```
<menu xmlns:android=
             "http://schemas.android.com/apk/res/android"
  xmlns:tools="http://schemas.android.com/tools"
  tools:context="com.example.myapplication.MainActivity" >

  <item
    android:id="@+id/action_settings"
    android:orderInCategory="100"
    android:showAsAction="never"
    android:title="Settings"/>

</menu>
```

The menu contains only one item, and in other parts of this app's code, you refer to that item by the name `action_settings`.

Android Studio's editor doesn't show you exactly what's in the `menu_main.xml` file. Where you see `android:title="Settings"` in Listing 4-4 (and in Android Studio's editor), the file really contains the text `android:title="@string/action_settings"`. The expression `@string/action_settings` has a value, and that value is the word `Settings`. For more information about `@string` expressions, see the "The res/values branch" section.

For more info about menus, see Book IV, Chapter 2.

The res/mipmap branch

The `res/mipmap` branch is like the `res/drawable` branch, except that the `res/mipmap` branch contains your app's icons. The term *mipmap* stands for *multum in parvo* mapping. And the Latin phrase *multum in parvo* means "much in little." A *mipmap* image contains copies of textures for many different screen resolutions.

The `mipmap` folder was introduced in Android 4.3, so you don't see it in older Android apps (including some of this book's apps).

The res/values branch

The files in the `values` branch describe miscellaneous things that an app needs to know. For example, Listing 4-3 shows you what's actually in your app's `activity_main.xml` file. In that file, the `@string/hello_world` attribute tells Android what text to display inside the TextView element. In Figure 4-1, these words happen to be Hello world! To find out how `@string/hello_world` gets turned into Hello world!, and how Hello world! gets to be displayed as part of your app, see Figure 4-4.

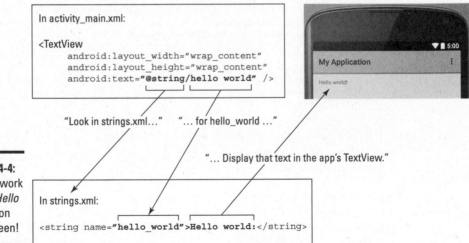

Figure 4-4: All this work to put *Hello world!* on the screen!

Why does the `activity_main.xml` file contain the following cryptic line?

```
android:text="@string/hello_world"
```

Why don't you simply code

```
android:text="Hello World!"
```

in the `activity_main.xml` file (the way the editor displays the file in Listing 4-2)?

Here's why: If you create a good Android app, people all around the world download your app. These people speak many different languages, so you don't put actual words (like *Hello world!*) in your app's Java code or even in your app's `activity_main.xml` layout file. Instead, you put `Hello world!` in your `res/values/strings.xml` file. Then, to localize your app for French, you put `Bonjour tout le monde!` in a `res/values-fr/strings.xml` file. To localize your app for Romanian, you put `Salut lume!` in a `res/values-ro/strings.xml` file.

Listing 4-5 shows the code in the simple `strings.xml` file.

Listing 4-5:   A Small strings.xml File

```xml
<?xml version="1.0" encoding="utf-8"?>
<resources>

    <string name="app_name">My Application</string>
    <string name="hello_world">Hello world!</string>
    <string name="action_settings">Settings</string>

</resources>
```

In Listing 4-5, the line

```xml
<string name="hello_world">Hello world!</string>
```

tells Android that, in other parts of the app's code, the expressions `@string/hello_world` and `R.string.hello_world` refer to the words *Hello world!*

In an Android app, one string of characters, such as `Hello world!` goes by many different names. Listing 4-5 describes a `"hello_world"` string containing the characters `Hello world!`. To refer to that `"hello_world"` string in Listing 4-1 (a `.java` file), you type **R.string.hello_world**. To refer to the same `"hello_world"` string in another XML file (such as the file in Listing 4-2), you type **@string/hello_world**. With either `@string/hello_world` or `R.string.hello_world`, you refer to the thing named `"hello_world"` (the thing in Listing 4-5). And, either way, you point to the words `Hello world!` in Figure 4-1. (Yes, it can be confusing. I've dealt with this string-naming business for several years, but I still have to stop and think about it.)

In Listing 4-5, expressions such as `@dimen/activity_horizontal_margin` work the same way as the `@string` expression. The `app/res/values` branch in the Project tool window contains a `dimens.xml` branch.

That `dimens.xml` branch typically contains two `dimens.xml` files. These `dimens.xml` files contain lines such as

```
<dimen name="activity_horizontal_margin">16dp</dimen>
```

When a device runs your app, the device substitutes an actual value (such as `16dp` — 16 device independent pixels) for the expression `@dimen/activity_horizontal_margin` in your `activity_main.xml` file. With this substitution trick, a single `activity_main.xml` file works for screens of many shapes and sizes. To accommodate a certain screen size, a device consults one of your app's `dimens.xml` files.

To read all about XML documents, like the ones in Listings 4-2 through 4-5, see Book II, Chapter 5.

Other files in an Android project

A simple Android app contains dozens of files. Many of these files appear in the Android view (in the Project tool window). Some of the files that don't appear are still worth knowing about.

The build.gradle file

Gradle is a software tool. When the tool runs, it takes a whole bunch of files and combines them to form a complete application. For example, a run of Gradle can use the files shown in Figure 4-2 to build a single `.apk` file for posting on Google's Play store. Of course, Gradle can combine files in many different ways, so to get Gradle to do things properly, someone has to provide Gradle with a script of some kind.

A new Android app comes with its own ready-made script. In Figure 4-2, that script appears in the branch labeled `build.gradle (Module: app)`.

Listing 4-6 shows the contents of a simple app's `build.gradle` file.

Listing 4-6:   A Little build.gradle File

```
apply plugin: 'com.android.application'

android {
    compileSdkVersion 21
    buildToolsVersion "21.1.2"

    defaultConfig {
        applicationId "com.example.myapplication"
        minSdkVersion 15
        targetSdkVersion 21
        versionCode 1
        versionName "1.0"
    }
```

```
buildTypes {
    release {
        minifyEnabled false
        proguardFiles getDefaultProguardFile
          ('proguard-android.txt'), 'proguard-rules.pro'
    }
  }
}

dependencies {
compile fileTree(dir: 'libs', include: ['*.jar'])
}
```

I cover some `build.gradle` code in the section "Your app's API levels,"
later in this chapter. So, in this section, I describe only a few of the listing's
highlights.

An app's versions

In Listing 4-6, the `versionCode` and `versionName` properties have similar
(but slightly different) meanings.

✦ The `versionCode` property is an integer. For publication on the Google
Play Store, the `versionCode` must increase from one version of your
app to another. The numbers don't have to be consecutive. So your
first published version can have `versionCode` 47, and the next
published version can be number 63. The app's user doesn't see the
`versionCode`.

✦ The `versionName` can be any string of characters, so this attribute's
value is largely cosmetic. The user sees the `versionName`.

Listing 4-6 contains values for an app's `compileSdkVersion`, `minSdk-`
`Version`, and `targetSdkVersion`. To find out what these SDK versions
are, see the section "Your app's API levels," later in this chapter.

What is ProGuard?

Obfuscation is a way of making your Java code difficult to understand (which
makes the code difficult to steal, difficult to modify, and difficult to infect),
and *ProGuard* is a tool that can obfuscate your Java programs. In order
to obfuscate your code, Android Studio needs to configure the ProGuard
tool. Listing 4-6 says that this configuration information lives in files named
`proguard-android.txt` and `progard-rules.pro`. (You can peek at the
`proguard-rules.pro` file by switching to the Project view in the Project
tool window.)

To read about ProGuard's role in Android app development, see Book VI,
Chapter 1.

Oh! For the good old days!

Before Android Studio came along, developers used Eclipse, and Eclipse didn't create `build.gradle` files. For that matter, Eclipse didn't use the Gradle build tool at all. Because of this, Eclipse's counterpart to the tree in Figure 4-2 looked quite different from what you see there. Eclipse organized files and folders differently from the structure in Figure 4-2. So an Android project built in the Eclipse days doesn't easily fit into the Android Studio IDE.

If you come across an old Eclipse Android project (a project with no `build.gradle` file), and you need to work with that project, you have two choices.

✔ **You can install Eclipse on your development computer.**

To do so, visit `http://eclipse.org` and download Eclipse for Java Developers. After installing Eclipse for Java Developers, follow the instructions at `http://developer.android.com/sdk/installing/installing-adt.html` to add the ADT (Android Developer Tools) to Eclipse.

✔ **You can import the Eclipse project into Android Studio.**

To do so, choose File ➪ Import Project from Android Studio's main menu. (Alternatively, you can select Import Project in Android Studio's Welcome screen.) Follow the steps in the resulting dialog boxes. (Browse to the directory on your hard drive where the older project resides. When in doubt, accept the defaults and simply click Next.)

The AndroidManifest.xml file

An app's `AndroidManifest.xml` file describes some of the things a device needs in order to run the app. (See Listing 4-7.)

Listing 4-7:   A Little AndroidManifest.xml File

```
<?xml version="1.0" encoding="utf-8"?>
<manifest xmlns:android=
          "http://schemas.android.com/apk/res/android"
  package="com.example.myapplication" >

  <application
    android:allowBackup="true"
    android:icon="@drawable/ic_launcher"
    android:label="@string/app_name"
    android:theme="@style/AppTheme" >
    <activity
```

```
android:name=
    "com.example.myapplication.MainActivity"
android:label="@string/app_name" >
<intent-filter>
  <action android:name=
              "android.intent.action.MAIN" />

  <category android:name=
              "android.intent.category.LAUNCHER" />
  </intent-filter>
</activity>
</application>

</manifest>
```

What you see in Android Studio's editor isn't the same as what I show in Listing 4-7. Some of the text composed by Android Studio changes from one version of Android Studio to the next. In addition, Android Studio's editor might display `android:label="My Application"` with `My Application` in light-gray text. But in place of that text, the `AndroidManifest.xml` file actually contains the reference `android:label="@string/app_name"`.

All Android apps have `AndroidManifest.xml` files. But only newer Android apps have `build.gradle` files. For older apps, information about `versionCode`, `versionName`, and SDK versions lives in the `AndroidManifest.xml` file:

```
<manifest xmlns:android=
  "http://schemas.android.com/apk/res/android"
    package="com.example.myapplication "
    android:versionCode="1"
    android:versionName="1.0">
  <uses-sdk android:minSdkVersion="15"/>
... Etc.
```

The <application> element

In Listing 4-7, the `application` element has several attributes, including `android:icon` and `android:label`. The user sees the application's icon and label on the device's Apps screen. The application's label (and sometimes the icon) appears when one of the app's activities is in the foreground. (See the words My Application in Figure 4-1.)

The <activity> element

In Listing 4-7, the `activity` element has an `android:label` attribute. An app's activity can have its own icon and label, overriding the app's icon and label.

One way or another, an `activity` element in an `AndroidManifest.xml` file must have an `android:name` attribute. The `android:name` attribute has either of the following values:

✦ **The fully qualified name of the activity class.**

In Listing 4-7, the fully qualified name is `com.example.myapplication.MainActivity`.

✦ **The abbreviated activity class name, preceded by a dot.**

The name *.SomeClass* stands for "the class named *SomeClass* in this project's package." So, in Listing 4-7, the following lines work just fine:

```
package="com.example.myapplication"
...
android:name= ".MainActivity"
```

The `manifest` element's `package` attribute isn't in the `android` namespace. In Listing 4-7, I type **package**, not **android:package**. For more information about XML namespaces, see Book II, Chapter 5.

Within an `activity` element, an `intent-filter` element describes the kinds of duties that this activity can fulfill. Intent filters consume an entire chapter (see Book III, Chapter 2). So in this section, I don't dare open the whole intent filter can of worms. But to give you an idea, action `android.intent.action.MAIN` indicates that this activity's code can be the starting point for an app's execution. And the category `android.intent.category.LAUNCHER` indicates that this activity's icon can appear in the device's Apps screen.

If you create a second activity for your app, you must declare the new activity in the app's `AndroidManifest.xml` file. If you don't, your app will crash with an `ActivityNotFoundException`.

The R.java file

Each Android project has an `R.java` file. Android Studio generates this file, and protects this file as if the file were made of gold. You, the developer, never create or modify the `R.java` file's text.

You don't see `R.java` in Figure 4-2 because the `R.java` file doesn't appear in the Android Project view. If you want to see the `R.java` file, switch the Project tool window to its Packages view. Follow the instructions on switching views in the sidebar "The many faces of Android Studio." When the Packages view replaces the Android Project view, visit the `app/com.example.myapplication/test/R` branch in the tree.

Listing 4-8 shows some of the lines in an R.java file.

Listing 4-8:   Don't Even Look at This File

```
/* AUTO-GENERATED FILE.  DO NOT MODIFY.
 *
 * This class was automatically generated by the
 * aapt tool from the resource data it found.  It
 * should not be modified by hand.
 */

package com.example.myapplication;

public final class R {
  public static final class attr {
  }
  public static final class drawable {
    public static final int ic_launcher=0x7f020000;
  }
  public static final class id {
    public static final int action_settings=0x7f080000;
  }
  public static final class layout {
    public static final int activity_main=0x7f030000;
  }
  public static final class menu {
    public static final int main=0x7f070000;
  }
  public static final class string {
    public static final int action_settings=0x7f050002;
    public static final int app_name=0x7f050000;
    public static final int hello_world=0x7f050001;
  }
  // ... There's more stuff here
}
```

The hexadecimal values in an R.java file are the jumping-off points for Android's resource management mechanism. Android uses these numbers for quick and easy loading of the things you store in the res branch. For example, the code in Listing 4-1 sets the look of your activity to R.layout. activity_main, and according to Listing 4-8, R.layout.activity_main has the hex value 0x7f030000.

Android's documentation tells you to put R.java and its hex values out of your mind, and that's probably good advice (advice that I break in this section). Anyway, here are two things to remember about the role of R.java in an Android app:

✦ **You cannot edit** R.java.

   Long after the creation of a project, your IDE continues to monitor (and if necessary, update) the contents of the R.java file. If you delete R.java, Android Studio re-creates the file. If you edit R.java, Android Studio undoes your edit.

✦ **Many of Android's pre-declared methods expect numbers in** `R.java` **as their parameters.**

This can lead to some confusion. Consider the following (very bad) chunk of code:

```
// THIS IS BAD CODE!
System.out.println("42");
System.out.println(42);

textView.setText("42");
textView.setText(42);
```

Java's two `System.out.println` calls (rarely used in Android apps) add text to a log file. In the bad code, the first `System.out.println` sends the string `"42"` to the file, and the second `System.out.println` converts the integer value `42` to the string `"42"` and then sends the string `"42"` to the log file. (Java's `System.out.println` is prepared to print a string, an integer, and various other types of values.) So far, there's nothing wrong with the code. So let's move on . . .

A text view's `setText` method accepts a string parameter or an integer parameter. In the bad code, the call `textView.setText("42")` is okay. But here's the *gotcha*: The integer version of `setText` doesn't convert the integer 42 into a string. Instead, `textView.setText(42)` looks for a resource with code number 42 (in `R.java`, hex value `0x0000002A`). When Android finds nothing with code number 42 in the `R.java` file, your app crashes.

The assets directory

When Android packages an app, a tool named aapt (short for *Android Asset Packaging Tool*) compiles the stuff in the app's `res` directory. In other words, aapt prepares the `res` directory's items for quick retrieval and use. So your application's access to items in the `res` directory is highly optimized.

But before there was Android, there was plain old Java, and plain old Java has its own ways to fetch images and strings. Using Java's techniques, you generally read byte by byte from the Internet or from a device's file system. To make your Android code grab an image or some other data using Java's standard tricks, put the image or data in the Android project's `assets` directory.

By default, an Android Studio project (the kind of project that's displayed in Figure 4-2) doesn't have an `assets` directory. To create such a directory, do the following:

1. **In the Project tool window (Figure 4-2) right-click the app branch at the top of the tree. (If you're a Mac user, control-click that branch.)**

A context menu appears.

2. **In the context menu, choose New ⇨ Folder ⇨ Assets Folder.**

   A dialog box appears.

3. **In the dialog box, click Finish.**

As a result, you see a new `assets` branch in the Android Project tree.

The android.jar archive

Each Android project's CLASSPATH includes Android's pre-declared Java code, and this pre-declared code lives in an `android.jar` archive file.

In Android Studio, you can see `android.jar` by switching to the Project view. Follow the instructions on switching views in the sidebar "The many faces of Android Studio." When the Project view replaces the Android Project view, visit the `External Libraries/Android API` branch of the tree.

A `.jar` file is a compressed archive containing a useful bunch of Java classes. In fact, a `.jar` file is a Zip archive. You can open any `.jar` file with WinZip, StuffIt Expander, or your operating system's built-in unzipping utility. (You may or may not have to change the file's name from *whatever*.`jar` to *whatever*.`zip`.) Anyway, an `android.jar` file contains Android's Java classes for a particular version of Android.

For more information about `.jar` files and `.zip` files, see Book II, Chapter 4.

The `android.jar` file contains code grouped into Java packages, and each package contains Java classes. (Figures 4-5 and 4-6 show only the tip of the `android.jar` iceberg.) The `android.jar` file contains classes specific to Android and classes that simply help Java to do its job. Figure 4-5 shows a bunch of Android-specific packages, and Figure 4-6 displays some all-purpose Java packages.

The APK file

Android puts the results of all its compiling, packaging, and other "ings" into a single file with the `.apk` extension. This *APK* file contains everything a user's device needs to know in order to run your app. When you install a new app on your Android device, you download and install a new APK file.

An important job of the Gradle tool is to combine your app's file into one APK file. This happens each time you choose Run ⇨ Run 'app' in Android Studio's main menu.

You can find an app's APK file using your Windows File Explorer or Macintosh Finder. For an Android Studio project, the APK file is in the project's `app/build/outputs/apk` subdirectory.

Figure 4-5:
Some of the packages and classes in android.jar.

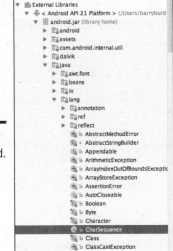

Figure 4-6:
The android.jar file includes general-purpose Java packages.

What Did I Agree To?

When you follow the instructions in Chapter 3 of this minibook, you create a new Android project. In doing so, you have lots of choices to make. The instructions in Chapter 3 tell you to accept a bunch of defaults. This section describes some of the "whys" and "wherefores" concerning those defaults.

What's in a name?

When you create a new application, you assign a bunch of names to things in your application. For example:

✦ You create an application name and a package name.

✦ You specify a project location, and in doing so, you name the directory that contains the app on your development computer's hard drive.

✦ You name an activity.

In Chapter 3 of this minibook, when you create your first application, I recommend accepting any default names that Android Studio flings at you. For example, you call your app My Application, and you use `example.com` as a company domain. Of course, in real life, default names aren't very helpful. Ordinary folks, like Joe and Jane User, will see your Application name in the Android device's launcher screen, and the name My Application isn't very inviting. If you're planning to market your app, your app's name should be short, sweet, and descriptive.

Here are some guidelines for naming things:

✦ When you create a new application, your project and application names may contain blank spaces, but your package name and your activity name must not contain blank spaces.

In general, I'm not a fan of blank spaces. Blank spaces can gum up the works when your software distinguishes the end of one name and the start of the next name. For example, in Windows, the folder name *Program Files* is a never-ending source of angst for me and other developers. My advice is, use blank spaces only where an app's cosmetics demand blank spaces. If things go wrong, be suspicious of any names with blank spaces.

✦ For your project name, you can type the name of any valid Java identifier. Make sure to start with a letter and then include only letters, digits, and underscores (_).

For the scoop on Java identifiers, see Book II, Chapter 2.

✦ Your activity is a Java class. So, to adhere to Java's stylistic conventions, start your activity's name with an uppercase letter. In the name, don't include any exotic characters (such as dots, blank spaces, dashes, dollar signs, or pictures of cows).

In Java, you normally group a bunch of related classes into a package, and you give the package a name. The name can be almost anything, but Java's rules of etiquette tell you how you should name a package:

✦ **Reverse your company's domain name.**

  For example, my company's domain name is allmycode.com. So, when I create a Java package, I start with `com.allmycode`.

  If you don't have a company, or if your company doesn't have a domain name, you can safely ignore this first rule.

✦ **Add a word that describes this particular package's purpose.**

  For example, I created a Java program to search for words in the user's input, so this Java program went in my `com.allmycode.wordsearch` package.

Android takes Java's package conventions one step further. In the Android world, a package contains the code for one and only one application. For example, I created a game named Hungry Burds, so my entire Hungry Burds game is in my `com.allmycode.hungryburds` package.

If you create many apps, keeping track of them all can drive you crazy. So it helps if you decide on a formula for naming your apps' packages, and then you stick to that formula as closely as you can.

For the technical story on Java packages and package names, see Book II, Chapter 2.

Your app's API levels

In Chapter 3 of this minibook, you create a new app and you select a minimum SDK. The acronym *SDK* stands for the term *Software Development Kit*. Like most authors (and like the people who created Android Studio), I often use the acronyms SDK and API (application programming interface) interchangeably. An *API level* (also known as an *SDK version*) is a bunch of code that you call upon in your own Android programs. For example, in Listing 4-1, when you write

```
extends Activity
```

you're referring to a bunch of code in Android's SDK. This code is known as Android's `Activity` class. In the same listing, when you write

```
setContentView(R.layout.activity_main)
```

you're calling a bunch of code known as the `setContentView` method. All this code lives in Android's SDK.

From time to time, the stewards of Android introduce improvements in the SDK. When they do, they mark the changes by creating a level number for the new and improved SDK. Level numbers increase as time goes on. That's why, when you create a new project, you select a minimum API level (minimum SDK version) for your new project.

In Chapter 3 of this minibook, when you select a minimum SDK version, Android Studio records your selection in a `build.gradle` file. (Refer to Listing 4-6. In that listing, your selection becomes the `minSdkVersion` number.) If `minSdkVersion` were the only version number in Listing 4-6, then life would be simple and this chapter would be finished. But life isn't so simple.

An Android app has several uses for API version numbers. For example, in Listing 4-6, the `minSdkVersion` is API 15, but the `targetSdkVersion` and `compileSdkVersion` numbers are both 21. What's the deal with all these SDK version numbers?

You design an Android app to run on a range of API versions. You can think informally of the minimum SDK (`minSdkVersion`) as the lowest version in the range, and the target SDK (`targetSdkVersion`) as the pinpoint focus of the range. If you select API 15 as the minimum and select 21 as the target, you design your app to run on Ice Cream Sandwich (API level 15), Jelly Bean (levels 16, 17, and 18), KitKat (levels 19 and 20), and Lollipop (level 21). You also say that your app *probably* runs on API levels 22, 23, and so on.

These informal notions of "lowest version in the range" and "pinpoint focus" are okay. But what do they mean when the rubber meets the road? And for that matter, why do you even bother specifying a range of SDK versions? Why not say "Every Android user can run my app"?

Here's the story: You can't put any old 1969 car part on a 2014 car, and you certainly can't put most 2014 car parts on an old 1969 car. In the same way, an app is as good as the system it runs on. My old Zenith Supersport computer (ca. 1990) had 5MB of memory and a 6 MHz processor. The Supersport can't run Microsoft Word 2013. And, despite the kinship between older and newer Microsoft operating systems, many of the programs from the Supersport's old disk drive don't run on newer Windows versions. (By the way, the Windows compatibility troubleshooter has never helped me with this problem. Not even once!)

In the old days, a system's underlying software was updated infrequently. When it was, users had to live with whatever consequences were caused by the change. But these days, changes in system software are fast and furious. Your computers and smartphones receive automatic updates over the network. To help you cope, software developers are mindful of *compatibility*.

At the very least, a system update shouldn't break an existing app. In other words, a system update can add new capabilities, but an update shouldn't mess up older capabilities. (This principle about maintaining older capabilities is called *backward compatibility.* The term emphasizes the direction from new systems back to older software.)

Android's official documentation reports that ". . . new versions of the platform are fully backward-compatible." So an app that runs correctly on API level 21 should run correctly on all levels higher than 21. (I write "should run correctly" because in practice, full backward compatibility is difficult to achieve. Anyway, if the Android team is willing to promise full backward compatibility, I'm willing to take my chances.)

One of the ways Android keeps track of system updates is with the software's API level. In November 2014, 30 percent of the world's working Android devices had API level 19, but about 50 percent had API levels 16, 17, or 18 (various incarnations of Android Jelly Bean), and a small percentage (about 0.6 percent) still ran API level 8 (Froyo).* So, no matter what API level you use to compile your app, someone will probably try to run it on a device with a different API level. To face the API levels problem head-on, Android stores several level numbers in your app's files.

Here's what these level numbers mean:

✦ **The minimum SDK (`midSdkVersion`) is the lowest system on which your app is (pretty much) guaranteed to run.**

Imagine putting the following code in your app:

```
SharedPreferences prefs =
  PreferenceManager.getDefaultSharedPreferences(this);
SharedPreferences.Editor editor = prefs.edit();
editor.putInt("amount", 100);
editor.apply();
```

In that last line of code, the word `apply` can cause trouble. Android didn't use the word `apply` this way until API level 9. So, when you create your app, you better specify level 9 or higher as the minimum SDK.

If you specify a minimum SDK level of 9, then when you publish your app on the Google Play Store, the store doesn't offer the app to users whose devices run API level 8 or lower.

An Android project's minimum SDK number is normally in the project's `build.gradle` file. For older projects (created before the Android Studio days), the minimum SDK number appears in the project's `AndroidManifest.xml` file.

*Source: `https://developer.android.com/about/dashboards`

✦ **Another number, the maximum SDK (**`maxSdkVersion`**), is the highest system on which your app is guaranteed to run.**

Listing 4-6 has no `maxSdkVersion` and hardly anyone ever specifies a maximum SDK version for an Android project. In fact, the maximum SDK value is a feature that the stewards of Android probably wish they had never created. The Android documentation discourages the use of a maximum SDK version. The docs warn that a maximum SDK version might cause an app to be uninstalled when the app is still usable.

✦ **The compile SDK (**`compileSdkVersion`**) is the SDK version used to turn your Java code into code that's ready to run.**

Put the earlier bullet's `editor.apply()` code in your app, and in the `build.gradle` file, specify a `compileSdkVersion` of 8. Android Studio immediately displays an error message, because the level 8 SDK doesn't understand this use of the word `apply`. (There's no danger that you'll run your app on a level 8 device because API level 8 can't even compile your app.)

Of course, you can try to sneak around the constraints by specifying level 8 as the minimum SDK and some higher level for the compile SDK. But then Android Studio warns you that you're treading on very thin ice. When you test your app on an API Level 9 device, everything is ducky. But when you test your app on an API Level 8 device, the app crashes.

An Android project's compile SDK version number is in the project's `build.gradle` file. You can change a project's compile SDK version by changing the number in that `build.gradle` file. For an older app (created before Android Studio became part of the picture), you might find the compile SDK number in a `project.properties` or `default.properties` file.

✦ **The target SDK (**`targetSdkVersion`**) is the API level of the system on which you intend to test your app.**

This notion of *intending* to test your app is an elusive concept. If you're a thorough developer, you test your app on many devices with many different API levels. Also, if a device or AVD with your app's target SDK isn't available, then Android Studio looks for another device that meets your app's minimum SDK requirement.

So the idea of a target SDK remains slippery. I'm sure that your IDE or your device uses this value somewhere in the app's lifecycle, but I'm not convinced that you should think about the target SDK too much. Most websites devoted to Android tips and techniques tell you to make the target SDK the same as the compile SDK, and to leave it at that.

An Android project's target SDK number is in the project's `build.gradle` file.

In addition to its backward compatibility concerns, Android has some forward compatibility features. An example of *forward compatibility* is when a system running API level 4 magically enters a time machine and runs an app with fragments — a feature that wasn't created until API level 11. (I don't know. Maybe an Android-enabled DeLorean can do this.)

In reality, forward compatibility in Android comes from things called support libraries. An Android *library* is an app that can't run on its own. A library exists only to help another app do its duties. And a *support library* is a library that helps an older system deal gracefully with a newer app's features. When you create a new project with fairly disparate minimum and target API levels, Android Studio adds a support library to your code. You often notice this when things named `android.support` and `appcompat` appear without warning as part of your code.

To read more about the ways Android keeps track of its versions, see Chapter 2 in this minibook. For more info on compilers, visit Book II, Chapter 2.

While I'm on the subject of versions numbers, I should describe the `buildToolsVersion` line in Listing 4-6. In spite of what I write elsewhere, remember that Android Studio is nothing but an IDE — a main window with a bunch of views, panels, tabs, and other visual aids. In its purest form, Android Studio doesn't create an Android app. Android Studio simply provides an interface to you, the developer. This interface is a go-between to help you work with the real, underlying Android development tools — the tools that actually compose skeletal code, compile the code, run Gradle, bundle up the icons, and package the whole business into a single APK file.

Those underlying tools are the real workhorses of Android development, and the folks at Google strive continuously to improve those tools. That's why, when you go to the main menu and choose Tools⇨Android⇨SDK Manager, you frequently see a check mark offering to update your Android SDK Build Tools software.

To help maintain compatibility, an Android Studio project keeps a record of the version of the tools that built the project. For the project that I describe in this chapter, the tools are Version 21.1.2. Your own first project is newer than the sample project in this chapter, so the project's build tools version number is likely to be higher. With a different build tools version, you might see some slightly different code. The skeletal Java class in Listing 4-1 might have a few more lines in it. One way or another, Android's basic principles apply to this chapter's example and to your own examples as well.

Chapter 5: Conjuring and Embellishing an Android App

In This Chapter

✔ Creating an app with check boxes and other widgets

✔ Making the app do something

✔ Finding bugs in your app (not that there are any, of course)

When I set out to learn something, I follow a "ready, set, go" approach. I don't "go" right into the detailed technical manuals. Instead, I get ready by examining the simplest example I can find. I work with a Hello World scenario like the one in Chapters 3 and 4 of this minibook. Then (. . . and here's where this chapter fits in . . .) I do some probing and poking; I explore some possibilities; I peek around corners; I try some experiments. These are my initial "ready, set" steps.

When I'm firm on my feet, I do the kind of stuff you do in Books III through VI. I "go." If you feel confident, "go" directly to Book III. But if you want more "ready, set" material, march on into this chapter.

Dragging, Dropping, and Otherwise Tweaking an App

A general guideline in app development tells you to separate logic from presentation. In less technical terms, the guideline warns against confusing what an app does with how an app looks. The guideline applies to many things in life. For example, if you're designing a website, have artists do the layout and have geeks do the coding. If you're writing a report, get the ideas written first. Later, you can worry about fonts and paragraph styles. (Melba, you're this book's copy editor. Do you agree with me about fonts and styles?)

The literature on app development has specific techniques and frameworks to help you separate form from function. But in this chapter, I do the simplest thing — I chop an app's creation into two sets of instructions. The first set is about creating an app's look; the second set is about coding the app's behavior.

Creating the "look"

To add buttons, boxes, and other goodies to your app, do the following:

1. **Launch Android Studio.**

If you followed the steps in Chapter 3 of this minibook, you created a skeletal Android Project. Maybe you finished by choosing File ⇨ Close Project, or maybe you simply quit the Android Studio app.

2. **If you didn't choose Close Project (or if you didn't even quit the Android Studio app), you see the project from Chapter 3 in Android Studio's main window. Select File ⇨ Close Project.**

The Android Studio's Welcome screen appears.

3. **In the Welcome screen, select Create New Project and then follow the remaining steps to create a project as in Chapter 3.**

In this section's listings and figures, I name the app `01_05_01`. I put the app in a package named `com.allmycode.p01_05_01`.

When you're finished creating a brand-new project, it appears in Android Studio's main window.

4. **In the new project's** `app/res/layout` **branch (in the main window's Project tool window), double-click** `activity_main.xml`**.**

Android Studio projects

In Steps 2 and 3, I encourage you to close your existing project and to work with the Welcome screen. You can do this over and over again, but you really don't have to. One alternative is to keep the Chapter 3 project open and to enhance that project with the instructions in this chapter. Another alternative is to keep the Chapter 3 project open and to create a second Android project.

With two projects open at the same time, your Android Studio app has two main windows. You can switch between the windows, minimize one of the windows, or do whatever you want with the two windows. One thing

you should definitely avoid doing is becoming confused and making changes in the wrong window. That's why I recommend closing any project that you're not actively developing.

To close an existing project, select File ⇨ Close Project in Android Studio's main menu.

To create a new project without closing one of your existing projects, select File ⇨ New Project in Android Studio's main menu. (When you do, you'll see the same Create New Project dialog boxes that you see when you choose New Project in the Welcome screen.)

The Project tool window appears on the left side of Android Studio's main window. The Project tool window has several different views, including the Project view, the Packages view, and the Android view. When you create a new project, the Android view appears by default. So if you're looking for the Project tool window, look for the word *Android* in a drop-down list in the main window's upper left corner. The tree that's immediately below this drop-down list is the Project tool window. (If you don't see anything like this, try clicking the *1: Project* tool button on the very left edge of the main window.) For more information about this, see Book II, Chapter 1.

As a result, Android Studio's Designer tool displays the contents of `activity_main.xml`. The Designer tool has two modes: design mode for drag-and-drop visual editing, and Text mode for XML code editing. So the bottom of the Designer tool has two tabs — a Design tab and a Text tab.

5. **Click the Design tab.**

   In Design mode, most of the Designer tool is taken up by the *palette* — a list of layouts, widgets, and other things that you can drag onto your app's screen — and the preview screen. (See Figure 5-1.)

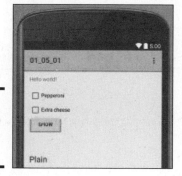

Figure 5-1:
You want to create this app.

If you don't see the palette, look for a little Palette button on the left edge of the Designer tool. If you click that button, the palette should appear.

The next several steps guide you through the creation of the app shown in Figure 5-1.

6. **In the palette's Widgets group, click to select CheckBox.**

7. **Click your mouse in the preview screen.**

   A check box appears where you clicked in the preview screen.

Instead of clicking twice, you can drag and drop from the palette to the preview screen. You don't need to do two separate clicks.

8. **Repeat Steps 6 and 7.**

   Now your app has two check boxes. Don't fuss too much about the positions of the two check boxes. Sure, it's good if the check boxes don't overlap. (If they do, you can drag one of the check boxes within the preview screen, but in my experience, dragging things in the preview screen doesn't always give you what you want.)

   With or without dragging, don't put much effort into making the layout look nice. You'll beautify the layout in Chapter 6 of this minibook.

9. **From the palette's Widgets group, put a Button on the preview screen.**

10. **Again from the palette's Widgets group, put a Large Text element on the preview screen.**

11. **Double-click the first check box in the preview screen.**

    As a result, a pop-up menu appears. (See Figure 5-2.)

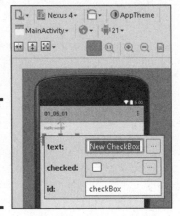

Figure 5-2: Changing the properties of a check box.

12. **In the field labeled *text*, type Pepperoni. (See Figure 5-3.)**

13. **Repeat Steps 11 and 12 a few times. Change the text entry of each component in the preview screen so that it looks like what you see in Figure 5-1.**

You might type Show (with mostly lowercase letters) in the text field for the button. Even so, newer Android devices will display the word *SHOW* (with all uppercase letters) on the face of the button. (Refer to Figure 5-1.) Some older devices will display Show. (See Figure 5-6.)

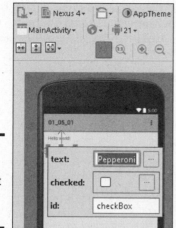

Figure 5-3:
Changing
the text that
labels a
check box.

To force lowercase letters onto the face of a button, start by selecting the button in the Preview screen. Look for the little filter icon in the upper right corner of the Properties panel in the Designer tool. Click that icon so that it appears to be pressed downward. This exposes some properties that aren't normally displayed (some "expert" properties). Look for the *textAllCaps* property and put a check mark in that property's check box. If you'd rather fuss with Java code, then ignore my instructions about the Properties panel and look for the `setTransformationMethod` method in Android's documentation.

14. **Choose File ⇨ Save All to save your work so far.**

With this section's steps, you edit your app visually. Behind the scenes, Android Studio is editing the text in your app's `activity_main.xml` document. You can see what changes Android Studio has made to your app's `activity_main.xml` document by selecting the Text tab at the bottom of Android Studio's editor. The `activity_main.xml` document is reproduced in Listing 5-1.

Whenever you want, you can change the look of your app by directly editing the text in `activity_main.xml`.

In Listing 5-1, the file `activity_main.xml` is modified from its original version. It's formatted to fit your page. In addition, the text in Listing 5-1 comes from my clicking and dragging within Android Studio's preview screen. Your own clicking and dragging might result in some different code. Finally, some of the text in Listing 5-1 appears differently in the Android Studio editor. Instead of `@string/hello_world` (the text in the `activity_main.xml` file), you see `Hello world!` in Android Studio's editor. And instead of `@dimen/activity_horizontal_margin` and `@dimen/activity_vertical_margin`, you see `16dp` in Android Studio's editor. To find out why the editor messes with your view of the `activity_main.xml` file's contents, visit Chapter 4 in this minibook.

Listing 5-1: The activity_main.xml Document

```xml
<RelativeLayout
    xmlns:android="http://schemas.android.com/apk/res/android"
    xmlns:tools="http://schemas.android.com/tools"
    android:layout_width="match_parent"
    android:layout_height="wrap_content"
    android:paddingBottom="@dimen/activity_vertical_margin"
    android:paddingLeft="@dimen/activity_horizontal_margin"
    android:paddingRight="@dimen/activity_horizontal_margin"
    android:paddingTop="@dimen/activity_vertical_margin"
    tools:context=".MainActivity">

    <TextView
        android:id="@+id/textView"
        android:layout_width="wrap_content"
        android:layout_height="wrap_content"
        android:text="@string/hello_world"/>

    <CheckBox
        android:id="@+id/checkBox"
        android:layout_width="wrap_content"
        android:layout_height="wrap_content"
        android:layout_alignParentStart="true"
        android:layout_alignParentLeft="true"
        android:layout_alignParentTop="true"
        android:layout_marginTop="37dp"
        android:checked="false"
        android:text="Pepperoni"/>

    <CheckBox
        android:id="@+id/checkBox2"
        android:layout_width="wrap_content"
        android:layout_height="wrap_content"
        android:layout_alignParentStart="true"
        android:layout_alignParentLeft="true"
        android:layout_alignParentTop="true"
        android:layout_marginTop="76dp"
        android:checked="false"
        android:text="Extra cheese"/>

    <Button
        android:id="@+id/button"
        android:layout_width="wrap_content"
        android:layout_height="wrap_content"
        android:layout_alignParentStart="true"
        android:layout_alignParentLeft="true"
        android:layout_below="@+id/checkBox2"
        android:text="Show"
        android:onClick="onButtonClick"/>
```

```
<TextView
    android:layout_width="wrap_content"
    android:layout_height="wrap_content"
    android:textAppearance=
        "?android:attr/textAppearanceLarge"
    android:text="Plain"
    android:id="@+id/textView2"
    android:layout_alignParentTop="true"
    android:layout_marginTop="214dp"
    android:layout_alignParentLeft="true"
    android:layout_alignParentStart="true"/>

</RelativeLayout>
```

Coding the behavior

Assuming you've followed the instructions in the section "Creating the 'look,'" what's next? Well, what's next depends on your app's minimum SDK version.

For minimum SDK version 4 or higher (Android 1.6 and beyond)

Android 1.6 introduced a cool `android:onClick` attribute that streamlines the coding of an app's actions. Here's what you do:

1. **Follow the steps in this chapter's "Creating the 'look'" section.**

2. **Make note of the labels on the branches in the Component tree.**

   The Component tree is on the right side of Android Studio's main window (to the right of the preview screen). Notice the labels on the branches of the tree. Each element on the screen has an *id* (a name to identify that element). In Figure 5-4, the ids of the screen's elements include *checkBox*, *checkBox2*, and *textView2*.

Figure 5-4:
The
Component
tree.

Android Studio assigns ids automatically, and you can change these ids if you wish. But in this example, I recommend accepting whatever you see in the Component tree. But before proceeding to the next step, make note of the ids in your app's Component tree. (They may not be the same as the ids in Figure 5-4.)

3. **In the preview screen, select the SHOW button. (Refer to Figure 5-1.)**

4. **Look for the Properties panel on the right side of the Designer tool. (See Figure 5-5.) In the Properties panel, change the** onClick **entry's value to** onButtonClick.

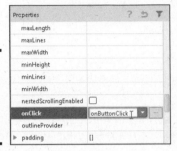

Figure 5-5:
Changing
an object's
onClick
property.

Actually, you can change the entry's value to anything you want, as long as it forms a valid Java method name.

5. **Inside the** app/java **branch of the Project tool window, double-click** MainActivity.

Of course, if you didn't accept the default activity name (MainActivity) when you created the new project, then double-click whatever activity name you used.

In the Project tool window, the MainActivity branch is located in a branch that's labeled with your app's package name (com. example.*somethingorother*). That package name branch is directly in the java branch, which is, in turn, in the app branch.

When you're finished with your double-clicking, the activity's code appears in Android Studio's editor.

6. **Modify the activity's code, as shown in Listing 5-2.**

The lines that you type are set in boldface in Listing 5-2.

In Listing 5-2, I assume that the branches on your app's Component tree have the same labels as the tree pictured in Figure 5-4. In other words, I assume that your app's check boxes have the ids checkBox and check-Box2, and that your Large Text element has the id textView2. If your app's widgets have different ids, change the code in Listing 5-2 accordingly. For example, if your first check box has the id checkBox1, change your first findViewById call to findViewById(R.id.checkBox1).

Listing 5-2: A Button Responds to a Click

```
package com.allmycode.p01_05_01;

import android.app.Activity;
import android.os.Bundle;
import android.view.Menu;
import android.view.MenuItem;
import android.view.View;
import android.widget.CheckBox;
import android.widget.TextView;


public class MainActivity extends Activity {
  CheckBox pepBox, cheeseBox;
  TextView textView;

  @Override
  protected void onCreate(Bundle savedInstanceState) {
    super.onCreate(savedInstanceState);
    setContentView(R.layout.activity_main);
    pepBox = (CheckBox) findViewById(R.id.checkBox);
    cheeseBox = (CheckBox) findViewById(R.id.checkBox2);
    textView = (TextView) findViewById(R.id.textView2);
  }

  public void onButtonClick(View view) {
    StringBuilder str = new StringBuilder("");
    if (pepBox.isChecked()) {
      str.append("Pepperoni ");

    }
    if (cheeseBox.isChecked()) {
      str.append("Extra cheese");
    }
    if (str.length() == 0) {
      str.append("Plain");
    }
    textView.setText(str);
  }
// You don't have to add any code below this point

  @Override
  public boolean onCreateOptionsMenu(Menu menu) {
    getMenuInflater().inflate(R.menu.menu_main, menu);
    return true;
  }

  @Override
  public boolean onOptionsItemSelected(MenuItem item) {
    int id = item.getItemId();

    if (id == R.id.action_settings) {
      return true;
    }

    return super.onOptionsItemSelected(item);
  }
}
```

Make Android Studio do the work

In Listing 5-2, you don't have to type the lines that start with the word `import`. You can tweak Android Studio's settings so that lines of this kind appear automatically whenever you type words like `View`, `CheckBox`, or `TextView`. Here's how:

1. **If you have a Window's PC, choose File ⇨ Settings.**

   If you have a Mac, choose Android Studio ⇨ Preferences.

   A dialog box appears. (The dialog box's title is either Settings or Preferences. Whatever!)

2. **In the panel on the left side of the dialog box, expand the Editor branch.**

3. **In the Editor branch, select Auto Import.**

   Several options appear in the main body of the dialog box. (See the figure.)

4. **In the drop-down list labeled *Insert Imports on Paste*, select All.**

5. **Put a check mark in the Optimize Imports on the Fly check box.**

6. **Put a check mark in the Add Unambiguous Imports on the Fly check box.**

7. **Click OK to commit to these changes.**

   Now, when you type a line like `TextView textView`, Android Studio automatically adds the required `import android.widget.TextView` line to your code. That's nice.

8. **Run the app.**

   When you click the app's button, you see one of the screens in Figure 5-6.

Concerning the code in Listing 5-2, a few words of explanation are in order:

Finding the check boxes and the text element

In Listing 5-2, the statement

```
pepBox = (CheckBox) findViewById(R.id.checkBox);
```

finds the first check box that you create in the steps in the section "Creating the 'look.'"

Wait a minute! What does it mean to "find" a check box, and how does a statement in Listing 5-2 accomplish that task? Figure 5-7 illustrates the situation.

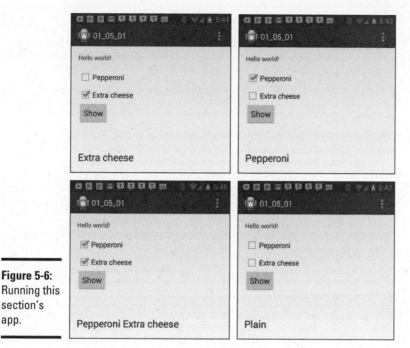

Figure 5-6:
Running this
section's
app.

When you do the stuff in the earlier section "Creating the 'look,'" you end up
with a file like the one in Listing 5-1. This file contains the lines

```
<CheckBox
    android:id="@+id/checkBox"
    . . .
    android:text="Pepperoni"/>
```

The Pepperoni check box's XML code contains a cryptic @+id/checkBox
attribute. Android Studio sees this @+id/checkBox attribute, and takes it as
an instruction to add a line to your app's R.java file:

```
public final class R {
  public static final class id {
    public static final int checkBox=0x7f050003;
```

Because of this Java code, the name R.id.checkBox stands for the number
0x7f050003.

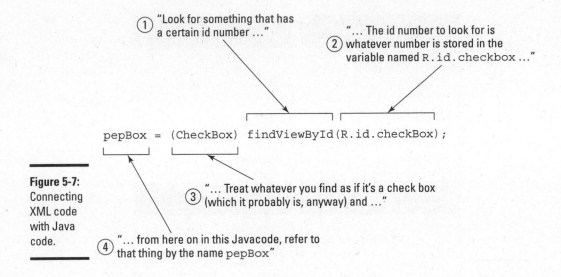

Figure 5-7:
Connecting
XML code
with Java
code.

So, if you look again at Figure 5-7, you see how a line of Java code says the following:

> *Look for something that has id number 2131034115. Treat whatever you find as if it's a check box, and from here on, in this Java code, refer to that thing by the name* pepBox.

This is how Android connects a widget that you create in the Designer tool with a name in your app's Java code.

In Listing 5-2, the lines

```
cheeseBox = (CheckBox) findViewById(R.id.checkBox2);
textView = (TextView) findViewById(R.id.textView2);
```

serve the same purpose for two of the other widgets that you added using the Designer tool.

The characters 0x7f050003 might not look much like a number but, in a Java program, the characters 0x7f050003 form the hexadecimal representation of what we ordinarily call 2131034115. If this number 2131034115 for a little check box seems arbitrary, then don't worry. It's *supposed* to be arbitrary. Android Studio generates the R.java file automatically from the things that you name in places like Listing 5-1. All the numbers in the R.java file are arbitrary. There's no reason for them not to be arbitrary.

Responding to a button click

The `onButtonClick` method in Listing 5-2 fulfills the promise that you make in Step 4 of this section's instructions. Setting the button's `onClick` property to `onButtonClick` gets Android Studio to add the attribute `android:onClick="onButtonClick"` to the button's start tag in `activity_main.xml`. As a result, Android calls your `onButtonClick` method whenever the user clicks the button.

In Listing 5-2, the first line of the method

```
public void onButtonClick(View view)
```

is the method's *heading*. Below the heading comes all the instructions to be performed whenever the user clicks the button. Here's what the instructions in Listing 5-2 tell Android to do when the user clicks the button:

```
Create an empty string.
If the pepBox is checked,
  add "Pepperoni " to the string.

If the cheeseBox is checked,
  add "Extra cheese" to the string.
If the string's length is still 0,
  add "Plain" to the string.
Set the textView's text to whatever is in the string.
```

In Android, any widget that appears on the device's screen is a kind of `View`. So in the method's heading, the `view` parameter is whatever object the user clicked. (Yes, you put the word `Button` in the name `onButtonClick`. But that doesn't mean that the thing the user clicked is a button. Instead of `onButtonClick`, you could have named this method `uqKgwlsdif`. It wouldn't mean that the item being clicked is a `Kgwlsdif`!)

In Listing 5-2, you don't use the method's `view` parameter, but the parameter is available nonetheless. In a more elaborate app, you might write instructions that say

```
if the view is the checkBox
  do one thing
if the view is checkBox2
  do something else
if view is the button
  do yet another thing
```

If you don't put a `View` parameter in your click-handling method, Android doesn't respond to the click.

You must put the word `public` in the `onButtonClick` method's heading. If you don't declare `onButtonClick` to be `public`, Android does nothing when a user clicks the button. The code that tries to call `onButtonClick` isn't a subclass of your activity and isn't in the same package. So, if your event-handling method isn't `public`, your efforts are thwarted.

I confess. I'm getting ahead of myself with all this talk about Java methods, parameters, and such. To read more about Java methods, see Book II, Chapter 2.

For any minimum SDK version

No matter what Android version you plan to use, this section's instructions get your app to respond to button clicks. You may never create an app whose minimum SDK is less than 4. Even so, the techniques in this section involve a very commonly used Java idiom. And many Android developers avoid using the `onClick` attribute (the previous section's technique). That technique sidesteps some issues having to do with the long-term maintenance of big Android projects. So to start right off with the most professional way of responding to button clicks, read on.

1. **Follow the steps in this chapter's "Creating the 'look'" section.**

2. **Modify the activity's code, as shown in Listing 5-3.**

   The lines that you type are set in boldface in Listing 5-3.

3. **Run the app.**

Listing 5-3: Event Handling (the Traditional Java Way)

```java
package com.example.myapplication;

import android.app.Activity;
import android.os.Bundle;
import android.view.Menu;
import android.view.MenuItem;
import android.view.View;
import android.view.View.OnClickListener;
import android.widget.Button;
import android.widget.CheckBox;
import android.widget.TextView;


public class MainActivity extends Activity
                    implements OnClickListener {
  CheckBox pepBox, cheeseBox;
  TextView textView;

  @Override
  protected void onCreate(Bundle savedInstanceState) {
    super.onCreate(savedInstanceState);
    setContentView(R.layout.activity_main);
```

```
    pepBox = (CheckBox) findViewById(R.id.checkBox);
    cheeseBox = (CheckBox) findViewById(R.id.checkBox2);
    textView = (TextView) findViewById(R.id.textView2);

    ((Button) findViewById(R.id.button))
                      .setOnClickListener(this);

}

public void onClick(View view) {
    StringBuilder str = new StringBuilder("");
    if (pepBox.isChecked()) {
        str.append("Pepperoni ");
    }
    if (cheeseBox.isChecked()) {
        str.append("Extra cheese");
    }
    if (str.length() == 0) {
        str.append("Plain");
    }
    textView.setText(str);
}

@Override
public boolean onCreateOptionsMenu(Menu menu) {
    getMenuInflater().inflate(R.menu.menu_main, menu);
    return true;
}

@Override
public boolean onOptionsItemSelected(MenuItem item) {
    int id = item.getItemId();

    if (id == R.id.action_settings) {
        return true;
    }

    return super.onOptionsItemSelected(item);
}
}
```

Listing 5-3 uses Java's traditional event-handling pattern. The button registers your activity as its click-event listener. Your activity declares itself to
be an OnClickListener and makes good on this click-listener promise by
implementing the onClick method.

You can program any of Java's well-known variations based on the event-
handling pattern in Listing 5-3. For example, you can create a separate class
to implement the OnClickListener interface, or you can implement the
interface with an inner class.

A Bit of Debugging

In a perfect world, you wake up refreshed and energetic every morning. Every app you write runs correctly on the first test. Every word you write in *Android Application Development All-in-One For Dummies, 2nd Edition* is *le mot juste*.

But the world isn't perfect. And often the first test of a new application forms a disappointing splat on your emulator's screen. So the next few sections contain some useful debugging techniques.

Try it!

To get a handle on Android debugging, follow these instructions:

1. **Create a new Android project.**

To cook up this section's figures and listings, I named the project `01_05_04`. I named the package `com.allmycode.p01_05_04`.

2. **Add a Large Text element to your project's** `activity_main.xml` **layout.**

For details, see the section "Creating the 'look.'"

After adding a Large Text element, the preview screen looks like the one in Figure 5-8, and Android Studio's Component tree contains a `textView2` branch.

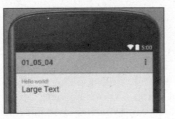

Figure 5-8: A layout containing a new text element.

3. **Open the new project's** `MainActivity` **for editing.**

The activity's `onCreate` method looks like this:

```
protected void onCreate(Bundle savedInstanceState) {
    super.onCreate(savedInstanceState);
    setContentView(R.layout.activity_main);
}
```

4. **Add two statements to the** `onCreate` **method, as in Listing 5-4.**

The statements that you add are set in bold type.

Listing 5-4:   A Misguided Attempt to Add a TextView to an Activity

```
// THIS IS BAD CODE!

protected void onCreate(Bundle savedInstanceState) {
    super.onCreate(savedInstanceState);
    TextView textView =
            (TextView) findViewById(R.id.textView2);
    setContentView(R.layout.activity_main);
    textView.setText("Oops!");
}
```

You can type **import android.widget.TextView** near the top of your code. But you can also get Android Studio to add this line automatically. To do so, follow the instructions in the sidebar "Make Android Studio do the work."

5. Run your app.

Your app comes crashing down with a big *01_05_04 Has Stopped* message. You click the message's OK button and give up in despair. Or . . .

6. Look at the lower portion of Android Studio's main window for a Logcat panel.

The Logcat panel displays the running emulator's log. (See Figure 5-9.)

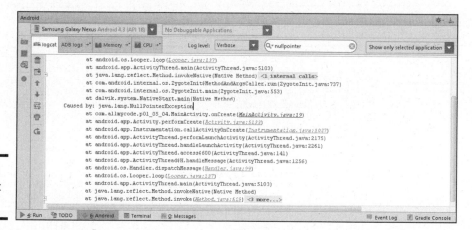

Figure 5-9:
The Logcat panel.

The Logcat panel is located in the *Logcat* tab, which is, in turn, part of the Android tool window. (Refer to Figure 5-9.) If you don't see the Logcat panel, click the Android tool button at the bottom of the main window. Doing so exposes (or hides) the Android tool window. In the Android tool window, click the *Logcat* tab. (And, while you're at it, make a mental note about the Android tool button's having nothing to do with the Android view in the Project tool window!)

7. In the Logcat panel, look for a Java stack trace.

The Java stack trace (plus a few of additional lines in the log) looks like the text in Listing 5-5.

Listing 5-5: Messages in the Logcat Pane

```
05-16 22:38:56.951 15403-15403/? D/dalvikvm: Late-enabling CheckJNI
05-16 22:38:57.025 15403-15403/com.allmycode.p01_05_04
  D/AndroidRuntime: Shutting down VM
05-16 22:38:57.033 15403-15403/com.allmycode.p01_05_04
  W/dalvikvm: threadid=1: thread exiting with uncaught exception
  (group=0x41c8a700)
05-16 22:38:57.040 15403-15403/com.allmycode.p01_05_04
  E/AndroidRuntime: FATAL EXCEPTION: main
 java.lang.RuntimeException: Unable to start activity ComponentInfo
  {com.allmycode.p01_05_04/com.allmycode.p01_05_04.MainActivity}:
  java.lang.NullPointerException
   at android.app.ActivityThread.performLaunchActivity(ActivityThread.ja
   at android.app.ActivityThread.handleLaunchActivity(ActivityThread.jav
   at android.app.ActivityThread.access$600(ActivityThread.java:141)
   at android.app.ActivityThread$H.handleMessage(ActivityThread.java:125
   at android.os.Handler.dispatchMessage(Handler.java:99)
   at android.os.Looper.loop(Looper.java:137)
   at android.app.ActivityThread.main(ActivityThread.java:5103)
   at java.lang.reflect.Method.invokeNative(Native Method)
   at java.lang.reflect.Method.invoke(Method.java:525)
   at com.android.internal.os.ZygoteInit$MethodAndArgsCaller.run(ZygoteI
   at com.android.internal.os.ZygoteInit.main(ZygoteInit.java:553)
   at dalvik.system.NativeStart.main(Native Method)
 Caused by: java.lang.NullPointerException
   at com.allmycode.p01_05_04.MainActivity.onCreate(MainActivity.java:19
   at android.app.Activity.performCreate(Activity.java:5133)
   at android.app.Instrumentation.callActivityOnCreate(Instrumentation.j
   at android.app.ActivityThread.performLaunchActivity(ActivityThread.ja
   at android.app.ActivityThread.handleLaunchActivity(ActivityThread.jav
   at android.app.ActivityThread.access$600(ActivityThread.java:141)
   at android.app.ActivityThread$H.handleMessage(ActivityThread.java:125
   at android.os.Handler.dispatchMessage(Handler.java:99)
   at android.os.Looper.loop(Looper.java:137)
   at android.app.ActivityThread.main(ActivityThread.java:5103)
   at java.lang.reflect.Method.invokeNative(Native Method)
   at java.lang.reflect.Method.invoke(Method.java:525)
   at com.android.internal.os.ZygoteInit$MethodAndArgsCaller.run(ZygoteI
   at com.android.internal.os.ZygoteInit.main(ZygoteInit.java:553)
   at dalvik.system.NativeStart.main(Native Method)
```

A log file always contains more information than you need. But if you look for the most recent bunch of words, you find the trace that you need.

8. In the stack trace, look for lines relating directly to the code in your app.

The *stack trace* shows which methods were calling which other methods when your app crashed. In this onslaught of details, you find a few lines containing names from your application — lines such as

```
at com.allmycode.p01_05_04.MainActivity.onCreate(MainActivity.java:19)
```

Above that line, you see the words `java.lang.NullPointer Exception`.

So your app caused a `NullPointerException` at line 19 of the `MainActivity.java` file.

9. **In Android Studio's editor, find the offending line in your app's code.**

In this section's example, the guilty line is `textView. setText("Oops!")` in your code's `MainActivity` class.

The Logcat panel's text contains hyperlinks. For example, in the message in Step 8, the text `MainActivity.java: 19` is a hyperlink. Click that link in the Logcat panel and Android Studio's editor jumps straight to the relevant line of code.

To make Android Studio's editor display line numbers, choose File➪Settings on Windows or Android Studio➪Preferences on a Mac. Under IDE Settings➪Editor➪Appearance, put a check mark in the Show Line Numbers check box.

10. **Figure out what part of the offending code might cause the error shown in the stack trace.**

Unfortunately, this step isn't always easy. You may need to make several guesses, try several possible solutions, or seek advice on some online forums.

Anyway, like a chef on a cooking show, I can quickly whip out a ready-made solution. When you call `textView.setText`, you get a `NullPointerException`. So `textView` is null. The problem in Listing 5-4 is the placement of the call to `findViewById`.

Until you set the activity's Content view, the app knows nothing about `R.id.textView2`. So, in Listing 5-4, calling `findViewById` before calling `setContentView` leads to disaster. To fix the problem, swap two statements as follows:

```
setContentView(R.layout.main);
TextView textView =
        (TextView) findViewById(R.id.textView2);
```

More than one way to skin a Logcat

With some clever use of Android's log, you can increase your chances of finding the source of an error.

Read your device's log file

If you connect a device to your development computer, you can see the device's log file in Android Studio's Logcat pane. But sometimes it's more convenient to view the log file right on the device. For example, you might want to debug an app when you're using it on the road.

The Google Play Store has apps to help you view your device's log file. I use an app called CatLog, but other apps might work well for you, too.

Filter the output

Android's logging has six *levels*. The levels, in decreasing order of seriousness, are ASSERT, ERROR, WARN, INFO, DEBUG, and VERBOSE. In general, only an ASSERT or ERROR entry is a showstopper. All other entries (WARN, INFO, and so on) are just idle chatter.

Android Studio's Logcat panel has a Log Level drop-down list. (Refer to Figure 5-9.) You select a level to filter out entries of lesser severity. For example, if you select the Error option, the Logcat pane displays only entries with levels ASSERT or ERROR.

You can filter entries in other ways. For example, to the right of the Log Level drop-down list, there's a little search field. (Refer to Figure 5-9.) If you type **Null** in that field, you see only the messages containing the word *Null*. In particular, you see messages containing the term NullPointerException — a very common error in Java programming. (Unfortunately, this filtering is of little help with the text in Listing 5-5, because the text in Listing 5-5 consists of only four messages, each beginning with 05-16, which stands for *May 16*. Only the last of the four messages contains the term NullPointerException, but that last message is about 30 lines long! Nonetheless, filtering for text can be very useful.)

In the upper-right corner of Figure 5-9, a drop-down list displays the text *Show only selected application*. This means that only messages pertaining to your com.allmycode.p01_05_04 package appear in the Logcat panel. You can see other messages by selecting No Filters in that drop-down list.

You can also select the drop-down list's Edit Filter Configuration option. When you do, you see a dialog box that offers more choices for filtering messages. (See Figure 5-10.) You can filter by Log Tag and by PID. You can pile additional criteria on top of existing filters by clicking the plus sign in the upper-right corner of the dialog box.

Every Logcat message has a *tag*. In Listing 5-5, the first three messages have the tag *art*, and the remaining two messages' tags are *AndroidRuntime*. (You get used to finding these tags if you spend enough time staring at Logcat messages.) If you type the letter **a** in the Log Tag field in Figure 5-10, you see several suggested tags, including *ActivityManager*, *AlarmMessengerService*, *AndroidRuntime*, and *art*.

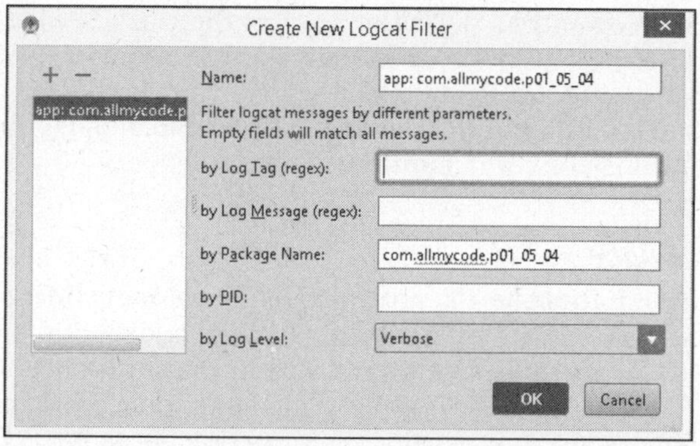

Figure 5-10:
The Create
New Logcat
Filter dialog
box.

In addition to its tag, every Logcat message belongs to one of the Android operating system's processes, and every process has its own *process identification number (PID)*. All the messages in Listing 5-5 come from the process whose PID is 15403. That's because, when I ran the 01_05_04 app to create Listing 5-5, the 01_05_04 app's process had PID 15403. (The next time I run the same 01_05_04 app, its PID is likely to be different.) To filter out all messages except those from process 15403, type **15403** in the PID field in the Create New Logcat Filter dialog box. (Once again, this does little good for the text in Listing 5-5. But filtering by PID can, at times, be very useful.)

Write to the log file

What? You don't trust my diagnosis of the problem in Listing 5-4? "Is textView really null?" you ask. You can peek at your program's variables with the Debug tool window, but for a quick answer to your question, you can write to Android's log file.

In Listing 5-4, add the following code before the textView.setText("Oops!") statement:

```
if (textView == null) {
    Log.i("READ ME!", "textView is null");
} else {
    Log.i("READ ME!",
          "-->" + textView.getText().toString());
}
```

The Log class's static i method creates an entry of level INFO in Android's log file. In this example, the entry's tag is READ ME!, and the entry's message is either textView is null or the characters displayed in the textView. When you run the app, you can check the Logcat pane to find out what this entry tells you.

By convention, a log entry's tag is the name of the class in which the log is created. For example, if your class's name is `MainActivity`, the first parameter of `Log.i` is the string `"MainActivity"`. In this section, I don't follow that formula. But, if other developers are involved in your project, coding conventions are very important.

Using the debugger

I have a confession to make. I'm not like most developers. Most developers use debugging tools to analyze behaviors in their code. I don't. I add logging statements to my code (the way you do in the earlier section "Write to the log file"). I do this because, for me, debugging tools don't make my life simpler. Debuggers give me too much information about a run of my app. Debuggers make my life more complicated.

Real developers make fun of people like me, and they're probably correct in doing so. But I don't care. I just continue sending messages to Android's Logcat and, when it's my duty to do so, I write in my books about debuggers — and this is one of those times when duty calls . . .

1. **Follow the steps in this chapter's "Try it!" section.**

   When you do, you have a buggy Android app.

2. **With** `MainActivity.java` **showing in the editor, click to the left of the** `textView.setText("Oops!")` **statement (in the editor's border).**

   When you do, Android Studio adds a red circle icon to the editor's border. (See Figure 5-11.) This icon represents a *breakpoint* — a place where your app will pause its run. During the pause, you can examine variables' values, change variables' values, and do other useful things.

```java
public class MainActivity extends Activity {

    @Override
    protected void onCreate(Bundle savedInstanceState) {
        super.onCreate(savedInstanceState);
        TextView textView =
            (TextView) findViewById(R.id.textView2);
        setContentView(R.layout.activity_main);
        textView.setText("Oops!");
    }
}
```

Figure 5-11: A breakpoint.

3. **In Android Studio's main menu, choose Run⇨Debug 'app'.**

   When you do, you see all the stuff that you'd see if you had chosen Run 'app'. Choosing Debug instead of Run doesn't change much until execution reaches the statement with the breakpoint. But when execution reaches the `textView.setText("Oops!")` statement, the Debug tool window appears. (See Figure 5-12.)

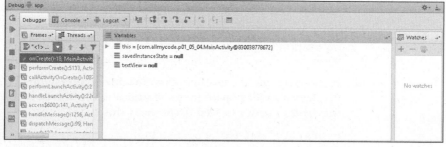

Figure 5-12:
The Debug
tool window.

Using Run⇨Debug 'app' instead of Run⇨Run 'app' can make your app run very slowly. Don't use Run⇨Debug 'app' routinely. Use Run⇨Debug 'app' only when you need Android Studio's debugging tool.

In the Debugger tab of the Debug tool window, you see a list of variables in your app's Java code. You may have to fish around for the variable that's giving you trouble. (You might have to expand the `this` branch of the tree in the Variables panel.) But in Figure 5-12, the situation is simpler. The value of `textView` is `null`. That's trouble, and it requires correcting. (To find out how to correct this problem, visit this chapter's "Try it!" section.

In the previous set of instructions, Android's debugger points immediately to the cause of my app's crash. (After writing this set of instructions, I'm wondering if my prejudice against debuggers is warranted.)

While I'm on a roll with debugging, I think I'll try a few more tricks.

1. **In an Android app's** `MainActivity.java` **file, replace the** `onCreate` **method with the following code:**

```
@Override
protected void onCreate(Bundle savedInstanceState) {
    super.onCreate(savedInstanceState);
    setContentView(R.layout.activity_main);
    int i = 7;
    int j = plusOne(i);
}

int plusOne(int i) {
    int temp = i;
    temp++;
    return temp;
}
```

I set the new code (the code that you should add) in boldface type.

2. **Click to the left of the** `int i = 7` **line to add a breakpoint at that line.**

3. **In Android Studio's main menu, choose Run ⇨ Debug 'app'.**

   The Debug tool window opens and the Variables panel appears in the tool window. The variable `i` doesn't appear in the list because Android hasn't yet executed the statement containing the breakpoint.

   Before proceeding to the next step, notice that the breakpoint statement, `int i = 7`, is highlighted in the editor.

4. **Hover over the icons above the Variables panel. One of these icons displays a small pop-up menu containing the words Step Over. Click this icon in order to step to the next statement.**

   In this case "step to the next statement" means executing the `int i = 7` statement. After clicking the icon, the variable `i` appears in the Variables panel. (See Figure 5-13.) The variable's value is `7`.

Figure 5-13: The variable `i` appears.

Notice how the statement after the breakpoint, `int j = plusOne(i)`, is highlighted in the editor.

5. **One of these icons displays a small pop-up menu containing the words Step Into. Click this Step Into icon.**

   Step Into means that, if the current statement contains a Java method call, pause the app's execution at the first statement inside the body of that method. The current statement contains a call to the `plusOne` method, so Android goes into the body of the `plusOne` method and pauses at the `int temp = i` statement.

6. **Click Step Over again.**

   After doing so, the current statement becomes `temp++`, and the Variables panel displays the `temp` variable. (See Figure 5-14.)

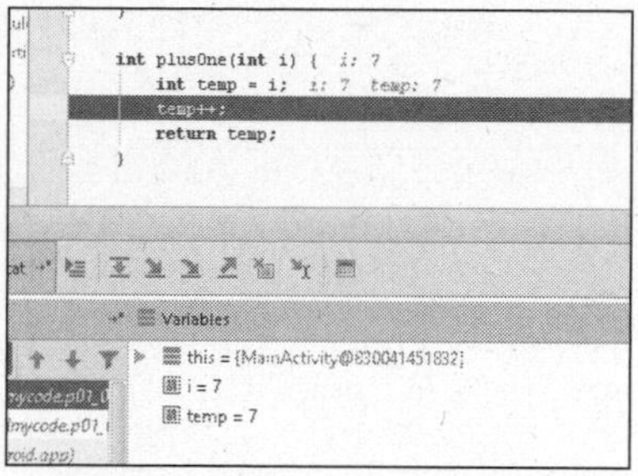

Figure 5-14:
The variable
`temp`
appears.

7. Click Step Over again.

Android executes `temp++`, so in the Variables panel, the value of `temp` changes to 8.

At this point, I don't want you to keep clicking Step Over. If you kept clicking, Android would return from the `plusOne` method call, and back in the `onCreate` method, the value of the `j` variable would become 8. That would be fine. But just for fun, let's mess with the value of `temp` instead.

8. Right-click (or on a Mac, Ctrl-click) the `temp` item in the Variables panel.

A contextual menu appears.

9. In the contextual menu, select Set Value.

An Edit field appears next to the `temp` variable in the Variables panel.

10. In the edit field, type the number 42, and then press Enter.

As a result, the `temp` variable's value changes to be 42.

11. Click Step Over two more times.

When you do, Android finishes executing the `plusOne` method and assigns the value returned from the `plusOne` call (the number 42) to the variable `j`. The variable `j`, with its value 42, appears in the Variables panel.

Chapter 6: Improving Your App

*F*ace it — the app in Chapter 5 of this minibook is boring! Really boring! Who wants to click a button to see the words *Pepperoni Extra Cheese* on a device's screen?

In this chapter, you improve on the app that you created in Chapter 5. I can't promise instant excitement, but with modest effort, you can add features to make the app more interesting. (I confess: In this chapter, the *real* reason for making the app interesting is to show you some additional Android developer tricks. Anyway, read on . . .)

Improving the Layout

In addition to being boring, the app in Chapter 5 is ugly. You can improve an app's look in two ways — the way it looks to a user and the way it looks to another developer. In this section, you do both. When you're done, you have a layout like the one in Figure 6-1.

Before creating the layout's code, I want to make some observations about the layout in Figure 6-1:

+ The button is below the pair of check boxes.

+ The check boxes are side-by-side.

+ The pair of check boxes is centered (side by side) on the screen.

+ The button is centered on the screen.

+ Taken as a group, the check boxes and the button don't fill the entire screen.

Figure 6-1:
Your
mission,
should you
decide to
accept it.

You may wonder why I make these five observations and not others. If so, read on.

1. **Launch Android Studio and create a new Android project.**

   For details on creating a new project, see Chapter 3 of this minibook.

2. **In the Designer tool's preview screen, select the Hello World! text view.**

   It's time to get rid of this silly text view.

3. **Press Delete.**

   Goodbye world!

   You want something that aligns objects vertically so that the button is below the pair of check boxes.

4. **Click the LinearLayout (Vertical) element in the palette's Layouts group. Then click in the preview screen.**

   As a result, the new LinearLayout (Vertical) element's outline appears on the preview screen.

5. **Click the Button element in the palette's Widgets group. Then click inside your vertical linear layout element in the preview screen.**

   Voilà! Your app has a button.

   Next, you want something that aligns objects horizontally so that the check boxes are side by side.

6. **Click the LinearLayout (Horizontal) element in the palette's Layouts group. Then click inside your vertical linear layout element in the preview screen.**

   Try to place the horizontal linear layout element above the button. If you have trouble doing that, go to the Component tree and drag the `LinearLayout (Horizontal)` branch so that it's above the `button` branch but still subordinate to the `LinearLayout (Vertical)` branch. (See Figure 6-2.)

Figure 6-2:
The
Component
tree (what
you have so
far, anyway).

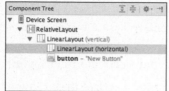

Next, you put the check boxes into your horizontal linear layout.

7. Click the CheckBox element in the palette's Widgets group. Then, click inside the horizontal linear layout element in the preview screen.

If you have trouble clicking inside the horizontal linear layout, place the check box anywhere on the preview screen. Then, in the Component tree, drag the `checkBox` branch so that it's subordinate to the `LinearLayout (Horizontal)` branch.

8. Click the CheckBox element in the palette's Widgets group again. Then click in the preview screen to the right of the first check box.

Like the first check box, this second check box is inside your horizontal linear layout.

The button and the two check boxes might not be centered side by side on the screen. You want to fix that, and I show you how in the next step.

9. In the Component tree, select your horizontal linear layout element.

You can try selecting this element in the preview screen but, for an element with nothing but a border, it's easier to do the selecting in the Component tree.

10. In the Properties panel, look for the `gravity` entry.

Don't confuse the `layout:gravity` entry with the `gravity` entry. They're two different rows in the Properties tree. One of them (the `layout:gravity` entry) is associated with an `android:layout_gravity` attribute in the layout's XML code. The other (the `gravity` entry) is associated with an `android:gravity` entry in the layout's XML code. (I know. This couldn't be more confusing. With any luck, the material in Book IV, Chapter 1 can help you sort it all out.)

11. In the Properties panel, the `gravity` entry is a branch of a tree. Expand this branch and put a check mark in the `center_horizontal` item within that branch.

The `gravity` property helps determine the positions of objects inside a layout (in this example, inside your horizontal linear layout element).

The `gravity` value `center_horizontal` centers objects side by side within the layout. After checking the `center_horizontal` item, notice that the two check boxes are centered (side by side) in the preview screen.

12. **In the Component tree, select your vertical linear layout element.**

13. **In the Properties panel, expand the vertical linear layout element's `gravity` branch. Put a check mark in the `center_horizontal` item within that branch.**

When you do this, the button snaps sideways to the center of the preview screen.

The vertical linear layout element holds the check boxes and the button, but there's another widget in Figure 6-1. (It's a TextView displaying the word Plain.) To make room for this additional widget, you want to tell Android that the vertical linear layout doesn't fill up the entire screen. The next step tells you how to do that.

14. **With the vertical linear layout element still selected, look for the `layout:height` entry in the Properties panel.**

15. **Click in the right column of the `layout:height` entry. In the drop-down list that appears, select `wrap_content`.**

As a result, your vertical linear layout element shrinks so that it's large enough for only the two check boxes and the button.

You have a bit more work to do, but the work isn't burdensome.

16. **Change the text on the check boxes and the button so that it matches what you see in Figure 6-1.**

Don't worry about the word Plain in Figure 6-1. You work on that in the section "Reusing a layout," later in this chapter.

For help changing the text, see to Chapter 5 of this minibook.

17. **Set the `onClick` property of the button to `onButtonClick`.**

For help setting the `onClick` property, see Chapter 5 of this minibook.

Creating a reusable layout

The check boxes and the button in Figure 6-1 are useful in more than one situation. You might place these widgets in an app with a confirmation word (such as the word Plain in Figure 6-1). You might use the same widgets in a different app with a picture of a pizza below the widgets. One way or another, it's worth your while to save the layout containing these widgets. You save these widgets in a new layout resource document (a `blahblah.xml` document in the res/layout directory). This section tells you how to do that.

1. **Open the project that you created in this chapter's "Improving the Layout" section.**

2. **In the preview screen, click in a neutral place inside the vertical linear layout that you created.**

   Make sure that you see the outline of the layout that contains both check boxes and the button. If you have trouble selecting this layout, you can ignore the preview screen and select the `LinearLayout (Vertical)` branch in the Component tree.

3. **In Android Studio's main menu, choose Refactor⇨Refactor This.**

   A pop-up menu containing the Style and Layout options appears.

4. **In the pop-up menu, select Layout.**

   An Extract Android Layout dialog box appears.

5. **In the dialog box's File Name field, type the name of your new resource document.**

   In Figure 6-3, I type **reusable_layout.xml**.

   The names of Android's resource files must not contain capital letters. You can use lowercase letters and underscores. You cannot use Java's customary "camelCase" naming convention with names like `reUsableLayout.xml`. And, yes, a layout filename must end with the extension `.xml`.

Figure 6-3:
The Extract
Android
Layout
dialog box.

6. **Click OK to close the dialog box.**

   The `app/res/layout` branch in the Project tool window now has a new item. If you named the file as I did in Step 5, the branch is labeled `reusable_layout.xml`.

7. **Double-click the** `reusable_layout.xml` **branch in the Project tool window.**

Android Studio displays the Designer tool for the `reusable_layout.xml` file.

8. **Make sure that the Designer tool is in Design mode (as opposed to Text mode).**

In Design mode, you can see the Component tree.

9. **Make note of the labels on the branches in the Component tree.**

Look for names like `checkBox`, `checkBox2`, and `button`. (See Figure 6-4.) You use these names (these id values) in the code that you write later in this chapter.

Figure 6-4:
The
Component
tree.

To change an element's id, double-click that element in the preview screen. The resulting pop-up menu has a text field labeled id. Change whatever is entered in that text field.

Congratulations! You have a group of widgets that you can use and reuse.

Reusing a layout

In the "Creating a reusable layout" section, you create a layout with check boxes and a button. You can reuse this layout in many of this chapter's examples. Here's how:

1. **Follow the steps in the "Creating a reusable layout" section.**

If you're impatient, you can skip a few of that section's steps, but be sure to create a `reusable_layout.xml` file and to populate the file with a few widgets.

2. **In the Project tool window, select the project's** `reusable_layout.xml` **file.**

3. **In Android Studio's main menu, choose Edit⇨Copy.**

You don't see much happening, but now your Clipboard contains a copy of the `reusable_layout.xml` file.

4. **Start a new Android project.**

5. **In the Project tool window, select the new project's** `app/res/layout`
branch.

6. **In Android Studio's main menu, choose Edit⇨Paste.**

Now the `app/res/layout` branch contains a `reusable_layout.xml` file.

7. **Open your project's** `res/layout/activity_main.xml` **file.**

When you do, you see your new project's preview screen (which is
mostly empty).

8. **In the Custom group in the Designer tool's palette, click the <include>**
item.

The palette has its own scroll bar. Use this scroll bar to find the palette's
Custom group.

When you do this, a Resources dialog box appears. (See Figure 6-5.)

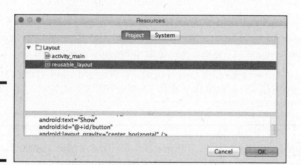

Figure 6-5:
The
Resources
dialog box.

9. **In the Resources dialog box, select your reusable layout — the one**
you named `reusable_layout.xml`**; then click OK.**

The Resources dialog box closes.

10. **Click in the Designer tool's preview screen.**

As if by magic, the stuff that you created in the "Creating a reusable
layout" section appears on the preview screen. (Well, anyway, it looks
like magic to me.) This stuff appears as one group, so you can drag that
group around in the preview screen.

11. **If necessary, reshape the newly included group (two check boxes and**
a button) by dragging its edges in the preview screen. Also, drag the
entire group so that it's centered inside the preview screen.

If all goes well, your layout looks like the stuff in Figure 6-1.

In the next step, you add the word *Plain* to your app's screen. (Refer to
Figure 6-1.)

12. **From the palette, place a Large Text element on the preview screen.**

13. **Replace the Large Text element's placeholder text with the word** Plain.

14. **(Optional) If you're very ambitious, follow the steps in Chapter 5 of this minibook for coding your app's behavior. Then run your app.**

Ambitious or not, you have a decent-looking layout with a reusable component. Nice work!

Starting Another Activity

As I mention in Chapter 4 of this minibook, an Android *activity* is one "screenful" of components. So juggling activities is a major endeavor for Android developers. This section's example does the simplest thing you can do with an activity — namely, make it run.

1. **Launch Android Studio and create a new project.**

In this section's listings, I name the application `01_06_01`, and I name the package `com.allyourcode.p01_06_01`.

2. **Follow the instructions in the earlier section "Reusing a layout" to include** `reusable_layout` **on your new app's screen.**

You have two check boxes and a button. When a user clicks the button, you want Android to display a different activity's screen. So you have to create another activity.

Let's get cracking . . .

3. **In the Project tool window, right-click or (on a Mac) Ctrl-click your project's** `app/java/`*your.package* **branch.**

In Listing 6-1, the package name is `com.allyourcode.p01_06_01`. So I Ctrl-click my project's `app/java/com.allyourcode.p01_06_01` branch.

4. **In the context menu that appears, choose New ⇨ Activity ⇨ Blank Activity.**

A dialog box appears. (You see this dialog box whenever you create a new blank activity. The dialog box is labeled Choose Options for Your New File.)

5. **In the dialog box, fill in the Activity Name and Layout Name fields.**

In Listings 6-1 and 6-2, I refer to `OtherActivity` and `other_layout`. So, if you're following along letter for letter with these instructions, type **OtherActivity** in the Activity Name field, and type **other_layout** in the Layout Name field. You can accept the defaults for all the other fields in the dialog box.

6. **Click Finish to close the dialog box.**

   Your new `other_layout` now appears in Android Studio's Designer tool.

7. **(Optional, but worth doing.) In this step, you don't have to do anything. Just look at something! In your project's `AndroidManifest.xml` file, notice the following code:**

   ```
   <activity
   android:name=".OtherActivity"
   android:label="OtherActivity" >
   </activity>
   ```

   Android Studio added this `<activity>` element when you created `OtherActivity` in Steps 3 through 6.

   Each activity in your application must have an `<activity>` element in the `AndroidManifest.xml` file. In an `<activity>` element, the `android:name` attribute points to the name of the activity's Java class. In this step, the attribute's value is "`.OtherActivity`". The initial dot refers to the application's package name (the name `com.allyourcode.p01_06_01` from Step 1). The rest of the attribute refers to the class name in Listing 6-2.

   Each activity in your application must have an `<activity>` element. If you're missing an `<activity>` element, the app can't start that activity. (Instead, the app crashes, and you see an *Unable to find explicit activity* message in the Logcat panel.)

8. **With other_layout showing in the preview screen, drag a Large Text element from the palette onto other_layout.**

   Now, other_layout has a TextView element (with large text).

   Your project has two activities (two Java files) and a layout for each activity (two XML files in the Project view's `app/res/layout` branch). In addition, your project has a `reusable_layout` that's included inside your main activity's layout. You can switch back and forth between the two activities and their layout files, but try to be mindful of the switching. Try not to be become confused by editing the wrong Java code or the wrong layout file (the way I often do).

9. **Look for your new TextView element in the Component tree.**

   Make note of the label on that element's branch of the tree. In my version of the app, the label is `textView3`.

   If you switch momentarily to the Designer tool's Text mode, you see the attribute `android:id="@+id/textView3"` inside the `TextView` tag. The id of this element is `textView3`.

To change an element's id, double-click that element in the preview screen. The pop-up menu that appears has a text field labeled *id*. Change whatever is entered in that text field.

10. **Modify your main activity's code, as shown in Listing 6-1.**

I set the code to be added in boldface type.

Listing 6-1:   Starting OtherActivity from the MainActivity

```
package com.allyourcode.p01_06_01;

import android.app.Activity;
import android.content.Intent;
import android.os.Bundle;
import android.view.Menu;
import android.view.MenuItem;
import android.view.View;
import android.widget.CheckBox;


public class MainActivity extends Activity {
  CheckBox pepBox, cheeseBox;

  @Override
  protected void onCreate(Bundle savedInstanceState) {
    super.onCreate(savedInstanceState);
    setContentView(R.layout.activity_main);

    pepBox = (CheckBox) findViewById(R.id.checkBox);
    cheeseBox = (CheckBox) findViewById(R.id.checkBox2);
}

  public void onButtonClick(View view) {
    Intent intent =
      new Intent(this, OtherActivity.class);
    intent.putExtra
      ("Pepperoni", pepBox.isChecked());
    intent.putExtra
      ("Extra cheese", cheeseBox.isChecked());
    startActivity(intent);
  }

  // You don't have to add any code below this point

  @Override
  public boolean onCreateOptionsMenu(Menu menu) {

  // . . . Et cetera
```

Double-check the expressions `R.id.checkBox` and `R.id.checkBox2` in Listing 6-1 against the names in the Component tree at the end of the "Creating a reusable layout" section. If the Component tree's labels aren't `checkBox` and `checkBox2`, change your Listing 6-1 code appropriately.

In the `MainActivity` (Listing 6-1), you have code that starts up the `OtherActivity`. You don't start an activity by calling the activity's methods. Instead, you create an intent. An *intent* is like an open-ended method call. In Listing 6-1, you create an *explicit intent* — an intent that invokes a specific class's code.

- The intent in Listing 6-1 invokes the code in a class named `OtherActivity` (or whatever you name your app's second activity).

- The intent in Listing 6-1 has two extra pieces of information. Each "extra piece" of information is a name/value pair. For example, if the user checks the Pepperoni box, `pepBox.isChecked()` is `true`, so the intent contains the extra pair `"Pepperoni", true`.

- In Listing 6-1, the call `startActivity(intent)` invokes the `OtherActivity` class's code.

This section's explanation of Android's *intent* mechanism shows you the tiniest tip of the iceberg. To read all about activities and intents, see Book III, Chapter 2.

Next up, your `OtherActivity` should have some code that responds to the fact that `OtherActivity` was started.

11. **In your new `OtherActivity` class, add the code in Listing 6-2.**

I set the code to be added in boldface type.

Listing 6-2:   The OtherActivity

```
package com.allyourcode.p01_06_01;

import android.app.Activity;
import android.content.Intent;
import android.os.Bundle;
import android.view.Menu;
import android.view.MenuItem;
import android.widget.TextView;


public class OtherActivity extends Activity {
  TextView textView;

  @Override
  protected void onCreate(Bundle savedInstanceState) {
    super.onCreate(savedInstanceState);
    setContentView(R.layout.other_layout);

    textView = (TextView) findViewById(R.id.textView3);

    Intent intent = getIntent();
    StringBuilder str = new StringBuilder("");
    if (intent.getBooleanExtra("Pepperoni", false)) {
      str.append("Pepperoni ");
    }
```

(continued)

Listing 6-2 *(continued)*

```
          if (intent.getBooleanExtra("Extra cheese", false)) {
            str.append("Extra cheese");
          }
          if (str.length() == 0) {
            str.append("Plain");
          }
          textView.setText(str);
      }

      // You don't have to add any code below this point

      @Override
      public boolean onCreateOptionsMenu(Menu menu) {

      // . . . Et cetera
```

In Listing 6-2, I assume that the `TextView` in the `other_layout.xml` file is `textView3`. (That is, I assume that, in the XML file itself, the TextView element has an attribute that reads `android:id="@+id/textView3"`.) If this TextView element has an id other than `textView3`, change the code in Listing 6-2 accordingly.

In Listing 6-2, the call to `getIntent` gets the stuff that started this activity running. So, by calling `getIntent` and `intent.getBooleanExtra`, the `OtherActivity` discovers the values of `pepBox.isChecked()` and `cheeseBox.isChecked()` from Listing 6-1. For example, the call

```
    intent.getBooleanExtra("Pepperoni", false)
```

returns `true` if the value of `pepBox.isChecked()` in Listing 6-1 is `true`. The call returns `false` if the value of `pepBox.isChecked()` in Listing 6-1 is `false`. The call's second argument is a default value. So, in Listing 6-2, the call to `intent.getBooleanExtra("Pepperoni", false)` returns `false` if the intent created in Listing 6-1 doesn't have an extra named `"Pepperoni"`.

12. **Run your app.**

When you click the app's button, you see a new activity like the one pictured in Figure 6-6.

Figure 6-6:
A new activity appears on the device's screen.

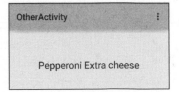

Localizing Your App

Words, words, words. The apps in this chapter have so many words. "Pepperoni" here; "Extra cheese" there! It's a wonder a developer can keep this stuff straight. It's too easy to type a word one way in one part of the code and misspell the word in a different part.

You can reduce the problem by creating string constants. For example, you can write

```
public final String pep = "Pepperoni";
```

at the top of your Java program and use the variable pep in place of the string "Pepperoni" throughout the code. But then, to change from the English word *pepperoni* to the Italian word *merguez,* you have to mess with your Java code. In a world where only six percent of all mobile phones are in the United States,* you don't want to edit Java code for dozens of countries.

The elegant solution to this problem is to use Android's *string externalization* feature. Here's what you do:

1. **Open the project that you created in this chapter's "Reusing a layout" section.**

   If you've messed with that project since you created it, or if you didn't faithfully execute each of my instructions in that section, don't despair. You can find that project in the stuff that you download from my website. Visit http://allmycode.com/android and follow the instructions in Chapter 3 of this minibook for running the downloaded examples.

2. **Open the project's** reusable_layout.xml **file and put the Designer tool in Text mode.**

   Notice lines such as

   ```
   android:text="Extra cheese"
   ```

   in the reusable_layout.xml file? What if the user isn't an English language speaker? A layout file describes the look of the app's screen. The look of the screen shouldn't depend on the user's being able to understand what Extra cheese means.

3. **In the editor, click inside the string** "Extra cheese".

*Source: http://en.wikipedia.org/wiki/List_of_countries_by_number_of_mobile_phones_in_use

4. Press Alt-Enter.

A pop-up menu appears. This menu is called an *intention action menu*. The menu contains a list of actions from which you can choose.

5. In the intention action menu, select Extract String Resource.

Well, wha' da' ya' know?! An Extract Resource dialog box appears! (See Figure 6-7.)

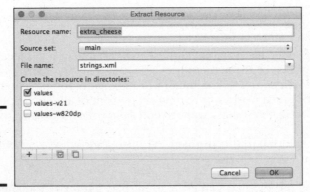

Figure 6-7: The Extract Resource dialog box.

6. In the Resource Name field, type extra_cheese.

A resource name must not contain blank spaces. In this step, `extra_cheese` is okay and `extracheese` is also okay. But `extra cheese` isn't okay.

7. Click OK.

Android Studio adds the following element to your `res/values/strings.xml` file:

```
<string name="extra_cheese">Extra cheese</string>
```

Android Studio also replaces `"Extra cheese"` in your layout's CheckBox element with an `@string` expression:

```
<CheckBox
    android:text="@string/extra_cheese"
```

8. (Optional, but very nice if you do it.) Repeat Steps 3 through 7 for the strings `"Pepperoni"`, `"Show"`, **and (in the** `activity_main.xml` **file)** `"Plain"`.

With your app's strings externalized, you're ready to go international.

9. Right-click (or on a Mac, Ctrl-click) the `strings.xml` **file in your project's** `res/values` **folder in the Project tool window.**

10. **In the context menu that appears, select Open Translations Editor.**

The Translations Editor appears in place of the Designer tool.
(See Figure 6-8.)

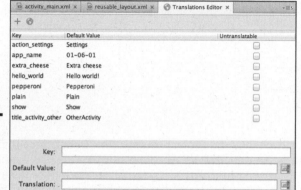

Figure 6-8:
The
Translations
Editor.

11. **Near the top of the Translations Editor, click the globe icon.**

A list of language locales appears. (See Figure 6-9.)

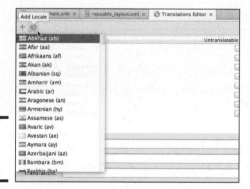

Figure 6-9:
Select a
language.

12. **Select a language locale from the list.**

For this exercise, I select *Italian (it)*. (I'd be disloyal to my buddy Steve if
I did otherwise.) For the full scoop on language locales, visit `www.iso.`
`org/iso/country_names_and_code_elements`.

As a result, the `strings.xml` branch in the Project tool window now
has two sub-branches. Both sub-branches sport the label `strings.xml`,
but the new sub-branch's icon is a tiny picture of the flag of Italy. (See
Figure 6-10.)

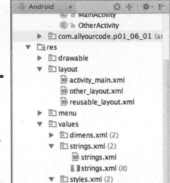

Figure 6-10:
Look! You
have two
`strings.`
`xml`
files.

Temporarily change the Project tool window from Android view to Project view. Your project's `res` folder now has a `values` subfolder and a `values-it` subfolder. The `values-it` subfolder contains its own `strings.xml` file. (Okay, you can go back to the Android view now!)

In the Translations Editor, the term `extra_cheese` is in red because you haven't yet translated `extra_cheese` into Italian. The same is true for other terms that you haven't yet translated.

13. **Double-click the Italian (it) column in the `extra_cheese` row. In that column, type** `Con più formaggio`, **and then press Enter.**

    (Sorry. The Translations Editor doesn't do any translating for you. The Translations Editor only adds code to your project when you type in the translations of words and phrases.)

14. **Repeat Step 13 for the *pepperoni*, *show*, and *plain* rows.**

    If your Italian is a bit rusty, copy the text from the `res/values-it/` `strings.xml` file in Listing 6-3.

Elenco 6-3: Benvenuto in Italia!

```
<?xml version="1.0" encoding="utf-8"?>
<resources>
    <string name="hello">
        Ciao mondo, la mia attività!</string>
    <string name="app_name">
        Il mio secondo progetto Android</string>
    <string name="extra_cheese">Con più formaggio</string>
    <string name="pepperoni">Merguez</string>
    <string name="plain">Semplice</string>
    <string name="show">Mostra</string>
</resources>
```

Book I
Chapter 6

Improving Your App

15. **Test your app.**

As with most devices, the emulator has a setting for Language & Input. Change this setting to Italiano (Italia), and suddenly, your app looks like the display in Figure 6-11.

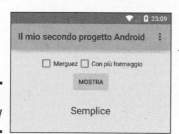

Figure 6-11:
Buongiorno!

Responding to Check Box Events

Why click twice when you can do the same thing by clicking only once? Think about the example in the previous section. Your app responds to the contents of check boxes when the user clicks a button. In a streamlined scenario, your app might respond as soon as the user checks a box. Listing 6-4 shows you how to make this happen.

Listing 6-4:   Responding to CheckBox Events

```
package com.allyourcode.p01_06_04;

import android.app.Activity;
import android.os.Bundle;
import android.view.Menu;
import android.view.MenuItem;
import android.widget.CheckBox;
import android.widget.CompoundButton;
import android.widget.CompoundButton.
                         OnCheckedChangeListener;
import android.widget.TextView;

public class MainActivity extends Activity
              implements OnCheckedChangeListener {

  TextView textView;

  @Override
  protected void onCreate(Bundle savedInstanceState) {
    super.onCreate(savedInstanceState);
    setContentView(R.layout.activity_main);
```

(continued)

Listing 6-4 *(continued)*

```
    ((CheckBox) findViewById(R.id.checkBox))
       .setOnCheckedChangeListener(this);
    ((CheckBox) findViewById(R.id.checkBox2))
       .setOnCheckedChangeListener(this);
    textView =
       (TextView) findViewById(R.id.textView);
  }


  @Override
  public void onCheckedChanged(CompoundButton box,
                               boolean isChecked) {
    StringBuilder str =
       new StringBuilder(textView.getText());
    CharSequence boxText = box.getText();
    if (isChecked) {
      str.append(" " + boxText);

    } else {
      int start = str.indexOf(boxText.toString());
      int length = boxText.length();
      str.replace(start, start + length, "");
    }
    textView.setText(str.toString().trim());
  }
//. . . Et cetera
```

Like a button, each check box listens for `onClick` events. So you can write this section's code very much like the code in Listing 6-1. But in this section's listing, I avoid using the `onClick` property and illustrate the use of a different event listener.

A check box listens for changes to its state (its "checked" versus "unchecked" state). So when the user touches a check box, Android fires an `onCheckedChanged` event. By registering `this` (the entire `MainActivity` instance) as each check box's `OnCheckedChangeListener`, you make Android call the `onCheckedChanged` method in Listing 6-4.

The `onCheckedChanged` method has two parameters — the component that was touched and the state of the component as a result of the touch. I've contrived the code in Listing 6-4 to make use of these two method parameters.

A `CompoundButton` is a widget with checked and unchecked states. The `CheckBox` class is a subclass of `CompoundButton`. Other subclasses of `CompoundButton` are `RadioButton` and `ToggleButton`. A `ToggleButton` is that cute little thing that lights when it's checked.

In Listing 6-4, the onCheckedChanged method's box parameter refers to whichever check box the user touches. That check box has a getText method, so in Listing 6-4, I use the getText method to help fill the textView element. I use the onCheckedChanged method's isChecked parameter to decide whether to add text to the textView element or delete text from the textView element.

Displaying Images

After designing an app and its variations in the previous sections, you may decide that your app needs some flair. How about designing your app so that when a user clicks a button, your app displays a picture of the pizza being ordered? The SHOW button in Figure 6-1 is perfect for this.

Android has all kinds of features for drawing images and displaying bitmap files. I cover many of these features in Book IV, Chapter 3. In this section, I cover one possible approach:

1. **Launch Android Studio and create a new project.**

   In this section's listings, I call the project 01_06_05, and I use the package com.allmycode.p01_06_05.

2. **Copy the** reusable_layout.xml **file from this chapter's "Creating a reusable layout" section to your new project's** app/res/layout **branch in the Project tool window.**

3. **Include** reusable_layout **in your project's** activity_main.xml **file.**

   For details, see Steps 7 through 11 in the section "Reusing a layout."

4. **Find four images — one for plain, one for pepperoni, one for extra cheese, and one for pepperoni with extra cheese.**

   Android's official documentation recommends the .png format for images. If you don't have .png images, Android's docs call the .jpg format "acceptable." If you don't have .png or .jpg, the docs tell you to hold your nose and use .gif. But remember, in this section, you're creating a practice application, not a work of art. Your images don't have to look good. They don't even have to look like pizzas. Besides, you can download my silly-looking drawings of pizzas from this book's website at www.allmycode.com/Android.

   In creating my project, I use the filenames plain.png, pepperoni. png, extracheese.png, and pep_extracheese.png.

   The names of Android's resource files must not contain capital letters. You can use only lowercase letters and underscores.

For working with image formats, the program IrfanView has always served me well. You can get this Windows program at `http://www.irfanview.com`. The program is free for noncommercial use.

5. **In your operating system's File Explorer or Finder, select the image files. Then, in the main menu, choose Edit⇨Copy.**

6. **In Android Studio's Project tool window, select the** `app/res/drawable` **branch.**

7. **In the main menu, choose Edit⇨Paste.**

   A Choose Destination Directory dialog box appears.

8. **In the Choose Destination Directory dialog box, select the** `drawable` **branch (as opposed to one of the** `drawable-dpi` **branches), and then click OK.**

   In a real-life app, you use the `drawable-dpi` directories as alternatives for devices with high, medium, extra-high, and extra-extra-high screen densities. But in this practice app, a default `drawable` folder is the easiest to use.

   The letters *dpi* stand for *dots per inch*. Android senses a device's screen density and uses the resources in the most appropriate `drawable-?dpi` folder. To find out what Android considers "most appropriate," visit `http://developer.android.com/guide/practices/screens_support.html`.

9. **Right-click (on Windows) or Ctrl-click (on a Mac) the** `app/res/drawable` **branch.**

10. **In the menu that appears, select New⇨File.**

    Once again, the Choose Destination Directory dialog box rears its ugly head.

11. **Select the** `drawable` **branch, and then click OK.**

    A New File dialog box appears. This dialog box has only one field — a field for the name of your new file. (See Figure 6-12.)

Figure 6-12:
The New
File dialog
box.

12. **In the New File dialog box's field, type** levels.xml.

13. **Click OK to dismiss the New File dialog box.**

14. **Use Android Studio's editor to populate your** levels.xml **file with the code in Listing 6-5.**

Listing 6-5: A Level-List Document

```xml
<?xml version="1.0" encoding="utf-8"?>
<level-list xmlns:android=
        "http://schemas.android.com/apk/res/android">
    <item android:drawable="@drawable/plain"
            android:maxLevel="0" />
    <item android:drawable="@drawable/pepperoni"
            android:maxLevel="1" />
    <item android:drawable="@drawable/extracheese"
            android:maxLevel="2" />
    <item android:drawable="@drawable/pep_extracheese"
            android:maxLevel="3" />
</level-list>
```

A *level-list* is a list of alternative drawables for a single image component to display. At any moment during an app's run, the image component has an integer level. You set the component's level using the setImageLevel method.

When your app calls setImageLevel, Android starts at the top of the level-list and looks for the first item whose android:maxLevel is greater than or equal to the new image level. You can also assign an android:minLevel attribute to an item. But in most situations, android:maxLevel is all you need.

15. **Add an ImageView element to your activity's layout.**

You can drag an ImageView element from the Widgets group in the Designer tool's palette, or you can add the following element to your app's activity_main.xml file:

```xml
<ImageView android:id="@+id/imageView1"
            android:layout_height="wrap_content"
            android:layout_width="wrap_content"
            android:src="@drawable/levels"></ImageView>
```

16. **Make sure that your ImageView element's** android:src **attribute refers to your new** levels.xml **file.**

In the src entry in the Properties view, look for the value @drawable/levels.

17. Code your project's activity file as in Listing 6-6.

In Listing 6-6, the onButtonClick method calls the setImageLevel method. The method parameter's value depends on the states of the activity's check boxes.

Listing 6-6:   Changing Images

```
package com.allmycode.p01_06_05;

import android.app.Activity;
import android.os.Bundle;
import android.view.Menu;
import android.view.MenuItem;
import android.view.View;
import android.widget.CheckBox;
import android.widget.ImageView;


public class MainActivity extends Activity {
  CheckBox pepBox, cheeseBox;
  ImageView imageView;

  @Override
  protected void onCreate(Bundle savedInstanceState) {
    super.onCreate(savedInstanceState);
    setContentView(R.layout.activity_main);

    pepBox =
        (CheckBox) findViewById(R.id.checkBox);
    cheeseBox =
        (CheckBox) findViewById(R.id.checkBox2);
    imageView =
        (ImageView) findViewById(R.id.imageView);
  }

  public void onButtonClick(View view) {
    int level = 0;

    if (pepBox.isChecked()) {
      level += 1;
    }
    if (cheeseBox.isChecked()) {
      level += 2;
    }
    imageView.setImageLevel(level);
  }

  // You don't have to add any code below this point

  @Override
  public boolean onCreateOptionsMenu(Menu menu) {

  // . . . Et cetera
```

18. **Run the app.**

The results, along with my beautiful drawings of pizza with toppings, are shown in Figure 6-13.

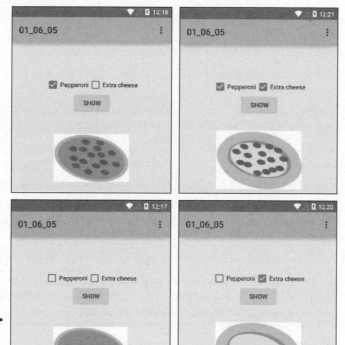

Figure 6-13:
What lovely drawings!

Sending in Your Order

If you've read any of this chapter's previous sections, you're probably very hungry. An app with nothing but pictures and the names of pizza toppings is a real tease.

So you'd better add some purchasing power to this chapter's example. Real e-commerce functionality is the subject of several other books. But in this book, you can get a small taste of the online pizza-ordering process (pun intended). You can submit your choice of toppings to an existing web server — Google's search engine, to be precise. It's not as good as biting into a tasty pizza, but the example shows you one way to send information from a mobile device.

In a real application, you might program your own server to respond intelligently to users' requests. For passing money back and forth, you might use the Google Play Store's in-app billing facilities.

Programming web servers isn't an Android-specific topic. To read all about servers, check out *Apache, MySQL, and PHP Web Development All-in-One Desk Reference For Dummies,* by Jeff Cogswell (John Wiley & Sons, Inc.).

1. **Launch Android Studio and create a new project.**

In this section's listing, I call the project 01_06_07, and I use the package com.allmycode.p01_06_07.

2. **Copy the** reusable_layout.xml **file from this chapter's "Creating a reusable layout" section to your new project's** app/res/layout **branch in the Project tool window.**

3. **Include** reusable_layout **in your project's** activity_main.xml **file.**

For details, see Steps 7 through 11 in the section "Reusing a layout."

4. **Get a WebView element from the Widgets group of the Designer tool's palette. Place that WebView element anywhere on your app's preview screen.**

A WebView is a mini web browser that you can add to an existing activity.

It doesn't matter how you position the WebView element on the screen. When the user visits a web page, the page will take up the entire screen. (If you want the page to appear below your check boxes and button, you'll have to see Chapter 1 in Book IV.)

5. **Code your project's activity file as in Listing 6-7.**

Listing 6-7:   Sending Info to a Server

```
package com.allmycode.p01_06_07;

import android.app.Activity;
import android.os.Bundle;
import android.view.Menu;
import android.view.MenuItem;
import android.view.View;
import android.webkit.WebView;
import android.widget.CheckBox;


public class MainActivity extends Activity {
    CheckBox pepBox, cheeseBox;
    WebView webView;
```

```
@Override
protected void onCreate(Bundle savedInstanceState) {
  super.onCreate(savedInstanceState);
  setContentView(R.layout.activity_main);

  pepBox = (CheckBox) findViewById(R.id.checkBox);
  cheeseBox = (CheckBox) findViewById(R.id.checkBox2);
  webView = (WebView) findViewById(R.id.webView);
}

  public void onButtonClick(View view) {
    StringBuilder str = new StringBuilder("");
    if (pepBox.isChecked()) {
      str.append("Pepperoni");
    }
    if (cheeseBox.isChecked()) {
      str.append("\"Extra cheese\"");
    }
    if (str.length() == 23) {
      str.insert(9, '+');
    }
    if (str.length() == 0) {
      str.append("Plain");
    }
    webView.loadUrl
      ("http://www.google.com/search?q="+str.toString());
}

// You don't have to add any code below this point

@Override
public boolean onCreateOptionsMenu(Menu menu) {

// . . . Et cetera
```

6. **Add the following element to your project's** `AndroidManifest.xml` **file:**

   ```
   <uses-permission
   android:name="android.permission.INTERNET" />
   ```

   Make this `uses-permission` element a direct sub-element of the document's `manifest` element.

   The `uses-permission` element grants your app permission to access the Internet. Access to the Internet will appear in the list the user sees before installing your app.

   When you create an app, don't forget to add the appropriate permissions to the app's `AndroidManifest.xml` file. In a recent survey of *For Dummies* book authors, all respondents reported that they frequently forget to add permissions to their apps' manifest files. (Survey sample size: one.)

7. **Run your app.**

   You might have to wait for the web page to load. When the page loads, your app looks something like the screen in Figure 6-14.

Figure 6-14: Your app sends stuff to a web server.

Book II
Android Background Material

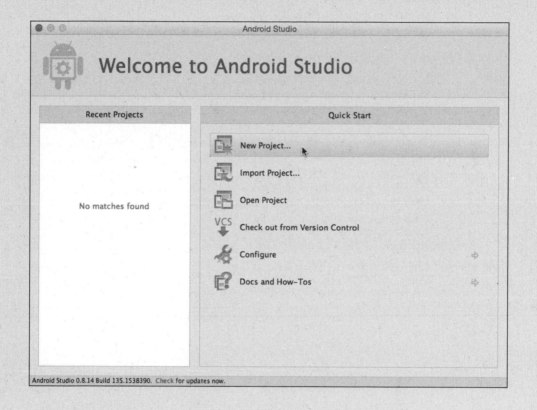

For more on Android's adb command, check out www.dummies.com/extras/androidappdevelopmentaio.

Contents at a Glance

Chapter 1: Using Android Studio

In This Chapter

✓ **Making sense of all that stuff in Android Studio's main window**

✓ **Getting the most out of Android Studio**

When you develop software, you have two options:

✦ **Be tough and use only command-line tools.**

Edit programs with plain text editors, such as UNIX vi, GNU Emacs, Windows Notepad, or Macintosh TextEdit. Issue commands to the Windows MS-DOS screen or in the Macintosh Terminal window.

✦ **Be wimpy and use an integrated development environment (an IDE).**

Execute commands by clicking menu items. Edit programs with a full-featured editor — an editor customized for whatever programming language you use. Change object values with code-aware property sheets. Create forms by dragging widgets from a palette to a visual layout.

I admire toughness, but wimpiness is more efficient. Being wimpy makes you more productive and less prone to error. Also, being wimpy helps you to concentrate on the app that you're creating instead of having to focus on the commands to create the app.

Don't get me wrong. Tough command-line tools are great in a pinch. When your IDE covers up subtle (but important) details, you need command-line tools to show you what's going on behind the scenes. But for most developers, most of the time, IDEs are great time-savers.

With or without Android, IntelliJ IDEA (the backbone of Android Studio) is a mature platform, with tools for Java development, C/C++ development, PHP development, modeling, project management, testing, debugging, and much more.

So this chapter covers Android Studio. I (naturally enough) focus on features that help you build Android apps, but keep in mind that Android Studio has hundreds of general-purpose software development features and many ways to access each feature.

Don't Read This Chapter

Several chapters in this book contain instructions for using Android Studio. Here are some highlights:

✦ In Book I, Chapter 2, you install Android Studio.

✦ In Book I, Chapter 3, you create and run an app using Android Studio.

✦ In Book I, Chapter 3, you download this book's code examples, and open them in Android Studio.

✦ In Book I, Chapter 5, you create the look of your app using Android Studio's Designer tool.

Many other chapters contain all the need-to-know Android Studio features. But some very useful things aren't need-to-know things. You can live a full life without knowing that Android Studio can fix your code's indentation. (You can fix the indentation yourself.) You can develop top-selling apps without knowing about the Project tool window's Floating mode.

For information about the need-to-know Android development tasks, skip to other chapters. But for the useful-to-know items (things that aren't absolutely required for getting the work done — the handy tricks that help you work more efficiently), check this chapter.

The Big Picture

Each Android app belongs to a project. A project can contain several modules. For example, an app that runs on Android Wear (an Android-enabled wristwatch) will have at least two modules. One module contains code that runs on a watch; the other module contains supporting code that runs on the user's smartphone. Figure 1-1 shows the structure of a project that contains two modules — a mobile module (for the smartphone) and a wear module (for the watch).

Most of this book's examples live in simple, one-module projects.

You can have dozens of projects on your computer's hard drive. When you run Android Studio, each of your projects is either *open* or *closed*. An open project appears in a window (its own window) on your computer screen. A closed project doesn't appear in a window.

Several of your projects can be open at the same time. You can switch between projects by moving from window to window. Each open project uses a chunk of your computer's precious RAM (random access memory). So, if you're not actively working on a particular project, it's best to close that project.

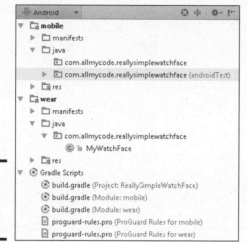

Figure 1-1:
A project
with two
modules.

I often refer to an open project's window as Android Studio's *main window*. This can be slightly misleading because, with several projects open at once, you have several main windows open at once. None of these windows is more "main" than the others.

If Android Studio is running, and no projects are open, Android Studio displays its Welcome screen. (See Figure 1-2.) The Welcome screen displays some recently closed projects. You can open a project by clicking its name on the Welcome screen. For an app that's not on the Recent Projects list, you can click the Welcome screen's Open an Existing Android Studio Project option.

If you have any open projects, Android Studio doesn't display the Welcome screen. In that case, you can open another project by choosing File➪Open, File➪Reopen Project, or File➪Open Recent in an open project's window. To close a project, you can choose File➪Close Project, or you can do whatever you normally do to close one of the windows on your computer. (On a PC, click the X in the window's upper-right corner. On a Mac, click the little red button in the window's upper-left corner.)

Android Studio remembers which projects were open from one run to the next. If any projects are open when you quit Android Studio, those projects open again (with their main windows showing) the next time you launch Android Studio. You can override this behavior (so that only the Welcome screen appears each time you launch Android Studio). To do so on a Windows computer, start by choosing File➪Settings➪System Settings. On a Mac, choose Android Studio➪Preferences➪System Settings. In either case, uncheck the Reopen Last Project on Startup check box.

Android Studio

Welcome to Android Studio

Recent Projects

01_05_01
~ \AndroidStudioProjects\01_05_01

ReallySimpleWatchFace
~ \AndroidStudioPr...llySimpleWatchFace

My Application
~ \AndroidStudioProjects\MyApplication4

My NDK App
~ \AndroidStudioProjects\MyNDKApp

CatalogBrowser
~ \AndroidStudioPr...cts\CatalogBrowser

C:\Users\Barry\AndroidStudioProjects\MyA...
~ \AndroidStudioProjects\MyApplication3

Quick Start

Start a new Android Studio project

Open an existing Android Studio project

VCS Check out project from Version Control

Import project (Eclipse ADT, Gradle, etc.)

Configure

Docs and How-Tos

Android Studio 1.2.1.1 Build 141.1903250. Check for updates now.

Figure 1-2:
The
Welcome
screen.

The main window

The main window is divided into several areas. Some of these areas can appear and disappear on your command. What comes next is a list of the areas, going from the top of the main window to the very bottom. (You can follow along in Figure 1-3.)

✦ The topmost area contains the main menu and the toolbars.

✦ Below the main window and the toolbars you'll see as many as three different areas:

• The leftmost of these areas contains the Project tool window.

   You use the Project tool window to navigate from one file to another within your Android app.

• The middle area contains the editor.

   The editor can have several tabs. Each tab contains a file that's open for editing. To open a file for editing, double-click the file's branch in the Project tool window. To close the file, click the little x next to the file's name in the editor tab.

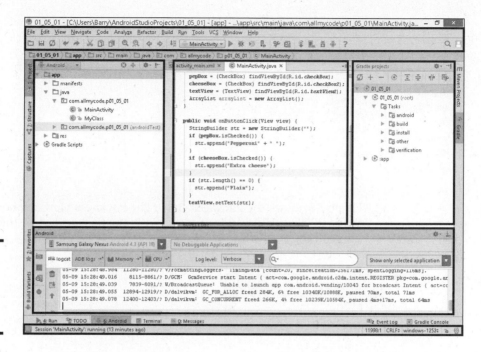

Book II
Chapter 1

Using Android
Studio

Figure 1-3:
The main
window
has several
areas.

- The rightmost area contains the Gradle tool window and the Maven Projects tool window.

    Gradle and *Maven* are tools for orchestrating the building of software projects (the combining of dozens of project files into one `.apk` file suitable for installation on a user's device). Gradle instructions are written in a language called Groovy; Maven instructions are written in XML.

    Android Studio creates Gradle scripts for each of your projects and executes these scripts as you develop your projects. If you have special requirements for a particular project, you can specify these requirements in the Gradle or Maven Projects tool window. (None of this book's examples require that kind of customization.)

At any given moment, the Project tool window displays one of several possible views. For example, back in Figure 1-3, the Project tool window displays its Android view. In Figure 1-4, I click the drop-down list and select the Packages view (instead of the Android view).

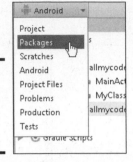

Figure 1-4:
Selecting the Packages view.

Figure 1-5 shows the Packages view. (The Packages view displays many of the same files as the Android view, but in the Packages view, the files are grouped differently.)

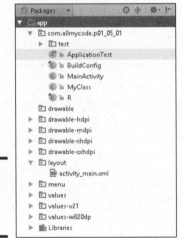

Figure 1-5:
The Packages view.

In Figure 1-3, to the left of the Project tool window, there's a Tool Window bar. The Tool Window bar contains three Tool Window buttons labeled "1: Project," "7: Structure," and "Captures." If the Project tool window is showing and you click the 1: Project tool button, the entire area consumed by the Project tool window disappears. (See Figure 1-6.) If you click the 1: Project tool button again, the area reappears with the Project tool window inside it.

You can move a tool window from one area to another by dragging the tool window's tool button. Try it!

If the Project tool window is showing and you click the 7: Structure tool button, the Structure tool window replaces the Project tool window in the rightmost area. (See Figure 1-7.)

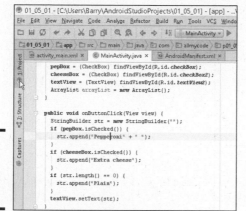

Figure 1-6: Look! No Project tool window!

Figure 1-7: The Structure tool window.

The same kind of thing happens when you click any of the Tool buttons:

- If the clicked tool button's window is showing, the window disappears, and its area shrinks to nothing.

- If the clicked tool button's area isn't showing, the area appears with the corresponding tool window inside it.

- If the clicked tool button's area is displaying a different tool window, the clicked button's tool window replaces whichever tool window is being displayed.

You can divide the Project tool window's area into two smaller areas. (See Figure 1-8.) To do so, click either the Build Variants or Favorites tool button. (You'll find these tool buttons in the main window's lower-left corner.) The reason this works is because the Build Variants and Favorites tool windows are in split mode. For more information about split mode, see the section "Viewing modes," later in this chapter.

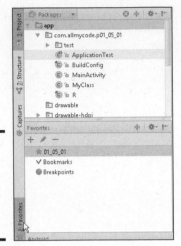

Figure 1-8:
Displaying the Favorites tool window.

Let's continue our tour of the areas in Figure 1-3:

✦ Below the middle three areas (that is, below the Project tool window, the editor, and the Gradle tool window) is another area that contains several tool windows.

• The Terminal tool window displays a PC's MS-DOS command prompt, a Mac's Terminal app, or some other text-based command screen that you specify. (See Figure 1-9.)

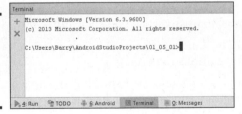

Figure 1-9:
The Terminal tool window on a PC.

• The Run tool window displays information about the launching of an Android app. (In Figure 1-10, phrases such as `Uploading file` refer to the movement of an app from your development computer to the emulator or physical device.)

The Run tool window appears automatically when you tell Android Studio to launch one of your projects.

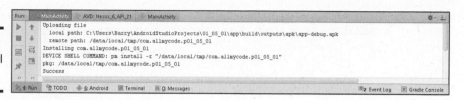

Figure 1-10:
The Run tool
window.

- The Android tool window displays information about the run of an Android app. This tool window appears automatically (replacing the Run tool window) when your app starts running on an emulator or a connected physical device.

  The Android tool window has several different panes — the Logcat pane, the ADB Logs pane, the Memory pane, the CPU pane, and possibly others. (Notice the tabs with these labels back in Figure 1-3.) The pane that I find most useful is the Logcat pane. In the Logcat pane, you see all the messages being logged by the running emulator or physical device. If your app isn't running correctly, you can filter the messages that are displayed and focus on the messages that are most helpful for diagnosing the problem.

- The Debug tool window appears in this area when you invoke Android Studio's debugger.

  For details on the use of the Logcat panel, the Debugger, and other nice toys, see Book I, Chapter 5.

You can force any of these tool windows to appear by clicking the corresponding tool button.

A particular tool button might not appear when there's nothing you can do with it. For example, if you're not trying to run an Android app, you might not see the Run tool button. You can see all the tool windows' names by choosing View⇨Tool Windows in Android Studio's main menu. The items whose tool buttons aren't visible are grayed out in the menu.

Finishing our tour of the areas in Figure 1-3 . . .

✦ The bottommost area contains the status bar.

  The status bar tells you what's happening now. For example, if your cursor is on the 37th character of the 11th line in the editor, you see *11:37* somewhere on the status line. When you tell Android Studio to run your app, you see `Gradle: Executing Tasks` on the status line. When Android Studio has finished executing Gradle tasks, you see `Gradle Build Finished` on the status line. Messages like these are helpful because they confirm that Android Studio is doing what you want it to do.

In addition to the areas that I mention in this section, other areas might pop up as the need arises. You can dismiss an area by clicking the area's Hide icon. (See Figure 1-11.)

Figure 1-11: Icons for hiding areas.

Viewing modes

The behavior that I describe in the previous section reflects tool windows in pinned, docked modes. You can change this behavior (and make other changes in the way tool windows behave) by clicking the gear icon in a tool window's upper right corner. (See Figure 1-12.)

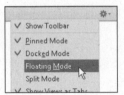

Figure 1-12: Selecting viewing modes.

There are four viewing modes — pinned mode, docked mode, floating mode, and split mode. For a particular tool window at a particular moment, each of the four modes is either on or off.

The viewing modes aren't mutually exclusive, and they aren't completely independent of one another. Whether one of the modes is on or off might make a difference in the way some other mode behaves. The default for many windows is pinned mode on, docked mode on, floating mode off, and split mode off.

Here's the meaning of each mode:

✦ **Pinned mode:** When pinned mode is off, the tool window disappears as soon as you click in a different area of the main window. To make that tool window reappear, click the corresponding tool button.

When pinned mode is on, clicking inside a different area doesn't make the tool window's area disappear.

✦ **Docked mode:** When docked mode is on, a tool window fits snugly inside its area. When docked mode is off, one of the edges must still line up with this tool window's tool window bar, but other edges of the tool window don't have to line up with an area's edges.

The tool window with docked mode off appears to live in a layer that's in front of the rest of the main window. Dragging the tool window's edges doesn't change the size of the main window's areas. (See Figures 1-13 and 1-14.)

Figure 1-13:
The undocked Project tool window is wide.

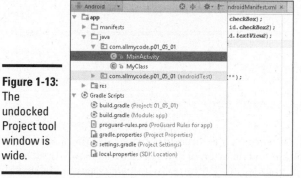

Figure 1-14:
The undocked Project tool window is narrow.

✦ **Floating mode:** A tool window with floating mode on is like one with docked mode off. The difference is, with floating mode on, none of the tool window's edges stay aligned with an area in the main window. The tool window appears to be an independent component floating above the main window. (See Figure 1-15.) You can drag the window's edges or drag the entire tool window.

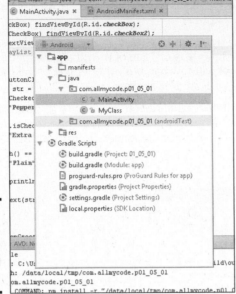

Figure 1-15:
The Project
tool window
with floating
mode on.

✦ **Split mode:** This mode works a bit differently from the others. A tool window with split mode on can appear in its area at the same time as a tool window with split mode off. (Both tool windows appear side by side or one above the other — see Figure 1-16.) In a particular area, at a particular time, if all of the area's tool windows have split mode off, then only one of the tool windows appears. (Similarly, if all of the area's tool windows have split mode *on,* then only one of the tool windows appears.)

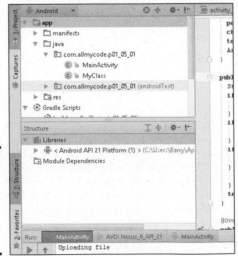

Figure 1-16:
The
Structure
tool window
in split
mode.

The Designer tool

When you edit a layout file (for example, the `activity_main.xml` file in the `res/layout` directory), Android Studio displays its Designer tool. The Designer tool has two modes: Design mode for drag-and-drop visual editing, and Text mode for XML code editing. (See Figures 1-17 and 1-18.) So the bottom of the Designer tool has two tabs — a Design tab and a Text tab.

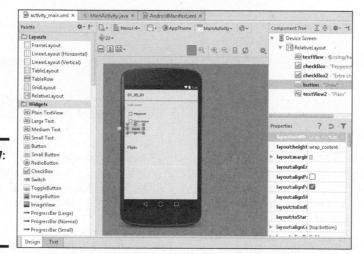

Figure 1-17: The Designer tool's Design mode.

Book II Chapter 1

Using Android Studio

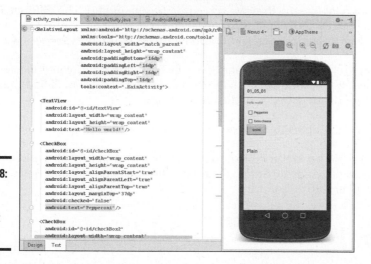

Figure 1-18: The Designer tool's Text mode.

In Design mode, you edit the layout by dragging and dropping widgets onto the Designer tool's Preview screen. In Text mode, you edit the same widgets by typing text in the XML file. When you use the Design mode's Preview screen, Android Studio automatically updates the XML file. And it works both ways. When you edit the XML file, Android Studio keeps the Preview screen up to date.

In Design mode, the Designer tool has three parts:

✦ The Preview screen in the middle is a place to drag and drop widgets. (Refer to Figure 1-18.)

✦ The palette on the left is a place to get the widgets that you drop onto the Preview screen.

✦ The combined Component tree and Properties pane on the right display facts about your activity's layout. You can change your layout by modifying the values that you find here.

You can hide the Preview screen or the Component tree with its Properties pane by clicking their respective Hide icons. (These icons look like the ones in Figure 1-11.) When you hide one of these parts, Android Studio creates a little tool button along the side of the Designer tool. Click the tool button to unhide one of the Designer tool's parts.

When the Designer tool is in Text mode, Android Studio displays its Preview tool window. (Refer to Figure 1-17.) The Preview tool window (in Text mode) looks a lot like the Preview screen (in Design mode). The difference is that the Preview tool window is only a viewer. It's not an editor. You can't modify the layout by dragging and dropping things in the Preview tool window.

If Android Studio's Designer tool is in Text mode, and you don't see the Preview tool window, click the Preview tool button. You'll find that button on the rightmost edge of the main window.

For details on using the Designer tool, see Book I, Chapter 5.

When you go to the Project tool window and double-click a file that's not a layout file, Android Studio dismisses the Designer tool and replaces it with the plain, old editor area.

The Things You Can Do

Android Studio has thousands of useful features. A typical developer uses a small percentage of all these features. This section covers some of the features that I use every day.

Finding things

You're probably familiar with a document editor's Find facilities. Using Pages, Microsoft Word, or some similar software, you search through a document to find a word or a phrase. Searching through a text document is a big job, but searching an entire Android project is even bigger. After all, an Android project has many folders, and each folder contains many files. It's a complicated bundle of data. But along with this complexity comes great opportunity. Each file has a known structure, and each word in each file has a very well-defined meaning. The potential for intelligent search is enormous.

Choosing Edit ⇨ Find in Android Studio's main menu gives you some hints about Android Studio's Find capabilities. (See Figure 1-19.)

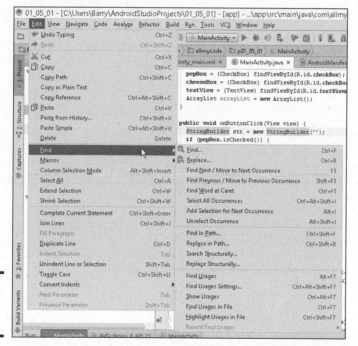

Figure 1-19:
Finding a
Find option.

The Find menu in Figure 1-19 has more than a dozen options. A long list describing the use of each option would be tedious for you to read. (What's more, it would be really boring for me to write!) So, in this section, I describe a few of my favorite options. If you want, you can set aside some time to poke around and explore the other options. When you do, you'll probably stumble on some favorites of your own.

Plain old Find

With the old Edit ➪ Find ➪ Find standby, you search for text in the current file (whatever file is currently visible in the editor). And, of course, when you choose Edit ➪ Find ➪ Replace, you replace occurrences of a word or phrase with another word or phrase.

TIP I'm not big on memorizing keyboard shortcuts, but I always use shortcuts for this simple version of Find. It's Ctrl+F on Windows and Cmd+F on a Mac. For the corresponding Replace action, it's Ctrl+R on Windows and Cmd+R on a Mac.

When you select the plain, old Find option, you get a Find panel. (See Figure 1-20.) This Find panel has some nice options to help you customize your search.

Figure 1-20:
The Find
panel.

With the up- and down-arrow icons, you can search upward or downward from your current position. With the Match Case check box, a search for `textView` doesn't find the capitalized name `TextView`. With the Words check box, you find whole words only (so that searching for `View` finds `android.view.Menu` but doesn't find `textView`).

With the Regex check box, you search for a regular expression match. Here are some examples:

✦ **A character followed by an asterisk matches zero or more of those characters.**

For example, if you search for `o*ps!`, you find `ps!`, `ops!`, `oops!`, `ooops!`, and so on.

✦ **A character followed by a plus sign matches one or more of those characters.**

For example, if you search for `o+ps!`, you find `ops!`, `oops!`, and `ooops!`. But you don't find `ps!`.

✦ **A dot matches any single character.**

The pattern `b.t` finds `bat`, `bet`, `bit`, `bot`, `but`, `bbt`, `bct`, `b@t`, `b.t`, and so on.

+ **A backslash followed by a dot matches a single dot character.**

  The pattern b\.t finds b.t, but it doesn't find bat, but, b..t or b\t.

+ **A dot followed by an asterisk matches any sequence of zero or more characters.**

  For example, b.*t matches bt, bat, boat, and the characters binge wat in the phrase binge watching.

+ **A bunch of characters enclosed in square brackets matches any one of the characters.**

  For example, b[aeiou]t finds bat, bet, bit, bot, but. It doesn't find bt, boat, or bbt.

Book II
Chapter 1

Using Android Studio

For the authoritative description of Android Studio's regular expression syntax, visit www.jetbrains.com/idea/help/regular-expression-syntax-reference.html.

Searching several files at once

When you choose Edit ⇨ Find ⇨ Find in Path, you get the dialog box shown in Figure 1-21. This is useful for finding all occurrences of a particular word in a project. Imagine that the name submitButton occurs somewhere in a project containing 100 .java files. You can find all files that mention submitButton using the Find in Path dialog box.

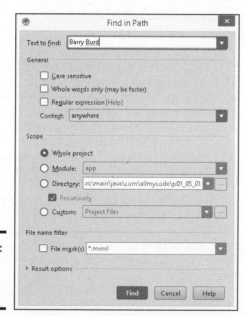

Figure 1-21: The Find in Path dialog box.

Here's another scenario: I've typed my first and last name in several of my project's files. At some point, I decide to add my middle initial. I can make the change automatically by choosing Edit ⇨ Find ⇨ Replace in Path. In a dialog box that's similar to the one in Figure 1-21, I type **Barry Burd** in the Text to Find field, and type **Barry A. Burd** in the Replace With field.

Highlighting usages

You want to find all occurrences of a variable named button1 in your activity. You can do an ordinary Find, but there's a better way. On a PC, choose File ⇨ Settings ⇨ Editor ⇨ General. (On a Mac, choose Android Studio ⇨ Preferences ⇨ Editor ⇨ General.) Look for the check box labeled Highlight Usages of Element at Caret. Put a check mark in that check box.

When you return to the editor, select any occurrence of the button1 variable. In response, the editor highlights all occurrences of that button1 variable. (See Figure 1-22.)

Figure 1-22:
The editor highlights occurrences of the button1 field.

The Java file in Figure 1-22 is so small that highlighting a few words hardly matters. But even in this tiny example, you can see how smart the highlighting feature is. The code in Figure 1-22 has four occurrences of the text button1, so if you were to do an ordinary Find for button1, you'd get four hits. But the code really contains two different button1 variables — the button1 field and the button1 parameter. These two button1 variables play two different roles in the example's code. (The two button1 variables are related to one another. But they're still two different variables.)

So look again at Figure 1-22. When you select the word button1 in this. button1, Android Studio highlights both occurrences of the button1 field. But occurrences of the button1 parameter are *not* highlighted. If you selected the button1 parameter instead of the button1 field, only the two button1 parameter uses would be highlighted. That's how smart the Highlight Usages feature is.

TIP

Normally, when you select a name in your code, Android Studio highlights all usages of that name in the file and removes the highlighting from previously highlighted names. You can override this behavior so that the highlighting of a name persists, even when you're no longer selecting an occurrence of that name. To do so, select a name in the editor. Then, in Android Studio's main menu, choose Edit⇨Find⇨Highlight Usages in File. All occurrences of that name will remain highlighted until you press Escape.

Navigating from place to place in your project

A method named computePrice gives you an answer that you don't expect. You're staring at the call to computePrice wondering why it gives you that answer. It would help to look at the declaration of the computePrice method. You can shuffle through your project's files to find the method's declaration, but it's easier to select the method call and then choose Navigate⇨Declaration. Android Studio jumps instantly to the declaration of the computePrice method. This works for methods, variables, and other names in Android's SDK, as well as for names that you declare in your own project.

The navigation trick has many variations. Consider the statement

```
pepBox = (CheckBox) findViewById(R.id.checkBox);
```

If you select pepBox and choose Navigate⇨Declaration, Android Studio jumps to a line of the following kind:

```
CheckBox pepBox;
```

But, if you select pepBox and choose Navigate⇨Type Declaration, Android Studio jumps to the declaration (in the SDK) of the CheckBox class. If you select MainActivity and choose Navigate⇨Super Method, you jump immediately to the declaration of the Activity method.

You can even jump quickly to the Android documentation. Select a name in your code in Android Studio's editor. Then choose View⇨Quick Documentation in the main menu. When you do, a pop-up menu appears. The pop-up menu contains a summary of the Javadoc for that name. The summary contains links. So, within the pop-up menu, you can go from MainActivity to Activity to setContentView and beyond.

Fixing code

In the previous section, you look but you don't touch. You find things in your project's code, but you don't make any changes. But this section is different. In this section, Android Studio helps you make changes to your code.

Intention actions

You're minding your own business, typing code, having a good time, and suddenly you see some commotion in the Editor window. A yellow lightbulb icon appears. The icon signals the presence of *intention actions* — proposals to make small changes to your code. In response to the icon's appearance, you press Alt+Enter. Doing so makes a pop-up menu appear. The pop-up menu contains a list of suggested changes. If you scroll to a list item and press Enter, Android Studio makes the change.

Figure 1-23 shows just such a pop-up menu.

Figure 1-23:
A list of intention actions.

+ **If you select Create Test, Android Studio writes a JUnit test for your** `MainActivity` **class.**

  The JUnit test class calls your activity's methods and checks the result against results that you expect.

+ **If you select Create Subclass, Android Studio does what the label suggests. It creates a subclass of your** `MainActivity` **class.**

  ```
  public class MainActivityImpl extends MainActivity {
  }
  ```

  The new subclass has an empty body. You add statements to that empty body.

+ **If you select Add Javadoc, Android Studio creates an empty Javadoc comment.**

  ```
  /**
   *
   */
  public class MainActivity extends Activity {
  ```

  You type lines inside the Javadoc comment.

+ **If you select Make Package-Local, Android Studio removes the word** `public` **from the start of the class declaration.**

  In this case, Android Studio is just offering to change whatever it finds in your code. If your class is public, the pop-up menu offers to remove the word `public`. But if your class isn't public, the pop-up menu includes a "Make 'public'" option.

  For a main activity, there's no good reason to remove the word `public`. In fact, your app won't run if the `MainActivity` class isn't public.

Code completion

When you type code in Android Studio, the editor guesses what you're trying to type and offers to finish typing it for you. In Figure 1-24, I type the letters `Log.` (ending with a dot). Android Studio reminds me that the `Log` class has static methods named `d`, `e`, `getStackTraceString`, and so on. I can select one of these by double-clicking the entry in the pop-up menu. Alternatively, I can select an entry in the pop-up menu and then press Enter or Tab.

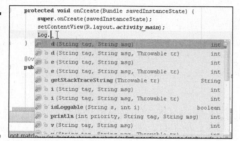

Figure 1-24: Android Studio displays the Log class's static members.

Book II Chapter 1

Using Android Studio

If I press Enter, the selected item goes between the cursor and any text that comes after the cursor. For example, I start with `Log.i(MYWHATEVER)`. I place the cursor after the letter `Y` and type an underscore. Now I have `Log.i(MY_WHATEVER)` with the suggestions `MY_TAG` and `MY_WORDS`. (See Figure 1-25.)

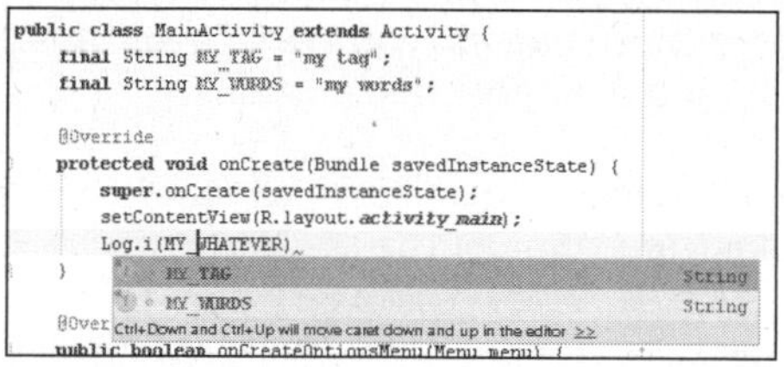

Figure 1-25: Android Studio suggests MY_TAG or MY_WORDS.

With the suggestion `MY_TAG` selected, I press Enter. Then Android Studio creates the text shown in Figure 1-26.

If I press Tab instead of Enter, the selected item *replaces* any text that comes after the cursor. Starting with the text shown in Figure 1-25, I end up with the text shown in Figure 1-27.

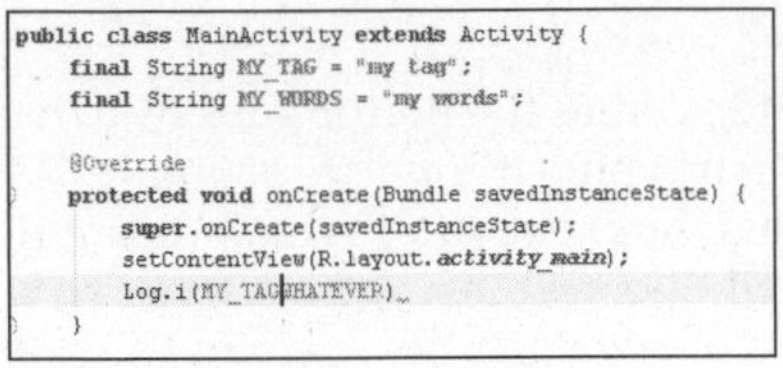

Figure 1-26:
After
pressing
Enter.

```
public class MainActivity extends Activity {
    final String MY_TAG = "my tag";
    final String MY_WORDS = "my words";

    @Override
    protected void onCreate(Bundle savedInstanceState) {
        super.onCreate(savedInstanceState);
        setContentView(R.layout.activity_main);
        Log.i(MY_TAGWHATEVER)
    }
```

Figure 1-26:
After
pressing
Enter.

```
public class MainActivity extends Activity {
    final String MY_TAG = "my tag";
    final String MY_WORDS = "my words";

    @Override
    protected void onCreate(Bundle savedInstanceState) {
        super.onCreate(savedInstanceState);
        setContentView(R.layout.activity_main);
        Log.i(MY_TAG)
    }
```

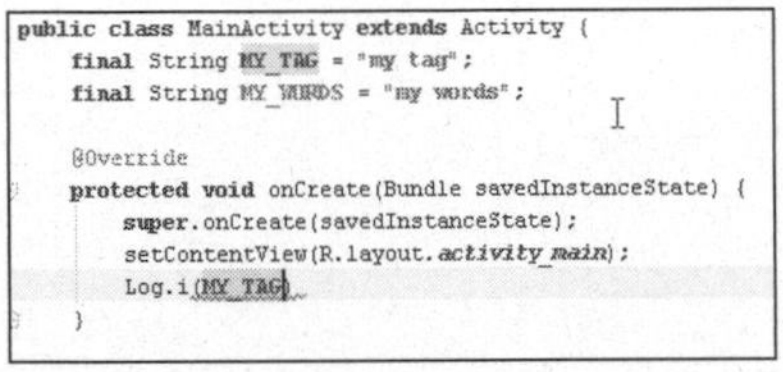

Figure 1-27:
After
pressing
Tab.

Optimizing imports

In Book I, Chapter 5, I describe a way to make Android Studio write all your import declarations. (On a PC, you put check marks in check boxes after choosing File ⇨ Settings ⇨ Editor ⇨ General ⇨ Auto Import. On a Mac, you do the same, but you start by choosing Android Studio ⇨ Preferences.) When you follow my instructions, Android Studio automatically adds and removes import declarations as you type. That can be a good thing. But sometimes, you want a bit more control.

So what happens if you ignore my instructions from Book I, Chapter 5? You still need import declarations, so you type all the import declarations yourself. But typing import declarations is a big pain. You might not remember the package names for all the classes and methods that you use in your code. Even if you remember these names, you have better things to do with your time than to type a bunch of import declarations.

To help you generate import declarations, Android Studio has several tricks. Here are two stories to illustrate some of the tricks:

✦ You type the name **Toast** (a name from the Android API). You haven't typed the required import declaration at the top of the Java file, so the name Toast appears in red letters. If you hover over the name, Android Studio says *Cannot resolve symbol 'Toast'*. (See Figure 1-28.)

Finally, you click your mouse on the word Toast. When you do, Android Studio suggests a fully qualified name. (See Figure 1-29.) You press Alt+Enter to accept this fully qualified name. As a result, Android Studio adds the appropriate import declaration to your code.

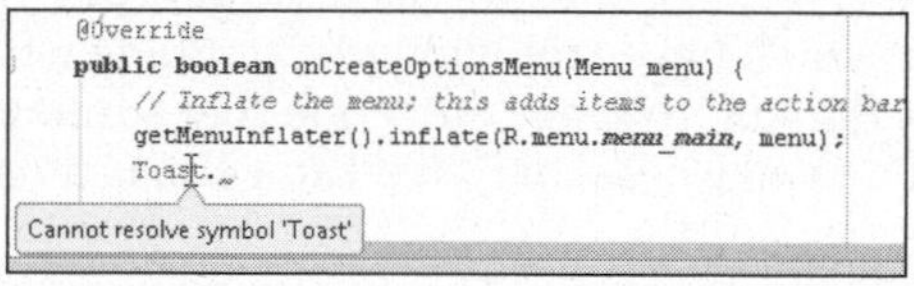

Figure 1-28:
Cannot
resolve
symbol.

```
@Override
public boolean onCreateOptionsMenu(Menu menu) {
    // Inflate the menu; this adds items to the action bar
    getMenuInflater().inflate(R.menu.menu_main, menu);
    Toast.
}
Cannot resolve symbol 'Toast'
```

Figure 1-29:
Do you
mean
android.
widget.
Toast?

```
        @Override
        public boolean onCreateOptionsMenu(Menu menu)
? android.widget.Toast? Alt+Enter    menu; this adds items to th
                getMenuInflater().inflate(R.menu.menu_main
            Toast.
```

✦ You use the name `Random`, and (one way or another) you add `import java.util.Random` to your code.

```
import java.util.Random;
...
Random random = new Random();
```

Sometime later, you change your mind and decide not to create an instance of the `Random` class. You delete the declaration of `random`, but you don't remove the import declaration. Android Studio changes the color of the import declaration from blue and black to a light gray.

You can delete the import declaration yourself, but you might have several other declarations to delete. You can delete all the unused import declarations in one fell swoop by choosing Code➪Optimize Imports in Android Studio's main menu.

Reformatting code

In these busy days, who isn't in a hurry sometimes? You're rushing to write code, and you type it in a sloppy fashion.

```
public class MyClass {
TextView textView;

    public void onButtonClick(View view) {
textView.setText("Hello");
}}
```

You figure you'll fix the indentation later, when you're not so pressed for time. But "later" keeps slipping away. Eventually, you have to bottle up your code and publish it on the Google Play Store. No worries! The code's poor formatting has no impact on its run.

But there's a big problem. The next time you look at this code (and that time will definitely come) you'll have trouble understanding what you wrote. Poorly formatted code is difficult to read. And code that's difficult to read is costly to maintain. What's even worse, hard-to-read code is annoying!

So how do you fix this quickly and easily? One solution is to avoid ever writing poorly formatted code. To some extent, Android Studio helps you in this goal. As you create new code, the editor positions your lines where they're supposed to go. Of course, you can override this automatic positioning. (Sometimes, you override the positioning without intending to do so.)

The good news is that Android Studio has a magic bullet. Click your mouse inside the editor. Then, in the main menu, choose Code ⇨ Reformat Code. *Et voilà!* Android Studio fixes your code's indentation.

```
public class MyClass {
    TextView textView;

    public void onButtonClick(View view) {
        textView.setText("Hello");
    }
}
```

Of course, you might not like the way Android Studio reformats code. I certainly don't. I have to squeeze long lines of code onto narrow 58-character-wide printed pages. For most of my examples, I need two-character indenting instead of four-character indenting. And I need spaces instead of tab characters because, on the printed page, spaces are more predictable.

Here's another example. Some people prefer the Allman style for positioning curly braces. In the Allman style, each brace has a line of its own:

```
public class MyClass
{
    TextView textView;

    public void onButtonClick(View view)
    {
        textView.setText("Hello");
    }
}
```

Can Android Studio help you with that?

Yes, it can. On a PC, choose File ⇨ Settings ⇨ Editor ⇨ Code Style ⇨ Java. (On a Mac, do the same, but start with Android Studio ⇨ Preferences.) When you do, you see hundreds (maybe thousands) of options for adjusting the way Android Studio formats your code. Change your code's line length, change the indentation, change the positioning of curly braces, and change so many other things.

In addition to all of its check boxes and drop-down menus, this dialog box shows you some sample Java classes. So when you make a change, you see immediately how the change affects the sample code. If you like the change, you can click Apply. If not, you can keep experimenting.

If you're one of those people who becomes obsessed with the positioning of curly braces, visit www.riedquat.de/prog/style. On that page, you find a thorough discussion of all the brace styles that people use.

Commenting and uncommenting

I have several lines of code that I don't particularly like. I want to experiment to find out what happens if these lines are gone. I can select these lines and press Delete, but I might not like the results of the experiment. I might want the lines back in my code. Instead of deleting these lines, I can turn them (perhaps temporarily) into comments.

Java has a few different kinds of comments, including block comments and end-of-line comments. (The language also has Javadoc comments, but you probably wouldn't use a Javadoc comment to temporarily disable lines of code.) To turn one or more statements into a comment, start by selecting those statements. Then, in the main menu, choose Code➪Comment with Line Comment or Code➪Comment with Block Comment. Whichever option you choose, Android Studio obliges by commenting out the lines that you selected. This trick is a lifesaver if you want end-of-line comments on many lines. But it also helps when you want to create a block comment.

Android Studio's commenting trick works both ways. Imagine that you've turned several statements into end-of-line comments, and you want to change them back to ordinary statements. (That is, you want to *uncomment* these lines.) First, select the lines. Then, in the main menu, choose Code➪Comment with Line Comment. The name of the option is a bit misleading. (You want to uncomment, not to comment.) Nevertheless, Android Studio sees that you've selected commented lines and removes the comment markers as you wish.

Generating code

Consider the humble Java class that I reformat in a previous section.

```
public class MyClass {
    TextView textView;

    public void onButtonClick(View view) {
        textView.setText("Hello");
    }
}
```

With your cursor positioned somewhere inside that class, choose
Code➪Generate. When you do, you see the pop-up menu shown in
Figure 1-30.

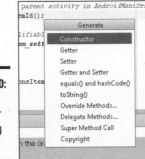

Figure 1-30:
Several
options for
generating
code.

If you select Constructor in the pop-up menu, you get another dialog box.
(See Figure 1-31.) This little `MyClass` example has only one field — namely,
the `textView` field. So you can either select or unselect that `textView` field.
If you select the field, Android Studio adds this constructor to your code:

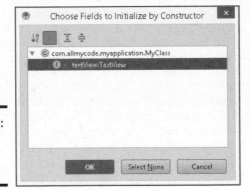

Figure 1-31:
Choose
fields to
initialize.

```
public MyClass(TextView textView) {
    this.textView = textView;
}
```

If you don't select the `textView` field, you get the empty constructor:

```
public MyClass() {
}
```

You can repeat the procedure to get as many constructors as you like.

Other options in Figure 1-30 include the Getter, the Setter, and the Getter and Setter options. When you select the Getter and Setter option, you see a dialog box that's similar to the one in Figure 1-31. The dialog box lists all the fields in your class and lets you select one of these fields. For the tiny `MyClass` code in this section, the only field is `textView`. So, when you double-click the `textView` entry, Android Studio generates the following new Getter and Setter methods:

```
public TextView getTextView() {
    return textView;
}

public void setTextView(TextView textView) {
    this.textView = textView;
}
```

Refactoring

In the parlance of computer programming, *refactoring* means improving the internal structure of your code without changing the code's behavior. Along with this concept come several *refactoring patterns*. Each pattern is a recipe for taking code that's structured a certain way and turning it into code that's structured differently.

For example, you're developing a game and writing several lines of code to make a ball bounce.

```
void doALot(Background backgr, Sprite sprite, Ball ball) {
    if (backgr.isCity()) {
        int steps = getSteps();
        sprite.move(steps);
        if (sprite.isNear(monster)) {
            sprite.changeFace(Sprite.PANIC);
            sprite.release(ball);
            double ballHeight = sprite.handHeight;
            while (ballHeight != 0) {
                double g = 9.807;
                double timeToDrop =
                        Math.sqrt(2 * ballHeight / g);
                double rebound =
                        ballHeight * ball.elasticity;
                ball.dropTo(0);
                ball.riseTo(rebound);
            }
        }
        int seconds = getLevel() + 2;
        showCar(seconds);
        makeNoise();
        // . . . Etc.
```

At some point, you realize that you'll be making balls bounce in other parts of your program. So you want to create a general `bounceBall` method with parameters such as `ball` and `ballHeight`.

You don't write the bounceBall method from scratch. Instead, you apply the Extract Method refactoring pattern. In the previous code sample, you select all the lines that I set in boldface. (These are the lines that make the ball bounce.) You move these lines outside of the method that currently houses them. You surround the lines with a method header and a closing brace. Then you write a method call where the lines used to live.

You can do all this work manually, but it's easier (and less error prone) if you get Android Studio to do the work for you. Here's how:

1. **Select the statements that will form the body of your new method.**

2. **In Android Studio's main menu, choose Refactor ⇨ Extract ⇨ Method.**

As a result, an Extract Method dialog box appears. (See Figure 1-32.)

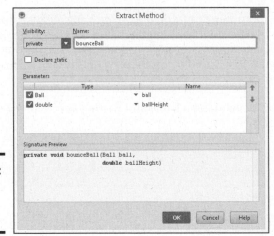

Figure 1-32:
The Extract
Method
dialog box.

3. **In the dialog box's Name field, type a name for your new method.**

In Figure 1-32, I type **bounceBall**.

4. **Click OK.**

As a result, Android Studio rewrites your code. For the bouncing ball example, the new code looks like this:

```
void doALot(Background backgr, Sprite sprite, Ball ball) {
    if (backgr.isCity()) {
        int steps = getSteps();
        sprite.move(steps);
        if (sprite.isNear(monster))
            sprite.changeFace(Sprite.PANIC);
        sprite.release(ball);
        double ballHeight = sprite.handHeight;
```

```
        bounceBall(ball, ballHeight);
    }
    int seconds = getLevel() + 2;
    showCar(seconds);
    makeNoise();
    // . . . Etc.

    }
}

private void bounceBall(Ball ball, double ballHeight) {
    while (ballHeight != 0) {
        double g = 9.807;
        double timeToDrop =
                Math.sqrt(2 * ballHeight / g);
        double rebound =
                ballHeight * ball.elasticity;
        ball.dropTo(0);
        ball.riseTo(rebound);
    }
}
```

Book II
Chapter 1

Using Android Studio

Android Studio supports about 30 refactoring patterns. You can find descriptions of these patterns almost anywhere on the web, so I don't describe all the patterns here. But I can't end this chapter without writing about my favorite pattern — the *Rename pattern*. Here's the story:

You're working with this section's game code and you want to change a name. It could be a variable name, a method name, or any other name in the project. For the purpose of this example, imagine replacing the method name isNear with the new name isCloseTo. To make the change manually, you have to edit the method header and then replace the name in each of the project's isNear method calls. If there are many such method calls, the change can take a long time.

So, instead of doing it manually, you select any occurrence of the method name isNear in your project. (The occurrence that you select doesn't have to be the one in the method header.) Then choose Refactor ➪ Rename. A list of suggested names appears. (See Figure 1-33.)

Figure 1-33: Renaming a method.

```
sprite.move(steps);
if (sprite.isNear(monster)) {
    sprite  isNear
    sprite  isnear
    double  Press Shift+F6 to show dialog with more options
    while (ballHeight != 0) {
        double g = 9.807;
```

You can accept one of the suggested names, but you can also start typing to replace the current name. As you type, every occurrence of the selected name changes throughout your project. When you press Enter, the renaming ends and all your isNear occurrences are now isCloseTo occurrences. It's simple. It's consistent. And it's free from manual typing errors. It's great!

Chapter 2: It's Java!

In This Chapter

✔ How computers, phones, and other devices run Java programs

✔ The parts of a typical Java program

*B*efore I became an Android guy, I was a Java guy. A *Java guy* is a person who revels in the workings of Java programs. I wrote Java programs, read about Java programs, went to Java user group meetings, and wore Java T-shirts. That's why I was thrilled to learn that Android's application programming language is Java.

In the early 1990s, James Gosling at Sun Microsystems created Java. He used ideas from many programming language traditions, including the object-oriented concepts in C++. He created an elegant platform with a wide range of uses. In mid-2014 (which is "now" as far as my chapter-writing goes), Java runs on 88 percent of all desktop computers in the United States, and on 97 percent of all enterprise desktops, with nine million Java developers worldwide.* Do you have a Blu-ray player? Under the hood, your player runs Java.

In this minibook (Book II), this chapter and Chapters 3 and 4 introduce the ins and outs of the Java programming language. But these chapters don't offer a comprehensive guide to Java. (To badly paraphrase Geoffrey Chaucer, "This book never yet no complete not Java coverage.") Instead, these chapters hit the highlights of Java programming. For a more complete introduction to Java, read *Java For Dummies,* 6th Edition or *Java Programming for Android Developers For Dummies* (both published by John Wiley & Sons, Inc.). (Yes, I wrote those books, too.)

From Development to Execution with Java

Before Java became popular, most programs went almost directly from the developer's keyboard to the processor's circuits. But Java added an extra translation layer, and then Android added yet another layer. This section describes the layers.

*Source: http://java.com/en/about

What is a compiler?

A Java program (such as an Android application program) goes through several translation steps between the time you write the program and the time a processor runs it. The reason for this is simple: What's convenient for processors to run is not convenient for people to write.

People can write and comprehend the code in Listing 2-1.

Listing 2-1:   Java Source Code

```
public void checkVacancy(View view) {
    if (room.numGuests == 0) {
        label.setText("Available");
    } else {
        label.setText("Taken :-(");
    }
}
```

The Java code in Listing 2-1 checks for a vacancy in a hotel. You can't run the code in Listing 2-1 without adding several lines. But at this stage of the game, those additional lines aren't important. What's important is that by staring at the code, squinting a bit, and looking past all the code's strange punctuation, you can see what the code is trying to do:

```
If the room has no guests in it,
    then set the label's text to "Available".
Otherwise,
    set the label's text to "Taken :-(".
```

The stuff in Listing 2-1 is *Java source code*.

The processors in computers, phones, and other devices don't normally follow instructions like the instructions in Listing 2-1. That is, processors don't follow Java source code instructions. Instead, processors follow cryptic instructions like these:

```
A3 86 01 00   2A 85 00 00   00 4D 00 00   00 50 00 00
00 55 55 55   55 00 00 00   02 4D 00 05   00 07 00 80
00 14 00 80   40 38 25 00   00 40 4D 40   00 00 40 32
45 00 80 40   14 6B 65 72   6E 65 6C 00   5F 70 75 74
49 6E 4D 65   6D 6F 72 79   00 5F 6D 61   6B 65 49 6E
74 65 72 72   75 70 74 32   31 00 5F 69   6E 74 65 72
72 75 70 74   32 31 53 65   72 76 69 63   65 52 6F 75
74 69 6E 65   00 69 6E 74   72 00 5F 69   6E 74 65 72
72 75 70 74   00 20 60 55   89 E5 1E 8B   46 04 8B 76
06 8A 4E 08   8E D8 88 0C   1F 5D C3 55   89 E5 8B 46
04 1E 8C CB   8E DB BE 02   80 32 00 57   88 44 01 1F
8B 46 06 8B   5E 08 8B 4E   0A 8B 56 0C   CD 00 B4 00
5D C3 BA 80   4D 00 52 1E   B8 00 00 8E   D8 BE 84 00
8C C8 89 44   02 89 14 1F   C3 00
```

To be fair, this gobbledygook that I call "instructions" isn't really numbers and letters. It's just 0s and 1s. So the first A3 in my "instructions" is short-hand for 10100011.

I once participated in a three-part translation conversation. I spoke English to my mother, who translated it into Yiddish for her cousin, who translated it into Russian for the cousin's husband. A similar kind of thing happens when you create an Android app. You start by writing Java source code, like the code in Listing 2-1. Your development computer translates the Java source code into Java bytecode. For a look at Java bytecode, see Listing 2-2.

Listing 2-2:   Java Bytecode

Book II
Chapter 2

```
 0 aload_0
 1 getfield #19 <com/allmycode/samples/MyActivity/room
Lcom/allmycode/samples/Room;>
 4 getfield #47 <com/allmycode/samples/Room/numGuests I>
 7 ifne 22 (+15)
10 aload_0
11 getfield #41 <com/allmycode/samples/MyActivity/label
Landroid/widget/TextView;>
14 ldc #54 <Available>
16 invokevirtual #56
 <android/widget/TextView/setText(Ljava/lang/CharSequence;)V>
19 goto 31 (+12)
22 aload_0
23 getfield #41 <com/allmycode/samples/MyActivity/label
Landroid/widget/TextView;>
26 ldc #60 <Taken :-(>
28 invokevirtual #56
 <android/widget/TextView/setText(Ljava/lang/CharSequence;)V>
31 return
```

It's Java!

When you write a Java program, you write source code instructions (like the instructions in Listing 2-1). After writing the source code, you run the code through a program — you apply a tool to your source code, in other words. The program is a compiler. The *compiler* translates your source code instructions into Java bytecode instructions. In other words, the compiler takes code that you can write and understand (such as the code in Listing 2-1) and translates your code into code that a computer can execute (such as the code in Listing 2-2).

You might put your source code in a file named HotelActivity.java. If so, the compiler probably puts the Java bytecode in another file named HotelActivity.class. Normally, you don't bother looking at the bytecode in the HotelActivity.class file. In fact, the compiler doesn't encode the HotelActivity.class file as ordinary text, so you can't examine the bytecode with an ordinary editor. If you try to open HotelActivity.class with Notepad, TextEdit, KWrite, or even Microsoft

Word, you see nothing but dots, squiggles, and other strange looking stuff. To create Listing 2-2, I had to apply yet another tool to my `HotelActivity.class` file. That tool displays a text-like version of a Java bytecode file. I used Ando Saabas's Java Bytecode Editor (`www.cs.ioc.ee/~ando/jbe`).

No one (except for a few crazy developers in some isolated labs in faraway places) writes Java bytecode. You run software (a compiler) to create Java bytecode. The only reason to look at Listing 2-2 is to understand what a hard worker your computer is.

Like the language relay involving me, my mother, and my mother's cousins, the translation from source code to 0s and 1s doesn't end with Listing 2-2. In 2007, Dan Bornstein at Google created *Dalvik bytecode* — another way of representing instructions for processors to follow. (To find out where some of Bornstein's ancestors come from, run your favorite Map application and look for Dalvik in Iceland.) Dalvik bytecode is optimized for the limited resources on a phone or a tablet device. Listing 2-3 contains some sample Dalvik instructions.*

Java bytecode instructions use a *stack machine* format. In contrast, Dalvik bytecode instructions use a *register machine* format. The upshot of this (for those who don't know much about machine language formats) is that a typical Dalvik instruction is longer and more complicated than a Java bytecode instruction. Despite what you see in Listings 2-2 and 2-3, a big Dalvik instruction normally replaces several little Java bytecode instructions.

When you create an Android app, Android Studio performs at least two compilations. The first compilation creates Java bytecode from your Java source files. (Your source filenames have the `.java` extension; the Java bytecode filenames have the `.class` extension.) The second compilation creates Dalvik bytecode from your Java bytecode files. (Dalvik bytecode filenames have the `.dex` extension.) To perform the first compilation, Android Studio uses a program named *javac,* or the *Java compiler*. To perform the second compilation, Android Studio uses a program named *dx* (known affectionately as *the dx tool*).

Android Studio compiles Java bytecode (Listing 2-2) to get Dalvik bytecode (Listing 2-3). Does the compiling end here? Not at all. When a user's mobile device gets ahold of some Dalvik bytecode, the device does even more compiling. One way or another, the device runs a virtual machine. "And what," you ask, "is a virtual machine?" It's funny that you should ask this question. Your question is the title of the very next section!

---

*To see the code in Listing 2-3, I used the Dedexer program. See `http://dedexer.sourceforge.net`.

Listing 2-3: Dalvik Bytecode

```
.method public checkVacancy(Landroid/view/View;)V
.limit registers 4
; this: v2 (Lcom/allmycode/samples/MyActivity;)
; parameter[0] : v3 (Landroid/view/View;)
.line 30
    iget-object
    v0,v2,com/allmycode/samples/MyActivity.room
    Lcom/allmycode/samples/Room;
; v0 : Lcom/allmycode/samples/Room; , v2 :
    Lcom/allmycode/samples/MyActivity;
    iget    v0,v0,com/allmycode/samples/Room.numGuests I
; v0 : single-length , v0 : single-length
    if-nez    v0,14b4
; v0 : single-length
.line 31
    iget-object
    v0,v2,com/allmycode/samples/MyActivity.label
    Landroid/widget/TextView;
; v0 : Landroid/widget/TextView; , v2 :
    Lcom/allmycode/samples/MyActivity;
    const-string    v1,"Available"
; v1 : Ljava/lang/String;
    invoke-virtual
    {v0,v1},android/widget/TextView/setText
    ; setText(Ljava/lang/CharSequence;)V
; v0 : Landroid/widget/TextView; , v1 : Ljava/lang/String;
14b2:
.line 36
    return-void
14b4:
.line 33
    iget-object
    v0,v2,com/allmycode/samples/MyActivity.label
    Landroid/widget/TextView;
; v0 : Landroid/widget/TextView; , v2 :
    Lcom/allmycode/samples/MyActivity;
    const-string    v1,"Taken :-("
; v1 : Ljava/lang/String;
    invoke-virtual
    {v0,v1},android/widget/TextView/setText ;
    setText(Ljava/lang/CharSequence;)V
; v0 : Landroid/widget/TextView; , v1 : Ljava/lang/String;
    goto    14b2
.end method
```

What is a virtual machine?

The instructions in Listings 2-2 and 2-3 are meant for processors to use, not for people to use. Even so, the processors in computers and mobile phones don't execute Java bytecode instructions (Listing 2-2) or Dalvik bytecode instructions (Listing 2-3). Instead, each kind of processor has its own set of executable instructions, and each operating system uses the processor's instructions in a slightly different way.

Imagine that you have two different devices — a smartphone and a tablet computer. The devices have two different kinds of processors. The phone has an ARM processor, and the tablet has an Intel Atom processor. (The acronym *ARM* once stood for *Advanced RISC Machine*. These days, *ARM* simply stands for ARM Holdings, a company whose employees design processors.) On the ARM processor, the *multiply* instruction is *000000*. On an Intel processor, the *multiply* instructions are D8, DC, F6, F7, and others. Many ARM instructions have no counterparts in the Atom architecture, and many Atom instructions have no equivalents on an ARM processor. An ARM processor's instructions make no sense to your tablet's Atom processor, and an Atom processor's instructions would give your phone's ARM processor a virtual headache.

So what's a developer to do? Does a developer provide translations of every app into every processor's instruction set? No.

Virtual machines create order from all this chaos. Dalvik bytecode is something like the code in Listing 2-3, but Dalvik bytecode isn't specific to one kind of processor or to one operating system. Instead, a set of Dalvik bytecode instructions runs on any processor. If you write a Java program and compile that Java program into Dalvik bytecode, your Android phone, your Android tablet, and even your grandmother's supercomputer can run the bytecode. (To do this, your grandmother must install *Android-x86,* a special port of the Android operating system, on her Intel-based machine.)

Both Java bytecode and Dalvik bytecode have virtual machines. With a virtual machine, you can take a bytecode file that you created for one Android device, copy the bytecode to another Android device, and then run the bytecode with no trouble at all. That's one of the many reasons why Android has become popular so quickly. This outstanding feature, which gives you the ability to run code on many different kinds of computers, is called *portability*.

Imagine that you're the Intel representative to the United Nations Security Council. (See Figure 2-1.) The ARM representative is seated to your right, and the representative from Texas Instruments is on your left. (Naturally, you don't get along with either of these people. You're always cordial to one another, but you're never sincere. What do you expect? It's politics!) The distinguished representative from Dalvik is at the podium. The Dalvik representative speaks in Dalvik bytecode, and neither you nor your fellow ambassadors (ARM and Texas Instruments) understand a word of Dalvik bytecode.

But each of you has an interpreter. Your interpreter translates from Dalvik bytecode to Intel instructions as the Dalvik representative speaks. Another interpreter translates from bytecode to ARM-ese. And a third interpreter translates bytecode into Texas Instruments speak.

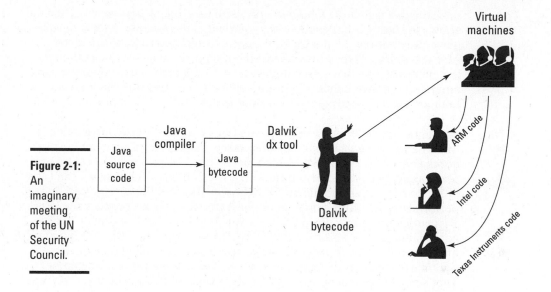

Figure 2-1:
An imaginary meeting of the UN Security Council.

Book II
Chapter 2

It's Java!

Think of your interpreter as a virtual ambassador. The interpreter doesn't really represent your country, but the interpreter performs one of the important tasks that a real ambassador performs. The interpreter listens to Dalvik bytecode on your behalf. The interpreter does what you would do if your native language was Dalvik bytecode. The interpreter pretends to be the Intel ambassador and sits through the boring bytecode speech, taking in every word, and processing each word in some way or other.

You have an interpreter — a virtual ambassador. In the same way, an Intel processor runs its own bytecode interpreting software. That software is a virtual machine.

A *virtual machine* is a proxy, an errand boy, a go-between. The virtual machine serves as an interpreter between run-anywhere bytecode and your device's own system. As it runs, a virtual machine walks your device through the execution of bytecode instructions. The virtual machine examines your bytecode, bit by bit, and carries out the instructions described in the byte-code. The virtual machine interprets bytecode for your ARM processor, your Intel processor, your Texas Instruments chip, or whatever kind of processor you're using. That's a good thing. It's what makes Java code and Dalvik code more portable than code written in any other language.

Back in 2007, along with Dalvik bytecode, the folks at Google created a Dalvik virtual machine. This virtual machine runs Android apps on devices running Cupcake, Donut, and all the desserts up to and including KitKat. But in 2013, Google announced a replacement for Dalvik called *ART*. (The acronym

ART stands for *Android RunTime*.) ART still uses Dalvik bytecode of the kind shown in Listing 2-3. (Despite what you read in the tabloids, Dalvik hasn't gone away entirely.) But after your code is translated to Dalvik bytecode, ART takes advantage of the enhanced horsepower in newer smartphones. In general, an app that's executed with ART runs much faster than the same app executed with Dalvik. By default, every app created for the Android Lollipop (and beyond) target runs on the newer ART virtual machine.

One of the big differences between the Dalvik and ART virtual machines is the time when a final translation step takes place. The Dalvik machine uses *just-in-time* (JIT) compilation, which means that the final translation takes place as needed while the app runs on a user's device. But wait! Doesn't that final translation take up time during the run? Doesn't the user notice slower performance while the phone does a last translation step on the code? Yes! JIT compilation slows down the run of an app. In contrast to Dalvik's JIT compilation, ART uses *ahead-of-time* (AOT) compilation. With AOT, an app's final translation takes place when the app is being installed on a device. By the time a user runs the app, the app's code has already been translated. That's one of the reasons why ART's virtual machine is faster than Dalvik's.

Grasping Java Code

When you create a new project, Android's tools create a small, no-nonsense Java class. I've copied the Java class in Listing 2-4.

Listing 2-4:   A Minimalistic Android Activity Class

```
package com.allmycode.samples;

import android.app.Activity;
import android.os.Bundle;
import android.view.Menu;
import android.view.MenuItem;


public class MyActivity extends Activity {

  @Override
  protected void onCreate(Bundle savedInstanceState) {
    super.onCreate(savedInstanceState);
    setContentView(R.layout.activity_my);
  }

  @Override
  public boolean onCreateOptionsMenu(Menu menu) {
    getMenuInflater().inflate(R.menu.my, menu);
    return true;
  }
```

```
@Override
public boolean onOptionsItemSelected(MenuItem item) {
  int id = item.getItemId();
  if (id == R.id.action_settings) {
    return true;
  }
  return super.onOptionsItemSelected(item);
}
}
```

This chapter covers the Java language features used in Listing 2-4. So in this chapter, `android.app.Activity` (from the second line of Listing 2-4) is only the name of something to import — nothing more. To read about the meaning of the word Activity and the word's implications for Android, see Book III, Chapter 1.

The Java class

Java is an object-oriented programming language. So, as a developer, your primary goal is to describe objects. Your closely related goal is to describe objects' close cousins — namely, classes.

In Java, nothing happens unless it happens inside an object or a class. The code in Listing 2-4 is a class. I created the code, so I get to make up a name for my new class. I chose the name `MyActivity` because the code in Listing 2-4 describes one screen full of stuff on an Android device (and in Android, a screen full of stuff is an *activity*). So the code in Listing 2-4 contains the words `public class MyActivity`.

The words `public` and `class` are Java keywords. What that means is that no matter who writes a Java program, the word `class` always has the same meaning. The same holds true of the word `public` (although some classes aren't declared to be `public`).

On the other hand, the word `MyActivity` in Listing 2-4 is an identifier. I made up the word `MyActivity` while I was creating the example for this chapter. (I could have changed the word to `MainActivity`, `YourActivity` or `BoopADoop` if I wanted to do so.) The word `MyActivity` is the name of a particular class — the class that I'm creating by writing this program.

A Java *identifier* can be any word containing only letters, digits, and underscores (_). An identifier must not begin with a digit. Other than that, there are no restrictions. Words like `MainActivity`, `LaFong3`, and `a_b_c` are valid Java identifiers. A word like `1Mississippi` isn't valid because it begins with a digit. A phrase like `my activity` isn't valid because it contains a blank space. A string like `one~two` is invalid because the tilde (~) isn't a letter, a digit, or an underscore.

tHE jAVA PROGRAMMING LANGUAGE IS cASe-sEnsITiVE. iF YOU CHANGE A lowercase LETTER IN A WORD TO AN UPPERCASE LETTER, YOU CHANGE THE WORD'S MEANING.

If you define a public class named `DogAndPony`, the class's Java code must go in a file named `DogAndPony.java`, spelled and capitalized exactly the same way as the class name is spelled and capitalized. If you define a class named `MySecretStuff` and write `class MySecretStuff` instead of `public class MySecretStuff`, you can put the `MySecretStuff` code in any file whose extension is `.java`. (Go ahead. Call your file `Urkshjk98t.java`. See if I care.)

Classes and objects

When you program in Java, you work constantly with classes and objects. Here's an analogy: A chair has a seat, a back, and legs. Each seat has a shape, a color, a degree of softness, and so on. These are the properties that a chair possesses. What I describe is *chairness* — the notion of something being a chair. In object-oriented terminology, I'm describing the `Chair` class.

In the preceding paragraph, I refer to the `Chair` class, not to the `chair` class. If you want to look like a very inexperienced developer, start the names of your Java classes with lowercase letters. With a class name such as `chair`, your code does what you want it to do, but you're committing a stylistic faux pas. Real Java developers start the names of their classes with uppercase letters.

Now peek over the edge of this book's margin and take a minute to look around your room. (If you're not sitting in a room right now, fake it.)

Several chairs are in the room, and each chair is an object. Each of these objects is an example of that ethereal thing called the `Chair` class. So that's how it works — the class is the idea of *chairness,* and each individual chair is an *object.*

A class isn't quite a collection of things. Instead, a class is the idea behind a certain kind of thing. When I talk about the class of chairs in your room, I'm talking about the fact that each chair has legs, a seat, a color, and so on. The colors may be different for different chairs in the room, but that doesn't matter. When you talk about a class of things, you're focusing on the properties that each of the things possesses.

It makes sense to think of an object as being a concrete instance of a class. In fact, the official terminology is consistent with this thinking. If you write a Java program in which you define a `Chair` class, each actual chair (the chair that you're sitting on, the empty chair right next to you, and so on) is called an *instance* of the `Chair` class.

Here's another way to think about a class. Imagine a table displaying three bank accounts. (See Table 2-1.)

Table 2-1	A Table of Accounts	
Name	*Address*	*Balance*
Barry Burd	222 Cyberspace Lane	24.02
John Q. Public	140 Any Way	−471.03
Jane Dough	800 Rich Street	247.38

Think of the table's column headings as a class, and think of each row of the table as an object. The table's column headings describe the Account class.

According to the table's column headings, each account has a name, an address, and a balance. Rephrased in the terminology of object-oriented programming, each object in the Account class (that is, each instance of the Account class) has a name, an address, and a balance. So, the bottom row of the table is an object with the name Jane Dough. This same object has the address *800 Rich Street* and a balance of *247.38*. If you opened a new account, you would have another object, and the table would grow an additional row. The new object would be an instance of the same Account class.

Java types

What does "six" mean? You can have six children, but you can also be six feet tall. With six children, you know exactly how many kids you have. (Unlike the average American family, you can't have 2.5 kids.) But if you're six feet tall, you could really be six feet and half an inch tall. Or you might be five feet eleven-and-three-quarter inches tall, and no one would argue about it.

A value's meaning depends on the value's *type*. If you write

```
int numberOfChildren = 6;
```

in a Java program, 6 means "exactly six." But if you write

```
double height = 6;
```

in a Java program, 6 means "as close to six as you care to measure." And if you write

```
char keystroke = '6';
```

in a Java program, '6' means "the digit that comes after the 5 digit."

In a Java program, every value has a *type*. Java has eight *primitive* types (types that are built into the language) and has as many *reference* types as you want to create.

Table 2-2 lists Java's eight primitive types.

Table 2-2	Java's Primitive Types	
Type Name	*What a Literal Looks Like*	*Range of Values*
Whole number types		
byte	(byte)42	−128 to 127
short	(short)42	−32768 to 32767
int	42	−2147483648 to 2147483647
long	42L	−9223372036854775808 to 9223372036854775807
Decimal number types		
float	42.0F	-3.4×10^{38} to 3.4×10^{38}
double	42.0	-1.8×10^{308} to 1.8×10^{308}
Character type		
char	'A'	Thousands of characters, glyphs, and symbols
Logical type		
boolean	true	true, false

A *literal* is an expression whose value doesn't change from one Java program to another. For example, the expression 42 means "the int value 42" in every Java program. Likewise, the expression 'B' means "the second upper-case letter in the Roman alphabet" in every Java program, and the word true means "the opposite of false" in every Java program.

In addition to its primitive types, Java has *reference types*. The code in Listing 2-4 contains the names of five reference types.

✦ **The reference type** android.app.Activity **is defined in the Android API (Android's enormous library of ready-made declarations).**

The reference types android.os.Bundle, android.view.Menu, and android.view.MenuItem are also defined in the Android API.

✦ **The reference type** MyActivity **is defined in Listing 2-4.**

How about that? Every class is a type!

When you write int numberOfChildren = 6, you declare the existence of a variable named numberOfChildren. The variable numberOfChildren has type int and has initial value 6.

But in Listing 2-4, android.os.Bundle, android.view.Menu, and android.view.MenuItem are also types. (They're reference types.) In fact, android.os.Bundle, android.view.Menu, and android.view.MenuItem are the names of classes that are declared as part of Android's API. So, just as you can write int numberOfChildren in a Java program, you can write Bundle savedInstanceState in Listing 2-4. (You can abbreviate android.os.Bundle to the simpler name Bundle because of the import declaration near the top of Listing 2-4.)

Because every class is a type, and because your newly declared MyActivity type is a class, you can add a line such as

```
MyActivity anActivity;
```

to the code in Listing 2-4. This new line declares that the name anActivity is a placeholder for a value (a value whose type is MyActivity). In case this idea muddies your mind, Listing 2-5 has another example.

Listing 2-5:   A Class Is a Type

```
public class Account {
    String name;
    String address;
    double balance;
}

Account myAccount = new Account();
Account yourAccount = new Account();

myAccount.name = "Burd";
yourAccount.name = "Dough";
myAccount.balance = 24.02;
```

Listing 2-5 doesn't contain a complete Java program. If you try to run the code in Listing 2-5 (without first adding some other stuff to the code), you get all kinds of error messages.

Listing 2-5 declares a class named Account. This blueprint for an account has three *fields*. The first field — the name field — refers to a Java String (a bunch of characters lined up in a row). The second field — the address field — refers to another Java String. The third field — the balance field — stores a double value. (Refer to Table 2-2.)

A *class* is "the idea behind a certain kind of thing." (I quote myself frequently.) An *object* is "a concrete instance of a class." So in Listing 2-5, the variable myAccount refers to an actual Account object, and the variable yourAccount refers to another Account object. The last statement in Listing 2-5 assigns the value 24.02 to the balance field of the object referred to by myAccount.

The Java method

A *method* is a chunk of code that performs some actions, and (possibly) produces a result. If you've written programs in other languages, you may know about functions, procedures, Sub procedures, or other such things. In Java, such things are called *methods*.

In Listing 2-4, the code

```
public boolean onCreateOptionsMenu(Menu menu) {
    getMenuInflater().inflate(R.menu.my, menu);
    return true;
}
```

declares the existence of a method. The method's name is onCreateOptionsMenu.

Real Java developers start the names of their methods with lowercase letters. You can ignore this convention. But if you ignore it, real Java developers will wince when they read your code.

Somewhere, buried deep inside the Android's virtual machine caverns, lives a line of code that looks something like this:

```
onCreateOptionsMenu(menu);
```

That line of code *calls* the onCreateOptionsMenu method of Listing 2-4. In other words, when the Android's virtual machine executes the onCreateOptionsMenu(Menu menu) statement, the flow of execution jumps to the first instruction inside the onCreateOptionsMenu method declaration in Listing 2-4.

A method declaration goes hand in hand with one or more calls. A method's declaration (such as the onCreateOptionsMenu declaration in Listing 2-4) defines the actions that a method eventually performs. The method doesn't perform any of its actions until some other piece of code executes a call to that method.

The onCreateOptionsMenu method's call hides inside some unseen Android system code. This situation isn't typical of methods and their calling statements. As an Android developer, you routinely declare a method in one part of your program and then call your own method in another part of the program.

The statements inside a method's declaration are collectively called the *method body*. Take, for example, the onCreate method in Listing 2-4. The onCreate method's body contains two statements (two instructions). The second statement, setContentView(R.layout.main), is a call to a method named setContentView. (The setContentView method's declaration comes with every Android implementation, so you don't declare the setContentView method yourself.)

Like any method call, the call setContentView(R.layout.main) starts with a method name. The stuff in parentheses after the method's name is a *parameter list*. For insight into parameter lists, consider the code in Listing 2-6.

Listing 2-6:   A Method and Two Method Calls

```
double monthlyPayment(double principal,
                      double percentageRate,
                      int years) {

  int numPayments = 12 * years;
  double rate = percentageRate / 100.00;
  double effectiveRate = rate / 12;
  return principal * (effectiveRate /
    (1 - Math.pow(1 + effectiveRate, -numPayments)));
}

double myPayment = monthlyPayment(100000.00, 5.25, 30);

double yourPayment = monthlyPayment(100000.00, 5.00, 15);
```

The code in Listing 2-6 isn't a complete Java program. You can't run the code without adding a bunch of stuff to it. Even so, the code illustrates some important ideas about methods and their parameters:

✦ **The name of the method declared in Listing 2-6 is** monthlyPayment.

✦ **In the body of the** monthlyPayment **method declaration, the processor computes the monthly payments on a mortgage.**

You can follow this description of methods and method parameters without understanding anything about the calculations in Listing 2-6.

✦ **The body of the** `monthlyPayment` **method uses certain names as place-holders.**

For example, in the body of the `monthlyPayment` method, the name `years` stands for the number of years in the mortgage's term. Likewise, the name `principal` stands for the total amount borrowed.

✦ **Some placeholders appear in parentheses at the beginning of the method's declaration.**

The names `principal`, `percentageRate`, and `years` are the method's *parameters*. Each parameter is destined to stand for a particular value. But a parameter doesn't stand for a value until an app executes a method call.

In Listing 2-6, the call `monthlyPayment(100000.00, 5.25, 30)` gives the method's first parameter (namely, `principal`) the value `100000.00`. That same call gives the method's second parameter (`percentageRate`) the value `5.25`. Finally, that method call gives the method's third parameter (`years`) the value `30`.

The next method call in Listing 2-6 gives the `monthlyPayment` method's parameters different values (again `100000.00` for `principal`, but `5.00` for `percentageRate` and `15` for years). Each time you call a method, you supply values for the method's parameters.

✦ **The types of parameters in a method call must match the types of the parameters in a method declaration.**

The declaration of method `monthlyPayment` in Listing 2-6 has a `double` parameter (`principal`), another `double` parameter (`percentageRate`), and an `int` parameter (`years`). Accordingly, the first method call in Listing 2-6 has two `double` parameters (`100000.00` and `5.25`) followed by an `int` parameter (`30`). The second method call in Listing 2-6 also has two `double` parameters followed by an `int` parameter.

You can declare the same method more than once, as long as each declaration has a different parameter list. For example, another method declaration in Listing 2-6 might have the same name `monthlyPayment` but only two parameters: `double monthlyPayment(double principal, double percentageRate)`. To call this alternative `monthlyPayment` method, you write something like `monthlyPayment (100000.00, 5.25)`. In this situation, the body of the alternative `monthlyPayment` method probably contains a statement like `years = 30`. You don't call this two-parameter method unless you know that the mortgage's term is 30 years.

✦ **A method call might stand for a value.**

The first method call in Listing 2-6 (in the listing's next-to-last line) stands for the `double` value `552.20` (or a value very close to the number `552.20`). The value `552.20` comes from all the calculations in the body of the `monthlyPayment` method when the `principal` is `100000.00`, the `percentageRate` is `5.25`, and the number of `years` is `30`. Near the end of the `monthlyPayment` method's body, the formula

```
principal * (effectiveRate /
    (1 - Math.pow(1 + effectiveRate, -numPayments)))
```

has the value `552.20`, and the word `return` says "send `552.20` back to the statement that called this method." So, in Listing 2-6, the end of the `monthlyPayment` method body effectively says

```
return 552.20;
```

and the next-to-last line in the listing effectively says

```
double myPayment = 552.20;
```

Similarly, the second method call in Listing 2-6 (the listing's last line) stands for the value `790.79`. Because of the second method call's parameter values, the end of the `monthlyPayment` method body effectively says

```
return 790.79;
```

and the last line in the listing effectively says

```
double yourPayment = 790.79;
```

Book II
Chapter 2

It's Java!

✦ **A method's declaration begins (much of the time) with the name of the return type.**

In Listing 2-6, the `monthlyPayment` method declaration begins with the type name `double`. That's good because the value returned at the end of the method's body (either `552.20` or `790.79`) is of type `double`. Also, the names `myPayment` and `yourPayment` store `double` values, so it's okay to assign the value of the call `monthlyPayment(100000.00, 5.25, 30)` to `myPayment`, and to assign the value of the call `monthlyPayment(100000.00, 5.00, 15)` to `yourPayment`.

Similarly, in Listing 2-4, the `onCreateOptionsMenu` and `onOptionsItemSelected` method declarations begin (more or less) with the type name `boolean`. The type `boolean` represents only one of two possible values — `true` or `false`. So the value returned at the end of the `onCreateOptionsMenu` method's body can be `true`. Also, if the Android's system's code contains a line like

```
boolean menuResult = onCreateOptionsMenu(someMenu);
```

then `menuResult` has type `boolean` so everything is hunky-dory.

✦ **A method call doesn't necessarily stand for a value.**

In Listing 2-1, the word `void` in the first line of the `checkVacancy` method indicates that a call to `checkVacancy` doesn't stand for a value. That is, a call to `checkVacancy` performs some actions, but the call doesn't calculate an answer of any kind.

Similarly, the method `onCreate` in Listing 2-4 doesn't return a value.

Objects and their constructors

Earlier, I introduce you to the Chair class example, and how it's the idea of *chairness,* and how each individual chair is an object . . . If you write a Java program in which you define a Chair class, each actual chair (the chair that you're sitting on, the empty chair right next to you, and so on) is called an *instance* of the Chair class. I also encourage you to think of the table's column headings as a class and to think of each row of the table as an object.

To drive this point home, consider the code in Listing 2-7.

Listing 2-7:   What Is an Account?

```
package com.allmycode.samples;

public class Account {
    public String name;
    public String address;
    public double balance;

    public Account(String name,
                   String address,
                   double balance) {
        this.name = name;
        this.address = address;
        this.balance = balance;
    }

    /** Called at the end of each month */
    public String infoString() {
        return name + " (" + address +
               ") has $" + balance;
    }
}
```

Listing 2-7 is a souped-up version of the code in Listing 2-5. In Listing 2-7, an Account has a name, an address, a balance, and an infoString method. The infoString method describes a way of composing a readable description of the account.

The variables name, address, and balance are *fields* of the Account class. In addition, the variables name, address, balance, and the method infoString are *members* of the Account class.

The Account class also has something that looks like a method, but isn't really a method. In Listing 2-7, the text beginning with public Account(String name is the start of a constructor. A *constructor* describes a way of creating a new instance of a class.

According to the code in Listing 2-7, each object created from the `Account` class has its own `name`, its own `address`, and its own `balance`. So, in Listing 2-7, the `Account` constructor's instructions say:

✦ `this.name = name;`

   When creating a new object (a new instance of the `Account` class), make `this` new object's `name` be whatever `name` has been passed to the constructor's parameter list. (See Figure 2-2.)

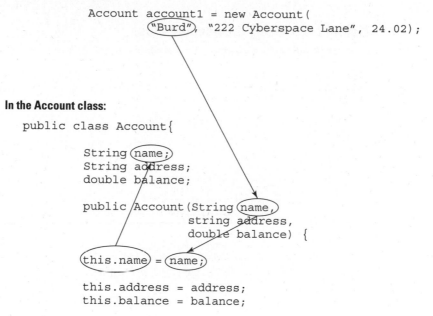

Elsewhere in your app:

```
Account account1 = new Account(
          "Burd", "222 Cyberspace Lane", 24.02);
```

In the Account class:

```
public class Account{

        String name;
        String address;
        double balance;

        public Account(String name,
                       string address,
                       double balance) {

        this.name = name;

        this.address = address;
        this.balance = balance;
```

Figure 2-2:
How an Account instance gets its name.

Book II Chapter 2

It's Java!

✦ `this.address = address;`

   When creating a new object (a new instance of the `Account` class), make `this` new object's `address` be whatever `address` has been passed to the constructor's parameter list.

✦ `this.balance = balance;`

   When creating a new object (a new instance of the `Account` class), make `this` new object's `balance` be whatever `balance` has been passed to the constructor's parameter list.

You can tell a constructor from a method by checking two things. First, the constructor's name is the same as the class's name. In Listing 2-7, both the class and the constructor have the name Account. Second, a constructor has no return type, not even void. In Listing 2-7, the infoString method has return type String. But the Account constructor has no return type.

Listing 2-8 shows you how to use the code in Listing 2-7. In Listing 2-8, the statement Account account1 = new Account("Burd", "222 Cyberspace Lane", 24.02) calls the constructor from Listing 2-7. As a result, the app has a brand-new instance of the Account class. The variable account1 refers to that new object.

Listing 2-8:   Using the Account Class

```
package com.allmycode.samples;

import android.app.Activity;
import android.os.Bundle;
import android.widget.TextView;

public class MyActivity extends Activity {
    TextView textView1;

    @Override
    public void onCreate(Bundle savedInstanceState) {
        super.onCreate(savedInstanceState);
        setContentView(R.layout.main);
        Account account1 = new Account(
                "Burd", "222 Cyberspace Lane", 24.02);

        textView1 =
            ((TextView) findViewById(R.id.textView1));
        textView1.setText(account1.infoString());
    }
}
```

Later in Listing 2-8, the text account1.infoString() calls the new account1 object's infoString method. The method returns a handsome-looking string of characters, which the activity displays on its screen.

To refer to a member belonging to an object, use the dot notation. For example, to call the account1 object's infoString method, write account1.infoString(). To refer to the account1 object's balance, write account1.balance. Method calls require parentheses, and field names don't use parentheses.

When you run the code in Listing 2-8, you get the screen shown in Figure 2-3.

Figure 2-3:
A run of
the app in
Listings 2-7
and 2-8.

Classes grow on trees

Listing 2-4 contains the words extends Activity. Apparently, the new
MyActivity class, declared in Listing 2-4, is some kind of extension of
something called Activity. So what's this all about?

You can download the Android source code (the Java code that comprises
Android's many pre-declared classes). When you do, you can open the
Activity.java file with your favorite editor. Listing 2-9 contains an
(admittedly unrepresentative) portion of the code in that file.

For more information about downloading Android's source code, visit
http://source.android.com/source/downloading.html.

Listing 2-9:   A Seriously Abridged Version of Android's Activity Class

```
package android.app;

public class Activity extends ContextThemeWrapper {

  protected void onCreate(Bundle savedInstanceState) {
    mVisibleFromClient =
      !mWindow.getWindowStyle().getBoolean(
        com.android.internal.R.styleable.
        Window_windowNoDisplay, false);
    mCalled = true;
  }

  protected void onDestroy() {
    mCalled = true;

    // dismiss any dialogs we are managing.
    if (mManagedDialogs != null) {
      final int numDialogs = mManagedDialogs.size();
      for (int i = 0; i < numDialogs; i++) {
        final ManagedDialog md =
          mManagedDialogs.valueAt(i);
        if (md.mDialog.isShowing()) {
          md.mDialog.dismiss();
        }
      }
      mManagedDialogs = null;
    }
```

(continued)

Listing 2-9 *(continued)*

```
  // Close any open search dialog
  if (mSearchManager != null) {
    mSearchManager.stopSearch();
  }
 }
}
```

The Android SDK comes with an `Activity` class, and the `Activity`
class contains methods named `onCreate` and `onDestroy`. (Actually, the
Android's `Activity` class contains at least 140 methods. But who's counting?) In Listing 2-4, the words `MyActivity extends Activity` establish a
relationship between the `MyActivity` class and Android's `Activity` class.
Among other things, the `MyActivity` class *inherits* fields and methods
belonging to the `Activity` class. So without adding any code to Listing 2-4,
you can rest assured that `MyActivity` has an `onDestroy` method. It's as if
you copied the `onDestroy` method declaration from Listing 2-9 and pasted
that declaration into Listing 2-4.

Aside from the `extends` terminology, Java has several names for the relationship between the `MyActivity` class and the `Activity` class:

✦ The `MyActivity` class is a **subclass** of the `Activity` class.

✦ The `MyActivity` class is a **child** of the `Activity` class.

✦ The `Activity` class is the **superclass** of the `MyActivity` class.

✦ The `Activity` class is the **parent** of the `MyActivity` class.

If all this parent/child business reminds you of a family tree, you're not
alone. Java developers draw upside-down trees all the time. For example, a
small part of the tree for the class in Listing 2-4 is pictured in Figure 2-4.

At the top of Figure 2-4, the tree's root is Java's ancestor of all classes —
the `Object` class. Android's `Context` class is a subclass of the `Object`
class. The `Context` class has many subclasses, two of which (`Application`
and `ContextWrapper`) are pictured in Figure 2-4. From there on,
`ContextWrapper` begets `ContextThemeWrapper`, which begets
`Activity`, which begets the main activity class in a typical Android app.

A class can have many subclasses, but a class has only one superclass.
The only class with no superclass is Java's `Object` class.

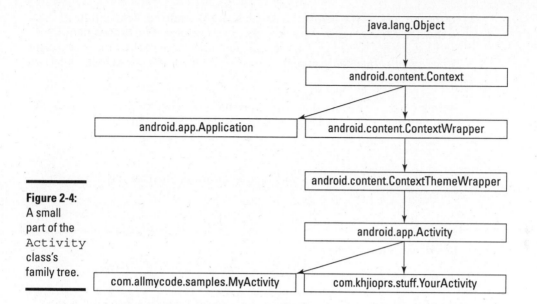

Figure 2-4:
A small
part of the
`Activity`
class's
family tree.

The Java package

Java has a feature that lets you lump classes into groups of classes. Each lump of classes is a *package*. The class in Listing 2-4 belongs to the `com.allmycode.samples` package because of the listing's first line of code.

In the Java world, developers customarily give packages long, dot-filled names. For instance, because I've registered the domain name `allmycode.com`, I name a package `com.allmycode.samples` or `com.allmycode.whateverIwant`. The Java API is actually a big collection of packages. The API has packages with names like `java.lang`, `java.util`, `java.awt`, `javax.swing`, and so on. The Android SDK is also a bunch of packages, with package names such as `android.app`, `android.view`, and `android.telephony.gsm`.

An `import` declaration starts with the name of a package and ends with either of the following:

✦ The name of a class within that package

✦ An asterisk (indicating all classes within that package)

For example, in the declaration

```
import android.app.Activity;
```

`android.app` is the name of a package in the Android SDK, and `Activity` is the name of a class in the `android.app` package. The dotted name `android.app.Activity` is the *fully qualified name* of the `Activity` class. A class's fully qualified name includes the name of the package in which the class is defined.

With an `import` declaration, you don't have to repeatedly use a class's fully qualified name. For example, in Listing 2-4, you *could* write

```
public class MyActivity extends android.app.Activity
```

but because of the Listing's `import` declaration, you can get away with plain old

```
public class MyActivity extends Activity
```

In a declaration such as

```
import android.app.*;
```

the asterisk refers to all classes in the `android.app` package. With this `import` declaration at the top of your Java code, you can use abbreviated names for all classes in the `android.app` package — names like `Activity`, `AlertDialog`, `Fragment`, `ListActivity`, and many others.

A public class

A class can be either public or non-public. If you see something like

```
public class SomeClass
```

you're looking at the declaration of a public class. But, if you see plain old

```
class SomeClass
```

the class that's being declared isn't public.

If a class is public, you can refer to the class from anywhere in your code. The following example illustrates the point.

In one file, you have

```
package com.allmycode.somepackage;

public class SomeClass {

}
```

And in another file, you have

```
package com.allmycode.someotherpackage;

import com.allmycode.somepackage.*;

//You CAN extend SomeClass:
class SomeOtherClass extends SomeClass {

    public void doStuff() {

        //This works too:
        SomeClass someObject = new SomeClass();
    }
}
```

If a class *isn't* public, you can refer to the class only from code within the class's package. The following code makes that crystal clear.

In one file, you have

```
package com.allyourcode.somepackage;

class SomeClass {

}
```

And in another file, you have

```
package com.allyourcode.someotherpackage;

import com.allyourcode.somepackage.*;

//You can't extend SomeClass:
class SomeOtherClass extends SomeClass {

    public void doStuff() {

        //This doesn't work either:
        SomeClass someObject = new SomeClass();
    }
}
```

Other public things

The *scope* of a name is the range of code in which you (the developer) can use the name. So, to sum up the preceding section's long-winded explanation:

✦ The scope of a **public** class's name includes all Java code.

✦ The scope of a **non-public** class's name is limited to the package in which the class is declared.

A public class's name doesn't really include *all* Java code. If I'm running a Java program on a computer at my moon base, and you're running a program on your phone while vacationing in orbit around Mars, your phone can't access my code's public classes. For code to access my public classes, that code must be running on the same Java virtual machine.

A class's members (the class's methods and fields) can also be public. For example, the class in Listing 2-7 has the public fields `name`, `address`, and `balance`, and has the public method `infoString`. In fact, the story for class members is a bit more involved. The word `public` is an *access modifier,* and a member of a class can be `public`, `private`, or `protected`, or have no access modifier. (For example, the `textView1` field in Listing 2-8 has no access modifier. The `onCreate` and `onDestroy` methods in Listing 2-9 have `protected` access.)

Your access modifier choices break down as follows:

✦ A `public` member's scope includes all Java code.

✦ A `private` member's scope includes the class in which the member is declared.

✦ A `protected` member's scope includes the class in which the member is declared. The scope also includes any subclasses of the class in which the member is declared and all classes belonging to the package in which the member is declared.

✦ The scope of a member with no access modifier includes the class in which the member is declared. The scope also includes all classes belonging to the package in which the member is declared.

I don't know about you, but I have trouble wrapping my head around the idea of `protected` access. One of the difficulties is that, contrary to my intuitions, sporting the word `protected` is less restrictive than sporting no access modifier at all. Anyway, when I encounter a member with `protected` access, I stop and think about it long enough for my queasiness to go away.

Defying your parent

In families, children often rebel against their parents' values. The same is true in Java. The `MyActivity` class (in Listing 2-4) is a child of the `Activity` class (in Listing 2-9). So at first glance, `MyActivity` should inherit the `onCreate` method declared in the `Activity` class's code.

But both the `Activity` and `MyActivity` classes have `onCreate` method declarations. And the two `onCreate` declarations have the same parameter list. In this way, the `MyActivity` class rebels against its parent. The `MyActivity` class says to the `Activity` class, "I don't want your stinking `onCreate` method. I'm declaring my own `onCreate` method."

So when you fire up an app, and your phone creates a `MyActivity` object, the phone executes the `MyActivity` version of `onCreate`, not the parent `Activity` version of `onCreate`.

Like all rebellious children, `MyActivity` can't break completely from its parent class's code. The first statement in the `MyActivity` class's `onCreate` method is a call to `super.onCreate`. (My kids don't usually refer to me as `super`, but a class refers to its parent that way.) Anyway, the statement `super.onCreate` calls the parent class's `onCreate` method. So, before the `onCreate` method in Listing 2-4 does anything else, the processor runs the `onCreate` method in Listing 2-9. (The creators of Android rigged things so that your `onCreate` method must call `super.onCreate`. If you forget to call `super.onCreate`, Android displays a blunt, annoying error message.)

Java annotations

Each `@Override` word in Listing 2-4 is an example of an annotation. An *annotation* tells Java something about your code. In particular, each `@Override` annotation in Listing 2-4 tells the Java compiler to be on the lookout for a common coding error. The annotation says, "Make sure that the method immediately following this annotation has the same stuff (the same name, the same parameters, and so on) as one of the methods in the `Activity` class. If not, display an error message."

So if I accidentally misspell a method's name, as in

```
@Override
public void nCreate(Bundle savedInstanceState)
```

the compiler reminds me that my new `nCreate` method doesn't really override anything that's in Android's pre-declared `Activity` class. Oops!

Java comments

A *comment* is part of a program's text. But unlike declarations, method calls, and other such things, a comment's purpose is to help people understand your code. A comment is part of a good program's documentation.

The Java programming language has three kinds of comments:

✦ **Block comments**

A *block* comment begins with `/*` and ends with `*/`. Everything between the opening `/*` and the closing `*/` is for human eyes only. No information between `/*` and `*/` is translated by the compiler.

A block comment can span across several lines. For example, the following code is a block comment:

```
/* This is my best
Android app ever! */
```

✦ **End-of-line comments**

An *end-of-line* comment starts with two slashes and goes to the end of a line of type. So in the following code snippet, the text `// A required call` is an end-of-line comment:

```
super.onCreate(savedInstanceState); // A required call
```

Once again, no text inside the end-of-line comment gets translated by the compiler.

✦ **JavaDoc comments**

A *JavaDoc* comment begins with a slash and two asterisks (`/**`). For example, in Listing 2-7, the text `/** Called at the end of each month */` is a JavaDoc comment.

A JavaDoc comment is meant to be read by people who never even look at the Java code. But that doesn't make sense. How can you see the JavaDoc comment in the Listing 2-7 comment if you never look at Listing 2-7?

Well, a certain program called `javadoc` (what else?) can find any JavaDoc comments in Listing 2-7 and turn these comments into a nice-looking web page. A page of this kind is shown in Figure 2-5.

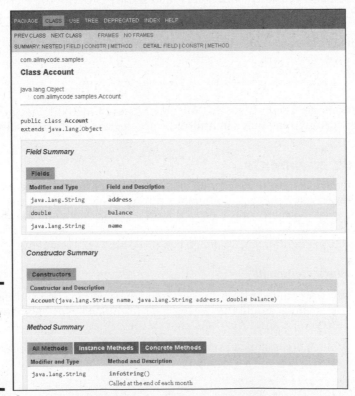

Figure 2-5:
A web page
created
from
JavaDoc
comments.

You can generate web pages like the one in Figure 2-5. Here's how:

1. **In Android Studio's main menu, choose Tools⇨Generate JavaDoc.**

   When you do, a dialog box appears. The title of the dialog box is Specify Generate JavaDoc Scope (a slightly awkward title).

2. **In the dialog box's Output Directory field, enter the name of the directory (on your computer's hard drive) where you want the new JavaDoc pages to live.**

   You can accept the defaults for other items in the dialog box.

3. **Click OK.**

   When you do, Android Studio runs the `javadoc` program to create web pages from the comments in your project. The main page opens in your default web browser.

Chapter 3: What Java Does (and When)

In This Chapter

↳ **Making decisions with Java statements**

↳ **Repeating actions with Java statements**

↳ **Adding exception handling**

Human thought centers on nouns and verbs. Nouns are the "stuff," and verbs are the stuff's actions. Nouns are the pieces, and verbs are the glue. Nouns are, and verbs do. When you use nouns, you say, "book," "room," or "stuff." When you use verbs, you say "Do this," "Do that," "Hoist that barge," or "Lift that bale."

Java also has nouns and verbs. Java's nouns include `String`, `ArrayList`, and `JFrame`, along with Android-specific things such as `Activity`, `Application`, and `Bundle`. Java's verbs involve assigning values, choosing among alternatives, repeating actions, and other courses of action.

This chapter covers some of Java's verbs. In Chapter 4 of this minibook, you bring in the nouns.

Making Decisions (Java if Statements)

When you're writing computer programs, you're constantly hitting forks in roads. Did the user correctly type his or her password? If yes, let the user work; if no, kick the bum out. So the Java programming language needs a way of making a program branch in one of two directions. Fortunately, the language has a way: It's called an `if` statement. The use of an `if` statement is illustrated in Listing 3-1.

Listing 3-1:   A Method with an if Statement

```
public void onClick(View v) {
    if (((CheckBox) v).isChecked()) {
        textview.setTextColor(Color.GREEN);
        textview.setText("Thank you!");
    } else {
        textview.setTextColor(Color.RED);
        textview.setText("No harm done.");
    }
}
```

Android calls the `onClick` method in Listing 3-1 when the user clicks a particular check box. (Android uses the parameter v to pass this check box to the `onClick` method. That's how the `onClick` method finds out which object the user clicked.) If clicking puts a check mark in the check box, the text view displays `Thank you!` in green letters. Otherwise, the text view displays `No harm done.` in red letters. (See the colorless Figure 3-1.)

Figure 3-1: Checking and unchecking in Listing 3-1.

An `if` statement has the following form:

```
if (condition) {
    statements to be executed when the condition is true
} else {
    statements to be executed when the condition is false
}
```

In Listing 3-1, the condition being tested is

```
((CheckBox) v).isChecked()
```

In this condition, variable v is the `onClick` method's parameter — the thing that Android passes to the `onClick` method. Listing 3-1 is far from being a complete Android app. But presumably, v is a check box. (See the sidebar, "Central casting.")

Central casting

In Listing 3-1, the variable v represents a View of some kind (or so says the onClick method's parameter list). Like all Java classes, the View class is part of a class family tree. The figure below shows some of the View class's nearest and dearest relatives. The lower you go in the tree, the more specific the class's characteristics are. For example, at the top of the tree, you have the very nebulous thing called Object. Below Object you have the View class. A View is something that you put on the user's screen (something the user sees). Not all View instances display text, so below View on the hierarchy are the more specific ImageView and TextView classes.

The CheckBox class is at the very bottom of the figure. A CheckBox is a specific kind of TextView — a TextView that's always in one of two states: checked or unchecked.

Meanwhile, back in Listing 3-1, the onClick method's v parameter is any kind of View.

This nonspecific "any kind of View" business comes because you never know what kind of View the user will click. Android's pre-declared onClick method (which you override in Listing 3-1) works with TextView instances, ImageView instances, Button instances, CheckBox instances, and all kinds of other instances.

Many kinds of View instances have no checked state and no unchecked state. For example, an ordinary TextView (displaying a line of text) is neither checked nor unchecked. So in Android's grand hierarchy of Object instances, View instances, and CheckBox instances, the humble View class has no isChecked method. If you replace the condition in Listing 3-1 with the simpler v.isChecked() condition, the modified code doesn't compile. Java realizes that v, being declared as a parameter of type View, might not have an isChecked method.

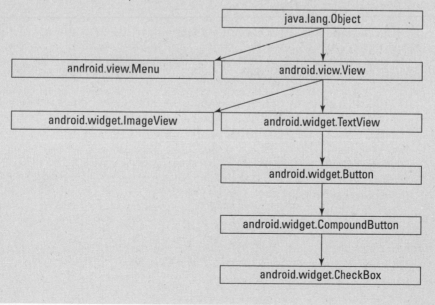

java.lang.Object

android.view.Menu → android.view.View

android.widget.ImageView → android.widget.TextView

android.widget.Button

android.widget.CompoundButton

android.widget.CheckBox

(continued)

(continued)

The issue in this example is the balance between generality and specificity. Android's `onClick` method must be prepared to work with any `View` instance, but for this particular app, you (the developer) know that the thing being clicked is a `CheckBox` instance. And in the Android API, every `CheckBox` instance has an `isChecked` method.

So what do you do? In Listing 3-1, you do *casting.* When you *cast* a value, you precede the value with a class's name in parentheses. The code `(CheckBox)  v` represents "v, when we think of v as a `CheckBox`." In other words, by writing `(CheckBox)  v`, the developer assures Java that when the time comes to execute this code, `v` will not only be a `View` of some kind or other. The `v` object will be a `CheckBox` and will have an `isChecked` method. So the condition `((CheckBox) v).isChecked()` is received warmly and graciously by the Java compiler.

Android's `isChecked` method returns either `true` or `false` — true when the v check box is checked; `false` when the v check box isn't checked.

The condition in an `if` statement must be enclosed within parentheses. The condition must be a `boolean` expression — an expression whose value is either `true` or `false`. (See Chapter 2 of this minibook for information about Java's primitive types, including the `boolean` type.) So, for example, the following condition is okay:

```
if (numberOfTries < 17) {
```

But the strange kind of condition that you can use in languages, such as C++, is not okay:

```
if (17) { //This is incorrect.
```

You can omit curly braces when only one statement comes between the condition and the word `else`. You can also omit braces when only one statement comes after the word `else`. For example, the following code is okay:

```
if (((CheckBox) v).isChecked())
    textview.setText("Thank you!");
else {
    textview.setTextColor(Color.RED);
    textview.setText("No harm done.");
}
```

An `if` statement can also enjoy a full and happy life without an `else` part. So the following code forms a complete `if` statement:

```
if (((CheckBox) v).isChecked()) {
    textview.setTextColor(Color.GREEN);
    textview.setText("Thank you!");
}
```

Testing for equality

Java has several ways to test for equality ("Is this value the same as that value?"). None of these ways is the first thing you'd think of doing. In particular, to find out whether the parameter v is the thing you call `check-box1`, you *don't* write if (v = checkbox1). Instead, you use a double equal sign (==). You write if (v == checkbox1). In Java, the single equal sign (=) is reserved for *assignment*. So n = 5 means "Let n stand for the value 5," and v = checkbox1 means "Let v stand for the `checkbox1` object."

Comparing two strings is yet another story. When you compare two strings with one another, you don't want to use the double equal sign. Using the double equal sign would ask, "Is this string stored in exactly the same place in memory as that other string?" That's usually not what you want to ask. Instead, you usually want to ask, "Does this string have the same characters in it as that other string?" To ask the second question (the more appropriate question), Java's `String` type has a method named `equals`:

```
if (response.equals("yes")) {
```

The `equals` method compares two strings to see whether they have the same characters in them. In this paragraph's tiny example, the variable response refers to a string, and the text "yes" refers to a string. The condition response.equals("yes") is true if response refers to a string whose letters are 'y', then 'e', and then 's'.

Like most programming languages, Java has the usual complement of comparison operators (such as < for "less than") and logical operators (such as && for "and"). For a list of such operators, visit http://download.oracle.com/javase/tutorial/java/nutsandbolts/opsummary.html.

Primitive and reference types

The `int` type is a primitive type. When you declare a variable to have type `int`, you can visualize what that declaration means in a fairly straightforward way. It means that, somewhere inside the computer's memory, a storage location is reserved for that variable's value. In that storage location is a bunch of bits. The arrangement of the bits ensures that a certain whole number is represented.

That explanation is fine for primitive types like `int` or `double`, but every Java class is a *reference* type. If you declare a variable to have some type that's not a primitive type, the variable's type is (most of the time) the name of a Java class.

What does it mean when you declare a variable to have a reference type? What does it mean to declare `response` to be of type `String` or to declare `v` to be of type `View`?

Because `String` is a class, you can create objects from that class. Each such object (each instance of the `String` class) is a sequence of characters. By declaring the variable `response` to be of type `String`, you're reserving the use of the name `response`. This reservation tells Java that `response` can refer to an actual `String`-type object. In other words, `response` can become a nickname for a sequence of characters. The situation is illustrated in the figure below, where the storage story for primitive types and reference types is told.

If you're familiar with other programming languages and you like talking about pointers, you can safely think of `String response` as a declaration whose meaning is "`response` stores a pointer to a sequence of characters."

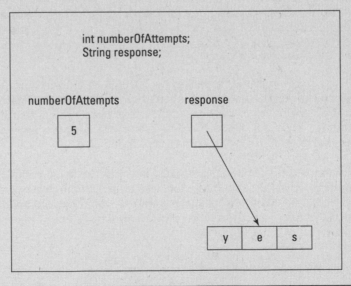

Choosing among many alternatives (Java switch statements)

I'm the first to admit that I hate making decisions. If things go wrong, I would rather have the problem be someone else's fault. Writing the previous sections (on making decisions with Java's `if` statement) knocked the stuffing right out of me. That's why my mind boggles as I begin this section on choosing among many alternatives.

Consider the code in Listing 3-2.

Listing 3-2: A Java switch Statement

```java
public void onClick(View v) {

    String message;
    Editable edit = textfield.getText();
    if (edit.length() != 0) {
        int number =
              Integer.valueOf(edit.toString());

        switch (number) {
        case 0:
            message = "none";
            break;
        case 1:
            message = "one";
            break;
        case 2:
            message = "two";
            break;
        case 3:
            message = "three";
            break;
        default:
            message = "many";
        }

        label.setText(message);
    }
}
```

**Book II
Chapter 3**

**What Java Does
(and When)**

The code in Listing 3-2 is part of an app, and the app's screen is pictured in Figure 3-2.

Figure 3-2:
A TextView object reports on an EditText object's content.

011|

many

The user clicks something or other (something not specified in Listing 3-2 or in Figure 3-2). As a result of the user's click, Android does the stuff in Listing 3-2. Some of that stuff involves a Java `switch` statement. The `switch` statement examines the characters in a text field. (In Figure 3-2, the text field contains `011`.) To make sure that the text field characters are all digits, I included the following element in the app's layout document:

```
<EditText android:layout_height="wrap_content"
    android:id="@+id/editText1"
    android:layout_width="match_parent"
    android:inputType="number"></EditText>
```

In the first line of the `switch` statement, `number` is a whole number. If `number` is 0, the code makes `message` be `"none"`. If `number` is 1, the code makes `message` be `"one"`. If `number` is not 0, 1, 2, or 3, the `default` part of the `switch` statement takes over, and the code makes `message` be `"many"`.

Each `break` statement in Listing 3-2 says, "Jump past any remaining cases." You can omit a `break` statement, but do so at your own peril! For example, if you write

```
case 2:
    message = "two";
case 3:
    message = "three";
default:
    message = "many";
}
```

and `number` is 2, Java executes three cases, one after another — namely, `message = "two"` followed by `message = "three"` followed immediately by `message = "many"`. The lack of `break` statements tells Java to *fall-through* from one case to the next. The end result is that the message is `"many"`, and that's probably not what you want.

A `switch` statement has the following form:

```
switch (expression) {
case constant1:
    statements to be executed when the
    expression has value constant1
case constant2:
    statements to be executed when the
    expression has value constant2
case . . .

default:
    statements to be executed when the
    expression has a value different from
    any of the constants
}
```

You can't put any old expression in a `switch` statement. The expression that's tested at the start of a `switch` statement must have

✦ One of the primitive types `char`, `byte`, `short`, or `int`, or

✦ One of the reference types `Character`, `Byte`, `Short`, or `Integer`, or

✦ An `enum` type

An `enum` type is a type whose values are limited to the few that you declare. For example, the code

```
enum TrafficSignal {GREEN, YELLOW, RED};
```

defines a type whose only values are `GREEN`, `YELLOW`, and `RED`. Elsewhere in your code, you can write

```
TrafficSignal signal;
signal = TrafficSignal.GREEN;
```

to make use of the `TrafficSignal` type.

Starting with Java 7, you can put a `String` type expression at the start of a `switch` statement, as follows:

```
String myString = "one";

// . . .
// Set the value of myString here
// . . .

switch (myString) {
case "one":
  textView.setText("1");
  break;
case "two":
  textView.setText("2");
  break;
default:
  break;
}
```

Repeating Instructions Over and Over Again

In 1966, the company that brings you Head & Shoulders shampoo made history. On the back of the bottle, the directions for using the shampoo read, "Lather, rinse, repeat." Never before had a complete set of directions (for doing anything, let alone shampooing your hair) been summarized so succinctly. People in the direction-writing business hailed this as a monumental achievement. Directions like these stood in stark contrast to others of the time. (For instance, the first sentence on a can of bug spray read, "Turn this can so that it points away from your face." Duh!)

Aside from their brevity, the thing that made the Head & Shoulders directions so cool was that, with three simple words, they managed to capture a notion that's at the heart of all instruction-giving — the notion of repetition. That last word, *repeat,* took an otherwise bland instructional drone and turned it into a sophisticated recipe for action.

The fundamental idea is that when you're following directions, you don't just follow one instruction after another. Instead, you take turns in the road. You make decisions ("If HAIR IS DRY, then USE CONDITIONER"), and you go into loops ("LATHER-RINSE and then LATHER-RINSE again"). In application development, you use decision-making and looping all the time.

Java while statements

In an Android app, a content provider feeds a *cursor* to your code. You can think of the cursor as a pointer to a row in a table. In Listing 3-3, each table row has three entries — an _id, a name, and an amount. Supposedly, the _id uniquely identifies a row, the name is a person's name, and the amount is a huge number of dollars owed to you by that person.

For the rundown on content providers, see Book III, Chapter 5.

Listing 3-3:   A while Loop

```
cursor.moveToFirst();

while (!cursor.isAfterLast()) {
    String _id = cursor.getString(0);
    String name = cursor.getString(1);
    String amount = cursor.getString(2);
    textViewDisplay.append(_id + " " +
                           name + " " + amount + "\n");
    cursor.moveToNext();
}
```

A cursor's moveToFirst method makes the cursor point to the first row of the table. Regardless of the row a cursor points to, the cursor's moveToNext method makes the cursor point to the next row of the table. The cursor's isAfterLast method returns true when, having tried to move to the next row, there's no next row.

In Java, an exclamation point (!) means "not," so `while (!cursor.`
`isAfterLast())` means "while it's not true that the cursor has reached past
the table's last row . . ." So the loop in Listing 3-3 repeatedly does the following:

```
As long as the cursor has not reached past the last row,
    get the string in the row's initial column and
        make _id refer to that string,
    get the string in the row's middle column and
        make name refer to that string,
    get the string in the row's last column and
        make amount refer to that string, and
append these strings to the textViewDisplay, and then
move the cursor to the next row in preparation
        for returning to the top of the while statement.
```

Imagine that a particular cursor's table has 100 rows. Then a processor
executes the statements inside Listing 3-3's `while` loop 100 times. Using the
official developer lingo, the processor performs 100 loop *iterations*.

A `while` statement has the following form:

```
while (condition) {
    statements to be executed
}
```

You can omit the curly braces when the loop has only one *statement to be
executed.*

In Listing 3-3, the characters \n form an *escape sequence.* When you put
\n inside a string, you're escaping from the normal course of things by
displaying neither a backslash nor a letter n. Instead, \n in a Java string
always means "Go to the next line." So in Listing 3-3, \n puts a line break
between one _id, name, amount group and the next.

Java for statements

Life is filled with examples of counting loops. And app development mirrors life — or is it the other way around? When you tell a device what to do,
you're often telling the device to display three lines, process ten accounts,
dial a million phone numbers, or whatever.

Listing 3-3 displays all the rows in a table full of data. Sometimes, all the data
is too much data. To get the idea of what the table has to offer, you might
want to display only the first ten rows of data. The code in Listing 3-4 does
the job.

Listing 3-4:   A for Loop

```
cursor.moveToFirst();

for (int i = 0; i < 10; i++) {
    String _id = cursor.getString(0);
    String name = cursor.getString(1);
    String amount = cursor.getString(2);
    textViewDisplay.append(i + ": " + _id + " " +
                              name + " " + amount + "\n");
    cursor.moveToNext();
}
```

Listing 3-4 declares an `int` variable named i. The starting value of i is 0. As long as the condition `i < 10` is true, the processor executes the instructions inside the `for` statement. In this example, the `for` statement's instructions include getting an `_id`, getting a `name`, getting an `amount`, and appending all that stuff to the `textViewDisplay`. In addition to that stuff, the `textViewDisplay` gets the value of i (be it 0, 1, 2, or any number less than 10).

To keep the ball rolling, the last instruction in the `for` statement moves the cursor to the next line. But wait! What happens when the processor goes to the beginning of the loop again? Before starting the loop anew, the processor does i++, which is Java-speak for "Add 1 to i." So after ten loop iterations, the value of i finally reaches 10 and the execution of the `for` loop's instructions comes to an end.

A `for` statement has the following form:

```
for (initialization ; condition ; update) {
    statements to be executed
}
```

✦ An *initialization* (such as `int i = 0` in Listing 3-4) defines the action to be taken before the first loop iteration.

✦ A *condition* (such as `i < 10` in Listing 3-4) defines the thing to be checked before an iteration. If the condition is `true`, the processor executes the iteration. If the condition is `false`, the processor doesn't execute the iteration and moves on to execute whatever code comes after the `for` statement.

✦ An *update* (such as `i++` in Listing 3-4) defines an action to be taken at the end of each loop iteration.

As always, you can omit the curly braces when the loop has only one *statement to be executed*.

Like the protagonist in an ancient Greek tragedy, the loop in Listing 3-4 has a fatal flaw. The loop comes crashing down if the cursor's table has fewer than ten rows. To remedy this (and to save the protagonist), you can add a check for "rowlessness" inside the loop:

```
for (int i = 0; i < 10; i++) {
    if (cursor.isAfterLast()) {
        break;
    }
    String _id = cursor.getString(0);
    String name = cursor.getString(1);
    String amount = cursor.getString(2);
    textViewDisplay.append(i + ": " + _id + " " +
                        name + " " + amount + "\n");
    cursor.moveToNext();
}
```

The `if` statement says "If there are no more rows (because the cursor is already positioned after the last row) then execute the `break` statement." And inside a loop (a `while` loop, a `for` loop, or some other kind of loop), a `break` statement says, "This looping is done" and "We're outta here." The processor moves on to execute whatever statement comes immediately after the loop's code.

Book II
Chapter 3

What Java Does
(and When)

Java do statements

To find a particular row of a cursor's table, you normally do a *query*. (For straight talk about queries, see Book IV.) You almost never perform a do-it-yourself search through a table's data. But just this once, look at a loop that iterates through row after row — the loop is in Listing 3-5.

Listing 3-5:   Leap Before You Look

```
cursor.moveToFirst();
String name;

do {
    String _id = cursor.getString(0);
    name = cursor.getString(1);
    String amount = cursor.getString(2);
    textViewDisplay.append(_id + " " +
                        name + " " + amount + "\n");
    cursor.moveToNext();
} while (!name.equals("Burd") && !cursor.isAfterLast());
```

With a `do` loop, the processor jumps right in, takes action, and then checks a condition to see whether the result of the action is what you want. If the result is what you want, execution of the loop is done. If not, the processor goes back to the top of the loop for another go-around.

In Listing 3-5, you're looking for a row with the name *Burd*. (After all, the bum owes you lots of money.) When you enter the loop, the cursor points to the table's first row. Before checking a row for the name *Burd,* you fetch that first row's data and add the data to the `textViewDisplay` where the user can see what's going on.

Before you march on to the next row (the next loop iteration), you check a condition to make sure that another row is worth visiting. (Check to make sure that you haven't yet found that Burd guy, and that you haven't moved past the last row of the table.)

To get the code in Listing 3-5 working, you have to move the declaration of `name` outside the `do` statement. A declaration that's inside a pair of curly braces (such as the `_id`, `name`, and `amount` declarations in Listing 3-4) cannot be used outside curly braces. So, in Listing 3-5, if you don't move the `name` declaration outside the loop, Java complains that `!name.equals("Burd")` is incorrect.

Arrays in Java

An *array* is a bunch of values of the same type. Each value in the array is associated with an *index*. For example, the following code puts 15.020999999999999 in an app's `textView1`:

```
double[] measurements = new double[3];
measurements[0] = 5.7;
measurements[1] = 9.32;
measurements[2] = 0.001;
textView1.setText(Double.toString(measurements[0]
        + measurements[1] + measurements[2]));
```

Arithmetic with `float` values and `double` values suffers from the woes of numeric errors. The sum 5.7 + 9.32 + 0.001 is 15.021, not 15.020999999999999. But computers use the bits 0 and 1 (instead of the digits 0 through 9) to store numbers internally. The use of zeros and ones, along with the fact that computers can't store infinitely long decimal expansions, leads inevitably to arithmetic errors. Sorry about that!

The following code puts *Barry Burd and Jane Dough* in an app's `textView1`:

```
String[] names = new String[3];
names[0] = new String("Barry Burd");
names[1] = new String("John Public");
names[2] = new String("Jane Dough");

textView1.setText(names[0] + " and " + names[2]);
```

You can step from value to value in an array using a `for` loop. For example, the following code puts *Barry Burd John Public Jane Dough* in an app's `text-View1`:

```
String[] names = new String[3];
names[0] = new String("Barry Burd ");
names[1] = new String("John Public ");
names[2] = new String("Jane Dough ");
textView1.setText("");
```

```
for (int i = 0; i < 3; i++) {
  textView1.append(names[i]);
}
```

Java's enhanced for statements

In the mid-1960s, a company advertised its product by announcing, "Our product used to be perfect. But now, our product is even better!"

In the mid-2000s, the newly created Java 5 specification had a brand-new kind of loop. This feature has been part of Java for several years, but it's still called the enhanced `for` loop. The following code uses an enhanced `for` loop to put *Barry Burd John Public Jane Dough* in an app's `textView1`:

Book II
Chapter 3

**What Java Does
(and When)**

```
String[] names = new String[3];
names[0] = new String("Barry Burd ");
names[1] = new String("John Public ");
names[2] = new String("Jane Dough ");
textView1.setText("");
for (String s : names) {
  textView1.append(s);
}
```

Here's another example. Suppose you have a cursor, and the cursor points to a table's row. (To keep this example simple, I assume that each column contains `String` data.) You don't know the table's column names, and you don't know how many columns the table has. Java's enhanced `for` statement provides an elegant way to deal with this kind of situation. Listing 3-6 shows you the story.

In Listing 3-6, a cursor's `getColumnNames` method returns an array of `String` values. The code assigns this array to the `columnNames` variable. Then the enhanced `for` loop creates a variable (`colName`) that steps through the `String` values in the array. The line

```
for (String colName : columnNames)
```

Listing 3-6:   An Enhanced for Loop

```
cursor.moveToFirst();

while (!cursor.isAfterLast()) {

    String[] columnNames = cursor.getColumnNames();

    for (String colName : columnNames) {
        int index = cursor.getColumnIndex(colName);
        textViewDisplay.append(colName + ":" +
                cursor.getString(index) + ", ");
    }

    textViewDisplay.append("\n");
    cursor.moveToNext();
}
```

says, "Repeat the instructions in the `for` statement once for each of the `String` values stored in the `columnNames` array. During each value in the array, let the variable `colName` stand for that value during one of the loop's iterations." So, for example, if the `columnNames` array contains the strings `_id`, `name`, and `amount`, the processor performs three iterations of the enhanced loop in Listing 3-6. During the first iteration, `colName` stands for `"_id"`. During the second iteration, `colName` stands for `"name"`. During the third iteration, `colName` stands for `"amount"`.

With or without enhanced loops, a cursor's `getString` method needs a column number. In Listing 3-5 (and in previous listings), I hand column numbers 0, 1, and 2 to the `getString` method. In Listing 3-6, I fetch these column numbers from the column names, using the cursor's `getColumnIndex` method.

An enhanced `for` statement has the following form:

```
for (TypeName variable : arrayOrCollection) {
    statements to be executed
}
```

The *TypeName* is the type of each element in the *arrayOrCollection*. The loop performs an iteration for each element of the *arrayOrCollection*. During each iteration, the variable refers to one of the elements in the *arrayOrCollection*.

Jumping Away from Trouble

The Java programming language has a mechanism called *exception handling*. With exception handling, a program can detect that things are about to go wrong and respond by creating a brand-new object. In the official terminology, the program is said to be *throwing* an exception. That new object, an instance of the `Exception` class, is passed like a hot potato from one piece of code to another until some piece of code decides to *catch* the exception. When the exception is caught, the program executes some recovery code, buries the exception, and moves on to the next normal statement as if nothing had ever happened.

The whole thing is done with the aid of several Java keywords. These keywords are as follows:

✦ `throw`: Creates a new exception object.

✦ `throws`: Passes the buck from a method up to whatever code called the method.

✦ `try`: Encloses code that has the potential to create a new exception object. In the usual scenario, the code inside a `try` clause contains calls to methods whose code can create one or more exceptions.

✦ `catch`: Deals with the exception, buries it, and then moves on.

For example, Java's `Integer.parseInt` method turns a `String` value into an `int` value. The value of `"279" + 1` is `"2791"`, but the value of `Integer.parseInt("279") + 1` is 280. A call to `Integer.parseInt` throws a `NumberFormat` Exception if the call's parameter isn't a whole number. So if your code calls `Integer.parseInt("3.5")`, your code has to deal with a `NumberFormat` Exception. (The String value `"3.5"` doesn't stand for a whole number.)

Book II
Chapter 3

Here's a simple method to add one to a number that's represented as a `String` value:

```
int increment(String str) {
  return Integer.parseInt(str) + 1;
}
```

What Java Does
(and When)

If you call `increment("985")`, you get 986. That's good.

But if you call `increment("2.71828")`, your code crashes, and your app stops running. Java leaves clues about the crash in the Logcat tab. The clues (which form a Java *stack trace*) look something like this:

```
Exception in thread "main" java.lang.NumberFormatException:
For input string: "2.71828"
    at java.lang.NumberFormatException.forInputString
    at java.lang.Integer.parseInt
```

If you add some exception handling code to the increment method, your code keeps running with or without the `increment("2.71828")` call.

```
int increment(String str) {
  try {
    return Integer.parseInt(str) + 1;
  } catch (NumberFormatException e) {
    return 0;
  }
}
```

With the `try` and `catch` in the revised method, Java attempts to evaluate `Integer.parseInt(str)`. If evaluation is successful, the method returns `Integer.parseInt(str) + 1`. But if `str` has a weird value, the call to `Integer.parseInt` throws a `NumberFormatException`. Fortunately, the revised `increment` method catches the `NumberFormatException`, returns the value 0, and continues running without bothering the user.

Chapter 4: Object-Oriented Programming in Java

In This Chapter

↙ **Using classes with finesse**

↙ **Working with Java's classes and interfaces**

↙ **Being part of Java's inner circle**

↙ **Putting your eggs (your file, that is) in a basket**

If you remember nothing else about Java, remember these ideas from Chapter 2 of this minibook:

> *Java is an object-oriented programming language. So, as a developer, your primary goal is to describe objects. Your closely related goal is to describe objects' close cousins — namely, classes. A class is the idea behind a certain kind of thing. An object is a concrete instance of a class.*

And if you remember nothing else about those ideas, remember the following two-word summary:

> *Classes; objects.*

Chapter 2 in this minibook covers the highlights of object-oriented programming in Java. This chapter covers some of object-oriented programming's finer points.

Static Fields and Methods

In Listing 4-1, I reproduce a small portion of the source code of Android's Toast class.

According to the code in Listing 4-1, the Toast class has a static field named LENGTH_LONG and a static method named makeText. Anything that's declared to be static belongs to the whole class, not to any particular instance of the class. When you create the static field, LENGTH_LONG, you create only one copy of the field. This copy stays with the entire Toast class. No matter how many instances of the Toast class you create — one, nine, or none — you have just one LENGTH_LONG field.

Listing 4-1: An Unrepresentative Sample of Android's Toast Class Code

```
public class Toast {

  public static final int LENGTH_LONG = 1;


  public static Toast makeText(Context context,
                               CharSequence text,
                               int duration) {
    Toast result = new Toast(context);

    LayoutInflater inflate = (LayoutInflater) context.
      getSystemService(Context.LAYOUT_INFLATER_SERVICE);
    View v = inflate.inflate
      (com.android.internal.
      R.layout.transient_notification, null);
    TextView tv = (TextView)v.findViewById
      (com.android.internal.R.id.message);
    tv.setText(text);

    result.mNextView = v;
    result.mDuration = duration;

    return result;
  }

  public void show() {
    if (mNextView == null) {
      throw new RuntimeException
        ("setView must have been called");
    }

    INotificationManager service = getService();

    String pkg = mContext.getPackageName();

    TN tn = mTN;

    try {
      service.enqueueToast(pkg, tn, mDuration);
    } catch (RemoteException e) {
      // Empty
    }
  }
}
```

Contrast this with the situation in Chapter 3 of this minibook. In that chapter, the Account class has fields name, address, and balance. The fields aren't static, so every instance of the Account class has its own name, its own address, and its own balance. One instance has name Barry Burd and balance 24.02, and another instance has name John Q. Public with balance –471.03. To refer to Burd's balance, you may write something like myAccount.balance, as in the following code:

```
Account myAccount = new Account();

myAccount.name = "Burd";
myAccount.address = "222 Cyberspace Lane";
myAccount.balance = 24.02;
```

To refer to a non-static member of a class, you write the name of an object (such as myAccount), followed by a dot, and then the name of the member (such as balance).

But the Toast class's LENGTH_LONG field is static. When you create a Toast instance, you don't create a new LENGTH_LONG field. The Toast class has one LENGTH_LONG field, and that's that. Accordingly, you refer to LENGTH_LONG by prefacing the field name with the Toast class name, followed by a dot:

**Book II
Chapter 4**

```
Toast.LENGTH_LONG
```

In fact, a typical use of Toast in an Android app refers to the static field LENGTH_LONG and the static method makeText:

**Object-Oriented
Programming
in Java**

```
Toast.makeText
  (getApplication(), "Whoa!", Toast.LENGTH_LONG).show();
```

A call to the Toast class's makeText method returns an actual object — an instance of the Toast class. (You can verify this by referring to the first line of the makeText method in Listing 4-1.) So in an Android app, an expression such as

```
Toast.makeText
  (getApplication(), "Whoa!", Toast.LENGTH_LONG)
```

stands for an object. And (again, according to Listing 4-1) each object created from the Toast class has its own non-static show method. That's why you normally follow a Toast.makeText call with .show().

Here's one final word about Listing 4-1: In addition to being static, the LENGTH_LONG field is also final. A final field is one whose value cannot be changed. In other words, when you declare LENGTH_LONG, you can initialize its value to 1 (as in Listing 4-1). But elsewhere in the code, you can't write LENGTH_LONG = 2. (For that matter, you can't even write LENGTH_LONG = 1 elsewhere in the code.)

Many programming languages use the word *constant* (or the abbreviation const) to refer to a variable whose value cannot be changed.

Interfaces and Callbacks

Listing 4-2 contains a snippet from Android's pre-declared Java code. The listing contains a Java *interface*.

Listing 4-2:   Android's OnClickListener Interface

```
public interface OnClickListener {
    void onClick(View v);
}
```

An interface is like a class, but it's different. (So, what else is new? A cow is like a planet, but it's quite a bit different. Cows moo; planets hang in space.) Anyway, when you hear the word *interface,* you can start by thinking of a class. Then, in your head, note the following things:

✦ **A class doesn't extend an interface. Instead, a class *implements* an interface.**

Later in this chapter, you can see the following line of code:

```
class MyListener implements OnClickListener
```

✦ **A class can extend only one parent class, but a class can implement more than one interface.**

For example, if you want `MyListener` objects to listen for long clicks as well as regular clicks, you can write

```
class MyListener implements OnClickListener,
                            OnLongClickListener {
```

A long click is what non-developers would probably call a touch-and-hold motion.

✦ **An interface can extend another interface.**

For example, in the following line of code, a homegrown interface named `SomeListener` extends Android's built-in `OnClickListener` interface:

```
public interface SomeListener extends OnClickListener {
```

✦ **An interface can extend more than one interface.**

✦ **An interface's methods have no bodies of their own.**

In Listing 4-2, the `onClick` method has no body — no curly braces and no statements to execute. In place of a body, there's just a semicolon.

A method with no body, like the method defined in Listing 4-2, is an *abstract method.*

Starting with Java 8, a method declared inside an interface can have a body. A method of this kind is called a *default method*. As an Android developer, you don't have to worry about this because Android doesn't support the new features in Java 8. From my mid-2015 perspective, Android works only with Java 5, 6, and 7.

✦ **When you implement an interface, you provide bodies for all the interface's methods.**

That's why the `MyListener` class in Listing 4-3 has an `onClick` method. By announcing that it will implement the `OnClickListener` interface, the `MyListener` class agrees that it will give meaning to the interface's `onClick` method. In this situation, *giving meaning* means declaring an `onClick` method with curly braces, a body, and maybe some statements to execute.

**Book II
Chapter 4**

**Object-Oriented
Programming
in Java**

Listing 4-3: Implementing Android's OnClickListener Interface

```
package com.allmycode.samples;

import android.app.Activity;
import android.os.Bundle;
import android.view.View;
import android.view.View.OnClickListener;
import android.widget.Button;

public class MyActivity extends Activity {

    Button button;

    @Override
    public void onCreate(Bundle savedInstanceState) {
        super.onCreate(savedInstanceState);
        setContentView(R.layout.main);

        button = ((Button) findViewById(R.id.button1));

        button.setOnClickListener(new MyListener(this));
    }
}

class MyListener implements OnClickListener {
    Activity activity;

    MyListener (Activity activity) {
        this.activity = activity;
    }

    @Override
    public void onClick(View arg0) {
        ((MyActivity) activity).button.setBackgroundColor
                        (android.graphics.Color.GRAY);
    }
}
```

Listing 4-3 doesn't illustrate the most popular way to implement the `OnClickListener` interface, but the listing presents a straightforward use of interfaces and their implementations.

When you announce that you're going to implement an interface (as in `class MyListener implements OnClickListener`), the Java compiler takes this announcement seriously. In the body of the class, if you fail to give meaning to any of the interface's methods, the compiler yells at you.

If you're really lazy, you can quickly find out what methods need to be declared in your interface-implementing code. Try to compile the code, and the compiler lists all the methods that you should have declared but didn't.

Chapter 3 in this minibook introduces the use of `@Override` — a Java annotation. Normally, you use `@Override` to signal the replacement of a method that's already been declared in a superclass. But from Java 6 onward, you can also use `@Override` to signal an interface method's implementation. That's what I do in Listing 4-3.

You can think of an interface as a kind of contract. When you write

```
class MyListener implements OnClickListener
```

you're binding `MyListener` to the contract described in Listing 4-2. That contract states, "You, the implementing class, hereby agree to provide a body for each of the abstract methods declared in the interface and to indemnify and hold harmless this interface for any damages, mishaps, or embarrassments from wearing pocket protectors."

As a member of society, you have exactly two biological parents, but you can enter into agreements with several companies. In the same way, a Java class has only one parent class, but a class can implement many interfaces.

The interface-implementing hierarchy (if you can call it a "hierarchy") cuts across the class-extension hierarchy. This idea is illustrated in Figure 4-1, where I display class extensions vertically and display interface implementations horizontally. (Android's `KeyboardView` class lives in the `android.inputmethodservice` package. Both `KeyboardView` and the homegrown `MyListener` class in Listing 4-3 implement Android's `OnClickListener` interface.)

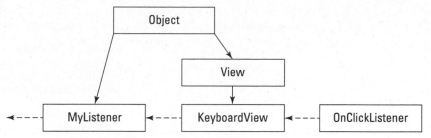

Figure 4-1:
The interface hierarchy cuts across the class hierarchy.

Event handling and callbacks

The big news in Listing 4-3, shown in the preceding section, is the handling of the user's button click. Anything the user does (such as pressing a key, touching the screen, or whatever) is an *event*. The code that responds to the user's press or touch is the *event-handling* code.

Some things that the user doesn't do are also events. For example, when you turn on a device's GPS sensor and the sensor gets its first fix, Android calls the onGpsStatusChanged event handler.

Listing 4-3 deals with the click event with three parts of its code:

✦ The MyListener class declaration says that this class implements OnClickListener.

✦ The activity's onCreate method sets the button's click handler to a new MyListener object.

✦ The code for the MyListener class has an onClick method.

Taken together, all three of these tricks make the MyListener class handle button clicks. Figure 4-2 illustrates the process.

When the user clicks the button, Android says, "Okay, the button was clicked. So, what should I do about that?" And the answer is, "Call an onClick method." It's as if Android has code that looks like this:

```
OnClickListener object1;
if (buttonJustGotClicked()) {
    object1.onClick(infoAboutTheClick);
}
```

Of course, behind every answer is yet another question. In this situation, the follow-up question is, "Where does Android find onClick methods to call?" And there's another question: "What if you don't want Android to call certain onClick methods that are lurking in your code?"

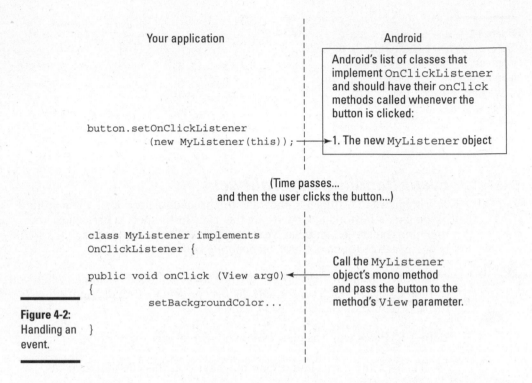

Your application

Figure 4-2:
Handling an
event.

Well, that's why you call the setOnClickListener method. In Listing 4-3, the call

```
button.setOnClickListener(new MyListener(this));
```

creates a new MyListener object. You tell Android, "Put the new object's onClick method on your list of methods to be called. Call this object's onClick method whenever the button is clicked."

And in response to this request, Android asks, "Oh, yeah? How do I know that your MyListener object has an onClick method that I can call?" And before you can answer the question, Android notices that your MyListener class implements the OnClickListener interface. So (because of the code in Listing 4-2), your MyListener object has an onClick method.

Of course, Android doesn't really ask, "How do I know that your MyListener object has an onClick method?" For one thing, Android doesn't say anything because Android doesn't have a mouth. And for another thing, Android's code to call onClick declares the object containing the onClick method to be of type OnClickListener. So, if your MyListener method doesn't implement OnClickListener, Java notices a type inconsistency (and Java complains vigorously).

So here's the sequence of events (follow along in Figure 4-2): Your app registers a listener with Android. Then your app goes about its business. When a relevant event takes place (such as the clicking of a button), Android calls back to your app's code. Android calls the `onClick` method inside whatever object you registered.

Android calls back to your app's code, so the term *callback* describes the mechanism that Android uses to handle events.

Starting with version 1.6 (also known as *Donut* or *API Level 4*), Android provides a way to respond to button clicks, keystrokes, and other things without all the complicated code in this chapter's listings. That is, you can handle certain events without implementing the `OnClickListener` interface. Even so, you can't write Java code without understanding events and callbacks. At many points in your Android development life, you have to write the kind of code that you find in this chapter.

For more information on handling events without implementing `OnClickListener`, see Book I, Chapter 5.

An object remembers who created it

In the preceding section, I raise several questions about the interaction between your app and Android's callback. But in that section, I miss one of the questions. The question is this: In the `onClick` method of Listing 4-3, how does the code know what `button` means? Listing 4-3 contains two classes — `MyActivity` and `MyListener`. Without jumping through some hoops, one class doesn't know anything about another class's fields.

In Listing 4-3, the keyword `this` sits inside the code that defines the `MyActivity` class:

```
button.setOnClickListener(new MyListener(this));
```

In Java, `this` refers to "the object that contains the current line of code." So, in Listing 4-3, the word `this` refers to an instance of `MyActivity` — the activity that's being displayed on the device's screen. The current `MyActivity` instance has a button. So far, so good.

Later in Listing 4-3, the `MyListener` constructor tucks a reference to the current activity into one of its fields. (See Figure 4-3.)

For more information about constructors and about the use of the word `this` inside a constructor, see Chapter 2 in this minibook.

In the MyActivity class:

```
button.setOnClickListener(new MyListener(this));
```

In the MyListener class:

```
class MyListener implements OnClickListener {
  Activity activity;

  Mylistener (Activity activity) {
      this.activity = activity;
  }
```

Figure 4-3:
How a
listener
remembers
its creator.

```
  @Override
  public void onClick(View arg0) {
        ((MyActivity) activity).button.setBackgroundColor
                    (android.graphics.Color.GRAY);
      }
}
```

Looking again at Figure 4-3, `MyListener` refers to an `activity`, and that
activity contains a button. When Android calls the `onClick` method, the
method executes an instruction that's very much like this one:

```
activity.button.setBackgroundColor
                    (android.graphics.Color.GRAY);
```

The instruction takes the referenced activity's button and sets the button's
background color to gray. (To make things work properly, you have to do
some casting in the `onClick` method of Listing 4-3, but you can worry about
the casting when you glance at Chapter 3 of this minibook.)

A less wordy way to implement an interface

If you read the preceding section and then you read this section, you'll
probably want to send me a nasty email message. The preceding section
describes an admittedly convoluted way to make a listener remember which
activity's button to tweak. It's important to know how Listing 4-3 works,
but if you modify Listing 4-3 so that the activity is its own listener, things
become much simpler. Listing 4-4 shows you how to do it.

Listing 4-4:   An Activity Eats Its Own Dog Food

```
package com.allmycode.samples;

import android.app.Activity;
import android.os.Bundle;
import android.view.View;
import android.view.View.OnClickListener;
import android.widget.Button;

public class MyActivity extends Activity
                        implements OnClickListener {

    Button button;

    @Override
    public void onCreate(Bundle savedInstanceState) {
        super.onCreate(savedInstanceState);
        setContentView(R.layout.main);

        button = ((Button) findViewById(R.id.button1));

        button.setOnClickListener(this);
    }

    @Override
    public void onClick(View arg0) {
        button.setBackgroundColor
                        (android.graphics.Color.GRAY);
    }
}
```

The earlier section starts with a question: "In the onClick method, how does the code know what button means?" In this section, that question goes away just as my lap goes away when I stand up.

In Listing 4-4, both the button and the onClick method are members inside the activity. So the onClick method has free-and-easy access to the button. You don't need an Activity field as in Listing 4-3, and you don't need any fancy casting from Activity to MyActivity.

You have to remind Android that MyActivity contains an onClick method; you do that by adding implements OnClickListener to the declaration of MyActivity. You must also remind Android to notify the current MyActivity object whenever the button gets clicked. You do this reminding by writing

```
button.setOnClickListener(this);
```

which, roughly speaking, translates to "Hey, Android! When someone clicks the button, call the onClick method that's inside this object (a MyActivity object, which fortunately implements OnClickListener)."

The pattern in Listing 4-4 (having an `Activity` implement whatever interface it requires) is a very common Java programming idiom.

Classes That Must (and Must Not) Be Extended

If a Java class isn't broken, don't fix it.

Suppose you want to add functionality to an existing Java class. You like Android's `Activity` class, but the pre-declared `Activity` class displays nothing on the screen. Do you rewrite Android's `Activity` class? No.

Instead of rewriting an existing class, you extend the class. Even in a do-nothing Android "Hello" application, you write

```
public class MyActivity extends Activity
```

Then, in the `MyActivity` class's declaration, you write

```
@Override
public void onCreate(Bundle savedInstanceState) {
    super.onCreate(savedInstanceState);
    setContentView(R.layout.main);
}
```

Your `MyActivity` class creates new functionality by extending most of Android's `Activity` functionality while overriding the `Activity` class's brain-dead `onCreate` method.

Java's final classes

In object-oriented programming, extending a class is the noblest thing you can do.

But some classes aren't meant to be extended. Take, for example, Java's `String` class. A `String` is a `String` is a `String`. You don't want somebody's `MyString.length` method to return the length of time it takes to scramble a string's characters. To prevent someone from doing something unexpected, unconventional, or unusual with a string's methods, the creators of Java made the `String` class final:

```
public final class String
```

Some of Android's pre-declared classes are also final, including the `Telephony` and `MediaStore` classes.

Java's abstract classes

Just as a final class hates to be extended, an *abstract class* insists on being extended. Android's `ViewGroup` is an example of an abstract class. (See Listing 4-5.)

Listing 4-5:   A Small Part of Android's ViewGroup Class

```
public abstract class ViewGroup {

    public void bringChildToFront(View child) {
        int index = indexOfChild(child);
        if (index >= 0) {
            removeFromArray(index);
            addInArray(child, mChildrenCount);
            child.mParent = this;
        }
    }

    protected abstract void onLayout(boolean changed,
            int l, int t, int r, int b);
}
```

Android's `ViewGroup.java` file is more than 3,700 lines long. So Listing 4-5 has only a tiny fraction of the file's code. But you can see from Listing 4-5 how a class becomes abstract. To no one's surprise, the word `abstract` precedes the word `class`. But the word `abstract` also starts the declaration of some methods belonging to the class.

The founders of Android decided that the idea of a `ViewGroup` is useful. They were correct because your favorite Android layouts (`LinearLayout`, `RelativeLayout`, and so on) are subclasses of `ViewGroup`. They also understood that from one kind of `ViewGroup` to another, some functionality doesn't change. For example, Listing 4-5 defines a `bringChildToFront` method, and subclasses of `ViewGroup` inherit this method.

But the founders also realized that some aspects of a `ViewGroup` make no sense unless you work with a particular kind of group. For example, a `LinearLayout` positions things one after another, and a `RelativeLayout` positions things above, below, and to the side of one another. So Listing 4-5 doesn't have a full-blown `onLayout` method. The `onLayout` declaration in Listing 4-5 has no method body. But Android requires each subclass of the `ViewGroup` class to declare its own `onLayout` method. Java enforces this requirement when (as in Listing 4-5) you declare method `onLayout` to be `abstract`.

As a developer, you can't create an object from an abstract class. If you write

```
ViewGroup group = new ViewGroup();
```

Java tells you that you're behaving badly. To do something useful with the `ViewGroup` class, you need a subclass of the `ViewGroup` class. The subclass has a concrete version of each abstract method in the `ViewGroup` class:

```
package com.allmycode.samples;

import android.content.Context;
import android.view.ViewGroup;

public class MyLayout extends ViewGroup {

    public MyLayout(Context context) {
        super(context);
    }

    @Override
    protected void onLayout(boolean changed,
                int l, int t, int r, int b);
    }
}
```

Inner Classes

Here's big news! You can define a class inside another class! Most classes don't live inside another class, and most classes don't contain other classes. But when the idea behind one class screams out to be part of another class, feel free to create a class within a class.

Named inner classes

For the user, Listing 4-6 behaves the same way as Listings 4-3 and 4-4. But in Listing 4-6, the `MyActivity` class contains its own `MyListener` class.

The `MyListener` class in Listing 4-6 is an *inner class*. An inner class is a lot like any other class. But within an inner class's code, you can refer to the enclosing class's fields. For example, the `onClick` method inside `MyListener` uses the name `button`, and `button` is defined in the enclosing `MyActivity` class.

Listings 4-4 and 4-6 are very similar. In both listings, you circumvent the complexities described in the section "An object remembers who created it," earlier in this chapter. For this chapter's example, the choice of Listing 4-4 or Listing 4-6 is largely a matter of taste.

Listing 4-6:   A Class within a Class

```
package com.allmycode.samples;

import android.app.Activity;
import android.os.Bundle;
import android.view.View;
import android.view.View.OnClickListener;
import android.widget.Button;

public class MyActivity extends Activity {

    Button button;

    @Override
    public void onCreate(Bundle savedInstanceState) {
        super.onCreate(savedInstanceState);
        setContentView(R.layout.main);

        button = ((Button) findViewById(R.id.button1));

        button.setOnClickListener(new MyListener());
    }

    class MyListener implements OnClickListener {

        @Override
        public void onClick(View arg0) {
            button.setBackgroundColor
                        (android.graphics.Color.GRAY);
        }
    }
}
```

Anonymous inner classes

Notice that the code in Listing 4-6 uses the `MyListener` class only once. (The only use is in a call to `button.setOnClickListener`.) So I ask, do you really need a name for something that's used only once? No, you don't. You can substitute the entire definition of the inner class inside the call to `button.setOnClickListener`. When you do this, you have an *anonymous inner class*. Listing 4-7 shows you how it works.

Inner classes are good for things like event handlers, such as the `onClick` method in this chapter's examples. The most difficult thing about an anonymous inner class is keeping track of the parentheses, the curly braces, and the indentation. So my humble advice is, start by writing code without any inner classes, such as the code in Listing 4-3 or Listing 4-4. Later, when you become bored with ordinary Java classes, experiment by changing some of your ordinary classes into inner classes.

Listing 4-7:   A Class with No Name (Inside a Class with a Name)

```
package com.allmycode.samples;

import android.app.Activity;
import android.os.Bundle;
import android.view.View;
import android.view.View.OnClickListener;
import android.widget.Button;

public class MyActivity extends Activity {

    Button button;

    @Override
    public void onCreate(Bundle savedInstanceState) {
        super.onCreate(savedInstanceState);
        setContentView(R.layout.main);

        button = ((Button) findViewById(R.id.button1));

        button.setOnClickListener(new OnClickListener() {

            @Override
            public void onClick(View arg0) {
                button.setBackgroundColor
                        (android.graphics.Color.GRAY);
            }
        });
    }

}
```

Gathering Your Files

An app might consist of several files — Java files, XML files, text files, images, and other things. When you create a single app from several files, you normally create a brand new file. The new file contains encoded versions of all the files needed to run the app. The new file is typically called an *archive,* even though this new file is neither yellowed nor dusty.

This section contains a brief rundown of some of the more popular archive file types.

✦ **ZIP files:** A file whose name ends with .zip can encode files of almost any kind.

   When you get back the files encoded in the .zip file, you're *unzipping,* *uncompressing,* or *expanding* the .zip archive. (All three terms have the same meaning. Take your pick.) In addition to encoding files, a .zip archive encodes the folder structure. So, when you unzip a file, you usually get a bunch of files inside several new folders.

In most operating systems, you can unzip a `.zip` file by double-clicking the `.zip` file's icon.

✦ **JAR files:** A file whose name ends with `.jar` encodes Java bytecode files.

Many of the files encoded in a `.jar` file are `.class` files. (See Chapter 2 in this minibook for more on `.class` files.) If you want to use someone else's code in your Java app, you typically put the other person's `.jar` file in a place where your app can find it.

Here's a tiny experiment: In Android Studio, change the Project tool window from Android view to Project view. (That is, just above the Project tool window, change the drop-down menu from *Android* to *Project*.) In the Project view, expand the External Libraries branch. If you dig deep enough, you'll see `android.jar` and `rt.jar` branches. The `android.jar` file contains the Android-specific part of Android's API. The `rt.jar` file contains the Java classes that apply to any system, including desktops, laptops, and other devices.

The JAR acronym stands for *Java ARchive*. (The acronym is also a pun. The word "Java" is slang for coffee, so you can think about putting coffee beans into a jar of some kind.) The encoding method used to create `.jar` files is the same method that's used to create `.zip` files.

✦ **APK files:** A file whose name ends with `.apk` encodes Android Dalvik bytecode files.

The APK acronym stands for Android PacKage. The encoding method used to create `.apk` files is the same method that's used to create `.zip` files.

When you create an Android project, your Android Studio gathers your project's files into an `.apk` file. When you publish your app on the Google Play Store (or on some other Android app store), you upload this `.apk` file to the store's server.

Chapter 5: A <brief> Look at XML

In This Chapter

- ✔ **What XML can do for you**
- ✔ **What goes into an XML document**
- ✔ **How XML handles the names of things**

Modern software takes on several forms:

- ✦ **Some software is *procedural*.**

    The software tells the computer to "Do this, then do that."

- ✦ **Some software is *declarative*.**

    The software says, "Here's what I want the form to look like" or "Here's a list of things my application should be allowed to do."

- ✦ **Some software is neither procedural nor declarative.**

    The software lists functions to be executed in the order in which they apply or lists logical rules to be checked for validity.

One way or another, a development platform should use the best software for the job. That's why the Android platform uses both procedural and declarative software.

- ✦ Android's **procedural** Java code tells a device what to do.

- ✦ Android's **declarative** XML code describes a layout, an application, a set of strings, a set of preferences, or some other information that's useful to a mobile device.

A typical Android application is a mix of Java code, XML code, and a few other things. So when you develop for Android, you write lots of Java code and you mess with XML code.

What? You "mess with" XML code? What does that mean?

The truth is, XML code is painful to type. A typical XML file involves many elements, each requiring very precise wording and all looking very much alike at first glance. So in the Android world, most XML files are generated automatically. You don't type all the file's angle brackets. Instead, you drop widgets from a palette onto a preview screen. You let Android Studio create the XML code on your behalf.

So, in many situations, you don't have to compose XML code. But I often encounter situations in which I want to bypass Android Studio's tools and tweak the XML code myself. Maybe the tools don't readily provide an option that I want to use in my XML code. Or maybe my app isn't behaving the way I want it to behave, and I read over the XML code to check for subtle errors.

For these reasons and others, you're best off understanding the fundamentals of XML. So this chapter covers XML basics.

XML Isn't Ordinary Text

You may already be familiar with *Hypertext Markup Language* (HTML) because HTML is the universal language of the World Wide Web. Choose View ▷ Source in your favorite web browser, and you'll see a bunch of HTML tags — tags like `<head>`, `<title>`, `<meta>`, and so on. An HTML document describes the look and layout of a web page.

An XML document is something like an HTML document. But an XML document differs from an HTML document in many ways. The two most striking ways are as follows:

✦ An XML file doesn't describe only look and layout. In fact, very few XML files describe anything visual at all. Instead, most XML files describe data — a list of stock trades; a hierarchical list of automobile makes and models; or a nested list of movements, measures, and notes in a Beethoven symphony.

✦ Certain rules describe what you can and cannot write in an HTML or an XML document. The rules for HTML are very permissive. The rules for XML are very strict.

In HTML, a missing character or word often goes unnoticed. In XML, a missing character or word can ruin your whole day.

The formal definitions of an XML document's parts can be daunting. But you can think of an XML document as a bunch of elements, with each element having one or two tags.

Of tags and elements

Tags and elements are the workhorses of XML. Here's the scoop:

✦ **A tag is some text surrounded by angle brackets.**

For example, Listing 5-1 contains a basic `AndroidManifest.xml` file. In this file, `<intent-filter>` is a tag, `</intent-filter>` (which comes a bit later in the file) is another tag. Text such as `<application android:icon="@drawable/icon" android:label="@string/app_name">` is also a tag.

Listing 5-1:   An AndroidManifest.xml File

**Book II
Chapter 5**

**A <brief> Look
at XML**

```xml
<?xml version="1.0" encoding="utf-8"?>
<manifest
    package="com.allmycode.droidcon"
    xmlns:android=
        "http://schemas.android.com/apk/res/android">

  <application
      android:allowBackup="true"
      android:icon="@drawable/ic_launcher"
      android:label="@string/app_name"
      android:theme="@style/AppTheme">
    <activity
        android:name=".MyActivity"
        android:label="@string/app_name">
      <intent-filter>
        <action android:name=
                "android.intent.action.MAIN"/>

        <category android:name=
                "android.intent.category.LAUNCHER"/>
      </intent-filter>
    </activity>
  </application>

</manifest>
```

Not everything with angle brackets qualifies as an XML tag. For example, the text `<This is my application.>` violates many of the rules of grammatically correct XML. For more about what an XML tag can and cannot contain, read on.

An XML document is *well formed* when its text obeys all the rules of grammatically correct XML.

✦ **An XML document may have three different kinds of tags:**

• A *start tag* begins with an open angle bracket and a name. The start tag's last character is a closing angle bracket.

In Listing 5-1, `<intent-filter>` is a start tag. The start tag's name is `intent-filter`.

- An *end tag* begins with an open angle bracket followed by a forward slash and a name. The end tag's last character is a closing angle bracket.

  In Listing 5-1, `</intent-filter>` is an end tag. The end tag's name is `intent-filter`.

- An *empty element tag* begins with an open angle bracket followed by a name. The empty element tag's last two characters are a forward slash, followed by a closing angle bracket.

  In Listing 5-1, the text

  ```
  <action android:name=
            "android.intent.action.MAIN"/>
  ```

  is an empty element tag. The tag's name is `action`.

  In this bullet's empty element tag, the text `android:name` isn't the tag's name! It's the name of an attribute, but the letters `name` in `android:name` have nothing to do with it being a name. For details about XML attributes, read on in this section.

I rattle on about tags a bit more in the next several paragraphs. But in the meantime, I want to describe an XML element.

✦ **An XML element either has both a start tag and an end tag, or it has an empty element tag.**

The document in Listing 5-1 contains several elements. For example, the document's `intent-filter` element has both a start tag and an end tag. (Both the start and end tags have the same name, `intent-filter`, so the name of the entire element is `intent-filter`.)

In Listing 5-1, the document's `action` element has only one tag — an empty element tag.

✦ **The names of XML elements are not cast in stone.**

In an HTML document, a `b` element creates boldface text. For example, the text `<b>Buy this!</b>` in an HTML document looks like **Buy this!** in your web browser's window.

In an HTML document, the element name `b` is cast in stone. But in XML documents, names like `manifest`, `application`, `activity`, and `intent-filter` are not cast in stone. An XML document has its own set of element names, and these names are likely to be different from the names in most other XML documents. You can create your own well-formed XML document as follows:

```
<pets>
    <cat>
        Felix
    </cat>
    <cat>
        Sylvester
    </cat>
</pets>
```

If your goal is to store information about kitty cats, your XML document is just fine.

The text in an XML document is case-sensitive. An element named `APPLICATION` doesn't have the same name as another element named `application`.

What element names can you use?

In HTML, the tags `<b>` and `</b>` surround text that appears in bold type. That's the way web pages are encoded.

But in XML, tags like `<cat>` and `</cat>` might represent a Windows security catalog, catenary-shaped wire hanging down from telephone poles, or a pet who's climbing on your computer keyboard (while you write *Android Application Development All-in-One For Dummies,* 2nd Edition, I might add).

How do you know whether the names in your XML document are meaningful?

The short answer is, "Meaning is as meaning does." (Whatever that means!) An element's name is meaningful as long as a computer program can do the things that you intend programs to do with that element. For example, a program that checks security catalogues to distinguish trustworthy from malicious downloads probably does nothing useful with an element like

```
<cat name="Felix" age="7" breed=
        "calico" />
```

On the other hand, a security catalog program may include instructions to deal with the following element:

```
<cat name="Firefox" verified="true"
        publisher="mozilla.org"
        version="7.0.1" />
```

Even so, the XML specs provide two ways to describe the names in a document. The older way is with a *DTD* (*Document Type Definition*). A DTD looks something like this:

```
<!ELEMENT CatThoughts (Image, Thought+)>
<!ATTLIST CatThoughts frequency CDATA
        #REQUIRED>

<!NOTATION JPEG SYSTEM "image/jpeg">
<!ENTITY CuteCat SYSTEM "weelie.jpg"
        NDATA JPEG>
<!ELEMENT Image EMPTY>
<!ATTLIST Image source ENTITY #REQUIRED>

<!ELEMENT Thought (#PCDATA)>
<!ENTITY meow "Feed me">
```

(continued)

(continued)

A DTD describes the names that you can use in a particular XML document (or in a bunch of XML documents) and describes the order in which you can use those names. But a DTD doesn't describe all the fine points of element-naming (like the fact that a name must refer to an integer value or to a date). So the newer way to describe the names in a document is with a *schema*. A schema looks something like this:

```
<?xml version="1.0"?>
<!-- Children.xsd -->

<xsd:schema xmlns:xsd="http://www.
            w3.org/2001/XMLSchema">
<xsd:element name="Children"
             type="xsd:integer"/>
</xsd:schema>
```

This schema says that a certain XML document (or a bunch of XML documents) uses the element name `Children`, and that the value stored in the `Children` element must be an integer. (A family can't have 2.5 children.) Even better, a schema is itself an XML document (with start tags, end tags, and everything else), so all the tools that you apply to ordinary XML documents can be applied to schema documents as well. (A DTD may look something like an XML document, but in a DTD, the exclamation points and the lack of end tags break the grammar rules of an XML document.)

Not every XML document is connected to a DTD or to a schema — and even if an XML document has a DTD or a schema, that document may or may not be valid. A *valid* XML document is a document whose names obey the rules described in the document's DTD or schema.

To test the validity of an XML document, use the online test application at `www.w3schools.com/XML/xml:validator.asp`.

+ **A non-empty XML element may contain *content*.**

The content is stuff between the start tag and the end tag. For example, in Listing 5-1, the `intent-filter` element's content is

```
<action android:name=
            "android.intent.action.MAIN" />
<category android:name=
            "android.intent.category.LAUNCHER" />
```

An element's content may include other elements. (In this example, the `intent-filter` element contains an `action` element and a `category` element.)

An element's content may also include ordinary text. For example, in Listing 5-2, the `resources` element contains two `string` elements, and each `string` element contains ordinary text.

You can even have mixed content. For example, between an element's start and end tags, you may have some ordinary text, followed by an element or two, followed by more ordinary text.

Listing 5-2:   An Android strings.xml File

```
<?xml version="1.0" encoding="utf-8"?>
<resources>
    <string name="app_name">droidcon</string>
    <string name="hello_world">Hello world!</string>
    <string name="action_settings">Settings</string>
</resources>
```

✦ **In some cases, two or more elements may have the same name.**

In Listing 5-2, two distinct elements have the name `string`. To find out more about the names used in an XML file, see the nearby sidebar "What element names can you use?"

✦ **Elements are either nested inside one another or they don't overlap at all.**

In Listing 5-1, the `manifest` element contains an `application` element. The `application` element contains an `activity` element, which in turn contains an `intent-filter` element, and so on.

```
<manifest>

    This code demonstrates element nesting.
    This code is NOT a real AndroidManifest.xml file.

    <application>

        <activity>
            <intent-filter>
                <action />
                <category />
            </intent-filter>
        </activity>

    </application>

</manifest>
```

In Listing 5-1 (and in the fake listing inside this bullet) the `action` and `category` elements don't overlap at all. But whenever one element overlaps another, one of the elements is nested completely inside the other.

For example, in Listing 5-1, the `intent-filter` element is nested completely inside the `activity` element. The following sequence of tags, with overlapping and not nesting, would be illegal:

```
<activity>
    <intent-filter>
    This is NOT well-formed XML code.
</activity>
    </intent-filter>
```

Near the start of this chapter, I announce that the rules governing HTML aren't as strict as the rules governing XML. In HTML, you can create non-nested, overlapping tags. For example, the code `<b>Use <i>irregular</b> fonts</i> sparingly` appears in your web browser as

Use *irregular* fonts sparingly

with "Use irregular" in bold and "irregular fonts" italicized.

Web browsers, such as Chrome, Firefox, and Microsoft Internet Explorer, are decent XML viewers. When you visit an XML document with most web browsers, you see a well-indented display of your XML code. The code's elements expand and collapse on your command. And if you visit an XML document that's not well-formed (for example, a document with overlapping, non-nested tags), the browser displays an error message.

✦ **Each XML document contains one element in which all other elements are nested.**

In Listing 5-1, the `manifest` element contains all other elements. That's good. The following outline would not make a legal XML document:

```
<manifest>
    <application>
    </application>

    This is NOT a well-formed XML document
    because another element comes after the
    following manifest end tag:
</manifest>

<manifest>
    <application>
    </application>
</manifest>
```

In an XML document, the single element that encloses all other elements is the *root* element.

✦ **Start tags and empty element tags may contain *attributes*.**

An *attribute* is a name-value pair. Each attribute has the form

```
name="value"
```

The quotation marks around the value are required.

In Listing 5-1, the start tags and empty element tags contain many attributes. For example, in the `manifest` start tag, the text

```
package="com.allmycode.droidcon"
```

is an attribute. In the same tag, the text

```
xmlns:android=
  "http://schemas.android.com/apk/res/android"
```

is an attribute. Later in Listing 5-1, the `application` start tag has four attributes, the `activity` start tag has two attributes, the empty element `action` tag has one attribute, and the empty element `category` tag has one attribute. Finally, the poor, lonely `intent-filer` start tag has no attributes. Sorry about that!

Other things you find in an XML document

There's more to life than tags and elements. This section describes all the things you can look forward to.

✦ **An XML document begins with an XML declaration.**

The declaration in Listing 5-1 is

```
<?xml version="1.0" encoding="utf-8"?>
```

The question marks distinguish the declaration from an ordinary XML tag.

This declaration announces that Listing 5-1 contains an XML document (big surprise!), that the document uses version 1.0 of the XML specifications, and that bit strings used to store the document's characters are to be interpreted with their meanings as UTF-8 codes.

In practice, you seldom have reason to mess with a document's XML declaration. For a new XML document, simply copy and paste the declaration in Listing 5-1.

The `version="1.0"` part of an XML declaration may look antiquated, but XML hasn't changed much since the initial specs appeared in 1998. In fact, the only newer version is XML 1.1, which developers seldom use. This reluctance to change is part of the XML philosophy — to have a universal, time-tested format for representing information about almost any subject.

✦ **An XML document may contain comments.**

A comment begins with the characters `<!--` and ends with the characters `-->`. For example, the lines

```
<!-- This application must be tested
     very, very carefully. -->
```

form an XML comment. A document's comments can appear between tags (and in a few other places that aren't worth fussing about right now).

Comments are normally intended to be read by humans. But programs that input XML documents are free to read comments and to act on the text within comments. Android doesn't normally do anything with the comments it finds in its XML files, but you never know.

✦ **An XML document may contain processing instructions.**

A processing instruction looks a lot like the document's XML declaration. Here's an example of a processing instruction:

```
<?chapter number="x" Put chapter number here ?>
```

A document may have many processing instructions, and these processing instructions can appear between tags (and in a few other places). But in practice, most XML documents have no processing instructions. (For reasons too obscure even for a Technical Stuff icon, the document's XML declaration isn't a processing instruction.)

Like a document's XML declaration, each processing instruction begins with the characters `<?` and ends with the characters `?>`. Each processing instruction has a name. But after the processing instruction's name, anything goes. The processing instruction near the start of this bullet has the name `chapter` followed by some free-form text. Part of that text looks like a start tag's attribute, but the remaining text looks like a comment of some sort.

You can put almost anything inside a processing instruction. Most of the software that inputs your XML document will simply ignore the processing instruction. (As an experiment, I added my chapter-processing instruction to the file in Listing 5-1. This change made absolutely no difference in the running of my Android app.)

So what good are processing instructions anyway? Well, if you stumble into one, I don't want you to mistake it for a kind of XML declaration. Also, certain programs may read specific processing instructions and get particular information from these instructions.

For example, a *style sheet* is a file that describes the look and the layout of the information in an XML document. Typically, an XML document and the corresponding style sheet are in two different files. To indicate that the information in your `pets.xml` document should be displayed using the rules in the `animals.css` style sheet, you add the following processing instruction to the `pets.xml` document:

```
<?xml-stylesheet SPihref="animals.css" type="text/css"?>
```

✦ **An XML document may contain entity references.**

I poked around among Android's official sample applications and found the following elements (spread out among different programs):

```
<Key android:codes="60" android:keyLabel="&lt;"/>
<Key android:codes="62" android:keyLabel="&gt;"/>
<Key android:codes="34" android:keyLabel="&quot;"/>
<string name="activity_save_restore">
    App/Activity/Save &amp; Restore State
</string>
```

The first element contains a reference to the < entity. You can't use a real angle bracket just anywhere in an XML document. An angle bracket signals the beginning of an XML tag. So, if you want to express that the name `three-brackets` stands for the string "`<<<`", you can't write

```
<string name="three-brackets"><<<</string>
```

The extra brackets will confuse any program that expects to encounter ordinary XML tags.

So, to get around XML's special use of angle brackets, the XML specs include the *entities* < and >. The first, <, stands for an opening angle bracket. The second, >, stands for the closing angle bracket. So to express that the name `three-brackets` stands for the string "`<<<`", you write

```
<string name="three-brackets">&lt;&lt;&lt;</string>
```

In the entity <, the letters `lt` stand for "less than." And after all, an opening angle bracket looks like the "less than" sign in mathematics. Similarly, in the entity >, the letters `gt` stand for "greater than."

What's in a Namespace?

The first official definition of XML was published in 1998 by the World Wide Web Consortium (W3C). This first standard ignored a sticky problem. If two XML documents have some elements or attributes with identical names, and if those names have different meanings in the two documents, how can you possibly combine the two documents?

Here's a simple XML document:

```
<?xml version="1.0" encoding="utf-8"?>
<banks>
    <bank>First National Bank</bank>
    <bank>Second Regional Bank</bank>
    <bank>United Trustworthy Trusty Trust</bank>
    <bank>Federal Bank of Fredonia (Groucho Branch)</bank>
</banks>
```

And here's another XML document:

```
<?xml version="1.0" encoding="utf-8"?>
<banks>
    <bank>Banks of the Mississippi River</bank>
    <bank>La Rive Gauche</bank>
    <bank>La Rive Droite</bank>
    <bank>The Banks of Plum Creek</bank>
</banks>
```

An organization with seemingly limitless resources aims to collect and combine knowledge from all over the Internet. The organization's software finds XML documents and combines them into one super, all-knowing document. (Think of an automated version of Wikipedia.)

But when you combine documents about financial institutions with documents about rivers, you get some confusing results. If both First National and the Banks of Plum Creek are in the same document's bank elements, analyzing the document may require prior knowledge. In other words, if you don't already know that some banks lend money and that other banks flood during storms, you might draw some strange conclusions. And unfortunately, computer programs don't already know anything. (Life becomes really complicated when you reach an XML element describing the Red River Bank in Shreveport, Louisiana. This river bank has teller machines in Shreveport, Alexandria, and other towns.)

To remedy this situation, members of the XML standards committee created XML namespaces. A *namespace* is a prefix that you attach to a name. You separate the namespace from the name with a colon (:) character. For example, in Listing 5-1, almost every attribute name begins with the android prefix. The listing's attributes include xmlns:android, android:allowBackup, android:icon, and more.

So to combine documents about lending banks and river banks, you create the XML document in Listing 5-3.

Listing 5-3: A Document with Two Namespaces

```xml
<?xml version="1.0" encoding="utf-8"?>

<banks xmlns:money=
            "http://schemas.allmycode.com/money"
       xmlns:river=
            "http://schemas.allmycode.com/river">

<money:bank>First National Bank</money:bank>
<money:bank>Second Regional Bank</money:bank>
<money:bank>
    United Trustworthy Trusty Trust
</money:bank>
<money:bank>
    Federal Bank of Fredonia (Groucho Branch)
</money:bank>

<river:bank>
    Banks of the Mississippi River
    </river:bank>
    <river:bank>La Rive Gauche</river:bank>
    <river:bank>La Rive Droite</river:bank>
    <river:bank>The Banks of Plum Creek</river:bank>

</banks>
```

In a name such as `android:icon`, the word `android` is a *prefix*, and the word `icon` is a *local name*.

At this point, the whole namespace business branches into two possibilities:

✦ **Some very old XML software is not namespace-aware.**

The original XML standard had no mention of namespaces. So the oldest XML-handling programs do nothing special with prefixes. To an old program, the names `money:bank` and `river:bank` in Listing 5-3 are simply two different names with no relationship to each other. The colons in the names are no different from the letters.

✦ **Newer XML software is namespace-aware.**

In some situations, you want the software to recognize relationships between names with the same prefixes and between identical names with different prefixes. For example, in a document containing elements named `consumer:bank`, `investment:bank`, and `consumer:confidence`, you may want your software to recognize two kinds of banks. You may also want your software to deal with two kinds of consumer elements.

Most modern software is namespace-aware. That is, the software recognizes that a name like `river:bank` consists of a prefix and a local name.

To make it easier for software to sort out an XML document's namespaces, every namespace must be defined. In Listing 5-3, the attributes

```
xmlns:money=
        "http://schemas.allmycode.com/money"
xmlns:river=
        "http://schemas.allmycode.com/river"
```

define the document's two namespaces. The attributes associate one URL with the `money` namespace and another URL with the `river` namespace. The special `xmlns` namespace doesn't get defined because the `xmlns` namespace has the same meaning in every XML document. The `xmlns` prefix always means, "This is the start of an XML namespace definition."

In Listing 5-3, each namespace is associated with a URL. So, if you're creating a new XML document, you may ask, "What if I don't have my own domain name?" You may also ask, "What information must I post at a namespace's URL?" And the surprising answers are "Make up one" and "Nothing."

The string of symbols doesn't really have to be a URL. Instead, it can be a URI — a *Universal Resource Identifier*. A URI looks like a URL, but a URI doesn't have to point to an actual network location. A URI is simply a name, a string of characters "full of sound and fury" and possibly "signifying nothing." Some XML developers create web pages to accompany each of their URIs. The web pages contain useful descriptions of the names used in the XML documents.

But most URIs used for XML namespaces point nowhere. For example, the URI `http://schemas.android.com/apk/res/android` in Listing 5-1 appears in almost every Android XML document. If you type that URI into the address field of your favorite web browser, you get the familiar `cannot display the webpage` or `Server not found` message.

An *unbound prefix* message indicates that you haven't correctly associated a namespace found in your XML document with a URI. Some very old software (software that's not namespace-aware) doesn't catch errors of this kind, but most modern software does.

For a more detailed description of URIs (including some really clever puns), see Book III, Chapter 2.

The package attribute

In Listing 5-1, the attribute name `package` has no prefix. So you might say, "What the heck! I'll change the attribute's name to `android:package` just for good measure." But this change produces some error messages. One message reads `Unknown attribute android:package`. What's going on here?

In an `AndroidManifest.xml` file, the `package` attribute has more to do with Java than with Android. (The `package` attribute points to the Java package containing the application's Java code.) So the creators of Android decided not to make this `package` attribute be part of the `android` namespace.

Each Android platform, from Cupcake onward, has a file named `public.xml` among the files you get when you download the Android SDK. If you open a `public.xml` file in a text editor, you see a list of names in the `android` namespace.

The style attribute

The same business about not being an `android` name holds for `style` and `package`. A *style* is a collection of items (or *properties*) describing the look of something on a mobile device screen. A style's XML document might contain

Android-specific names, but the style itself is simply a bunch of items, not an Android property in its own right.

To see how this works, imagine creating a very simple app. The XML file describing the app's basic layout may look like the code in Listing 5-4.

Listing 5-4:   Using the style Attribute

```
<?xml version="1.0" encoding="utf-8"?>
<LinearLayout xmlns:android=
  "http://schemas.android.com/apk/res/android"
    android:orientation="vertical"
    android:layout_width="match_parent"
    android:layout_height="match_parent"
    >
<TextView
    android:layout_width="match_parent"
    android:layout_height="wrap_content"
    android:text="@string/callmom"
    style="@style/bigmono"
    />
</LinearLayout>
```

In Listing 5-4, all attribute names except `style` (and the name `android` itself) are in the `android` namespace. The value `"@style/bigmono"` points Android to an XML file in your app's `res/values` folder. Listing 5-5 contains a very simple file named `styles.xml`.

Listing 5-5   A File with Style

```
<?xml version="1.0" encoding="utf-8"?>
<resources>
    <style name="bigmono">
        <item name="android:textSize">50dip</item>
        <item name="android:typeface">monospace</item>
    </style>
</resources>
```

Again, notice the mix of words that are inside and outside of the `android` namespace. The words `android:textSize` and `android:typeface` are in the `android` namespace, and the other words in Listing 5-5 are not.

The style in Listing 5-5 specifies a whopping 50 density-independent pixels for the size of the text and monospace (traditional typewriter) font for the typeface. When Android applies the style in Listing 5-5 to the layout in Listing 5-4, you see the prominent message in Figure 5-1.

Figure 5-1:
Be a good
son or
daughter.

For more information about styles, layouts, density-independent pixels, and the use of XML to describe these things, see Book IV, Chapter 1.

Book III
The Building Blocks

Using a ContentProvider

EMPTY THE NAMES_AMOUNTS DATA

ADD SAM 100; JEN 300

UPDATE SAM 500

SHOW SILLY_STUFF

1 Sam 500
2 Jennie 300

For a closer look at Android Studio's Navigation Editor, check out a great online article at www.dummies.com/extras/androidappdevelopmentaio.

Contents at a Glance

Chapter 1: Android Activities

In This Chapter

✔ **Launching an activity**

✔ **Going through an activity's lifecycle**

✔ **Getting information from an activity**

On a desktop computer, everything starts with a window. Open a window, and run a word processor. Open another window, and read your email. Move a window, minimize a window, resize a window. It's a very familiar story.

But mobile devices aren't desktop computers. A smartphone has a relatively small screen, and if by chance you *could* open several windows at once, the phone's processor would fall over from exhaustion. On a mobile phone, the "window" metaphor would lead to nothing but trouble.

Tablet devices have larger screens and better processors than their telephone cousins. You can probably squeeze a few windows on a tablet screen, but the power that you would allocate to window-handling could be put to better use.

So where does that leave you? The earliest computers had no windows and no multitasking. You can't have that. Without some kind of multitasking, "smartphones" wouldn't be smart.

Android's first and foremost answer to all windowing questions is the *activity*. In other chapters, I refer to an activity as "one *screenful* of components." I liken activities to online forms, such as "a form for entering information to make a purchase on a website." I write, "Unlike most online forms, Android activities don't necessarily have text boxes — places for the user to type credit card numbers and such. But Android activities have a lot in common with online forms." I love quoting myself.

All about Activities

Here's what the official Android docs say about an activity:

> *An activity is a single, focused thing that the user can do. Almost all activities interact with the user, so the Activity class takes care of creating a window for you in which you can place your UI with* `setContentView(View)`. *While activities are often presented to the user as full-screen windows . . .*

The `android.app.Activity` class's code is a complete, official definition describing what an activity is and what an activity isn't. But from an app designer's point of view, no formal definition of *activity* paints the complete picture. So maybe the way to describe an activity is behaviorally. Here's my informal description:

At some point during the run of an app, an app designer fills up the screen with stuff. At that point, the designer thinks, "I have to move all this stuff out of the way so the user can deal sensibly with whatever has become most important." So the designer creates a new screen layout, codes the layout's behavior, and refers to the whole business (the layout and its behavior) as a new activity.

At that (newer) point, the designer has two different activities — the original activity that filled up the screen with stuff and the new activity that deals with whatever has become most important. On a smaller device (a smartphone as opposed to a tablet), each activity fills the entire screen. The original activity invokes the new activity and then the new activity covers the original activity.

Under normal circumstances, the two activities form part of a *stack* — a *first in, last out* structure. Imagine that Activity A invokes Activity B, which in turn invokes Activity C. Then the activities A, B, and C form a stack, with Activity C being on top of the stack (and visible to the user). When the user presses the Back button, Activity C pops off the stack to reveal Activity B. When the user presses the Back button again, Activity B pops off the stack to reveal Activity A.

A stack of Android activities is called a *task*. So now you have apps, activities, and tasks. Unfortunately, these words have different meanings for Android developers than they have for the rest of the world.

An *application* is a collection of things meant to accomplish a particular user goal. Some of the things belonging to an app are activities.

The other things belonging to an app are services, broadcast receivers, and content providers. I cover these things in Chapters 3, 4, and 5 of this minibook.

Each application runs in its own Android Linux process, with its own user ID. This is one of Android's security strengths. Separate processes don't share memory. So in effect, each application is sandboxed from the rest of the system, with very narrowly defined (tightly guarded) paths of communication between one application and another. If an application does something wrong (either maliciously or unintentionally), the chance of that wrongdoing affecting the rest of the system is limited. As a developer, you create an application using the XML `<application>` element in the app's `AndroidManifest.xml` file.

Applications and processes

A typical operating system (Android included) has users, processes, and threads.

✔ **Each person who logs onto the system is a *user.* But the system may also create virtual users — things that the operating system treats as separate users but that don't correspond to people tapping screens or using keyboards.**

With users who aren't real people, a system can create specialized pathways for access to resources. For example, a database might be the only "user" with permission to access certain data. A human user gets the data indirectly. The human user logs in to the database and asks the database to fetch the data on his or her behalf.

Each user on a system (a session conducted by a real person or a virtual user) has a *user identification number (UID).*

Throughout most of this book, I refer to the person who touches the device's screen as "the user." I don't worry too much about virtual users.

✔ **The operating system divides its work into *processes.***

Each process has its own memory space, separate from the space belonging to other processes. Processes interact with one another only through narrow, well-policed pathways.

The system schedules the running of processes. To do this, the system executes a sequence of statements in one process, then a sequence of statements in another process, then a sequence in a third, eventually returning to the place where the first process left off.

Each process has a *process identification number (PID).*

✔ **A process may divide its work into *threads*.**

The operating system schedules threads in an interleaved fashion. In this respect, a thread is a lot like a process. But a single process's threads share the process's memory space. So a single process's threads can communicate freely with one another.

(continued)

(continued)

With Android, each app runs in its own process and bears its own PID and UID. (Apps don't hold onto their PIDs or UIDs from one run to another. The operating system assigns these numbers at the start of a run and then dumps them at the end of the run. The system assigns new numbers for the app's next run.)

Android assigns PIDs incrementally as new processes are created. So when your app starts running, it may have PID 1900. Later, your device may be running low on memory. Android might notice that none of your app's components are needed in the short term. (For example, the device is displaying a different app's activity, and your app contains no long-running services.) To save space, Android might kill your app's process. Poof! The process is gone.

Of course, the user knows nothing of this process assassination. (I'm referring to the human user, not some virtual figment of the system's imagination.) The user simply wanders away from your app's activities by invoking another activity, by pressing Home, by answering a phone call, or some other way. So at some point, the user says, "Hey, wait! I want to get back to what I was doing a few minutes ago." The user navigates back to one of your process's activities. So Android (clever operating system that it is) starts a new process to run your application, re-creates your app's activity as it was before the murder, and displays the activity as if nothing unusual happened. Now your application has a new PID (maybe 1921) because Android created several other processes between the time of your app's murder and the time of your app's rebirth.

An activity can (and frequently does) invoke activities belonging to other apps. (For example, an email message might contain a link. So an email app's activity might invoke a web browser app's activity.) That means that a particular task might contain activities from several applications. (See Figure 1-1.)

The scenario often works this way:

1. The user starts an app. (Call it Application 1.)

   Android creates a new process for the app, creates an instance of the app's main activity, and puts the main activity onto a brand-new task stack. (Call it Task 1.)

2. From the app's main activity, the user invokes another activity (say, a secondary activity belonging to the same app).

   Android creates a new instance of the secondary activity. Android pushes the secondary activity onto the task stack. (See Figure 1-2.) The device's screen displays only the secondary activity. (Think of the app's main activity as being hidden underneath the secondary activity. Call the main activity Activity 1; call the secondary activity Activity 2.)

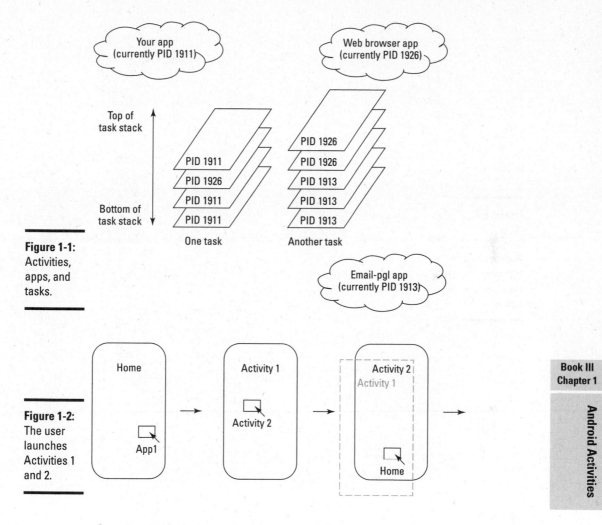

Figure 1-1: Activities, apps, and tasks.

Figure 1-2: The user launches Activities 1 and 2.

3. The user presses Home.

Android moves Task 1 off the screen and displays the Home screen, as shown in Figure 1-3.

4. The user starts a second app. (How about calling it Application 2?)

With Task 1 still waiting in the wings, Android creates a second task (Task 2) with the second app's main activity.

5. The user presses Home again and presses the icon for Application 1.

See Figure 1-4. Android displays the top of the Task 1 stack. Activity 2 is still at the top of Task 1. So the user sees Activity 2. Happily, Activity 2 is in the same state as it was when the user first pressed Home. Text fields still have whatever text the user previously entered, and so on.

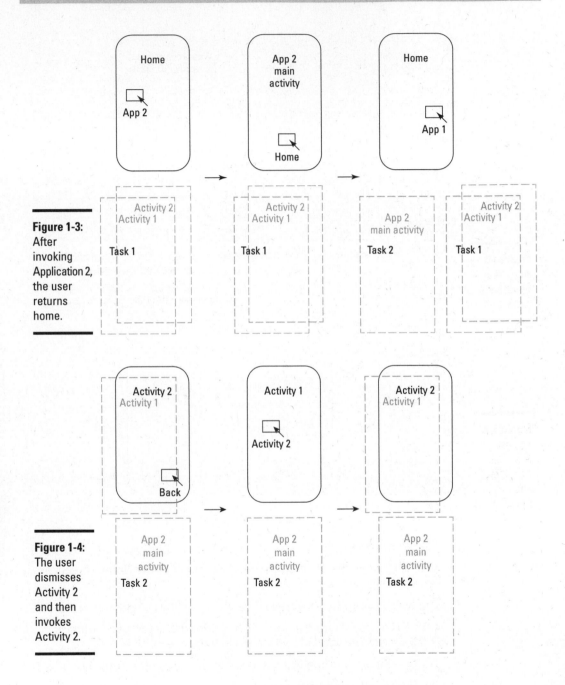

Figure 1-3:
After invoking Application 2, the user returns home.

Figure 1-4:
The user dismisses Activity 2 and then invokes Activity 2.

6. The user presses the Back button.

   Android pops Activity 2 off the Task 1 stack and destroys this instance of Activity 2. The user sees Activity 1, which is in the same state as it was immediately before Android covered up Activity 1 with Activity 2.

7. From Activity 1, the user again invokes the secondary activity belonging to Application 1.

   Android creates a brand-new instance of the secondary activity. Android pushes the secondary activity onto the task stack. The device's screen displays only the secondary activity. This new instance is *not* in the same state that Activity 2 was in when Activity 2 was destroyed. This new instance is initialized with new values (which is normal for brand-new objects).

The scenario in these steps can have many variations. For starters, the user doesn't necessarily press buttons and icons in the order described in the steps. For another thing, a developer can change the way in which activities pile onto tasks. (See Chapter 2 in this minibook.) And Android has *fragments,* which are like activities but take up only part of a tablet device's screen. (See Chapter 1 in Book V for more on fragments.)

State your intention

The Android programming model is based on the use of scarce resources. Compared to a desktop or laptop computer, a smartphone has a small screen, limited memory, and a wimpy processor. With that in mind, the original creators of Android focused on reuse.

Imagine that my app includes a link to my website. When the user clicks the link, Android opens a web browser. But which browser does Android open? Android comes with its own browser (a close cousin of Google's Chrome browser). But the user might have also installed Firefox for Android, Opera Mini, or any number of other web browsers.

In the Windows and Mac operating systems, the choice of browser depends on filename extensions and protocol associations. For example, if I double-click the icon for a file named `something.html`, the Chrome browser opens. But if I double-click the icon for a `somethingElse.torrent` file, the Opera browser opens.

In Android, the developer invokes a browser by issuing an intent.

In Android development, an *intent* is like an open-ended method call. Instead of coding something like

**Book III
Chapter 1**

Android Activities

```
firefox("http://www.google.com");
```

or

```
android_built_in_browser("http://allmycode.com/android");
```

you code the following:

```
String url = "http://allmycode.com/android";
Intent intent = new Intent(Intent.ACTION_VIEW);
intent.setData(Uri.parse(url));
startActivity(intent);
```

In this example, calling `startActivity(intent)` is like throwing an I-want-to-browse ball into the air and expecting another app's activity to catch it. Another app announces its intentions to catch the I-want-to-browse ball by putting an element of the following kind in the app's `AndroidManifest.xml` file:

```
<activity android:name=".Catcher"
          android:label="Catcher">
  <intent-filter>
    <action
      android:name="android.intent.action.VIEW" />
    <category
      android:name="android.intent.category.DEFAULT" />
    <category
      android:name="android.intent.category.BROWSABLE" />
    <data android:scheme="http" />
  </intent-filter>
</activity>
```

Again, I quote Android's official documentation:

> *An intent is an abstract description of an operation to be performed. It can be used with* `startActivity` *to launch an* `Activity`. . . . *An Intent provides a facility for performing late runtime binding between the code in different applications. Its most significant use is in the launching of activities, where it can be thought of as the glue between activities. It is basically a passive data structure holding an abstract description of an action to be performed.*

In truth, Android has two kinds of intents — *implicit* and *explicit* intents.

✦ The kind of intent that I describe in the previous paragraphs (to start any activity claiming to be a web browser) is an *implicit* intent. An implicit intent doesn't call for a particular activity to be launched. Instead, an implicit intent names an action to be taken, along with other information required to fulfill the intent.

The intent

```
Intent intent = new Intent(Intent.ACTION_VIEW);
intent.setData(Uri.parse(url));
```

is an implicit intent.

I cover implicit intents in Chapter 2 of this minibook.

✦ An *explicit* intent actually names an activity class whose instance is to be launched.

In this chapter's examples, I use explicit intents to launch activities. So the next section covers explicit intents.

The explicit intent

To use an explicit intent, you can write something like the code in Listing 1-1.

Listing 1-1:   Calling Your Own App's Activity Using an Explicit Intent

```
package my.pack;

import android.app.Activity;
import android.os.Bundle;

public class SomeActivity extends Activity {
  // ... code of some sort belongs here

  Intent intent = new Intent();
  intent.setClassName("my.pack", "my.pack.OtherActivity");
  startActivity(intent);
}
```

In Listing 1-1, the intent's `setClassName` method takes two `String` parameters. The first parameter is the name of the package containing the target activity, and the second parameter is the activity's *fully qualified* class name. So in Listing 1-1, the call to `setClassName` has two strings containing `"my.pack"`. (There may be a reasonable way to avoid repetition, where you'd write something like `setClassName("my.pack", "OtherActivity")`. But if there is one, no one's told *me* about it.)

To invoke another app's activity, you can write something like the code in Listing 1-2.

Listing 1-2: Calling Another App's Activity Using an Explicit Intent

```
package my.pack;

import android.app.Activity;
import android.os.Bundle;

public class SomeActivity extends Activity {
  // ... code of some sort belongs here

  intent = new Intent();
  intent.setClassName("other.pack",
                      "other.pack.OtherAppActivity");
  startActivity(intent);
}
```

Listing 1-2 is almost exactly like Listing 1-1. The only difference is that in Listing 1-2, the two activities (the invoking and the invoked activities) belong to two different applications. *Different applications* means different packages. So Listing 1-1 has "my.pack", and Listing 1-2 has "other.pack".

If one project's activity invokes another project's activity, you must install both apps on your emulator or test device. If you forget to do so, your app crashes with the message *Unable to find explicit activity* in the Logcat panel. And when you see such a message, screaming "Whadaya mean, Unable to Find Activity?" won't solve the problem.

If one project's activity invokes a second project's activity, that second activity isn't necessarily a main activity. (In technical terms, that second activity's element in the AndroidManifest.xml file might not contain the <action android:name="android.intent.action.MAIN" /> element.) In many scenarios, the second project doesn't even have a main activity of its own. When you choose Run⇨Run 'app' for a project with no main activity, you see an Edit Configuration dialog box. In that case, select the Do Not Launch Activity option, and then click the Run button.

Using a context

Another way to start a specific activity is with a context. A *context* is an "interface to global information about an application environment." (Again, I'm quoting the Android docs.) Informally, a context is the background information that you might want to know about the things that are actually happening. For an Android app, the Context Java object might include the app's package name, the theme, the wallpaper, the names of files associated with the app, and pointers to location services, to user account services, and to other info. All this stuff is available programmatically by way of a Java Context object.

The word *programmatically* describes something that you can access (and maybe even modify) in your project's Java code.

An Android activity runs in a certain context. That makes sense. But here's an idea that's always been difficult for me to embrace: An activity *is* a context. It's a context for two reasons (one being technical; the other being somewhat intuitive):

✦ In the Android SDK, the class `android.app.Activity` is a subclass of `android.content.Context`.

✦ An activity has all the things that any context has — namely, the app's package name, the theme, the wallpaper, the names of files associated with the app, and pointers to location services, to user account services, and other info.

In Listing 1-3, an activity calls another activity within the same application.

Listing 1-3:   Calling Your Own App's Activity Using an Explicit Intent with a Context

```
package my.pack;

import android.app.Activity;
import android.os.Bundle;

public class SomeActivity extends Activity {
  // ... code of some sort belongs here

  Intent intent =
    new Intent(this, OtherActivity.class);
  startActivity(intent);
}
```

In Listing 1-3, the last two statements are really saying, "With `this` activity's own context, start running an instance of `OtherActivity`." (If all goes well, the class `OtherActivity` extends Android's `Activity` class, and you're good to go.)

In Listing 1-3, the `Intent` class's constructor takes two parameters — a context and a Java class. The word `this` represents the enclosing `SomeActivity` instance. That's good, because the constructor's first parameter is of type `Context`, and Android's `Activity` class is a subclass of the abstract `Context` class.

Compare Listings 1-2 and 1-3. In Listing 1-2, the intent learns the `OtherActivity`'s package name from a call to `intent.setClassName`. But in Listing 1-3, the `Intent` constructor gets the `OtherActivity`'s package name from `this` — the `SomeActivity` object's context.

**Book III
Chapter 1**

Android Activities

Each activity is part of an application, and an `Application` instance is also a context. So in many programs, you can use any of the following method calls (instead of `this`) to obtain a `Context` instance:

```
getContext()
getApplicationContext()
getBaseContext()
```

The `getApplicationContext` and `getBaseContext` methods have limited, specialized uses in Android programs. In this book's examples, you'll never need to call `getApplicationContext` or `getBaseContext`.

In Listing 1-4, an activity from one app uses a context to call another app's activity.

Listing 1-4:   Calling Another App's Activity Using an Explicit Intent with a Context

```
package my.pack;

import android.app.Activity;
import android.os.Bundle;

public class SomeActivity extends Activity {
  // ... code of some sort belongs here

  try {
    otherContext =
      createPackageContext("other.pack",
      Context.CONTEXT_IGNORE_SECURITY |
      Context.CONTEXT_INCLUDE_CODE);
  } catch (NameNotFoundException e) {
    e.printStackTrace();
  }
  Class<?> otherClass = null;
  try {
    otherClass = otherContext.getClassLoader().
      loadClass("other.pack.OtherAppActivity");
  } catch (ClassNotFoundException e) {
    e.printStackTrace();
  }
  Intent intent = new Intent(otherContext, otherClass);
  startActivity(intent);
}
```

Listing 1-4 is more complicated than Listing 1-3. But most of the complexity comes from the way Java loads classes. One way or another, Listing 1-4 creates an intent from a context and a class name, and then starts the intent's activity.

The Activity Lifecycle

"And one man in his time plays many parts, His acts being seven ages."

— from *As You Like It,* by William Shakespeare

The human lifecycle is infancy, childhood, adolescence, young adulthood, middle age, old age, and finally, the end.

Android activities have a lifecycle, too. Here are the stages:

✦ **Active (or Running):** The activity is in the foreground on the device's screen at the top of a task stack. The user can interact with the activity.

✦ **Stopped:** The activity is on a task stack, but the activity isn't visible. Maybe the activity isn't at the top of its stack and other activities on the stack are covering up that activity. Alternatively, the activity isn't visible because the device's screen displays something that's not part of this activity's stack.

✦ **Paused:** The Paused state is a kind of limbo between Active and Stopped. Officially, an activity is paused if it's on the currently active stack but it's partially obscured by another activity (such as a transparent activity or a non-full-screen activity that's at the top of the stack).

In practice, an activity that's transitioning from Active to Stopped goes through a brief period of being Paused, even if the user doesn't see a "partially obscured" phase.

✦ **Destroyed:** How sad! But wait! *Destroyed* doesn't mean "dead and gone forever." Android might destroy an activity in order to revive it with a different configuration. Or Android might temporarily clobber an activity while the user isn't actively using that activity.

Lifecycle methods

Most cultures have rites of passage. A *rite of passage* is something that you do when you transition from one life stage to another. For example, where I come from, a child does the following when transitioning to adolescence: "Ye shall stand at the highest point in all of thy land (which is normally the Dauphin Street station of the Frankford El train) and swing a raw fish thrice over thy head. All the while, thou shalt exclaim, 'I shall be a troublesome, raving lunatic for the next few years.'"

Android activities have their own rites of passage, dubbed *lifecycle methods.* Figure 1-5 illustrates the methods.

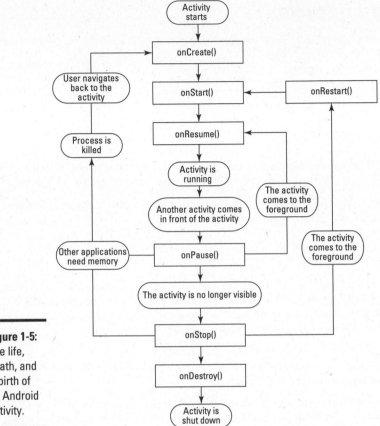

Figure 1-5:
The life, death, and rebirth of an Android activity.

Unlike people, activities don't step predictably from one stage to the next. For example, a typical activity goes back and forth from being Active to Stopped and back to Active again, with several interludes of being Paused. And when Destroyed, an activity can unceremoniously be revived. For an activity, destruction and reconstruction are parts of the normal course of events.

An Android activity has seven lifecycle methods — namely, `onCreate`, `onRestart`, `onStart`, `onResume`, `onPause`, `onStop`, and `onDestroy`. In addition, an activity has a few *onSomething* methods (such as `onSaveInstanceState`) that aren't formally part of the lifecycle and aren't guaranteed to be called. Anyway, Listing 1-5 contains a bunch of these methods.

Listing 1-5: Add Some Logging to Your Activity

```
package com.allmycode.demo1;

import android.app.Activity;
import android.content.res.Configuration;
import android.os.Bundle;
import android.view.View;

public abstract class MyActivity extends Activity {

    abstract void logStuff(String message);

    public void addBreak(View view) {
        logStuff("------");

    }

    /** Called when the activity is created (either
     *  for the first time or after having been
     *  Destroyed. */
    @Override
    public void onCreate(Bundle savedInstanceState) {
        super.onCreate(savedInstanceState);
        logStuff("onCreate");
    }

    /** Called when the activity transitions to
     *  Paused (on its way to Active) after having
     *  been Stopped.
     */
    @Override
    public void onRestart() {
        super.onRestart();
        logStuff("onRestart");
    }

    /** Called when the activity transitions to
     *  Paused (on its way to Active), either for
     *  the first time or after the activity has
     *  been Stopped.
     */
    @Override
    public void onStart() {
        super.onStart();
        logStuff("onStart");
    }

    /** Called when the activity transitions
     *  from Paused to Active.
     */
    @Override
    public void onResume() {
        super.onResume();
        logStuff("onResume");
    }
```

(continued)

Listing 1-5 *(continued)*

```java
/** Never called unless you set
 * android:configChanges in the
 * AndroidManifest.xml file.
 */
@Override
public void onConfigurationChanged
                          (Configuration config) {
    super.onConfigurationChanged(config);
    logStuff("onConfigurationChanged");
}

/** Usually (but not always) called during the
 *  transition from Active to Paused, or during
 *  the transition from Paused to Stopped.
 */
@Override
public void onSaveInstanceState(Bundle state) {
    super.onSaveInstanceState(state);
    logStuff("onSaveInstanceState");
}

/** Called when the activity transitions from
 *  Active to Paused.
 */
@Override
public void onPause() {
    super.onPause();
    logStuff("onPause");
}

/** Called when the activity transitions from
 *  Paused to Stopped.
 */
@Override
public void onStop() {
    super.onStop();
    logStuff("onStop");
}

/** Called when the activity transitions from
 *  Stopped to Destroyed.
 */
@Override
public void onDestroy() {
    super.onDestroy();
    logStuff("onDestroy");
}
}
```

My goal in creating Listing 1-5 is to provide logging that helps you see the lifecycle methods in action. You can drop Listing 1-5 into almost any app to get a Burd's-eye view of your activities and their transitions. To this end, I've created an app that lets you bounce back and forth among different kinds of activities. Listings 1-6, 1-7, and 1-8 describe the app's main activity, and Figure 1-6 shows the main activity's screen.

Listing 1-6: The com.allmycode.demo1.Demo1Activity Class

```
package com.allmycode.demo1;

import android.content.Intent;
import android.os.Bundle;
import android.util.Log;
import android.view.View;

public class Demo1Activity extends MyActivity {

    @Override
    public void onCreate(Bundle savedInstanceState) {
        super.onCreate(savedInstanceState);
        setContentView(R.layout.main);
    }

    @Override
    void logStuff(String message) {
        Log.i("Demo1Activity", message);
    }

    public void startOtherActivity(View view) {
        Intent intent = new Intent();
        intent.setClassName("com.allmycode.demo1",
            "com.allmycode.demo1.OtherActivity");
        startActivity(intent);
    }
    public void startOtherAppActivity(View view) {
        Intent intent = new Intent();
        intent.setClassName("com.allmycode.demo1A",
            "com.allmycode.demo1A.OtherAppActivity");
        startActivity(intent);
    }

    public void startTransparentActivity(View view) {
        Intent intent = new Intent();
        intent.setClassName("com.allmycode.demo1",
            "com.allmycode.demo1.TranslucentActivity");
    startActivity(intent);
    }
}
```

**Book III
Chapter 1**

Android Activities

Listing 1-7: The Activity's Layout File

```
<?xml version="1.0" encoding="utf-8"?>
<LinearLayout xmlns:android=
        "http://schemas.android.com/apk/res/android"
    android:orientation="vertical"
    android:layout_width="fill_parent"
    android:layout_height="fill_parent">

    <TextView android:layout_width="fill_parent"
            android:layout_height="wrap_content"
            android:text="@string/hello" />
```

(continued)

Listing 1-7 *(continued)*

```xml
<Button android:layout_width="wrap_content"
        android:id="@+id/button1"
        android:onClick="startOtherActivity"
        android:layout_height="wrap_content"
        android:text="@string/start_this_app_other">
</Button>

<EditText android:layout_height="wrap_content"
        android:id="@+id/editText"
        android:layout_width="match_parent"
        android:hint="Type anything here">
    <requestFocus></requestFocus>
</EditText>

<include android:id="@+id/include1"
        android:layout_width="wrap_content"
        layout="@layout/add_break"
        android:layout_height="wrap_content">
</include>

<Button android:id="@+id/button2"
        android:layout_width="wrap_content"
        android:layout_height="wrap_content"
        android:onClick="startOtherAppActivity"
        android:text="@string/start_other_app">
</Button>

<Button android:id="@+id/button3"
        android:layout_width="wrap_content"
        android:layout_height="wrap_content"
        android:onClick="startTransparentActivity"
        android:text="@string/start_translucent">
</Button>

</LinearLayout>
```

Listing 1-8:   The add_break.xml File

```xml
<?xml version="1.0" encoding="utf-8"?>
<LinearLayout xmlns:android=
        "http://schemas.android.com/apk/res/android"
    android:orientation="vertical"
    android:layout_width="match_parent"
    android:layout_height="match_parent"
    android:gravity="center">

    <Button android:id="@+id/button1"
            android:layout_width="wrap_content"
            android:layout_height="wrap_content"
            android:onClick="addBreak"
            android:text="@string/add_break">
    </Button>

</LinearLayout>
```

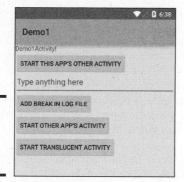

Figure 1-6:
The main
activity's
screen.

I cover most of the Android coding tricks from Listings 1-6, 1-7, and 1-8 in Book I, Chapters 4 through 6. But these listings form the basis for an app that lets you experiment with the activity lifecycle. The next section describes what the widgets in Figure 1-6 (and a few other buttons) do.

The next section describes a number of experiments involving the code in Listings 1-6, 1-7, 1-8, and 1-9, and some other Android code. To try the experiments yourself, download all the code from this book's website (www.allmycode.com/android).

Taking an activity lifecycle through its paces

No two lives are the same, so it would make sense that there is an infinite variety as well to the lifecycles of individual activities. If you dutifully followed my advice about downloading the code from Listings 1-6, 1-7, 1-8, and 1-9 from this book's website, you can follow along as I demonstrate the kinds of curveballs I can throw at an activity lifecycle.

Starting another activity in the same app

In Figure 1-6, you can click the Start This App's Other Activity button to cover up the main activity with another activity from the same application. When you click the button, Android Studio's Logcat panel displays the following entries:

```
1416-1416/com.allmycode.demo1 I/Demo1Activity: onPause
1416-1416/com.allmycode.demo1 W/OtherActivity: onCreate
1416-1416/com.allmycode.demo1 W/OtherActivity: onStart
1416-1416/com.allmycode.demo1 W/OtherActivity: onResume
1416-1416/com.allmycode.demo1 I/Demo1Activity:
                              onSaveInstanceState
1416-1416/com.allmycode.demo1 I/Demo1Activity: onStop
```

An `OtherActivity` instance goes from not existing to being Active, and the `Demo1Activity` instance goes from being Active to being Stopped.

In Listing 1-6, I code `Demo1Activity`'s `logStuff` method with an `i` for *INFO*. And in the `OtherActivity` (which you can download from this book's website), I code `logStuff` with a `w` for *WARN*. I don't mean to imply that `OtherActivity`'s methods are more important than `Demo1Activity`'s methods. I use INFO and WARN because Android Studio's Logcat panel displays different levels (such as INFO and WARN) with different colors. So, on your computer screen, you can distinguish one activity's entries from another with a casual glance. In this book, instead of asking for four-color printing, I set some of the entries in boldface type.

By default, Android Studio filters entries in the Logcat panel so you see only your own app's entries. To change or remove this filter, see Book I, Chapter 5.

Taking a break

In Figure 1-6, you can click the Add Break in Log File button to add an entry whose message is a dashed line. Press this button to help keep track of the parts in a long log file.

The Back button

Your device's Back button pops an activity off the task stack.

Imagine that with `Demo1Activity` and `OtherActivity` on the stack, you press the Back button. As a result, Android Studio's Logcat panel displays the following entries:

```
1416-1416/com.allmycode.demo1 W/OtherActivity: onPause
1416-1416/com.allmycode.demo1 I/Demo1Activity: onRestart
1416-1416/com.allmycode.demo1 I/Demo1Activity: onStart
1416-1416/com.allmycode.demo1 I/Demo1Activity: onResume
1416-1416/com.allmycode.demo1 W/OtherActivity: onStop
1416-1416/com.allmycode.demo1 W/OtherActivity: onDestroy
```

Notice that pressing the Back button destroys the `OtherActivity` instance.

Saving (and not saving) an activity's state

In Figure 1-6, the Type Anything Here text field helps you understand when an activity's state is preserved (and when it's not).

Try this experiment:

1. **Type something in the text field and then click the Start This App's Other Activity button.**

   `OtherActivity` obscures `Demo1Activity`, and `Demo1Activity` is Stopped.

2. Dismiss `OtherActivity` **with the Back button.**

The `Demo1Activity` reappears with your typed characters still in the text field. In spite of `Demo1Activity`'s being stopped, Android has preserved the state of `Demo1Activity`.

Try another experiment:

1. Type something in the text field and then click the Home button.

The Home screen appears, and `Demo1Activity` is Stopped.

2. Find the Demo1 icon and touch the icon to invoke `Demo1Activity`.

The `Demo1Activity` reappears with your typed characters still in the text field. Android has preserved the state of the `Demo1Activity`.

Pressing Home is like telling Android, "I want to do something else while the current activity goes into 'suspended animation.'"

Here's another experiment:

1. Type something in the text field and then click the Back button.

The `Demo1Activity`'s screen goes away. In the Logcat panel, you see `Demo1Activity` execute its `onPause`, `onStop`, and `onDestroy` methods.

2. Find the Demo1 icon and touch the icon to invoke `Demo1Activity`.

The `Demo1Activity` reappears, but the Type Anything Here text field has been reinitialized. Android hasn't preserved the `Demo1Activity`'s state.

Pressing Back is like saying to Android, "I'm done with this activity. Get me out 'a' here!"

In the next experiment, you create a workaround for the behavior of Android's Back button.

1. Modify the first several lines of the `Demo1Activity` **as follows:**

```
package com.allmycode.demo1;

import android.content.Intent;
import android.content.SharedPreferences;
import android.os.Bundle;
import android.util.Log;
import android.view.View;
import android.widget.EditText;

public class Demo1Activity extends MyActivity {
EditText editText;
```

```
@Override
public void onCreate(Bundle savedInstanceState) {
  super.onCreate(savedInstanceState);
  setContentView(R.layout.main);

  editText = (EditText) findViewById(R.id.editText);
}

@Override
public void onPause() {
  super.onPause();
  SharedPreferences prefs =
      getPreferences(MODE_PRIVATE);
  SharedPreferences.Editor editor = prefs.edit();
  editor.putString("EditTextString",
      editText.getText().toString());
  editor.commit();
}

@Override
public void onResume() {
  super.onResume();
  SharedPreferences prefs =
      getPreferences(MODE_PRIVATE);
  String str = prefs.getString("EditTextString", "");
  editText.setText(str);
}

    // You don't have to add any code below this point

@Override
void logStuff(String message) {

    // ... Et cetera
```

2. **Choose Run ⇨ Run 'app'.**

   The app starts running with your modified `Demo1Activity` code.

3. **Type something in the text field and then click the Back button.**

   The `Demo1Activity`'s screen goes away. In the Logcat panel, you see `Demo1Activity` execute its `onPause`, `onStop`, and `onDestroy` methods.

4. **Find the Demo1 icon and touch the icon to invoke** `Demo1Activity`.

   The `Demo1Activity` reappears with your typed characters still in the text field. Android didn't automatically preserve the `Demo1Activity`'s state, but you used `SharedPreferences` to save the state and then to restore the state.

To save an activity's relevant information, put your `SharedPreferences` code in the `onPause` method. Don't wait to save the information in the `onStop` or `onDestroy` method.

The code in this experiment uses `SharedPreferences`. For more about `SharedPreferences`, see Chapter 3 in this minibook.

Here's your next experiment:

1. **If you followed the previous set of instructions and added** `SharedPreferences` **code, remove that code.**

   You can remove the entire `onPause` method. Remove the `onResume` method, too.

2. **Choose Run ⇨ Run 'app' to get the app running again.**

3. **When the app starts running, type something in the text field.**

4. **Turn your device sideways.**

   If you're running an emulator, you can do a virtual turn by pressing Ctrl+F11. Your activity's screen adjusts (from portrait to landscape or vice versa), and your typed characters are still in the text field.

   But when you look at Android Studio's Logcat panel, you see the following entries:

   ```
   1437-1437/com.allmycode.demo1 I/Demo1Activity: onPause
   1437-1437/com.allmycode.demo1 I/Demo1Activity:
                                     onSaveInstanceState
   1437-1437/com.allmycode.demo1 I/Demo1Activity: onStop
   1437-1437/com.allmycode.demo1 I/Demo1Activity:
                                     onDestroy
   1437-1437/com.allmycode.demo1 I/Demo1Activity: onCreate
   1437-1437/com.allmycode.demo1 I/Demo1Activity: onStart
   1437-1437/com.allmycode.demo1 I/Demo1Activity: onResume
   ```

Surprise! In order to rotate your activity's screen, Android destroys and then re-creates the activity. And between destruction and subsequent creation, Android preserves your activity instance's state. The text field's content is restored.

This leads you to another experiment:

1. **Add the following attribute to the** `Demo1Activity`**'s** `<activity>` **element in the** `AndroidManifest.xml` **file:**

   ```
   android:configChanges="orientation|screenSize"
   ```

2. **Run the app and change the orientation of the emulator or the device.**

   You see the following entry in Android Studio's Logcat panel:

   ```
   8556-8556/com.allmycode.demo1 I/Demo1Activity:
                                     onConfigurationChanged
   ```

The `android:configChanges="orientation|screenSize"` attribute tells Android to notify the activity about changes in the device's orientation or the size of the screen. So, if you tilt the device sideways, Android doesn't do the usual routine of destroying and re-creating the activity. Instead, Android calls the activity's `onConfigurationChanged` method. In Listing 1-5, a call to the `onConfigurationChanged` method creates a log entry to record the event.

In the expression `orientation|screenSize`, the character between the words `orientation` and `screenSize` is your keyboard's *pipe symbol*. When used this way, the pipe symbol stands for the word *or*. That is, Android calls the activity's `onConfigurationChanged` method if either the device's orientation changes *or* the size of the screen changes. Starting with API Level 13, Android considers a tilt of the device to be a change in screen size. So, if you want your activity to handle its own orientation changes, you must put both `orientation` and `screenSize` in the activity's `android:configChanges` attribute.

Using the `android:configChanges` attribute, you intercept Android's default actions when the user tilts the device. You can then handle the orientation change with your own `onConfigurationChanged` method. But the official documentation recommends against doing this. And, in giving this advice, the Android docs are probably correct. Here's one reason why:

With very little tinkering, you can specify two different layouts for your activity — a portrait mode layout and a landscape mode layout. (For details, see Book IV, Chapter 1.) When the user tilts the device, Android can automatically switch from one layout to the other. This ensures that your app looks good no matter how the user holds the device. The trouble is, if you override the default behavior using the `android:configChanges` attribute, the system doesn't automatically switch layouts. You have to remember to switch layouts in your activity's `onConfigurationChanged` method. At best, this means more coding work for you. At worst, you forget to modify the `onConfigurationChanged` method, and your app looks crummy when the user tilts the device.

Here's one more experiment:

1. **If you followed the previous set of instructions and added an** `android:configChanges` **attribute in the** `AndroidManifest.xml` **file, remove that attribute.**

   Actually, any newly created Android project will do just fine.

2. **Add the following method to your** `MainActivity` **code.**

   ```
   @Override
   public void onDestroy() {
     super.onDestroy();
     Log.i("MainActivity", Boolean.toString(isFinishing()));
   }
   ```

3. **Run the app.**

4. **On the emulator or the physical device, tap the Back button.**

   When you do, you see I/MainActivity: true in the Logcat panel. Android calls your activity's onDestroy method, and a call to the onFinishing method returns true.

5. **Run the app again.**

6. **Tilt the emulator sideways (by pressing Ctrl+F11) or tilt the physical device sideways.**

   When you do, you see I/MainActivity: false in the Logcat panel. Android calls your activity's onDestroy method, but a call to the onFinishing method returns false.

   By calling the onFinishing method, you can distinguish a device-tilt onDestroy call from a Back button onDestroy call. That's nice.

Starting another app's activity

In Figure 1-6, you can click the Start Other App's Activity button to cover up the main activity — you essentially cover the main activity with an activity from a different application. When you click the button, Android Studio's Logcat panel displays the following entries:

```
4150-4150/com.allmycode.demo1 I/Demo1Activity: onPause
4150-4150/com.allmycode.demo1 I/Demo1Activity:
                                     onSaveInstanceState
4150-4150/com.allmycode.demo1 I/Demo1Activity: onStop

4471-4497/com.allmycode.demo1A V/OtherAppActivity: onCreate
4471-4497/com.allmycode.demo1A V/OtherAppActivity: onStart
4471-4497/com.allmycode.demo1A V/OtherAppActivity: onResume
```

Book III
Chapter 1

Android Activities

To see the OtherActivity lines in the Logcat panel, look for a drop-down list displaying a package name (probably com.allmycode.demo1) just above that panel. In that drop-down list, select the package containing OtherActivity (most likely, the package com.allmycode.demo1A). And, by the way, if you see No Debuggable Applications in the drop-down list, choose Tools ➪ Android ➪ Enable ADB Integration in Android Studio's main menu.

One difference between these entries and the entries in previous examples is that these entries use two PID numbers. In this example, the Demo1Activity has PID 4150, and the OtherAppActivity has PID 4471. As promised, two different apps run in two different operating system processes, and each process has its own PID. You can get independent verification of this fact by examining the Devices panel in the Android Device Monitor.

To see the Devices panel, do the following:

1. **Choose Tools ⇨ Android ⇨ Android Device Monitor.**

2. **In the Android Device Monitor's menu, choose Window ⇨ Open Perspective ⇨ DDMS (default).**

   With the DDMS perspective open, the Devices panel is on the right side of the Android Device Monitor.

Figure 1-7 shows you the Devices panel.

Figure 1-7:
The Devices panel.

In Figure 1-7, the process running `Demo1Activity` (in package `com.allmycode.demo1`) has PID `4150`. And the process running `OtherApp Activity` (in package `com.allmycode.demo1A`) has PID `4471`.

Overloading the system

As the sun sets on the "Starting another app's activity" section, you're running two `com.allmycode` processes. (Refer to Figure 1-7.) On your emulator's screen, the `com.allmycode.demo1.Demo1Activity` is obscured by the `com.allmycode.demo1A.OtherAppActivity`.

So you can conduct another experiment:

1. **Get your emulator (or device) in the state described at the end of the "Starting another app's activity" section.**

   To do so, start the app whose main activity is in Listing 1-6. Then click the Start Other App's Activity button.

2. **Press the emulator's Home button.**

   See Figure 1-8. You're not pressing the Back button, so you're not backing out of the `OtherAppActivity` or the `Demo1Activity`. Those two activities are Stopped, not Destroyed. (You can verify this by looking at the Android Studio's Logcat panel.)

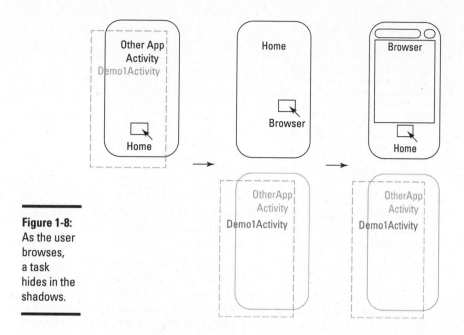

Figure 1-8:
As the user browses, a task hides in the shadows.

3. **In Android Studio, open the Hog app that I've included in the download for this book. Run that Hog app in the same emulator or device that you used in Step 1.**

   My Hog app's sole purpose is to inundate your emulator with processes. The Hog app displays a button with a number on it. (See Figure 1-9.) The button's number tells you how many processes the Hog has launched. When you click the button, the app starts a new process running on your emulator and increments the number on the button.

Figure 1-9:
The Hog app.

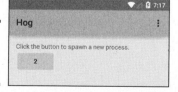

4. **Keep an eye on Android Studio's Devices panel as you repeatedly click the Hog app's button.**

   You can see a list of Hog processes in the Devices panel. (See Figure 1-10.)

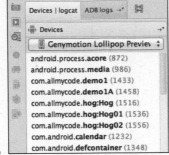

Figure 1-10:
The Devices panel shows you some Hog processes.

To flood the emulator with processes, my Hog app adds an `android:process` attribute to each of the app's activities. I also use some really messed-up, repetitive code.

At some point, you see the `com.allmycode.demo1` process disappear from the Devices pane. (For me, this happens when I start the 16th process, but your mileage may vary. See Figure 1-11.) Android has reclaimed memory by killing off a process. After all, the `com.allmycode.demo1.Demo1Activity` instance is Stopped, so Android figures it can destroy that activity. The `com.allmycode.demo1A.OtherAppActivity` is also Stopped. But the last time you saw `OtherAppActivity`, that activity was at the top of a task stack.

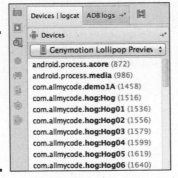

Figure 1-11:
The package com. allmycode. demo1 has dis-appeared.

Android kills a process in order to reclaim space, and the user has no clue that the process has been killed. This is business as usual for the Android operating system.

At this point in the experiment, the `Demo1Activity` is Stopped, the activity's process has been killed, and the activity isn't on top of its current task.

5. **Press Home and then the Apps button to return to the emulator's Apps screen, and click the Demo1 icon (the icon for the** `com.allmycode.demo1.Demo1Activity` **instance).**

The `OtherAppActivity` reappears on the screen. (See Figure 1-12.) Android interprets your click as a wish to return to the *top of the task stack* containing `Demo1Activity`, and not to `Demo1Activity` itself. In the Logcat panel, `OtherAppActivity` has been created, started, and resumed.

```
1796-1796/com.allmycode.demo1A V/OtherAppActivity:
                                        onCreate
1796-1796/com.allmycode.demo1A V/OtherAppActivity:
                                        onStart
1796-1796/com.allmycode.demo1A V/OtherAppActivity:
                                        onResume
```

In Android Studio's Devices pane, you still don't see `com.allmycode.demo1`.

The Logcat panel might be filtering for the `com.allmycode.hog` app, in which case, you don't see `com.allmycode.demo1` or `com.allmycode.demo1A` entries. If this is the case, select No Filters in the drop-down box in the upper-right corner of the Logcat panel. Then, to filter for `demo1` and `demo1A` entries, type `demo` in the search field immediately above the Logcat panel.

6. **Press the emulator's Back button.**

Android remembers that `com.allmycode.demo1.Demo1Activity` was hidden (conceptually) underneath `OtherAppActivity` on the task stack. Because the `com.allmycode.demo1` process no longer exists, Android creates a new process with a new PID to run the `com.allmycode.demo1.Demo1Activity` code.

As a result, `Demo1Activity` appears on your emulator's screen, `com.allmycode.demo1` reappears in Android Studio's Devices panel with a new PID, and the following entries appear in Android Studio's Logcat panel:

```
1796-1796/com.allmycode.demo1A V/OtherAppActivity:
                                        onPause
1819-1819/: V/Demo1App: onCreate
1819-1819/: I/Demo1Activity: onCreate
1819-1819/: I/Demo1Activity: onStart
1819-1819/: I/Demo1Activity: onResume
1796-1796/com.allmycode.demo1A V/OtherAppActivity:
                                        onStop
1796-1796/com.allmycode.demo1A V/OtherAppActivity:
                                        onDestroy
```

Unbeknownst to the user, Android has restored the `Demo1Activity` in a new process.

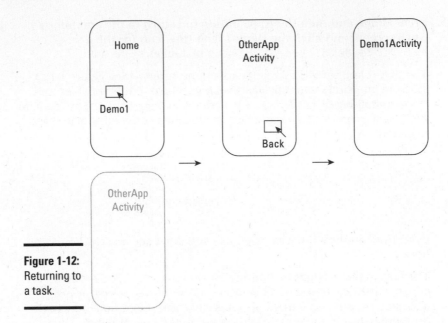

Figure 1-12:
Returning to
a task.

Partially covering an activity

In Figure 1-6, clicking the Start Translucent Activity button does what you think it should do. The button makes Android invoke a see-through activity. (App development terminology tends to blur the difference between "translucent" and "transparent." Get it? "Blur" the difference?) Of course, you can't invoke a translucent activity unless you have a translucent activity to invoke. So Listing 1-9 shows you how to create a translucent activity.

Listing 1-9   The AndroidManifest.xml File for One of This Chapter's Big Projects

```xml
<?xml version="1.0" encoding="utf-8"?>
<manifest xmlns:android=
    "http://schemas.android.com/apk/res/android"
    package="com.allmycode.demo1"
    android:versionCode="1"
    android:versionName="1.0">
    <uses-sdk android:minSdkVersion="8" />

    <application android:icon="@drawable/icon"
                android:label="@string/app_name"
                android:name=".Demo1App">
```

```
<activity android:name=".Demo1Activity"
        android:label="@string/app_name" >
    <intent-filter>
        <action android:name=
            "android.intent.action.MAIN" />
        <category android:name=
            "android.intent.category.LAUNCHER" />
    </intent-filter>
</activity>

<activity android:name=".OtherActivity" />
<activity android:name=".TranslucentActivity"
        android:theme=
            "@android:style/Theme.Translucent" />
</application>

</manifest>
```

To create a translucent activity, create a Java class that extends Android's `Activity` class. Then, in your `AndroidManifest.xml` file, declare the activity's `theme` to be Android's predefined `Theme.Translucent` style.

My `TranslucentActivity` class has only one button — an Add Break in Log File button in the center of the activity. So, after pressing the Start Translucent Activity button in Figure 1-6, I see the stuff in Figure 1-13. True to its word, Android superimposes the Translucent Activity's button on top of the next activity on the stack.

**Book III
Chapter 1**

Android Activities

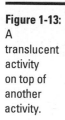

Figure 1-13:
A translucent activity on top of another activity.

Referring to the list of activity states described at the beginning of this section, one of the Paused state's duties is to house activities that are partially obscured. So, if you look at Android Studio's Logcat panel after clicking the Start Translucent Activity button, you see the following entries:

```
1419-1419/com.allmycode.demo1 I/Demo1Activity: onPause
1419-1419/com.allmycode.demo1 W/TranslucentActivity: onCreate
1419-1419/com.allmycode.demo1 W/TranslucentActivity: onStart
1419-1419/com.allmycode.demo1 W/TranslucentActivity: onResume
1419-1419/com.allmycode.demo1 I/Demo1Activity:
                                        onSaveInstanceState
```

`Demo1Activity` pauses but doesn't stop.

Getting Results Back from an Activity

In Book I, Chapter 6, I compare an intent to a method call. To start an activity, you don't call a method. Instead, you fire up an intent.

So far, so good. But what feature of an intent takes the place of a method call's return value? Listings 1-10 and 1-11 have the answer.

Listing 1-10:   An Activity Asks for a Result

```java
package com.allmycode.results;

import android.app.Activity;
import android.content.Intent;
import android.os.Bundle;
import android.view.View;
import android.widget.TextView;

public class GetResultActivity extends Activity {
  final int MY_REQUEST_CODE = 42;
  TextView textView;

  @Override
  public void onCreate(Bundle savedInstanceState) {
    super.onCreate(savedInstanceState);
    setContentView(R.layout.main);
    textView = (TextView) findViewById(R.id.textView);
  }

  public void onButtonClick(View v) {
    Intent intent = new Intent();
    intent.setClassName("com.allmycode.results",
      "com.allmycode.results.GiveResultActivity");
    startActivityForResult(intent, MY_REQUEST_CODE);
  }

  @Override
  protected void onActivityResult(int requestCode,
                                  int resultCode,
                                  Intent intent) {

    if (requestCode == MY_REQUEST_CODE &&
                        resultCode == RESULT_OK) {
      textView.setText(intent.getStringExtra("text"));

    }
  }
}
```

Listing 1-11:   An Activity Provides a Result

```
package com.allmycode.results;

import android.app.Activity;
import android.content.Intent;
import android.os.Bundle;
import android.view.View;
import android.widget.EditText;

public class GiveResultActivity extends Activity {

  EditText editText;

  @Override
  public void onCreate(Bundle state) {
    super.onCreate(state);

    setContentView(R.layout.giver);
    editText = (EditText) findViewById(R.id.editText);

  }

  public void onButtonClick(View arg0) {
    Intent intent = new Intent();
    intent.putExtra
      ("text", editText.getText().toString());

    setResult(RESULT_OK, intent);
    finish();
  }
}
```

The actions of Listings 1-10 and 1-11 take place in three stages. First, the user sees the `GetResultActivity` in Listing 1-10. (See Figure 1-14.)

Figure 1-14:
The
activity in
Listing 1-10.

When the user clicks the Get A Result button, Android calls `startActivityForResult(intent, MY_REQUEST_CODE)`.

The `startActivityForResult` method takes an intent and a request code. In Listing 1-10, the intent points explicitly to the activity being started. The request code is any `int` value. The request code identifies the return result when the result arrives. (You can call `startActivityForResult` more than once before you get any results. When results arrive, you use the request code to distinguish one result from another.)

After clicking the button in Figure 1-14, the user sees the `GiveResultActivity` in Listing 1-11. (See Figure 1-15.)

Figure 1-15: The activity in Listing 1-11.

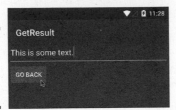

The user types text into the text field in Figure 1-15 and then clicks the Go Back button. The button click causes the code in Listing 1-11 to create an intent. The intent has extra information — namely, the user's text input.

The call to `setResult` sends a result code (`RESULT_OK`, `RESULT_CANCELED`, or any positive `int` value that's meaningful to the receiver) along with the intent full of useful information.

At the end of Listing 1-11, the `finish` method call ends the run of the activity shown in Figure 1-15. The screen returns to the `GetResultActivity`. (See Figure 1-16.)

Figure 1-16: The activity in Listing 1-10 after getting a result.

At this point, Android calls the `onActivityResult` method in Listing 1-10. The method uses the result in some way or other. (In this example, the `onActivityResult` method simply displays the result in a `TextView` element.)

Applications Don't Feel Left Out

In any operating system, things come and things go. Users log on and log off, and activities are created and destroyed. But what about applications? Applications are created and terminated.

If you check Listing 1-9, you see an `application` element with an `android:name=".Demo1App"` attribute. An app doesn't need an `android:name` attribute, but if it has one, you must create a class with the name that you specify. You can keep track of an app's global values (values that transcend the app's individual activities) with this class. Listing 1-12 sheds light on the situation.

Listing 1-12   An Android Application

```java
package com.allmycode.demo1;

import android.app.Application;
import android.content.res.Configuration;
import android.util.Log;

public class Demo1App extends Application {
    private static final String CLASSNAME = "Demo1App";

    @Override
    public void onCreate() {
        Log.v(CLASSNAME, "onCreate");
    }

    @Override
    public void onConfigurationChanged
                        (Configuration config) {
        Log.v(CLASSNAME, "onConfigurationChanged");
    }

    @Override
    public void onLowMemory() {
        Log.v(CLASSNAME, "onLowMemory");
    }

    @Override
    public void onTerminate() {
        Log.v(CLASSNAME, "onTerminate");
    }
}
```

Android's `Application` class has only four of its own methods — the methods declared in Listing 1-12. In previous sections, I didn't draw attention to the log entries from Listing 1-12. But in this section, you can watch for the name "Demo1App" as you follow these instructions:

1. **Open this chapter's example project (the project from this chapter's "Lifecycle methods" section).**

Even if you stopped working with this project a while ago, the project might still be consuming part of your emulator's memory. In this section, you want to start afresh. So, if the project is still in memory, you want to remove it. Here's how:

2. **In the Devices panel, look for** `com.allmycode.demo1` **and** `com.allmycode.demo1A.`

If you don't see `com.allmycode.demo1` or `com.allmycode.demo1A` in the Devices panel, that's okay. In fact, the reason you're looking for them is to get rid of them if they're there.

The Devices panel is part of the Android Device Monitor. For help finding the Devices panel, refer to the section "Starting another app's activity," earlier in this chapter.

3. **If you see** `com.allmycode.demo1` **in the Devices panel, select that entry. Look to the left of the Devices panel for an icon displaying a Stop sign. (See Figure 1-17.) Click that icon to terminate the** `com.allmycode.demo1` **process.**

Figure 1-17:
Using the Devices panel to terminate a process.

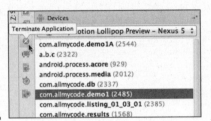

4. **Repeat Step 3, this time looking for a** `com.allmycode.demo1A` **entry.**

   Be ruthless if you must.

5. **In Android Studio's main menu, choose Run ➪ Run 'app' to run the project anew.**

   When the app starts running, you see the following entry in the Logcat panel:

   ```
   1701-1701/com.allmycode.demo1 V/Demo1App: onCreate
   ```

   The entry appears because Android calls the `onCreate` method in Listing 1-12.

   Android calls the `onCreate` method in Listing 1-12 only if your `AndroidManfest.xml` file's application tag has an `android:name` attribute.

   ```
   <application
               ...
               android:name=".Demo1App"
   ... Etc.
   ```

   If you have trouble finding a `Demo1App` entry in the Logcat panel, you can quickly filter the entries. To do so, type **Demo1App** in the text field immediately above the Logcat panel.

6. Change your emulator's orientation (from portrait to landscape, for example).

As a result, you see the following entry in the Logcat panel:

```
1701-1701/com.allmycode.demo1 V/Demo1App:
                         onConfigurationChanged
```

Android has notified your app about the device's configuration change.

7. Press the emulator's Home button. Then start a new app (the Phone app, for example).

Your app's activity is Stopped, so you don't see evidence of the app's run on your emulator's screen. But if you check Android Studio's Devices panel, you still see a `com.allmycode.demo1` entry. The application is still alive.

8. Change your emulator's orientation (from landscape to portrait, for example).

Again, you see the following `onConfigurationChanged` entry in the Logcat panel:

```
1701-1701/com.allmycode.demo1 V/Demo1App:
                         onConfigurationChanged
```

Android has notified all running apps about the device's configuration change.

9. Restart or return to the Hog app (the app from this chapter's section "Overloading the system").

If the Hog app is still running in your emulator, use the emulator's Recents button to return to the Hog app. Otherwise, choose Run⇨Run 'app' in Android Studio's main menu.

10. Click the Hog app's button until `com.allmycode.demo1` disappears from Android Studio's Devices panel.

If you don't do too much filtering in the Logcat panel, you see messages from Android about the termination of `com.allmycode.demo1`.

```
553-947/system_process I/ActivityManager:
  Killing 1365:com.allmycode.demo1/u0a70 (adj 14):
  cached #17
553-605/system_process W/InputDispatcher:
  channel '2c2e3292
  com.allmycode.demo1/com.allmycode.demo1.Demo1Activity
  (server)' ~ Consumer closed input channel or an error
  occurred.  events=0x9
553-605/system_process E/InputDispatcher:
  channel '2c2e3292
  com.allmycode.demo1/com.allmycode.demo1.Demo1Activity
  (server)' ~ Channel is unrecoverably broken and will
  be disposed!
```

Book III
Chapter 1

Android Activities

```
553-941/system_process I/WindowState: WIN DEATH:
  Window{2c2e3292 u0
  com.allmycode.demo1/com.allmycode.demo1.Demo1Activity}
```

But here's a surprise. You see none of the log messages from Listing 1-12 (not even when Android kills your apps' processes). If you read the fine print in Android's docs, you see the following:

While the exact point at which this [onLowMemory method] will be called is not defined, generally it will happen around the time all background process have [sic] been killed. . . . [The onTerminate method] will never be called on a production Android device, where processes are removed by simply killing them; no user code (including this callback) is executed when doing so.

During my run of this chapter's apps, Android never calls either onLowMemory or onTerminate.

Some of Android's doc entries are concisely worded. This makes the docs easy to misinterpret. Your confidence in a doc entry's interpretation should be proportional to your experience using and testing that entry's claims.

11. **Return to your original app's task (as in Step 5 of the earlier section "Overloading the system").**

You see the OtherApp startup entries:

```
1899-1899/com.allmycode.demo1 V/Demo1App: onCreate
1899-1899/com.allmycode.demo1 I/Demo1Activity: onCreate
1899-1899/com.allmycode.demo1 I/Demo1Activity: onStart
1899-1899/com.allmycode.demo1 I/Demo1Activity: onResume
```

One of your "other" app's activities is on top of the stack. So Android creates a new process (with a new PID) for your other app.

Chapter 2: Intents and Intent Filters

In This Chapter

✔ **Making a match**

✔ **Getting the lowdown on intents and intent filters**

✔ **Practicing with intents on an emulator or device**

✔ **Stacking up your activities and tasks**

You can judge people's mental ages by the kinds of foods they eat. For example, one of my friends seeks out new tastes from strange and exotic lands. Mentally, he's a mature adult. As for me, I like cheeseburgers and chocolate. Mentally, I'm 12 years old.

So here's an experiment: Put a meal on a table and then put a bunch of people in the room. Each person has a list of foods that he is willing to eat. Now use the people's lists to figure out who is (and who isn't) willing to eat the meal.

Things can become complicated. I love cheeseburgers . . . but no toppings, please! . . . unless the topping is mayonnaise. Yes, I want fries with that, but not if they're sweet potato fries. And above all, if the food's slimy, or if you have to explain where it comes from, I'm not eating it.

How to Make a Match

Android has two kinds of intents — explicit and implicit:

✦ An *explicit* intent names an activity class whose instance is to be launched.

✦ An *implicit* intent doesn't call for a particular activity to be launched. Instead, an implicit intent describes some work to be done. An implicit intent names an action to be taken, along with other information required to perform the action.

I cover explicit intents in Chapter 1 of this minibook.

Android's use of implicit intents is like the meal-in-a-room experiment in this chapter's introduction. An intent is like a meal. An *intent filter* is like a person's list of acceptable foods.

First, an activity sends an intent. Then the system compares that intent with other activities' intent filters to find out which activities have filters that match the intent (which activities can perform the desired action). See Figure 2-1.

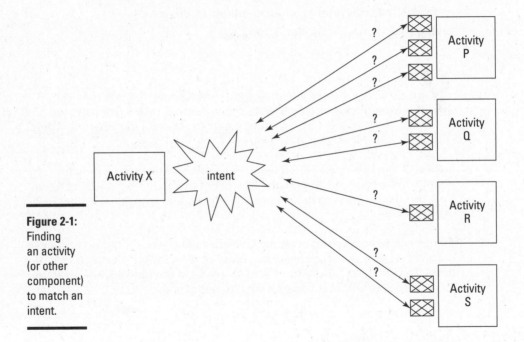

Figure 2-1: Finding an activity (or other component) to match an intent.

In Figure 2-1, Android checks for a match between the intent and the first of Activity P's filters. If the intent doesn't match Activity P's first filter, Android checks for a match between the intent and the second Activity P filter. If Android finds a match in one of Activity P's filters, Android marks Activity P as one possible way to fulfill the intent (one possible component that may perform the work described by the intent).

Still in Figure 2-1, Android proceeds to test Activity Q's, Activity R's, and Activity S's filters. Android keeps a list of all the activities that have at least one matching filter.

✦ If exactly one activity has a matching intent filter, that activity starts running.

✦ If no activities have any matching intent filters, the app throws an exception.

✦ If more than one activity has a matching intent filter, the system chooses among the matching activities, or the system displays a menu asking the user to choose among the matching activities.

Android's `startActivity`, `startService`, `bindService`, and `sendBroadcast` methods all take arguments of type `Intent`. So a component that matches an intent can be an activity, a service, or a broadcast receiver. For most of this chapter's examples, you can safely think *activity* when you read the word *component*. Sometimes I blur the terminology and use *activity* as an example, even though a more complete explanation would use the word *component*.

In this minibook, I cover services in Chapter 3 and broadcast receivers in Chapter 4.

The parts of an intent

Figure 2-2 shows you the parts of an implicit intent. An intent has an action, data, categories, extras, and flags. Some of these things might be omitted, but Android sets stiff restrictions about what may or may not be omitted, and when.

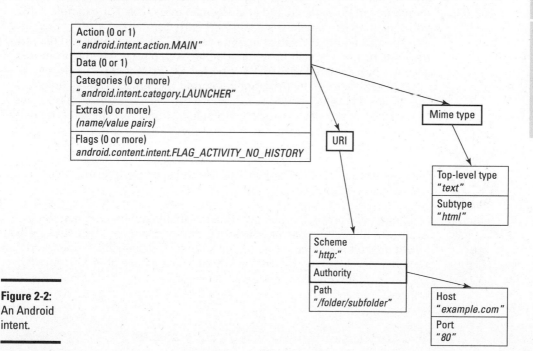

Figure 2-2:
An Android intent.

Book III
Chapter 2

Intents and
Intent Filters

Each item in Figure 2-2 consists of one or more values. Some typical sample values are in italics.

✦ In Figure 2-2, the string `"android.intent.action.MAIN"` is a value that an action might have.

✦ Also in Figure 2-2, the predeclared `android.content.Intent.FLAG_ ACTIVITY_NO_HISTORY` Java constant is a value that a flag might have. That Java constant stands for the number 1073741824 (which is the same as hexadecimal 40000000).

The conventions surrounding Android intents make it difficult to distinguish between strings and predeclared constants. In Figure 2-2, `"android. intent.action.MAIN"` is a string and `android.content.Intent. FLAG_ACTIVITY_NO_HISTORY` is a predeclared constant (a static final field named `FLAG_ACTIVITY_NO_HISTORY` in the `android.content.Intent` class). Oddly, the dots in the string `"android.content.intent.MAIN"` don't mean very much. There's no member named `MAIN` in any `android. content.intent` class.

Figure 2-2 indicates that an intent's data parts come in two flavors — URI and MIME type. An intent may have neither of these, one of the two, or both.

Still looking at Figure 2-2, the *MIME* in MIME type stands for *Multipurpose Internet Mail Extensions.* The original MIME standard describes the kinds of data that can be encoded and sent in email messages. For example, when your email program receives a message with `Content-Type: text/html`, your program interprets the message as an HTML document and displays the content the way web browsers display web pages. When a program receives bits declared with MIME type `audio/mp3`, `image/jpeg`, or `application/zip`, the program interprets the bits as sounds, images, or ZIP files. In each case, the word before the slash is a *top-level type,* and the word after the slash is a *subtype.* Familiar top-level-type/subtype pairs include `text/plain`, `text/html`, `text/xml`, `image/png`, `image/jpeg`, and `image/gif`.

Many of the names in Android's SDK use the shortened term *type* instead of the full name *MIME type.*

Unlike the use of MIME types in ordinary email handling, the matching of Android's MIME types is case-sensitive. So, for example, `TEXT/PLAIN` in an intent doesn't match `text/plain` in a filter. Android's developer guidelines recommend using only lowercase letters in the names of MIME types.

A *Uniform Resource Locator (URL)* is any familiar web address that you dictate when someone asks, "Where can I find that on the web?" A *Uniform Resource Identifier (URI)* looks like a URL, but URIs describe more than just web pages. Every URL is a URI, but a URI isn't necessarily a URL.

In Android, a URI has from one to four parts, depending on how you count and on what you choose to omit. Figure 2-3 has some examples.

```
http:
```
scheme only

```
http://project.example.com
```
scheme · host
authority

```
http://project.example.com:80
```
scheme · host · port
authority

```
http://project.example.com/folder/subfolder
```
scheme · host · path
authority

```
http://project.example.com:80/folder/subfolder
```
scheme · host · port · path
authority

Figure 2-3: Uniform Resource Identifiers.

Book III
Chapter 2

Intents and
Intent Filters

The kind of URI that I illustrate in Figure 2-3 is a *hierarchical* URI. The alternative to a hierarchical URI is an *opaque* URI. An opaque URI, such as `tel:6502530000` or `mailto:android@allmycode.com`, has a single colon instead of `://`. Also, in an opaque URI, what comes after the colon varies widely depending on the scheme. In fact, what comes after the colon in an opaque URI is the URI's *scheme-specific part*. So, for example, in the URI `mailto:android@allmycode.com`, the scheme is `mailto` and the scheme-specific part is `android@allmycode.com`. An opaque URI has neither an authority nor a path.

What r u?

If you don't live under a rock, you've used hundreds of URLs (*U*niform *R*esource *L*ocators). As the name suggests, a URL locates something. For example, the URL `www.panynj.gov:80/path` locates the main page of the website for the Port Authority Trans-Hudson Corporation — the organization in charge of trains that run between New Jersey and New York City. This URL's scheme is `http`. Its host is `www.panynj.gov`. Its port is `80`. Its authority is `www.panynj.gov:80`. Its path happens to be `/path`.

Every URL is a URI (*U*niform *R*esource *I*dentifier), but a URI isn't necessarily a URL. Some URIs don't locate anything. For example, every `AndroidManifest.xml` document contains the attribute `xmlns:android="http://schemas.android.com/apk/res/android"`. The URI's scheme is `http`. Both the host and authority are `schemas.android.com`. (This URI has no port.) The URI's path is `/apk/res/android`.

If you type **http://schemas.android.com/apk/res/android** into your web browser's address field, your browser goes nowhere. The URI `http://schemas.android.com/apk/res/android` doesn't locate anything. Like the URIs that start many XML documents, this URI is nothing but a name. This URI is a URN (*U*niform *R*esource *N*ame).

According to the Internet Engineering Task Force document RFC 3986, URNs "are required to remain globally unique and persistent even when the resource ceases to exist or becomes unavailable. . . ." In other words, a URN names something — something whose name always applies — something that might never need to be found.

Here's another example. The Android SDK comes with a folder full of sample apps. One of the apps (the SearchableDictionary example) uses the URI `content://com.example.android.searchabledict.DictionaryProvider/dictionary`. The URI's scheme is `content`, and so on. This URI doesn't work in a web browser's address field. But within Android's SearchableDictionary example, the URI locates a particular content provider (in this case, a provider of dictionary words and definitions). The things that a URI locates don't have to be web pages.

The World Wide Web Consortium is currently working on IRIs (*I*nternationalized *R*esource *I*dentifiers). An IRI is like a URI except that an IRI's characters aren't restricted to characters in the Roman alphabet. The following figure has an example of an IRI.

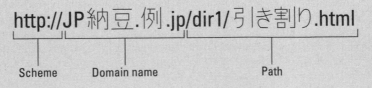

http://JP納豆.例.jp/dir1/引き割り.html

Scheme   Domain name   Path

The parts of an intent filter

Your app creates an intent and then calls `startActivity(intent)`. Then what happens? Android has a list of activities installed on the device, and each activity has its intent filters. Android tries to match the intent with each intent filter. If an activity has any matching intent filters, that activity goes on the list of possible responders to the `startActivity` method call.

An activity's non-matching filters don't harm the activity's chances of going on the list. Even if only one of an activity's filters matches, the activity still goes on the list of possible responders.

So what constitutes a match between an intent and an intent filter? Funny you should ask! The answer is far from simple.

An intent filter can have actions, data entries, and categories. (Unlike an intent, an intent filter can have more than one action and more than one data entry. Like an intent, an intent filter can have more than one category.) Intent filters don't have extras or flags. (See Figure 2-4.)

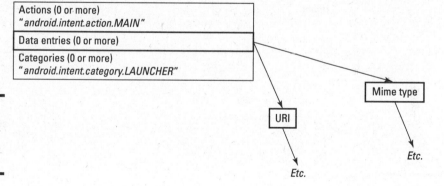

Figure 2-4:
The parts
of an intent
filter.

To find a match between an implicit intent and an intent filter, Android performs three tests:

✦ Android tests the intent's action for a match with the filter's actions.

✦ Android tests the intent's categories for a match with the filter's categories.

✦ Android tests the intent's data for a match with the filter's data.

Android's rules for matching an intent's action with a filter's action are fairly straightforward. And the rules for matching the intent's categories with the filter's categories are okay. But neither of these rules is a memorable, one-sentence slogan. And the rules for matching the intent's data with the filter's data are quite complicated. Unfortunately, the official documentation about filter matching (`http://developer.android.com/guide/topics/intents/intents-filters.html`) is ambiguous and contains some errors.

So, to help you understand how intents match intent filters, I take a multifaceted approach. (That's a fancy way to say that I explain matching a few times in a few different ways.)

Matching: The general idea using a (silly) analogy

Two kinds of people sign up to participate in a speed-dating event. On one side of the room, each participant represents a part of an Android intent. (So one person is an action, the next two people are categories, and so on. I warned you that this analogy would be silly!) On the other side of the room, each participant represents a part of a filter. (See Figure 2-5.)

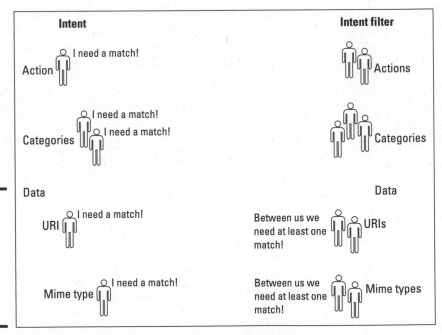

Figure 2-5: Intent elements and filter elements in a speed-dating event.

Like all dating situations, the room might be imbalanced. The filter might have more actions or more categories. The intent might have more data. It's almost never a fairy tale, one-to-one mix of people.

In this arena, some people are needier than others. For example, on the intent side, you have an action that absolutely insists on finding a match among the filters. On the filter side, you have a category that's speed dating only to keep a friend company. This nonchalant category doesn't need to find a match among the intent's categories.

As a quick (and not entirely accurate) rule, the entire intent matches the entire filter if and only if each needy person finds a match. Anyone who isn't needy doesn't have to be matched. That is, the whole speed-dating event is successful even if no one who's along only for the ride finds a match. Non-needy parts don't derail the overall match between the intent and the filter.

So who's needy and who isn't? Figure 2-5 gives you a rough idea.

The matching rules in Figures 2-5, 2-6, and 2-7 are general guidelines. The official rules include some important exceptions. For more info, see the next few sections.

The real story

An intent filter has three parts — actions, categories, and data. Android tests each part to determine whether a particular intent matches a particular filter. Each part consists of one or more Java strings. So, roughly speaking, an intent's part matches a filter's part if and only if `intent_part.equals(filter_part)`. In this situation, `equals` is Java's `String` comparison method.

In the preceding paragraph, I write "roughly speaking" because Android's rules for matching actions aren't quite the same as the rules for matching categories, which in turn are different from the rules for matching data entries. How do you decide whether the one action in an intent matches the many actions in a filter? And what do you do with each part of a URI? Stay tuned, because the next several sections answer these questions.

In the next few sections, be aware of the many kinds of matching — an intent with a filter, an intent with an activity, an intent action with a filter action, a scheme with an entire URI, and several other kinds of matching.

Java methods and XML elements

An intent's Java methods include the following:

- ✦ `setAction`: Sets the intent's action.
- ✦ `addCategory`: Adds a category to the intent.
- ✦ `setData`: Sets the intent's URI and removes the intent's MIME type (if the intent has a MIME type).

✦ setType: Sets the intent's MIME type and removes the intent's URI (if the intent has a URI).

✦ setDataAndType: Sets both the intent's URI and the intent's MIME type. According to the docs, "This method should very rarely be used."

You can describe an intent filter in an AndroidManifest.xml document or in Java code. In an AndroidManifest.xml document, the <intent-filter> element has <action>, <category>, and <data> subelements.

```
<action android:name="string" />

<category android:name="string" />

<data android:scheme="string"
      android:host="string"
      android:port="string"
      android:path="string"
      android:pathPattern="string"
      android:pathPrefix="string"
      android:mimeType="string" />
```

The intent methods and the data element's attributes aren't parallel. For example, with an intent's setAction method, you set an intent's one and only action (if you want the intent to have an action). But with a filter's <action> element, you add one of possibly many actions to the filter. With an intent's setData method, you set an intent's one and only URI (if you want the intent to have a URI). But with a filter's <data> elements, you add individual pieces of a URI.

You typically set a filter's values in the AndroidManifest.xml file. But in Java code, the android.content.IntentFilter class has lots of useful methods. I list a few here:

✦ addAction: Adds an action to the filter.

✦ addCategory: Adds a category to the filter.

✦ addDataScheme: Adds a scheme to the filter.

✦ addDataAuthority: Adds an authority to the filter.

✦ addDataPath: Adds a path to the filter.

✦ addDataType: Adds a MIME type to the filter.

As was the case with the intent methods and the data element's attributes, the intent methods and the filter methods aren't parallel. An intent's setAction method does the obvious — it sets an intent's action (if you want the intent to have an action). A filter's addAction method, however, lets you add one of possibly many actions to the filter. An intent's setData method sets an intent's URI (if you want the intent to have a URI). A filter's addDataScheme, addDataAuthority, and addDataPath methods, on the other hand, let you separately add pieces of a URI.

Matching actions

According to Figure 2-5, an intent's action must be matched with one of the filter's actions. That makes sense because an intent's action says, "I want a component that can do *such-and-such*." And the filter's action says, "I can do *such-and-such*." The filter might have other actions (be able to do other things), but having additional filter actions doesn't prevent an intent from matching with a filter.

Exactly what is an action? The simplest answer is that an *action* is a string. You can create your own action string `"thisismyaction"` or `"allmycode.intent.action.DO_THIS"` — Android's docs recommend the latter form. But Android also has a bunch of standard actions — actions reserved for certain kinds of work. For example, when a developer creates an activity that can display something (a document, a web page, an image, or whatever), the developer includes `"android.intent.action.VIEW"` in the activity's filter. Then, when you want someone else's activity to display something, you put the string `"android.intent.action.VIEW"` (or the constant `android.content.Intent.ACTION_VIEW`, whose value is the string `"android.intent.action.VIEW"`) in your intent.

Table 2-1 lists some of my favorite standard actions.

Book III
Chapter 2

Intents and
Intent Filters

Table 2-1	Some Standard Actions for Activities	
String Value	*Constant Name*	*An Activity with This Action in One of Its Filters Can . . .*
`"android.intent.action.MAIN"`	`Intent.ACTION_MAIN`	Be the first activity in a brand-new task stack (the task's *root* activity).
`"android.intent.action.VIEW"`	`Intent.ACTION_VIEW`	Display something.
`"android.intent.action.GET_CONTENT"`	`Intent.ACTION_GET_CONTENT`	Show the user a certain kind of data and then let the user choose an item from the displayed data. With this action, you don't specify the source (URI) of the data.

(continued)

Table 2-1 *(continued)*

String Value	Constant Name	An Activity with This Action in One of Its Filters Can . . .
"android. intent.action. PICK"	Intent.ACTION_ PICK	Show the user a certain kind of data and then let the user choose an item from the displayed data. With this action, you specify the source (URI) of the data.
"android. intent.action. INSERT_OR_EDIT"	Intent.ACTION_ INSERT_OR_EDIT	Same as Intent. ACTION_PICK except that the user can create a new item.
"android. intent.action. EDIT"	Intent.ACTION_ EDIT	Edit something.
"android. intent.action. INSERT"	Intent.ACTION_ INSERT	Add a new empty item to something. (You fill the item later.)
"android. intent.action. DELETE"	Intent.ACTION_ DELETE	Delete something.
"android. intent.action. PASTE"	Intent.ACTION_ PASTE	Paste something from the Clipboard.
"android. intent.action. SEARCH"	Intent.ACTION_ SEARCH	Search for something.
"android. intent. category. ALTERNATIVE"	Intent.ACTION_ WEB_SEARCH	Search for something on the Internet.
"android. intent.action. ANSWER"	Intent.ACTION_ ANSWER	Handle an incoming call.

String Value	Constant Name	An Activity with This Action in One of Its Filters Can . . .
`"android. intent.action. CALL"`	`Intent.ACTION_ CALL`	Make a phone call.
`"android. intent.action. DIAL"`	`Intent.ACTION_ DIAL`	Launch a dialer with a particular phone number in place, but let the user press the Dial button.
`"android. intent.action. SYNC"`	`Intent.ACTION_ SYNC`	Do data synchronization.
`"android. intent.action. SEND"`	`Intent.ACTION_ SEND`	Send data to a recipient (with the recipient "to be determined" after the activity is launched).
`"android. intent.action. SENDTO"`	`Intent.ACTION_ SENDTO`	Send data to a recipient (with the recipient specified as part of the intent).

For a complete list of Android's standard actions, visit `http:// developer.android.com/reference/android/content/ Intent.html`.

Here's a useful experiment:

1. **Create a new Android project with two activities — the main activity and a second** `OtherActivity.java` **activity.**

   For help creating an app's second activity, see Book 1, Chapter 6.

2. **Modify the second** `activity` **element in the project's** `AndroidManifest.xml` file **so that it reads as follows:**

```
<activity android:name=".OtherActivity">
  <intent-filter>
    <action
      android:name="com.allmycode.action.MY_ACTION" />
    <category
      android:name="android.intent.category.DEFAULT" />
  </intent-filter>
</activity>
```

3. **In the main activity, add the following code:**

```
final String THE_ACTION =
    "com.allmycode.action.MY_ACTION";
Intent = new Intent();
intent.setAction(THE_ACTION);
startActivity(intent);
```

   Add this code after the call to `setContentView` in the activity's `onCreate` method.

4. **Using Android Studio's Designer tool, change the layout of the other activity.**

   Any change is okay. The only reason for changing the other activity's layout is to help you recognize which of the two activities (the main activity or the other activity) is on the emulator's screen.

5. **Run the project.**

   As soon as your emulator executes the code in Step 3, Android launches the other activity. The intent's `"com.allmycode.action.MY_ACTION"` matches the filter's `"com.allmycode.action.MY_ACTION"`, so the other activity starts running.

   Real Android developers use a standard action (such as the actions in Table 2-1), or they make up dotted action names, such as `"com.allmycode.action.MY_ACTION"`. Real developers type that `"com.allmycode.action.MY_ACTION"` string in the `AndroidManifest.xml` file (because they must). But in the Java code, real developers create a constant value to represent the string (because it's good programming practice).

   The `category` element in Step 2 of this section's instructions is an anomaly that I cover in the later section "The fine print." If you don't want to skip to that section, simply add the category `"android.intent.category.DEFAULT"` to each filter in your `AndroidManifest.xml` file.

   Continuing the experiment . . .

6. **Comment out (or delete) the following element from your project's** `AndroidManifest.xml` **file:**

```
<action
  android:name="com.allmycode.action.MY_ACTION" />
```

7. **Run your project again.**

   When your emulator executes the Java code in Step 3, your app crashes. The filter has no action matching your intent's `"com.allmycode.action.MY_ACTION"`, and (in all likelihood) no other activity on your emulator has a filter containing `"com.allmycode.action.MY_ACTION"`.

In Step 7, your app intentionally crashes. Crashes make good learning experiences, but users tend not to appreciate such learning experiences. To avoid the kind of disaster you see in Step 7, call the `PackageManager` class's `queryIntentActivities` method before attempting to call `startActivity`. Alternatively, you can put your `startActivity` call in a try/catch block with the `ActivityNotFoundException`:

```
try {
  startActivity(intent);
} catch (ActivityNotFoundException e) {
  e.printStackTrace();
}
```

Working through these particular lines of code, note that they start out by telling Java to *try* `startActivity` — to call it, in other words. If Android can't start an activity (that is, if Android can't find an activity to match the `intent`), Java jumps to the statement `e.printStackTrace()`, which displays error information in Android Studio's Logcat panel. After displaying the information, Java marches on to execute whatever code comes after the attempt to call `startActivity`. Therefore, the app doesn't crash — the error has been *caught*.

For more on try/catch blocks, see Book II, Chapter 3.

8. **Uncomment the element that you commented out in Step 6.**

9. **Modify the other activity's element in the** `AndroidManifest.xml` **file as follows:**

```
<activity android:name=".OtherActivity">
  <intent-filter>
    <action
      android:name="com.allmycode.action.MY_ACTION" />
    <action
      android:name="com.allmycode.action.X_ACTION" />
    <category
      android:name="android.intent.category.DEFAULT" />
  </intent-filter>
</activity>
```

10. **Run the project again.**

When your emulator executes the Java code in Step 3, Android launches the other activity. The intent's `"com.allmycode.action.MY_ACTION"` matches the filter's `"com.allmycode.action.MY_ACTION"`, and the filter's additional `"com.allmycode.action.X_ACTION"` doesn't require a match.

Following this example's steps for each intent and filter that you want to test can become very tedious. So to help you test matches, I've created a special Android app. For details, see the "Practice, Practice, Practice" section, later in this chapter.

Matching categories

According to Figure 2-5, each of an intent's categories must be matched with one of the filter's categories. That makes sense because an intent's category says, "I want a component of *such-and-such* kind." And the filter's category says, "I'm a *such-and-such* kind of component." The filter might have other categories, but having additional filter categories doesn't prevent an intent from matching with a filter.

Exactly what is a category? Like an action, a *category* is a string. You can create your own category string "thisismycategory" or "allmycode.intent.category.THIS_KIND"; Android's docs recommend the latter form. But Android also has a bunch of standard categories — categories reserved for certain kinds of components. Table 2-2 lists some of my favorites.

Table 2-2	Some Standard Categories	
String Value	*Constant Name*	*An Activity with This Category in One of Its Filters Is . . .*
"android.intent.category.DEFAULT"	Intent.CATEGORY_DEFAULT	Able to respond to user actions and to be launched by calls to the startActivity and startActivityForResult methods.
"android.intent.category.BROWSABLE"	Intent.CATEGORY_BROWSABLE	Able to work in a web browser.
"android.intent.category.LAUNCHER"	Intent.CATEGORY_LAUNCHER	Displayed as an icon on the device's app launcher screen.
"android.intent.category.ALTERNATIVE"	Intent.CATEGORY_ALTERNATIVE	When the system offers the user a choice of activities to do a job, the system lists activities with filters possessing this category.
"android.intent.category.CAR_DOCK"	Intent.CATEGORY_CAR_DOCK	Launched when the user inserts the device into the dock of an automobile dashboard.

String Value	Constant Name	An Activity with This Category in One of Its Filters Is . . .
`"android.intent.category.MONKEY"`	`Intent.CATEGORY_MONKEY`	Able to run with automated software testing tools.
`"android.intent.category.APP_MARKET"`	`Intent.CATEGORY_APP_MARKET`	Able to browse and download new apps.
`"android.intent.category.HOME"`	`Intent.CATEGORY_HOME`	Launched when the device first boots.

Consider the kitty-cat intent created with the following Java code:

```
final String THE_ACTION =
       "com.allmycode.action.MY_ACTION";
final String THE_CATEGORY =
       "com.allmycode.category.KITTY";
Intent intent = new Intent();
intent.setAction(THE_ACTION);
intent.addCategory(THE_CATEGORY);
startActivity(intent);
```

This kitty-cat intent matches a filter with the following XML code:

```
<activity android:name=".OtherActivity">
  <intent-filter>
    <action
      android:name="com.allmycode.action.MY_ACTION" />
    <category
      android:name="com.allmycode.category.KITTY" />
    <category
      android:name="android.intent.category.DEFAULT" />
  </intent-filter>
</activity>
```

The kitty-cat intent also matches the following intent because (in the language of speed dating) *filter* categories aren't needy.

```
<activity android:name=".OtherActivity">
  <intent-filter>
    <action
      android:name="com.allmycode.action.MY_ACTION" />
    <category
      android:name="com.allmycode.category.KITTY" />
    <category
      android:name="Otto.Schmidlap" />
    <category
      android:name="android.intent.category.DEFAULT" />
  </intent-filter>
</activity>
```

The kitty-cat intent does not match the following intent because *an intent's* categories are needy:

```
<activity android:name=".OtherActivity">
  <intent-filter>
    <action
      android:name="com.allmycode.action.MY_ACTION" />
    <category
     android:name="Otto.Schmidlap" />
    <category
     android:name="android.intent.category.DEFAULT" />
  </intent-filter>
</activity>
```

Matching data

Figure 2-5 illustrates an interesting relationship between an intent's data and a filter's data:

+ If an intent has a URI or if a filter has a URI, one of the filter's URIs must match the intent's URI.

+ If an intent has a MIME type or if a filter has a MIME type, one of the filter's MIME types must match the intent's MIME type.

These rules have some corollaries:

+ An intent without a URI cannot match a filter with a URI. A filter without a URI cannot match an intent with a URI.

+ An intent without a MIME type cannot match a filter with a MIME type. A filter without a MIME type cannot match an intent with a MIME type.

How does all this stuff about URIs and MIME types make sense? The deal is, data doesn't perform the same role as an action or a category in matching a filter with an intent. Imagine that an intent announces, "I want a component to perform `android.intent.action.VIEW`", and a certain activity's filter announces, "I can perform `android.intent.action.VIEW`". The intent doesn't care if the filter announces that it can perform other actions.

But what if an intent announces, "I want a component to handle the URI `tel:6502530000`"? (The URI `tel:6502530000` places a call to Google's corporate headquarters in Mountain View, California.) An appropriate filter contains the `tel` scheme. (See Figure 2-6.) Now, imagine another intent with no `tel:` URI and a filter whose only scheme is the `tel` scheme. (Again, see Figure 2-6.) In this case, the filter says, "I can do something useful with a telephone number, and when I'm invoked, I expect to receive a telephone number." If the intent has no `tel:` URI, a match isn't appropriate.

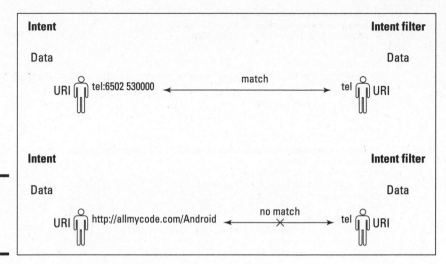

So the coupling between an intent's and a filter's data is stronger than the coupling between actions or the coupling between categories. With the URI part of the data, both the intent and the filter are needy. The same is true of the data's MIME types.

The following intent and filter form a match:

```
final String THE_ACTION =
        "com.allmycode.action.MY_ACTION";
Intent intent = new Intent();
intent.setAction(THE_ACTION);
intent.setData(Uri.parse("http:"));
startActivity(intent);

<intent-filter>
  <action
    android:name="com.allmycode.action.MY_ACTION" />
  <category
    android:name="android.intent.category.DEFAULT" />
  <data android:scheme="http" />
  <data android:scheme="mymadeupscheme" />
</intent-filter>
```

The same intent with a slightly modified filter does *not* form a match because the set of MIME types in a filter is needy:

```
<intent-filter>
  <action
    android:name="com.allmycode.action.MY_ACTION" />
  <category
    android:name="android.intent.category.DEFAULT" />
```

**Book III
Chapter 2**

**Intents and
Intent Filters**

```
  <data android:scheme="http" />
  <data android:scheme="mymadeupscheme" />
  <data android:mimeType="text/html" />
</intent-filter>
```

To match this modified filter, you need either of the following intents:

```
final String THE_ACTION =
        "com.allmycode.action.MY_ACTION";
Intent intent = new Intent();
intent.setAction(THE_ACTION);
intent.setDataAndType(Uri.parse("http:"), "text/html");
startActivity(intent);
final String THE_ACTION =
        "com.allmycode.action.MY_ACTION";
Intent intent = new Intent();
intent.setAction(THE_ACTION);
intent.setDataAndType
    (Uri.parse("mymadeupscheme:"), "text/html");
startActivity(intent);
```

Finally, the following intent and filter form a match because the MIME type in the intent matches one of the MIME types in the filter:

```
final String THE_ACTION =
        "com.allmycode.action.MY_ACTION";
Intent intent = new Intent();
intent.setAction(THE_ACTION);
intent.setType("text/html");
startActivity(intent);
```

```
<intent-filter>
  <action
    android:name="com.allmycode.action.MY_ACTION" />
  <category
    android:name="android.intent.category.DEFAULT" />
  <data android:mimeType="abc/xyz" />
  <data android:mimeType="text/html" />
</intent-filter>
```

Matching parts of the data

The section "Java methods and XML elements," earlier in this chapter, lists methods and XML elements. With an intent's setData method, you set an intent's URI (if you want the intent to have a URI). With a filter's <data> elements, you add individual pieces of a URI. The filter's pieces don't have to fit together. For example, the following intent and filter form a match:

```
final String THE_ACTION =
        "com.allmycode.action.MY_ACTION";
Intent intent = new Intent();
intent.setAction(THE_ACTION);
intent.setData(Uri.parse("abc://example.com:2222"));
startActivity(intent);
```

```
<intent-filter>
  <data android:scheme="xyz" android:host="example.com" />
  <data android:port="2222" />
  <action
    android:name="com.allmycode.action.MY_ACTION" />
  <category
    android:name="android.intent.category.DEFAULT" />
  <data android:scheme="abc" />
</intent-filter>
```

A filter can have schemes `"abc"` and `"xyz"`, and authority `"example.com"`. Then the filter's data matches both intent data `"abc://example.com"` and intent data `"xyz://example.com"`. This works even if you lump `"xyz"` and `"example.com"` in the same `<data>` element.

With a filter's `addDataScheme`, `addDataAuthority`, and `addDataPath` methods, you separately add pieces of a URI. For example, the following intent and filter form a match:

```
final String THE_ACTION =
        "com.allmycode.action.MY_ACTION";
Intent intent = new Intent();
intent.setAction(THE_ACTION);
intent.setData(Uri.parse("abc://example.com:2222"));

final IntentFilter filter = new IntentFilter();
filter.addAction(THE_ACTION);
// Constant com.content.Intent.CATEGORY_DEFAULT has
//   value "android.intent.category.DEFAULT"
filter.addCategory(Intent.CATEGORY_DEFAULT);
filter.addDataScheme("abc");
filter.addDataScheme("xyz");
filter.addDataAuthority("example.com", "2222");
```

At this point, a few observations are in order:

✦ An intent has three similar methods @@ `setData`, `setDataAndType`, and `setType`. You call `setData` for an intent with a URI but no MIME type. You call `setType` for an intent with a MIME type but no URI. You call `setDataAndType` only for an intent with both a URI and a MIME type.

✦ You don't pass a string to the `setData` method or to the first parameter of the `setDataAndType` method. Instead, you pass an instance of the `android.net.Uri` class. You do this by applying the method `Uri.parse` to a string of characters.

✦ Here's a silly but important detail: A call to `intent.setData(Uri.parse("http:"))` with a colon after `http` matches the filter element `<data android:scheme="http" />` *without* a colon after the `http`. Other combinations of colon/no-colon for a URI scheme fail to make a match.

Matching URIs

Figure 2-5 illustrates an imaginary speed-dating event for the parts of an intent and an intent filter. The figure doesn't address the matching of one URI with another. So imagine that the URIs in Figure 2-5 bring their darling little children (their schemes, authorities, and paths) to the speed-dating event. As the evening begins, the kids go off to a separate room for a speed-dating event of their own. (Sure, they're too young to date. But it's good practice for adolescence.) Figure 2-7 illustrates the neediness situation in the kids' event.

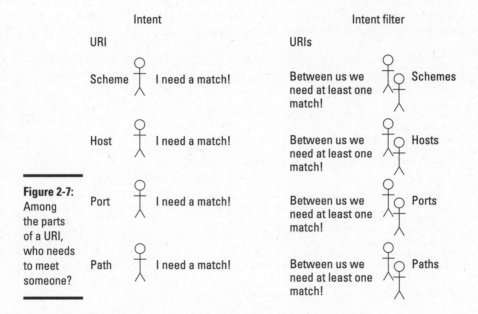

Figure 2-7: Among the parts of a URI, who needs to meet someone?

The situation with the URI's kids is similar to the situation with all data. Everybody's happy as long as each thing on the intent side matches something on the filter side. For example, the following intent and filter form a match:

```
final String THE_ACTION =
      "com.allmycode.action.MY_ACTION";
Intent intent = new Intent();
intent.setAction(THE_ACTION);
intent.setData(Uri.parse("abc://example.com:2222"));
startActivity(intent);
<intent-filter>
  <action
    android:name="com.allmycode.action.MY_ACTION" />
  <category
    android:name="android.intent.category.DEFAULT" />
  <data android:scheme="abc" />
</intent-filter>
```

But with the same intent, the following filter isn't a match:

```
<intent-filter>
  <action
    android:name="com.allmycode.action.MY_ACTION" />
  <category
    android:name="android.intent.category.DEFAULT" />
  <data android:scheme="abc" />
  <data android:host="example.com" />
  <data android:port="2222" />
  <data android:path="/some/stuff" />
</intent-filter>
```

The fine print

With all the fuss about filter matching in the previous sections, you'd think the issue was covered and done with. But the work is never done. Here's a list of filter matching's most important gotchas and exceptions:

✦ Android treats activities differently from other components (such as services and broadcast receivers).

You can create an implicit intent with no actions. If you do, a call to `startActivity(intent)` doesn't find a match among any activity filters. However, calls to `sendBroadcast(intent)` or to `bindService(intent,...)` may find matches.

✦ With respect to categories, Android treats activities differently from other components.

When you try to start an activity, Android behaves as if the intent contains the `"android.intent.category.DEFAULT"` category. (Android does this even if you don't execute code to add that category to the intent.) Because of this, an activity filter without the `"android.intent.category.DEFAULT"` category never matches an intent. Broadcast receivers and services don't suffer from this anomaly.

The activity that starts when the user first presses an app's icon is the app's *main activity*. A main activity's filter normally contains the action `"android.intent.action.MAIN"` and the category `"android.intent.category.LAUNCHER"`. If you want an activity to function only as a main activity (and never be started by an app's call to `startActivity`), you can safely omit `"android.intent.category.DEFAULT"` from the activity's filter.

✦ Flip back to Figure 2-3 to see the kinds of URIs you can create. A URI with an authority must have a scheme, and a URI with a path must have an authority and a scheme. Also, a port without a host is ignored. So the following strings are not valid URIs:

• `example.com`: Has an authority but no scheme.

• `http:///folder/subfolder`: Has a path but no authority.

**Book III
Chapter 2**

Intents and
Intent Filters

The official Android docs provide the following loophole: " . . . if a host is not specified, the port is ignored." So a URI like `http://:2000/folder` is strange but valid. I've created such URIs in captivity, but I've never encountered one in the wild.

✦ A filter URI with nothing but a scheme matches any intent URI with the same scheme. Take, for example, the intent URI to call Google's corporate headquarters, `tel:6502530000`. An appropriate filter probably contains the `tel` scheme but not the number `6502530000`. (A filter whose sole URI is `tel:6502530000` can call *only* Google's corporate headquarters. The filter would be useful only for an Unsatisfied Google Customer app.)

In the same way, a filter URI with a scheme, an authority, and no path matches any intent filter with the same scheme and the same authority.

✦ The schemes `content` and `file` get special treatment. If the intent's URI has scheme `content` or scheme `file`, and the intent has a MIME type, you can omit the scheme from the filter. (You must still have a match between the intent's MIME type and one of the filter's MIME types.) Someday this rule will make sense to me.

✦ Certain parts of the data may contain wildcards or simplified regular expressions. Here are a few examples:

- The type `text/*` matches `text/plain`. The type `text/*` also matches `text/html` and `text/whatever`. The type `text/*` matches `text/` (with a slash and no subtype) but does not match `text` (with no slash and no subtype).

- The type `*/*` matches `text/plain`. The type `*/*` also matches `image/jpeg`, and so on.

- The type `*` (one wildcard with no slash) and `*/html` don't seem to match anything.

- The type `text/ht*` doesn't match `text/html`. (With a top-level type or a subtype, the wildcard must be "all or nothing.")

- Paths use a simplified regular expression form. (In other words, paths can include wildcards and other funky symbols.) For example, the intent URI `http://example.com/folder` matches the filter URI with scheme `http`, authority `example.com`, and path pattern `/fol.*`. In the `AndroidManifest.xml` file, the data element's `android:path`, `android:pathPrefix`, and `android:pathPattern` attributes distinguish among the various possibilities.

For more information about path expressions, visit `http://developer.android.com/guide/topics/manifest/data-element.html`.

- With the exception of the host name, the strings in an intent and its filter are case-sensitive. So `text/html` doesn't match `TEXT/HTML`, and `HTTP` doesn't match `http`. But `http://example.com` matches `http://EXAMPLE.com`. Android's docs recommend using mostly lowercase letters.

Practice, Practice, Practice

If I had a nickel for every time I misinterpreted something in Android's Intent Filters documentation, I'd have enough to fill my tank with gas. (That's pretty impressive, isn't it?) I want to believe that this chapter's sections on intent and filter matching are clear and unambiguous. But in my heart, I know that almost all spoken-language sentences are moving targets. Take, for example, the following sentences:

Put Mommy in the car behind us.

I want David Copperfield to read.

I'll put the bandage on myself.

Everything shouldn't be blue.

Chew one tablet three times a day until finished.

I saved everyone five dollars.

Cars towed at owner's expense.

Our cream is so gentle that it never stings most people, even after shaving.

I hope someday that you love me as much as Amy.

If he were to learn that wild bears are related to dogs, and never hurt people, then he'd be happier.

The best test of your understanding is not the way you nod while you read this book's paragraphs. Instead, the best test is when you try your own examples on an emulator or a device. If you can accurately predict the results much of the time, you understand the subject.

Unfortunately, testing intent and filter matching can be tedious. For every change, you have to edit Java code, then edit the `AndroidManifest.xml` file, and then reinstall your app. Some time ago, after many hours of such testing, I was "mad as hell and I wasn't going to take it anymore." I wrote an app to test filter matches one after another without modifying files or reinstalling anything. I named it the Intentsity app (because, as an author, I'm tired of worrying about things being spelled correctly). Needless to say, the app is available for your use through this book's website — `www.allmycode.com/android`. (You can thank me later.)

The upper half of the app's main screen is shown in Figure 2-8.

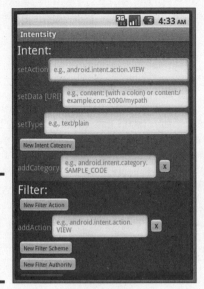

Figure 2-8:
A screen
for entering
intent and
intent filter
strings.

The Intentsity app's screen has an Intent part and a Filter part. Both parts have EditText fields for filling in `String` values. Each EditText field represents an `Intent` instance method or an `IntentFilter` instance method. (For a list of such methods, see the section "Java methods and XML elements," earlier in this chapter.)

Android has no features for setting an activity's intent filter using Java code. But you can create another component — a broadcast receiver — and set the broadcast receiver's filter using Java code. (You use the `IntentFilter` method calls described in the "Java methods and XML elements" section.) Accordingly, my Intentsity app tests the values you type in the EditText fields by attempting to communicate with a broadcast receiver. The fields in the lower part of the app (the Filter fields) match with the Java methods for creating an `IntentFilter` object, not with the attributes in the `AndroidManifest.xml` document. To keep things as faithful as possible to Android's real behavior, my app respects the fact that a broadcast receiver's filter can do without the category `"android.intent.category.DEFAULT"`. So, when you move from the Intentsity app to your own project, remember to add `"android.intent.category.DEFAULT"` to your activities' filters.

The section "Java methods and XML elements," earlier in this chapter, lists methods like `setAction` and `addCategory`. Methods beginning with `set` are for things like an intent's action because an intent can't have more than one action. Methods beginning with `add` are for things like an intent's category, because an intent can have more than one category.

Figure 2-8 shows a New Intent Category button. When you click this button, the app creates an additional `addCategory` row.

Figure 2-9 shows the bottom of the Intentsity app's scrolling screen.

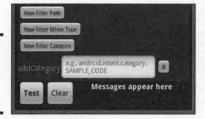

Figure 2-9: Press Test to check for a match.

After filling in some EditText fields, click the Test button, and the app does what it does best:

✦ The app calls the `Intent` class's methods to compose an intent from your Intent fields' entries.

✦ The app calls the `IntentFilter` class's methods to compose a filter from your Filter fields' entries.

✦ The app calls `registerReceiver(myReceiver, filter)` to create a broadcast receiver with the new filter.

✦ The app calls `sendBroadcast(intent)` to shout out to all the system's broadcast receivers.

If the receiver's filter matches your intent, the receiver displays a screen like the one in Figure 2-10.

With or without a match, the app displays `toString` versions of your intent and intent filter. Figure 2-11 shows the display for a failed attempt to match.

The Intentsity app doesn't want you to type variables in the EditText fields. In your own Java code, the call `setAction(Intent.ACTION_VIEW)` sets the intent's action to the string `"android.intent.action.VIEW"`. But in the Intentsity app, typing `Intent.ACTION_VIEW` in the topmost field sets the intent's action to the string `"Intent.ACTION_VIEW"`, which is not equal to (and therefore doesn't match) a filter string `"android.intent.action.VIEW"`.

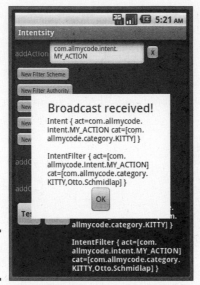

Figure 2-10:
It's a match!

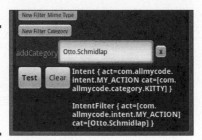

Figure 2-11:
The app
displays the
values in an
intent and a
filter.

Activities and Stacks

The activity that starts when the user first presses an app's icon is the app's *main activity*. When the user first presses the app's icon, this main activity becomes the *root activity* in a new task stack. At first, the root activity is the only activity on the task stack. (In Figure 2-12, the app is named App A, and the app's main activity is named A1.)

For an introduction to Android's tasks, see Chapter 1 of this minibook.

Imagine that the main activity displays a button. When the user presses that button, Android launches another of Application A's activities. As a task stack grows, the root activity remains at the bottom of the task stack. (See Figure 2-13.)

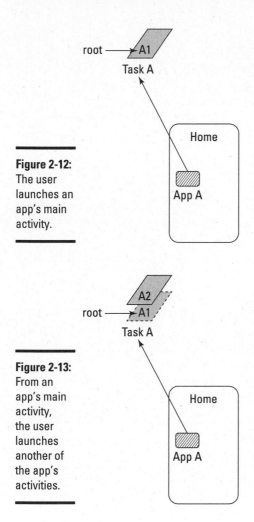

Figure 2-12:
The user launches an app's main activity.

Figure 2-13:
From an app's main activity, the user launches another of the app's activities.

At this point, the user sees activity A2. (Activity A1 isn't visible. Activity A1 has been Stopped. Think of Activity A1 as being hidden beneath Activity A2.)

Now imagine that the user presses the device's Home button. Then, on the Home screen, the user touches another app's icon (the icon for Application B). This creates a brand new task stack (Task B in Figure 2-14).

At this point, the user sees activity B1. (Task A has been placed on the back burner.) Of course, actions taken in Application B can launch other activities of Application B. Each new activity goes on top of the Task B stack. (See Figure 2-15.)

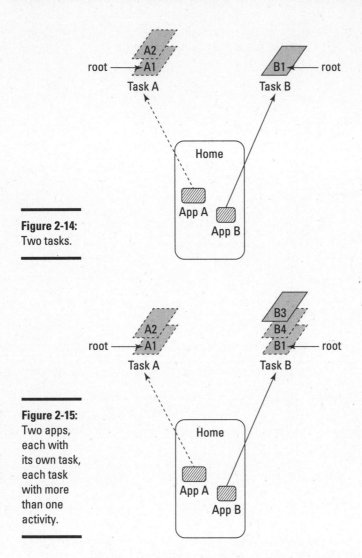

Figure 2-14:
Two tasks.

Figure 2-15:
Two apps,
each with
its own task,
each task
with more
than one
activity.

Look again at Figure 2-15. When Activity B3 starts up, the user sees Activity B3 on the device's screen. Activities B4 and B1 are waiting behind B3, and the whole of Task A is sitting silently somewhere in Android's virtual holding space.

If an app has several activities, those activities don't necessarily come in any particular order. In Figure 2-15, I emphasize this point by starting activities B1, B4, and then B3. If Application B has an activity named B2, I skip that activity entirely.

If the user presses the device's Back button, Activity B3 pops off of the Task B stack, and Activity B4 reappears. (See Figure 2-16.)

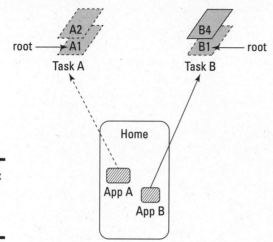

Figure 2-16:
Activity B3
has been
destroyed.

But imagine that the user presses the device's Home button followed by Application A's icon. Task A belongs to Application A, so Android shifts its attention back to Task A. The user sees Activity A2 (the activity on top of the Task A stack) on the device's screen. (See Figure 2-17.)

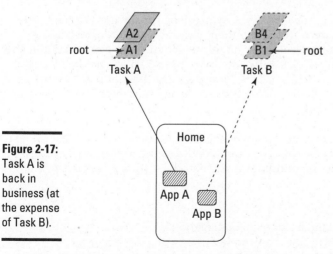

Figure 2-17:
Task A is
back in
business (at
the expense
of Task B).

But here's an interesting wrinkle. A call to `startActivity` in Activity A's code can launch an activity belonging to a different app (Application B, for example). When this happens, Android launches Activity B by pushing

Activity B onto Activity A's task stack. So one task may contain activities belonging to more than one application. (See Figure 2-18.)

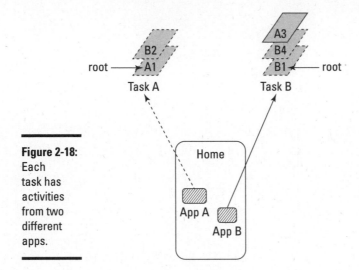

Figure 2-18:
Each task has activities from two different apps.

How does Android keep all this straight (without driving Joe User crazy)? Here's how: Each task stack is associated with a single application — namely, the app containing the task stack's root activity. And, typically, that single application has an icon on the device's Home screen or Apps screen.

The user can switch between tasks by pressing the device's Home button (and maybe the Apps button) and then pressing the icon whose app is associated with the desired task. Alternatively, the user can find the desired app by pressing the device's Recents button (also known as the *Overview* button). Look again at Figure 2-18. After pressing the A app's icon, the user sees whatever is at the top of A's task stack, and that might be an activity belonging to the B app.

The user has task-level control over the device's behavior. The user doesn't have activity-level control. (For example, the user can't routinely return to an activity that's in the middle [rather than the top] of a task stack.)

Fly the flag

An intent can contain six kinds of information:

✦ The name of a component to be invoked (making the intent an *explicit* intent rather than an *implicit* intent)

✦ A set of extras

✦ One action

✦ A set of categories

✦ Some data (one URI and/or one MIME type)

✦ A set of flags

I cover the first two kinds of information in Chapter 1 of this minibook, and I beat the third, fourth, and fifth kinds of information to death in this chapter's previous sections. So this section deals with the sixth kind of information — namely, flags.

A *flag* tells Android how to deal with a component. In most cases, the component is an activity that you're launching by calling `startActivity` or `startActivityForResult`. A typical programming pattern is as follows:

```
Intent = new Intent();
intent.setAction(someActionString);
intent.addCategory(someCategoryString);
intent.addFlags(int_value_representing_one_or_more_flags);
startActivity(intent);
```

Examples of Android's standard flags include the following:

✦ `Intent.FLAG_ACTIVITY_NO_ANIMATION`: When starting the new activity, don't animate the activity's entrance. That is, if the norm is to slide the new activity over the existing activity, don't slide it. Just make the new activity "poof" onto the screen.

✦ `Intent.FLAG_ACTIVITY_NO_HISTORY`: Start the new activity, but destroy this new activity as soon as the user navigates away from it. For example, if the user presses Home and then returns to this task, restore the task as if this new activity had never been added. (See Figure 2-19.)

✦ `Intent.FLAG_ACTIVITY_SINGLE_TOP`: If an instance of the activity is already on top of the activity stack, don't start another instance of that activity. Instead, use the instance that's already on top of the stack. (See Figure 2-20.)

✦ `Intent.FLAG_ACTIVITY_CLEAR_TOP`: If the activity being started already has an instance somewhere on the task stack, don't add a new instance at the top of the task stack. Instead, grab all activities above the existing instance, and pop them off the stack. (Yes, destroy them.) See Figure 2-21.

✦ `Intent.FLAG_ACTIVITY_NEW_TASK`: Each task is associated with an application. Imagine that you have two applications — App A and App B — and that the currently active task is associated with App A. Inside this task, you call `startActivity` to launch an activity in the other app — App B. What happens?

Without FLAG_ACTIVITY_NO_HISTORY:

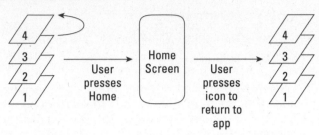

With FLAG_ACTIVITY_NO_HISTORY:

Figure 2-19:
The effect
of adding
FLAG_
ACTIVITY_
NO_
HISTORY.

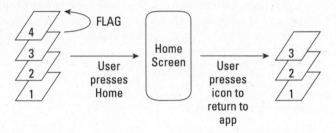

Without FLAG_ACTIVITY_SINGLE_TOP:

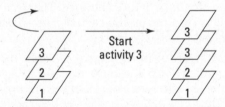

Figure 2-20:
The effect
of adding
FLAG_
ACTIVITY_
SINGLE_
TOP.

With FLAG_ACTIVITY_SINGLE_TOP:

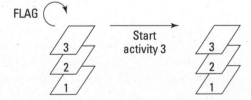

✦ Without the FLAG_ACTIVITY_NEW_TASK flag, Android pushes the newly starting activity on top of the current stack. (See Figure 2-22.) But with the FLAG_ACTIVITY_NEW_TASK flag, Android looks for a task associated with App B.

• *If Android finds such a task,* Android pushes the newly starting activity onto that task.

• *If Android doesn't find such a task,* Android creates a task associated with App B. (Refer to Figure 2-22.)

With or without a previously existing App B task, Android displays the newly started activity on the user's screen.

Without FLAG_ACTIVITY_CLEAR_TOP:

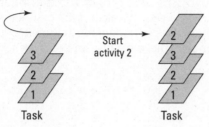

With FLAG_ACTIVITY_CLEAR_TOP:

Figure 2-21:
The effect of adding FLAG_ ACTIVITY_ CLEAR_TOP.

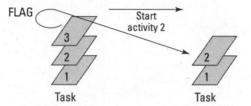

Without FLAG_ACTIVITY_NEW_TASK:

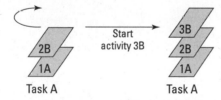

Installed applications:
com.example.A
com.example.B

With FLAG_ACTIVITY_NEW_TASK:

Figure 2-22:
The effect of adding FLAG_ ACTIVITY_ NEW_TASK.

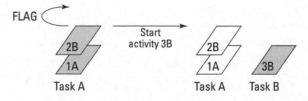

✦ `Intent.FLAG_ACTIVITY_EXCLUDE_FROM_RECENTS`: Don't display this activity's app when the user presses the device's Recents button.

Android creates a `"Recents"` item when you create a new task. Combining `FLAG_ACTIVITY_EXCLUDE_FROM_RECENTS` with `FLAG_ACTIVITY_NEW_TASK` suppresses the creation of a new `"Recents"` item.

✦ `Intent.FLAG_ACTIVITY_CLEAR_TASK`: When used with `FLAG_ACTIVITY_NEW_TASK` and the new activity is already part of a task, make the task containing the activity be the active task *and* obliterate all other activities currently on that task. (See Figure 2-23.)

Without flags:

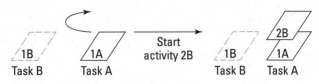

With FLAG_ACTIVITY_NEW_TASK:

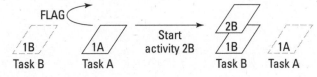

Figure 2-23:
The effect
of adding
FLAG_
ACTIVITY_
CLEAR_
TASK.

With FLAG_ACTIVITY_NEW_TASK and FLAG_ACTIVITY_CLEAR_TASK:

The `FLAG_ACTIVITY_CLEAR_TASK` feature joined Android's SDK with the release of Honeycomb. If your minimum SDK is older than Honeycomb, don't try to use `FLAG_ACTIVITY_CLEAR_TASK`.

✦ `Intent.FLAG_ACTIVITY_REORDER_TO_FRONT`: If an instance of the activity being started is already part of the current task, reorder the task's activities so that the instance is on top. (See Figure 2-24.)

✦ `Intent.FLAG_EXCLUDE_STOPPED_PACKAGES`: When searching for an activity to start, consider only activities that are currently active or paused.

Without FLAG_ACTIVITY_REORDER_TO_FRONT:

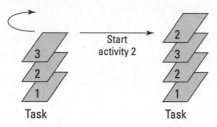

Start
activity 2

Task   Task

Figure 2-24:
The effect
of adding
FLAG_
ACTIVITY_
REORDER_
TO_FRONT.

With FLAG_ACTIVITY_REORDER_TO_FRONT:

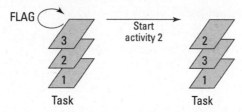

FLAG

Start
activity 2

Task   Task

Each of these flags has a Java int value, and you can combine two or more flags with Java's bitwise OR operator (|). For example, you can write

```
intent.addFlags(FLAG_ACTIVITY_NEW_TASK |
                FLAG_ACTIVITY_CLEAR_TASK);
```

The result is 0x10000000 | 0x00008000, which is 0x10008000.

The FLAG_ACTIVITY_CLEAR_TASK feature joined Android's SDK with the release of Honeycomb. If you try to use this flag's numeric value (0x00008000) on a pre-Honeycomb system, you don't get a compile-time error. After all, the compiler thinks 0x00008000 is a perfectly good hexadecimal number, even when you pass the number to the addFlags method. But at runtime, a pre-Honeycomb system says, "I can't do addFlags(0x00008000), so I think I'll display a rude application has stopped unexpectedly message." So to catch such errors before runtime, always use the constant name FLAG_ACTIVITY_CLEAR_TASK as well as other SDK constants.

Keeping an eye on activities and tasks

To test your intent flags, you must keep track of the apps, tasks, and activities as they run on your emulator or device. This isn't always straightforward.

Fortunately, Android's dumpsys command can show you a snapshot of the current state of affairs. Here's how:

1. **In Android Studio's main menu, choose Run⇨Run 'app'.**

An app starts running on an emulator or device of your choosing.

2. **At the bottom of Android Studio's main window, click the Terminal tool button.**

As a result, your development computer's Terminal or Command Prompt (MS-DOS) window appears in the lower portion of the Android Studio window.

3. **In the Terminal panel, type** adb shell.

As a result, you see the pound sign (#) prompt. This prompt comes from the Android system (the emulator or the real device). Whatever command you type next goes directly to the running Android system.

4. **Type** dumpsys activity.

A lot of text whizzes by very quickly in the Terminal panel. Fortunately, you can scroll to see text that raced off the screen.

If you do a bit of scrolling, you see something like this:

```
ACTIVITY MANAGER ACTIVITIES (dumpsys activity activities)
Display #0 (activities from top to bottom):
  Stack #1:
  Task id #268
    TaskRecord{ae33feb #268 A=com.allyourcode.appb U=0 sz=1}
    Intent { act=android.intent.action.MAIN
    cat=[android.intent.category.LAUNCHER] flg=0x10000000
    cmp=com.allyourcode.appb/.MainActivity }
    Hist #0: ActivityRecord{e150d7c u0
    com.allyourcode.appb/.MainActivity t268}
      Intent { act=android.intent.action.MAIN
    cat=[android.intent.category.LAUNCHER] flg=0x10000000
     cmp=com.allyourcode.appb/.MainActivity }
      ProcessRecord{28bf81bb 1447:com.allyourcode.appb/u0a89}
  Task id #267
    TaskRecord{3afe0148 #267 A=com.allyourcode.appa U=0 sz=2}
    Intent { act=android.intent.action.MAIN
    cat=[android.intent.category.LAUNCHER] flg=0x10000000
    cmp=com.allyourcode.appa/.MainActivity }
    Hist #1: ActivityRecord{1dc06f54 u0
    com.allyourcode.appa/.Activity2A t267}
      Intent { cmp=com.allyourcode.appa/.Activity2A }
      ProcessRecord{4b366d8 1388:com.allyourcode.appa/u0a88}
    Hist #0: ActivityRecord{2e0b1892 u0
    com.allyourcode.appa/.MainActivity t267}
      Intent { act=android.intent.action.MAIN
    cat=[android.intent.category.LAUNCHER] flg=0x10000000
    cmp=com.allyourcode.appa/.MainActivity }
      ProcessRecord{4b366d8 1388:com.allyourcode.appa/u0a88}
```

```
Running activities (most recent first):
  TaskRecord{ae33feb #268 A=com.allyourcode.appb U=0 sz=1}
  Run #2: ActivityRecord{e150d7c u0
  com.allyourcode.appb/.MainActivity t268}
  TaskRecord{3afe0148 #267 A=com.allyourcode.appa U=0 sz=2}
  Run #1: ActivityRecord{1dc06f54 u0
  com.allyourcode.appa/.Activity2A t267}
  Run #0: ActivityRecord{2e0b1892 u0
  com.allyourcode.appa/.MainActivity t267}

mResumedActivity: ActivityRecord{e150d7c u0
  com.allyourcode.appb/.MainActivity t268}

Stack #0:
Task id #266
  TaskRecord{83aabe1 #266 A=com.android.launcher3 U=0 sz=1}
  Intent { act=android.intent.action.MAIN
  cat=[android.intent.category.HOME] flg=0x10000000
  cmp=com.android.launcher3/.Launcher }
  Hist #0: ActivityRecord{3bf784bb u0
  com.android.launcher3/.Launcher t266}
    Intent { act=android.intent.action.MAIN
  cat=[android.intent.category.HOME] flg=0x10000000
  cmp=com.android.launcher3/.Launcher }
    ProcessRecord{1941462e 807:com.android.launcher3/u0a37}

  Running activities (most recent first):
    TaskRecord{83aabe1 #266 A=com.android.launcher3 U=0 sz=1}
    Run #0: ActivityRecord{3bf784bb u0
    com.android.launcher3/.Launcher t266}
```

With some careful experimentation, you'll be able to decipher the output of the `dumpsys activity` command and to use the output to gain a deeper understanding of Android's activities, tasks, and intent flags.

Needless to say, I created an app to help you experiment with intent flags. My flag-testing app is very much like the Intentsity app that I describe previously in this chapter. You can download the Flagacity app and its source code from this book's website — www.allmycode.com/android.

Chapter 3: Services

In This Chapter

↳ **Running code without bothering the user**

↳ **Running code when a device starts**

↳ **Starting, binding, and querying**

↳ **Sending messages from one process to another**

Some things are of no concern to the user of an Android device. Imagine seeing a pop-up message saying, "A process on your phone is checking for email right now," followed immediately by the message, "Nope, no new email. Sorry about the interruption. Get back to what you were doing. You'll hear from me again in exactly one minute." One of my phones actually did this! Such notices are intrusive and unnecessary, especially on a device with limited screen real estate.

To do something behind the scenes, you don't want an Android activity. An activity normally has a layout file, and the user deals with the layout's gizmos on the screen. Instead, you want the kind of component that runs quietly in the background. In other words, you want an Android service.

A Very Simple Service

I start this chapter with an embarrassingly simple example — a service that doesn't do anything. This lazy service simply illustrates the minimum service source code requirements.

The service

Listing 3-1 contains the good-for-nothing service.

In truth, the service in Listing 3-1 has more code than is absolutely necessary. As a subclass of the abstract `android.app.Service` class, the only required method in Listing 3-1 is `onBind`. Still, the listing's `onStartCommand` and `onDestroy` methods are a bit more useful than the methods that would be inherited from the `android.app.Service` class.

Listing 3-1: An Un-Weather Service

```
package com.allyourcode.p03_03_01;

import android.app.Service;
import android.content.Intent;
import android.os.IBinder;
import android.widget.Toast;

public class MyWeatherService extends Service {

  @Override
  public IBinder onBind(Intent intent) {
    Toast.makeText(this, R.string.service_bound,
                         Toast.LENGTH_SHORT).show();
    return null;
  }

  @Override
  public int onStartCommand(Intent intent,
                            int flags, int startId) {
    Toast.makeText(this, R.string.service_started,
                         Toast.LENGTH_SHORT).show();
    return START_NOT_STICKY;
  }

  @Override
  public void onDestroy() {
    Toast.makeText(this, R.string.service_destroyed,
                         Toast.LENGTH_SHORT).show();
  }
}
```

The required `onBind` method in Listing 3-1 returns `null`. Normally, the object returned by an `onBind` method implements the `android.os.IBinder` interface, and an object that implements `IBinder` allows one process to exchange information with another process. That's nice, but in this simple example, the service doesn't exchange information.

I put the service from Listing 3-1 in its own Android Studio project, with its own package name. So this service runs as its own application on an emulator or a device. The service has no user interface (and, therefore, no layout file). The application's `AndroidManifest.xml` file has no `<activity>` element but instead has the `<service>` element shown in Listing 3-2.

In Listing 3-2, the attribute `android:exported="true"` is not optional. Starting with Android's Lollipop version, an intent that starts a service must be an explicit intent. So, to start this section's service from an activity that's not in the `com.allyourcode.p03_03_01` package, you must include `android:exported="true"` in the service's `AndroidManifest.xml` file.

Listing 3-2: The Un-Weather Service's AndroidManifest.xml File

```xml
<?xml version="1.0" encoding="utf-8"?>
<manifest
  package="com.allyourcode.p03_03_01"
  xmlns:android="http://schemas.android.com/apk/res/android">

  <application
    android:allowBackup="true"
    android:icon="@drawable/ic_launcher"
    android:label="@string/app_name"
    android:theme="@style/AppTheme">
    <service
      android:name=".MyWeatherService"
      android:enabled="true"
      android:exported="true">
    </service>
  </application>

</manifest>
```

When you install an app with no main activity (like the app in Listings 3-1 and 3-2), Android Studio prompts you with an Edit Configuration dialog box. In this dialog box, check the Do Not Launch Activity radio button, and then press Run.

A client activity

To start the service in Listing 3-1, other components refer to the name of Java class. Listing 3-3 shows you how.

The activity in Listing 3-3 has two buttons — a Start button and a Stop button. (See Figure 3-1.)

Figure 3-1:
Start and
stop a
service.
How simple
is that?

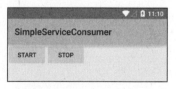

Again, starting with Android's Lollipop version, an intent that starts a service must be an explicit intent. That's why you call `intent.setClassName` in Listing 3-3.

Listing 3-3: A Client for the Un-Weather Service

```
package com.allyourcode.p03_03_03;

import android.app.Activity;
import android.content.Intent;
import android.os.Bundle;
import android.view.View;

public class ServiceConsumerActivity extends Activity {
  Intent intent = new Intent();

  @Override
  public void onCreate(Bundle savedInstanceState) {
    super.onCreate(savedInstanceState);
    setContentView(R.layout.activity_main);
    intent.setClassName("com.allyourcode.p03_03_01",
        "com.allyourcode.p03_03_01.MyWeatherService");
  }

  public void onStartClick(View view) {
    startService(intent);
  }

  public void onStopClick(View view) {
    stopService(intent);
  }
}
```

The code in Listing 3-3 makes use of the code in Listing 3-1, and the code in these two listings belong to two different projects. Before running the code in Listing 3-3, you must install both projects on your emulator or physical device.

In creating the layout for this section's project, I took the liberty of assigning listener method names to the two buttons:

```
<Button android:id="@+id/button"
  android:onClick="onStartClick"
  android:text="@string/start"
  android:layout_width="wrap_content"
  android:layout_height="wrap_content">
</Button>
<Button android:id="@+id/button2"
  android:onClick="onStopClick"
  android:text="@string/stop"
  android:layout_width="wrap_content"
  android:layout_height="wrap_content">
</Button>
```

So clicking the Start button calls `startService(intent)`, and clicking the Stop button calls `stopService(intent)`. In addition to starting and stopping the service, each click displays a `Toast` view.

For a brief treatise on Android's `Toast` class, see the section "Informing the user," later in this chapter.

A service's primary purposes are to run in the background (independent of any obvious user interaction) and to offer help to other apps. So, if the code in Listing 3-1 represented a useful service, this code would be doing something about the weather. (For code that does something useful, see the section "Talking about the Weather," later in this chapter.)

In the previous paragraph, the phrase "run in the background" means "run without displaying an activity." It specifically does *not* mean "run as part of a process or thread that's different from the main process or thread." This subtle point has important consequences, which you can read about in this chapter's "Getting Real Weather Data" section.

Here's what happens when you play with the buttons in Figure 3-1:

✦ **Press Start and then press Stop.**

After pressing Start, you see the Service Started toast. Then, after pressing Stop, you see the Service Destroyed toast. No surprises here!

✦ **Press Stop twice in a row.**

If the service is running, the first call to `stopService` (in Listing 3-3) destroys the service. The second call to `stopService` doesn't display a Service Destroyed toast because a component that's not running can't be destroyed.

✦ **Press Start twice in a row and then press Stop twice in a row.**

As a result, you see two Service Started toasts followed by only one Service Destroyed toast. Each `startService` call (from Listing 3-3) triggers a call to `onStartCommand` in Listing 3-1. But the first `stopService` call (again, from Listing 3-3) destroys the service. Subsequent `stopService` calls have no effect.

✦ **Press Start and then press the emulator's Back button.**

When you press the Back button, you *don't* see a Service Destroyed toast. And that's the essence of an Android service. A service can live on after the activity that started the service has been destroyed.

To confirm that the service is still running, use Android's Recents list (also known as the *Overview* list) to restart the client activity. Then, in the client activity, don't press the Start button. The service is still running, so simply press the Stop button. When you press the Stop button, the running service gets destroyed. So you see the Service Destroyed toast.

Services start, stop, and start again

A service has no user interface, and it may continue to run after you destroy the service's starting activity. That can be a dangerous combination of traits. Services without interfaces can hang around indefinitely like Rasputin — the mad monk of czarist Russia that no one could kill. If developers don't include code to manage their services, the services clog up the system. No one's happy.

Of course, Android can kill services in order to reclaim needed memory. The `http://developer.android.com/reference/android/app/Service.html` page lists all the situations in which Android kills or doesn't kill a service, and it doesn't make for light reading.

One insight about the lifetime of a service comes from the `onStartCommand` method in Listing 3-1. The `onStartCommand` method takes an `Intent` parameter. The parameter's value points to whatever `Intent` object the `startService` method sends. (See Listing 3-3.) The `onStartCommand` method returns an `int` value. In Listing 3-1, the `int` value is `START_NOT_STICKY` (a constant in the `android.app.Service` class). This constant value tells Android how to restart the service at a certain time interval after killing it. The alternative `int` values are as follows:

✦ `START_STICKY`: If Android kills the service, Android waits for a certain time interval and then restarts the service. Upon restart, Android feeds the service the intent from whatever `startService` call is next in the queue of such commands. If no `startService` calls are waiting to start this particular service, Android feeds `null` to the `onStartCommand` method's `Intent` parameter.

✦ `START_REDELIVER_INTENT`: If Android kills the service, Android waits for a certain time interval and then restarts the service. Upon restart, Android feeds the service the intent that came as a parameter in the current call to `onStartCommand`.

✦ `START_NOT_STICKY`: If Android kills the service, Android doesn't automatically restart the service. Android restarts the service if and when the next `startService` call queues up to start this particular service.

✦ `START_STICKY_COMPATIBILITY`: If Android kills the service, Android tries to restart the service the way `START_STICKY` restarts services. But Android doesn't promise to restart the service.

The bottom line is, be proactive in starting and stopping your own service. Don't be a memory hog by relying on the system to clean up after you. Be aware of your service's lifespan, and destroy your service when it's no longer needed. Add a `stopService` call to your activity's `onPause` or `onDestroy` method if it makes sense to do so. And, if a service knows that it's no longer useful, have the service call its own `stopSelf` method.

Android calls an activity's `onDestroy` method whenever the user turns the device (from portrait to landscape, for example). If you put a `stopService` call in an activity's `onDestroy` method, you must deal with all possible situations in which the service halts. For details, see this chapter's "Talking about the Weather" section.

Running a Service at Boot Time

How important is your service? Does your service start on rare occasions when the user presses a certain button? Or does your service start when the device powers up?

If Android users can't survive without running your service, you can start the service at boot time. To do so, you create another kind of component — a broadcast receiver.

A *broadcast receiver* responds to intents that you fling into the air using the `sendBroadcast` or `sendOrderedBroadcast` method. Android provides special treatment for an intent sent with either of these methods.

✦ **When you call** `startActivity` **or** `startService`, **Android looks for** *one* **component to satisfy the intent.**

If the system finds more than one suitable activity (two installed web browsers, for example), Android displays a dialog box prompting the user to choose among the alternatives.

✦ **When you call** `sendBroadcast` **or** `sendOrderedBroadcast`, **Android fires up** *all* **the receivers whose filters satisfy the intent.**

With `sendOrderedBroadcast`, Android runs receivers one after the other. Each receiver can pass the intent on to the next receiver in line or can break the chain by calling its `abortBroadcast` method.

With `sendBroadcast`, Android may interleave the running of several receivers. In this scenario, having a receiver abort a broadcast doesn't make sense.

For an example, consider the Weather service in Listing 3-1. In the same application, create a Java class with the code from Listing 3-4.

When `MyBootReceiver` runs, it starts an instance of the `MyWeatherService` class. The not-too-difficult trick is to make `MyBootReceiver` run when the emulator or device starts.

Listing 3-5 shows you the mechanics of launching the receiver in Listing 3-4.

**Book III
Chapter 3**

Services

Listing 3-4:   A Simple Broadcast Receiver

```
package com.allyourcode.p03_03_01;

import android.content.BroadcastReceiver;
import android.content.Context;
import android.content.Intent;

public class MyBootReceiver extends BroadcastReceiver {

  @Override
  public void onReceive(Context context, Intent intent) {
    Intent serviceIntent = new Intent();
    serviceIntent.setClassName(
        "com.allyourcode.p03_03_01",
        "com.allyourcode.p03_03_01.MyWeatherService");

    context.startService(serviceIntent);
  }
}
```

Listing 3-5:   Manifest for the Receiver in Listing 3-4

```xml
<?xml version="1.0" encoding="utf-8"?>
<manifest
  package="com.allyourcode.p03_03_01"
  xmlns:android="http://schemas.android.com/apk/res/android">

  <uses-permission android:name=
      "android.permission.RECEIVE_BOOT_COMPLETED"/>

  <application
    android:allowBackup="true"
    android:icon="@drawable/ic_launcher"
    android:label="@string/app_name"
    android:theme="@style/AppTheme">
    <service
      android:name=".MyWeatherService"
      android:enabled="true"
      android:exported="true">
    </service>
    <receiver
      android:name=".MyBootReceiver"
      android:enabled="true"
      android:exported="true" >
      <intent-filter>
        <action android:name=
            "android.intent.action.BOOT_COMPLETED" />
        <category android:name=
            "android.intent.category.HOME" />
      </intent-filter>
    </receiver>

  </application>

</manifest>
```

The `<uses-permission>` element in Listing 3-5 grants this app permission to receive `"android.intent.action.BOOT_COMPLETED"` broadcasts. And, in the receiver's `<action>` element, the `android:name` attribute says, "Wake me up if anyone hollers `android.intent.action.BOOT_ COMPLETED"`.

The Java constant `ACTION_BOOT_COMPLETED` in the `Intent` class has String value `"android.intent.action.BOOT_COMPLETED"`.

When you launch your emulator or you turn on your device, Android runs through its normal boot sequence and then sends an intent containing `ACTION_BOOT_COMPLETED`. At that point, Android finds the receiver in Listing 3-4 and calls the receiver's `onReceive` method. In turn, the `onReceive` method in Listing 3-4 gooses the Weather service in Listing 3-1.

A broadcast receiver lives long enough to run its `onReceive` method, and then the receiver stops running. A receiver doesn't have any `onCreate` or `onDestroy` methods, or any of the lifecycle methods belonging to other kinds of components. A broadcast receiver does its work and then hides in the shadows until the next relevant broadcast comes along.

To add a broadcast receiver to an existing project, right-click (or on a Mac, Ctrl-click) the package name in the Project tool window. Then, in the context menu that appears, select New ➪ Other ➪ Broadcast Receiver.

Testing the boot-time service

You can download this section's example from the book's website. To test the code, install the app on an emulator. Then shut down the emulator and restart the emulator. Ay, there's the rub! Starting an emulator once is annoying enough. Starting it several times (because you got some detail wrong the first few times) is a pain in the class.

Your code can't test Listing 3-4 by creating an `ACTION_BOOT_COMPLETED` intent. Android reserves `ACTION_BOOT_COMPLETED` for system-level code only. By using the Android Debug Bridge, though, you can launch an intent as a Linux shell superuser. When you do, your emulator or device does what looks like a partial reboot, and this saves a bit of time. Here's what you do:

1. **Install this section's code onto an emulator.**

2. **Launch a command window by clicking the Terminal tool button at the bottom of Android Studio's main screen.**

3. **In the Terminal window, issue the `cd` command to make the** `ANDROID_HOME/platform-tools` **directory your working directory.**

For examples of the use of the `cd` command, and for help finding your `ANDROID_HOME/platform-tools` directory, see Book I, Chapter 2.

4. **Type the following command (but type it all on one line):**

```
adb shell am broadcast
        -a android.intent.action.BOOT_COMPLETED
```

Using Android's `am` command, you can call `startActivity`, `startService`, and `sendBroadcast` as if you were Android itself (or himself, or herself, or whomever). When you issue the command in Step 4, Android behaves as if the system is just finishing its boot sequence.

5. **Using Run ⇨ Run 'app' or the Recents button on the emulator, restart the client app (from Listing 3-3).**

When the app starts running, don't touch the Start button. You're trying to find out if the service is already running.

6. **In the client app's activity, press the Stop button.**

Hooray! The Service Destroyed message appears on your emulator's screen.

You can see all the `am` command's options by typing **adb shell am** in the Terminal window.

For more information about the Android Debug Bridge, see Book I, Chapter 2. For more information about broadcast receivers, see Chapter 4 in this minibook.

Starting and Binding

You can do two kinds of things with a service:

✦ **You can start and stop a service.**

You do this by calling the `Context` class's `startService` and `stopService` methods. Also, a service can take the bull by the horns and call its own `stopSelf` or `stopSelfResult` method.

When you call `startService`, you create only a momentary relationship with the service. Android creates an instance of the service if no instances are already running. In addition, Android calls the service's `onStartCommand` method. (See Listing 3-1.)

Calls to `startService` don't pile up. To illustrate the point, consider this sequence of method calls, along with their resulting Android responses:

```
Activity A calls startService to start MyService.
    Android instantiates MyService and
        calls the instance's onStartCommand method.
```

```
Activity B calls startService to start MyService.
      Android calls the existing instance's
         onStartCommand method.

Activity A calls stopService to stop MyService.
      Android destroys the MyService instance.

Activity B calls stopService to stop MyService.
      Android says "The joke's on you." There's no
         instance of MyService to stop.
```

✦ **You can bind to and unbind from a service.**

You do this by calling the Context class's bindService and unbindService methods. Between binding and unbinding, you have an ongoing connection with the service. Through this connection, you can send messages to the service and receive messages from the service. That's useful!

When you call bindService, Android creates an instance of the service if no instances are running already. In addition, Android calls the service's onBind method. (For an example, skip ahead to Listings 3-6 and 3-7.)

When you call bindService, Android doesn't call the service's onStartCommand method.

Calls to bindService pile up. A service can have many bindings at once, each to a different activity. Your service's code can keep track of all this hubbub by maintaining a collection of binding objects (an ArrayList, or whatever). When you call unbindService, you don't destroy the service instance. Android keeps the service alive as long as any activities are bound to the service.

Services can receive Start requests and Bind requests all at the same time. When all bound activities unbind themselves from a particular service, the system checks whether anybody started the service this time around. If so, the system waits for somebody to call stopService before destroying the service.

Android can terminate activities to reclaim memory. If I were a service and Android terminated the activities that were bound to me, I'd be afraid for my own survival. Test your apps for unwanted results from the untimely termination of activities and their services. If, in testing, you experience any unexpected behavior due to the early termination of a service, please fix the code.

The previous sections' examples started and stopped a service. The rest of this chapter binds and unbinds with a service.

Talking about the Weather

Every Android book needs a Weather Service example, and this book is no exception. In this section, your activity binds to a service, which in turn reaches out for weather information over the Internet.

A service

I build the example in stages. The first stage is *essence de service*. An activity binds to the service, gets back some fake responses to nonsense queries, and then unbinds. Listing 3-6 contains the service.

Listing 3-6:   A Weather Service with a Fear of Commitment

```
package com.allyourcode.p03_03_06;

import android.app.Service;
import android.content.Intent;
import android.os.Bundle;
import android.os.Handler;
import android.os.IBinder;
import android.os.Message;
import android.os.Messenger;
import android.os.RemoteException;
import android.widget.Toast;

public class MyWeatherService extends Service {

  Messenger messengerToClient = null;

  MyIncomingHandler myIncomingHandler =
      new MyIncomingHandler();
  Messenger messengerToService =
      new Messenger(myIncomingHandler);

  @Override
  public IBinder onBind(Intent intent) {
    doToast(R.string.service_bound);
    return messengerToService.getBinder();
  }

  class MyIncomingHandler extends Handler {

    @Override
    public void handleMessage(Message incomingMessage) {
      messengerToClient = incomingMessage.replyTo;

      Bundle reply = new Bundle();
      reply.putString("weather", "It's dark at night.");
      Message replyMessage = Message.obtain();
      replyMessage.setData(reply);
      try {
        messengerToClient.send(replyMessage);
      } catch (RemoteException e) {
        e.printStackTrace();
      }
```

```
      doToast(R.string.message_handled);
    }
  }

  @Override
  public boolean onUnbind(Intent intent) {
    doToast(R.string.service_stopped_itself);
    stopSelf();
    return false;
  }

  @Override
  public void onDestroy() {
    myIncomingHandler = null;
    doToast(R.string.service_destroyed);
  }

  void doToast(int resource) {
    Toast.makeText(this, resource,
        Toast.LENGTH_SHORT).show();
  }
}
```

The flow of control in Listing 3-6 isn't simple, so I created Figure 3-2 to help you understand what's going on. The first thing to notice in Figure 3-2 is that the service doesn't interact directly with a client application. Instead, the service gets calls indirectly through the Android operating system.

MyWeather Service

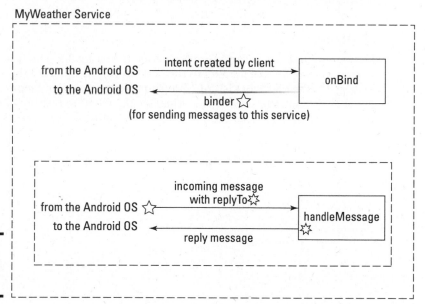

Figure 3-2:
Binding and
messaging.

Like many other communication regimens, the talk between a client and a service has two phases:

✦ The first phase (the binding phase) establishes a line of communication.

✦ In the second phase, the client and the service exchange useful information via messages. In general, the client sends a request for information and the service sends a reply.

To bind to a service, a client sends an intent. Android hands this intent to the service's onBind method. In response, the onBind method returns a *binder* — an object that implements the IBinder interface. (Refer to Listing 3-6 and Figure 3-2.) The binder is like a business card. By returning a binder, the service says, "Android, tell the client application that it can reach me at this address." That's why, in Listing 3-6, the service creates the binder from an instance of MyIncomingHandler. (It's the same as printing a business card from an instance of "my answering machine's phone number.")

Android delivers the binder to the client app. Eventually, the client app queries the service. The query contains a request for specific information. But the query also contains a replyTo field. The service's inner class (in this example, MyIncomingHandler) uses the replyTo information to send an answer back to the client app. In Listing 3-6, I keep things simple by replying It's dark at night no matter what query the client sends. (A weather report like this is always correct.)

A client

Listing 3-7 contains a client for the service in Listing 3-6. The first several lines of Listing 3-7 are parallel to the code in Listing 3-6. Like the service in Listing 3-6, the client in Listing 3-7 has messengers and an incoming handler class. But unlike the service in Listing 3-6, the client in Listing 3-7 spans three printed pages. So, in this section, I describe Listing 3-7 one piece at a time.

Listing 3-7: A Client for the Service in Listing 3-6

```
package com.allyourcode.p03_03_07;

import android.app.Activity;
import android.content.ComponentName;
import android.content.Context;
import android.content.Intent;
import android.content.ServiceConnection;
import android.content.SharedPreferences;
import android.os.Bundle;
import android.os.Handler;
import android.os.IBinder;
import android.os.Message;
import android.os.Messenger;
import android.os.RemoteException;
```

```java
import android.view.View;
import android.widget.Button;
import android.widget.EditText;
import android.widget.TextView;
import android.widget.Toast;

public class ServiceConsumerActivity extends Activity {

  Messenger messengerToService = null;

  MyIncomingHandler myIncomingHandler =
      new MyIncomingHandler();
  Messenger messengerFromService =
      new Messenger(myIncomingHandler);

  ServiceConnection connection =
      new MyServiceConnection();
  SharedPreferences prefs;
  boolean isBound = false;

  void bind() {
    Intent intent = new Intent();
    intent.setClassName("com.allyourcode.p03_03_06",
        "com.allyourcode.p03_03_06.MyWeatherService");
    isBound =
        bindService(intent, connection,
            Context.BIND_AUTO_CREATE);
  }

  public void queryService() {
    if (isBound) {
      Bundle bundle = new Bundle();
      bundle.putString("location", "19122");
        // 19122 is the zip code of the neighborhood
        // where I grew up. Philadelphia's El train
        // passed right by my bedroom window.

      Message message = Message.obtain();
      message.replyTo = messengerFromService;
      message.setData(bundle);
      try {
        messengerToService.send(message);
      } catch (RemoteException e) {
        e.printStackTrace();
      }
    } else {
      textView.setText(R.string.report_appears_here);
      doToast(R.string.service_not_bound);
    }
  }

  class MyIncomingHandler extends Handler {
    @Override
    public void handleMessage(Message msg) {
      Bundle bundle = msg.getData();
      textView.setText(bundle.getString("weather"));
    }
  }
```

Book III
Chapter 3

Services

(continued)

Listing 3-7 *(continued)*

```java
void unbind() {
  if (isBound) {
    unbindService(connection);
    isBound = false;
  }
}

class MyServiceConnection implements ServiceConnection {
  public void onServiceConnected(
      ComponentName className, IBinder binder) {
    messengerToService = new Messenger(binder);
    doToast(R.string.service_connected);
  }
  public void onServiceDisconnected(ComponentName n) {
    messengerToService = null;
    doToast(R.string.service_crashed);
  }
}

void doToast(int resource) {
  Toast.makeText(this, resource,
      Toast.LENGTH_SHORT).show();
}

@Override
public void onDestroy() {
super.onDestroy();

  prefs = getSharedPreferences("PREFS", MODE_PRIVATE);
  SharedPreferences.Editor editor = prefs.edit();
  editor.putBoolean("isBound", isBound);
  editor.putString("report", textView.getText()
      .toString());
  editor.commit();


  unbind();
}

@Override
public void onCreate(Bundle savedInstanceState) {
  super.onCreate(savedInstanceState);
  setContentView(R.layout.activity_service_consumer);
  prefs = getSharedPreferences("PREFS", MODE_PRIVATE);
  if (prefs != null) {
    textView = (TextView) findViewById(R.id.textView);

    textView.setText(prefs.getString("report",
      getString(R.string.report_appears_here)));
    if (prefs.getBoolean("isBound", false)) {
      bind();
    }
  }

  bindButton = (Button) findViewById(R.id.buttonBind);
  locationText =
      (EditText) findViewById(R.id.editText);
  queryButton = (Button) findViewById(R.id.buttonQuery);
```

```
        unbindButton =
            (Button) findViewById(R.id.buttonUnbind);
    }

    public static TextView textView;
    Button bindButton, queryButton, unbindButton;
    EditText locationText;

    public void onButtonClick(View view) {
        if (view == bindButton) {
            bind();
        } else if (view == queryButton) {
            queryService();
        } else if (view == unbindButton) {
            unbind();
        }
    }
}
```

Figure 3-3 shows a layout that I created for the activity in Listing 3-7. The bind, queryService, and unbind methods in Listing 3-7 handle the button clicks in Figure 3-3. (This section's service doesn't care what city you're in, so, in Figure 3-3, the EditText view set up for a United States postal code doesn't serve any purpose. It's a placeholder for user input in subsequent examples.)

In the activity's layout file, I set each button's onClick attribute to onButtonClick. Then, in the Java code (Listing 3-7), the onButton-Click method tests to find out which of the three buttons experienced the click event.

Book III
Chapter 3

Services

Figure 3-3:
A user
interface for
the activity
in Listing 3-7.

Informing the user

Near the bottom of Figure 3-3, there's a capsule-shaped pop-up containing the words *Message handled.* The rectangle illustrates the use of Android's `Toast` class. A *toast* is an unobtrusive little view that displays some useful information for a brief period of time. A `Toast` view pops up on the screen, the way a hot piece of bread pops up from a toaster. (Rumor has it that the Android class name `Toast` comes from this goofy analogy.)

A `Toast` view typically displays a message for the user to read. So Android developers often talk about *toast messages.* In principle, there's nothing wrong with the term *toast message.* But much of this chapter deals with instances of the `android.os.Message` class — messages sent between a service and its client. And near the bottom of Figure 3-3, the words *Message handled* refer to a message between a service and its client, not to a toast message. So in Figure 3-3, a toast message informs the user about a completely different kind of message. What's an author to do? In this chapter, I use the word *message* to refer to communication between a service and its client. In other chapters, I throw around the words *toast message* without worrying about the problem.

The `Toast` class has two extremely useful methods: `makeText` and `show`.

✦ **The static** `Toast.makeText` **method creates an instance of the** `Toast` **class.**

The `makeText` method has three parameters:

- The first parameter is a context (the word `this` in Listing 3-7).

- The second parameter is either a resource or a sequence of characters (a `String`, for example).

    If you call `makeText` with a `String`, the user sees the `String` when Android displays the toast. If you call `makeText` with a resource, Android looks for the resource in your app's `res` directory. In Listing 3-7, the code calls `makeText` twice — once with resource `R.string.service_connected` and once with `R.string.service_crashed`.

    If you use an `int` value (42, for example) for the second parameter of the `makeText` method, Android doesn't display the characters *42* in the `Toast` view. Instead, Android looks for a resource whose value in `R.java` is 42. Your `R.java` file probably doesn't contain the number 42. So, instead of a `Toast` view, you get a `ResourceNotFound` exception. Your app crashes, and you groan in dismay.

- The `makeText` method's third parameter is either `Toast.LENGTH_LONG` or `Toast.LENGTH_SHORT`. With `LENGTH_LONG`, the `Toast` view appears for about four seconds. With `LENGTH_SHORT`, the `Toast` view appears for approximately two seconds.

✦ **The** `show` **method tells Android to display the** `Toast` **view.**

In Listing 3-7, notice that I call both `makeText` and `show` in one Java statement. If you forget to call the `show` method, the `Toast` view doesn't appear. You stare in disbelief wondering why you don't see the `Toast` view. ("Who stole my toast?" you ask.) When you finally figure out that you forgot to call the `show` method, you feel foolish. (At least that's the way I felt when I forgot earlier today.)

Binding to the service

In Listing 3-7, the call to `bindService` takes three parameters — an intent, a service connection, and an `int` value representing flags.

✦ **The intent helps determine which service to invoke.**

In Listing 3-7, the intent has class name `com.allyourcode.` `p03_03_06.MyWeatherService`. That points to the code in Listing 3-6.

✦ **The connection is the virtual rope between the client and the service.**

The `connection` parameter in Listing 3-7 implements the `android.content.ServiceConnection` interface. I declare the `MyServiceConnection` class later in Listing 3-7.

Notice that in one of the `MyServiceConnection` class's methods, Android hands the service's business card (the binder) to the client. This is a bit different from the code in Listing 3-6, where the service gets `replyTo` information from each incoming message. The difference stems from the way the client and the service talk to each other. The client initiates communications, and the service twiddles its virtual thumbs waiting for communications.

Another thing to notice about `MyServiceConnection` is the peculiar role of the `onServiceDisconnected` method. As the toast implies, Android doesn't call `onServiceDisconnected` unless the service takes a dive prematurely.

✦ **The flags provide additional information about the run of the service.**

When Android needs more memory, Android terminates processes. In Listing 3-7, the flag `BIND_AUTO_CREATE` tells Android to avoid terminating the service's process while your activity runs. An alternative, `BIND_` `NOT_FOREGROUND`, tells Android not to consider your activity's needs when deciding whether to terminate the service's process.

Querying the service

In Listing 3-7, the `queryService` method asks the service for the answer to a question. Here's what the `queryService` method does:

1. The `queryService` method obtains a blank message from the `android.os.Message` class.

2. The `queryService` method adds a question (the *bundle*) to the message.

3. The `queryService` method tells a messenger to send the message to the service.

A *bundle* (an instance of `android.os.Bundle`) is something that a process can write to and that another process can read from. You see a bundle in every activity's `onCreate` method. In the world of data communications, sending a message is likened to writing data. So, in Listing 3-7, the code juggles bundles.

✦ The `queryService` method puts a bundle on a message and then "writes" the message to an Android message queue.

✦ The `handleMessage` method in the `MyIncomingHandler` class "reads" a message from an Android message queue and then gets the message's bundle for display on the device's screen.

Using shared preferences to restart a connection

Listing 3-7 contains an important lesson about the life of a service. A service that's bound to another component (an activity, for example) tends to stay alive. If developers don't explicitly unbind from services, the services build up and start clogging Android's pipes. So a good citizen does the housekeeping to unbind services.

So, in Listing 3-7, the `onDestroy` method unbinds the service. So far, so good. But what happens when the user turns the device sideways? Chapter 1 of this minibook reminds you what happens when the user reorients the device — Android destroys the current activity and re-creates the activity in the new orientation. So, if you're not careful, the user loses the service just by turning the device sideways. That's probably not what you want.

To defend against this problem, use *shared preferences*. With shared preferences, you can store information. Later, your app (or, if you want, someone else's app) can retrieve the information.

Here's how you wield a set of shared preferences:

✦ **To create shared preferences, call the** `android.content.Context` **class's** `getSharedPreferences` **method.**

For parameters, feed a name and a mode to the method call. In Listing 3-7, the name is the string `"PREFS"`, and the mode is the `int` value `android.content.Context.MODE_PRIVATE`. The alternatives are

- *MODE_PRIVATE:* No other process can read from or write to these preferences.

- *MODE_WORLD_READABLE:* Other processes can read from these preferences.

- *MODE_WORLD_WRITEABLE:* Other processes can write to these preferences.

- *MODE_MULTI_PROCESS:* Other processes can write to these preferences even while a process is in the middle of a read operation. Weird things can happen with this much concurrency. So watch out!

You can combine modes with Java's bitwise `or` operator. So a call such as

```
getSharedPreferences("PREFS",
    MODE_WORLD_READABLE | MODE_WORLD_WRITEABLE);
```

makes your preferences both readable and writable for all other processes.

✦ **To add values to a set of shared preferences, use an instance of the** `android.content.SharedPreferences.Editor` **class.**

In Listing 3-7, the `onDestroy` method creates a new editor object. Then the code uses the editor to put information for safe keeping into the shared preferences. Each piece of information is a (*name, value*) pair, such as (`"isBound"`, `isBound`) or (`"report"`, `textView.getText().toString()`). For putting information into shared preferences, the `Editor` class has methods such as `putInt`, `putString`, `putStringSet`, and so on.

✦ **To make Android remember the information in shared preferences, call the editor's** `commit` **method.**

Again, see Listing 3-7.

✦ **To retrieve an existing set of shared preferences, call** `getShared-Preferences`, **using the same name as the name you used to create the preferences.**

Can you guess which listing contains an example of this code? Yes! Listing 3-7. Look at the listing's `onCreate` method.

✦ **To read values from an existing set of shared preferences, call** `getBoolean`, `getInt`, `getFloat`, **or one of the other** `get` **methods belonging to the** `SharedPreferences` **class.**

In Listing 3-7, the call to `getBoolean` takes two parameters. The first parameter is the name in whatever (`name`, `value`) pair you're trying to get. The second parameter is a default value. So, when you call `prefs.getBoolean("isBound", false)`, if `prefs` has no pair with name `"isBound"`, the method call returns `false`.

In Listing 3-7, the `onDestroy` method saves the value of `isBound`. Then, when Android revives the activity, the `onCreate` method retrieves the `isBound` value. In effect, the `onCreate` method "finds out" whether the service was bound before the activity was destroyed. If the service was bound, the code renews its connection, making another call to the `bindService` method.

The `SharedPreferences` code in Listing 3-7 saves the weather report and the `isBound` value no matter how the activity is destroyed. This includes times when the user reorients the device, but it also includes times when the user presses Android's Back button. The trouble is, a press of the Back button probably means "I'm finished with this activity. The next time I use this activity, I will have forgotten all about this moment's weather conditions." So, when the user presses the Back button, you might not want to save the current weather report. What you need is a way to distinguish between Back-button `onDestroy` calls and other kinds of `onDestroy` calls. To do this, use the `Activity` class's `isFinishing` method. For details, see Chapter 1 in this minibook.

Using attributes in an app's `AndroidManifest.xml` document, you can keep Android from destroying an activity when the user reorients the device. But the Android docs recommend against doing this. For information, see Chapter 1 of this minibook.

Getting Real Weather Data

In this section, you supplement the code in Listings 3-6 and 3-7 so that your app retrieves real weather data. Here's what you do:

✦ **In the client app, get the user's input from the EditText widget and send this input to the service.**

That is, change the statement

```
bundle.putString("location", "19122");
```

in Listing 3-7 to a statement such as

```
bundle.putString("location",
locationText.getText().toString().trim());
```

✦ **In the service, send the incoming message's text to the Weather Underground server.**

That is, change the statement

```
reply.putString("weather", "It's dark at night.");
```

in Listing 3-6 to a statement such as

```
reply.putString("weather", actualWeatherString);
```

The Weather Underground server takes a city name or a U.S. postal code (a zip code) and returns a JSON document describing the weather at that location. (To keep the example simple, I use only U.S. postal codes in this section's listings.)

Listing 3-8 contains an abridged version of a response from the Weather Underground server.

Listing 3-8:   JSON Response from the Weather Underground

```
{
  "response": {
    "version":"0.1",
    "features": {
      "conditions": 1
    }
  }
  ,
  "current_observation": {
    "weather":"Overcast",
    "temperature_string":"62.4 F (16.9 C)",
    "temp_f":62.4,
    "temp_c":16.9,
    "relative_humidity":"88%",
    "wind_dir":"SSE",
    "wind_degrees":150,
    "wind_mph":6.0,
  }
}
```

✦ **In the service, sift information from the Weather Underground server's response.**

This section's code ferrets out the Fahrenheit temperature and the weather condition from the Weather Underground's response. (I apologize in advance to non-U.S., non-Belize readers for the use of the Fahrenheit scale. Bad habits are difficult to break.)

✦ **As a final step, your service gets the data obtained from the Weather Underground server and forwards that information to the client app.**

**Book III
Chapter 3**

Services

What is JSON?

JSON stands for JavaScript Object Notation. JSON is a universally agreed-upon way to represent structured data. JSON notation involves name:value pairs. For example:

- In `"weather":"Overcast"`, `"weather"` is a name, and the string `"Overcast"` is its value.

- In `"temp_f":62.4`, `"temp_f"` is a name, and the number `62.4` is its value.

  JSON values can have type number (integer or floating point), string, Boolean, array, object, or null.

- In its broadest outline, Listing 3-8 consists of two name:value pairs. The first name is `"response"`, and the second name is `"current_observation"`.

- In the following JSON code

  ```
  "current_observation": {
    "weather":"Overcast",
    "temperature_string":"62.4 F
        (16.9 C)",
    "temp_f":62.4,
    "temp_c":16.9,
    "relative_humidity":"88%",
    "wind_dir":"SSE",
    "wind_degrees":150,
    "wind_mph":6.0,
  }
  ```

  `"current_observation"` is a name, and the rest of the text (enclosed in curly braces) is its value. (The rest of the text is a value of type *object* — a comma separated list of name:value pairs.)

- In the code

  ```
  "response": {
    "version":"0.1",
    "features": {
      "conditions": 1
    }
  }
  ```

  the value of `"response"` is an object. That object contains two name:value pairs (the two names being `"version"` and `"features"`). The value of `"features"` is itself an object containing only one name:value pair (the pair `"conditions"`: 1).

JSON is like XML, but JSON text is much less verbose than XML text.

You don't have to guess about the JSON code that comes from the Weather Underground server. You can see this JSON code in your web browser by typing **http://api.wunderground.com/api/***your_key_id***/conditions/q/94103.json** in the web browser's address field. (In place of your_key_id, you type an id string that you get when you sign up at wunderground.com.)

You must have a Weather Underground account in order to run this section's code. But don't fret. For up to 500 queries per day, Weather Underground's service is free. You can get an account by visiting www.wunderground.com/weather/api/.

In the old days, before JSON or XML were commonly used, your app would be screen scraping. *Screen scraping* refers to the practice of fishing for data in an ordinary web page. In the era before JSON or XML, your code had to eliminate the page's colors, font tags, advertisements, and any other irrelevant material. Then your code had to search the page for the current Fahrenheit temperature, making every effort to avoid grabbing next week's forecast or the cost of a subscription to *Weather and Wine Weekly*. Then you hoped that any future changes in the website's layout didn't spoil the correctness of your code. Undoubtedly, reading JSON or XML is more reliable.

Dealing with JSON

This section presents an alternative to the fake weather service in Listing 3-6. As you might expect, a real service is more complicated than a fake service. So it helps to digest this section's code in pieces. The first piece is in Listing 3-9.

Listing 3-9:   A Real Weather Service: Part I

```
package com.allyourcode.p03_03_09;

import android.app.Service;
import android.content.Intent;
import android.os.AsyncTask;
import android.os.Bundle;
import android.os.Handler;
import android.os.IBinder;
import android.os.Message;
import android.os.Messenger;
import android.os.RemoteException;
import android.widget.Toast;

import org.json.JSONException;
import org.json.JSONObject;

import java.io.BufferedReader;
import java.io.IOException;
import java.io.InputStream;
import java.io.InputStreamReader;
import java.net.HttpURLConnection;
import java.net.URL;

public class MyWeatherService extends Service {

  Messenger messengerToClient = null;

  MyIncomingHandler myIncomingHandler =
      new MyIncomingHandler();
  Messenger messengerToService =
      new Messenger(myIncomingHandler);

  @Override
  public IBinder onBind(Intent intent) {
```

(continued)

Listing 3-9 *(continued)*

```
    doToast(R.string.service_bound);
    return messengerToService.getBinder();
}

class MyIncomingHandler extends Handler {

    @Override
    public void handleMessage(Message incomingMessage) {
        messengerToClient = incomingMessage.replyTo;
        new MyAsyncTask().execute
            (incomingMessage.getData().getString("location"));
    }
}

@Override
public boolean onUnbind(Intent intent) {
    doToast(R.string.service_stopped_itself);
    stopSelf();
    return false;
}

@Override
public void onDestroy() {
    myIncomingHandler = null;
    doToast(R.string.service_destroyed);
}

void doToast(int resource) {
    Toast.makeText(this, resource, Toast.LENGTH_SHORT).show();
}

// ... More to come in Listings 3-10 and 3-11
```

Looking at Listing 3-9, you may have a distinct sense of *déjà vu*. In fact, Listing 3-9 is almost identical to Listing 3-6. The only difference is the body of the handleMessage method. (Come to think of it, that's not too surprising. Both listings need the plumbing for responding to binding requests and queries. The only difference is the way the two listings get their weather data.)

In Listing 3-6, the handleMessage method composes a fake reply and sends the reply back to the client. But in Listing 3-9, handleMessage delegates the work to a mysterious-looking thing called an AsyncTask. Listing 3-10 contains your weather service's AsyncTask code.

Listing 3-10:   A Real Weather Service: Part II

```
// ... Continued from Listing 3-9

class MyAsyncTask extends AsyncTask<String, Void, String> {

    @Override
    protected String doInBackground(String... locations) {
        return getWeatherFromInternet(locations[0]);
    }
```

```
@Override
protected void onPostExecute(String actualWeatherString) {
  sendWeatherToClient(actualWeatherString);
  doToast(R.string.message_handled);
}

}
// ... More to come in Listing 3-11
```

The class in Listing 3-10 is an inner class of the `MyWeatherService` class. I have a lot more to say about the `AsyncTask` construct in Book IV, Chapter 3. In this chapter, I make only two points:

✦ **An** `AsyncTask` **runs in a thread of its own.**

That's important because a service runs in the same thread as the client that invokes the service. Your service has to reach out along the Internet to Weather Underground's servers. That takes time, time that the client's busy user interface code might not have.

Imagine putting a request to Weather Underground right inside the `handleMessage` method. The `handleMessage` method (and everything else inside the service's code) runs inside the same thread as the client activity. So the client activity, with its `EditText` field and buttons, can do nothing while the `handleMessage` method waits to get information back from Weather Underground. If the user presses a button, nothing happens. The button's shade doesn't even change to show that it's been pressed. That's bad.

Before Honeycomb, a developer was free to issue Internet requests inside an activity's thread. It was bad programming practice, but Android would let you do it. Starting with Honeycomb, requests of this kind are strictly forbidden. A call for network data from the service's regular code throws a `NetworkOnMainThreadException`, and the app's request is not fulfilled.

To fix this problem, Listing 3-10 executes an `AsyncTask`. An `AsyncTask` operates outside of its originator's thread, so an `AsyncTask` can make Internet requests on its originator's behalf.

✦ **The execution of an** `AsyncTask` **proceeds in distinct phases.**

The code in Listing 3-10 has two methods — namely, `doInBackground` and `onPostExecute`.

● **In an** `AsyncTask`**, the** `doInBackground` **method is where all the heavy lifting occurs.**

In Listing 3-10, the `doInBackground` method reaches out to the Internet (via method calls) and actually waits for the response from Weather Underground. This step can be time-consuming, but because the `AsyncTask` isn't blocking the client activity's responses, the wait is tolerable.

At the end of its execution, the `doInBackground` method returns a value. In Listing 3-10, this value is a `String` such as `"31.7° F Overcast"` — a value obtained through a request sent over the Internet.

- **In an** `AsyncTask`, **the** `onPostExecute` **method starts running only after the** `doInBackground` **method has finished whatever it has to do.**

The `onPostExecute` method's parameter is whatever value the `doInBackgroud` method returned. So, in Listing 3-10, the value of `actualWeatherString` is something like `"31.7° F Overcast"`. The job of the `onPostExecute` method is to bundle this information into a reply and send that reply back to the client.

The rest of this section's code makes good on the promises made inside Listing 3-10 — namely, to implement the `getWeatherFromInternet` and `sendWeatherToClient` methods.

Listing 3-11:   A Real Weather Service: Part III

```
// ... Continued from Listing 3-10

  private static final String WEATHER_UNDERGROUND_URL =
      "http://api.wunderground.com/" +
        "api/your_key_id/conditions/q/";
  private static final String CONDITION = "weather";
  private static final String TEMP_F = "temp_f";

  String getWeatherFromInternet(String location) {
    String temperature = "", condition = "", weatherString;

    URL url;

    if (location != null && !location.equals("")) {
      try {
      url = new URL
        (WEATHER_UNDERGROUND_URL + location + ".json");

      HttpURLConnection connection =
          (HttpURLConnection) url.openConnection();
      connection.setDoInput(true);
      connection.connect();

      InputStream input = connection.getInputStream();
      BufferedReader reader = new BufferedReader
                    (new InputStreamReader(input));

      String oneLineFromInternet;
      String wholeReplyFromInternet = "";
      while ((oneLineFromInternet = reader.readLine())
                                        != null) {
```

```
        wholeReplyFromInternet +=
                        oneLineFromInternet + " ";
      }

      JSONObject jsonObject =
            new JSONObject(wholeReplyFromInternet);
      JSONObject current_observation =
       jsonObject.getJSONObject("current_observation");
      temperature = current_observation.getString(TEMP_F);
      condition = current_observation.getString(CONDITION);

      } catch (JSONException | IOException e) {
        e.printStackTrace();
      }

      weatherString = temperature
          + (char) 0x00B0 + "F " + condition;
    } else {
      weatherString = "It's dark at night.";
    }
    return weatherString;
  }

  void sendWeatherToClient(String actualWeatherString) {
    Bundle reply = new Bundle();
    reply.putString("weather", actualWeatherString);
    Message replyMessage = Message.obtain();
    replyMessage.setData(reply);
    try {
      messengerToClient.send(replyMessage);
    } catch (RemoteException e) {
      e.printStackTrace();
    }
  }

}
```

Listing 3-11 contains a lot of code, but most of it either comes straight from Listing 3-6 or is boilerplate Java code (not Android-specific code).

✦ **The stuff about** `HttpURLConnection`**,** `InputStream`**, and** `BufferedReader` **is the way Java sends a URL to an Internet server.**

The `while` loop in Listing 3-11 gets the server's response, line by line, and appends this response to its own `wholeReplyFromInternet` string. When all is said and done, that string looks something like the JSON code in Listing 3-8. (Of course, in real life, that response string is quite a bit longer.)

✦ **The business about** `JSONObject` **is Java's way of sifting values from a JSON string.**

Notice the nesting in Listing 3-8. The whole listing has two parts: a `"response"` part and a `"current_observation"` part. And the `"current_observation"` part has several parts of its own, two of which are the `"weather"` and `"temp_f"` parts.

(As far as I'm concerned, the name `"weather"` is an unfortunate choice. The whole thing is about weather. The pair `"weather":"Overcast"` in Listing 3-8 is only a small piece of the overall weather picture. But `"weather":"Overcast"` is what the Weather Underground server deals to me, so `"weather":"Overcast"` is what I must use. In Listing 3-11, I create an alias `CONDITION` for this strange use of the name `"weather"`.)

In Listing 3-11, I extract the `"weather"` and `"temp_f"` values from the code in Listing 3-8. Because of the nesting in Listing 3-8, I perform the extraction in three steps:

1. **Using the** `JSONObject` **constructor, I get something that I can analyze with Java's JSON methods.**

   I put this thing in the `jsonObject` variable.

2. **I call the** `jsonObject` **variable's** `getJSONObject` **method to sift the** `"current_observation"` **part from the server's response.**

   I put this `"current_observation"` part into the `observation` variable.

3. **I call the** `observation` **variable's** `getString` **method to sift the** `"temp_f"` **and** `"weather"` **values out of the** `"current_ observation"` **part.**

   I put these values into the `temperature` and `condition` variables.

As a final *coup de grâce*, I combine the `temperature` and `condition` strings into one `weatherString`. I return that `weatherString` so that, down the line in the code, the `weatherString` can be returned to the client code and displayed on the user's screen.

In Listing 3-11, the only other excitement comes from the `(char) 0x00B0` value. The hex value `B0` (decimal value 176) is the Unicode representation for the degree symbol. (See the text view in Figure 3-4.)

If an app's code fetches data from the Internet (as this section's service does), then the app's `AndroidManifest.xml` file must have the `<uses-permission-android:name="android.permission.INTERNET"/>` element.

Dealing with XML

In your Android-related travels, you might not always get JSON back from an Internet server. Another popular format for data interchange is XML. Because Weather Underground offers both JSON and XML, I can illustrate the use of XML by translating the previous section's example.

For some tips on deciphering the contents of XML documents, see Book II, Chapter 5.

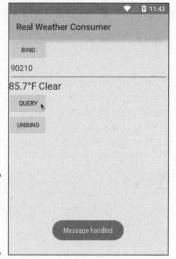

Figure 3-4:
Displaying
weather
information.

To get weather data from Weather Underground, you send a URL. If the URL ends with `.json`, you get a response like the stuff in Listing 3-8. But if the URL ends with `.xml`, you get something like the response in Listing 3-12.

Book III
Chapter 3

Services

Listing 3-12:   XML Response from the Weather Underground

```
<response>
  <version>0.1</version>
  <features>
    <feature>conditions</feature>
  </features>
  <current_observation>
    <weather>Mostly Cloudy</weather>
    <temperature_string>65.7 F (18.7 C)</temperature_string>
    <temp_f>65.7</temp_f>
    <temp_c>18.7</temp_c>
    <relative_humidity>71%</relative_humidity>
    <wind_dir>South</wind_dir>
    <wind_degrees>177</wind_degrees>
    <wind_mph>15.2</wind_mph>
  </current_observation>
</response>
```

There are two popular ways to get information from an XML document — DOM and SAX:

✦ DOM (*D*ocument *O*bject *M*odel) picks apart an entire XML document, loads all this information into memory, and then lets you query the parser for values anywhere in the document. "What are the characters inside the `<temp_f>` element in the `<current_conditions>`

element?" you ask. The DOM parser answers, but only after analyzing the entire document.

DOM works much like the code in Listing 3-11, but tends to consume lots and lots of memory.

✦ SAX (*Simple API for XML*) scans an XML document one piece at a time, keeping only the current piece in memory. At every step, a SAX parser offers to report its findings. "I found a start tag" or "I found some characters between start and end tags," says the parser. This section's SAX code monitors parser findings for relevant data and adds any useful data to an instance of the `Weather` class.

SAX isn't as memory-intensive as DOM.

The SAX code to monitor the response from Weather Underground is in Listing 3-13.

Listing 3-13: Your Very Own SAX Handler

```
package com.allyourcode.p03_03_13;

import org.xml.sax.Attributes;
import org.xml.sax.SAXException;
import org.xml.sax.helpers.DefaultHandler;

public class MySaxHandler extends DefaultHandler {

  private static final String CONDITION = "weather";
  private static final String TEMP_F = "temp_f";

  private Weather weather = new Weather();

  private boolean isInTemp_f = false;
  private boolean isInCondition = false;

  public Weather getWeather() {
    return weather;
}

  @Override
  public void startElement(String namespaceURI,
                           String localName,
                           String qName,
                           Attributes attributes)
                                throws SAXException {
    if (localName.equals(TEMP_F)) {
      isInTemp_f = true;
    } else if (localName.equals(CONDITION)) {
      isInCondition = true;
    }
  }
```

```
@Override
public void characters(char[] ch,
                       int start,
                       int length) {
  if (isInTemp_f) {
    weather.temperature =
                    new String(ch, start, length);
  } else if (isInCondition) {
    weather.condition = new String(ch, start, length);
  }
}

@Override
public void endElement(String namespaceURI,
                       String localName,
                       String qName)
                            throws SAXException {
  if (localName.equals(TEMP_F)) {
    isInTemp_f = false;
  } else if (localName.equals(CONDITION)) {
    isInCondition = false;
  }
}
}
```

The SAX handler makes use of a tiny `Weather` class shown in Listing 3-14.

Listing 3-14:   (Not much to see, here!)

```
package com.allyourcode.p03_03_13;

public class Weather {

  String temperature = "0.0";
  String condition = "";

}
```

The code in Listing 3-13 has more to do with XML than with Android, so I don't go into detail about the code in Listing 3-13.

Listing 3-15 contains the XML/SAX alternative to the `getWeatherFromInternet` method in Listing 3-11.

Listing 3-15:   Getting Weather the XML/SAX Way

```
String getWeatherFromInternet(String location) {
  Weather weather = null;
  String weatherString;

  URL url;
```

(continued)

Listing 3-15 *(continued)*

```
if (location != null && !location.equals("")) {
  try {
    url = new URL
      (WEATHER_UNDERGROUND_URL + location + ".xml");

    SAXParser parser =
      SAXParserFactory.newInstance().newSAXParser();
    XMLReader reader = parser.getXMLReader();
    MySaxHandler saxHandler = new MySaxHandler();
    reader.setContentHandler(saxHandler);

    reader.parse(new InputSource(url.openStream()));

    weather = saxHandler.getWeather();

  } catch (SAXException |
           ParserConfigurationException |
           IOException e) {
    e.printStackTrace();
  }

  weatherString = weather.temperature
      + (char) 0x00B0 + "F " + weather.condition;
} else {
  weatherString = "It's dark at night.";
}
  return weatherString;
}
```

The method in Listing 3-15 does what Java programs do when they get a response from a web server and submit the response to a SAX parser. I review the steps briefly because the code is mostly boilerplate. You can paste it into your own app with barely any changes.

1. **Create a URL pointing to Weather Underground's weather server.**

2. **Create a** `SAXParser` **instance and then use the parser to get an** `XMLReader` **instance (whatever an** `XMLReader` **instance is).**

3. **Create a** `MySaxHandler` **instance (refer to Listing 3-10) and feed the** `MySaxHandler` **instance to the** `XMLReader` **instance.**

4. **Connect to Weather Underground by creating** `newInputSource` `(url.openStream())`**.**

5. **Call the reader's** `parse` **method, feeding Weather Underground's response to the reader.**

6. **Get a** `Weather` **instance from the SAX handler.**

Whew!

Talking to a Service as if You're Right Next Door

Where I come from, you're thought to be sophisticated if you're multilingual. Do you speak a foreign language? If so, you're cool.

Learning a second language is easy. Just find something whose acronym ends with the letter *L,* and learn how to use it. In this section, you read about *AIDL* — the *Android Interface Definition Language.*

Aside from being a language, AIDL is a programming idiom. AIDL is a way of rewriting some of your Java code to make it more natural and more straightforward.

In Listings 3-6 and 3-7, a service and its client pass messages back and forth. The message-passing paradigm is nice, but wouldn't life be simpler if the client could simply call one of the service's methods? That's exactly what AIDL does for your code.

Using AIDL

Here's how AIDL works:

1. **Create two projects.**

   One project has the service; the other project has the client. The service project has no activity; the client project starts with a blank activity.

   In this section's listings, the service's package name is `com.allyourcode.aidlservice`, and the client's package name is `com.allyourcode.aidlclient`.

2. **In the Project tool window of the service project, right-click (or on a Mac, Ctrl-click) the** `app` **branch.**

3. **In the context menu that appears, select New⇨AIDL⇨AIDL File.**

   A dialog box appears. The dialog box has an Interface Name field. In this set of instructions, I accept the default name `IMyAidlInterface`.

4. **Click Finish.**

   As a result, the Project tool window has a new branch — an `app/aidl` branch containing an `IMyAidlInterface.aidl` item. In the editor, you see the text inside the new `IMyAidlInterface.aidl` file.

5. **Modify the** `IMyAidlInterface.aidl` **file's text, as shown in Listing 3-16.**

Listing 3-16:   An AIDL file

```
package com.allyourcode.aidlservice;

interface IMyAidlInterface {

    String fetchWeather(in String location);

}
```

The `.aidl` file describes the kind of information to be passed between the service and the client. The file is almost a plain old Java source file. The big difference is the use of the non-Java keyword `in`. This `in` keyword tells the world that the service's code receives a `String` value (instead of sending out a `String` value).

6. **In the service project's main menu, choose Build⇨ Make Project.**

   This forces Android Studio to create some Java code. The new Java code implements some of the things that are described in your AIDL file.

7. **Find the Java code that was generated in Step 6.**

   To do so, switch the Project tool window from the Android view to the Project view. Then expand the `app/build/generated/source/aidl/ debug/com.allyourcode.aidlservice` branch. Inside this branch, you see an `IMyAidlInterface` branch.

   The `IMyAidlInterface.java` file is long and complicated. You can look at the `IMyAidlInterface.java` file by double-clicking the Project view's `IMyAidlInterface` branch, but you'll be just as happy if you don't.

   Both the service and the client must have copies of the AIDL information. So your next step is to put a copy of the `IMyAidlInterface` stuff in the client project.

8. **Go to the Android view in the Project tool window in the client project.**

9. **Right-click (or on a Mac, Ctrl-click) the** `app/java` **branch. In the resulting context menu, select New⇨ Package.**

   A Choose Destination Directory dialog box appears. Most likely, the dialog box wants you to choose between `main` and `androidTest`.

10. **In the dialog box, select** `main`, **and then click OK.**

    A New Package dialog box appears.

11. **In the dialog box's Enter New Package Name field, type the name of the service app's package. Then click OK.**

    If you're following these instructions to the letter, the service app's package name is `com.allyourcode.aidlservice`.

Now, in addition to its `aidlclient` branch, the client's Project tool window contains an `aidlservice` branch. The `aidlservice` branch is a sub-branch of the `app/java/com.allyourcode` branch.

12. **Right-click (or on a Mac, Ctrl-click) the `aidlservice` branch. Then, in the resulting context menu, choose New ⇨ AIDL ⇨ AIDL File.**

As in Step 3, a dialog box appears. For the Interface Name, type the same name that you typed in Step 3.

13. **Click Finish.**

As in Step 4, the Project tool window has a new *app/aidl* branch containing an `IMyAidlInterface.aidl` item. In the editor, you see the text inside the new `IMyAidlInterface.aidl` file.

14. **Modify the `IMyAidlInterface.aidl` file's text, as shown in Listing 3-16.**

Now both the service and the client have `IMyAidlInterface.aidl` files, and both of these files belong to the `com.allyourcode.aidlservice` package.

15. **In the client project's main menu, choose Build ⇨ Make Project.**

As a result, both the service and the client have `IMyAidlInterface.java` files.

Now it's time to add some regular Java code (along with layout files and `strings.xml` files) to your two projects. The Java code in this section is very much like the service and client classes in Listings 3-6 and 3-7. But in this section's code, you don't worry about messengers and binders. The automatically generated `IMyAidlInterface.java` code takes care of that messy stuff on your behalf.

16. **In the service app's Project tool window, right-click the `com.allyourcode.service` branch.**

As usual, Ctrl-click if you're using a Mac.

17. **In the resulting context menu, select New ⇨ Service ⇨ Service.**

A dialog box appears. The dialog box has a Class Name field and two check boxes. The default class name is `MyService`. The Exported and Enabled check boxes are checked.

18. **Click Finish to accept the defaults.**

When the dust settles, you see a new `MyService` class in Android Studio's editor.

19. **Modify the `MyService` class's code, as shown in the upcoming Listing 3-17.**

The code in Listing 3-17 is quite a bit simpler than the code in Listing 3-6. The `WeatherFetcher` class in Listing 3-17 takes the place of the messengers and the handler in Listing 3-6.

20. **In the client project, modify the `ActivityMain` class's code, as shown momentarily in Listing 3-18.**

    Notice the call to `reporter.fetchWeather` in Listing 3-18. Back in Listing 3-7, the client code passes a message to the service. But with the code in Listing 3-18, the client uses an ordinary method call to get data from the service. That's much simpler than message passing.

21. **Add layout and `strings.xml` files to the client project.**

    You can reuse the files you used for Listing 3-7.

22. **Install the service and client apps on an emulator or a real device.**

23. **Run the client app.**

    The client communicates with the service through the AIDL mechanisms. The weather report appears on your screen, and the experiment is a success!

The code in Listing 3-6 has a messenger and an incoming message handler. The message handler sends a message to be delivered to the client. In contrast, the code in Listing 3-12 has a `fetchWeather` method, which simply returns a `String` value. The class in Listing 3-12 can't shoot the messenger because the class doesn't even see the messenger.

In Listings 3-17 and 3-18, the developer is free of the messy messaging business when one process communicates with another. So the developer — that's you! — can concentrate instead on the underlying application logic. Nice stuff!

Listing 3-17:   The Service Code Using AIDL

```
package com.allyourcode.aidlservice;

import android.app.Service;
import android.content.Intent;
import android.os.IBinder;

public class MyService extends Service {

  @Override
  public IBinder onBind(Intent intent) {
    return new WeatherFetcher();
  }

  class WeatherFetcher extends IMyAidlInterface.Stub {
    public String fetchWeather(String city) {
```

```
      String weatherString = null;
      if (city != null) {
        weatherString = "It's dark at night.";
      }
      return weatherString;
    }
  }

  @Override
  public boolean onUnbind(Intent intent) {
    stopSelf();
    return false;
  }
}
```

Listing 3-18:   The Client Code Using AIDL

```java
package com.allyourcode.aidlclient;

import android.app.Activity;
import android.content.ComponentName;
import android.content.Context;
import android.content.Intent;
import android.content.ServiceConnection;
import android.content.SharedPreferences;
import android.os.Bundle;
import android.os.IBinder;
import android.os.RemoteException;
import android.view.View;
import android.widget.Button;
import android.widget.EditText;
import android.widget.TextView;

import com.allyourcode.aidlservice.IMyAidlInterface;

public class MainActivity extends Activity {

  IMyAidlInterface reporter;
  ServiceConnection connection = new MyServiceConnection();
  SharedPreferences prefs;
  boolean isBound = false;

  void bind() {
    Intent intent = new Intent();
    intent.setClassName("com.allyourcode.aidlservice",
        "com.allyourcode.aidlservice.MyService");
    isBound = bindService(intent, connection,
      Context.BIND_AUTO_CREATE);
  }

  public void queryService() {
    if (isBound) {
      try {
        String report = reporter
          .fetchWeather(locationText.getText()
            .toString());
        textView.setText(report);
```

(continued)

Listing 3-18 *(continued)*

```
        } catch (RemoteException e) {
          e.printStackTrace();
        }
      } else {
        textView.setText(R.string.service_not_bound);
      }
    }

    void unbind() {
      if (isBound) {
        unbindService(connection);
        isBound = false;
      }
    }

    class MyServiceConnection implements ServiceConnection {
      public void onServiceConnected(
          ComponentName className, IBinder binder) {
        reporter = IMyAidlInterface.Stub
          .asInterface(binder);
      }

      public void onServiceDisconnected(ComponentName n) {
      }
    }

// For rest of this listing, copy the code from
// Listing 3-7 (from the onDestroy method,
// downward).
```

Chapter 4: Broadcast Receivers

In This Chapter

✔ **Creating broadcast receivers**

✔ **Organizing data from broadcast receivers**

✔ **Restricting a receiver's access**

Chapter 3 of this minibook introduces a broadcast receiver for the purpose of running code at boot time. Here's a summary of that chapter's broadcast receiver news:

✦ When you send a broadcast, Android fires up all the receivers whose filters satisfy the intent.

✦ A broadcast receiver runs long enough to execute the code in the receiver's onReceive method. A receiver has no onCreate, onDestroy, or *onAnythingElse* methods — only onReceive. After Android finishes executing the onReceive method's code, the broadcast receiver becomes dormant, doing nothing until an app sends another matching broadcast.

This chapter describes broadcast receivers in more detail.

Receivers 101

This chapter's first example contains the world's simplest broadcast receiver. To be precise, Listing 4-1 contains the receiver class (MyReceiver, which extends BroadcastReceiver), Listing 4-2 contains code to broadcast to the receiver, and Listing 4-3 contains the example's AndroidManifest. xml file.

Listing 4-1: A Simple Broadcast Receiver

```
package com.allmycode.rec1;

import android.content.BroadcastReceiver;
import android.content.Context;
import android.content.Intent;
import android.util.Log;

public class MyReceiver extends BroadcastReceiver {
```

(continued)

Listing 4-1 *(continued)*

```
@Override
public void onReceive(Context arg0, Intent arg1) {
    Log.i("MyReceiver", "Received a broadcast");
}
}
```

A class that extends `android.content.BroadcastReceiver` must implement the `onReceive` method. The class in Listing 4-1 says, "When I receive a broadcast, I'll write an entry in Android's log file."

Listing 4-2:   A Simple Broadcaster

```
package com.allmycode.rec1;

import android.app.Activity;
import android.content.Intent;
import android.os.Bundle;
import android.view.View;

public class MyActivity extends Activity {

    @Override
    public void onCreate(Bundle savedInstanceState) {
        super.onCreate(savedInstanceState);
        setContentView(R.layout.main);
    }

    public void onButtonClick(View view) {
        Intent intent = new Intent();
        intent.setAction("com.allmycode.ACTION");

        sendBroadcast(intent);
    }
}
```

In Listing 4-2, the `onButtonClick` method sends a broadcast. The method creates an intent and then feeds the intent to the `sendBroadcast` broadcast method.

In Listing 4-3, the receiver's action is `"com.allmycode.ACTION"`. And, sure enough, in Listing 4-2, the broadcast intent's action is also `"com.allmycode.ACTION"`. With no other constraints in either listing, the broadcast matches the receiver. So, when you run the code in Listings 4-1, 4-2, and 4-3, Android calls the receiver's `onReceive` method. The method writes an entry to Android's log file.

You can get the layout file for this example (and for all the book's examples) at my web site — `www.allmycode.com/android`.

Listing 4-3:   Declaring a Broadcast Receiver

```xml
<?xml version="1.0" encoding="utf-8"?>
<manifest xmlns:android=
    "http://schemas.android.com/apk/res/android"
  package="com.allmycode.rec1">

  <application android:icon="@drawable/icon"
               android:label="@string/app_name">

    <activity android:name=".MyActivity"
              android:label="@string/app_name">
      <intent-filter>
        <action android:name=
          "android.intent.action.MAIN" />
        <category android:name=
          "android.intent.category.LAUNCHER" />
      </intent-filter>
    </activity>

    <receiver android:name=".MyReceiver">
      <intent-filter>
        <action android:name="com.allmycode.ACTION" />
      </intent-filter>
    </receiver>

  </application>
</manifest>
```

Creating a receiver on the fly

Of Android's four components (`Activity`, `Service`, `BroadcastReceiver`, and `ContentProvider`), the `BroadcastReceiver` is the only component that doesn't require its own `AndroidManifest.xml` element. Instead of creating a `<receiver>` element the way I do in Listing 4-3, you can register a broadcast receiver on the fly in your code. Listing 4-4 shows you how.

Listing 4-4:   Registering a New Broadcast Receiver

```java
public void onButtonClick(View view) {
  IntentFilter filter = new IntentFilter();
  filter.addAction("com.allmycode.ACTION");
  registerReceiver(new MyReceiver(), filter);

  Intent intent = new Intent();
  intent.setAction("com.allmycode.ACTION");
  sendBroadcast(intent);
}
```

With the bold code in Listing 4-4, you eliminate the need for the `<receiver>` element in Listing 4-3. So if you're typing your own code, comment out that `<receiver>` element.

To comment out a line of XML code, surround the line with <!-- and -->.

Juggling receivers and broadcasts

You can create several instances of a broadcast receiver and send several broadcasts. Listings 4-5 and 4-6 illustrate the situation.

Listing 4-5: Registering Several Receivers

```
public void onButtonClick(View view) {
  IntentFilter filter = new IntentFilter();
  filter.addAction("com.allmycode.ACTION");
  MyReceiver receiver = new MyReceiver();

  registerReceiver(receiver, filter);
  registerReceiver(receiver, filter);
  registerReceiver(new MyReceiver(), filter);

  Intent intent = new Intent();
  intent.setAction("com.allmycode.ACTION");
  sendBroadcast(intent);

  Log.i("MyActivity",
      "Sent a broadcast; about to send another...");

  sendBroadcast(intent);
}
```

Listing 4-6: Entries in the Log

```
I/MyActivity? Sent a broadcast; about to send another...
I/MyReceiver? Received a broadcast 1422812727126
I/MyReceiver? Received a broadcast 1422812727127
I/MyReceiver? Received a broadcast 1422812727126
I/MyReceiver? Received a broadcast 1422812727127
```

Listing 4-5 contains an alternative to the onButtonClick method in Listing 4-2, and Listing 4-6 shows the output (using the MyReceiver class from Listing 4-1). Here's how it all works:

✦ **Listing 4-5 registers two instances of** MyReceiver.

Sure, the code in Listing 4-5 calls registerReceiver three times. But the second call is redundant because it contains the same MyReceiver instance as the first registerReceiver call.

✦ **Listing 4-5 sends two broadcasts.**

No argument about that.

✦ **After sending the first of the two broadcasts, the activity logs the words "Sent a broadcast; about to send another."**

But in Listing 4-6, you see log entries in a different order. In Listing 4-6, you see the activity bragging about having sent one broadcast. Then you see two broadcasts landing on two receivers (for a total of four log entries).

Remember that a broadcast isn't a method call. *Sending a broadcast* means flinging a message to the Android operating system. The system then calls `onReceive` methods in its own good time. So calls to `onReceive` (and their corresponding log entries) arrive out of sync with the sender's code. That asynchronous effect happens even if the sender and receiver classes belong to the same app.

How to unregister a receiver

You can unregister, reregister, and re-unregister broadcast receivers. You can even un-re-un-re-unregister broadcast receivers. Listings 4-7 and 4-8 illustrate all this with some code.

Listing 4-7:   Registering and Unregistering

```
package com.allmycode.rec1;

import android.app.Activity;
import android.content.Intent;
import android.content.IntentFilter;
import android.net.Uri;
import android.os.Bundle;
import android.util.Log;
import android.view.View;

public class MyActivity extends Activity {
  MyReceiver receiver1 = new MyReceiver(1);
  MyReceiver receiver2 = new MyReceiver(2);
  Intent intent = new Intent();

  IntentFilter filter = new IntentFilter();

  @Override
  public void onCreate(Bundle savedInstanceState) {
    super.onCreate(savedInstanceState);
    setContentView(R.layout.main);
  }

  public void onButtonClick(View view) {
    Log.i("MyActivity",
          "The user clicked the first button.");

    filter.addAction("com.allmycode.ACTION");
    filter.addDataScheme("letter");

    registerReceiver(receiver1, filter);
    registerReceiver(receiver2, filter);
```

(continued)

Book III
Chapter 4

Broadcast
Receivers

Listing 4-7 *(continued)*

```
    intent.setAction("com.allmycode.ACTION");
    intent.setData(Uri.parse("letter:A"));
    sendBroadcast(intent);
  }

  public void onClickOfSecondButton(View view) {
    Log.i("MyActivity", "---------------");
    Log.i("MyActivity",
          "The user clicked the second button.");

    unregisterReceiver(receiver1);

    sendBroadcast(intent);

    intent.setData(Uri.parse("letter:B"));
    sendBroadcast(intent);

    registerReceiver(receiver1, filter);
  }


}
```

In Listing 4-7, I break the activity's behavior into two clicks (of two different buttons). I do this to make sure that the unregistering of `receiver1` doesn't happen too quickly. (You can read more about this strategy later in this section.)

Also in Listing 4-7, I create two receivers and, in each receiver's constructor call, I give the receiver its own `int` value. This helps the receiver identify itself in a log entry.

I also add identifying letters to the code's intents. I could paste these letters as extras in the intents. But instead, I create my own URI scheme (the Letter scheme) and send an opaque URI along with each intent.

An *opaque URI* is a URI that has no particular structure to the right of the first colon. I describe opaque URIs in Chapter 2 of this minibook.

Listing 4-8 contains the receiver's code. The receiver writes its number and the broadcast's letter to each log entry.

Listing 4-8:   A More Verbose Broadcast Receiver

```
package com.allmycode.rec1;

import android.content.BroadcastReceiver;
import android.content.Context;
```

```
import android.content.Intent;
import android.util.Log;

public class MyReceiver extends BroadcastReceiver {
  private int number;

  public MyReceiver(int number) {
    this.number = number;
  }

  @Override
  public void onReceive(Context context, Intent intent) {
    String letter =
        intent.getData().getSchemeSpecificPart();
    Log.i("MyReceiver", number + " Received a broadcast "
        + letter);
  }
}
```

What's the log output of the code in Listings 4-7 and 4-8? Listing 4-9 has the answer.

Listing 4-9:   Entries in the Log

```
I/MyActivity? The user clicked the first button.
I/MyReceiver? 1 Received a broadcast A
I/MyReceiver? 2 Received a broadcast A
I/MyActivity? ---------------
I/MyActivity? The user clicked the second button.
I/MyReceiver? 2 Received a broadcast A
I/MyReceiver? 2 Received a broadcast B
```

Here's what happens when you run the code in Listing 4-7:

✦ **The user clicks the first button, so the code registers two instances of** `MyReceiver`, **numbered 1 and 2.**

✦ **The code sends a broadcast with letter** A.

   Both receivers get the broadcast. (See the first two lines in Listing 4-9.)

✦ **The user clicks the second button, so the code unregisters** `receiver1`.

   At this point, only `receiver2` is registered.

✦ **The code sends another broadcast with letter** A.

   Only `receiver2` gets the broadcast. (See the third line in Listing 4-9.)

✦ **The code sends another broadcast with letter** B.

   Again, `receiver2` gets the broadcast. (See the last line in Listing 4-9.)

✦ **The code reregisters** `receiver1`.

Too late. All the broadcasts have propagated through the system, and each broadcast has died its own quiet death. So `receiver1` doesn't get a broadcast, and nothing new appears in Listing 4-9.

A receiver can continue to receive until you unregister the receiver. (Notice how `receiver2` gets all three broadcasts in this section's example.)

In contrast, Android wipes away a broadcast after the broadcast reaches all currently registered receivers. (At the end of this section's example, reregistering `receiver1` has no visible effect because all the code's broadcasts have run their course.)

The preceding paragraph says, "Android wipes away a broadcast after the broadcast reaches all currently registered receivers." That's a half-truth. You can send a broadcast that sticks around on the system long after the broadcast has finished reaching all currently registered receivers. In other words, you can create a *sticky* broadcast. To find out more about it, skip ahead to the "How to be a stickler" section.

When I write "registered receivers," I include any receivers declared in the `AndroidManifest.xml` file. You don't call `registerReceiver` to start these manifest file broadcast receivers. Android registers an instance of each manifest file receiver when you install the file's app. If you happen to call `registerReceiver` for a receiver that you've declared in the `AndroidManifest.xml` file, Android responds by registering an additional instance of your broadcast receiver class.

In this example, the timing of things can make a big difference. Imagine merging the code in Listing 4-7 so that it's all performed in one button click.

```
registerReceiver(receiver1, filter);
registerReceiver(receiver2, filter);
sendBroadcast(intent);
unregisterReceiver(receiver1);
// ... Etc.
```

The code flings a broadcast into the air, and two receivers (`receiver1` and `receiver2`) are prepared to get the broadcast. But these receivers might not get the broadcast immediately. While the broadcast percolates through the system, the code marches on relentlessly and unregisters `receiver1`. So `receiver1` might be unregistered before it ever receives the broadcast. Things don't always happen this way. (Sometimes, `receiver1` might get the broadcast and respond before being unregistered.) But you have no way of knowing which things will happen in which order. That's why, in Listing 4-7, I create two separate buttons.

Broadcast receivers and contexts

Like the `startActivity` and `startService` methods, the `sendBroadcast` method belongs to the class `android.content.Context`. The familiar `Activity` class is a subclass of the `Context` class, so an activity's code can call `startActivity`, `startService`, and `sendBroadcast`. Android's `Service` class is also a subclass of the `Context` class. But the `BroadcastReceiver` class isn't a subclass of the `Context` class. So a broadcast receiver's code can't directly call `startActivity` or any of the other methods that require a context. For a workaround, have the broadcast receiver use the `context` parameter in its `onReceive` method:

```
@Override
public void onReceive(Context context, Intent intent) {
  Intent newIntent = new Intent();
  newIntent.setClassName("com.allmycode.rec3",
      "com.allmycode.rec3.OtherActivity");
  newIntent.addFlags(Intent.FLAG_ACTIVITY_NEW_TASK);
  context.startActivity(newIntent);
}
```

Beyond the Fundamentals

The earlier section of this chapter deals with some minimalist, no-nonsense broadcast receiver examples. This section covers some additional broadcast receiver features.

Managing receivers

The previous section's code is nice and simple. At least I think it's nice because I'm a teacher, both by profession and in spirit. I like the little examples, even if they're not sturdy enough to survive real-world use.

But some hard-core developers don't agree with me. They'd call Listings 4-4, 4-5, and 4-7 "bad and simple" because (and I'm being painfully honest) the code in these listings can't take a beating in the real world. In fact, the code in these listings probably wouldn't survive gentle petting. To find out why, read on.

What's the problem?

Try the following experiment:

1. **Create a brand-new Android project.**

2. **In the** `AndroidManifest.xml` **file, declare a receiver (refer to Listing 4-3).**

3. **In the main activity's layout file, add a button.**

4. **In the main activity's Java code, add a method to handle the button click.**

   For the method's body, use the body of the `onButtonClick` method in Listing 4-4.

5. **Restart your emulator.**

   If you've been testing this chapter's examples on a real Android device, restart the device. Restarting things ensures that you don't have any receivers lurking in the background as you begin this section's experiment.

6. **Run the app.**

7. **Click the button on the app's screen, and look at the resulting entries in Android Studio's Logcat panel.**

   You see two `MyReceiver Received a broadcast` entries because Android is running two `MyReceiver` instances. One instance comes from the `<receiver>` element in the `AndroidManifest.xml` document. The other receiver comes from the `registerReceiver` method call in your app's main activity.

   You might not see both `Received a broadcast` entries right away. If not, be patient.

   Having two `MyReceiver` instances isn't bad. But in most cases, it's probably not what you want. Observing these two instances is a side benefit that comes from performing this experiment.

8. **While the app is still running, press the emulator's Back button, and look again at the Logcat panel.**

   In the Logcat panel, you see a big, ugly activity has leaked an IntentReceiver error message. The message tells you that Android has destroyed your activity. In doing so, Android noticed that you didn't unregister the receiver that you registered in Listing 4-4, so Android unregisters this receiver for you. (In essence, Android behaves like your mother when you don't clean your room. Android says, "If you refuse to clean up after yourself, I'll clean up for you. I'll terminate your broadcast receiver. And just like your mother, I'll show my disapproval by writing an entry to the log file." If only Mom had been so even-tempered!)

   The problem is, you're getting rid of your activity and leaving your registered receiver in limbo. If other developers do the same thing, the user's Android device can have all kinds of broadcast receivers floating around after their parent activities have been destroyed. The device experiences its own *Night of the Living Broadcast Receivers*.

Android doesn't like the `MyReceiver` instance that I register and don't unregister in Listing 4-4. But Android isn't upset about the `MyReceiver` instance from the `AndroidManifest.xml` file (refer to Listing 4-3). Android expects receivers declared this way to have a life of their own, surviving past the lifetime of any activities in the application.

The error message `activity has leaked IntentReceiver` hints that Android's SDK has an `IntentReceiver` class. But that's misleading. The name `IntentReceiver` is an artifact from Android's early history. What used to be called an `IntentReceiver` is now a `BroadcastReceiver`.

You might not be impressed by Step 9's `activity has leaked IntentReceiver` message. After all, Android doesn't alert the user, so your app doesn't look bad. And when the user clicks the Back button, you probably don't mind that Android terminates your broadcast receiver. So what's the big deal? Well, try the next few steps . . .

9. **In Android Studio's main menu, choose Run ⇨ Run 'app' to restart this section's app.**

10. **Again, press the button on the activity's screen to invoke the code in Listing 4-4.**

11. **While the app is still running, turn the emulator sideways by pressing Ctrl+F11.**

    Of course, if you're testing on a real device, simply turn the device sideways.

    In Android Studio's Logcat panel, look again for the insulting `activity has leaked IntentReceiver` error message. Unless you override the default behavior, Android destroys and re-creates your activity when the device's orientation changes. As far as the user is concerned, the activity is still alive and well. But unbeknownst to the user, Android killed the broadcast receiver and hasn't revived it. You've lost a broadcast receiver just by tilting the device. It's difficult to imagine a scenario in which you want that to happen.

What's the solution?

In most of this chapter's simple examples, I register and unregister receivers in one or more `onButtonClick` methods. I do it to illustrate a step-by-step progression of registrations, broadcasts, receipts of broadcasts, and so on. It's okay if I include logic to deal with the nasty things that happen in the previous section's example.

But the logic to avoid the previous section's pitfalls can become complicated, and it's easy to make mistakes. That's why it's best to do receiver registering and unregistering in an activity's lifecycle methods. Listing 4-10 shows you what to do.

Listing 4-10: Dealing with the Component Lifecycle

```
package com.allmycode.rec1;

import android.app.Activity;
import android.content.Intent;
import android.content.IntentFilter;
import android.os.Bundle;
import android.view.View;

public class MyActivity extends Activity {
  MyReceiver receiver = new MyReceiver();

  @Override
  public void onCreate(Bundle savedInstanceState) {
    super.onCreate(savedInstanceState);
    setContentView(R.layout.main);
  }

  @Override
  public void onResume() {
    super.onResume();
    IntentFilter filter = new IntentFilter();
    filter.addAction("com.allmycode.ACTION");

    registerReceiver(receiver, filter);
  }

  @Override
  public void onPause() {
    super.onPause();
    unregisterReceiver(receiver);
  }

  public void onButtonClick(View view) {
    Intent intent = new Intent();
    intent.setAction("com.allmycode.ACTION");
    sendBroadcast(intent);
  }
}
```

I can state the big message in Listing 4-10 very simply: Make things in an activity's onResume method and then get rid of these things in the activity's onPause method. If you want things to live longer, make things in the activity's onCreate method and get rid of these things in the activity's onDestroy method. That's it. (And yes, I'm aware that I wrote the whole "Managing receivers" section to pontificate about something that I can summarize at the end in only two sentences. Thanks for noticing!)

How to be a stickler

An ordinary broadcast disintegrates after it's sent to all the matching, currently running receivers. But another kind of broadcast — a *sticky* broadcast — hangs on until someone or something explicitly removes the broadcast. To remove a sticky broadcast, you can call removeStickyBroadcast. Alternatively, you can turn off your device, hit your device with a hammer, or do other unpleasant things. Listing 4-11 contains some informative code.

Listing 4-11: Sending a Sticky Broadcast

```
package com.allmycode.rec1;

import android.app.Activity;
import android.content.Intent;
import android.content.IntentFilter;
import android.net.Uri;
import android.os.Bundle;
import android.view.View;
import android.widget.Button;

public class MyActivity extends Activity {
  MyReceiver receiver1 = new MyReceiver(1);
  MyReceiver receiver2 = new MyReceiver(2);
  MyReceiver receiver3 = new MyReceiver(3);
  Intent intent = new Intent();
  IntentFilter filter = new IntentFilter();
  Button button, button2, button3, button4, button5;

  @Override
  public void onCreate(Bundle savedInstanceState) {
    super.onCreate(savedInstanceState);
    setContentView(R.layout.main);

    button = (Button) findViewById(R.id.button);
    button2 = (Button) findViewById(R.id.button2);
    button3 = (Button) findViewById(R.id.button3);
    button4 = (Button) findViewById(R.id.button4);
    button5 = (Button) findViewById(R.id.button5);

  }

  public void onButtonClick(View view) {
    if (view == button) {

      filter.addAction("com.allmycode.ACTION");
      filter.addDataScheme("letter");
      registerReceiver(receiver1, filter);

    } else if (view == button2) {

      intent.setAction("com.allmycode.ACTION");
      intent.setData(Uri.parse("letter:A"));
      sendStickyBroadcast(intent);

    } else if (view == button3) {

      registerReceiver(receiver2, filter);

    } else if (view == button4) {

      removeStickyBroadcast(intent);

    } else if (view == button5) {

      registerReceiver(receiver3, filter);

    }
  }
}
```

This section's experiment involves so many buttons that I decided to put all button-clicking code into one big method. In the activity's layout file, I set each button's `onClick` attribute to `onButtonClick`. Then in the Java code (Listing 4-11), the `onButtonClick` method tests to find out which of the five buttons experienced the click event.

Imagine that the user clicks `button`, `button2`, `button3`, and so on, in order one after another. With the receiver that I set up back in Listing 4-8, Android logs the entries shown in Listing 4-12.

Listing 4-12:   Log File Entries

```
I/MyReceiver? 1 Received a broadcast A
I/MyReceiver? 2 Received a broadcast A
```

By clicking the first and second buttons, I register `receiver1` and then send the broadcast. So `receiver1` receives the broadcast, and you get the first line in Listing 4-12. No big deal here.

At this point in the run of Listing 4-11, `receiver1` is the only currently registered receiver, and `receiver1` has received the broadcast. But the broadcast is sticky, so the broadcast lives on. When I click the third button, I register `receiver2`, and at that point, `receiver2` receives the broadcast. That's what stickiness does.

By pressing the last two buttons, I remove the sticky broadcast (with a method call, not with turpentine), and I register `receiver3`. Because I've removed the only matching broadcast, `receiver3` receives nothing.

A component that calls `sendStickyBroadcast` (or calls the closely related `sendStickyOrderedBroadcast` method) must have the `<uses-permission android:name="android.permission.BROADCAST_STICKY" />` element in its app's `AndroidManifest.xml` document. A component that calls `sendBroadcast` (or its friend, the `sendOrderedBroadcast` method) doesn't need permission to do so.

For a bare-bones `<uses-permission>` example (one that doesn't involve broadcast receivers), see Book I, Chapter 6.

Using receiver intents

At some point, you might have several receivers and several sticky broadcasts vying for attention in a multiprocess, nondeterministic fashion. Sounds like fun, doesn't it? You may also be dealing with broadcasts from other apps and from the system itself. To help you keep track of the comings and goings, the `registerReceiver` method returns an intent. This intent comes from one of the (possibly many) broadcasts that the newly registered receiver catches.

In Listing 4-13, I register two receivers and fling two sticky broadcasts ("letter:A" and "letter:O") into the air. For each receiver registration, Listing 4-13 logs an intent caught by the receiver.

Listing 4-13:   Getting an Intent from a Receiver's Registration

```
package com.allmycode.rec1;

import android.app.Activity;
import android.content.Intent;
import android.content.IntentFilter;
import android.net.Uri;
import android.os.Bundle;
import android.util.Log;
import android.view.View;
import android.widget.Button;

public class MyActivity extends Activity {
  Button button, button2, button3, button4, button5;
  IntentFilter filter = new IntentFilter();
  MyReceiver receiver1 = new MyReceiver(1);
  MyReceiver receiver2 = new MyReceiver(2);
  Intent returnedIntent, intentAct, intentOth;

  @Override
  public void onCreate(Bundle savedInstanceState) {
    super.onCreate(savedInstanceState);
    setContentView(R.layout.main);
    button = (Button) findViewById(R.id.button);
    button2 = (Button) findViewById(R.id.button2);
    button3 = (Button) findViewById(R.id.button3);
    button4 = (Button) findViewById(R.id.button4);
    button5 = (Button) findViewById(R.id.button5);
  }

  public void onButtonClick(View view) {
    if (view == button) {

      filter.addAction("com.allmycode.ACTION");

      filter.addAction("com.allmycode.OTHER_ACTION");
      filter.addDataScheme("letter");
      returnedIntent = registerReceiver(receiver1, filter);
      Log.i("MyActivity", getStatus(returnedIntent));

    } else if (view == button2) {

      intentAct = new Intent();
      intentAct.setAction("com.allmycode.ACTION");
      intentAct.setData(Uri.parse("letter:A"));
      sendStickyBroadcast(intentAct);
```

(continued)

Listing 4-13 *(continued)*

```
    } else if (view == button3) {

        intentOth = new Intent();
        intentOth.setAction("com.allmycode.OTHER_ACTION");
        intentOth.setData(Uri.parse("letter:O"));
        sendStickyBroadcast(intentOth);

    } else if (view == button4) {

        returnedIntent = registerReceiver(receiver2, filter);
        Log.i("MyActivity", getStatus(returnedIntent));

    } else if (view == button5) {

        removeStickyBroadcast(intentAct);
        removeStickyBroadcast(intentOth);
        unregisterReceiver(receiver1);
        unregisterReceiver(receiver2);

    }
}

private String getStatus(Intent returnedIntent) {
    if (returnedIntent == null) {
        return "null";
    } else {
        return returnedIntent.toString();
    }
}
}
```

Listing 4-14 shows the results of a run of Listing 4-13's code (using the receiver in Listing 4-8, and pressing the buttons in order during the run). The first registration returns `null` rather than an actual intent. This happens because no broadcast is alive when the code executes this first registration.

Listing 4-14:   Log This!

```
I/MyActivity? null
I/MyReceiver? 1 Received a broadcast A 1422834917781
I/MyReceiver? 1 Received a broadcast O 1422834917781
I/MyActivity?
  Intent { act=com.allmycode.ACTION dat=letter:A flg=0x10 }
I/MyReceiver? 2 Received a broadcast A 1422835011653
I/MyReceiver? 2 Received a broadcast O 1422835011653
```

The second receiver registration returns the `"com.allmycode.ACTION"` intent. The receiver's filter has both `"com.allmycode.ACTION"` and `"com.allmycode.OTHER_ACTION"`, and both of these actions belong to active sticky broadcasts. But the call to `registerReceiver` returns only one of the broadcasts' intents. One way or another, two receivers catch two broadcasts.

Ordered broadcasts

Android takes a regular broadcast and throws it into the air. Then the receivers with matching filters jump like basketball players, catching the broadcast in no particular order. This "no particular order" behavior can be nice because it frees up the system to make the most of any available processing time.

But occasionally you want a predictable sequence of `onReceive` calls. To achieve such behavior, you assign priorities to the receivers' intent filters and then send an *ordered* broadcast.

In this chapter's log listings, receivers seem to form a first-come/first-served waiting line to catch broadcasts. That's fine. But in general, Android makes no promises about this polite behavior. In fact, Android might run two receivers at once. You never know.

Listing 4-15 prioritizes receivers and sends an ordered broadcast.

Listing 4-15:   Set Your Priorities

```
public void onButtonClick(View view) {
    IntentFilter filter = new IntentFilter();
    filter.addAction("com.allmycode.ACTION");
    filter.addDataScheme("letter");

    IntentFilter filter1 = new IntentFilter(filter);
    IntentFilter filter2 = new IntentFilter(filter);
    IntentFilter filter3 = new IntentFilter(filter);

    filter1.setPriority(17);
    filter2
        .setPriority(IntentFilter.SYSTEM_HIGH_PRIORITY - 1);
    filter3.setPriority(-853);

    MyReceiver receiver1 = new MyReceiver(1);
    MyReceiver receiver2 = new MyReceiver(2);
    MyReceiver receiver3 = new MyReceiver(3);

    registerReceiver(receiver1, filter1);
    registerReceiver(receiver2, filter2);
    registerReceiver(receiver3, filter3);

    Intent intent = new Intent();
    intent.setAction("com.allmycode.ACTION");
    intent.setData(Uri.parse("letter:A"));

    sendOrderedBroadcast(intent, null);
    Log.i("MyActivity",
        "Now watch the log entries pour in...");
}
```

From a single intent filter, Listing 4-15 stamps out three copies. Then the code assigns a priority to each copy. Priorities are int values, ranging from @nd999 to 999. Android reserves the values –1000 (IntentFilter. SYSTEM_LOW_PRIORITY) and 1000 (IntentFilter.SYSTEM_HIGH_ PRIORITY) for its own private use.

You can set an intent filter's priority in an app's AndroidManifest.xml document. Do so with an attribute, such as android:priority="17".

After registering three receivers (one for each of the three filters), Listing 4-15 sends an ordered broadcast and lets the chips fall where they may. The chips fall in Listing 4-16.

Listing 4-16:   Yet Another Log

```
I/MyActivity? Now watch the log entries pour in...
I/MyReceiver? 2 Received a broadcast A 1422835783590
I/MyReceiver? 1 Received a broadcast A 1422835783613
I/MyReceiver? 3 Received a broadcast A 1422835783618
```

Listing 4-16 confirms that receiver2 — the receiver with the highest priority — receives the broadcast first. Poor receiver3 — the receiver with the lowest priority — receives the broadcast last.

Stopping a broadcast in its tracks

In the preceding section, an ordered broadcast travels from one receiver to another. The sequence of receivers depends on their relative priorities.

In this section, you play a nasty trick on all but one of the receiver instances. To do so, change the MyReceiver class's code, as in Listing 4-17.

Listing 4-17:   Aborting a Broadcast

```
package com.allmycode.rec1;

import android.content.BroadcastReceiver;
import android.content.Context;
import android.content.Intent;
import android.util.Log;

public class MyReceiver extends BroadcastReceiver {
  private int number;

  public MyReceiver(int number) {
    this.number = number;
  }
```

```
   @Override
   public void onReceive(Context context, Intent intent) {
     String letter =
         intent.getData().getSchemeSpecificPart();
     Log.i("MyReceiver", number + " Received a broadcast "
         + letter);
     abortBroadcast();
   }
}
```

With the call to `abortBroadcast` in Listing 4-17, a run of the code in Listing 4-15 creates only two log entries:

```
I/MyActivity? Now watch the log entries pour in...
I/MyReceiver? 2 Received a broadcast A
```

The second log entry comes from an instance of the receiver in Listing 4-17. The listing's call to `abortBroadcast` stops the ordered broadcast in its tracks. Other instances of `MyReceiver` never see the broadcast.

The `abortBroadcast` method works only with ordered broadcasts. Normally, you have a `MyReceiver` instance abort a broadcast so that some other receiver (maybe a `YourReceiver` instance) doesn't get the broadcast. But in this chapter's examples, I keep things simple by creating only one `MyReceiver` class and several instances of the class.

Getting results from receivers

What will they think of next? You have sticky broadcasts and ordered broadcasts. Why not have a broadcast that's both sticky and ordered? Developers typically use sticky, ordered broadcasts to collect results from several broadcast receivers.

Listing 4-18 contains a receiver on steroids.

Listing 4-18:   A Receiver Manages Data

```
package com.allmycode.rec1;

import java.util.ArrayList;

import android.app.Activity;
import android.content.BroadcastReceiver;
import android.content.Context;
import android.content.Intent;
import android.os.Bundle;
import android.util.Log;
```

(continued)

**Book III
Chapter 4**

**Broadcast
Receivers**

Listing 4-18 *(continued)*

```
public class MyReceiver extends BroadcastReceiver {
  private int number;
  private boolean INTENTIONALLY_FAIL = false;

  public MyReceiver(int number) {
    this.number = number;
  }

  @Override
  public void onReceive(Context context, Intent intent) {
    String letter =
        intent.getData().getSchemeSpecificPart();
    Log.i("MyReceiver", number + " Received a broadcast "
        + letter);

    if (INTENTIONALLY_FAIL) {
      setResultCode(Activity.RESULT_CANCELED);
      return;
    }

    if (getResultCode() == Activity.RESULT_OK) {
      Bundle bundle = getResultExtras(true);
      ArrayList<Integer> receiverNums =
          bundle.getIntegerArrayList("receiverNums");
      if (receiverNums != null) {
        receiverNums.add(new Integer(number));

      }
      setResultExtras(bundle);
    }
  }
}
```

An ordered broadcast goes to an ordered chain of receiver instances. Along with the broadcast, each receiver instance gets *result extras* from the previous receiver in the chain. These result extras take the form of a bundle.

For the lowdown on bundles, see Chapter 3 of this minibook.

An instance of the receiver in Listing 4-18 gets a bundle containing an `ArrayList` of integers. This `ArrayList` happens to contain the numbers of all the previous receiver instances in the ordered broadcast's chain. The instance in Listing 4-18 adds its own number to the `ArrayList` and then sets its own result to be the newly enhanced `ArrayList`. The next receiver instance in the chain gets this newly enhanced `ArrayList`.

Notice the `getResultCode` and `setResultCode` method calls in Listing 4-18. For an ordered broadcast, each receiver gets a result code from the previous receiver in the chain, and sets a result code for the next receiver in the chain. In Listing 4-18, the call to `getResultCode` checks for the `android.app.Activity.RESULT_OK` code. (The value of `android.app.Activity.RESULT_OK` happens to be @nd1, but you never test if (getResultCode() == -1). You always test if (getResultCode() == Activity.RESULT_OK).) Any receiver instance in the chain can mess up the works with a result code that's not OK.

In Listing 4-18, I add an extra INTENTIONALLY_FAIL constant to test undesirable situations. Changing the constant's value to true forces Listing 4-18 to set the result code to android.app.Activity.RESULT_CANCELED. After that, any result from the ordered broadcast can't be trusted.

Always remove testing and debugging code (such as the INTENTIONALLY_ FAIL code in Listing 4-18) before you publish your app.

Listing 4-19 puts the receiver in Listing 4-18 through its paces.

Listing 4-19: Dealing with the Result from a Chain of Receivers

```
package com.allmycode.rec1;

import java.util.ArrayList;

import android.app.Activity;
import android.content.BroadcastReceiver;
import android.content.Context;
import android.content.Intent;
import android.content.IntentFilter;
import android.net.Uri;
import android.os.Bundle;
import android.util.Log;
import android.view.View;

public class MyActivity extends Activity {

  @Override
  public void onCreate(Bundle savedInstanceState) {
    super.onCreate(savedInstanceState);
    setContentView(R.layout.main);
  }

  public void onButtonClick(View view) {
    IntentFilter filter = new IntentFilter();
    filter.addAction("com.allmycode.ACTION");
    filter.addDataScheme("letter");

    IntentFilter filter1 = new IntentFilter(filter);
    IntentFilter filter2 = new IntentFilter(filter);
    IntentFilter filter3 = new IntentFilter(filter);

    MyReceiver receiver1 = new MyReceiver(1);
    MyReceiver receiver2 = new MyReceiver(2);
    MyReceiver receiver3 = new MyReceiver(3);

    registerReceiver(receiver1, filter1);
    registerReceiver(receiver2, filter2);
    registerReceiver(receiver3, filter3);
```

Book III
Chapter 4

Broadcast
Receivers

(continued)

Listing 4-19 *(continued)*

```
    Intent intent = new Intent();
    intent.setAction("com.allmycode.ACTION");
    intent.setData(Uri.parse("letter:A"));

    MyEndResultReceiver resultReceiver =
        new MyEndResultReceiver();
    ArrayList<Integer> receiverNums =
        new ArrayList<Integer>();
    Bundle bundle = new Bundle();
    bundle.putIntegerArrayList("receiverNums",
        receiverNums);

    sendStickyOrderedBroadcast(intent, resultReceiver,
        null, Activity.RESULT_OK, null, bundle);
  }
}

class MyEndResultReceiver extends BroadcastReceiver {

  final static String CLASSNAME = "MyEndResultReceiver";

  @Override
  public void onReceive(Context context, Intent intent) {
    if (getResultCode() == Activity.RESULT_OK) {
      Bundle bundle = getResultExtras(true);
      ArrayList<Integer> receiverNums =
          bundle.getIntegerArrayList("receiverNums");
      Log.i(CLASSNAME, receiverNums.toString());
    } else {
      Log.i(
          CLASSNAME,
          "Result code: "

    }
  }
}
```

In Listing 4-19, the call to `sendStickyOrderedBroadcast` takes a boatload of parameters. The official signature of method `sendStickyOrderedBroadcast` is as follows:

```
public void
sendStickyOrderedBroadcast(Intent intent,
                           BroadcastReceiver resultReceiver,
                           Handler scheduler,
                           int initialCode,
                           String initialData,
                           Bundle initialExtras)
```

✦ **The `intent` parameter plays the same role as any other broadcast's intent.**

The `intent` presents a list of criteria to test against receivers' filters.

✦ **The** `resultReceiver` **is the last instance in the ordered broadcast's calling chain.**

By specifying the result receiver, you know where to look for the accumulated results.

✦ **The** `scheduler` **(if it's not** `null`**) handles messages coming from the** `resultReceiver`.

✦ **The** `initialCode` **is the starting value for the sequence of result codes passed from one receiver to the next.**

In most apps, the `initialCode`'s value is `Activity.RESULT_OK`. You give the `initialCode` a different value only when you're making up your own custom result code values. When you do such a thing, you program your app to respond sensibly to each of the made-up values.

✦ **The** `initialData` **(if it's not** `null`**) is a starting value for a string that's passed from receiver to receiver in the chain.**

An ordered broadcast carries a bundle (the result extras) and a code (an `int` value, such as `Activity.RESULT_OK`). In addition, an order broadcast carries *result data* — a `String` value that can be examined and modified by each receiver instance in the chain.

✦ **The** `initialExtras` **is a starting value for the broadcast's bundle of extra stuff.**

In Listing 4-19, the `initialExtras` bundle is an empty `ArrayList`. Each receiver instance that gets the broadcast adds its number to this `ArrayList`.

Listing 4-20 shows the output of the code in Listings 4-18 and 4-19.

Listing 4-20: More Log Entries

```
I/MyReceiver? 1 Received a broadcast A
I/MyReceiver? 2 Received a broadcast A
I/MyReceiver? 3 Received a broadcast A
I/MyEndResultReceiver? [1, 2, 3]
```

The broadcast ends its run at an instance of `MyEndResultReceiver` — the instance named *last in the chain* by the `sendStickyOrdered` `Broadcast` call in Listing 4-19. When this last receiver does it stuff, the receiver logs `[1, 2, 3]` — the accumulated `ArrayList` of receiver numbers.

Using permissions and other tricks

To send a broadcast, you toss an intent into the ether. A broadcast receiver gets the intent if the receiver's filter matches the intent. And that's the whole story. Or is it?

When you send a broadcast, you can also specify a permission. Permissions come from those `<uses-permission>` elements that you put in your `AndroidManifest.xml` document (after first forgetting to do it and getting an error message).

In Listing 4-21, the `sendBroadcast` call's second parameter is a permission.

Listing 4-21:   Requiring a Permission

```
public void onButtonClick(View view) {
  Intent intent = new Intent();
  intent.setAction("THIS_ACTION");

  sendBroadcast(intent,
      android.Manifest.permission.INTERNET);
}
```

The receiver declared in Listing 4-22 catches the broadcast in Listing 4-21.

Listing 4-22:   Declaring That an App Has a Permission

```
<?xml version="1.0" encoding="utf-8"?>
<manifest xmlns:android=
    "http://schemas.android.com/apk/res/android"
        package="com.allmycode.receiver2"
        android:versionCode="1"
        android:versionName="1.0">

  <uses-sdk android:minSdkVersion="8" />

  <uses-permission
    android:name="android.permission.INTERNET" />

  <application android:icon="@drawable/icon"
              android:label="@string/app_name">

    <receiver android:name=
      "com.allmycode.receiver2.MyReceiverWithPermission">

      <intent-filter>
        <action android:name="THIS_ACTION" />
      </intent-filter>
    </receiver>

  </application>
</manifest>
```

Another receiver that's in an app whose manifest doesn't have the `<uses-permission>` element can't receive the broadcast from Listing 4-21.

Android's built-in `android.Manifest.permission.INTERNET` constant (used in Listing 4-21) has `String` value `"android.permission.INTERNET"`. At the risk of being gauche, you can use the quoted string `"android.permission.INTERNET"` in the Java code of Listing 4-21. But you can't use the `android.Manifest.permission.INTERNET` constant in Listing 4-13 or in any other `AndroidManifest.xml` document.

Android has all kinds of mechanisms for shielding components from other components. For example, you can add an attribute to the `<receiver>` start tag in Listing 4-22:

```
<receiver android:name=
    "com.allmycode.receiver2.MyReceiverWithPermission"
    android:exported="false">
```

If you do, no component outside the receiver's app can send a broadcast to this receiver.

Standard Broadcasts

Chapter 2 of this minibook contains a list of some standard actions for starting activities. Android's SDK also contains standard actions for sending broadcasts. Table 4-1 has a list of some actions that your app can broadcast.

Table 4-1	Some Standard Broadcast Actions	
String Value	*Constant Name*	*A Broadcast Receiver with This Action in One of Its Filters Can . . .*
`"android.intent. action.CAMERA_ BUTTON"`	`Intent.ACTION_ CAMERA_BUTTON`	Respond to the user pressing the camera button.
`"android.intent. action.HEADSET_ PLUG"`	`Intent.ACTION_ HEADSET_PLUG`	Respond to a wired headset being plugged or unplugged.
`"android.intent. action.DATE_ CHANGED"`	`Intent.ACTION_ DATE_CHANGED`	Respond to the system's date being changed.
`"android.intent. action.TIME_SET"`	`Intent.ACTION_ TIME_CHANGED`	Respond to the system's time being changed.
`"android.intent. action.INPUT_ METHOD_CHANGED"`	`Intent.ACTION_ INPUT_METHOD_ CHANGED`	Respond to a change of the device's input method.

(continued)

Table 4-1 *(continued)*

String Value	Constant Name	A Broadcast Receiver with This Action in One of Its Filters Can . . .
`"android.intent. action.MEDIA_ MOUNTED"`	`Intent.ACTION_ MEDIA_MOUNTED`	Respond to the insertion of an SD card (or some other media).
`"android.intent. action.MEDIA_ EJECT"`	`Intent.ACTION_ MEDIA_EJECT`	Respond to a request to allow media to be removed.
`"android.intent. action.MEDIA_ REMOVED"`	`Intent.ACTION_ MEDIA_REMOVED`	Respond to the proper removal of media.
`"android.intent. action.MEDIA_ BAD_REMOVAL"`	`Intent.ACTION_ MEDIA_BAD_ REMOVAL`	Respond to the improper removal of an SD card (or some other media).

The actions in Table 4-1 are both *libre* and *gratis*. Or, to paraphrase Richard Stallman, the actions are free as in "free speech" and free as in "free beer."* Whatever metaphor you prefer, you can broadcast or receive intents with the actions in Table 4-1.

The actions in Table 4-2 resemble beer more than they resemble speech. In your app's code, a broadcast receiver's filter can include these actions. But your app can't broadcast an intent having any of these actions. Only the operating system can broadcast intents that include the actions in Table 4-2.

As an Android developer, you can test the effect of broadcasting any of the actions in Table 4-2. To do so, you become superuser on the Android shell and issue an am command. (In Linux, a *superuser* has administrative privileges. A consumer becomes superuser when he or she *roots* a device.) For an example of the use of the am command, see Chapter 3 of this minibook.

For a complete list of Android's standard actions, visit `http:// developer.android.com/reference/android/content/Intent. html`.

*From "The Free Software Definition," `www.gnu.org/philosophy/free-sw.html`.

Table 4-2	Some Standard System Broadcast Actions	
String Value	*Constant Name*	*A Broadcast Receiver with This Action in One of Its Filters Can . . .*
"android. intent.action. SCREEN_OFF"	Intent.ACTION_ SCREEN_OFF	Respond to the device going to sleep (whether or not the screen turns off).
"android. intent.action. SCREEN_ON"	Intent.ACTION_ SCREEN_ON	Respond to the device waking up (whether or not screen turns on).
"android. intent.action. DREAMING_ STARTED"	intent.ACTION_ DREAMING_ STARTED	Respond when the device starts dreaming. (Yes, this is for real!)
"android. intent. action.BOOT_ COMPLETED"	Intent.ACTION_ BOOT_COMPLETED	Respond to the end of system startup.
"android. intent.action. BATTERY_LOW"	Intent.ACTION_ BATTERY_LOW	Respond to a low-battery condition.
"android. intent.action. BATTERY_OKAY"	Intent.ACTION_ BATTERY_OKAY	Respond to the battery's condition no longer being low.
"android. intent.action. DEVICE_ STORAGE_LOW"	Intent.DEVICE_ STORAGE_LOW	Respond to memory becoming low.
"android. intent.action. DEVICE_ STORAGE_OK"	Intent.DEVICE_ STORAGE_OK	Respond to memory no longer being low.
"android. intent.action. ACTION_POWER_ CONNECTED"	Intent. ACTION_POWER_ CONNECTED	Respond to a power cord being connected.
"android. intent.action. ACTION_POWER_ DISCONNECTED"	Intent. ACTION_POWER_ DISCONNECTED	Respond to a power cord being removed.

(continued)

Table 4-2 *(continued)*

String Value	Constant Name	A Broadcast Receiver with This Action in One of Its Filters Can . . .
"android. intent.action. LOCALE_ CHANGED"	Intent.LOCALE_ CHANGED	Respond to a change in locale (from the United States to the United Kingdom, for example).
"android. intent.action. TIMEZONE_ CHANGED"	Intent.ACTION_ TIMEZONE_ CHANGED	Respond to the system's time zone being changed.
"android. intent.action. TIME_TICK"	Intent.ACTION_ TIME_TICK	Respond when the system broadcasts this TIME_ TICK action once each minute.
"android. intent.action. NEW_OUTGOING_ CALL"	Intent.NEW_ OUTGOING_CALL	Respond to the start of an outgoing call.

Chapter 5: Content Providers

*I*n his introduction to *Napalm & Silly Putty* (Hyperion Books), George Carlin wrote, "For the next few hundred pages, I will be your content provider." Carlin was poking fun at business-speak phrases and other phrases that seem artificially lofty or commercially sanitized. Little did he know that a few years later, the introduction to his book would compare him to an Android SDK component.

Databases: From the Stone Age to the Present Day

A *database* is a place to store lots of data. Nobody's surprised about that. A *database management system* is a bunch of software for creating the data, finding the data, and doing other useful things with the data.

Until the mid-1970s, people didn't agree on the best structure for storing data in a database. Some argued for hierarchical structures, whereas others swore that networked structures were the only way to go. But in the 1970s, Edgar Codd (working at IBM) published papers on relational structures for storing data. Since the mid-1980s, the relational database has been the all-around favorite.

A *relational database* is a bunch of *tables.* Like a table in this book, a database table has *rows* and *columns.* Each row represents an instance (a customer, an employee, an appointment, or whatever), and each column represents a property of some kind (such as the customer's name, the employee's salary, or the appointment's time). Table 5-1 is a table in this book, but it might as well be a table in a relational database.

A Java programmer might compare a database table to a Java class. Each instance is a row, and each public field is column. In fact, this similarity between tables and classes has been apparent to people for quite a while. Many software frameworks specialize in *object-relational mapping (ORM)*, in which the software automatically manages the correspondence between Java objects and relational database tables.

Table 5-1		Customers	
Account Number	*Name*	*Outstanding Balance*	*Comment*
001	Boris Bleeper	25.00	Valued, long-time customer
002	Barry Burd	454.21	Deadbeat
003	Jane Q. Customer	0.00	Valued, long-time customer

These days, database systems without tables are all the rage. Such systems are called NoSQL databases. Instead of tables, such systems have documents, graph structures, and other things. You can talk to a NoSQL database from an Android app. But in this chapter, I stick with plain, old relational databases.

A *database management system (DBMS)* stores database data and provides access to the data for administrators and users. A *database administrator (DBA)* is a person who keeps the DBMS software running. A *user* is a person who gets information from the database and (with the right privileges) modifies values stored in the database. A user might directly or indirectly add rows to a table, but a user doesn't add columns to a table or change a table's structure in any way.

A database management system uses sophisticated data structures and algorithms to efficiently store and retrieve data. So the data in a database seldom lives in a flat file.

A *flat file* is an ordinary bunch of data on a hard drive, with no special pointers or indices to important places inside the file. Database management systems offer the option to store data in flat files, but only as a necessary evil for quick-and-dirty data storage. With database tables in a flat file, the DBMS has to chug slowly and inefficiently through the file for any data that you need.

Database management systems come from many different vendors, with many different price ranges and many different feature sets. The big commercial players are IBM (with its DB2 software), Microsoft (with its Access and SQL Server products), and Oracle (with its aptly named Oracle Database). Some popular noncommercial products include MySQL (owned by Oracle), PostgreSQL, and SQLite. Each Android device comes with SQLite software.

In general, you communicate with a database in the following way:

✦ You connect to the database (whatever that means).

✦ You query the database, asking for rows and columns matching criteria that you specify.

In response, the database management system hands you a cursor. A *cursor* is a minitable; it's a table of the rows and columns that match your query. The database management system distills the information in the database in order to deliver the cursor to you.

Like a regular database table, a cursor consists of rows and columns. At any point in time, the cursor points to one of the rows in the table (or to the never-never land after the table's last row).

✦ You step from row to row with the cursor, doing whatever you need to do with each row of data.

✦ Finally (and not unimportantly), you close the connection to the database.

Depending on your permissions, you can also create a table, modify the values in rows of the table, insert rows into the table, and do other things. The four major table operations go by the name *CRUD,* which stands for *C*reate, *R*ead, *U*pdate, and *D*elete.

The most common way of issuing commands to a DBMS is with SQL — the *S*tructured *Q*uery *L*anguage. (Depending on your mood, you can pronounce the SQL acronym *ess-kyoo-el* or *sequel.*) An SQL statement looks something like this:

```
SELECT * FROM CUSTOMER_TABLE WHERE COMMENT-'Deadbeat';
```

Each database management system has its own dialect of SQL, so the only way to study SQL in detail is to work exclusively with one DBMS. With Android's SDK, you can add strings containing SQL commands to your code. But you can also call methods that compose SQL commands on your behalf.

For the rules governing SQLite's use of SQL, visit `http://sqlite.org/lang.html`.

Working with a Database

With Android's SDK, an app has two ways to access a database:

✦ An app can access its own database directly with commands to SQLite. (See Figure 5-1.)

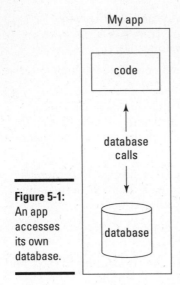

Figure 5-1:
An app
accesses
its own
database.

✦ An app can access another app's database indirectly with commands to
the other app's content provider. (See Figure 5-2.)

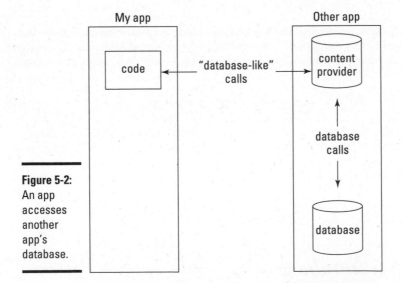

Figure 5-2:
An app
accesses
another
app's
database.

In the interest of full disclosure, I must write that content providers don't
work exclusively with databases. A content provider is a bridge between an
app's code and another app's data. The other app's data doesn't have to be
part of a database. But the content provider's publicly exposed methods

look like database calls. So to anyone living outside the provider's app, the provider's data looks like database data. (See Figure 5-3.) The provider creates an abstract database-like view of whatever data lives underneath it.

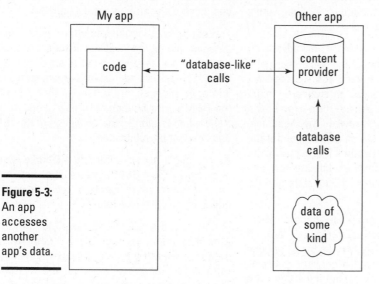

Figure 5-3:
An app
accesses
another
app's data.

Book III
Chapter 5

Content Providers

The rest of this chapter consists of two examples. The first example demonstrates an app creating its own SQLite database and making calls directly to that database. In the second example, an app makes data available using a content provider, and another app accesses the first app's data through the provider.

As you compare the first and second examples, you'll notice some striking similarities. The second example is very much like the first. To get the second example, I (figuratively) tear the first example in half, giving half of the first example's code to the new content provider and giving the other half of the first example's code to a brand-new app.

Coding for SQLite using Android's SDK

Listing 5-1 contains code to access an SQLite database. When the activity begins running, the code inserts data, then modifies the data, and then deletes the data. To keep things simple, I intentionally omit much of the fail-safe checking that database code normally has. I also have a dirt-simple user interface. The activity's screen has only one widget — a text view for displaying data at various stages of processing.

Headaches involving concurrency

Any computing device worth its salt runs several processes simultaneously. In other words, the processes are *concurrent*.

Concurrency is great for taking full advantage of a device's resources, but if two or more processes write to a database at the same time, nasty things can happen. For example, I might discover that Table 5-1 has three rows, and decide to add a fourth row. In the meantime, you might discover the same thing and issue your own command to add a fourth row. In the end, the table has only one additional row, and the row contains a mix of your data and my data. Ouch!

To combat the two-process-writing problem, database management systems have locks. A *lock* enforces read-only status for all but one process at a time. So two processes can't perform write operations at the same time. The trick for the database management system (and sometimes for the developer) is to choose options that maintain the data's integrity while locking the smallest chunk of data for the smallest amount of time. Long-lived, widely applied locks tend to slow down the system.

Another possible pitfall with database handling is the danger of incomplete write operations. Imagine that my rich uncle calls the company to pay my bill in Table 5-1. A representative keys in the new information for account number 002 — my rich uncle's name; the new 0.00 balance; and the Valued, Long-time Customer comment. The DBMS changes the name and the new balance, but the network connection fails before the DBMS receives the request to change the comment. Then account number 002 has values `Rich Burd`, `0.00`, `Deadbeat`. You may not think much of my uncle, but he's certainly not a deadbeat!

To fight against incomplete write operations, database management systems perform transactions. A *transaction* is a collection of operations to be performed in all-or-nothing fashion. "Either do them all, or do none of them," says the DBMS. The collection of operations in a transaction is *atomic;* the collection of operations cannot be subdivided.

As you might guess, enforcing atomicity isn't easy. How does a DBMS ensure all-or-nothing writing when some heinous network error gums up the whole system?

Fortunately, the mechanisms used to enforce atomicity aren't your problem if you are a database user. If your app requires atomicity (and if the database management system doesn't automatically enforce atomicity), you simply write a sequence of regular database commands. At the end of an all-or-nothing sequence, you issue a special `commit` command or a special `rollback` command. A `commit` command says, "Cast all the changes in this sequence of operations in stone," and a `rollback` command says, "Discard all the changes in this sequence." The database management system implements the special `commit` and `rollback` commands cleanly and reliably.

(In case you're wondering, these `commit` and `rollback` commands normally belong in alternative branches within your code. Most of the time, you `commit`. Once in a while, you're forced to `rollback`.)

Listing 5-1:   Sending Commands to a Database

```
package com.allmycode.db1;

import android.app.Activity;
import android.content.ContentValues;
import android.database.Cursor;
import android.database.sqlite.SQLiteDatabase;
import android.os.Bundle;
import android.widget.TextView;

public class MyActivity extends Activity {

  TextView textView;
  Cursor cursor = null;
  DBHelper helper = null;
  SQLiteDatabase db = null;
  ContentValues values = null;

  @Override
  public void onCreate(Bundle savedInstanceState) {
    super.onCreate(savedInstanceState);
    setContentView(R.layout.main);

    textView = (TextView) findViewById(R.id.textView1);

    helper = new DBHelper(this, "simple_db", null, 1);
    db = helper.getWritableDatabase();
    values = new ContentValues();

    values.put("name", "Barry");
    values.put("amount", "100");
    db.insert("simpletable", "", values);
    values.clear();
    values.put("name", "Harriet");
    values.put("amount", "300");
    db.insert("simpletable", "", values);

    addToTextView();

    values.clear();
    values.put("amount", "500");
    db.update("simpletable", values, "name='Barry'", null);

    addToTextView();

    db.delete("simpletable", "1", null);

    addToTextView();
  }

  @Override
  public void onDestroy() {
    super.onDestroy();
    helper.close();
  }

  void addToTextView() {
    cursor =
        db.rawQuery("SELECT * FROM simpletable;", null);

    if (cursor != null && cursor.moveToFirst()) {
```

Book III
Chapter 5

Content Providers

(continued)

Listing 5-1 *(continued)*

```
    String name;
    do {
      String _id = cursor.getString(0);
      name = cursor.getString(1);
      int amount = cursor.getInt(2);
      textView.append(_id + " " + name + " " + amount
        + "\n");
    } while (cursor.moveToNext());
  }
  textView.append("-----------\n");
  }
}
```

In Listing 5-1, I make a meager attempt to be tidy by closing the helper in the activity's `onDestroy` method. But in practice, manually closing and reopening database resources can be much more complicated.

The first new and exciting statement in Listing 5-1 is the call to a `DBHelper` constructor. My `DBHelper` class (to be unveiled in Listing 5-2) extends the abstract `android.database.sqlite.SQLiteOpenHelper` class. The purpose of such a class is to manage the creation and modification of an SQLite database. In particular, the code in Listing 5-1 uses the helper to grab hold of an actual database.

Details about the friendly helper class

Listing 5-2 contains my `DBHelper` code.

Listing 5-2:   A Subclass of the SQLiteOpenHelper Class

```
package com.allmycode.db1;

import android.content.Context;
import android.database.sqlite.SQLiteDatabase;
import android.database.sqlite.SQLiteOpenHelper;

public class DBHelper extends SQLiteOpenHelper {

  public DBHelper(Context context, String dbName,

      SQLiteDatabase.CursorFactory factory, int version) {
    super(context, dbName, factory, version);
  }

  @Override
  public void onCreate(SQLiteDatabase db) {
    String createString =
        "CREATE TABLE IF NOT EXISTS simpletable "
          + "( _id INTEGER PRIMARY KEY AUTOINCREMENT, "
          + "name TEXT NOT NULL, "
          + "amount INTEGER NOT NULL);";
    db.execSQL(createString);
  }
```

```
@Override
public void onUpgrade(SQLiteDatabase db,
    int oldVersion, int newVersion) {
  String dropString =
    "DROP TABLE IF EXISTS simpletable;";
  db.execSQL(dropString);
  onCreate(db);
  }
}
```

In Listing 5-2, I implement the parent class's abstract methods (as I must). I also create a constructor that takes the lazy way out, passing all its parameters to the parent constructor.

The most important part of Listing 5-2 is the helper's `onCreate` method. You never call this method directly. Instead, Android calls the method on your behalf when you set up a helper the way I do in Listing 5-1.

Android delays the call to the helper's `onCreate` method until your code actually uses the database. That bodes well for your app's performance.

Android hands the `onCreate` method an *SQLite database* (a database belonging to the app in which the helper is located). That SQLite database (called `db` in the `onCreate` method's parameter list) has an `execSQL` method. Listing 5-2 calls the database's `execSQL` method, feeding the method an ordinary Java string. Luckily for me, this ordinary Java string happens to be an SQL command.

In Listing 5-2's `onCreate` method, lots of good things happen without much fanfare. If the database doesn't already exist, Android creates one. If the database doesn't already have a table named `simpletable`, SQLite creates one. If the database already exists and has a `simpletable`, the `onCreate` method doesn't rock the boat.

Databases normally live on after the hosting process terminates. If you run this example's code in March and then turn off your device for three months, the database still exists (along with any data that you added in March) when you turn on the device again in June.

I don't cover SQL commands in this book. I'd go crazy trying to cover them all. But fortunately, other authors have covered SQL without going crazy. So to read all about SQL commands, buy either the standard *SQL For Dummies* or the supersize version *SQL All-in-One For Dummies*, both by Allen G. Taylor (John Wiley & Sons, Inc.).

SQL is more readable than some other languages, so with or without a thorough introduction, you can probably make sense of most of the SQL commands in this book. The SQL command midway through Listing 5-2, for example, says the following:

```
If the database doesn't have a table named simpletable,
   create simpletable with three columns, called
   _id, name, and amount.
      The _id column stores an integer value,
            which serves to identify its row,
            and is incremented by 1 for each newly added row,
      The name column stores a string value
            which cannot be null, and
      The amount column stores an integer value
            which cannot be null.
```

Android's SDK wants you to use the name _id for a table's auto-incremented primary key. I haven't experimented with other column names, but from what I've read, something will break if I try it.

An `SQLiteOpenHelper`'s `onUpgrade` method deals with new versions of the database. For example, when I modify the database in Listing 5-2 so that each row has an additional column (a *Comment* column, perhaps), I'm changing the table's structure. A change of this kind requires me to obliterate the existing table (that is, to *drop* the table) and to create another table as if from scratch. In a helper's `onUpgrade` method, you manage this (admittedly delicate) procedure.

Details about the mainstream SQLite code

In Listing 5-1, after the call to `getWritableDatabase`, the code performs some fairly commonplace operations — namely, inserting, updating, deleting, and querying.

Inserting

Each call to `db.insert` adds a row of values to the `simpletable`. Each *value* is actually a name/value pair, the name being a database column name and the value being something to stuff into that column.

The `put` method belonging to the `ContentValues` class takes two `String` parameters. In the call `values.put("amount", "100")`, the first parameter is a column name. The second parameter is the value to be placed into that column in the current row. Notice that the second parameter `"100"` is a Java `String` even though the database's *amount* column stores an integer. That's just the way it works. Oh, and while you're remembering things, don't forget to call `values.clear()` between using one set of values and assembling another.

In Listing 5-1, the `insert` method takes three parameters — a table name, a null column hack, and a set of values constituting the newly created row. The *null column hack* is a value that you add to deal with the possibility of a completely empty insert. SQLite behaves badly if you try to insert a row containing no data.

As a result of the calls to `insert` in Listing 5-1, the activity's screen contains the first two lines in the text view of Figure 5-4.

Figure 5-4:
Running
the code in
Listing 5-1.

Updating

In Listing 5-1, the call to `db.update` takes four parameters. The first two parameters — a table name and a set of values — are old hat. The `update` method's third parameter is part of an SQL `WHERE` clause. A *WHERE clause* tells SQLite which rows should be chosen for processing. For example, the `WHERE` clause in the section "Databases: From the Stone Age to the Present Day" tells SQLite to select only those rows whose Comment column contains the value `Deadbeat`.

For the third parameter in an `update` method call, you supply a string containing the entire `WHERE` clause, but you omit the word *WHERE*. So in Listing 5-1, the `update` method call generates an SQL statement containing `WHERE name = 'Barry'`. At this point in the game, it's easy to become confused with nested single quotes and double quotes. The SQL command rules require a value such as `'Barry'` to be quoted, and a Java string must be double-quoted. If things become more complicated, you have to use escape sequences and other tricks.

In Listing 5-1, the `update` method's last parameter is a set of `WHERE` *arguments* — values to plug into the holes in your `WHERE` clause. For example, you can gain some flexibility (and in some cases, slightly better performance) by substituting the following two statements for the `update` call in Listing 5-1:

```
String[] whereArgs = {"Barry"};
db.update("simpletable", values, "name=?", whereArgs);
```

Deleting

The `delete` method call in Listing 5-1 takes three parameters — a table name, a `WHERE` clause, and a set of `WHERE` arguments. The `WHERE` clause is normally something like `"name='Barry'"`. (Get rid of that deadbeat!) But in Listing 5-1, the `WHERE` clause is `"1"` — the SQL code for *everything*. In Listing 5-1, the `delete` method removes every row in the database table.

Querying

After each change to the database, the code in Listing 5-1 adds text to the activity's text view. To do this, the code executes a *query*. The database's `rawQuery` method takes two parameters — an SQL command string and a (possibly null) set of `WHERE` arguments.

In Listing 5-1, the call to `rawQuery` returns a cursor. The `cursor.moveToFirst` call returns `true` as long as the attempt to reach the cursor table's first row is successful. (Failure typically means that the table has no rows.)

For an introduction to database cursors, see the section "Databases: From the Stone Age to the Present Day," earlier in this chapter.

From that point on, the code in Listing 5-1 loops from row to row, moving the cursor to the next table row each time through the loop. The `cursor.moveToNext` call returns `false` when there's no next row to move to.

Every time through the loop, the code uses the cursor to get the values in each of the table's three columns. The columns' indices start at 0 and increase in the order in which I declare the columns in Listing 5-2. Notice how I call `get` methods particular to the types of data in the database. Nothing good can happen if, for one column or another, I use a `get` method with the wrong type.

As the code in Listing 5-1 takes its last breath, the activity's `onDestroy` method closes the helper instance. Doing so shuts down the entire database connection and frees up resources for use by other apps. As is the case with all `onDestroy` methods, you should eschew my overly simple code. Before calling the helper's `close` method, make sure that the helper isn't `null`. Also include code to handle the possibility that the Android is temporarily destroying (and later re-creating) the activity. For some help with that, see Chapter 3 of this minibook.

How to find out what's really going on

SQLite expects each SQL command to end with a semicolon. So, for example, near the end of the `onCreate` method in Listing 5-2, a line contains two semicolons — one to end the SQL command and another to end the Java statement. Android's methods let you omit an SQL command's ending semicolon. So the line in Listing 5-2 works just as well if you write `"amount INTEGER NOT NULL)";` with only one semicolon. But I like to include the extra semicolon. That way, I remember SQLite's punctuation rules when I'm not composing Java code.

And when do I write SQL commands without Java code? I'm glad you asked! Imagine that I'm testing some of this section's code. I'm using an emulator or a real, Android-powered device attached to my development computer. Before installing this section's code, I comment out the `delete` method call in Listing 5-1. (That way, the database has two rows when the code finishes its run.)

The figure nearby shows a session in my development computer's command window.

✔ **I invoke Android's `adb` command with the `shell` option.**

This deposits me into the emulator's Linux command interface. On the emulator, the prompt is the pound sign (`#`).

✔ **I issue the Linux `cd` command four times.**

As a result, my working directory is `/data/data/com.allmycode.db1/databases`. Notice that my humble little app has a directory for its own databases.

✔ **The Linux `ls` command lists files in my working directory.**

The directory contains a file that stores the `simple_db` database (the database created by the code in Listing 5-1).

✔ **I invoke the `sqlite3` executable — a program to help me explore and modify an SQLite database.**

The `sqlite3` program displays the `sqlite>` prompt. My next several commands are specific to the `simple_db` database. Commands that start with a dot are instructions to the sqlite3 program. (These may include instructions such as `.help`, `.log`, and `.exit`.)

Commands that don't start with a dot are actual SQL commands. These SQL commands read and update the `simple_db` database.

✔ **Two times during the session, I type the `SELECT * FROM simpletable;` SQL command.**

When I issue this command, I see exactly what's in the `simple_db` database. I can use this information to help me debug my Java code (Not that my Java code ever needs debugging . . .)

✔ **In the nearby figure, when I type an SQL `INSERT` command, I forget to end the command with a semicolon.**

As a result, the sqlite3 program prompts me with `. . . >`. To complete the command, I type the required semicolon and press Enter. (Is it time for me to say, "I told you so?")

✔ **I type `.exit` to terminate the sqlite3 program and then type `exit` to end the emulator's shell session.**

(continued)

(continued)

All things considered, it's a very enlightening session. Communicating directly with the database management system can be extremely helpful.

```
C:\>\android-sdk\platform-tools\adb shell
# cd data
cd data
# cd data
cd data
# pwd
pwd
/data/data
# cd com.allmycode.db1
cd com.allmycode.db1
# cd databases
cd databases
# ls
ls
simple_db
# sqlite3 simple_db
sqlite3 simple_db
SQLite version 3.6.22
Enter ".help" for instructions
Enter SQL statements terminated with a ";"
sqlite> .tables
.tables
android_metadata    simpletable
sqlite> .schema
.schema
CREATE TABLE android_metadata (locale TEXT);
CREATE TABLE simpletable ( _id INTEGER PRIMARY KEY AUTOINCREMENT, name TEXT NOT
NULL, amount INTEGER NOT NULL);
sqlite> SELECT * FROM simpletable;
SELECT * FROM simpletable;
1|Barry|500
2|Harriet|300
sqlite> INSERT INTO simpletable ("name", "amount") VALUES ("Alex", "29")
INSERT INTO simpletable ("name", "amount") VALUES ("Alex", "29")
   ...> ;
;
sqlite> SELECT * FROM simpletable;
SELECT * FROM simpletable;
1|Barry|500
2|Harriet|300
3|Alex|29
sqlite> .exit
.exit
# exit
exit
C:\>_
```

Creating and Using a Content Provider

A *content provider* is a gateway to an app's data. Other apps approach the gateway as if it's a database. But under the hood, the data can take many different forms.

This section's example involves two apps — an app with a content provider and a separate client app. (Refer to Figures 5-2 and 5-3.) The client app's code is in Listing 5-3.

Listing 5-3:   Getting Data from a Content Provider

```
package a.b.c;

import android.app.Activity;
import android.content.ContentResolver;
import android.content.ContentValues;
import android.content.CursorLoader;
import android.content.Loader;
import android.content.Loader.OnLoadCompleteListener;
import android.database.Cursor;
import android.net.Uri;
import android.os.Bundle;
import android.view.View;
import android.widget.Button;
import android.widget.TextView;


public class MainActivity extends Activity {

  ContentValues values = null;
  ContentResolver resolver = null;
  CursorLoader loader = null;

  Button button, button2, button3, button4;
  TextView textView;

  Uri CONTENT_URI = Uri.parse
     ("content://com.allmycode.db/names_amounts");
  Uri SILLY_URI = Uri.parse
     ("content://com.allmycode.db/silly_stuff");

  @Override
  public void onCreate(Bundle b) {
    super.onCreate(b);
    setContentView(R.layout.activity_main);

    values = new ContentValues();
    resolver = getContentResolver();

    textView = (TextView) findViewById(R.id.textView);
    button = (Button) findViewById(R.id.button);
    button2 = (Button) findViewById(R.id.button2);
    button3 = (Button) findViewById(R.id.button3);
    button4 = (Button) findViewById(R.id.button4);
  }

  public void onButtonClick(View view) {

    if (view == button) {

      resolver.delete(CONTENT_URI, "1", null);
      showStuffFrom(CONTENT_URI);

    } else if (view == button2) {

      values.clear();
      values.put("name", "Sam");
      values.put("amount", "100");
```

(continued)

**Book III
Chapter 5**

Content Providers

Listing 5-3 *(continued)*

```
          resolver.insert(CONTENT_URI, values);
          values.clear();
          values.put("name", "Jennie");
          values.put("amount", "300");
          resolver.insert(CONTENT_URI, values);
           showStuffFrom(CONTENT_URI);

      } else if (view == button3) {

          values.clear();
          values.put("amount", "500");
          resolver.update(CONTENT_URI, values,
              "name='Sam'", null);
          showStuffFrom(CONTENT_URI);

      } else if (view == button4) {

          showStuffFrom(SILLY_URI);

      }
    }

    void showStuffFrom(Uri uri) {
      loader =
        new CursorLoader(this, uri, null, "1", null, null);
      loader.registerListener(42,
        new MyOnLoadCompleteListener());
      loader.startLoading();
    }

    class MyOnLoadCompleteListener implements
      OnLoadCompleteListener<Cursor> {

      @Override
      public void onLoadComplete(Loader<Cursor> loader,
                                 Cursor cursor) {
        textView.setText("");
        if (cursor != null && cursor.moveToFirst()) {
          do {
            String _id = cursor.getString(0);
            String name = cursor.getString(1);
            int amount = cursor.getInt(2);
            textView.append(_id + " " + name + " " + amount
                + "\n");
          } while (cursor.moveToNext());
        }
      }
    }
  }
}
```

The activity in Listing 5-3 has four buttons:

✦ **If you click the first button, you empty the content provider of any and all** names_amounts **data. (See Figure 5-5.)**

If view == button is true, you call a delete method. The method's second parameter contains an SQL WHERE clause. And (oddly enough) the number 1 happens to be a complete `WHERE` clause. As a `WHERE` clause, 1 means *all rows*.

Figure 5-5:
The
activity in
Listing 5-3
(after
pressing the
first button).

✦ **If you click the second button, you add two rows to the content provider's** `names_amounts` **data. (See Figure 5-6.)**

Figure 5-6:
The
activity in
Listing 5-3
(after
pressing
the second
button).

If you click the first button once, and then click the second button two times, the content provider has four rows of data (a `Sam` row, a `Jennie` row, and then another `Sam` row and another `Jennie` row).

✦ **If you click the third button, you change Sam's amount to 500. (See Figure 5-7.)**

The content provider might have more than one `Sam` row. The value in every `Sam` row changes to 500.

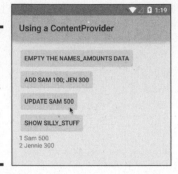

Figure 5-7:
The
activity in
Listing 5-3
(after
pressing
the third
button).

The content provider has at least two kinds of data — `names_amounts` data and `silly_stuff` data. If you click the fourth button, you display the content provider's `silly_stuff` data. (See Figure 5-8.)

Figure 5-8:
The
activity in
Listing 5-3
(after
pressing
the fourth
button).

There's nothing mysterious about a content provider with two kinds of data. If you're curious, look ahead to Listing 5-5.

Using a content resolver

In Listing 5-3, the client app has no direct communication with the provider's database. Instead, the client app talks to the database through a *content resolver.*

A content resolver has methods to insert data, update data, delete data, and so on. Each content resolver method takes a URI — a reference to some data offered by a content provider. Here's what happens when your code calls a content resolver method:

✦ **Android examines the URI's scheme and finds the** `content:` **scheme.**

The `content:` scheme tells Android to look for a matching content provider.

✦ **Android compares the URI's authority with the authorities in the intent filters of available content providers. (See Figure 5-9.)**

A content provider must declare one or more authorities in its app's `AndroidManifest.xml` document. Listing 5-4 has the `AndroidManifest.xml` document for this section's example. Notice that in this example, the app containing the content provider has no activity. The app has no direct interface to the user.

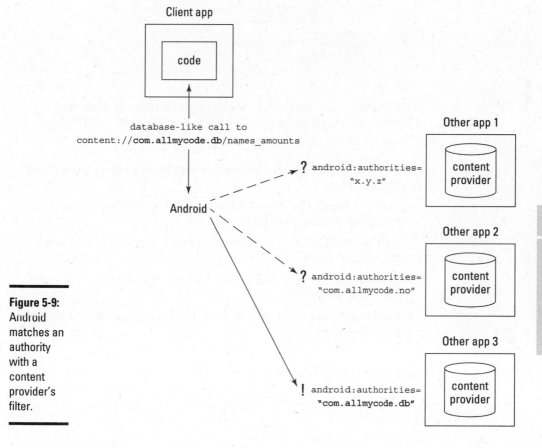

Figure 5-9:
Android matches an authority with a content provider's filter.

Listing 5-4:   A Content Provider's XML Element

```
<manifest xmlns:android=
          "http://schemas.android.com/apk/res/android"
         package="com.allmycode.db">

   <application android:allowBackup="true"
              android:label="@string/app_name"
              android:icon="@drawable/ic_launcher"
              android:theme="@style/AppTheme">

      <provider android:name=".MyContentProvider"
              android:authorities="com.allmycode.db"
              android:exported="true">
      </provider>

   </application>

</manifest>
```

If an `android:authorities` attribute contains more than one authority, you separate authorities from one another using semicolons:

```
android:authorities="this.is.one;this.is.another"
```

So far, so good. Here's what happens when Android finds a matching content provider:

- **Android hands the client's database-like call (URI and all) to the matching content provider.**

  After Android hands the call to a content provider, the ball is in the content provider's court.

- **The content provider parses the URI's path to further refine the client app's request.**

- **The content provider uses its own app's data to fulfill the client app's request.**

Using a cursor loader

To get data from a content provider, Listing 5-3 uses a *cursor loader*. The `CursorLoader` constructor has six parameters. The parameters are as follows:

- ✦ `Context context`: In Listing 5-3, the context (`this`) is the activity itself.

  To read about Android's `Context` class, see Chapter 1 in this minibook.

- ✦ `Uri uri`: A reference to some data offered by a content provider.

✦ `String[] projection`: A list of columns from the table. (If you pass `null`, you're saying "gimme' all the columns.")

✦ `String selection`: An SQL `WHERE` clause. (See this chapter's "Updating" section.)

✦ `String[] selectionArgs`: The `WHERE` string can include question marks. The question marks are placeholders for actual values that you place in the `selectionArgs` array. (See this chapter's "Updating" section.)

✦ `String sortOrder`: The order in which the rows come from the table. (A SQL statement can have an `ORDER BY` clause. Put that clause, minus the words `ORDER BY`, in this parameter.) A `null` value means "use the default order, whatever that is."

From the constructor call onward, the activity's thread registers a callback listener (the `MyOnLoadCompleteListener`) and calls the loader's `startLoading` method. This means that the parent thread (the code in Listing 5-3) doesn't stop and wait for the `startLoading()` call to return. Instead, the activity's code continues on its merry way.

In the meantime, the cursor loader does its thing in a separate thread, and the callback listener (`OnLoadCompleteListener`) listens for the cursor loader to get its results. When at last the loading of the data is complete (that is, the cursor is done being loaded), Android calls the `onLoadComplete` method inside the `OnLoadCompleteListener` instance. This `onLoadComplete` method can do whatever you want done with the cursor's data. (In Listing 5-3, the `onLoadComplete` method displays data in your activity's text view.)

Like a teenager off to college, a `CursorLoader` instance manages itself by leaving its parent thread, going out on its own, and eventually returning with the desired result. Like any real teenager, a `CursorLoader` instance, with all its asynchronous behavior, can behave in strange and surprising ways. Be mindful of your use of the `CursorLoader` class.

The code in Listing 5-3 works with Honeycomb (Android 3.0) and later. Before Honeycomb, Android used a `startManagingCursor` method instead of the `CursorLoader` in Listing 5-3. Android's documentation says that older devices can use the newer `CursorLoader` code as long as you include a compatibility package along with your app. This means importing the package `android.support.v4.content.CursorLoader`.

At last! A content provider!

Listing 5-5 contains a content provider for this section's ongoing example.

Listing 5-5:   Look: It's a Content Provider

```
package com.allmycode.db;

import android.content.ContentProvider;
import android.content.ContentUris;
import android.content.ContentValues;
import android.content.UriMatcher;
import android.database.Cursor;
import android.database.MatrixCursor;
import android.database.sqlite.SQLiteDatabase;
import android.net.Uri;

public class MyContentProvider extends ContentProvider {
  public static final Uri CONTENT_URI = Uri
      .parse("content://com.allmycode.db/names_amounts");
  public static final Uri SILLY_URI = Uri
      .parse("content://com.allmycode.db/silly_stuff");

  private static final String SIMPLE_DB = "simple_db";
  private static final String SIMPLETABLE = "simpletable";


  DBHelper helper = null;
  SQLiteDatabase db = null;
  ContentValues values = null;
  UriMatcher uriMatcher = null;
  {

    uriMatcher = new UriMatcher(UriMatcher.NO_MATCH);
    uriMatcher.addURI("com.allmycode.db",
                               "names_amounts", 1);
    uriMatcher.addURI("com.allmycode.db",
                               "silly_stuff", 2);
  }

  @Override
  public boolean onCreate() {
    try {
      helper =
          new DBHelper(getContext(), SIMPLE_DB, null, 1);
      db = helper.getWritableDatabase();
      values = new ContentValues();
      return true;
    } catch (Exception e) {
      return false;
    }
  }

  @Override
  public Uri insert(Uri ure, ContentValues values) {
    long id = db.insert(SIMPLETABLE, "", values);
    return ContentUris.withAppendedId(CONTENT_URI, id);
  }
```

```java
@Override
public int update(Uri uri, ContentValues values,
    String whereClause, String[] whereArgs) {

  int numOfChangedRows =
      db.update(SIMPLETABLE, values, whereClause,
          whereArgs);

  return numOfChangedRows;
}

@Override
public int delete(Uri uri, String whereClause,
    String[] whereArgs) {
  int numOfChangedRows =
      db.delete(SIMPLETABLE, whereClause, whereArgs);
  return numOfChangedRows;
}

@Override
public Cursor query(Uri uri, String[] columns,
    String whereClause, String[] whereArgs,
    String sortOrder) {
  Cursor cursor = null;
  int code = uriMatcher.match(uri);
  if (code == 1) {

    cursor =
        db.query(SIMPLETABLE, columns, whereClause,
            whereArgs, null, null, sortOrder);

  } else if (code == 2) {
    String[] columnNames = { "_id", "name", "amount" };
    String[] rowValues = { "Table ", "4 ", "2" };
    MatrixCursor matrixCursor =
        new MatrixCursor(columnNames);
    matrixCursor.addRow(rowValues);
    cursor = matrixCursor;
  }
  return cursor;
}

@Override
public String getType(Uri uri) {
  return null;
}
}
```

Listing 5-5 implements the six abstract methods declared in the `android.
content.ContentProvider` class. The implementation code bears a strik-
ing resemblance to some of the code in Listing 5-1.

✦ Both `onCreate` methods use `DBHelper` (which extends Android's
`SQLiteOpenHelper` class) to get a writable database.

✦ Both listings call the database's `insert`, `update`, and `delete` methods.

✦ Both listings issue a query to the database.

Actually, Listing 5-1 uses the `rawQuery` method and an SQL command string. In contrast, Listing 5-5 uses the `query` method with a bunch of parameters. The difference has nothing to do with content providers. It's just my whim in using different methods to illustrate different ways of issuing a query.

The bottom line is this: A content provider does with its app's data what an ordinary activity does with its own app's data.

Listing 5-5 has some features that I choose not to use in Listing 5-1. For example, Android's `update` and `delete` methods return `int` values. In Listing 5-1, I simply ignore the return values. But in Listing 5-5, I pass each method's return value back to the client code. (Don't congratulate me on my diligence. I pass on each value because the content provider's abstract `update` and `delete` methods must have `int` return values.)

Listing 5-5 also has some features that are unique to content providers. For example, to effectively dish out data, a content provider must manage URIs. Normally, a content provider examines each method's incoming URI and uses the information to decide on its next move. In Listing 5-5, I keep things simple with only a minor bit of URI handling in the `query` method.

Outside the Android world, the use of URIs to connect to databases is commonplace. For example, in a Java JDBC program, you may connect to a database with a statement, such as `DriverManager.getConnection("jdbc :derby:AccountDatabase")`. In this statement's opaque URI, the scheme `jdbc:` forwards a request to another scheme — namely, the `derby:` scheme.

In Listing 5-5, the `query` method calls on a `UriMatcher` instance to distinguish one path from another. As it's defined near the start of Listing 5-5, the `UriMatcher` instance returns 1 for the `names_amounts` path and returns 2 for the `silly_stuff` path.

A return value of 1 makes the `query` method do its regular old database query. But a return value of 2 does something entirely different. To show that I can do it, I respond to a URI's `silly_stuff` path without consulting a real database. Instead, I use arrays to concoct something that looks like a `simpletable` row. I squish the arrays into a `MatrixCursor` (a cursor built from an array rather than a database), and I send the cursor back to the client.

The `insert` method in Listing 5-5 returns a URI. What's that all about? Each row associated with the `content:` scheme has its own individual URI. For example, in a run of this section's code, the first two row insertions have URIs `content://com.allmycode.db/names_amounts/1` and `content://com.allmycode.db/names_amounts/2`. The `android. content.ContentUris` class's `withAppendedId` method fetches the URI for a particular database row. The client can use this row-specific URI to refer to one database row at a time.

Book IV

Programming Cool Phone Features

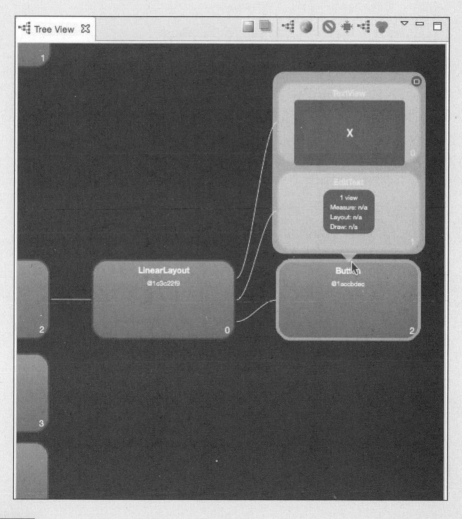

For a closer look at Android emulators, check out the online article at www.dummies.com/extras/androidappdevelopmentaio.

Contents at a Glance

Chapter 1: Laying Out Your Stuff

In This Chapter

✔ Organizing the widgets on the device's screen

✔ Dealing with colors, sizes, and positions

✔ Working with various layouts

Which description do you prefer?

✦ *In my entire line of sight, I see a polygon with convex vertices at the points (1.5, 0), (0, 1.2), (3, 1.2), (0.6, 3), (2.4, 3), and with concave vertices at the points (1.15, 1.2), (1.85, 1.2), (0.95, 1.8), (2.05, 1.8), (1.5, 2.2). The units are in inches.*

✦ *In my entire line of sight, I see a five-pointed star.*

The first description is more precise, but the first is also more brittle. As I type this introduction, I anticipate the email messages from readers: "You got one of the numbers wrong in the first description."

The second description is also more versatile. The second description makes sense whether you describe an image on a laptop screen or on a highway billboard. In a world with all kinds of mobile devices, all kinds of screen sizes, screen resolutions, display qualities, refresh rates, and who-knows-what-other variations, the big picture is often more useful than the picky details. When you describe your app's screen, you should avoid measurements in favor of concepts.

Android supports several layout concepts, including linear layout, relative layout, table layout, and frame layout. In many cases, choosing one kind of layout over another is a matter of taste. A table layout with only one row looks like a horizontal linear layout. A set of nested linear layouts may look exactly like a complicated relative layout. The possibilities are endless.

Android Layouts

The game with Android's layouts is to place visible things into a container in an orderly way. In a typical scenario, one of these "visible things" is a *view,* and one of these "containers" is a *view group.*

The formal terminology is a bit hazy. But fortunately, the fine distinctions between the terms aren't terribly important. Here's some formal terminology:

✦ A *view* appears on the user's screen and (either directly or indirectly) involves user interaction. The word *view* often refers to an instance of the `android.view.View` class. A broader use of the word *view* includes any class or interface in the `android.view` package.

✦ A *widget* appears on the user's screen and (either directly or indirectly) involves user interaction. (Sounds a lot like a view, doesn't it?) The word *widget* commonly refers to a class or interface in the `android.widget` package.

Views can be widgets, and widgets can be views. As long as your `import` declarations work and your method parameter types match, the distinction between widgets and views is unimportant.

Commonly used widgets and views include buttons, check boxes, text views, toasts, and more exotic things such as digital clocks, sliding drawers, progress bars, and other good junk.

(Android or no Android, I think *widget* is a wonderful word. The playwrights George S. Kaufman and Marc Connelly made up the word "widget" for dialogue in their 1924 comedy *Beggar on Horseback*. I learned about widgets from the fictitious Universal Widgets company — an enterprise featured in *The Wheeler Dealers* from 1963.)

✦ A *view group* (an instance of `android.view.ViewGroup`) is a view that contains other views (including other view groups). The views contained in a view group are the view group's *children*.

Examples of view groups are the linear layouts, relative layouts, table layouts, and frame layouts mentioned at the beginning of this chapter, as well as some more special-purpose things such as the list view and the scroll view.

One way or another, I usually write about putting a "view" on a "layout."

Linear Layout

Linear layouts have either vertical or horizontal orientation. Views in a vertical linear layout line up one beneath the other. Views in a horizontal linear layout line up one beside the other. (See Figure 1-1.)

You can create the layout in Figure 1-1 with the XML code in Listing 1-1.

Figure 1-1:
Four
buttons in a
horizontal
linear
layout.

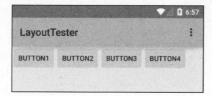

Listing 1-1: A Horizontal Linear Layout

```xml
<?xml version="1.0" encoding="utf-8"?>
<LinearLayout xmlns:android=
     "http://schemas.android.com/apk/res/android"
    android:layout_width="match_parent"
    android:layout_height="match_parent"
    android:orientation="horizontal">

    <Button android:text="Button1"
        android:layout_height="wrap_content"
        android:layout_width="wrap_content"
        android:id="@+id/button1">
    </Button>

    <Button android:text="Button2"
        android:layout_height="wrap_content"
        android:layout_width="wrap_content"
        android:id="@+id/button2">
    </Button>

    <Button android:text="Button3"
        android:layout_height="wrap_content"
        android:layout_width="wrap_content"
        android:id="@+id/button3">
    </Button>

    <Button android:text="Button4"
        android:layout_height="wrap_content"
        android:layout_width="wrap_content"
        android:id="@+id/button4">
    </Button>

</LinearLayout>
```

You can also create the layout in Figure 1-1 by dragging and dropping views onto the Preview screen in Android Studio's Designer tool.

Linear layouts don't wrap, and they don't scroll. So, if you add six buttons to a horizontal layout and the user's screen is wide enough for only five of the buttons, the user sees only five buttons. (See Figure 1-2.)

**Book IV
Chapter 1**

Laying Out Your Stuff

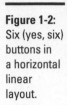

Figure 1-2:
Six (yes, six)
buttons in
a horizontal
linear
layout.

Attributes (A Detour)

Using XML attributes, you can change a layout's default behavior. This section has several examples.

android:layout_width and android:layout_height

You can tweak the size of a view using the android:layout_width and android:layout_height attributes. Listing 1-2 has some code, and Figure 1-3 shows the resulting layout.

Listing 1-2:   Setting a View's Width and Height

```xml
<?xml version="1.0" encoding="utf-8"?>
<LinearLayout xmlns:android=
    "http://schemas.android.com/apk/res/android"
  android:orientation="vertical"
  android:layout_width="match_parent"
  android:layout_height="match_parent">

  <Button
    android:layout_width="match_parent"
    android:layout_height="wrap_content"
    android:text=
      "1. android:layout_height is wrap_content\n
       android:layout_width is match_parent ">
    android:id="@+id/button1"
  </Button>

  <Button
    android:layout_width="wrap_content"
    android:layout_height="wrap_content"
    android:text="2. wrap/wrap">
    android:id="@+id/button2"
  </Button>

  <Button
    android:layout_width="60dp"
    android:layout_height="wrap_content"
    android:text="3. width 60dp">
    android:id="@+id/button3"
  </Button>
```

```
<Button
  android:layout_width="160dp"
  android:layout_height="wrap_content"
  android:text="4. android:layout_width is 160dp">
  android:id="@+id/button4"
</Button>

<Button
  android:layout_width="wrap_content"
  android:layout_height="match_parent"
  android:text="5. width wrap_content\n
             height match_parent"
  android:id="@+id/button5">
</Button>

</LinearLayout>
```

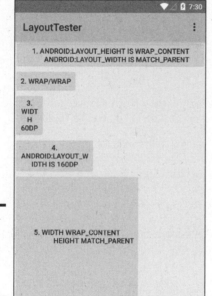

Figure 1-3:
Buttons
of various
widths and
heights.

You can describe a view's size using general guidelines or numbers of units, as spelled out in the next two sections.

Using general size guidelines

To create general guidelines, use the `"wrap_content"`, `"match_parent"`, or `"fill_parent"` value. (Refer to Listing 1-2.) With `"wrap_content"`, Android shrinks a view's width or length so that the view tightly encloses whatever it contains. With `"match_parent"` and `"fill_parent"`, Android expands a view's width or length so that the view fits tightly inside its container.

What it means to "tightly enclose" something or "fit tightly inside" something depends on the amount of breathing room you specify for the boundaries around things. This breathing room comes in two forms — padding and margins. (If you want, you can look ahead to this chapter's section on padding and margins.)

The strings `"match_parent"` and `"fill_parent"` have the same meaning. Before API Level 8, only `"fill_parent"` works. Starting with API Level 8, the string `"fill_parent"` is deprecated in favor of `"match_parent"`. According to Java's official documents, deprecated features are obsolete and "are supported only for backwards compatibility." In the Java world, a feature that's deprecated might be unavailable in future software versions. But Java's deprecated features tend to linger on for years. Both `"fill_parent"` and `"match_parent"` work up to (and possibly beyond) API Level 21 (Lollipop).

In Listing 1-2, the first button has attributes `android:layout_width="match_parent"` and `android:layout_height="wrap_content"`. So in Figure 1-3, the top button is as wide as it can be and only tall enough to contain the words displayed on the button's face.

In Listing 1-2, look for `\n` inside quoted strings of characters. The `\n` business is called an *escape sequence*. It means "go to the next line."

Using numbers of units

In Listing 1-2, I describe the third button's width in units. The value *60dp* stands for 60 *density-independent pixels.* A density-independent pixel is a measurement based on a 160 pixels-per-inch benchmark.

"And what," you ask, "is a 160 pixels-per-inch benchmark?" A *pixel* is a single dot on a device's screen. A pixel can be invisible, glow brightly, or anything in between.

Different devices have different pixel densities. For example, a low-density screen might have 120 pixels per inch, and an extra-extra-high-density screen might have 480 pixels per inch. To adjust for these differences, each Android screen has several metrics. Each *metric* is a numeric value describing some characteristic of the display:

✦ `widthPixels` (an `int` value): The number of pixels from the left edge to the right edge of the screen.

✦ `heightPixels` (an `int` value): The number of pixels from the top to the bottom of the screen.

✦ `xdpi` (an `int` value): The number of pixels from left to right along one inch of the screen.

✦ ydpi (an int value): The number of pixels from top to bottom along one inch of the screen. (In a square inch, some screens stuff more pixels across than up and down, so xdpi isn't necessarily the same as ydpi.)

✦ densityDpi (an int value): A general measure of the number of pixels per inch. For screens with equal xdpi and ydpi values, densityDpi is the same as xdpi and ydpi. For screens with unequal xdpi and ydpi values, somebody figures out what the screen's densityDpi is (but they don't tell me how they figure it out).

✦ density (a float value): The number of pixels per inch, divided by 160.

✦ scaledDensity (a float value): Another take on the density measure, but this time with some extra stretching or squeezing to account for any default font size chosen by the user. (Some versions of Android don't let the user adjust the default font size, but with some third-party apps, a user can get around the limitation.)

When you specify 160dp (as in Listing 1-2), you're telling Android to display density × 160 pixels. So, on my tiny screen, a width of 160dp is one inch, and on the Android home theater that you transport through time from the year 2055, a width of 160dp is one inch. Everybody gets the inch that they want.

The letters *dpi* stand for *dots per inch*. Your Android project might have folders named res/drawable-xhdpi, res/drawable-hdpi, res/drawable-ldpi, and so on. At runtime, Android senses a device's or emulator's screen density and uses the resources in the most appropriate res/drawable-dpi folder. For more info, see this chapter's "Using configuration qualifiers" section.

Another handy unit of measurement is *sp* — *scale-independent pixels*. Like the dp unit, the size of an sp unit adjusts nicely for different screens. But the size of an sp unit changes in two ways. In addition to changing based on the screen's pixel density, the sp unit changes based on the user's font size preference settings.

The abbreviations *dp* and *dip* are interchangeable. Both stand for *density-independent pixels*. But sp is always sp. Android has no unit named *sip*.

If you want to be ornery, you can use physical units. For example, value 2in stands for two inches. Other unsavory physical units include *mm* (for millimeters), *pt* (for points, with 1 point being $\frac{1}{1000}$ of an inch), and *px* (for pixels — actual dots on the device's screen). In almost all situations, you should avoid physical units. Use dp to specify a view's size, and use sp to specify a text font size.

Figures 1-4 and 1-5 illustrate the relationship between pixels and density-independent pixels. The screen in Figure 1-4 has density 0.75. So an inch-wide button consumes $0.75 \times 160 = 120$ pixels. You can confirm this by comparing the sizes of the 160dp and 160px buttons. The 160dp button is roughly three quarters the width of the 160px button.

This book's figures might have stretched or shrunk in printing. Objects may be larger than they appear. What measures an inch across in this book's pages or on your e-reader's screen isn't necessarily an inch on an Android device's screen.

The screen in Figure 1-5 has a density 1.5, so in Figure 1-5, a 160dp button is 1.5 times as wide as a 160px button.

The XML document describing the layout in Figures 1-4 and 1-5 is shown in Listing 1-3.

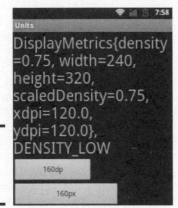

Figure 1-4:
A low-density display.

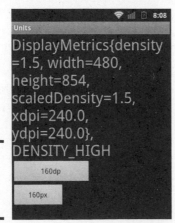

Figure 1-5:
A high-density display.

Listing 1-3   Using Size Units

```xml
<?xml version="1.0" encoding="utf-8"?>
<LinearLayout xmlns:android=
     "http://schemas.android.com/apk/res/android"
    android:orientation="vertical"
    android:layout_width="fill_parent"
    android:layout_height="fill_parent">

    <TextView android:textSize="30sp"
        android:layout_width="wrap_content"
        android:layout_height="wrap_content"
        android:id="@+id/textView1"></TextView>

    <Button android:layout_width="160dp"
        android:text="160dp"
        android:layout_height="wrap_content"
        android:id="@+id/button1"></Button>

    <Button android:layout_width="160px"
        android:text="160px"
        android:layout_height="wrap_content"
        android:id="@+id/button2"></Button>

</LinearLayout>
```

Look again at Figures 1-4 and 1-5, and at Listing 1-3. In a real-life app, you probably don't want things like 160dp to appear on the user's screen. You can specify text that appears only while you test your app (and not after you've prepared your app for publication). To do so, add the xmlns:tools="http://schemas.android.com/tools" attribute to your layout file's root element. Then replace android:text="160dp" with tools:text="160dp". (Your Button component can even have both attributes — a tools:text attribute for when you develop your app, and an android:text attribute for when you publish the app.)

Notice the metric information in the text view in Figures 1-4 and 1-5. To display this information, I use the android.util.DisplayMetrics class in my app's main activity:

```java
package com.allmycode.screen;

import android.app.Activity;
import android.os.Bundle;
import android.util.DisplayMetrics;
import android.widget.TextView;

public class ScreenActivity extends Activity {
  TextView textView;
  DisplayMetrics metrics;
  String densityDpiConstant;

  @Override
  public void onCreate(Bundle savedInstanceState) {
    super.onCreate(savedInstanceState);
    setContentView(R.layout.main);
```

```
textView = (TextView) findViewById(R.id.textView1);

metrics = new DisplayMetrics();
getWindowManager().getDefaultDisplay().
  getMetrics(metrics);

switch (metrics.densityDpi) {
case DisplayMetrics.DENSITY_LOW:
  densityDpiConstant = "DENSITY_LOW";
  break;
case DisplayMetrics.DENSITY_MEDIUM:
  densityDpiConstant = "DENSITY_MEDIUM";
  break;
case DisplayMetrics.DENSITY_HIGH:
  densityDpiConstant = "DENSITY_HIGH";
  break;
case DisplayMetrics.DENSITY_XHIGH:
  densityDpiConstant = "DENSITY_XHIGH";
  break;
case DisplayMetrics.DENSITY_XXHIGH:
  densityDpiConstant = "DENSITY_XXHIGH";
  break;
default:
  densityDpiConstant = "densityDpi is " +
                              metrics.densityDpi;
  break;
}

textView.setText(metrics.toString()
    + ", " + densityDpiConstant);
  }
}
```

android:padding and android:margin

Objects on a screen need room to breathe. You can't butt one text field right up against another. If you do, the screen looks horribly cluttered. So Android has things called *padding* and *margin:*

✦ A view's *padding* is space between the view's border and whatever is contained inside the view.

✦ A view's *margin* is space between the view's border and whatever is outside the view.

In Figure 1-6, I superimpose labels onto a screen shot from an emulator. The rectangle with eight little squares along its perimeter is the text view's border. Think of the border as the text view's clothing. The padding keeps the clothing from being too tight, and the margins determine how much "personal space" the text view wants.

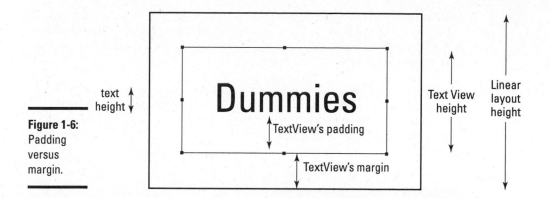

Figure 1-6:
Padding
versus
margin.

Listing 1-4 contains the code that generates the layout in Figure 1-6.

Listing 1-4:   Using Margin and Padding

```
<?xml version="1.0" encoding="utf-8"?>
<LinearLayout xmlns:android=
    "http://schemas.android.com/apk/res/android"
    android:orientation="vertical"
    android:layout_width="match_parent"
    android:layout_height="match_parent"
    android:gravity="center">

<LinearLayout android:id="@+id/LinearLayout1"
    android:layout_height="wrap_content"
    android:layout_width="wrap_content"
    android:background="@color/opaque_white">

    <TextView android:text="Dummies"
        android:layout_margin="30dip"
        android:padding="30dip"
        android:textSize="30sp"

        android:layout_height="wrap_content"
        android:layout_width="wrap_content"

        android:id="@+id/textView1"
        android:textColor="@color/opaque_black">
    </TextView>
</LinearLayout>

</LinearLayout>
```

android:gravity and android:layout_gravity

I once asked a button what it wanted to be when it grows up. The button
replied, "I want to be an astronaut." So I placed the button inside a layout

with attribute `android:layout_gravity="center"`. A layout with this attribute is like the International Space Station. Things float in the middle of it. (Well, they don't actually bob to and fro the way things do in the space-station videos, but that's beside the point.)

Android has two similarly named attributes, and it's very easy to confuse them with one another. The `android:gravity` attribute tells a layout how to position the views within it. The `android:layout_gravity` attribute tells a view how to position itself within its layout. Figure 1-7 illustrates the idea.

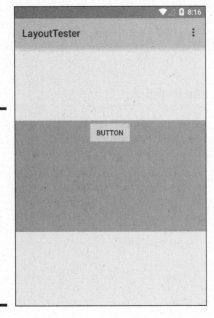

Figure 1-7: The gray layout gravitates to the center of the screen; the button gravitates to the top of the gray layout.

The screen in Figure 1-7 contains a shortened linear layout and a button. The linear layout is only 220dip tall, and its `android:layout_gravity` is `center_vertical`. (See Listing 1-5.) So the gray linear layout floats downward to the center of the screen. But the layout's `android:gravity` attribute is `center_horizontal`. So the button within the layout shimmies horizontally to the layout's center. The button hangs along the top edge of the layout because, by default, things rise to the top and hug the left.

Listing 1-5: Using layout_gravity and gravity

```xml
<?xml version="1.0" encoding="utf-8"?>
<LinearLayout xmlns:android=
        "http://schemas.android.com/apk/res/android"

    android:layout_gravity="center_vertical"
    android:gravity="center_horizontal"

    android:background="#F999"
    android:orientation="vertical"
    android:layout_width="match_parent"
    android:layout_height="220dip">

    <Button android:text="Button"
        android:id="@+id/button1"
        android:layout_width="wrap_content"
        android:layout_height="wrap_content">
    </Button>

</LinearLayout>
```

Figures 1-8 through 1-11 illustrate some other `android:gravity` attribute values.

Figure 1-10 shows what you can do by combining gravity values using Java's `bitwise or` operator (|).

Figure 1-8:
LinearLayout with android: gravity= "center_ vertical"

Figure 1-9:
LinearLayout with android: gravity= "center"

Figure 1-10: LinearLayout with android: gravity= "bottom| right"

Figure 1-11: LinearLayout with no explicit android: gravity attribute.

Don't gloss over the word *layout*

In the Designer view's Text mode, look for attributes named `android:gravity` and `android:layout_grav-ity`. And while you're checking for text, look for `android:layout_width` and `android:layout_height` attributes. You probably won't find the simple `android:width` attribute, but some layout files contain this attribute.

When I first started developing Android apps, I ignored the difference between `gravity` and `layout_gravity`. I wish someone had told me to be mindful of the difference.

✔ **A component's** `gravity` **determines what the component does to the things inside of it.**

The options include `top`, `bottom`, `left`, `right`, `center`, `fill`, `center_` `horizontal`, `center_vertical`, `fill_horizontal`, `fill_verti-cal`, and a few others.

Think of `gravity` as something that the Earth has. If the Earth had a name for its `gravity` attribute, that name would be `down`.

✔ **A component's** `layout_gravity` **determines how the component is situated within the component that contains it.**

The options are the same as the `gravity` attribute's options. If an airplane pilot had a name for his or her `layout_gravity` property, that name might be `30000_` `feet_above_ground`.

✔ **A component's** `layout_width` **and** `layout_height` **attributes describe the width and height of the component.**

You can specify `layout_width` and `layout_height` as a certain number of pixels, but this way of describing size can be very tricky. (For the lowdown on pixels, see the "Using numbers of units" section.) A simpler way to specify `layout_width` is to write

```
android:layout_width="wrap_content"
```

or

```
android:layout_width="match_parent"
```

The value `wrap_content` means "shrink so that you're large enough to show what's inside of you," and the value `match_parent` means "grow to fill whatever contains you."

The same `wrap_content` and `match_parent` options can apply to a component's `layout_height` attribute. In addition, Android has a `fill_parent` option that developers don't use anymore. (If you use the `fill_parent` option, it has the same meaning as the newer `match_parent` option.)

✔ **A** `TextView` **item can have a** `width` **attribute. A** `TextView` **item's** `width` **attribute is the same as its** `layout_width` **attribute except that you can't specify** `wrap_content` **or** `match_parent` **for the** `width` **attribute.**

The `android:width` attribute isn't very useful. But if you see this attribute in a layout file, at least you'll know what it means.

While I'm on the subject, here's one more attribute that you'll find in Android's layout files:

✔ **A component's** `layout_weight` **attribute tells Android how much room to allocate to that component. This applies only if the component is inside something that has room to spare.**

Imagine creating three `TextView` components inside a `LinearLayout`. For one `TextView` component, you don't specify an `android:layout_weight` property in the layout file. By default, that component's `layout_weight` is 0. For the second `TextView` component, you specify

```
android:layout_weight="1"
```

in the layout file. For the third component, you specify

```
android:layout_weight="2"
```

in the layout file. If the `LinearLayout` has room to spare, the `TextView` with `layout_weight` 2 is considered to be the most important, so that `TextView` takes up more of the spare space than the other two `TextView` components. The `TextView` with `layout_weight` 0 is considered to be the least important, so that `TextView` takes up less of the spare space than the other two components.

android:color

You can apply colors to all kinds of things — things such as text, backgrounds, shadows, links, and other stuff. In Listing 1-5, I use the attribute `android:background="#F999"`, making a layout's background one quiet, dignified shade of gray.

As an Android developer, the most grown-up way to create a color is to declare it in a res/values/colors.xml file. The file looks something like the stuff in Listing 1-6.

Listing 1-6:   A colors.xml File

```
<?xml version="1.0" encoding="utf-8"?>
<resources xmlns:android=
    "http://schemas.android.com/apk/res/android">
  <color name="bright_red">#F00</color>
  <color name="bright_red2">#FF00</color>
  <color name="bright_red3">#FF0000</color>
  <color name="translucent_red">#7F00</color>
  <color name="invisible_good_for_nothing_red">
    #00FF0000
  </color>
  <color name="white">#FFF</color>
  <color name="black">#000</color>
  <color name="puce">#CC8898</color>
</resources>
```

A color value begins with a pound sign (#) and then has three, four, six, or eight hexadecimal digits. With three digits, the leftmost digit is an amount of redness, the middle digit is an amount of greenness, and the rightmost digit is an amount of blueness. (The colors always come in that order — red, then green, and then blue. It's called *RGB* color.) So, for example, the color value #F92 stands for a decent-looking orange color — 15 units of red, 9 units of green, and 2 units of blue, each out of a possible 16 units.

With only three hexadecimal digits, you can't express fine color differences. So Android permits you to express a color as a sequence of six hex digits. For example, the value #FEF200 is a good approximation to the yellow on this book's cover. It's 254 units of red, 242 units of green, and no blue, each out of a possible 255 units.

With three RGB digits, you can add a fourth *alpha* digit immediately after the pound sign. And with six RGB digits, you can add two additional alpha digits immediately after the pound sign. The alpha value is the amount of opaqueness, with 15 being fully opaque and 0 being completely transparent. So the value #7F00 in Listing 1-6 is partially transparent red ("translucent red," if you will). Against a black background, the value #7F00 is a dull, depressing reddishness.

```
<?xml version="1.0" encoding="utf-8"?>
<LinearLayout xmlns:android=
    "http://schemas.android.com/apk/res/android"
  android:background="@color/black"
  android:id="@+id/linearLayout1"
  android:layout_height="wrap_content"
```

```
    android:layout_width="match_parent"
    android:orientation="vertical">

    <Button android:background="@color/translucent_red"
        android:layout_width="match_parent"
        android:layout_height="wrap_content"
        android:text="Button"
        android:id="@+id/button8"></Button>
</LinearLayout>
```

Against a white background, the value #7F00 looks like elementary-school pink.

A hexadecimal digit is an ordinary decimal digit or one of the letters *A, B, C, D, E,* or *F.* (Either uppercase or lowercase letters are okay.) The letter *A* stands for 10, *B* stands for 11, and so on up to *F,* which stands for 15. A two-digit hex number stands for "the right digit, plus 16 times the left digit." For example, A5 stands for $5 + (16 \times 10)$, which is 165. With only one hex digit, you can represent the `int` values from 0 to 15, inclusive. With two hex digits, you can represent the `int` values from 0 to 255, inclusive.

android:visibility

An Android view has one of three visibility values — `android.view.View.VISIBLE`, `android.view.View.INVISIBLE`, or `android.view.View.GONE`. The first value — `VISIBLE` — is self-explanatory. The difference between `INVISIBLE` and `GONE` is as follows: An `INVISIBLE` view takes up space; a view that's `GONE` takes up no space. For example, in Figure 1-12, an `INVISIBLE` view (Button2) separates Button1 from Button3. If I change Button2's visibility to `GONE`, Button1 butts up against Button3. (See Figure 1-13.)

Figure 1-12: Button2 is INVISIBLE.

Figure 1-13: Button2 is GONE.

In Figure 1-13, Button2 is gone but not forgotten. See this chapter's "Frame Layout" section for more details.

Using Configuration Qualifiers (Another Detour)

You may have noticed folders with names like `drawable-xhdpi` and `layout-sw300dp`. In Android Studio's Project tool window, they appear as items inside the `drawable` and `layout` branches. But in your system's File Explorer or Finder, these are separate folders containing image files, XML files, and other kinds of files. You can also find branches in the Project tool window with names like `values-it` (values for the Italian language locale). In your File Explorer or Finder, the corresponding folders contain `strings.xml` files, and other locale-specific files.

To find out how to use localization folders such as `values-it`, refer to Chapter 6 in Book I.

In a `res` subfolder name, characters that start with a dash (characters such as `-xhdpi`, `-sw300dp`, and `-it`) are *configuration qualifiers*. The general idea is to specify certain folders for particular device configurations. If the device is configured to display text in Italian, Android uses files from the `res/values-it` folder instead of from the default `res/values` folder. If the device has an extra-high-density screen (no big deal by today's standards), Android uses files from the `res/layout-xhdpi` folder. (That is, Android uses files from the `res/layout-xhdpi` folder if the project has such a folder.)

When you run an app, Android checks the device screen's characteristics. A screen with dpi value 240 is considered to be high density. This can be called `hdpi` or `DisplayMetrics.DENSITY_HIGH`, depending on where you refer to it in your project. So, if the screen's dpi value is close to 240 (whatever "close to" means), Android looks for folders named `res/layout-hdpi`, `res/drawable-hdpi`, and so on. The `res/layout-hdpi` folder (if your app has one) contains files named `activity_main.xml` and other files describing the layout of your app's screens. The `res/drawable-hdpi` folder (if your app has such a folder) contains images. For a high-density device or emulator, Android uses files that it finds in these `-hdpi` folders. If your app doesn't have such folders, Android uses files in the default folders (the plain old `res/layout` and `res/drawable` folders).

Table 1-1 contains some of Android's dpi names and their corresponding dpi values.

Table 1-1	**Android Screen Densities**		
Name	*Acronym*	*Approximate* Number of Dots per Inch (dpi)*	*Fraction of the Default Density*
DENSITY_LOW	ldpi	120	¾
DENSITY_MEDIUM	mdpi	160	1
DENSITY_HIGH	hdpi	240	1½
DENSITY_XHIGH	xhdpi	320	2
DENSITY_XXHIGH	xxhdpi	480	3
DENSITY_XXXHIGH	xxxhdpi	640	4

*When the screen density of a device doesn't match a number in Column 3 of Table 1-1, Android does its best with the existing categories. For example, Android classifies density 265 dpi in the hdpi group.

Fun facts: DENSITY_XHIGH is used for 1080p high-definition televisions in the United States. A seldom-used Android density, DENSITY_TV with 213 dpi, represents 720p television. The ultra-large DENSITY_XXXHIGH might be useful for displaying graphics on the newest 4K television screens.

You can combine configuration qualifiers. For example, the folder with the name drawable-en-land is for the English language when the device is in landscape mode. When you do this, you must list the qualifiers in a certain order. For details, see http://developer.android.com/guide/topics/resources/providing-resources.html.

Specifying exact dpi values

When I was young, products were available in sizes small, medium, and large. But the U.S. economy was doing well, and people were buying more and more stuff. So companies started selling extra-large items. After a while, people were no longer buying small sizes. Eventually, the three choices in supermarket shelves were large, extra-large, and jumbo. Nothing was available in small or medium sizes.

The same kind of thing has happened with Android screen sizes. People don't write apps for DENSITY_LOW screens anymore. And the trend toward higher and higher densities isn't stopping. By the time Android 3.2 was released, the stewards of Android were tired of making up new names for higher and higher screen densities. So they came up with a more versatile scheme. They called for folders with names such as layout-sw300dp.

In the Android documentation, such folders are named sw<*N*>dp folders. The letters *sw* stand for *smallest width* (the width of your activity when the activity has its narrowest width — typically the activity's width in portrait mode). If the screen width available to your activity is ever smaller than whatever number you substitute in place of *N*, Android doesn't look inside this sw<*N*>dp folder. For example, if the screen width available to your activity is ever smaller than 600dp, Android doesn't look inside the layout-sw600dp folder, the drawable-sw600dp, or any other -sw600dp folders.

An activity's smallest width doesn't change when you flip from portrait to landscape mode, because "smallest width" really means "smallest possible width in any mode — landscape, portrait, or whatever other mode there might be."

Here's an experiment for you to try:

1. **Create a new Android project.**

2. **Using your system's File Explorer or Finder, create a subfolder of the project's** res **folder. Name the new folder** layout-sw300dp **(for example).**

3. **Still using your system's File Explorer or Finder, copy your app's** activity_main.xml **file from the** res/layout **folder to the new** res/layout-sw300dp **folder.**

   Now your main activity has two layout files — one for emulators and devices that have 300dp or more for an activity and another for all other screens.

4. **Modify one of the** activity_main.xml **files so that you can determine which is being used during a run of the app.**

   For me, the easiest thing to do is to take the text view that comes with every new app. In that text view, change the characters in one of the activity_main.xml files.

5. **Run your app on two emulators — one relatively new and another that's fairly old.**

   I ran this app on a 768 × 1280 Nexus 4, and a 480 × 800 Nexus One. The Nexus 4 displayed the layout from the res/layout-sw300dp folder. But the Nexus One defaulted to the layout from the res/layout folder. That's how these sw<*N*>dp folders work.

Specifying screen orientation

In the previous section, you name different layout files for different screen sizes. The screen sizes depend on the device's dpi (dots per inch) value. This is very useful, but when you're trying to make an app look nice, dots per inch don't tell the whole story.

Suppose you want different layouts for the device in portrait and landscape modes. You can make that happen by creating a res/layout-land folder. Here are the details:

1. **Create a new Android project.**

2. **Using your system's File Explorer or Finder, create a subfolder of the project's** `res` **folder. Name the new folder** `layout-land`.

3. **Still using your system's File Explorer or Finder, copy your app's** `activity_main.xml` **file from the** `res/layout` **folder to the new** `res/layout-land` **folder.**

   Now your main activity has two layout files — one for landscape mode on your emulator or device (`res/layout-land/activity_main.xml`) and another for portrait mode (`res/layout /activity_main.xml`).

4. **Modify one of the** `activity_main.xml` **files so that you can determine which is being used during a run of the app.**

   For me, the easiest thing to do is to take the text view that comes with every new app. In that text view, change the characters in one of the `activity_main.xml` files.

5. **Run your app.**

6. **Change the emulator or device back and forth between portrait and landscape mode.**

   Notice how the layout changes automatically from one XML file to the other.

   To switch an emulator between portrait and landscape modes, press Ctrl+F11.

Some other configuration qualifiers

This chapter emphasizes the `dpi`, `sw<N>dp`, and `land` configuration qualifiers. But Android has many other configuration qualifiers. Table 1-2 contains a brief list.

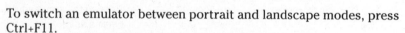

Table 1-2	Configuration Qualifiers	
Name	*Examples*	*Meaning*
Language and region	`-en`, `-it`	In what language (and for what country or region) is this device configured?
Layout direction	`-ldrtl`, `-ldltr`	In which direction does writing go on this device? Right-to-left (as in Hebrew or Arabic) or left-to-right (as in many other languages)?

(continued)

Table 1-2 *(continued)*

Name	Examples	Meaning
Smallest width	-sw300dp	No matter how the device is oriented, what's the smallest width (in density-independent pixels) that's available to your activity?
Available width	-w720dp	For the device's current orientation, what's the width (in density-independent pixels) that's available to your activity?
Available height	-h1024dp	For the device's current orientation, what's the height (in density-independent pixels) that's available to your activity?
Pixel density	-hdpi, -xhdpi	How many density-independent pixels does the device's screen have?
Orientation	-port, -land	How is the device currently oriented? Portrait or landscape?
UI mode	-car, -desk, -watch, -television, -appliance	What kind of a device is running your app?
Night mode	-night, -notnight	Are you (or aren't you) currently in the Earth's shadow?
Touchscreen type	-notouch, -finger	Does the screen respond to the user's touch?
API level	-v4, -v7	Which API level does this device support?

I occasionally become sloppy and write that the choice of sw<*N*>dp, w<*N*>dp, and h<*N*>dp folders depends on a device's screen size. This is mostly true, but sometimes, it's worth being picky. To be painfully precise, measurements such as sw300dp and h1024dp don't really refer to the entire screen. They refer to whatever part of the screen is available for use by your activity. For example, the Back, Home and Recents buttons that appear at the bottom of a phone's screen are not part of an activity's layout. So the space taken by these elements doesn't count when Android decides about using an h<*N*>dp folder. If the screen has 1060dp with these buttons but only 900dp when you don't count the height of these buttons, then on this device, Android doesn't use an h1024dp folder's file. (If there's a surprise in this story, it concerns the Action bar. The Action bar counts as part of the activity's screen space. So, if you have 1060dp with the Action bar and only 900dp without the Action bar, Android can use the h1024dp folder's files.)

Relative Layout

When you create a new Android project, Android Studio fills your main activity's layout with a relative layout. A relative layout describes the placement of each view compared with other views. For example, in a relative layout, you might place Button2 beneath Button1 and place Button3 to the right of Button1. Listing 1-7 has some code, and Figure 1-14 shows the resulting screen.

Listing 1-7: Using a Relative Layout

```xml
<?xml version="1.0" encoding="utf-8"?>
<RelativeLayout xmlns:android=
      "http://schemas.android.com/apk/res/android"
    android:orientation="vertical"
    android:layout_height="match_parent"
    android:layout_width="match_parent">

    <Button android:layout_alignParentTop="true"
            android:layout_alignParentLeft="true"

        android:text="Button1" android:id="@+id/button1"
        android:layout_height="wrap_content"
        android:layout_width="wrap_content"></Button>

    <Button android:layout_alignParentLeft="true"
            android:layout_below="@+id/button1"

        android:text="Button2" android:id="@+id/button2"
        android:layout_height="wrap_content"
        android:layout_width="wrap_content"></Button>

<Button android:layout_alignParentTop="true"
            android:layout_toRightOf="@+id/button1"

        android:text="Button3" android:id="@+id/button3"
        android:layout_height="wrap_content"
        android:layout_width="wrap_content"></Button>

    <Button android:layout_below="@+id/button2"
            android:layout_alignLeft="@+id/button3"

        android:text="Button4" android:id="@+id/button4"
        android:layout_height="wrap_content"
        android:layout_width="wrap_content"></Button>

</RelativeLayout>
```

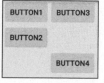

Figure 1-14:
Buttons in
a relative
layout.

Coding Android's relative layouts can be complicated. I have trouble remembering which `android:id` goes with which view's `android:layout_toRightOf`. I can easily goof by creating a circular reference. But don't give up on relative layouts! To avoid relative layouts, people try creating vast nests of linear layouts within other linear layouts. Things go well until someone runs the code. Excessive nesting of linear layouts slows down a processor.

Android has tools to help wean you away from nested linear layouts. One is the hierarchy viewer. The hierarchy viewer's tree displays the nesting of your layout's objects. To use the hierarchy viewer, do the following:

1. **Choose Tools ⇨ Android ⇨ Android Device Monitor.**

2. **In the Android Device Monitor's menu, choose Window ⇨ Open Perspective ⇨ Hierarchy View.**

3. **When the hierarchy view opens, look for the Windows tab at the upper-left corner of the viewer. (See Figure 1-15.)**

4. **In the viewer's Windows tab, double-click the item corresponding to your app.**

If you're not a total geek, you won't get the hierarchy viewer to work on a real device. The tool normally works only on an emulator.

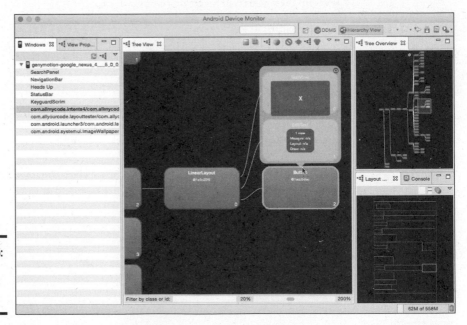

Figure 1-15:
The
hierarchy
viewer.

Figure 1-15 contains a revealing (okay, okay, a personally embarrassing) hierarchy viewer analysis of one of my recent projects. Look at the Tree Overview in the upper-right panel. Each rounded rectangle represents a view (a layout, for example). The length of the tree (from left to right) shows how deep the nesting goes for this particular project. Some of the tree's branches are nine levels deep, and the processor can't draw a view without first calculating the views to its left along the tree's branches. So the processor chugs slowly as it tries to render the whole scene.

A run of the hierarchy viewer tells you how deeply nested your layouts are. With the viewer's tree in mind, you can look for ways to eliminate some of the nesting.

Table Layout

A table layout has rows, and each row contains some views. If you do nothing to override the defaults, the views line up to form columns.

For example, the table layout in Figure 1-16 has three table rows. Each table row contains buttons.

```xml
<?xml version="1.0" encoding="utf-8"?>
<TableLayout xmlns:android=
  "http://schemas.android.com/apk/res/android"
        android:layout_width="match_parent"
        android:layout_height="match_parent">

  <TableRow>
    <Button android:text="Button"/>
    <Button android:text="Button"/>
    <Button android:text="Button"/>
  </TableRow>

  <TableRow>
    <Button android:text="Button"/>
    <Button android:text="Wide button"/>
  </TableRow>

  <TableRow>
    <Button android:text="Button"/>
    <Button android:text="Btn."/>
    <Button android:text="Button"/>
  </TableRow>

</TableLayout>
```

In Figure 1-16, notice how each column widens to accommodate the largest item in the column. Notice also how each item expands to fill its entire column.

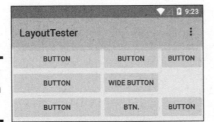

Figure 1-16:
Buttons in a
table layout.

What? You say you want the leftmost column to be wider? Just add the
`android:stretchColumns` attribute to your `<TableLayout>` start tag:

```
<TableLayout xmlns:android=
              "http://schemas.android.com/apk/res/android"
        android:layout_width="match_parent"
        android:layout_height="match_parent"
        android:stretchColumns="0">
```

The leftmost column has number 0, so when you write `stretchColumns="0"`,
you get a layout like the one in Figure 1-17.

Figure 1-17:
Stretching a
column.

Do you want more than one column to be stretched? Then name several
column numbers in your `stretchColumns` attribute:

```
<TableLayout xmlns:android=
              "http://schemas.android.com/apk/res/android"
        android:layout_width="match_parent"
        android:layout_height="match_parent"
        android:stretchColumns="0,1,2">
```

When you do, you get the layout shown in Figure 1-18.

You can move the Wide button back in Figure 1-16 to the rightmost column:

```
<TableRow>
  <Button android:text="Button"/>
  <Button android:text="Wide button"
        android:layout_column="2"/>
</TableRow>
```

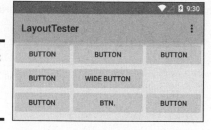

Figure 1-18:
Stretching
several
columns.

The resulting layout is shown in Figure 1-19.

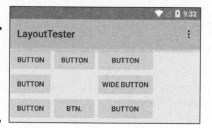

Figure 1-19:
Putting a
widget in a
particular
column.

You can make a cell in the table span several columns:

```
<TableRow>
  <Button android:text="Button"/>
  <Button android:text="Wide button"
        android:layout_span="2"/>
</TableRow>
```

When you do, you get the layout shown in Figure 1-20.

Figure 1-20:
Spanning
across
columns.

Grid Layout

Like a table layout, a *grid layout* arranges things in rows and columns. But some features make grid layouts different from table layouts. For one thing, you don't use TableRow elements (or anything like TableRow elements) in a grid layout. Instead, you specify the number of rows and columns in the `GridLayout` start tag:

```
<GridLayout xmlns:android=
            "http://schemas.android.com/apk/res/android"
         android:layout_width="match_parent"
         android:layout_height="match_parent"
         android:columnCount="3"
         android:rowCount="3">

    <Button android:text="Button"/>
    <Button android:text="Button"/>
    <Button android:text="Button"/>
    <Button android:text="Button"/>
    <Button android:text="Wide button"/>
    <Button android:text="Button"
         android:layout_row="2"
         android:layout_column="0"/>
    <Button android:text="Btn."/>
    <Button android:text="Button"/>
</GridLayout>
```

This code gives you the layout shown in Figure 1-21. Notice how the `layout_row` and `layout_column` attributes force all the buttons after the Wide button into the bottommost row.

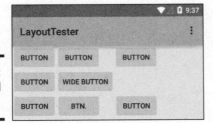

Figure 1-21:
Using a grid
layout.

Notice also how the buttons in Figure 1-21 don't expand to fill their respective columns. Android's `layout_width` attribute doesn't play nicely with the grid layout. So, if you want an item in a grid layout to expand to fill its column, use the `android:layout_gravity` attribute:

```
<Button android:text="Button"
         android:layout_row="2"
         android:layout_column="0"/>

<Button android:layout_gravity="fill_horizontal"
         android:text="Btn."/>

<Button android:text="Button"/>
```

The resulting layout is shown in Figure 1-22.

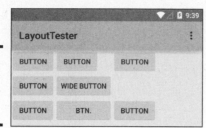

Figure 1-22:
Filling a
column in a
grid layout.

Frame Layout

A frame layout displays one view. What good is that?

Well, to be more precise (and less sensational), a frame layout displays views one in front of another. (Put on your 3D glasses and think of a frame layout as an outward-pointing linear layout.) Because views tend to cover the stuff behind them, a frame layout normally displays only one view — namely, whatever's in front.

Frame layouts usually serve one of two purposes:

✦ A frame layout might display a small view superimposed on a larger view (such as text on an image).

✦ A frame layout might store several views, only one of which is visible at any point in time. Using the frame layout, you change what appears in a certain place on the screen.

This section's example illustrates both ideas. You start with a word superimposed on an image, which is, in turn, supcrimposed on top of another image. (See Figure 1-23.)

Figure 1-23:
Three
widgets
on a frame
layout.

When the user touches the screen, two of the three items disappear. (See Figure 1-24.) The screen cycles through the three images, changing the image whenever the user touches the screen. (See Figures 1-25 and 1-26.)

Figure 1-24: Meow!

Figure 1-25: The largest of three images.

Figure 1-26: The midsize image.

(I know what you're thinking: "The author looks for excuses to show pictures of his cats." That's only partly true. I include lots of illustrations to help you visualize the code's behavior. Anyway, pictures of cats make perfect clip art. Cats don't complain when you use their least favorite profiles. Pictures of cats are better than pictures of your family members because readers seldom stalk cats. Best of all, no one's figured out how to patent the domestic cat. I can't be sued for putting cat pictures in my book. Not yet, anyway.)

Listing 1-8 shows you the XML code for the app in Figures 1-23 to 1-26.

Listing 1-8:   Creating a Frame Layout

```xml
<?xml version="1.0" encoding="utf-8"?>

<FrameLayout xmlns:android=
        "http://schemas.android.com/apk/res/android"
    android:id="@+id/mainlayout"
    android:layout_height="fill_parent"
    android:layout_width="fill_parent"
    android:orientation="vertical"
    android:onClick="rotate">

    <ImageView android:src="@drawable/calico"

        android:layout_height="wrap_content"
        android:layout_width="wrap_content"
        android:padding="5px"

        android:layout_gravity="center"
        android:id="@+id/imageViewCalico"/>

    <ImageView android:src="@drawable/burmese"

        android:layout_height="wrap_content"
        android:layout_width="wrap_content"
        android:padding="5px"

        android:layout_gravity="center"
        android:id="@+id/imageViewBurmese"/>

    <TextView android:text="@string/meow"

        android:textColor="#FFF"
        android:textSize="15sp"
        android:layout_width="wrap_content"
        android:layout_height="wrap_content"
        android:layout_gravity="center"
        android:id="@+id/textView"/>

</FrameLayout>
```

The only important business in Listing 1-8 is the order in which I declare the views. The largest image (the Calico) is the `FrameLayout` element's first child. So, in Figure 1-23, the Calico appears behind the other images. If the Burmese's image was as large as the Calico's image, you wouldn't see the edges of the Calico's image in Figure 1-23. The last element in Listing 1-8 is the text view, so in Figure 1-23, the text is superimposed on top of the other elements.

Listing 1-9 has the code that rotates from image to image.

When the app starts running, all three views (the two images and the text view) are visible. But then Listing 1-9 cycles from one view to another. Each call to the `rotate` method makes one view visible and makes the other two views invisible.

Listing 1-9:   Coding Java with a Frame Layout

```java
package com.allmycode.layouts;

import android.app.Activity;
import android.os.Bundle;
import android.view.View;
import android.widget.ImageView;
import android.widget.TextView;

public class LayoutTesterActivity extends Activity {
  ImageView imageCalico, imageBurmese;
  TextView textView;

  @Override
  public void onCreate(Bundle savedInstanceState) {
    super.onCreate(savedInstanceState);
    setContentView(R.layout.frame);
    imageCalico =
        (ImageView) findViewById(R.id.imageViewCalico);
    imageBurmese =
        (ImageView) findViewById(R.id.imageViewBurmese);
    textView = (TextView) findViewById(R.id.textView);
  }

  int count = 0;

  public void rotate(View view) {
    switch (count++ % 3) {
    case 0:
      textView.setVisibility(View.VISIBLE);
      imageCalico.setVisibility(View.INVISIBLE);
      imageBurmese.setVisibility(View.INVISIBLE);
      break;
    case 1:
      textView.setVisibility(View.INVISIBLE);
      imageCalico.setVisibility(View.VISIBLE);
      imageBurmese.setVisibility(View.INVISIBLE);
      break;
    case 2:
      textView.setVisibility(View.INVISIBLE);
      imageCalico.setVisibility(View.INVISIBLE);
      imageBurmese.setVisibility(View.VISIBLE);
      break;
    }
  }
}
```

Using a ScrollView

Sometimes, an activity's screen takes up more space than is available on a
mobile phone. If that's likely to happen, you can enclose the activity's screen
in a ScrollView. As its name suggests, a ScrollView lets the user slide
things onto the screen as other things slide off. Listing 1-10 shows you some
code, and Figure 1-27 shows you the results.

Listing 1-10:   How to Scroll

```
<?xml version="1.0" encoding="utf-8"?>
<ScrollView xmlns:android=
            "http://schemas.android.com/apk/res/android"
            android:layout_width="match_parent"
            android:layout_height="wrap_content">

  <LinearLayout
    android:layout_width="match_parent"
    android:layout_height="wrap_content"
    android:orientation="vertical">

    <TextView
      android:layout_width="match_parent"
      android:layout_height="wrap_content"
      android:text="0\n1\n2\n3\n4\n5\n6\n7\n8\n9"
      android:textSize="40sp"/>

    <TextView
      android:layout_width="match_parent"
      android:layout_height="wrap_content"
      android:text="10\n11\n12\n13\n14"
      android:textSize="40sp"/>

    <TextView
      android:layout_width="match_parent"
      android:layout_height="wrap_content"
      android:text="15\n16\n17\n18\n19"
      android:textSize="40sp"/>

  </LinearLayout>

</ScrollView>
```

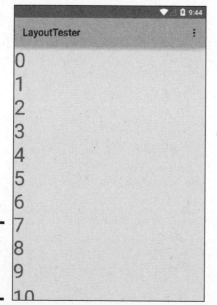

Figure 1-27:
The screen
in Listing
1-10.

In truth, Figure 1-27 doesn't show you the whole story. If the user slides a finger upward along the screen, the numbers in Figure 1-27 move upward. The smaller numbers scroll off the top of the screen, and larger numbers scroll up onto the bottom of the screen.

Inside a quoted string of characters, \n stands for *newline*. So, in Listing 1-10, "10\n11\n12\n13\n14" means *10, go to the next line, 11, go to the next line, and so on.*

The big restriction on a ScrollView is that a ScrollView may contain only one direct child. So, in Listing 1-10, you can't put three TextView elements directly inside a ScrollView element. Instead, you put the three TextView elements inside some other element (in Listing 1-10, a LinearLayout element) and then put that other element inside the ScrollView.

Defining a Layout in Java Code

XML files are good for describing layouts because XML is *declarative.* In an XML file, you declare, once and for all, a layout's characteristics. You declare the presence of a text field and a button. You don't think of these widgets as actions ("Put a text field here and, sometime later, put a button there"), so you don't say "Do this, and later, do that" the way you say things in a Java program.

But sometimes, a layout's look has to change. Imagine an activity in which you have one row consisting of two items — a text field and a button. (See Figure 1-28.)

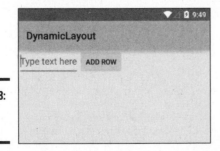

Figure 1-28: A row of widgets.

When you click the button, you want an additional row to appear. (See Figure 1-29.)

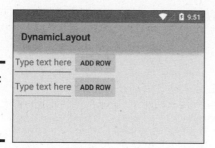

Figure 1-29:
One row
turns into
two rows.

To make this happen, you start with a regular, old XML layout. (See Listing 1-11.)

Listing 1-11:   The Starting Layout

```
<LinearLayout xmlns:android=
    "http://schemas.android.com/apk/res/android"
        android:orientation="vertical"
        android:id="@+id/linear_layout"
        android:layout_width="match_parent"
        android:layout_height="match_parent">

  <LinearLayout
    android:orientation="horizontal"
    android:layout_width="fill_parent"
    android:layout_height="wrap_content">

    <EditText
      android:layout_width="wrap_content"
      android:layout_height="wrap_content"
      android:hint="@string/type_text_here"/>

    <Button
      android:id="@+id/button"
      android:layout_width="wrap_content"
      android:layout_height="wrap_content"
      android:text="@string/add_a_row"/>
  </LinearLayout>

</LinearLayout>
```

The layout in Listing 1-11 describes the screen shown earlier in Figure 1-28.

In your main activity, you respond to button clicks. The code is in Listing 1-12.

In Listing 1-12, in the onCreate method, you identify the outmost linear layout and the button that's currently displayed in that layout. You assign these items to the variables rootLayout and firstButton. You make this very activity be the listener for button clicks. Accordingly, this activity implements the OnClickListener interface and has an onClick method. The onClick method responds when the user clicks the button.

**Book IV
Chapter 1**

Laying Out Your Stuff

Listing 1-12:   Creating a New Row of Widgets.

```java
package com.allyourcode.dynamiclayout;

import android.app.Activity;
import android.os.Bundle;
import android.view.View;
import android.widget.Button;
import android.widget.EditText;
import android.widget.LinearLayout;
import android.widget.LinearLayout.LayoutParams;

public class MainActivity extends Activity
                      implements View.OnClickListener {
  LinearLayout rootlayout;

  @Override
  protected void onCreate(Bundle savedInstanceState) {
    super.onCreate(savedInstanceState);
    setContentView(R.layout.activity_main);
    rootlayout =
        (LinearLayout) findViewById(R.id.linear_layout);
    Button firstButton = (Button) findViewById(R.id.button);
    firstButton.setOnClickListener(this);
  }

  @Override
  public void onClick(View view) {
    LayoutParams editTextLayoutParams =
        new LayoutParams(LayoutParams.WRAP_CONTENT,
                         LayoutParams.WRAP_CONTENT);
    LayoutParams buttonLayoutParams =
        new LayoutParams(LayoutParams.WRAP_CONTENT,
                         LayoutParams.WRAP_CONTENT);
    LayoutParams rowLayoutParams =
        new LayoutParams(LayoutParams.MATCH_PARENT,
                         LayoutParams.WRAP_CONTENT);

    EditText editText = new EditText(this);
    editText.setLayoutParams(editTextLayoutParams);
    editText.setHint(R.string.type_text_here);

    Button button = new Button(this);
    button.setLayoutParams(buttonLayoutParams);
    button.setText(R.string.add_a_row);
    button.setOnClickListener(this);

    LinearLayout newRow = new LinearLayout(this);
    newRow.setLayoutParams(rowLayoutParams);
    newRow.setOrientation(LinearLayout.HORIZONTAL);

    newRow.addView(editText);
    newRow.addView(button);

    LinearLayout currentRow =
                    ((LinearLayout) view.getParent());
    int currentIndex =
        ((LinearLayout) currentRow.getParent())
                      .indexOfChild(currentRow);
    rootlayout.addView(newRow, currentIndex + 1);
  }

}
```

For a review of the use of `OnClickListener` and `setOnClickListener`, refer to Chapter 5 in Book I.

In the body of the `onClick` method, you do five things:

✦ **You create instances of the** `LayoutParams` **class.**

Each instance sets the width and height for one of the items that you'll be adding to the user's screen.

✦ **You create a new** `EditText` **and a new** `Button`.

You set the properties of these two new items. In particular, you make this activity listen for clicks of your new button.

✦ **You create a new row.**

The row has a horizontal linear layout.

✦ **You add the** `EditText` **and the** `Button` **to the new row.**

✦ **Finally, you add the new row to the** `rootLayout`.

If you call

```
rootlayout.addView(newRow);
```

then the new row gets added after all other rows in the `rootLayout`. In some situations, this is okay. But presumably, in this example, a new row goes immediately below whichever button the user pressed.

Accordingly, before adding a new row, you want to find out which row contains the button that the user pressed. That's what this bit of Listing 1-12 code does:

```
LinearLayout currentRow =
                ((LinearLayout) view.getParent());
int currentIndex =
    ((LinearLayout) currentRow.getParent())
                    .indexOfChild(currentRow);
```

With `currentIndex` equal to the position number of the row containing the pressed button, you call

```
rootlayout.addView(newRow, currentIndex + 1);
```

You add the `newRow` one position after the current row.

Sometimes, you need both (XML and Java code)

At the end of Chapter 6 in Book I, I present an activity that has a few check boxes and a button. When the user clicks the button, a web page takes over the entire screen. This behavior is surprising because you call

```
webView.loadUrl("http://blah-blah-blah");
```

and the `webView` in question is only one element in the activity's layout. Why don't the other elements stay on the screen?

In early versions of Android, the web page didn't consume the entire screen, and it would be nice if those good old days weren't gone forever. To keep the web page from consuming all of the screen's real estate, declare the `webView`'s position in the activity's relative layout.

```
<!-- Disclaimer: This code conveys the general idea
     but this code isn't real XML. (Sorry about that!) -->

<RelativeLayout . . .>

  <include
    android:id="@+id/checkboxes_and_button"
    ... />

  <WebView
    android:layout_below="@id/checkboxes_and_button"
    ... />

</RelativeLayout . . .>
```

In addition, you have to sneak back to the main activity's Java file and add code of the following kind:

```
webView.setWebViewClient(new WebViewClient() {

  @Override
  public boolean shouldOverrideUrlLoading
                 (WebView webView, String url) {
    webView.loadUrl(url);
    return true;
  }
});
```

This extra Java code overrides the default behavior by letting your activity control the loading of the new URL. The `webView` in your activity's layout displays the web page, and the good old days are here again.

Chapter 2: Menus, Lists, and Notifications

In This Chapter

⌐ **Building options menus and context menus**

⌐ **Connecting lists with activities**

⌐ **Adding notifications to the status bar**

Sure, I wish I were down at my favorite cheap restaurant, ordering something that a gourmet would never eat. Alas, I am not. As much as I would prefer to talk about menus dealing with food, I'm actually going to talk about menus inside an Android application!

All about Menus

Android provides several ways for you to add menus to your applications. With Android's help, you can add the following types of menus:

✦ **Options menu:** An activity's options menu is the activity's main menu. On a device running Android 3.0 or greater, the options menu is a bunch of icons on the activity's action bar. The action bar normally appears across the top of the activity screen. (See Figure 2-1.)

Figure 2-1: The action bar (on Honeycomb or later).

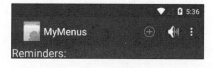

On a pre-Honeycomb device, items in the options menu appear when the user presses the Menu key. (See Figure 2-2.)

Figure 2-2:
An options
menu on
Gingerbread
(or earlier).

✦ **Context menu:** A context menu is a list of menu items. The list appears
when a user long-presses something. (See Figure 2-3.)

Context menus come in two flavors — the floating context menu
(Figure 2-3) and the contextual action mode (Figure 2-4).

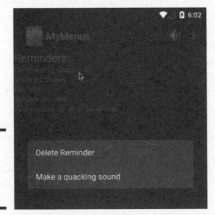

Figure 2-3:
A floating
context
menu.

Figure 2-4:
A context
menu with
contextual
action
mode.

✦ **Pop-up menu:** A pop-up menu is a list of menu items that appears when
the user taps a widget (a text view, an image, or whatever) on the activity's screen. The pop-up menu appears near the widget that the user
taps. Figure 2-5 shows a pop-up menu that's associated with an image
widget.

Figure 2-5:
A pop-up
menu.

In this chapter, you create options menus, context menus, pop-up menus, and some other fun things.

Creating an Options Menu

The action bar back in Figure 2-1 contains four elements:

✦ **On the left is the *app icon*.**

The app icon identifies your application. The same icon (along with your app's text label) appears no matter which of your app's activities is showing.

✦ **The plus sign and volume icons are called *action icons* or *action items*.**

When the user presses an action icon, the activity takes some action. (This isn't surprising. What else would you expect something called an "action item" to do? Of course, it's up to you, the developer, to write code that makes the action happen.) The look and number of these icons vary from one activity to another. Some activities have lots of action items; other activities have no action items.

✦ **The three dots aligned vertically are called the *overflow icon* or *action overflow*.**

When the user presses this icon, Android shows a list with some additional action icons. (See Figure 2-6.) When the user presses one of these additional action icons, the activity takes some action. (Again, it's up to you, the developer, to write code to make this happen.) You use the overflow when there are too many actions to fit individually in the action bar, or when some actions aren't important enough to appear on their own in the action bar.

Figure 2-6:
Some
overflow
items.

Using the app icon

The app icon is the little picture in the upper-right corner of Figure 2-1. This app icon doesn't appear without some coaxing. To make it appear, you add

```
getActionBar().setDisplayShowHomeEnabled(true);
```

to your activity's `onCreate` method. (You do this for API level 11 and above.)

With some additional code, you can program your app icon for *upward navigation*. You start by coding a hierarchy of activities in your app's `AndroidManifest.xml` file. For example, when the user presses an item in a list of books, your app replaces the list with an activity showing details about the selected book. So, in the `AndroidManifest.xml` file, you designate the list activity as being above the book detail activity.

```
<activity
    android:name="com.allyourcode.bookapp.Booklist" ...>
    ...
</activity>
<activity
    android:name="com.allmycode.bookapp.Bookdetail"
    android:parentActivityName=
                "com.allyourcode.bookapp.Booklist" ...>
    ...
</activity>
```

So imagine that the user is viewing the details about a particular book. When the user touches the app icon, Android moves upward in the hierarchy, from details about the selected book back to the list of books. The app icon is like the Back button except that the Back button's behavior depends on chronology — the order in which activities appeared recently on the task stack. In contrast, the app icon's behavior depends on the hierarchy of activities declared in the app's `AndroidManifest.xml` file.

Starting with Android's Ice Cream Sandwich version, you can put more complicated things (called action views) in your app's action bar. For example, Figure 2-7 shows a search view inside the action bar.

Figure 2-7:
A search
view in the
action bar.

You can use Java code or an XML document to create a menu. If you use XML, your document lives in a `res/menu` directory. The preferred method of creating menus is to define menus through XML. This helps separate the menu definition from the actual application code.

Defining the XML file

When you create a new project, Android Studio creates a `res/menu` directory containing a `menu_main.xml` file. Listing 2-1 contains the `menu_main.xml` file for Figures 2-1 and 2-6.

Listing 2-1:   Description of a Menu

```xml
<?xml version="1.0" encoding="utf-8"?>
<menu xmlns:android=
    "http://schemas.android.com/apk/res/android">
  <item android:id="@+id/menu_insert"
      android:icon="@android:drawable/ic_menu_add"
      android:title="@string/menu_insert"
      android:showAsAction="ifRoom|withText" />
  <item android:id="@+id/make_noise"
      android:icon=
        "@android:drawable/ic_lock_silent_mode_off"
      android:title="@string/honk"
      android:showAsAction="ifRoom|withText" />
  <item android:id="@+id/settings"
      android:title="Settings" />
  <item android:id="@+id/about"
     android:title="About"/>
</menu>
```

The values `@android:drawable/ic_menu_add` and `@android:drawable/ic_lock_silent_mode_off` are built-in Android icons. You don't have to provide these bitmaps in your `res/drawable` folders. The icon comes with the Android SDK in the `android.R.drawable` class.

All resources in the `android.R` class are available for you to use in your application and are recommended because they give your application a common and consistent user interface and user experience with the Android platform. To view other resources available to you, peruse the `android.R` documentation here: `http://developer.android.com/reference/android/R.html`.

In Listing 2-1, the attribute `android:showAsAction="ifRoom|withText"` tells Android two things:

✦ `ifRoom`: **Show this icon in the action bar if there's room for it.**

   If there isn't enough room, reveal this icon when the user presses the overflow icon.

✦ `withText`: **Show this item's title in the action bar if there's room for it.**

   If there isn't enough room, don't show the title.

Compare Figure 2-1 with Figure 2-8. In Figure 2-8, I turn the device from portrait to landscape orientation. Because the landscape screen is much wider, the two titles appear in the action bar.

Figure 2-8:
Titles
appear
when
there's
enough
room.

The vertical line character (|) between `ifRoom` and `withText` is called the *pipe character*. In Java, the pipe character performs the *or* operation between the bits in its two operands. In binary, the value of `ifRoom` is 001, and the value of `withText` is 100. So the value of `ifRoom|withText` is 101. (The middle bit is 0 because that middle bit isn't 1 in either 001 *or* 100.) When your app runs, Android interprets 101 as *"yes" to* `ifRoom`; *"yes" to* `withText`. (If the middle bit were 1, Android would interpret the 1 as *"yes" to always*.)

In addition to `ifRoom` and `withText`, you can use the following values:

✦ `always`: **Show the icon on the action bar whether there's room or not.**

  If there isn't enough room, the screen is very ugly.

✦ `never`: **Don't show the icon on the action bar, even if there's room.**

  Reveal this icon in the overflow list only. The skeletal app that Android Studio creates has a Settings item, and this item's `showAsAction` value is `never`.

✦ `collapseActionView`: **When there's no room for the entire action view, shrink the view so that it's represented by an icon.**

  This value applies to action views such as the search view in Figure 2-7.

Listing 2-1 is very nice, but the `menu_main.xml` file in Listing 2-1 isn't enough to put icons in your app's action bar. For that, you need to inflate the XML file. That's why Android Studio adds the following method to your app's main activity.

```
@Override
public boolean onCreateOptionsMenu(Menu menu) {
  getMenuInflater().inflate(R.menu.menu_main, menu);
  return true;
}
```

When you *inflate* an XML document, Android turns the XML code into something resembling Java code (a Java object, perhaps).

In the preceding code, you get a `MenuInflater` that's capable of inflating menus from XML resources. Then you inflate the XML code to get a real live Java object.

When you implement the `onCreateOptionsMenu` method, you must return either `true` or `false`. If you return `false`, Android doesn't display your menu! How rude!

Handling user actions

In the section entitled "Defining the XML file," you create a menu and display it on your app's action bar. Now you want to perform some type of action when it's clicked. To do this, add the method in Listing 2-2 to your app's main activity.

Listing 2-2:   Responding to a Menu Item Click

```
@Override
public boolean onOptionsItemSelected(MenuItem item) {

  switch (item.getItemId()) {

    case R.id.menu_insert:
      createReminder();
      return true;

    case R.id.make_noise:
      MediaPlayer mediaPlayer =
        MediaPlayer.create(this, R.raw.honk);
      mediaPlayer.start();
      return true;

    case R.id.settings:
      // TODO: Write code to display settings
      return true;

    case R.id.about:
      // TODO: Write code to display "about" info
      return true;

  }
  return super.onOptionsItemSelected(item);
}
```

In your `onOptionsItemSelected` method, you do the old switcheroo to find out exactly which item the user clicks. You match the clicked item's ID with the ID of the items in your menu's XML document. In this example, your menu has four items. One item creates a reminder, and the others are placeholders. (In this example app, the `make_noise`, `settings`, and `about` items simply show you how to deal with menus. Nothing that's the least bit useful happens when the user clicks those items.)

**Book 4
Chapter 2**

Menus, Lists, and
Notifications

To get Listing 2-2 to compile, you still have to define the `createReminder` method, but in the meantime, you can add a sound to your project. To add a sound, first create a `res/raw` folder and then copy an MP3 file into that `res/raw` folder. After renaming the file `honk.mp3`, you're ready to make some noise.

The method in Listing 2-2 returns `true`. This `true` value tells Android that you've finished handling the user's selection. If you return `false`, Android passes the selection event to whatever other code might be waiting for it.

Creating a reminder

The method in Listing 2-3 responds to a call in Listing 2-2. You add Listing 2-3's code to your project's main activity.

Listing 2-3:   Calling an Activity to Create a New Reminder

```
private static final int ACTIVITY_CREATE = 0;

private void createReminder() {
  Intent intent =
      new Intent(this, ReminderEditActivity.class);
  startActivityForResult(intent, ACTIVITY_CREATE);
}
```

The `createReminder` method starts an instance of `ReminderEdit Activity`. The `startActivityForResult` call allows you to get a result back from the `ReminderEditActivity`. In this app, you use the result to repopulate a list with the newly added reminder.

For straight talk about the `startActivityForResult` method, see Book III, Chapter 1.

Listing 2-4 contains an embarrassingly simple `ReminderEditActivity` class.

Listing 2-4:   Creating a Reminder

```
package com.allmycode.menus;

import android.app.Activity;
import android.content.Intent;
import android.os.Bundle;
import android.view.View;
import android.widget.EditText;

public class ReminderEditActivity extends Activity {
  EditText editText;

  @Override
  public void onCreate(Bundle b) {
```

```
        super.onCreate(b);
        setContentView(R.layout.reminder_edit);
        editText = (EditText) findViewById(R.id.editText1);
    }

    public void onPostButtonClick(View view) {
        Intent intent = new Intent();
        intent
            .putExtra("reminder_text", editText.getText().toString());
        setResult(Activity.RESULT_OK, intent);
        finish();
    }
}
```

When the user clicks a button, the `ReminderEditActivity` sets its result and finishes its run. The result comes from the activity's `EditText` widget.

To add an additional activity to an app, right-click (or on a Mac, Ctrl-click) the package's branch in the Project tool windows. In the resulting context menu, select New ⇨ Activity ⇨ Blank Activity. When you do this, Android Studio adds a Java class to your project and adds an `<activity>` element to your project's `AndroidManifest.xml` file. You can bypass these steps and create a Java class on your own. The new Java class might even extend Android's `Activity` class. But if you don't do New ⇨ Activity ⇨ Blank Activity, you must edit the XML document and type your own `<activity>` element. If you forget (and, believe me, I've forgotten), your new activity doesn't start, and your app crashes.

My no-nonsense layout for the activity in Listing 2-4 is shown in Listing 2-5. The activity's screen is shown in Figure 2-9.

Listing 2-5:   A Layout for the Activity in Listing 2-4

```xml
<?xml version="1.0" encoding="utf-8"?>
<LinearLayout xmlns:android=
        "http://schemas.android.com/apk/res/android"
    android:orientation="vertical"
    android:layout_width="match_parent"
    android:layout_height="match_parent"
    android:gravity="center_horizontal">

    <EditText android:layout_height="wrap_content"
            android:id="@+id/editText1"
            android:layout_width="match_parent"
            android:hint="Type a reminder here.">
        <requestFocus></requestFocus>
    </EditText>

    <Button android:layout_height="wrap_content"
            android:id="@+id/button1"
            android:layout_width="wrap_content"
            android:text="@string/post"
            android:onClick="onPostButtonClick"></Button>

</LinearLayout>
```

Book 4
Chapter 2

Menus, Lists, and
Notifications

Figure 2-9:
Adding a
reminder.

Putting the new reminder in a list

To do what is spelled out in this section's title — putting the new reminder
in a list — add the code in Listing 2-6 to your project's main activity.

Listing 2-6:   Using Another Activity's Result

```
ListView listView;
ArrayList<String> listItems = new ArrayList<String>();
ArrayAdapter<String> adapter;

@Override
public void onCreate(Bundle savedInstanceState) {
  super.onCreate(savedInstanceState);
  setContentView(R.layout.activity_main);

  listView = (ListView) findViewById(R.id.listView1);
  adapter =
    new ArrayAdapter<String>(this,
        R.layout.my_list_layout, listItems);
  listView.setAdapter(adapter);
}

@Override
protected void onActivityResult(int requestCode,
    int resultCode, Intent intent) {
  if (resultCode == RESULT_OK) {
    listItems.add(intent
        .getStringExtra("reminder_text"));

    adapter.notifyDataSetChanged();
  }
}
```

The code in Listing 2-6 refers to two new resources — namely, R.id.
listView1 and R.layout.my_list_layout. The first is a ListView
widget. You create it by adding a <ListView> element to your main
activity's layout file. The following element works just fine:

```
<ListView android:id="@+id/listView1"
          android:layout_height="wrap_content"
          android:layout_width="match_parent">
</ListView>
```

The `R.layout.my_list_layout` resource in Listing 2-6 is new and different. This layout describes an item in the list view. Android uses this layout many times (as many times as there are items in the list view). So, if you're creating this app as you read along, create a `res/layout/my_list_layout.xml` file, and put the code from Listing 2-7 into the file.

Listing 2-7:   The res/layout/my_list_layout.xml File

```
<?xml version="1.0" encoding="utf-8"?>
<TextView xmlns:android=
       "http://schemas.android.com/apk/res/android"
    android:id="@+id/identView"
    android:layout_width="wrap_content"
    android:layout_height="wrap_content">
</TextView>
```

According to the code in Listing 2-7, each list view item has its own text view.

With the Android SDK, you don't add an item directly to an onscreen list. Instead, you add items to a Java list (an `ArrayList`, for example). Then you tie the Java list to the onscreen list using an adapter. An *adapter* separates your code's business logic from the app's visible presentation. The adapter also smooths the look of changes in the onscreen list.

In Listing 2-6, I create a new adapter using three parts:

✦ The ever-present context — namely, `this`

✦ The list view's layout — namely, `R.layout.my_list_layout`

✦ An `ArrayList` of items

The `ArrayList` of items contains Java `String` objects, each of which is a reminder for me to do something (such as `Pay your taxes`, `Take out the trash`, or `Finish writing Chapter 2`). The new adapter contains enough information to connect the `ArrayList` with the visible `listView` object. Then, still in Listing 2-6, I marry the `ArrayList` to the `listView` by calling `listView.setAdapter(adapter)`.

When the code in Listing 2-4 finishes running, Android calls the `onActivityResult` method in Listing 2-6. The `onActivityResult` method grabs the newly created result and adds that result to the code's `ArrayList` (the `listItems` object). Finally, to make sure that the screen knows about this addition, the code calls `adapter.notifyDataSetChanged()`.

WARNING! Calling `setAdapter` (as in Listing 2-6) binds a Java list to an onscreen list. The call does *not* bind one variable name to another. So, for example, in Listing 2-6, if you follow the `listView.setAdapter(adapter)` call with a second `adapter = new ArrayAdapter` statement, the second assignment has no noticeable effect.

The code in Listing 2-6 overrides an onActivityResult method. For several nice paragraphs about Android's onActivityResult method, see Book III, Chapter 1.

After all is said and done (or after all is written and read; or after all is developed, published, and then downloaded), the user sees a screen like the one in Figure 2-10.

Figure 2-10: A list of items created by this section's example.

Figure 2-10 shows what happens when the user selects ADD REMINDER or presses the plus icon several times. (Refer to Figure 2-8.) The menu in this example has another item — a HONK item. When the user clicks the HONK item, the app makes a honking sound. I thought for a while about ways to demonstrate that action. My only idea was to ask Wiley to add a little speaker to this page, like one of those greeting cards that plays "Somewhere My Love" when you open it. But in the end, I didn't have the nerve to make that request. What do you think? It's a very practical idea, isn't it?

Doing more on the action bar

Once you've tasted a delicious Ice Cream Sandwich, the action bar shown earlier in Figure 2-1 is boring, boring, boring! You can add lots more pizazz to your action bar. In particular, you can put things that implement the CollapsibleActionView interface on your action bar. Android's SDK provides a readymade thing of this kind. It's called a *search view*.

Figure 2-7 shows you how a search view typically looks. When you add this thing to the action bar, your app's search functionality doesn't cover up other important items on your activity's screen. To add a search view to the action bar, put the following element in the res/menu directory's XML file:

```
<item android:id="@+id/action_search"
      android:title="@string/action_search"
      android:icon="@android:drawable/ic_menu_search"
      android:showAsAction="ifRoom|collapseActionView"
      android:actionViewClass=
                  "android.widget.SearchView" />
```

With only this `<item>` element, your action bar has a search view, but the search view doesn't do anything. To make the search view do something, add the following code to your main activity. Put it in the `onCreateOptions-Menu` method (after the statement that calls the `getMenuInflater` method).

```
SearchView searchView = (SearchView) menu.findItem
                (R.id.action_search).getActionView();
searchView.setQueryHint("Type your query here");
searchView.setOnQueryTextListener
                (new SearchView.OnQueryTextListener() {

  @Override
  public boolean onQueryTextSubmit(String query) {
    Toast.makeText(MainActivity.this,
                "I found what you're looking for!",
                Toast.LENGTH_LONG).show();
    return true;
  }

  @Override
  public boolean onQueryTextChange(String newText) {
    return true;
  }

});
```

When the user enters text in the search view, this code responds with a happy toast message. *I found what you're looking for*, says the toast message. It doesn't really search for anything, but at least it's cheerful! In general, responding to a search query involves things like content providers, which I cover in Book III, Chapter 5.

Creating a Context Menu

When the user long-presses a view, Android displays a context menu. The context menu displays options for the user. (Refer to Figures 2-3 and 2-4.)

Describing the menu

Listing 2-8 contains the XML document describing this section's context menu.

Listing 2-8:   The res/menu/list_menu_item_longpress.xml Document

```
<?xml version="1.0" encoding="utf-8"?>
<menu xmlns:android=
      "http://schemas.android.com/apk/res/android">
    <item android:id="@+id/menu_delete"
          android:title="@string/menu_delete" />
    <item android:id="@+id/make_noise2"
          android:title="Make a quacking sound" />
</menu>
```

Notice that I don't put any `icon` attributes in this menu. Context menus normally don't have icons.

I've seen web posts containing tricks for adding icons to context menus. I haven't tried any of these tricks, but I'm sure that some of them work.

Floating context menus

From Honeycomb onward, Android has two ways of handling context menus. The older way (not entirely obsolete) is called a *floating context menu*. Here's how it works:

You want Android to inflate Listing 2-8's menu when the user long-presses a list view item. To achieve this, you make two connections:

✦ Connect the `listView` object (declared in Listing 2-6) with context menus in general. You do this by adding one statement to Listing 2-6's `onCreate` method.

```
registerForContextMenu(listView);
```

✦ Connect context menus in general with the menu in Listing 2-8. Listing 2-9 shows you how.

Listing 2-9:   Handling a Long Press

```
@Override
public void onCreateContextMenu(ContextMenu menu,
    View view, ContextMenuInfo menuInfo) {
  super.onCreateContextMenu(menu, view, menuInfo);
  MenuInflater inflater = getMenuInflater();
  inflater.inflate
        (R.menu.list_menu_item_longpress, menu);
}
```

Listing 2-9 is very much like the `onCreateOptionsMenu` method in the "Defining the XML file" section. The method name is different, and the method in Listing 2-9 doesn't return a `boolean` value. Other than that, it's the same old stuff.

Handling item selections

To handle the selection of a context menu item, add the code from Listing 2-10 to your main activity.

Listing 2-10:   Responding to a Context Menu Click

```
@Override
public boolean onContextItemSelected(MenuItem item) {

  switch (item.getItemId()) {

  case R.id.menu_delete:
    deleteReminder(item);
    return true;

  case R.id.make_noise2:
    MediaPlayer mediaPlayer =
        MediaPlayer.create(this, R.raw.quack);
    mediaPlayer.start();
    return true;

  }
  return super.onContextItemSelected(item);
}

void deleteReminder(MenuItem item) {
  AdapterContextMenuInfo info =
      (AdapterContextMenuInfo) item.getMenuInfo();
  listItems.remove(info.position);
  adapter.notifyDataSetChanged();
}
```

Listing 2-10 looks a lot like Listings 2-2 and 2-3. The most significant difference is in the code to delete a list view item. Listing 2-10 doesn't start a secondary activity, so you don't need an intent, and you don't need an onActivityResult method like the one in Listing 2-6.

Grabbing information about the selected list view item is one step more complicated than you might expect. The reason for this is that you're dealing with two different items — the list view item that the user long-pressed and the context menu item that the user clicked.

In Listing 2-10, I call getMenuInfo to create an AdapterContextMenuInfo instance. Then I use the instance's public position field to tell me which list view item the user long-pressed. I remove the list view item corresponding to the info.position value.

Contextual action mode

In Honeycomb and later Android versions, you can use contextual action mode to deal with context menus. With contextual action mode, menu items don't float in a separate group on the screen. Instead, these items appear in a *contextual action bar* (CAB) — a list that hangs at the top of the screen like the activity's regular action bar. (Refer to Figure 2-4.)

Listing 2-11 shows you how to use contextual action mode.

Listing 2-11:   Using Contextual Action Mode

```
ListView listView;

ArrayList<String> listItems = new ArrayList<String>();
ArrayAdapter<String> adapter;

@Override
public void onCreate(Bundle savedInstanceState) {
  super.onCreate(savedInstanceState);
  setContentView(R.layout.main);

  listView = (ListView) findViewById(R.id.listView1);
  adapter = new ArrayAdapter<String>
                (this, R.layout.my_list_layout, listItems);
  listView.setAdapter(adapter);
  listView.setChoiceMode
                    (ListView.CHOICE_MODE_MULTIPLE_MODAL);

  listView.
   setMultiChoiceModeListener(new MultiChoiceModeListener() {

    int positionOfLongPressedItem;

    @Override
    public boolean onActionItemClicked
                        (ActionMode mode, MenuItem item) {
      switch (item.getItemId()) {

        case R.id.menu_delete:
          deleteReminder(positionOfLongPressedItem);
          mode.finish();

          break;
        case R.id.make_noise2:
          MediaPlayer mediaPlayer = MediaPlayer.create
                        (MyMenusActivity.this, R.raw.quack);
          mediaPlayer.start();
          break;
      }
     return true;
    }

    @Override
    public boolean onCreateActionMode
                        (ActionMode mode, Menu menu) {
      MenuInflater inflater = mode.getMenuInflater();
      inflater.inflate
                (R.menu.list_menu_item_longpress, menu);
      return true;
    }

    @Override
    public void onItemCheckedStateChanged
                    (ActionMode mode, int position,
                          long id, boolean checked)   {
      positionOfLongPressedItem = position;
    }
```

```
    @Override
    public void onDestroyActionMode(ActionMode mode) {
    }

    @Override
    public boolean onPrepareActionMode
                          (ActionMode mode, Menu menu) {
        return false;
    }
  });
}

void deleteReminder(int  positionOfLongPressedItem) {
  listItems.remove(positionOfLongPressedItem);
  adapter.notifyDataSetChanged();
}
```

Listing 2-11 begins the way Listing 2-6 begins — by declaring a list view
(a list of reminders, for example) and assigning an adapter for the list view.
But in Listing 2-11, you set the list view's choice mode to CHOICE_MODE_
MULTIPLE_MODAL and create a MultiChoiceModeListener.

✦ **When the user long-presses a list item, Android calls the listener's**
onItemCheckedStateChanged **and** onCreateActionMode **methods.**

The onActionItemClicked method records the position of the item
that the user long-pressed. For example, if the list view contains the
items shown earlier in Figure 2-10, and the user taps the *Finish writing
Chapter 2* item, the position number is 0. For the *Wash the dishes* item,
the position number is 1. And so on.

The onCreateActionMode method inflates the options menu (the
menu in Listing 2-8). This menu appears in the contextual action bar.
(Refer to Figure 2-4.)

✦ **When the user taps an item in the contextual action bar, Android calls
the listener's** onActionItemClicked **method.**

In Listing 2-11, the onActionItemClicked method responds differently
depending on which menu item was tapped. For the menu_delete item,
the method calls the deleteReminder method.

The deleteReminder method in Listing 2-11 is a bit simpler than the corresponding method in Listing 2-10. In Listing 2-10, the deleteReminder
method calls the menu item's getMenuInfo method to determine the
position of the item in the menu. But in Listing 2-11, that position number
is already stored in the positionOfLongPressedItem field. So the
deleteReminder method simply removes the item in that position.

In the deleteReminder method in Listing 2-11, the call to notify-
DataSetChanged is *not* optional. If you omit this call, the listItems
collection list loses an element, but the adapter doesn't respond to
the change. So the item doesn't disappear from the user's screen. In
Listing 2-11, after calling deleteReminder, I call mode.finish().

**Book 4
Chapter 2**

**Menus, Lists, and
Notifications**

The `finish` method removes the contextual action bar so that the user no longer sees Figure 2-4's DELETE REMINDER menu item. (To see DELETE REMINDER again, the user must long-press one of the remaining reminders.)

More Stuff about Lists

The previous sections describe list views, but there are tons more to lists than list views. This section covers Android's `ListActivity` class and shows more tricks you can do with lists.

Creating a list activity

On a typical phone screen, you might not have room to add a list view to an existing activity's layout. An alternative is to create a separate activity containing nothing but the list. This strategy is so commonly used that the makers of Android created a special class for it. A `ListActivity` instance is an activity whose sole purpose is to display a list.

And speaking of lists, Listing 2-12 lists a `ListActivity`'s code.

Listing 2-12:   An Activity That's Also a List

```
package com.allmycode.lists;

import java.util.ArrayList;

import android.app.ListActivity;
import android.content.Intent;
import android.os.Bundle;
import android.widget.ArrayAdapter;

public class MyListActivity extends ListActivity {

  public void onCreate(Bundle savedInstanceState) {
    super.onCreate(savedInstanceState);
    Intent intent = getIntent();
    String isChecked =
      intent.getData().getSchemeSpecificPart();

    ArrayList<Integer> listItems =
      new ArrayList<Integer>();
    for (int i = 0; i < 5; i++) {
      if (isChecked.charAt(i) == '1') {
        listItems.add(i);
      }
    }
```

```
setListAdapter(new ArrayAdapter<Integer>(this,
    R.layout.my_list_layout, listItems));
    }
}
```

The code in Listing 2-12 extends `android.app.ListActivity`, which is a subclass of `Activity`. So the listing's `MyListActivity` class is an Android activity. But notice that Listing 2-12 has no `setContentView` call. Instead, a `ListActivity` instance gets its layout from the call to `setListAdapter`. This `setListAdapter` call is strikingly similar to some code in Listing 2-6, and that's no accident. After all, a list is a list is a list (whatever that means).

Anyway, Listings 2-6 and 2-12 even use the same `R.layout.my_list_ layout` resource — the layout described in Listing 2-7. Like a `ListView` instance's layout, a `ListActivity` instance's layout describes only one list item.

I don't envision `MyListActivity` (the code in Listing 2-12) as a project's main activity. The main activity calls `startActivity` to get `MyListActivity` going. In the call to `startActivity`, the main activity passes an intent containing a URI of the following kind:

```
checked:01011
```

I made up this opaque URI format in order to pass five yes-or-no values from the main activity to the list activity. With the `01011` URI, the list activity's screen looks like the stuff in Figure 2-11.

Figure 2-11:
The result
of sending
checked:
01011 to this
section's list
activity.

**Book 4
Chapter 2**

**Menus, Lists, and
Notifications**

The sequence `01011` is my way of representing "no" 0, "yes" 1, "no" 2, "yes" 3, and "yes" 4. So the numbers 1, 3, and 4 appear as items in the list. The loop in Listing 2-12 picks the 0s and 1s out of the incoming intent's URI.

Here's one more thing to remember about this section's list activity. The activity's incoming intent has my made-up `checked` data scheme. So, in the project's `AndroidManifest.xml` document, I specify the `checked` scheme in the list activity's intent filter:

```
<activity android:name=".MyListActivity">
  <intent-filter>
    <action android:name="action_required_but_not_used" />
    <data android:scheme="checked" />
  </intent-filter>
</activity>
```

The intent filter must have an `<action>` element, but in this example, I use an explicit intent to start `MyListActivity`. So I never use the `<action>` element's name anywhere else in the project.

A client for the list activity

Listing 2-13 contains the code for a main activity. This main activity gives the user a way to fire up the app's list activity.

Listing 2-13:   Code to Trigger the List Activity

```
package com.allmycode.lists;

import android.app.Activity;
import android.content.Intent;
import android.net.Uri;
import android.os.Bundle;
import android.view.View;
import android.widget.CheckBox;

public class MainActivity extends Activity {
    CheckBox[] checkBoxes = new CheckBox[5];

    @Override
    public void onCreate(Bundle savedInstanceState) {
        super.onCreate(savedInstanceState);
        setContentView(R.layout.activity_main );
        checkBoxes[0] = (CheckBox) findViewById(R.id.a);
        checkBoxes[1] = (CheckBox) findViewById(R.id.b);
        checkBoxes[2] = (CheckBox) findViewById(R.id.c);
        checkBoxes[3] = (CheckBox) findViewById(R.id.d);
        checkBoxes[4] = (CheckBox) findViewById(R.id.e);
    }

    public void onShowListClick(View view) {
      Intent intent =
          new Intent(this, MyListActivity.class);

      StringBuffer isChecked = new StringBuffer("");
```

```
    for (CheckBox box : checkBoxes) {
      isChecked.append(box.isChecked() ? "1" : "0");
    }
    intent.setData(Uri.parse("checked:"
        + isChecked.toString()));

    startActivity(intent);
  }
}
```

Listing 2-13 maintains an array of `CheckBox` instances. A loop composes a string of 0s and 1s from the states of the five boxes. Then Listing 2-13 wraps these 0s and 1s in an intent's URI and passes the intent to the list activity.

Listing 2-14 describes the main activity's layout, and Figure 2-12 shows the layout as it appears on the user's screen.

Listing 2-14: The res/layout/activity_main.xml File

```xml
<?xml version="1.0" encoding="utf-8"?>
<LinearLayout xmlns:android=
      "http://schemas.android.com/apk/res/android"
    android:layout_width="match_parent"
    android:layout_height="match_parent"
    android:gravity="center_horizontal"
    android:orientation="vertical" >

    <TextView
        android:id="@+id/textView1"
        android:layout_width="wrap_content"
        android:layout_height="wrap_content"
        android:text="@string/main_activity" >
    </TextView>

    <CheckBox
        android:id="@+id/a"
        android:layout_width="wrap_content"
        android:layout_height="wrap_content"
        android:text="@string/box0" >
     </CheckBox>

    <CheckBox
        android:id="@+id/b"
        android:layout_width="wrap_content"
        android:layout_height="wrap_content"
        android:text="@string/box1" >
    </CheckBox>

    <CheckBox
        android:id="@+id/c"
        android:layout_width="wrap_content"
        android:layout_height="wrap_content"
        android:text="@string/box2" >
    </CheckBox>
```

(continued)

Listing 2-14 *(continued)*

```
<CheckBox
   android:id="@+id/d"
   android:layout_width="wrap_content"
   android:layout_height="wrap_content"
   android:text="@string/box3" >
</CheckBox>

<CheckBox
   android:id="@+id/e"
   android:layout_width="wrap_content"
   android:layout_height="wrap_content"
   android:text="@string/box4" >
</CheckBox>

<Button
   android:id="@+id/button1"
   android:layout_width="wrap_content"
   android:layout_height="wrap_content"
   android:onClick="onShowListClick"
   android:text="@string/show_list" >
</Button>

</LinearLayout>
```

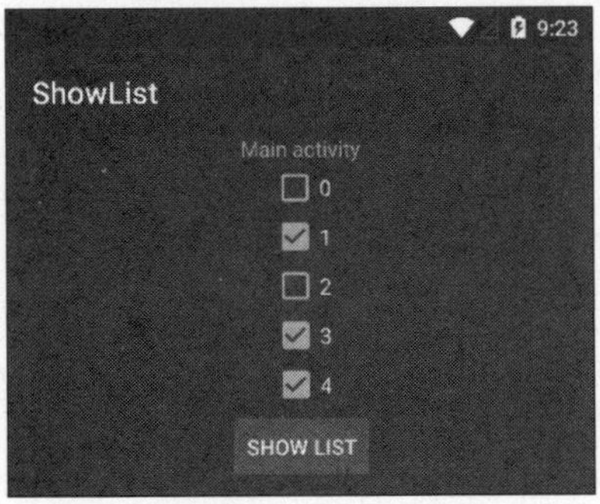

Figure 2-12: The user selects values to send to the list activity.

Displaying two (or more) values in a list item

When you display a list on the user's screen, you often display more than one value per entry. Maybe each entry has a title and a subtitle, or a keyword and an icon. Anyway, the preceding section's list has only one value in each list entry. Displaying more than one value is both easy and difficult. (Huh?)

It's easy because switching from single-value entries to multi-value entries doesn't involve any large strategy changes in your code. You still have a

Java list, an onscreen list, and an adapter. Whatever tricks you use to pass data to a list activity work equally well with both single- and multi-value entries.

Displaying more than one value is difficult because you have to wield a complicated data structure in which the Java list meshes with the onscreen list. Figure 2-13 describes the situation.

A Java *map* is a list of key/value pairs. To create an adapter, you create a Java list of maps. Each map in the Java list represents one entry in the onscreen list.

So now the trick is to tell Android how one map turns into one onscreen entry. To do this, you create two arrays — an array containing the map key names and an array containing an entry's views. Android associates the key names with the views as though they're partners in a contra dance. Listing 2-15 contains the code.

The Java data structure
Adapter:

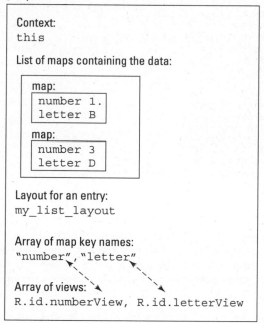

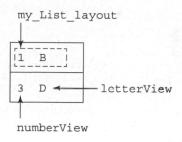

On the screen

my_List_layout

letterView

numberView

Figure 2-13:
An adapter
for the
list in this
section's
code.

**Book 4
Chapter 2**

Menus, Lists, and
Notifications

Listing 2-15: Putting Two Values in Each List Entry

```
package com.allmycode.lists;

import java.util.ArrayList;
import java.util.HashMap;

import android.app.ListActivity;
import android.content.Intent;
import android.os.Bundle;
import android.widget.SimpleAdapter;

public class MyListActivity extends ListActivity {

  public void onCreate(Bundle savedInstanceState) {
    super.onCreate(savedInstanceState);
    Intent intent = getIntent();
    String isChecked =
        intent.getData().getSchemeSpecificPart();

    ArrayList<HashMap<String, String>> data =
     new ArrayList<HashMap<String, String>>();

    for (int i = 0; i < 5; i++) {
      if (isChecked.charAt(i) == '1') {
        HashMap<String, String> map =
            new HashMap<String, String>();
        map.put("number", Integer.toString(i));
        map.put("letter",
            (new Character((char) (i + 65))).toString());

        data.add(map);
      }
    }

    String[] columnNames = { "number", "letter" };
    int[] textViews = new int[2];
    textViews[0] = R.id.numberView;
    textViews[1] = R.id.letterView;

    setListAdapter(new SimpleAdapter(this, data,
        R.layout.my_list_layout, columnNames, textViews));
  }

}
```

This section's example uses the main activity from Listing 2-13. Other than the enhanced list activity in Listing 2-15, the only other change from single-valued to double-valued entries is the use of a new layout. The new layout for a list entry (see Listing 2-16) has two text views instead of one.

Listing 2-16:   A res/layout/my_list_layout.xml Document with Two Text Views

```xml
<?xml version="1.0" encoding="utf-8"?>
<LinearLayout xmlns:android=
      "http://schemas.android.com/apk/res/android"
    android:layout_width="match_parent"
    android:layout_height="match_parent"
    android:orientation="horizontal">

    <TextView android:id="@+id/numberView"
        android:layout_width="wrap_content"
        android:layout_height="wrap_content"></TextView>

    <TextView android:id="@+id/letterView"
        android:layout_width="wrap_content"
        android:layout_height="wrap_content"
        android:padding="20dp"></TextView>

</LinearLayout>
```

Listing 2-15 puts into code what Figure 2-13 illustrates with a drawing. The most noteworthy feature in Listing 2-15 is the use of a `SimpleAdapter`. Unlike the `ArrayAdapter` of Listing 2-12, a `SimpleAdapter` can handle multi-value list entries.

To connect an onscreen list with the rows in a database table, use the `android.widget.SimpleCursorAdapter`.

Figure 2-14 shows the result of sending the numbers 1, 3, and 4 to this section's list activity. To keep the example tidy, I don't do anything fancy to associate a second value with each number. Instead, I use `new Character((char) (i + 65))).toString()`. This code converts from `int` values 0, 1, 2, 3, and 4 to `char` values 'A', 'B', 'C', 'D', and 'E'.

Figure 2-14:
A list with two values in each entry.

**Book 4
Chapter 2**

Menus, Lists, and Notifications

Creating a Pop-Up Menu

A pop-up menu is a list of menu items that appears when the user taps a widget (a text view, an image, or whatever) on the activity's screen. The pop-up menu appears near the widget that the user taps. Like many of Android's newer features, pop-up menus popped up in API 11 (Honeycomb).

To associate a pop-up menu with a widget, add an `android:onClick` attribute to the widget's element in the layout file.

```
<ImageButton
    android:layout_width="wrap_content"
    android:layout_height="wrap_content"
    android:src="@drawable/ic_launcher"
    android:onClick="showPopup" />
```

The `android:onClick` attribute's value is the name of a method to be called when the user clicks the widget. Listing 2-17 has just such a method.

Listing 2-17:   Making a Pop-Up Menu Pop Up

```
package com.allmycode.popup;

import android.app.Activity;
import android.os.Bundle;
import android.view.MenuItem;
import android.view.View;
import android.widget.PopupMenu;
import android.widget.Toast;


public class MainActivity extends Activity {

  @Override
  protected void onCreate(Bundle savedInstanceState) {
    super.onCreate(savedInstanceState);
    setContentView(R.layout.activity_main);
  }

  public void showPopup(View v) {
    PopupMenu popup = new PopupMenu(this, v);

    popup.setOnMenuItemClickListener
        (new PopupMenu.OnMenuItemClickListener() {

      @Override
      public boolean onMenuItemClick(MenuItem item) {
        int id = item.getItemId();

        if (id == R.id.action_1) {
          Toast.makeText(MainActivity.this, "Pop!",
                         Toast.LENGTH_LONG).show();
        } else if (id == R.id.action_2) {
          Toast.makeText(MainActivity.this, "Snap!",
                         Toast.LENGTH_LONG).show();
        }
```

```
        return true;
      }
  });

  //Before API Level 14, use this:
  //MenuInflater inflater = popup.getMenuInflater();
  //inflater.inflate(R.menu.menu_popup, popup.getMenu());
  popup.inflate(R.menu.menu_popup);
  popup.show();
}

}
```

In Listing 2-17, the `showPopup` method creates a pop-up menu and then creates a listener for the pop-up menu. The listener's `onMenuItemClick` method handles clicks of the pop-up menu's items.

To complete this example, you need a layout file for the pop-up menu. Here's a file for the menu shown earlier in Figure 2-5.

```
<menu xmlns:android=
      "http://schemas.android.com/apk/res/android"
      xmlns:tools="http://schemas.android.com/tools"
      tools:context=".MainActivity">

    <item android:id="@+id/action_1"
          android:title="@string/pick_me"/>
    <item android:id="@+id/action_2"
          android:title="@string/no_pick_me"/>
</menu>
```

In the pop-up, each menu item has an `id`. So, in Listing 2-17, you use the `id` to decide which item has been clicked.

Notifying the User

One of Android's cool features is its status bar. The status bar appears at the top of the screen. The user drags the bar downward to see all the current notifications. (See Figure 2-15.)

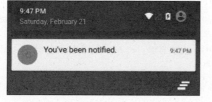

Figure 2-15: Android notifies the user.

In this section, you add notifications to the device's status bar.

Book 4
Chapter 2

Menus, Lists, and
Notifications

Simple notification

If you want to notify the user and you don't need any bells or whistles along with the notification, Listing 2-18 is for you.

Listing 2-18:   Notification, and Nothing Else

```
package com.allyourcode.simplenotificaton;

import android.app.Activity;
import android.app.Notification;
import android.app.NotificationManager;
import android.content.Context;
import android.os.Bundle;
import android.view.View;

public class MainActivity extends Activity {

  @Override
  protected void onCreate(Bundle savedInstanceState) {
    super.onCreate(savedInstanceState);
    setContentView(R.layout.activity_main);
  }

  public void onButtonClick(View view) {
    Notification.Builder builder =
        new Notification.Builder(this);
    builder.setSmallIcon
        (android.R.drawable.ic_menu_info_details);
    builder.setContentTitle("You've been notified.");

    Notification notification = builder.build();

    NotificationManager notificationMgr =
        (NotificationManager)
        getSystemService(Context.NOTIFICATION_SERVICE);

    notificationMgr.notify(1, notification);
  }

}
```

Listing 2-18 is a no-frills activity. When the user clicks a button, Android creates the notification shown in Figure 2-15. To do this, Listing 2-18 uses three classes — `Notification.Builder`, `Notification`, and `NotificationManager`. Here's the scoop on these three classes:

✦ **As the name suggests, you use the** `Notification.Builder` **class to build a notification object.**

In Listing 2-18, you call the builder's `setSmallIcon` and `setContentTitle` methods.

- The `setSmallIcon` method specifies an icon to appear on the notification.

- The `setContentTitle` method specifies the large text that appears on the notification. (Compare the method call in Listing 2-18 with the text in Figure 2-15.)

The `Notification.Builder` class is an inner class of the `android.app.Notification` class. For info about Java's inner classes, refer to Chapter 4 in Book II.

✦ **You call the** `build` **method of the** `Notification.Builder` **class to create an actual** `Notification` **object.**

The `builder.build()` method that's called in Listing 2-18 isn't available until API Level 16. If your project's minimum SDK is lower than 16, call `builder.getNotification()` instead.

✦ **A** `NotificationManager` **object handles notifications for the user's device.**

In particular, the `notify` method belonging to a `Notification Manager` posts a notification on the user's device. In Listing 2-18, you call `notify` to post the notification that you create a few statements earlier.

The notify method has two parameters.

- The `notify` method's first parameter is an `int` value. This `int` value (a value of your choosing) identifies the notification for future reference. For example, the call

  ```
  notificationMgr.cancel(1)
  ```

  would get rid of the notification that I create in Listing 2-18 because, in Listing 2-18, I call `notify` with parameter value 1.

- The method's second parameter is the notification that's being posted.

Notifications normally don't jump out on the device's screen. To see a notification, the user has to swipe down from the top of the screen (and some users hardly ever do this). But starting with Android Lollipop, you can grab the user's attention with a *heads-up notification*. A heads-up notification appears on the screen as soon as your code calls `notify`.

To create a heads-up notification in this section's example, add

```
builder.setPriority(Notification.PRIORITY_MAX);
builder.setDefaults(Notification.DEFAULT_VIBRATE);
```

to the code in Listing 2-18.

Book 4
Chapter 2

Menus, Lists, and
Notifications

To turn an ordinary notification into a heads-up notification, you call two methods — `setPriority` and `setDefaults`. The particular `setPriority` call that you add to Listing 2-18 says "This builder creates notifications with the highest possible priority." The `setDefaults` call that you add says "Make the device vibrate." (Someone at Google thinks that you shouldn't have a heads-up notification without making the device vibrate. So, after wondering why the call to `setPriority` asking for the highest possible priority isn't sufficient, and after checking several online forums for an answer, I added this `setDefaults` call specifying the vibrating business.)

A not-so-simple notification

In the section entitled "Creating a list activity," you create a list from a bunch of check boxes. The items in the list are passive. If the user clicks an item in the list, nothing happens. Later, in the "Simple notification" section, you create a notification. But again, the notification doesn't do anything. If the user taps the notification, nothing happens. (Well, the user smudges the screen at bit, but that doesn't count.)

This section adds code to the activity in Listing 2-12. With the new code, tapping a list item creates a notification, and tapping that notification starts a new activity. (See Figures 2-16 and 2-17.)

Figure 2-16: Tapping a notification (on the emulator using a mouse).

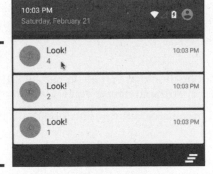

Figure 2-17: After tapping a notification, you see another activity.

The replacement for Listing 2-12 is in Listing 2-19.

Listing 2-19: Every Click Counts!

```
package com.allmycode.lists;

import android.app.ListActivity;
import android.app.Notification;
import android.app.NotificationManager;
import android.app.PendingIntent;
import android.content.Context;
import android.content.Intent;
import android.net.Uri;
import android.os.Bundle;
import android.view.View;
import android.widget.ArrayAdapter;
import android.widget.ListView;

import java.util.ArrayList;

public class MyListActivity extends ListActivity {
  int notificationNumber = 0;
  NotificationManager notificationMgr;

  /* Code copied from Listing 2-14... */

  public void onCreate(Bundle savedInstanceState) {
    super.onCreate(savedInstanceState);
    Intent intent = getIntent();
    String isChecked =
        intent.getData().getSchemeSpecificPart();

    ArrayList<Integer> listItems =
        new ArrayList<Integer>();
    for (int i = 0; i < 5; i++) {
      if (isChecked.charAt(i) == '1') {
        listItems.add(i);
      }
    }

    setListAdapter(new ArrayAdapter<Integer>(this,
        R.layout.my_list_layout, listItems));
  }

  /* Code to respond to a list item click... */

  @Override
  public void onListItemClick(ListView listView,
      View view, int position, long id) {

    makeNewNotification(listView, position);
  }

  /* Code to create a status bar notification... */

  private void makeNewNotification
                  (ListView listView, int position) {
```

(continued)

Listing 2-19 *(continued)*

```
String numberValue =
    listView.getItemAtPosition(position).toString();

Notification.Builder builder =
    new Notification.Builder(this);
builder.setSmallIcon
    (android.R.drawable.ic_menu_info_details);
builder.setContentTitle("Look!");
builder.setContentText(numberValue);
builder.setAutoCancel(true);

Intent intent =
    new Intent(this, YetAnotherActivity.class);
intent.setData(Uri.parse("number:" + numberValue));
intent.addFlags(Intent.FLAG_ACTIVITY_NEW_TASK);
PendingIntent pendingIntent =
    PendingIntent.getActivity(this, 0, intent, 0);

builder.setContentIntent(pendingIntent);

Notification notification = builder.build();

notificationMgr = (NotificationManager)

    getSystemService(Context.NOTIFICATION_SERVICE);
notificationMgr.notify
                (notificationNumber++, notification);
}

/* Goodbye, cruel world... */

@Override
public void onDestroy() {
  super.onDestroy();
  for (int i = 0; i <= notificationNumber; i++) {
    notificationMgr.cancel(i);
  }
}
}
```

To respond to a list item click, simply add an `onListItemClick` method to your code. This section's example uses two of the method's four parameters — namely, the list view that the user clicked and the position number of the clicked entry. In Listing 2-19, I pass those parameters' values to my homegrown `makeNewNotification` method.

Here's what happens inside the `makeNewNotification` method:

✦ Using the list view's `getItemAtPostion` method, I find the number value of the list item that the user clicked. I store this value for safekeeping in my `numberValue` string.

✦ I create a `NotificationBuilder` instance, and set some of the instance's properties.

- The `setSmallIcon` method's `int` parameter refers to one of Android's standard icons.

- The title is the large text that appears on the notification.

  In Listing 2-19, the title is *Look!* (Refer to Figure 2-16.)

- The text is whatever smaller text appears on the notification.

  In Listing 2-19, this text is the position number of the list item that the user clicked. Again, refer to Figure 2-16.

- The call to `setAutoCancel` tells Android to remove the notification after the user clicks the notification.

✦ Continuing on the tour of Listing 2-19, the next step in displaying a notification is to create an intent.

- The intent's purpose is to invoke `YetAnotherActivity`.

- The intent has a URI, such as `number:3`, indicating that the user clicked either the topmost or bottommost notification in Figure 2-15.

The intent's purpose is to invoke `YetAnotherActivity`, but this invocation doesn't happen right away. In fact, the code in Listing 2-19 does *not* start an instance of `YetAnotherActivity`. Instead, the code attaches this intent to the notification that's being built. The intent won't be used for starting `YetAnotherActivity` until the user views (and then taps) the notification.

✦ The code in Listing 2-19 turns the `YetAnotherActivity` intent into a pending intent. A *pending intent* is an intent that one component asks another component to execute.

In this example, the code in Listing 2-19 asks the notification to execute the intent. (To be more precise, with the call to `setContentIntent`, Listing 2-19 tells the notification "Wait until the user taps you. Then execute this intent.")

✦ As in Listing 2-18, the code builds a notification and feeds the notification to a `notify` method. Calling the `notify` method places the notification in the device's status bar.

In this example, the user can click more than one list item. So the app might call `makeNewNotification` more than once. In the call to `notify`, the `int` parameter gets 1 added to it each time. So each notification has its own identification number.

**Book 4
Chapter 2**

**Menus, Lists, and
Notifications**

Notifications' identification numbers don't cross application boundaries. If two different applications create notifications with identification number 1, there's no conflict. But within an application, identification numbers shouldn't conflict. If your app calls `notificationMgr.notify` twice with the same `int` parameter value, Android replaces the first notification with the second. Only one of the two notifications appears in the status bar.

The last method in Listing 2-19 is the `onDestroy` method. This `onDestroy` method deletes any notifications that the code created. By the time Android calls the `onDestroy` method in Listing 2-19, some of the original notifications may have already been canceled. (The call to `setAutoCancel` does some of that housekeeping.) Fortunately, nothing bad happens when you try to cancel a nonexistent notification.

In case you're wondering, Listing 2-20 contains my `YetAnotherActivity` code. In the `YetAnotherActivity` class, I grab the notification's identification number and display it on the screen.

Listing 2-20:   Using the Result of the Pending Intent

```
package com.allmycode.lists;

import android.app.Activity;
import android.content.Intent;
import android.os.Bundle;
import android.widget.TextView;

public class YetAnotherActivity extends Activity {
  TextView textView;

  @Override
  public void onCreate(Bundle b) {
    super.onCreate(b);
    setContentView(R.layout.yet_another_layout);
    textView = (TextView) findViewById(R.id.textView1);

    Intent intent = getIntent();

    String numberValue =
        intent.getData().getSchemeSpecificPart();

    textView.setText("You selected " + numberValue + ".");
  }
}
```

Chapter 3: An Android Potpourri

In This Chapter

✓ Programming Android to make phone calls

✓ Working with text messages and device sensors

✓ Responding to multi-touch events

✓ Drawing things

✓ Distracting the user with a progress bar

✓ Putting Java threads to good use

A *potpourri* is an assortment — a little of this and a little of that. It's a mixture of pleasant things related in one way or another, but not dependent upon one another. It's a medley of songs or a bunch of nice-smelling dried plants. It's a salmagundi with meats, eggs, vegetables, fruits, and nuts. It's a pastiche such as Queen's "Bohemian Rhapsody." It's a plate of gefilte fish with a mix of carp, pike, perch, salmon, mullet, whitefish, and other things whose odors form an orange haze that spreads throughout the house. But in this book, a potpourri is a collection of useful programming goodies.

Making Phone Calls

Before smartphones came along, the most techno-savvy people around carried personal digital assistants (PDAs). A PDA (a PalmPilot or an iPAQ with Windows CE) did many of the things that today's smartphones do. But the early PDAs didn't make phone calls. So they didn't catch on with the general public.

An explosion in mobile device usage came when companies merged computing with telephony. In retrospect, it's not surprising. After all, communication is a "killer app." People need to share. People talk to friends, arrange meetings, send photos, and post recommendations. Exchanging ideas is one of humanity's greatest strengths.

This section puts the *phone* in *smartphone*.

Two ways to initiate a call

Making a phone call requires two steps:

1. *Dial* a phone number.

2. Press the *Call* button.

Accordingly, Android has two intent actions — one for dialing and another for calling. This section's code, shown in Listing 3-1 illustrates both situations.

Listing 3-1:   Dialing and Calling

```
package com.allmycode.samples;

import android.app.Activity;
import android.app.AlertDialog;
import android.content.Context;
import android.content.DialogInterface;
import android.content.Intent;
import android.net.Uri;
import android.os.Bundle;
import android.telephony.TelephonyManager;
import android.view.View;

public class MyActivity extends Activity {

  @Override
  public void onCreate(Bundle savedInstanceState) {
    super.onCreate(savedInstanceState);
    setContentView(R.layout.main);
  }

  public void onButtonClick(View view) {
    boolean isOk = true;
    Intent intent = new Intent();

    if (!deviceIsAPhone()) {
     displayAlert();
     isOk = false;
    }

    if (isOk) {
      switch (view.getId()) {
      case R.id.dialButton:
        intent.setAction(Intent.ACTION_DIAL);
        break;
      case R.id.callButton:
        intent.setAction(Intent.ACTION_CALL);
        break;
      default:
        isOk = false;
      }
      intent.setData(Uri.parse("tel:234-555-6789"));
    }
```

```
    if (isOk) {
      startActivity(intent);
    }
  }

  boolean deviceIsAPhone() {
    TelephonyManager manager = (TelephonyManager)
        getSystemService(Context.TELEPHONY_SERVICE);
    return manager.getPhoneType() !=
                  TelephonyManager.PHONE_TYPE_NONE;
  }

  void displayAlert() {
    AlertDialog.Builder alertBuilder =
        new AlertDialog.Builder(this);
    alertBuilder
      .setTitle("Not a telephone!")
      .setMessage("This device can't phone make calls!")
      .setPositiveButton("OK", new MyDialogListener())
      .show();
  }

  class MyDialogListener implements
      DialogInterface.OnClickListener {

    public void onClick(DialogInterface dialog,
                        int whichButton) {
    }

  }
}
```

Before testing the code in Listing 3-1, I lay out the main activity's screen, as shown in Figure 3-1.

Figure 3-1:
The main layout for the code in Listing 3-1.

When I run the code and press the activity's Dial button, I see my phone's familiar dialer. The dialer has my fake phone number 234-555-6789 at the top of the screen, just waiting for me to press the little phone icon. (See Figure 3-2.)

Figure 3-2:
The result of
clicking the
Dial button.

(If your ego needs a lift, dialing a phone number with the fake 555 exchange makes you feel like an actor in a Hollywood movie.)

Pressing the activity's Call button is another story. Pressing the Call button in Figure 3-1 takes me immediately to the calling screen in Figure 3-3.

Figure 3-3:
The result of
clicking the
Call button.

REMEMBER

To start an activity with `Intent.ACTION_CALL`, your app must have the following element in its `AndroidManifest.xml file`:

```
<uses-permission
        android:name="android.permission.CALL_PHONE" />
```

The basic strategy in Listing 3-1 isn't complicated. You create an intent with action `Intent.ACTION_DIAL` (or `Intent.ACTION_CALL`). You add a `tel` URI to the intent and then call `startActivity`.

In Listing 3-1, you can modify the `tel` URI so that the URI has no scheme-specific part:

```
intent.setData(Uri.parse("tel:"));
```

CROSS-REFERENCE

To read more than you ever wanted to know about URIs and scheme-specific parts, see Book III, Chapter 2.

```
intent.setData(Uri.parse("tel:"));
```

Modifying the `tel` URI in this fashion changes the way `Intent.ACTION_DIAL` works. Now the phone launches the dial screen with no phone number. (See Figure 3-4.) The user enters a phone number and then presses the Call button.

Figure 3-4:
A blank
dialer.

If you combine `"tel:"` with `Intent.ACTION_CALL`, Android tries to place a call with no phone number. (It's a call to "nowhere" — the stuff science-fiction plots are made of.) On some phones, you get no response. On other phones, you see a dialog box warning you that something's very wrong. (See Figure 3-5.)

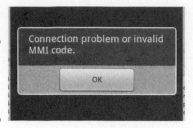

Figure 3-5:
Trying to
dial no one
in particular.

Oops! No phone

Some Android devices aren't phones. Running the preceding section's example on a 10-inch tablet is like trying to call Paris using a can opener. You might expect users to know this, but life is complicated, and users have other things to think about. (Doesn't everyone?)

It's best to anticipate the worst and to remind users when they press the wrong buttons. So, in Listing 3-1, I add code to check for "phone-ness." I display an alert if the user tries to make a call from an Android-based dishwasher.

What kind of phone is this?

In Listing 3-1, the `deviceIsAPhone` method gets a `TelephonyManager`. Then the method uses the `TelephonyManager` to check the device's phone type.

The phone type options are `PHONE_TYPE_GSM`, `PHONE_TYPE_CDMA`, `PHONE_TYPE_SIP`, and `PHONE_TYPE_NONE`.

✦ **Global System for Mobile Communications (GSM):** It's used by most of the world's carriers, including AT&T and T-Mobile in the United States.

✦ **Code Division Multiple Access (CDMA):** It's used in the United States by the carriers Sprint and Verizon.

✦ **Session Initiation Protocol (SIP):** It's a telephone standard based on Internet packets. SIP isn't commonly used on commercial mobile phones.

✦ **The value `PHONE_TYPE_NONE`** applies to devices with no telephony capabilities. It's the telephone standard used by tablet devices, rocks, table lamps, ham sandwiches, and other things that neither place nor receive phone calls.

I need your attention

In Listing 3-1, the `displayAlert` method creates the dialog box shown in Figure 3-6.

Figure 3-6:
An alert
dialog box.

An alert dialog box can have one, two, or three buttons. If you use the `AlertDialog.Builder` class to construct an alert dialog box, the buttons' names are `positive`, `negative`, and `neutral`. (So, for example, to create a NO button, you call `alertBuilder.setNegativeButton`.)

If you skip the `AlertDialog.Builder` class and instead call the `AlertDialog` class's methods, the corresponding method calls are `setButton`, `setButton2`, and `setButton3`.

The `displayAlert` method in Listing 3-1 illustrates an interesting feature of Android's builder classes. A builder has setter methods, and each setter method returns a newly modified builder. For example, you start with a vanilla `new AlertDialog.Builder(this)`. You assign the new builder to your `alertBuilder` variable. Then you call `alertBuilder.setTitle`, which returns a builder whose title is `"Not a telephone!"` To this enhanced builder, you apply `setMessage`, returning a builder with the title `"Not a telephone!"` and the message `"This device can't make phone calls!"`

The chain continues until you feed a builder to the `show` method. The `show` method displays the dialog box created by the builder.

An example in Chapter 2 of this minibook uses the `Notification.Builder` class. In that example, I don't use the result returned by each of the builder's setter methods. The choice to use (or not use) a builder's return results is simply a matter of taste.

In the preceding Listing 3-1, I check for the presence of telephony hardware using Android's `TelephonyManager`. In the first draft of this section's code, I relied on the `PackageManager` class as follows:

```
PackageManager manager = getPackageManager();
ComponentName name = intent.resolveActivity(manager);
return name != null;
```

As strategies go, this first draft wasn't a bad one. An intent's `resolve-Activity` method tells you which activity, if any, has an intent filter matching the intent. But the plan stumbled when I learned that my device's Contacts app matches the phone intents. When I ran the code on a tablet device, I expected to see the `"Not a telephone!"` dialog box. Instead, the device offered to add the new phone number to my Contacts list. Okay. No harm done.

On being a dialer

In Listing 3-1, you call `startActivity` to invoke the default Android dialer. You can also *become* a dialer by adding stuff to your activity's intent filter. (See Listing 3-2.) A quick search on Google's Play Store shows that many developers create alternatives to the standard system dialer. I see dialers integrated with enhanced contacts lists, dialers customized for particular businesses, old-style rotary dialers, dialers designed for sliding your fingers across the keys, dialers that play music, and many more.

Listing 3-2:   Responding to a Dial Intent

```
<activity android:name=".DialerActivity">
  <intent-filter>
    <action android:name="android.intent.action.DIAL" />
    <category
      android:name="android.intent.category.DEFAULT" />
    <data android:scheme="tel" />
  </intent-filter>
</activity>
```

The value of the constant `Intent.ACTION_DIAL` (used in Listing 3-1) is the string `"android.intent.action.DIAL"`.

In Java code, you can use either the constant `Intent.ACTION_DIAL` or the string `"android.intent.action.DIAL"`. But in the `AndroidManifest.xml` document, you must use the string.

Listing 3-2 also contains a `<data>` element, and without this `<data>` element, the code is worthless. Any app that invokes a dialer sends dialing information (empty or not) as part of the intent. The dialing information is a URI with the `tel` scheme. If an intent's data has a scheme, a matching intent filter must have the same scheme.

To read all about the matching of intents and intent filters, see Book III, Chapter 2.

Keep an eye on the phone

The `android.telephony` package has a useful `PhoneStateListener` class. With this class, you can "listen in" on a phone's state transitions. Here's a code snippet:

```
PhoneStateListener listener = new PhoneStateListener() {
  private static final String CLASSNAME =
      "PhoneStateListener";

  @Override
  public void onCallStateChanged(int state,
      String incomingNumber) {
    String stateString = "N/A";
    switch (state) {
    case TelephonyManager.CALL_STATE_IDLE:
      stateString = "Idle";
      break;
    case TelephonyManager.CALL_STATE_OFFHOOK:
      stateString = "Off Hook";
      break;
    case TelephonyManager.CALL_STATE_RINGING:
      stateString = "Ringing";
      break;
    }
    Log.i(CLASSNAME, stateString);
  }
};

TelephonyManager manager =
  (TelephonyManager) getSystemService(TELEPHONY_SERVICE);
manager.listen(listener, PhoneStateListener.LISTEN_CALL_STATE);
```

Android calls the listener's `onCallStateChanged` method when an interesting event occurs.

To make this code snippet work, you must add `<uses-permission android:name="android.permission.READ_PHONE_STATE" />` to your project's `AndroidManifest.xml` file.

The listener's other useful methods include `onCellLocationChanged`, `onDataActivity`, `onDataConnectionStateChanged`, and `onSignal-StrengthsChanged`. To use any of these methods, you must add the following element to your `AndroidManifest.xml` document:

```
<uses-permission
android:name="android.permission.READ_PHONE_STATE">
</uses-permission>
```

How to call a nonexistent phone

Sometimes, you want to test what happens when the user's device receives a phone call. When you test with a real device, you place a call to the device. But how to place a call to an emulator? If you're using Android's standard emulator, do the following:

1. **Launch the emulator.**

2. **In Android Studio's main menu, choose Tools ⇨ Android ⇨ Android Device Monitor.**

   The Android Device Monitor (a separate program) starts running.

3. **Look for the Devices list on the left side of the Android Device Monitor.**

   The Devices list shows the emulators and physical devices currently running, along with the processes that are running on these devices. If the Android Device Monitor looks nothing like what you see in the figure in this sidebar, go

to the Monitor's main menu and choose Window ⇨ Open Perspective ⇨ DDMS (default).

4. **In the Devices list, select the device that will receive the incoming call.**

   You can't skip this step (even if only one device is running).

5. **In the main body of the Android Device Monitor window, select the Emulator Control tab.**

   You see a bunch of options, including an Incoming Number field.

6. **In this field, type a telephone number.**

   Again, see the sidebar figure.

7. **In the Emulator Control tab, press Call.**

   To see the incoming call, switch to the emulator window on your development computer.

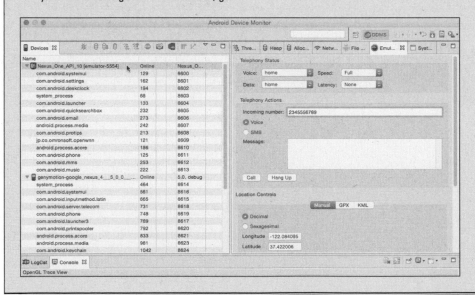

Sending a Text Message

Where I come from, people send "text messages" to one another. Apparently, the rest of the world calls this SMS (*S*hort *M*essaging *S*ervice). Whatever you call it, the business of sending brief, phone-to-phone messages is an important feature of today's communications.

Listing 3-3 shows you how an Android program sends a text message.

Listing 3-3:   Sending Text

```
SmsManager smsMgm = SmsManager.getDefault();

smsMgm.sendTextMessage("2345556789", null,
    "Hello world", null, null);
```

The sendTextMessage method has five parameters:

+ **The first parameter, a Java string, is the destination's phone number.**

+ **The second parameter, a Java string, is a *service center* address (see the nearby sidebar).**

   The value null in Listing 3-3 says, "I don't care how the message gets to its destination. Just send it!"

+ **The third parameter, also a Java string, is the message content.**

+ **The fourth and fifth parameters are pending intents.**

   Android uses both intents to send broadcasts. The fourth parameter's broadcast notifies the system when the message is sent. The fifth parameter's broadcast notifies the system when the message is received.

For an introduction to pending intents, see Chapter 2 in this minibook.

To run the code in Listing 3-3, your app must have android.permission. SEND_SMS.

What's an SMS service center?

When you send a text message, the message goes first to a service center. The service center stores the message before forwarding it to the desired recipient.

This *store and forward* mechanism might sound cumbersome. But the reality is, text messages aren't synchronous. When you talk on the phone, you interact in real time with another voice. But when you send a text message, the other person might not read the message immediately. Indeed, the recipient's phone might be turned off.

Because of this gap in timing, text messaging requires a buffer — a service center. If it weren't for this buffer, messages that weren't processed immediately would never be delivered. Text messaging would require careful coordination between the sender and the receiver.

Working with Device Sensors

A full-featured Android device is more than just a telephone. To emphasize this point, I include a list of constants from the `android.content.PackageManager` class:

```
FEATURE_BLUETOOTH
FEATURE_CAMERA
FEATURE_CAMERA_AUTOFOCUS
FEATURE_CAMERA_FLASH
FEATURE_CAMERA_FRONT
FEATURE_FAKETOUCH
FEATURE_FAKETOUCH_MULTITOUCH_DISTINCT
FEATURE_FAKETOUCH_MULTITOUCH_JAZZHAND
FEATURE_LIVE_WALLPAPER
FEATURE_LOCATION
FEATURE_LOCATION_GPS
FEATURE_LOCATION_NETWORK
FEATURE_MICROPHONE
FEATURE_NFC
FEATURE_SCREEN_LANDSCAPE
FEATURE_SCREEN_PORTRAIT
FEATURE_SENSOR_ACCELEROMETER
FEATURE_SENSOR_BAROMETER
FEATURE_SENSOR_COMPASS
FEATURE_SENSOR_GYROSCOPE
FEATURE_SENSOR_LIGHT
FEATURE_SENSOR_PROXIMITY
FEATURE_SIP
FEATURE_SIP_VOIP
FEATURE_TELEPHONY
FEATURE_TELEPHONY_CDMA
```

```
FEATURE_TELEPHONY_GSM
FEATURE_TOUCHSCREEN
FEATURE_TOUCHSCREEN_MULTITOUCH
FEATURE_TOUCHSCREEN_MULTITOUCH_DISTINCT
FEATURE_TOUCHSCREEN_MULTITOUCH_JAZZHAND
FEATURE_USB_ACCESSORY
FEATURE_USB_HOST
FEATURE_WIFI
```

Some of these constants are self-explanatory, but others need some clarification. For example, with FAKETOUCH, a device without a real touchscreen has some support for touch events. (For the FAKETOUCH_MULTITOUCH constants, DISTINCT stands for simulation of two-finger touches, and JAZZHAND stands for simulation of five-finger touches.)

A device can sense LOCATION in several ways. A crude way is to guess location using the known locations of nearby cellphone towers. Using GPS (*G*lobal *P*ositioning *S*ystem) is much more accurate.

Among all the PackageManager's FEATURE constants, my favorite is FEATURE_SENSOR_BAROMETER. I can't imagine shopping for a phone and thinking, "That model isn't good enough. I can't use it to measure barometric pressure."

Anyway, when you start programming a device's sensors, you grapple with new kinds of problems. What's the underlying physics of the sensor measurement? How do you handle the necessary mathematics? How do you deal with tiny adjustments in an inherently analog world? The GPS sensor notices a location change. Should my code do processing in its onLocation-Changed method, or is the change so small that I should call it background noise and ignore it?

Quantifying location and orientation

You're probably familiar with the terms *latitude* and *longitude,* but just in case:

✦ **Latitude** is 0 on the Earth's equator, 90 degrees at the North Pole, and –90 degrees at the South Pole.

✦ **Longitude** is 0 at the Royal Observatory in Greenwich, UK. Longitude is negative to the west of Greenwich and positive to the east of Greenwich. Longitude is 180 degrees at the International Date Line in the Pacific Ocean.

**Book IV
Chapter 3**

An Android Potpourri

In the Android world, the term *orientation* has two different (but closely related) meanings:

+ The **screen's orientation** can be either *portrait* or *landscape*.

+ The **device's orientation** is a measurement consisting of three numbers — yaw, pitch, and roll.

Usually, when people talk about orientation (or write about orientation), they don't say "screen orientation" or "device orientation." They simply say, "orientation." Fortunately, you can distinguish the two kinds of orientation from the surrounding terminology:

+ If you hold the device so that the screen's height is greater than the screen's width, the screen's orientation is *portrait*.

+ If you hold the device so that the screen's width is greater than the screen's height, the screen's orientation is *landscape*.

You can use most Android devices in either portrait or landscape mode. So as a developer, you must design your app's interface with both modes in mind. True, users tend to hold phones in portrait mode and hold tablets in landscape mode. But when you define an activity's layouts, you must consider all possibilities. Does your app look good when a user lies flat on a couch and looks up at the device?

+ If you lay the device flat on the ground so that the top of the device points to the Earth's magnetic North Pole, the device's yaw, pitch, and roll values are all 0. (This assumes that the ground is perfectly horizontal.)

If you keep the device flat on the ground while you turn the device, you're changing the *yaw*. If you lift the top of the device (while the bottom of the device still touches the ground) you're changing the *pitch*. If you lift one side of the device (while the other side still touches the ground) you're changing the *roll*.

Android doesn't use degrees to measure yaw, pitch, and roll. Instead, Android's methods return *radian* measure. A half turn of the device is Π radians. A full 360-degree turn is 2Π radians. The easiest way to convert between degrees and radians is as follows:

+ To change degrees into radians, multiply the number of degrees by 0.01745327777777777778.

+ To change radians into degrees, multiply the number of radians by 57.2958279087977743754.

Don't fret at the number of digits in each of the conversion factors. Use fewer digits if you want. No matter how many digits you use, the numbers aren't completely accurate.

Sending location and orientation

The program in Listing 3-4 displays a device's location and orientation. The program's run is shown in Figure 3-7.

Listing 3-4:   Sensing Device Orientation

```
package com.allmycode.sensor;

import static android.hardware.Sensor.TYPE_ACCELEROMETER;
import static android.hardware.Sensor.TYPE_MAGNETIC_FIELD;
import android.app.Activity;
import android.content.Context;
import android.hardware.Sensor;
import android.hardware.SensorEvent;
import android.hardware.SensorEventListener;
import android.hardware.SensorManager;
import android.location.Location;
import android.location.LocationListener;
import android.location.LocationManager;
import android.os.Bundle;
import android.widget.TextView;
import android.widget.Toast;

public class MyActivity extends Activity {
  SensorManager sensorManager;
  Sensor magFieldSensor, accelerometer;
  SensorEventListener sensorListener;
  LocationListener locationListener;
  LocationManager locationManager;
  TextView orientationView, locationView;

  private float[] gravityValues = new float[3];
  private float[] geoMagnetValues = new float[3];
  private float[] orientation = new float[3];
  private float[] rotationMatrix = new float[9];

  @Override
  protected void onCreate(Bundle savedInstanceState) {
    super.onCreate(savedInstanceState);

    setContentView(R.layout.main);
    sensorManager = (SensorManager)
      getSystemService(Context.SENSOR_SERVICE);
    magFieldSensor = sensorManager
          .getDefaultSensor(TYPE_MAGNETIC_FIELD);

    accelerometer = sensorManager
          .getDefaultSensor(TYPE_ACCELEROMETER);

    sensorListener = new MySensorEventListener();

    locationListener = new MyLocationListener();
    locationManager = (LocationManager)
      getSystemService(Context.LOCATION_SERVICE);
```

(continued)

**Book IV
Chapter 3**

An Android Potpourri

Listing 3-4 *(continued)*

```java
    orientationView =
        (TextView) findViewById(R.id.orientationView);
    locationView =
        (TextView) findViewById(R.id.locationView);
}

@Override
protected void onResume() {
    super.onResume();
    sensorManager.registerListener(sensorListener,
        magFieldSensor, SensorManager.SENSOR_DELAY_UI);
    sensorManager.registerListener(sensorListener,
        accelerometer, SensorManager.SENSOR_DELAY_UI);

    locationManager.requestLocationUpdates
    (LocationManager.GPS_PROVIDER,
        0, 0, locationListener);
}

@Override
protected void onPause() {
    super.onPause();
    sensorManager.unregisterListener(sensorListener);
    locationManager.removeUpdates(locationListener);
}

class MySensorEventListener implements SensorEventListener {

    @Override
    public void onSensorChanged(SensorEvent event) {

        int sensorEventType = event.sensor.getType();
        if (sensorEventType == Sensor.TYPE_ACCELEROMETER) {
            System.arraycopy
                (event.values, 0, gravityValues, 0, 3);

        } else if (sensorEventType ==
                            Sensor.TYPE_MAGNETIC_FIELD) {
            System.arraycopy
                (event.values, 0, geoMagnetValues, 0, 3);

        } else {
         return;
        }

        if (SensorManager.getRotationMatrix(rotationMatrix,
            null, gravityValues, geoMagnetValues)) {

            SensorManager.getOrientation(rotationMatrix,
                orientation);

            orientationView.setText
                ("Yaw:   " + orientation[0] + "\n"
                + "Pitch: " + orientation[1] + "\n"
                + "Roll:  " + orientation[2]);
        }
    }
```

```
    @Override
    public void onAccuracyChanged(Sensor sensor,
        int accuracy) {
      if (accuracy <= 1) {
        Toast.makeText(MyActivity.this, "Please shake the " +
          "device in a figure eight pattern to " +
          "improve sensor accuracy!", Toast.LENGTH_LONG)
          .show();
      }
    }
  }
}

class MyLocationListener implements LocationListener {

  @Override
  public void onLocationChanged(Location location) {
    locationView.setText
        ("Latitude:  " + location.getLatitude() + "\n"
      + "Longitude: " + location.getLongitude());
  }

  @Override
  public void onProviderDisabled(String provider) {
  }

  @Override
  public void onProviderEnabled(String provider) {
  }

  @Override
  public void onStatusChanged(String provider,
      int status, Bundle extras) {
  }
}
}
```

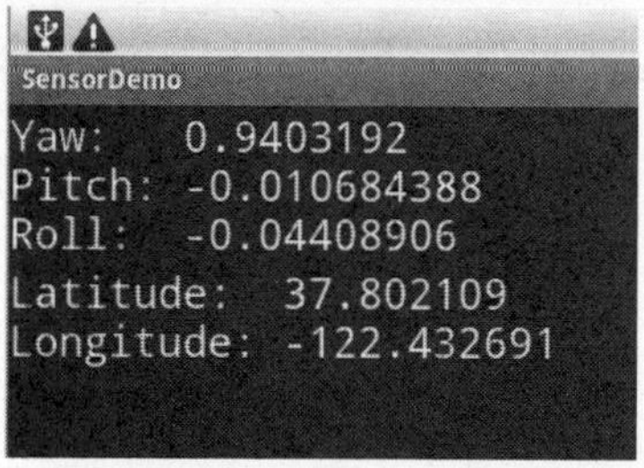

Figure 3-7: Displaying orientation and location.

SensorDemo
```
Yaw:     0.9403192
Pitch:  -0.010684388
Roll:   -0.04408906
Latitude:   37.802109
Longitude: -122.432691
```

Listing 3-4 illustrates a bunch of sensor features — some that are specific to location and orientation, and others that apply to sensors in general. One way or another, most sensors use the same programming constructs:

✦ Instances of the `Manager` classes connect your code to the device's hardware sensors.

In Listing 3-4, calling `getSystemService` provides access to sensor managers. The managers belong to `android.hardware.SensorManager` and `android.location.LocationManager`.

The `LocationManager` isn't in the `android.hardware` package because sensing location is abstracted for various sensing techniques. The `LocationManager` class represents GPS readings, cell tower usage, and other things. You can estimate a device's location based on Wi-Fi hotspot usage, the device's IP address, user queries, last known location, and readings borrowed from nearby mobile devices. The `LocationManager` deals generically with places on Earth, not specifically with GPS hardware.

✦ Instances of `android.hardware.Sensor` represent the sensors themselves.

In Listing 3-4, calls to the `getDefaultSensor` method return values for `magFieldSensor` and for `accelerometer`.

✦ Objects that implement `Listener` interfaces receive notice of changes to sensor values.

In Listing 3-4, instances of `MySensorEventListener` and `MyLocationListener` fill these roles. I register the listeners in the activity's `onResume` method and unregister the listeners in the activity's `onPause` method.

Your app should stop listening when the activity pauses. If you forget to unregister, the user's battery might die of exhaustion.

The code to get useful values from sensor events depends on the kind of event. In Listing 3-4, getting location information means simply calling `location.getLatitude()` and `location.getLongitude()`. For orientation, the story is more complicated. One way or another, you feed values from the device's level gravity sensor or the device's magnetometer into the `SensorManager.getRotationMatrix` method.

A few miscellaneous tidbits in Listing 3-4 are worth noting:

✦ To sense the device's location, your app must have "`android.permission.ACCESS_FINE_LOCATION`". Sensing orientation requires no particular permission. (Hackers rarely benefit from knowing the tilt of the user's device.)

✦ When you test this section's app, you probably tilt your device in several directions. By default, this tilting can change the display from portrait to landscape and back. Oddly enough, these display changes can be very annoying. (With most apps, your mind zones out while you're turning the device. But with this app, the turning motion is the app's *raison d'être*.)

To keep changes in screen orientation from driving you crazy, add either `android:screenOrientation="landscape"` or `android:screenOrientation="portrait"` to the `<activity>` element in the `AndroidManifest.xml` document.

✦ Calls to `registerListener` in Listing 3-4 have delay parameters. The delay parameter's value tells the device how often to check the sensor's value. The choices are `SENSOR_DELAY_FASTEST`, `SENSOR_DELAY_GAME`, `SENSOR_DELAY_NORMAL`, and `SENSOR_DELAY_UI`. The `SENSOR_DELAY_GAME` value is appropriate for game playing, and the `SENSOR_DELAY_UI` value is best for displaying the information. Of course, to figure out what's best for your app, ignore the guidelines and do lots of testing.

✦ When you implement the `SensorEventListener` interface, you must create an `onAccuracyChanged` method. The predefined accuracy values are `SENSOR_STATUS_UNRELIABLE` with `int` value 0, `SENSOR_STATUS_ACCURACY_LOW` with `int` value 1, `SENSOR_STATUS_ACCURACY_MEDIUM` with `int` value 2, and `SENSOR_STATUS_ACCURACY_HIGH` with `int` value 3. For some reason, shaking the device in a figure-eight pattern tends to improve orientation sensitivity.

Finally, notice the austere-looking typeface in Figure 3-7. I added `android:typeface="monospace"` to each of the `TextView` start tags in the app's `AndroidManifest.xml` document. A font that's *monospace* reserves the same width for each character. So, for example, with a mono-space font, the letter *i* consumes as much width as the letter *m,* and each blank space is as wide as the letter *m.*

In this section's example, I use monospace to help align the numeric values. So in the preceding Figure 3-7, the three orientation numbers form a column, and the two location numbers form a column. Without a monospace font, the display would have the jagged look you see in Figure 3-8.

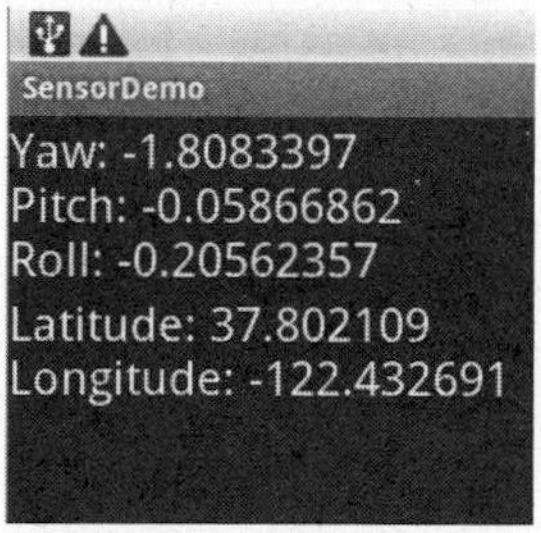

Figure 3-8:
The display from this section's app without a monospace font.

SensorDemo
Yaw: -1.8083397
Pitch: -0.05866862
Roll: -0.20562357
Latitude: 37.802109
Longitude: -122.432691

I could have aligned the numbers by creating separate text views and specifying the width of each text view. Alternatively, I could try adding tabs to my single text view:

```
locationView.setText
        ("Latitude:\t\t" + location.getLatitude() + "\n"
    + "Longitude:\t" + location.getLongitude());
```

The escape sequence \t tells Java to space to the next tab stop. If you use tabs, the display looks like the stuff in Figure 3-9.

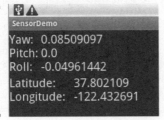

Figure 3-9:
The display from this section's app using tabs.

When I'm tempted to use tabs, I stop and remember how flakey tabs can be. For example, in Figure 3-9, the word *Latitude* is narrower than the word *Longitude*. So my code snippet compensates by having two tabs after the word *Latitude* and only one tab after the word *Longitude*. The extra tab works fine on my test device, but with different font settings on another user's device, the same tabs might throw the numbers out of alignment.

Drawing, Dragging, and Zooming

No doubt about it — touchscreens are cool. You press plain old glass, and the device responds! (Okay. It's not plain old glass. But it's still mysterious.) When you slide your finger, a drawing of some kind moves! And with multi-touch screens, you can zoom things, rotate things, and reshape things.

Android's software supports events involving up to 256 fingers. That's about two-and-one-half centipedes walking on the screen at the same time. Of course, humans seldom apply more than two fingers to a device's screen.

The big picture

Listing 3-5 demonstrates the handling of touch events. A *touch event* is a lot like a click. The most important difference is that touch events may involve motion — the sliding of your finger (or stylus) along the screen's surface.

Listing 3-5:   Handling Touch Events

```
package com.allmycode.draw;

import android.app.Activity;
import android.content.Context;
import android.graphics.Canvas;
import android.graphics.Color;
import android.graphics.Paint;
import android.graphics.Rect;
import android.os.Bundle;
import android.util.DisplayMetrics;
import android.view.MotionEvent;
import android.view.View;
import android.view.View.OnTouchListener;

public class DrawStuffActivity extends Activity implements
    OnTouchListener {

  MyView myView;
  int numberOfFingers = 0;
  float oldX[] = new float[2], oldY[] = new float[2];
  Rect rectangle = new Rect(0, 0, 100, 100);
  DisplayMetrics metrics = new DisplayMetrics();

  @Override
  public void onCreate(Bundle savedInstanceState) {
    super.onCreate(savedInstanceState);

    myView = new MyView(this);
    setContentView(myView);
    myView.setOnTouchListener(this);

    getWindowManager().getDefaultDisplay().
      getMetrics(metrics);
  }

@Override
public boolean onTouch(View view, MotionEvent event) {
    switch (event.getActionMasked()) {
    case MotionEvent.ACTION_DOWN:
      numberOfFingers = 1;
      oldX[0] = event.getX(0);
      oldY[0] = event.getY(0);
      break;
    case MotionEvent.ACTION_POINTER_DOWN:
      numberOfFingers = 2;
      oldX[1] = event.getX(1);
      oldY[1] = event.getY(1);
      break;
    case MotionEvent.ACTION_MOVE:
      handleMove(event);
      break;
    case MotionEvent.ACTION_POINTER_UP:
    case MotionEvent.ACTION_UP:
      numberOfFingers--;
      break;
    }
```

(continued)

Listing 3-5 *(continued)*

```
    view.invalidate();
    return true;
  }
  // The handleMove method is in Listing 3-6.

  class MyView extends View {
    Paint whitePaint = new Paint();

    MyView(Context context) {
      super(context);
      whitePaint.setColor(Color.WHITE);
    }

    @Override
    public void onDraw(Canvas canvas) {
      canvas.drawRect(rectangle, whitePaint);
    }
  }
}
```

The activity in Listing 3-5 isn't complete. It has a big byte taken out of it. The remaining piece comes in Listing 3-6.

Figure 3-10 has an unexciting screen shot from a run of this section's example.

Figure 3-10: Believe me! You can move and resize the white rectangle.

Listing 3-5 has the basic outline of most other Android activity classes. The onCreate method sets the activity's content view and registers a listener. But unlike most of the examples scattered through this book's various minibooks, the content view in Listing 3-5 isn't a resource. Instead, Listing 3-5 gets its content view from an object constructed in the code.

The content view is an instance of the MyView class, which I define at the end of Listing 3-5. The MyView class isn't fancy. The class's primary purpose is to override the View class's onDraw method. When Android draws a `MyView` instance, Android places a white rectangle on a canvas. The rectangle itself (an instance of Android's `Rect` class) has four properties: `left`, `top`, `right`, and `bottom`. (See Figure 3-11.) Each property is a number of pixels.

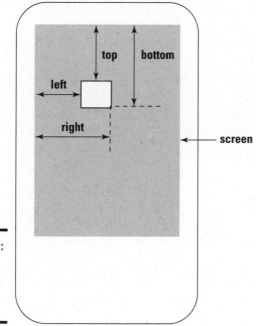

Figure 3-11:
The properties of a Rect instance.

In Listing 3-5, the `onTouch` method responds to motion events. The motion event's `getActionMasked` method returns the type of motion:

+ Android fires `MotionEvent.ACTION_DOWN` when the user places one finger on the screen.

+ Android fires `MotionEvent.ACTION_POINTER_DOWN` when the user places a second finger on the screen.

+ Android fires `MotionEvent.ACTION_UP` when the user lifts the first finger off the screen.

+ Android fires `MotionEvent.ACTION_POINTER_UP` when the user lifts the second finger off the screen.

+ Android fires `MotionEvent.ACTION_MOVE` when the user drags one or more fingers along the screen's surface.

Android has constants, such as ACTION_POINTER_2_UP and ACTION_POINTER_3_DOWN, but these names are deprecated. To distinguish among three or more fingers, look for MotionEvent.ACTION_POINTER_INDEX_MASK in Android's SDK documentation.

The onTouch method in Listing 3-5 records the pixel coordinates where the user's fingers land on the screen:

✦ The getX method returns the number of pixels from the screen's left edge.

✦ The getY method returns the number of pixels from the top of the screen.

✦ In the calls to getX and getY, the 0 parameter represents the first finger that the user places on the screen.

✦ The 1 parameter represents the second finger that the user places on the screen.

Aside from this quick bookkeeping, the onTouch method defers to the handleMove method for most of the code's calculations. (The handleMove method in Listing 3-6 — shown later in this chapter — computes the white rectangle's new size and position.)

Near the end of the onTouch method, I call view.invalidate(). This tells Android that the rendering of this view on the screen is no longer valid. Thus, Android must redraw the view. That is, Android must call the view's onDraw method.

At the end of the onTouch method, the return value true indicates that the method has handled the motion event once and for all. Any other methods that think they're going to handle the motion event can go fly a kite.

This section's app shouldn't respond to a tilt of the screen. To keep the screen in landscape mode, add android:screenOrientation="landscape" to the activity's start tag in the AndroidManifest.xml document.

The details

Moving gizmos on a screen can involve some interesting math. In fact, most graphics packages use matrix transformations to adjust items' shapes and sizes. But in this section, I compromise. Instead of using the concise mathematical tools in Android's SDK, I do some simpler (and maybe more intuitive) measurements. Listing 3-6 has the code.

Listing 3-6: Dragging and Zooming

```
float newX[] = new float[2], newY[] = new float[2];
int xChange[] = new int[2], yChange[] = new int[2];
int diffX, diffY;
int newLeft = rectangle.left, newTop = rectangle.top,
    newRight = rectangle.right,
    newBottom = rectangle.bottom;

void handleMove(MotionEvent event) {
  newX[0] = Math.round(event.getX(0));
  newY[0] = Math.round(event.getY(0));
  xChange[0] = Math.round(newX[0] - oldX[0]);
  yChange[0] = Math.round(newY[0] - oldY[0]);
  oldX[0] = newX[0];
  oldY[0] = newY[0];

  switch (numberOfFingers) {
  case 1:

    newLeft = rectangle.left + xChange[0];
    newTop = rectangle.top + yChange[0];
    newRight = rectangle.right + xChange[0];
    newBottom = rectangle.bottom + yChange[0];
    if (newLeft < 0 || newRight > metrics.widthPixels) {
      newLeft = rectangle.left;
      newRight = rectangle.right;
    }
    if (newTop < 0 || newBottom > metrics.heightPixels) {
      newTop = rectangle.top;
      newBottom = rectangle.bottom;
    }
    rectangle =
      new Rect(newLeft, newTop, newRight, newBottom);

    break;

  case 2:
    newX[1] = Math.round(event.getX(1));
    newY[1] = Math.round(event.getY(1));

    diffX =
        Math.abs(Math.round(newX[1] - newX[0]))
          - Math.abs(Math.round(oldX[1] - oldX[0]));
    diffY =
        Math.abs(Math.round(newY[1] - newY[0]))
          - Math.abs(Math.round(oldY[1] - oldY[0]));

    oldX[1] = newX[1];
    oldY[1] = newY[1];

    newLeft = rectangle.left - diffX / 2;
    newTop = rectangle.top - diffY / 2;
    newRight = rectangle.right + diffX / 2;
    newBottom = rectangle.bottom + diffY / 2;
    rectangle =
        new Rect(newLeft, newTop, newRight, newBottom);
    break;
  }
}
```

The code in Listing 3-6 compares the most recent motion event's coordinates with the previous event's coordinates. With this information, the code computes the distances and directions of the user's finger movements. The code uses these values to calculate the change in the rectangle's position, size, and shape. With this information (and with the rectangle's current `left`, `top`, `right`, and `bottom` properties), the code computes new values for the rectangle's four properties.

Finally, if you do nothing to constrain the rectangle's motion, it could happen that you slide the rectangle away from the screen's visible area. To keep this from happening, I add a few `if` statements to the one-finger code. In those `if` statements, the `metrics` variable tells me the screen's width and height in pixels. (The `metrics` variable gets its values in the `onCreate` method in Listing 3-5.)

Notice the use of `float` values in Listing 3-6. Android's `MotionEvent` methods work with all kinds of devices, and some devices report touch-event locations as fractions of a pixel. After all, the touch-sensing hardware on a screen's surface is different from the light-producing hardware in the screen's guts. If the touch-sensing hardware has higher resolution than the light-producing hardware, the device can report movement in fractions of a pixel.

On the Importance of Waiting Patiently

This section deals with an important multitasking issue. Suppose your app has a feature that can take a long time to complete. For example, you create an app that displays an image on the screen. The image normally lives on a website, so your app reaches out with a URL.

While the user waits for a response from the website, your app must not appear to be frozen. The user doesn't want an interface that's unresponsive until the image appears on the screen.

Almost any part of your app's code can open an HTTP connection and request an image from the web. But if you're not careful, the request takes place in your app's main thread (the so-called *UI thread*). Like any other thread, the main thread is a one-lane road. While your HTTP request waits at a stoplight, none of your app's other features can move forward. Parts of the display don't get updated, buttons are unresponsive, and all the while, the user dreams up nasty things to write on the Play Store's app ratings page.

You may be familiar with the use of Java threads. A piece of code can spawn a new thread. With two threads of execution (the main thread and the newly spawned thread), your code can do two things at once. One thread waits for a web page while the other thread handles button clicks and other user-related events. The new thread is like a side road. While a big truck clogs up this side road, cars continue to flow along the main highway.

But spawning new Java threads doesn't entirely solve the problem. Android's threading rules dictate that no thread other than the main thread can update an application's user interface. So, for example, your secondary thread can wait to get an image from the web. But after the image has been downloaded, the secondary thread can't easily display the image.

To fix this problem once and for all, Android has an abstract `AsyncTask` class. An `AsyncTask` does your app's time-consuming work in a separate thread and returns useful results to your app's main thread. In addition, an `AsyncTask` has methods that structure the code in a sensible, fill-in-the-blanks way.

Of course, the kinds of work that you do with an `AsyncTask` come in many forms and flavors. That's why the `AsyncTask` class has generic type parameters.

In spite of the naming, Android's `AsyncTask` class has little in common with a stack of activities that form a task. True, I sometimes use the word *task* for either a stack of activities or an `AsyncTask` instance. But the two kinds of tasks are quite different. For a refresher course on activity stacks, see Book III, Chapters 1 and 2.

Creating an AsyncTask

The `AsyncTask` in Listing 3-7 fetches an image from the web. In the meantime, the code updates a progress bar that appears on the device's screen.

Listing 3-7:   Getting an Image from a Website

```
class MyAsyncTask extends
    AsyncTask<String, Integer, Bitmap> {

  int progress;

  @Override
  protected void onPreExecute() {
    progress = 0;
    button.setClickable(false);
  }
```

(continued)

Listing 3-7 *(continued)*

```java
@Override
protected Bitmap doInBackground(String. . . urlArray) {
  try {
    URL url = new URL(urlArray[0]);
    HttpURLConnection connection =
        (HttpURLConnection) url.openConnection();
    connection.setDoInput(true);
    connection.connect();

    progress += 50;
    publishProgress(progress);

    InputStream input = connection.getInputStream();
    Bitmap bitmap = BitmapFactory.decodeStream(input);

    progress += 50;
    publishProgress(progress);

    return bitmap;
  } catch (IOException e) {
    e.printStackTrace();
    return null;
  }
}

@Override
protected void onProgressUpdate(Integer. . . progressArray) {
  progressBar.setProgress(progressArray[0]);
}

@Override
protected void onPostExecute(Bitmap result) {
  imageView.setImageBitmap(result);
  button.setClickable(true);
}
}
```

The code in Listing 3-7 is an inner class; it should be nestled inside an app's main activity (or inside some other class in your app).

When you extend `AsyncTask`, you must supply three generic parameters (in this example, `<String, Integer, Bitmap>`) and four methods:

✦ **The first generic parameter (`String` in Listing 3-7) describes the type of input to the task's `doInBackground` method.**

  Think of this as the type of input that the task needs in order to do its work. In Listing 3-7, the `doInBackground` method's parameter is a variable-length array of strings. The method body uses only one string (the value stored in the `urlArray`'s initial element). The code uses this string the way you'd use any web address — to fetch a web page (or in this example, an image).

In Java, when you use three dots in a parameter list, you create a *varargs* parameter. (In Listing 3-7, the declaration `doInBackground(String...urlArray)` has a varargs parameter.) The `doInBackground` method is prepared to receive not one `String` value, but many `String` values. If you call `execute` with only one `String` value, the `doInBackground` method treats that `String` value as `urlArray[0]`. If you call `execute` with two `String` values, the `doInBackground` method ends up with an array containing two elements — `urlArray[0]` and `urlArray[1]`. And so on. That's what the three dots mean in the `doInBackground` method's parameter list.

✦ **The second generic parameter (`Integer` in Listing 3-7) describes the type of input to the task's `onProgressUpdate` method.**

Think of this as the type of information that describes the state of the progress bar. In Listing 3-7, the `onProgressUpdate` method's parameter is a variable-length array of `Integer` values. The method body uses only one integer (the value stored in the `progressArray`'s initial element). The code calls the progress bar's `setProgress` method to make the progress bar display the current status.

✦ **The third generic parameter (`Bitmap` in Listing 3-7) describes the result type of the task's `doInBackground` method, which is also the type of input to the task's `onPostExecute` method.**

Think of this as the type of information that's created by a run of the task. In Listing 3-7, the `onPostExecute` method feeds a bitmap (the bitmap obtained from a website) to the activity's `imageView` object.

When you create an `AsyncTask`, any or all of the three generic parameters can be `Void`. (Java's `Void` class stores the primitive `void` type — the type that refers to nothing.) When a parameter is `Void`, the `AsyncTask` doesn't use the corresponding information. For example, an `AsyncTask` with no progress bar has a middle parameter that's `Void`.

Multithreaded code, with its threads and its callbacks, can be very complicated. The `AsyncTask` class is nice because it provides preinstalled *plumbing code*. This plumbing code relieves the developer of much of the multithreaded programming burden.

Using a progress bar

I heard a story a long time ago. I don't know where I heard it. So, if you're the story's originator, please contact me via email, and I'll give you credit in the next edition. (And whatever you do, please don't sue me for using the story.)

Anyway, the story takes place in a tall office building with too few elevators. People would wait impatiently to go from the lobby to one of the higher floors. The building's owner got estimates for the cost of adding more elevators, and the price was staggering.

So, to solve the problem, the owner installed wall-to-wall mirrors beside each of the elevators. As a result, people didn't get faster service. But everyone stopped to check their appearance in the mirrors. So, from then on, no one complained about the elevators' being too slow.

Clearly, this story has an important moral. The moral is, you don't necessarily have to speed up a process. But you must keep the user busy while the process chugs along.

That's what progress bars are for. Figure 3-12 displays the progress bar in this section's example.

Figure 3-12: A horizontal progress bar.

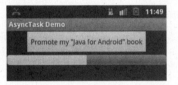

I define this example's progress bar with the following code:

```
<ProgressBar android:id="@+id/progressBar1"
    style="?android:attr/progressBarStyleHorizontal"
    android:max="100"

    android:layout_width="match_parent"
    android:layout_height="wrap_content"/>
```

Android's built-in `android.R.attr.progressBarStyleHorizontal` resource describes the progress bar in Figure 3-12. The `android:max="100"` attribute tells your app to display a completed progress bar when you call `progressBar.setProgress(100)` and to display a partially completed progress bar for values between `0` and `100`.

For this section's example, I might have done better using `style="?android:attr/progressBarStyleLarge"`, which displays a spinning circle with no progress percentage. But I chose the horizontal style to illustrate the usage of progress updates. In Listing 3-7, I start with progress value `0` in the task's `onPreExecute` method. Then, at certain points in the task's `doInBackground` method, I call `publishProgress`. A call to `publishProgress` automatically triggers a call to the `onProgressUpdate` method. And in Listing 3-7, my `onProgressUpdate` method refreshes the progress bar's display.

In Listing 3-7, I select two points in the `doInBackground` method to change the progress value and update the progress bar's display. I do this to illustrate the use of a horizontal progress bar. But in truth, the progress bar in Listing 3-7 might easily annoy the user. A bar with only three values (`0, 50, 100`) doesn't give the user much useful information. And besides, the timing of the work in Listing 3-7's `doInBackground` method probably isn't a 50/50 split. When you create a real app, think carefully about updates to the progress bar. Try as hard as you can to make them reflect the task's expected timing. And, if the timing is unpredictable, use `progressBar-StyleSmall`, `progressBarStyleLarge`, or one of the other percentage-free types in the `android.R.attr` class. You can also avoid a percentage display by putting a progress bar into *indeterminate mode*. For more info, check the `ProgressBar` class's `setIndeterminate` method and the `android:indeterminate` XML attribute.

Using an AsyncTask

Listing 3-8 contains the code to use the task in Listing 3-7. To form a complete code example, paste the task from Listing 3-7 into the `MyActivity` class of Listing 3-8. (That is, make `MyAsyncTask` be an inner class of the `MyActivity` class.)

Listing 3-8:   The Main Activity Uses an AsyncTask

```
package com.allmycode.samples;

import java.io.IOException;
import java.io.InputStream;
import java.net.HttpURLConnection;
import java.net.URL;

import android.app.Activity;
import android.graphics.Bitmap;
import android.graphics.BitmapFactory;
import android.os.AsyncTask;
import android.os.Bundle;
import android.view.View;
import android.widget.Button;
import android.widget.ImageView;
import android.widget.ProgressBar;

public class MyActivity extends Activity {

  Button button;
  ImageView imageView;
  ProgressBar progressBar;

  @Override
  public void onCreate(Bundle savedInstanceState) {
    super.onCreate(savedInstanceState);
    setContentView(R.layout.main);
```

(continued)

**Book IV
Chapter 3**

An Android Potpourri

Listing 3-8 *(continued)*

```
    button = ((Button) findViewById(R.id.button1));

    imageView = (ImageView) findViewById(R.id.imageView1);
    progressBar =
        (ProgressBar) findViewById(R.id.progressBar1);
    progressBar.setProgress(0);
}

    public void onButtonClick(View view) {
        new MyAsyncTask().execute
            ("http://allmycode.com/Java4Android/" +
                "JavaProgrammingForAndroidDevelopers.jpg");
    }

    // The MyAsyncTask class is in Listing 3-7.

}
```

When the user clicks a button, the code in Listing 3-8 executes a new `MyAsyncTask` instance. The result (a shameless plug for one of my Java books) is shown in Figure 3-13.

Figure 3-13:
The
completion
of the task.

This section's example gets a bitmap from the web. So, to run this section's code, add `<uses-permission android:name="android.permission.INTERNET"></uses-permission>` to the application's `AndroidManifest.xml` file.

Chapter 4: An Android Social Media App

In This Chapter

↙ **Posting on Twitter with Android code**

↙ **Tweeting with your app on a user's behalf**

A reader from Vancouver (in British Columbia, Canada) writes:

"Hello, Barry. I just thought I would ask that you include the area that seems to get attention from app developers: programs connecting with social sites. I look forward to reading the new book! Best regards, David."

Well, David, you've inspired me to create a Twitter app. This chapter's example does two things: It posts a new tweet, and it gets a Twitter user's timeline. The app can perform many more Twitter tasks — for example, search for tweets, look for users, view trends, check friends and followers, gather suggestions, and do lots of other things that Twitter users want done. For simplicity, though, I have the app perform only two tasks: tweet and display a timeline.

I can summarize the essence of this chapter's Twitter code in two short statements. To post a tweet, the app executes

```
twitter.updateStatus("This is my tweet.");
```

And, to display a user's timeline, the app executes

```
List<twitter4j.Status> statuses =
    twitter.getUserTimeline("allmycode");
```

Of course, these two statements only serve as a summary, and a summary is never the same as the material it summarizes. Imagine standing on the street in Times Square and shouting the statement "Twitter dot update status: 'This is my tweet.'" Nothing good happens because you're issuing the correct command in the wrong context. In the same way, the context surrounding a call to `twitter.updateStatus` in an app matters an awful lot.

This chapter covers all the context surrounding your calls to `twitter.updateStatus` and `twitter.getUserTimeline`.

The Twitter App's Files

You can import this chapter's code from my website (http://allmycode.com/Android) by following the instructions in Book I, Chapter 3. As is true for any Android app, this chapter's Android Studio project contains about 100 files and about 170 different folders. In this chapter, I concentrate on the project's MainActivity.java file. But a few other files require some attention.

The Twitter4J API jar file

Android has no built-in support for communicating with Twitter. Yes, the raw materials are contained in Android's libraries, but to deal with all of Twitter's requirements, someone has to paste together those raw materials in a useful way. Fortunately, several developers have done all the pasting and made their libraries available for use by others. The library that I use in this chapter is Twitter4J. Its website is http://twitter4j.org.

Chapter 4 in Book II describes the role of .jar files in Java program development. For this chapter's example to work, your project must include a .jar file containing the Twitter4J libraries. If you've downloaded the code from this book's website and opened the 04_04_01 project, you have everything you need. (The project that you downloaded contains the required .jar file.)

If you're creating this chapter's example on your own, or if you're having trouble with the project's existing .jar files, you can add the Twitter4J libraries by following these steps:

1. **Visit** http://twitter4j.org.

2. **Find the link to download the latest stable version of Twitter4J.**

   To run this chapter's example, I use Twitter4J version 4.0.2. If you download a later version, it'll probably work. But I make no promises about the backward compatibility, forward compatibility, or sideward compatibility of the various Twitter4J versions. If my example doesn't run properly for you, you can search the Twitter4J site for a download link to version 4.0.2.

3. **Click the link to download the Twitter4J software.**

   The file that I downloaded is twitter4j-4.0.2.zip.

4. **Look for a twitter4j-core.jar file in the downloaded .zip file.**

   In the .zip file that I downloaded, I found a file named twitter4j-core-4.0.2.jar.

5. **Extract the twitter4j-core.jar file to this project's app/build directory.**

   Use your operating system's File Explorer or Finder to do the extracting and copying.

6. **In Android Studio's main menu, choose File⇨Project Structure.**

7. **In the Project Structure dialog box, in the panel on the left side, select** `app` **(in the Modules group).**

   See Figure 4-1.

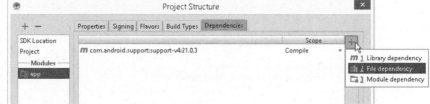

Figure 4-1: Adding a dependency.

8. **In the main body of the Project Structure dialog box, select the Dependencies tab.**

   You want to add the `twitter4j-core.jar` file to the list of dependencies.

9. **Click the plus sign that's to the right of the Dependencies list.**

   A little pop-up menu appears. (Refer to Figure 4-1.)

10. **In the pop-up menu, select File Dependency.**

    Android Studio displays a Select Path dialog box.

11. **In the Select Path dialog box, expand the** `build` **directory and select the** `twitter4j-core.jar` **file.**

    What I refer to as your `twitter4j-core.jar` file is probably named `twitter4j-core-4.0.2.jar` or something similar.

12. **Click OK to close the Select Path dialog box.**

    Doing so adds your `twitter4j-core.jar` file to the list of items on the Dependencies tab.

13. **In the Project Structure dialog box, click OK.**

    Now Twitter4J's `.jar` file is part of your project. (See Figure 4-2.)

Figure 4-2: Your project depends on Twitter4J.

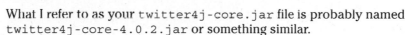

Book IV Chapter 4

An Android Social Media App

The manifest file

Listing 4-1 contains the `AndroidManifest.xml` file for this chapter's Twitter app.

Listing 4-1:   The AndroidManifest.xml File

```
<?xml version="1.0" encoding="utf-8"?>
<manifest xmlns:android=
    "http://schemas.android.com/apk/res/android"
 package="com.allmycode.twitter">

<uses-permission android:name=
    "android.permission.INTERNET"/>

<application
  android:allowBackup="true"
  android:icon="@drawable/ic_launcher"
  android:label="@string/app_name"
  android:theme="@style/AppTheme" >
  <activity
    android:name="com.allmycode.twitter.MainActivity"
    android:label="@string/app_name"
    android:windowSoftInputMode="adjustPan" >
    <intent-filter>
      <action android:name=
          "android.intent.action.MAIN" />
      <category android:name=
          "android.intent.category.LAUNCHER" />
    </intent-filter>
  </activity>
  </application>

</manifest>
```

In Listing 4-1, you find the same stuff that you find in other `AndroidManifest.xml` files. In addition, you find the following:

✦ **The** `uses-permission` **element warns Android that my app requires Internet connectivity.**

✦ **The** `windowSoftInputMode` **attribute tells Android what to do when the user activates the onscreen keyboard.**

   The `adjustPan` value tells Android not to squash together all my screen's widgets. (Take my word for it: The app looks ugly without this `adjustPan` value.)

The main activity's layout file

The layout file for this chapter's example has no extraordinary qualities. I include it in Listing 4-2 for completeness. As usual, you can import this

chapter's code from my website (`http://allmycode.com/Android`).
But if you're living large and creating the app on your own from scratch,
you can copy the contents of Listing 4-2 to the project's `res/layout/`
`activity_main.xml` file. Alternatively, you can use Android Studio's
Designer tool to drag and drop, point and click, or type and tap your way
to the graphical layout shown in Figure 4-3.

Listing 4-2:   The Layout File

```
<RelativeLayout xmlns:android=
    "http://schemas.android.com/apk/res/android"
xmlns:tools="http://schemas.android.com/tools"
android:layout_width="match_parent"
android:layout_height="match_parent"
android:paddingBottom="@dimen/activity_vertical_margin"
android:paddingLeft="@dimen/activity_horizontal_margin"
android:paddingRight=
    "@dimen/activity_horizontal_margin"
android:paddingTop="@dimen/activity_vertical_margin"
tools:context=".MainActivity" >

<TextView
   android:id="@+id/textView2"
   android:layout_width="wrap_content"
   android:layout_height="wrap_content"
   android:layout_alignBaseline="@+id/editTextUsername"
   android:layout_alignBottom="@+id/editTextUsername"
   android:layout_alignLeft="@+id/editTextTweet"
   android:text="@string/at_sign"
   android:textAppearance=
       "?android:attr/textAppearanceLarge" />

<EditText
   android:id="@+id/editTextUsername"
   android:layout_width="wrap_content"
   android:layout_height="wrap_content"
   android:layout_above="@+id/timelineButton"
   android:layout_toRightOf="@+id/textView2"
   android:ems="10"
   android:hint="@string/type_username_here" />

<TextView
   android:id="@+id/textViewTimeline"
   android:layout_width="wrap_content"
   android:layout_height="wrap_content"
   android:layout_alignLeft="@+id/timelineButton"
   android:layout_below="@+id/timelineButton"
   android:maxLines="100"
   android:scrollbars="vertical"
   android:text="@string/timeline_here" />

<Button
   android:id="@+id/timelineButton"
   android:layout_width="wrap_content"
   android:layout_height="wrap_content"
   android:layout_alignLeft="@+id/textView2"
```

(continued)

Listing 4-2 *(continued)*

```
      android:layout_centerVertical="true"
      android:onClick="onTimelineButtonClick"
      android:text="@string/timeline" />

  <Button
      android:id="@+id/tweetButton"
      android:layout_width="wrap_content"
      android:layout_height="wrap_content"
      android:layout_above="@+id/editTextUsername"
      android:layout_alignLeft="@+id/editTextTweet"
      android:layout_marginBottom="43dp"
      android:onClick="onTweetButtonClick"
      android:text="@string/tweet" />

  <EditText
      android:id="@+id/editTextTweet"
      android:layout_width="wrap_content"
      android:layout_height="wrap_content"
      android:layout_above="@+id/tweetButton"
      android:layout_alignParentLeft="true"
      android:layout_marginLeft="14dp"
      android:ems="10"
      android:hint="@string/type_your_tweet_here" />

  <TextView
      android:id="@+id/textViewCountChars"
      android:layout_width="wrap_content"
      android:layout_height="wrap_content"
      android:layout_alignBaseline="@+id/tweetButton"
      android:layout_alignBottom="@+id/tweetButton"
      android:layout_toRightOf="@+id/timelineButton"
      android:text="@string/zero" />

</RelativeLayout>
```

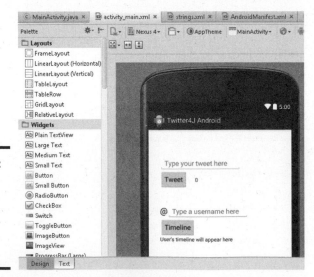

Figure 4-3:
The graphical layout of the main activity's screen.

How to Talk to the Twitter Server

Listing 4-3 contains a snippet of code from the main activity in this chapter's example.

Listing 4-3:   Some Fake Java Code (Yes, It's Fake!)

```
Twitter twitter;

// . . . Some code goes here

ConfigurationBuilder builder =
                    new ConfigurationBuilder();
builder
  .setOAuthConsumerKey("01qedaqsdtdemrVJIkU1dg")
  .setOAuthConsumerSecret("TudeMgXgh37Ivq173SNWnRIhI")
  .setOAuthAccessToken("1385541-ueSEFeFgJ8vUpfy6LBv6")
  .setOAuthAccessTokenSecret("G2FXeXYLSHI7XlVdMsS2e");

TwitterFactory factory =
    new TwitterFactory(builder.build());
twitter = factory.getInstance();
```

The code in Listing 4-3 creates an instance of the `Twitter` class.

Here's some information regarding the Twitter4J API:

✦ **A** `Twitter` **object is a gateway to the Twitter servers.**

   A call to one of the methods belonging to a `Twitter` object can post a brand-new tweet, get another Twitter user's timeline, create favorites, create friendships, create blocks, search for users, and do other cool things.

✦ `TwitterFactory` **is a class that helps you create a new** `Twitter` **object.**

   As the name suggests, `TwitterFactory` is a factory class. In Java, a *factory* class is a class that can call a constructor on your behalf.

✦ **Calling the** `getInstance` **method creates a new** `Twitter` **object.**

   A factory method, such as `getInstance`, contains the actual constructor call.

The `ConfigurationBuilder`, `TwitterFactory`, and `Twitter` classes belong to the Twitter4J API. If, instead of using Twitter4J, you use a different API to communicate with Twitter servers, you'll use different class names. What's more, those classes probably won't match up, one for one, with the Twitter4J classes.

Using OAuth

When you run this chapter's example, the code has to talk to Twitter on your behalf. And normally, to talk to Twitter, you supply a username and password. But should you be sharing your Twitter password with any app that comes your way? Probably not. Your password is similar to the key to your house. You don't want to give copies of your house key to strangers, and you don't want an Android app to remember your Twitter password.

So how can your app post a tweet without having your Twitter password? One answer is *OAuth,* a standardized way to have apps log on to host computers.

The big, ugly strings in Listing 4-3 are OAuth strings. You get strings like this from the Twitter website. If gobbledygook of the kind you see in Listing 4-3 is copied correctly, your app acquires revocable permission to act on behalf of the Twitter user. And the app never gets hold of the user's password.

Now, here come the disclaimers:

✦ **A discussion of how OAuth works, and why it's safer than using ordinary Twitter passwords, is far beyond the scope of this book.**

I don't pretend to explain OAuth and its mysteries in this chapter.

✦ **True app security requires more than what you see in Listing 4-3.**

The goal of this chapter is to show how an app can talk to a social media site. In this chapter's code, I use OAuth and Twitter4J commands to achieve that goal as quickly as I can, without necessarily showing you the "right" way to do it. For more comprehensive coverage of OAuth, visit `oauth.net`: the official website for OAuth developers.

✦ **The codes in Listing 4-3 don't work.**

I'm not prepared to share my own OAuth codes with the general public, so to create Listing 4-3, I took the general outline of my real `ConfigurationBuilder` code and then ran my fingers over the keyboard to replace most of the characters in the OAuth strings.

To run this chapter's app, you must create your own set of OAuth keys and copy them into your Java code. The section entitled "Getting OAuth codes" outlines the steps.

Making a ConfigurationBuilder

In Listing 4-3, the chaining of `set` method calls, one after another, is called the *builder pattern.*

Here's the basic idea. A configuration builder has lots of properties, and you can imagine several different ways of setting those properties. For example, you could have one enormous constructor:

```
// This is not correct Twitter4J code:

ConfigurationBuilder builder = new ConfigurationBuilder(
  "01qedaqsdtdemrVJIkU1dg", "TudeMgXgh37Ivq173SNWnRIhI",
  "1385541-ueSEFeFgJ8vUpfy6LBv6", "G2FXeXYLSHI7XlVdMsS2e");
```

This approach is really cumbersome because you must remember which string belongs in which position. In fact, it gets worse. A configuration builder has 46 different properties, and you may want to set more than four of these properties. However, a constructor with 46 parameters would be really awful.

Another possibility is to create a blank-slate configuration builder and then set each of its properties with separate method calls.

```
// This is not correct Twitter4J code:

ConfigurationBuilder builder = new ConfigurationBuilder();
builder.setOAuthConsumerKey("01qedaqsdtdemrVJIkU1dg");
builder.setOAuthConsumerSecret
                 ("TudeMgXgh37Ivq173SNWnRIhI");
builder.setOAuthAccessToken
                 ("1385541-ueSEFeFgJ8vUpfy6LBv6");
builder.setOAuthAccessTokenSecret
                 ("G2FXeXYLSHI7XlVdMsS2e");
```

This is less awkward than having a giant constructor, but there's a better way. In the Twitter4J API, the `ConfigurationBuilder` class has 46 `set` methods. Each method applies to an existing `ConfigurationBuilder` instance. And each method returns, as its result, a new `ConfigurationBuilder` instance. So, in Listing 4-3, the statement

```
ConfigurationBuilder builder =
                 new ConfigurationBuilder();
```

creates a blank-slate configuration builder. The next piece of code

```
builder
  .setOAuthConsumerKey("01qedaqsdtdemrVJIkU1dg")
```

applies to the blank-slate instance. But the value of this piece of code is an instance with a particular OAuth consumer key. To this enhanced instance you apply

```
.setOAuthConsumerSecret("TudeMgXgh37Ivq173SNWnRIhI")
```

The combined code's value is an even better instance — one with a particular OAuth consumer key and an OAuth consumer secret. And so on. Each application of a `set` method takes an existing instance and yields an instance with more and better properties. This elegant way of adding properties to an object is the builder pattern. It's the idea behind the code in Listing 4-3.

Getting OAuth codes

For your Android app to communicate with Twitter servers, you need your own OAuth codes. To get them, follow this section's steps.

The following instructions apply to the Twitter web pages for developers at the time of this book's publication. Twitter might change the design of its website at any time without notice. (At any rate, Twitter won't notify me!)

1. **Sign in to your Twitter user account (or register for an account if you don't already have one).**

2. **Visit** `https://apps.twitter.com/app/new`.

   If the stars are aligned harmoniously, you should see Twitter's Create an Application page.

3. **On the Create an Application page, fill in all required fields along with the (misleadingly optional) Callback URL field.**

   When I visit the page, I see the Name field, the Description field, the Website field, and the Callback URL field. All but the Callback URL field are listed as being required.

   Making up an application name (for the Name field) isn't challenging. But what do you use for the other fields? After all, you aren't creating an industrial-strength Android app. You're creating only a test app — an app to help you see how to use Twitter4J.

   The good news is that almost anything you type in the Description field is okay. The same is true for the Website and Callback URL fields, as long as you type things that look like real URLs.

   I've never tried typing a `twitter.com` URL in either the Website or Callback URL fields, but I suspect that typing a `twitter.com` URL doesn't work.

   To communicate with Twitter via an Android app, you need a callback URL. In other words, for this chapter's example, the callback URL isn't optional. Neither the Website field nor the Callback URL field has to point to a real web page. But you must fill in those two fields.

This chapter's app doesn't work through a web browser. But, using OAuth, you can log a user into Twitter through a web browser. When the log in is successful, the user's browser visits a particular page, and that page's URL is the callback URL.

The Callback URL field isn't marked as being required. Nevertheless, you must type a URL (such as `http://www.example.com`) in the Callback URL field.

4. **After agreeing to the terms, and doing the other stuff to prove that you're a good person, click the Create Your Twitter Application button.**

    Doing so brings you to a page where you see some details about your new application — the Details tab, in other words. For this example, the two most important items are your app's access level and its consumer key.

In the OAuth world, an app whose code communicates with Twitter's servers is a *consumer*. To identify itself as a trustworthy consumer, an app must send passwords to Twitter's servers. In OAuth terminology, these passwords are called the *consumer key* and the *consumer secret*.

5. **On that same web page, select your application's Permissions tab.**

    In the Permissions tab, you see a choice of access types.

6. **Change your app's access from Read Only (the default) to Read, Write and Access Direct Messages.**

    For this toy application, you select Read, Write and Access Direct Messages — the most permissive access model that's available. This option prevents your app from hitting brick walls because of access problems. But when you develop a real-life application, you do the opposite — you select the least permissive option that suits your application's requirements.

First change your app's access level, and then create the app's access token (as explained in Step 9). Don't create the access token before changing the access level. If you try to change the access level after you've created the access token, your app won't work. What's worse, the `dev.twitter.com` page won't warn you about the problem. Believe me — I've wasted hours of my life on this Twitter quirk.

7. **Click the button that offers to update your application's settings.**

    Doing so changes your app's access level to Read, Write and Access Direct Messages.

8. **On that same web page, select the Keys and Access Tokens tab.**

    After selecting that tab, you see some new stuff on the page.

9. **Click the Create My Access Token button.**

   After doing so, your app's Keys and Access Tokens tab displays your app's access token and the access token secret, in addition to your app's access level, consumer key, and consumer secret.

10. **Copy the four codes (Consumer Key, Consumer Secret, Access Token, and Access Token Secret) from your app's Details tab to the appropriate lines in your app's main activity.**

    The main activity is in this book's very next section.

The Application's Main Activity

Listing 4-4 contains the Twitter app's Java code.

Listing 4-4: The MainActivity.java File

```java
package com.allmycode.twitter;

import android.app.Activity;
import android.os.AsyncTask;
import android.os.Bundle;
import android.text.Editable;
import android.text.TextWatcher;
import android.text.method.ScrollingMovementMethod;
import android.view.View;
import android.widget.EditText;
import android.widget.TextView;

import java.util.List;

import twitter4j.Twitter;
import twitter4j.TwitterException;
import twitter4j.TwitterFactory;
import twitter4j.conf.ConfigurationBuilder;

public class MainActivity extends Activity {
  TextView textViewCountChars, textViewTimeline;
  EditText editTextTweet, editTextUsername;

  Twitter twitter;

  @Override
  protected void onCreate(Bundle savedInstanceState) {
    super.onCreate(savedInstanceState);
    setContentView(R.layout.activity_main);
    editTextTweet =
        (EditText) findViewById(R.id.editTextTweet);
    editTextTweet.addTextChangedListener
        (new MyTextWatcher());
    textViewCountChars =
        (TextView) findViewById(R.id.textViewCountChars);
```

```
    editTextUsername =
        (EditText) findViewById(R.id.editTextUsername);
    textViewTimeline =
        (TextView) findViewById(R.id.textViewTimeline);
    textViewTimeline.setMovementMethod
        (new ScrollingMovementMethod());

    ConfigurationBuilder builder =
                        new ConfigurationBuilder();
    builder
      .setOAuthConsumerKey("01qedaqsdtdemrVJIkU1dg")
      .setOAuthConsumerSecret("TudeMgXgh37Ivq173SNWnRIhI")
      .setOAuthAccessToken("1385541-ueSEFeFgJ8vUpfy6LBv6")
      .setOAuthAccessTokenSecret("G2FXeXYLSHI7X1VdMsS2e");

    TwitterFactory factory =
        new TwitterFactory(builder.build());
    twitter = factory.getInstance();
}

// Button click listeners

public void onTweetButtonClick(View view) {
  new MyAsyncTaskTweet().execute
      (editTextTweet.getText().toString());
}

public void onTimelineButtonClick(View view) {
  new MyAsyncTaskTimeline().execute
      (editTextUsername.getText().toString());
}

// Count characters in the Tweet field

class MyTextWatcher implements TextWatcher {

  @Override
  public void afterTextChanged(Editable s) {
    textViewCountChars.setText
        ("" + editTextTweet.getText().length());
  }

  @Override
  public void beforeTextChanged
    (CharSequence s, int start, int count, int after) {
  }

  @Override
  public void onTextChanged
    (CharSequence s, int start, int before, int count) {
  }

}

// The AsyncTask classes

public class MyAsyncTaskTweet
    extends AsyncTask<String, Void, String> {
```

Book IV
Chapter 4

An Android Social
Media App

(continued)

Listing 4-4 *(continued)*

```java
    @Override
    protected String doInBackground(String. . . tweet) {
      String result = "";

      try {

        twitter.updateStatus(tweet[0]);
        result =
            getResources().getString(R.string.success);

      } catch (TwitterException twitterException) {
        result = getResources().
            getString(R.string.twitter_failure);
      } catch (Exception e) {
        result = getResources().
            getString(R.string.general_failure);
      }

      return result;
    }


    @Override
    protected void onPostExecute(String result) {
      editTextTweet.setHint(result);
      editTextTweet.setText("");
    }
  }

public class MyAsyncTaskTimeline
    extends AsyncTask<String, Void, String> {

    @Override
    protected String doInBackground(String. . . username) {
      String result = new String("");

      List<twitter4j.Status> statuses = null;

      try {

        statuses = twitter.getUserTimeline(username[0]);

      } catch (TwitterException twitterException) {
        result = getResources().
            getString(R.string.twitter_failure);
      } catch (Exception e) {
        result = getResources().
            getString(R.string.general_failure);
      }

      for (twitter4j.Status status : statuses) {

        result += status.getText();
        result += "\n";
      }
      return result;
    }
```

```
@Override
protected void onPostExecute(String result) {
  editTextUsername.setText("");
  textViewTimeline.setText(result);
  }
 }
}
```

 Twitter's network protocols require that the device that runs this chapter's app is set to the correct time. I don't know how correct the "correct time" has to be, but I've had lots of trouble running the app on emulators. Either my emulator is set to get the time automatically from the network (and it gets the time incorrectly) or I set the time manually and the *seconds* part of the time isn't close enough. One way or another, the error message that comes back from Twitter (usually specifying a null authentication challenge) isn't helpful. So I avoid lots of hassle by avoiding emulators whenever I test this code. Rather than run an emulator, I set my phone or tablet to get the network time automatically. Then I run this chapter's app on that phone or tablet. I recommend that you do the same.

When you run the app, you see two areas. One area contains a Tweet button; the other area contains a Timeline button, as shown in Figure 4-4.

**Book IV
Chapter 4**

**An Android Social
Media App**

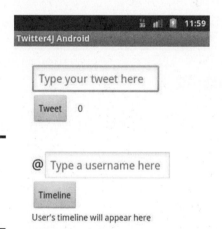

Figure 4-4:
The main
activity in
its pristine
state.

In Figure 4-4, the text in both text fields is light gray. This happens because I use `android:hint` attributes in Listing 4-2. A *hint* is a bunch of characters that appear only when a text field is otherwise empty. When the user clicks inside the text field, or types any text inside the text field, the hint disappears.

Type a tweet into the text field on top; then press the Tweet button, as shown in Figure 4-5. If your attempt to tweet is successful, the message Success! replaces the tweet in the text field, as shown in Figure 4-6. If, for one reason or another, your tweet can't be posted, a message such as "Failed to tweet" replaces the tweet in the text field, as shown in Figure 4-7.

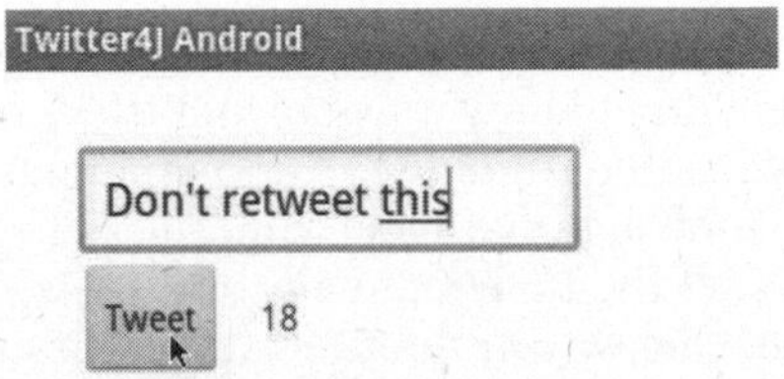

Figure 4-5:
The user types a tweet.

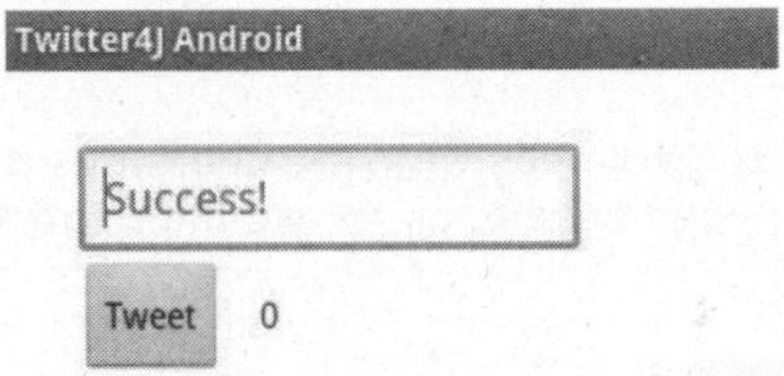

Figure 4-6:
The app indicates a successful tweet.

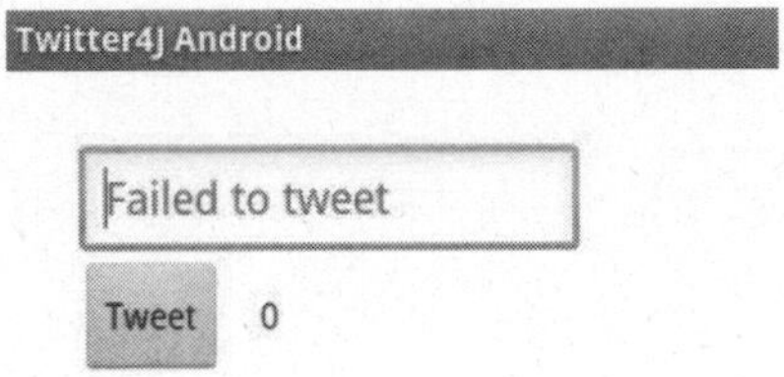

Figure 4-7:
The app brings bad tidings to the user.

Next, type a username in the lower text field and click Timeline. If all goes well, a list of the user's most recent tweets appears below the Timeline button, as shown in Figure 4-8. You can scroll the list to see more of the user's tweets.

The onCreate method

The `onCreate` method in Listing 4-4 makes a `MyTextWatcher` instance to listen for changes in the field where the user types a tweet. Android notifies

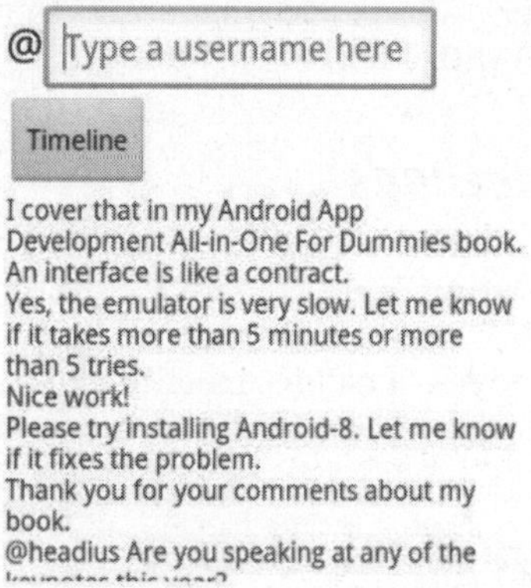

I cover that in my Android App
Development All-in-One For Dummies book.
An interface is like a contract.
Yes, the emulator is very slow. Let me know
if it takes more than 5 minutes or more
than 5 tries.
Nice work!
Please try installing Android-8. Let me know
if it fixes the problem.
Thank you for your comments about my
book.
@headius Are you speaking at any of the
keynotes this year?

Figure 4-8:
A user's
timeline.

the `MyTextWatcher` instance whenever the user types characters in (or deletes characters from) the app's `editTextTweet` field. Later in Listing 4-4, the actual `TextChangedListener` class's `afterTextChanged` method counts the number of characters in the `editTextTweet` field. The method displays the count in the tiny `textViewCountChars` field. (With the advent of Twitter, the number 140 has become quite important.)

This chapter's app doesn't do anything special if a user types more than 140 characters into the `editTextTweet` field. In a real-life app, I'd add code to handle 141 characters gracefully, but when I create sample apps, I like to keep the code as uncluttered as possible.

Android actually notifies the `MyTextWatcher` instance three times for each text change in the `editTextTweet` field — once before changing the text, once during the change of the text, and once after changing the text. In Listing 4-4, I don't make `MyTextWatcher` execute any statements before or during the changing of the text. In `MyTextWatcher`, the only method whose body contains statements is the `afterTextChanged` method. Even so, in order to implement Android's `TextWatcher` interface, the `MyTextWatcher` class must provide bodies for the `beforeTextChanged` and the `onTextChanged` methods.

Also, in the `onCreate` method, the call to `setMovementMethod(new ScrollingMovementMethod())` permits scrolling on the list of items in a user's timeline.

For another way to make things scroll on the user's screen, visit Chapter 1 in this minibook.

Book IV
Chapter 4

An Android Social
Media App

The last several lines in the `onCreate` method set up the `Twitter` object for communicating with Twitter's server. To read about that, refer to this chapter's "How to Talk to the Twitter Server" section.

The button listener methods

Listing 4-2 describes two buttons, each with its own `onClick` method. I declare the two methods in Listing 4-4 — the `onTweetButtonClick` method and the `onTimelineButtonClick` method. Each of the methods has a single statement in its body — a call to execute a newly constructed `AsyncTask` of some kind. Believe me, this is where the fun begins!

My Twitter app's AsyncTask classes

In Chapter 3 of this minibook, I describe Android's `AsyncTask`. An `AsyncTask` is what you use when something takes too much time during the run of your app. For example, the user requests a web page. Who knows how long it takes to fetch the page? The service that hosts the web page might be experiencing high volume. Or the user might be on a train passing through a tunnel. All kinds of things might slow down the page's retrieval. And during this retrieval, the user might want to click buttons, scroll a document, or do something else that demands a response from your app.

You can't stop the show while your app waits for a web page, fetches a Twitter timeline, or updates the user's Twitter status. That's why you code the network request inside an `AsyncTask`.

Android's `AsyncTask` is versatile enough to deal with all types of values. In fact, the documentation defines an `AsyncTask` this way:

```
android.os.AsyncTask<Params,Progress,Result>
```

The definition has three generic type placeholders — `Params`, `Progress`, and `Result`. When you create your own `AsyncTask`, you "fill in the blanks" by specifying actual types in place of `Params`, `Progress`, and `Result`. Listing 4-4 contains two `AsyncTask` classes — one to post the user's tweet, and another to get a Twitter user's timeline. This gives you two opportunities to specify `Params`, `Progress`, and `Result` types. (Don't you love the way I call them "opportunities"?)

Posting a new tweet

To add a tweet on behalf of the user, you grab a `Twitter` object (the instance that you made with `factory.getInstance()`), and you call the instance's `updateStatus` method. You don't want this network request to interrupt the flow of your main activity, so you put the request inside an `AsyncTask`. In Listing 4-4, the task's name is `MyAsyncTaskTweet`. The task's three generic types are as follows: `String`, `Void`, and `String`:

```
public class MyAsyncTaskTweet
            extends AsyncTask<String, Void, String> {
```

✦ **The first type (`String`) represents a 140-character tweet.**

The code

```
execute(editTextTweet.getText().toString())
```

grabs a string of characters from one of the activity's text fields and passes that string to `MyAsyncTaskTweet`. Inside `MyAsyncTaskTweet`, the `doInBackground` method calls that string `tweet[0]` and uses that `tweet[0]` string to update the user's status.

In Listing 4-4, the parameter to the `updateStatus` method is an array element. That's because, in the `doInBackground` method's header, `tweet` is a varargs parameter. The word *varargs* means "variable number of arguments." You can pass as many values to `doInBackground` as you want. In the body of the method, you treat `tweet` as though it's an ordinary array. The first `tweet` value is `tweet[0]`. If there were a second `tweet` value, it would be `tweet[1]`, and so on.

✦ **The second type (`Void`) stands for a value (or values) that mark the background thread's progress in completing its work.**

This chapter's example has no progress bar, nor a progress indicator of any kind. So in Listing 4-4, the second type name is `Void`.

In Java, the `Void` class is a wrapper class for the void value. Put that in your black hole of nothingness!

✦ **The third type (`String`) stands for a phrase such as Success! or Failed to tweet.**

The `doInBackground` method finds the string associated with either `R.string.success`, `R.string.twitter_failure`, or `R.string.general_failure` and returns this string as its result. Then the `onPostExecute` method displays this string in the screen's `editTextTweet` field.

Figure 4-9 summarizes the way generic type names influence the methods' types in Listing 4-4, and Figure 4-10 summarizes how values move from one place to another in the `MyAsyncTaskTweet` class of Listing 4-4.

```
new MyAsyncTaskTweet().execute(editTextTweet.getText().toString())


public class MyAsyncTaskTweet extends AsyncTask<String, Void, String> {

    @override
    protected String doInBackground(String... tweet) {
      String result = "";

      try {
        twitter.updateStatus(tweet[0]);
        result =
          getResources().getString(R.string.success);
      } catch (TwitterException twitterException) {
        result = getResources().
           getString(R.string.twitter_failure);
      } catch (Exception e) {
        result = getResources().
           getString(R.string.general_failure);
      }
      return result;
    }

    @override
    protected void onPostExecute(String result) {
      editTextTweet.setHint(result);
      editTextTweet.setText("");
    }
}
```

Figure 4-9:
The use
of types in
MyAsync
TaskTweet.

Getting a user's timeline

If you've seen one AsyncTask, you've seen 'em all! In Listing 4-4, the
MyAsyncTaskTimeline class is almost identical to the MyAsyncTask
Tweet. The only differences are as follows:

✦ In MyAsyncTaskTweet, the parameter passed to doInBackground is
  treated as a tweet. But in MyAsyncTaskTimeline, the parameter passed
  to doInBackground is a username. The code passes this username to
  the getUserTimeline method.

✦ In MyAsyncTaskTweet, the value returned from doInBackground is
  a success or failure message. But in MyAsyncTaskTimeline, the value
  returned from doInBackground is a string full of tweets (a timeline).

In Listing 4-4, the code to fetch a user's timeline looks something like this:

```
List<twitter4j.Status> statuses = null;

statuses = twitter.getUserTimeline(username[0]);
```

```
new MyAsyncTaskTweet().execute(editTextTweet.getText().toString())


public class MyAsyncTaskTweet extends AsyncTask<String, Void, String> {

    @override
    protected String doInBackground(String... tweet) {
      String result = "";

      try {
        twitter.updateStatus(tweet[0]);
        result =
           getResources().getString(R.string.success);
      } catch (TwitterException twitterException) {
        result = getResources().
            getString(R.string.twitter_failure);
      } catch (Exception e) {
        result = getResources().
            getString(R.string.general_failure);
      }
      return result;
    }

    @override
    protected void onPostExecute(String result) {
      editTextTweet.setHint(result);
      editTextTweet.setText("");
    }
}
```

Figure 4-10:
The flow of
values in
MyAsync
TaskTweet.

Book IV
Chapter 4

An Android Social
Media App

A fellow named Yusuke Yamamoto developed Twitter4J (or at least, Yusuke Yamamoto was the Twitter4J project leader), and at some point, Mr. Yamamoto decided that the getUserTimeline method returns a collection of twitter4J.Status objects. (Each twitter4J.Status instance contains one tweet.) So, to honor the contract set by calling the getUserTimeline method, the code in Listing 4-4 declares statuses to be a collection of twitter4J.Status objects.

A few lines later in the code, an enhanced for statement steps through the collection of statuses values and appends each value's text to a big result string. The loop adds "\n" (Java's go-to-the-next-line character) after each tweet for good measure. In the onPostExecute method, the code displays the big result string in the screen's textViewTimeline field.

In Listing 4-4, in the second doInBackground method, I use the fully qualified name twitter4j.Status. I do this to distinguish the twitter4J.Status class from Android's own AsyncTask.Status class (an inner class of the AsyncTask class).

In Java, an inner class is a class declared inside of another class. For more insight into Java's inner classes, refer to Chapter 4 in Book II.

An `AsyncTask` can be fairly complicated. But when you compare Android's `AsyncTask` to the do-it-yourself threading alternatives, the `AsyncTask` idea isn't bad at all. In fact, when you get a little practice and create a few of your own `AsyncTask` classes, you get used to thinking that way. The whole business starts to feel quite natural.

Chapter 5: Hungry Burds: A Simple Android Game

In This Chapter

✔ **Coding an Android game**

✔ **Using Android animation**

✔ **Creating random play**

What started as a simple pun involving the author's last name has turned into this minibook's Chapter 5 — the most self-indulgent writing in the history of technical publishing.

The scene takes place in south Philadelphia in the early part of the twentieth century. My father (then a child) sees his father (my grandfather) handling an envelope. The envelope has just arrived from the old country. My grandmother grabs the envelope out of my grandfather's hands. The look on her face is one of superiority. "I open the letters around here," she says with her eyes.

While my grandmother opens the letter, my father glances at the envelope. The last name on the envelope is written in Cyrillic characters, so my father can't read it. But he notices a short last name in the envelope's address. Whatever the characters are, they're more likely to be a short name like Burd than a longer name like Burdinsky or Burdstakovich.

The Russian word for bird is *ptitsa*, so there's no etymological connection between my last name and our avian friends. But as I grew up, I would often hear kids yell "Burd is the word" or "Hey, Burdman" from across the street. Today, my one-person Burd Brain Consulting firm takes in a small amount of change every year.

Introducing the Hungry Burds Game

When the game begins, the screen is blank. Then, for a random amount of time (averaging one second), a Burd fades into view, as shown in Figure 5-1.

Figure 5-1:
A Burd
fades into
view.

If the user does nothing, the Burd disappears after fading into full view. But if the user touches the Burd before it disappears, the Burd gets a cheeseburger and remains onscreen, as shown in Figure 5-2.

Figure 5-2:
You've fed
this Burd.

After ten Burds have faded in (and the unfed ones have disappeared), the screen displays a text view, showing the number of fed Burds in the current run of the game. The text view also shows the high score for all runs of the game, as shown in Figure 5-3.

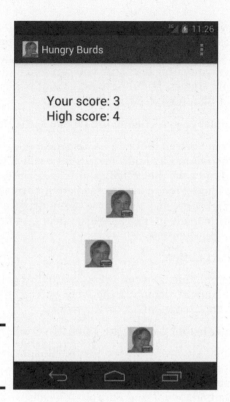

Figure 5-3:
The game ends.

For many apps, timing isn't vitally important: For them, a consistently slow response is annoying but not disabling. But for a game like Hungry Burds, timing makes a big difference. Running Hungry Burds on a slow emulator feels more like a waiting game than an action game. If your emulator is slow, run the app on a real-life device.

The Hungry Burds Java code is about 140 lines long. (Compare this with one of the Android game developer's books that I bought. In that book, the simplest example has 2,300 lines of Java code.) To keep the Hungry Burds code from consuming dozens of pages, I've omitted some features that you might see in a more realistically engineered game.

✦ **The Hungry Burds game doesn't access data over a network.**

The game's leaderboard doesn't tell you how well you did compared with your friends or with other players around the world. The leaderboard applies to only one device — the one you're using to play the game.

Google Play Game Services is a collection of network-enabled tools to help you add leaderboards, achievements, and multiplayer features to your game app. Game Services belongs to a category of things called *back-end services*. When you publish an app, you can sign up for one or more of these back-end services. For information about publishing and back-end services, visit Chapter 1 in Book VI.

✦ **The game restarts whenever you change the device's orientation.**

If you tilt the device from Portrait mode to Landscape mode, or from Landscape mode to Portrait mode, Android calls the main activity's lifecycle methods. Android calls the activity's `onPause`, `onStop`, and `onDestroy` methods. Then it reconstitutes the activity by calling the activity's `onCreate`, `onStart`, and `onResume` methods. As a result, whatever progress you've made in the game disappears, and the game starts itself over again from scratch.

✦ **The game has no Restart button.**

To play the game a second time, you can press Android's Back button and then touch the game's launcher icon. Alternatively, you can tilt the device from Portrait mode to Landscape mode, or vice versa.

✦ **The screen measurements that control the game are crude.**

Creating a visual app that involves drawing, custom images, or motion of any kind involves some math. You need math to make measurements, estimate distances, detect collisions, and complete other tasks. To do the math, you produce numbers by making Android API calls, and you use the results of your calculations in Android API library calls.

To help me cut quickly to the chase, my Hungry Burds game does only a minimal amount of math, and it makes only the API calls I believe to be absolutely necessary. As a result, some items on the screen don't always look their best. (This happens particularly when the device is in Landscape mode.)

✦ **The game has no settings.**

The number of Burds displayed, the average time of each Burd's display, and the minimal length of time for each Burd's display are all hard-coded in the game's Java file. In the code, these constants are `NUMBER_OF_BURDS`, `AVERAGE_SHOW_TIME`, and `MINIMUM_SHOW_TIME`. As a developer, you can change the values in the code and reinstall the game. But the ordinary player can't change these numbers.

✦ **The game isn't challenging with the default** `NUMBER_OF_BURDS`, `AVERAGE_SHOW_TIME`, **and** `MINIMUM_SHOW_TIME` **values.**

I admit it: On this front, I'm at a distinct disadvantage. I'm a lousy game player. I remember competing in video games against my kids when they were young. I lost every time. At first it was embarrassing; in the end, it was ridiculous. I could never avoid being shot, eaten, or otherwise squashed by my young opponents' avatars.

I don't presume to know what values of NUMBER_OF_BURDS, AVERAGE_ SHOW_TIME, and MINIMUM_SHOW_TIME are right for you. And if no values are right for you (and the game isn't fun to play no matter which values you have), don't despair. I've created Hungry Burds as a teaching tool, not as a replacement for Super Mario.

The Project's Files

The project's build.grade file is nothing special. The only thing you have to watch for is minSdkVersion. The minSdkVersion has to be 13 or higher. That's because the Java code calls the Display class's getSize method, and that method isn't available in Android API levels below 13.

If you have to get a layout's measurements in an app that runs in API Level 12 or lower, check the documentation for Android's ViewTreeObserver. OnPreDrawListener class.

The project's activity_main.xml file is almost empty, as shown in Listing 5-1. I put a TextView somewhere on the screen so that, at the end of each game, I can display the most recent statistics. I also add an android:id attribute to the RelativeLayout element. Using that android:id element, I can refer to the screen's layout in the Java code.

Listing 5-1: The Main Activity's Layout File

```
<RelativeLayout xmlns:android=
    "http://schemas.android.com/apk/res/android"
  xmlns:tools="http://schemas.android.com/tools"
  android:id="@+id/relativeLayout"
  android:layout_width="match_parent"
  android:layout_height="match_parent"
  android:paddingBottom=
      "@dimen/activity_vertical_margin"
  android:paddingLeft=
      "@dimen/activity_horizontal_margin"
  android:paddingRight=
      "@dimen/activity_horizontal_margin"
  android:paddingTop=
      "@dimen/activity_vertical_margin"
  tools:context=".MainActivity" >

<TextView
  android:id="@+id/textView1"
  android:layout_width="wrap_content"
  android:layout_height="wrap_content"
```

(continued)

Book IV
Chapter 5

Hungry Burds:
A Simple Android
Game

Listing 5-1 *(continued)*

```
android:layout_alignParentLeft="true"
android:layout_alignParentTop="true"
android:layout_marginLeft="42dp"
android:layout_marginTop="34dp"
android:text="@string/nothing"
android:textAppearance=
    "?android:attr/textAppearanceLarge" />

</RelativeLayout>
```

In the `res` directory of my Hungry Burds project, I have ten `.png` files —
two files each for several of Android's generalized screen densities. (See
Figure 5-4.)

For a look at Android screen densities, see Chapter 1 in this minibook.

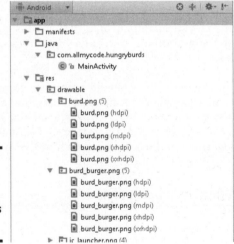

Figure 5-4:
Images
in the
project's res
directory.

Each `burd.png` file is a picture of me. Each `burd_burger.png` file is a
picture of me with a cheeseburger. When Android runs the game, Android
checks the device's specs and decides, on the spot, which of the five screen
densities to use.

The Main Activity

The Hungry Burds game has only one activity: the app's main activity. So
you can digest the game's Java code in its entirety in one big gulp. To make
this gulp palatable, I start with an outline of the activity's code. The outline

is in Listing 5-2. (If outlines don't work for you, and you want to see the code in its entirety, see Listing 5-3.)

Listing 5-2:   An Outline of the App's Java Code

```java
package com.allmycode.hungryburds;

public class MainActivity extends Activity
    implements OnClickListener, AnimationListener {

  // Declare fields

  /* Activity methods */

  @Override
  public void onCreate(Bundle savedInstanceState) {
    super.onCreate(savedInstanceState);
    setContentView(R.layout.activity_main);

    // Find layout elements

    // Get the size of the device's screen
  }

  @Override
  public void onResume() {
    showABurd();
  }

  /* Game methods */

  void showABurd() {
    // Add a Burd in some random place
    // At first, the Burd is invisible

    // Create an AlphaAnimation to make the Burd
    // fade in (from invisible to fully visible).
    burd.startAnimation(animation);
  }

  private void showScores() {
    // Set up SharedPreferences to deal with high scores
    // Get high score from SharedPreferences
    // Display high score and this run's score
  }

  /* OnClickListener method */

  public void onClick(View view) {
    countClicked++;
    // Change the image to a Burd with a cheeseburger
  }
```

**Book IV
Chapter 5**

**Hungry Burds:
A Simple Android
Game**

(continued)

Listing 5-2 *(continued)*

```
/* AnimationListener methods */

public void onAnimationEnd(Animation animation) {
  if (++countShown < NUMBER_OF_BURDS) {
    showABurd(); // Again!
  } else {
    showScores();
  }
}

}
```

The heart of the Hungry Burds code is the code's game loop, as shown in the following example:

```
public void onResume() {
  showABurd();
}

void showABurd() {
  // Add a Burd in some random place.
  // At first, the Burd is invisible . . .

  burd.setVisibility(View.INVISIBLE);

  // . . . but the animation will make the
  // Burd visible.

  AlphaAnimation animation =
      new AlphaAnimation(0.0F, 1.0F);
  animation.setDuration(duration);
  animation.setAnimationListener(this);
  burd.startAnimation(animation);
}

public void onAnimationEnd(Animation animation) {
  if (++countShown < NUMBER_OF_BURDS) {
    showABurd(); // Again!
  } else {
    showScores();
  }
}
```

When Android executes the onResume method, the code calls the showABurd method. The showABurd method does what its name suggests, by animating an image from alpha level 0 to alpha level 1. (Alpha level 0 is fully transparent; alpha level 1 is fully opaque.)

In the onCreate method, you put code that runs when the activity comes into existence. In contrast, in the onResume method, you put code that runs when the user begins interacting with the activity. The user isn't aware of the difference because the app starts running so quickly. But for you, the developer, the distinction between an app's coming into existence and starting to interact is important. In Listings 5-2 and 5-3, the onCreate method contains code to set the layout of the activity, assign variable names to screen widgets, measure the screen size, and prepare for storing high scores. The onResume method is different. With the onResume method, the user is about to touch the device's screen. So in Listings 5-2 and 5-3, the onResume method displays something for the user to touch: the first of several hungry Burds.

When the animation ends, the onAnimationEnd method checks the number of Burds that have already been displayed. If the number is less than ten, the onAnimationEnd method calls showABurd again, and the game loop continues.

By default, a Burd returns to being invisible when the animation ends. But the main activity implements OnClickListener, and when the user touches a Burd, the class's onClick method makes the Burd permanently visible, as shown in the following snippet:

```
public void onClick(View view) {
  countClicked++;
  ((ImageView) view).setImageResource
                    (R.drawable.burd_burger);
  view.setVisibility(View.VISIBLE);
}
```

The code, all the code, and nothing but the code

Following the basic outline of the game's code in the previous section, Listing 5-3 contains the entire text of the game's MainActivity.java file.

Listing 5-3:   The App's Java Code

```
package com.allmycode.hungryburds;

import java.util.Random;

import android.app.Activity;
import android.content.SharedPreferences;
import android.graphics.Point;
import android.os.Bundle;
import android.view.Display;
import android.view.Menu;
import android.view.View;
import android.view.View.OnClickListener;
import android.view.animation.AlphaAnimation;
import android.view.animation.Animation;
import android.view.animation.Animation.AnimationListener;
import android.widget.ImageView;
import android.widget.RelativeLayout;
import android.widget.RelativeLayout.LayoutParams;
import android.widget.TextView;
```

(continued)

Listing 5-3 *(continued)*

```java
public class MainActivity extends Activity
    implements OnClickListener, AnimationListener {

  final int NUMBER_OF_BURDS = 10;
  final long AVERAGE_SHOW_TIME = 1000L;
  final long MINIMUM_SHOW_TIME = 500L;
  TextView textView;
  int countShown = 0, countClicked = 0;
  Random random = new Random();

  RelativeLayout relativeLayout;
  int displayWidth, displayHeight;

  /* Activity methods */

  @Override
  public void onCreate(Bundle savedInstanceState) {
    super.onCreate(savedInstanceState);
    setContentView(R.layout.activity_main);

    textView = (TextView) findViewById(R.id.textView1);
    relativeLayout = (RelativeLayout)
        findViewById(R.id.relativeLayout);

    Display display =
        getWindowManager().getDefaultDisplay();
    Point size = new Point();
    display.getSize(size);
    displayWidth = size.x;
    displayHeight = size.y;
  }

  @Override
  public boolean onCreateOptionsMenu(Menu menu) {
    getMenuInflater().inflate(R.menu.main, menu);
    return true;
  }

  @Override
  public void onResume() {
    super.onResume();
    countClicked = countShown = 0;
    textView.setText(R.string.nothing);
    showABurd();
  }

  /* Game methods */

  void showABurd() {
    long duration =
        random.nextInt((int) AVERAGE_SHOW_TIME)
        + MINIMUM_SHOW_TIME;

    LayoutParams params = new LayoutParams
                    (LayoutParams.WRAP_CONTENT,
                     LayoutParams.WRAP_CONTENT);
```

```
    params.leftMargin =
        random.nextInt(displayWidth) * 7 / 8;
    params.topMargin =
        random.nextInt(displayHeight) * 4 / 5;

    ImageView burd = new ImageView(this);
    burd.setOnClickListener(this);
    burd.setLayoutParams(params);
    burd.setImageResource(R.drawable.burd);
    burd.setVisibility(View.INVISIBLE);

    relativeLayout.addView(burd);

    AlphaAnimation animation =
        new AlphaAnimation(0.0F, 1.0F);
    animation.setDuration(duration);
    animation.setAnimationListener(this);
    burd.startAnimation(animation);
  }

  private void showScores() {
    SharedPreferences prefs =
        getPreferences(MODE_PRIVATE);
    int highScore = prefs.getInt("highScore", 0);

    if (countClicked > highScore) {
      highScore = countClicked;
      SharedPreferences.Editor editor = prefs.edit();
      editor.putInt("highScore", highScore);
      editor.commit();
    }

    textView.setText("Your score: " + countClicked +
                     "\nHigh score: " + highScore);
  }

  /* OnClickListener method */

  public void onClick(View view) {
    countClicked++;
    ((ImageView) view).setImageResource
                         (R.drawable.burd_burger);
    view.setVisibility(View.VISIBLE);
  }

  /* AnimationListener methods */

  public void onAnimationEnd(Animation animation) {
    if (++countShown < NUMBER_OF_BURDS) {
      showABurd();
    } else {
      showScores();
    }
  }

  public void onAnimationRepeat(Animation arg0) {
  }

  public void onAnimationStart(Animation arg0) {
  }
}
```

Random

A typical game involves random choices. (You don't want Burds to appear in the same places every time you play the game.) Truly random values are difficult to generate. But an instance of Java's `Random` class creates what appear to be random values (*pseudorandom* values) in ways that the programmer can help determine.

For example, a `Random` object's `nextDouble` method returns a `double` value between 0.0 and 1.0 (with 0.0 being possible but 1.0 being impossible). The Hungry Burds code uses a `Random` object's `nextInt` method. A call to `nextInt(10)` returns an `int` value from 0 to 9.

If `displayWidth` is 720 (which stands for 720 pixels), the call to `random.nextInt(displayWidth)` in Listing 5-3 returns a value from 0 to 719. And because `AVERAGE_SHOW_TIME` is the `long` value `1000L`, the expression `random.nextInt((int) AVERAGE_SHOW_TIME)` stands for a value from 0 to 999. (The casting to `int` helps fulfill the promise that the `nextInt` method's parameter is an `int`, not a `long` value.) By adding back `MINIMUM_SHOW_TIME` (refer to Listing 5-3), I make `duration` be a number between 500 and 1499. A Burd takes between 500 and 1499 milliseconds to fade into view.

Measuring the display

Android's `Display` object stores information about a device's display. How complicated can that be? You can measure the screen size with a ruler, and you can determine a device's resolution by reading the specs in the user manual.

Of course, Android programs don't have opposable thumbs, so they can't use plastic rulers. And a layout's characteristics can change depending on several runtime factors, including the device's orientation (portrait or landscape) and the amount of screen space reserved for Android's notification bar and buttons. If you don't play your cards right, you can easily call methods that prematurely report a display's width and height as zero values.

Fortunately, the `getSize` method in Android API level 13 and higher gives you some correct answers in an activity's `onCreate` method. So, here and there in Listing 5-3, you find the following code:

```
public class MainActivity extends Activity {

  int displayWidth, displayHeight;

  public void onCreate(Bundle savedInstanceState) {

    Display display =
        getWindowManager().getDefaultDisplay();
    Point size = new Point();
    display.getSize(size);
```

```
      displayWidth = size.x;
      displayHeight = size.y;

  }

  void showABurd() {

    LayoutParams params;
    params = new LayoutParams(LayoutParams.WRAP_CONTENT,
                              LayoutParams.WRAP_CONTENT);
    params.leftMargin =
        random.nextInt(displayWidth) * 7 / 8;
    params.topMargin =
        random.nextInt(displayHeight) * 4 / 5;

  }
```

An instance of Android's `Point` class is basically an object with two components: an x component and a y component. In the Hungry Burds code, a call to `getWindowManager().getDefaultDisplay()` retrieves the device's display. The resulting display's `getSize` method takes an instance of the `Point` class and fills its x and y fields. The x field's value is the display's width, and the y field's value is the display's height, as shown in Figure 5-5.

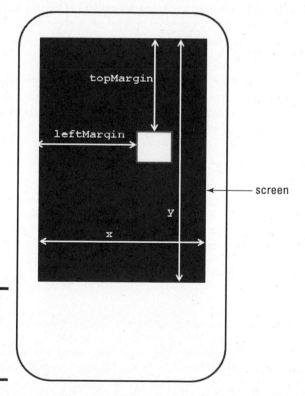

Figure 5-5:
Measuring
distances
on the
screen.

A LayoutParams object stores information about the way a widget should appear as part of an activity's layout. (Each kind of layout has its own LayoutParams inner class, and the code in Listing 5-3 imports the RelativeLayout.LayoutParams inner class.) A LayoutParams instance has a life of its own, apart from any widget whose appearance the instance describes. In Listing 5-3, I construct a new LayoutParams instance before applying the instance to any particular widget. Later in the code, I call

```
burd.setLayoutParams(params);
```

to apply the new LayoutParams instance to one of the Burds.

A LayoutParams instance's leftMargin field stores the number of pixels between the left edge of the display and the left edge of the widget. Similarly, a LayoutParams instance's topMargin field stores the number of pixels between the top edge of the display and the top edge of the widget. (Refer to Figure 5-5.)

In Listing 5-3, I use random values to position a new Burd. A Burd's left edge is no farther than ⅞ths of the way across the screen, and the Burd's top edge is no lower than ⅘ of the way down the screen. If you don't multiply the screen's width by ⅞ (or some such fraction), an entire Burd can be positioned beyond the right edge of the screen. The user sees nothing while the Burd comes and goes. The same kind of thing can happen if you don't multiply the screen's height by ⅘.

The fractions ⅞ and ⅘, which I use to determine each widget's position, are crude guesstimates of a portrait screen's requirements. A more refined app would carefully measure the available turf and calculate the optimally sized region for positioning new Burds.

Constructing a Burd

Android's ImageView class represents objects that contain images. Normally, you put an image file (a .png file, a .jpg file, or a .gif file) in one of your project's res/drawable directories, and a call to the ImageView object's setImageResource method associates the ImageView object with the image file. In Listing 5-3, the following lines fulfill this role:

```
ImageView burd = new ImageView(this);

burd.setImageResource(R.drawable.burd);
```

Because of the R.drawable.burd parameter, Android looks in the project's res/drawable directories for files named burd.png, burd.jpg, or burd.gif. (Refer to Figure 5-4.) Android selects the file whose resolution best suits the device and displays that file's image on the ImageView object.

The statement

```
burd.setVisibility(View.INVISIBLE);
```

makes the Burd be completely transparent. The next statement

```
relativeLayout.addView(burd);
```

normally makes a widget appear on the user's screen. But with the `View.INVISIBLE` property, the Burd doesn't show up. It's not until I start the code's fade-in animation that the user begins seeing a Burd on the screen.

Android has two kinds of animation: view animation and property animation. The Hungry Burds code uses view animation. An object's `visibility` property doesn't change when a view animation makes the object fade in or fade out. In this chapter's example, a Burd starts off with `View.INVISIBLE`. A fade-in animation makes the Burd appear slowly on the screen. But when the animation finishes, the Burd's `visibility` field still contains the original `View.INVISIBLE` value. So normally, when the animation ends, the Burd simply disappears.

Listing 5-3 contains the statement

```
burd.setOnClickListener(this);
```

So, when the user clicks on a Burd, Android calls the `onClick` method in Listing 5-3. The `onClick` method's `view` parameter represents the `ImageView` object that the user clicked. In the body of the `onClick` method, the statement

```
((ImageView) view).setImageResource
                    (R.drawable.burd_burger);
```

assures Java that `view` is indeed an `ImageView` instance and changes the picture on the face of that instance from a hungry author to a well-fed author. The `onClick` method also sets the `ImageView` instance's visibility to `View.VISIBLE`. That way, when this Burd's animation ends, the happy Burd remains visible on the user's screen.

Android animation

Android has two types of animation:

✦ **View animation:** An older system in which you animate with either tweening or frame-by-frame animation, as described in this list:

   • *Tweening:* You tell Android how an object should look initially and how the object should look eventually. You also tell Android how to change from the initial appearance to the eventual appearance. (Is

Book IV
Chapter 5

Hungry Burds:
A Simple Android
Game

the change gradual or sudden? If the object moves, does it move in a straight line or in a curve of some sort? Will it bounce a bit when it reaches the end of its path?)

With tweening, Android considers all your requirements and figures out exactly how the object looks *between* the start and the finish of the object's animation.

- *Frame-by-frame animation:* You provide several snapshots of the object along its path. Android displays these snapshots in rapid succession, one after another, giving the appearance of movement or of another change in the object's appearance.

  Movie cartoons are the classic example of frame-by-frame animation, even though, in modern moviemaking, graphics specialists use tweening to create sequences of frames.

✦ **Property animation:** A newer system (introduced in Android 3.0, API Level 11) in which you can modify any property of an object over a period of time.

With property animation, you can change anything about any kind of object, whether the object appears on the device's screen or not. For example, you can increase an `earth` object's average temperature from 15° Celsius to 18° Celsius over a period of ten minutes. Rather than display the `earth` object, you can watch the way average temperature affects water levels and plant life, for example.

Unlike view animation, the use of property animation changes the value stored in an object's field. For example, you can use property animation to change a widget from being invisible to being visible. When the property animation finishes, the widget remains visible.

The Hungry Burds code uses view animation, which includes these specialized animation classes:

✦ `AlphaAnimation`: Fades into view or fades out of view.

✦ `RotateAnimation`: Turns around.

✦ `ScaleAnimation`: Changes size.

✦ `TranslateAnimation`: Moves from one place to another.

In particular, the Hungry Burds code uses `AlphaAnimation`.

The statement

```
AlphaAnimation animation =
    new AlphaAnimation(0.0F, 1.0F);
```

creates a fade-in / fade-out animation. An alpha level of 0.0 indicates complete transparency, and an alpha level of 1.0 indicates complete opaqueness. (The `AlphaAnimation` constructor expects its parameters to be float values, so I plug the `float` values `0.0F` and `1.0F` into the constructor call.)

The call

```
animation.setAnimationListener(this);
```

tells Java that the code to respond to the animation's progress is in this main activity class. Indeed, the class header at the top of Listing 5-3 informs Java that the `HungryBurds` class implements the `AnimationListener` interface. And to make good on the implementation promise, Listing 5-3 contains bodies for the methods `onAnimationEnd`, `onAnimationRepeat`, and `onAnimationStart`. (Nothing happens in the `onAnimationRepeat` and `onAnimationStart` methods. That's okay.)

The `onAnimationEnd` method does what I describe earlier in this chapter: The method checks the number of Burds that have already been displayed. If the number is less than ten, the `onAnimationEnd` method calls `showABurd` again, and the game loop continues.

Shared preferences

When a user finishes a game of Hungry Burds, the app displays the score for the current game and the high score for all games. (Refer to Figure 5-3.) The high-score display applies to only one device — the device that's running the current game. To remember the high score from one run to another, I use Android's Shared Preferences feature. For a careful look at Android's Shared Preferences feature, refer to Chapter 3 in Book III.

Chapter 6: Going Native

In This Chapter

✔ **Connecting C code to Java code**

✔ **Creating an Android app with native code**

Sometimes, you have to get your hands dirty. You have to pop the hood and figure out why smoke comes out of your car. You have to bake a cake for that special friend who's allergic to the ingredients in store-bought cakes. Or, in order to build the perfect mobile app, you must bypass Android's comfortable Java coating and dig deep to find your true inner geek. You must create part of an app in the primitive, nuts-and-bolts, down-and-dirty language called C.

Book II, Chapter 2 explains how Java puts a virtual machine between your processor's hardware and a running application. Java programs don't turn directly into sets of instructions that your processor can then run. Instead, your processor runs another set of instructions; namely, a virtual machine. (Your Android device runs the Android Runtime; your laptop computer runs the Java Virtual Machine.) The virtual machine interprets a Java program's instructions and carries out these instructions on your processor's behalf.

Anyway, this added layer of software (between the Java instructions and your processor's circuits) has both benefits and drawbacks. Isolation from the hardware enhances portability and security. But the added software layer might slow down a program's execution. The layer also prevents Java from micromanaging the processor.

Imagine solving your allergic friend's problem by ordering a cake directly from a local bakery. "My friend has a wheat allergy. Can you make the cake without using any wheat products?" At a classy establishment, the baker knows how to avoid wheat gluten. But your friend is also allergic to *carrageenan with polysorbate 80,* an emulsifier found in many commercial food products. "Please don't use any carrageenan polysorbate 80," you say. And the person behind the bakery counter says, "We'll try our best. We can't check for every chemical in every ingredient that we use."

So you leave the bakery without completing the order. For the sake of your friend's health, you need complete control over the baking process. Delegating some of the work to a baker in the back room (or to a virtual machine executing instructions on behalf of your device's processor) just isn't good enough.

Another potent reason for using non-Java code is to avoid rewriting code that you already have — code written in another programming language. Imagine having a thousand-line C program that reliably computes a decent daily investment strategy. (No, I don't have such a program, in case you're wondering.) The program does lots of fancy calculations, but the program has no user-friendly interface. The code has no windows, no buttons, and nothing nice for the user to click. You want to package this program inside an Android application. The app presents choices to the user, computes today's investment strategy with its complicated formulas, and then displays details of the strategy (in a friendly, colorful way) on the user's screen.

You can try rewriting the C program in Java. But translating between two closely related languages (such as C and Java) is a virtual rat's nest. The translation is often messy and unreliable. A better plan is to write the user interface as an Android Java app and let your Java app defer to your existing C program only for the intricate investing strategy calculations. All you need is a way to exchange information between a Java program and a C program.

The Native Development Kit

The creators of Android realized that developers would want to use non-Java code. So Android has a framework that mediates between Java and other languages. As you might have guessed from this section's title, that framework is *NDK* — Android's *Native Development Kit*. With Android's NDK, you can write code that executes directly on a mobile device's processor without relying on a virtual machine to carry out the instructions.

Getting the NDK

The NDK doesn't come as part of Android's standard Software Development Kit — its *SDK*. In fact, you don't get the NDK by checking for available packages in the Android SDK Manager. The NDK is a separate archive file, available for download at `http://developer.android.com`. (If I'm lucky, the particular URL will still be `http://developer.android.com/tools/sdk/ndk` when you read this chapter.) On Windows, the NDK download is usually an `.exe` file. For Mac or Linux, the NDK download is usually a `.bin` file. The downloaded file is a self-extracting archive file. When you execute the file, your development computer extracts all the files stored in the archive.

To be more precise, the computer creates a new subdirectory of the directory containing the downloaded file. If you execute `android-ndk-r10d.exe` while it's in your `xyz` directory, you get a new `xyz/android-ndk-r10d` directory. So your first step is to move the downloaded file to a place where you want your new `android-ndk-whatever` directory to live. It hardly matters where you move the file, as long as you remember where you move it.

The NDK files don't like to be inside folders with blank spaces in their names. For example, in Windows, don't move your android-ndk-*whatever*.exe file to the C:\Program Files directory, or to any subdirectory of the C:\Program Files directory.

The way you expand the NDK download's contents depends on your development computer's operating system.

✦ **On Windows, double-click the** android-ndk-*whatever*.exe **file's icon.**

✦ **On Linux or on a Mac, do the following:**

1. **Click the Terminal button at the bottom of Android Studio's main window.**

   A Terminal window opens in the lower portion of Android Studio's main window.

2. **In the Terminal window, use the Change Directory command (cd) to navigate to the directory containing the downloaded NDK archive.**

   For example, if you moved the downloaded file to the /Users/JaneQReader directory, type

   ```
   cd /Users/JaneQReader
   ```

3. **Type the command**

   ```
   ls ndk*
   ```

   and look for the name of the downloaded NDK archive. (It's probably android ndk-r10c-darwin-x86_64.bin, or something like that.)

4. **Assuming that the downloaded file's name is** android-ndk-r10c-darwin-x86_64.bin, **type the following two commands:**

   ```
   chmod a+x android-ndk-r10c-darwin-x86_64.bin
   ./android-ndk-r10c-darwin-x86_64.bin
   ```

When you follow these steps, your computer creates an android-ndk-*something-or-other* directory and puts a few files and subfolders into the directory. By "a few files and folders," I mean approximately 50,000 files in more than 4,000 folders. The extracted files consume more than three gigabytes of space. (The expanding takes about fifteen minutes on one of my favorite computers.)

Make note of the folder containing your extracted NDK materials. In later sections, I refer to this folder as your *NDK_HOME* directory.

Book IV
Chapter 6

Going Native

Creating an Application

An NDK-enabled application is almost exactly like an ordinary Android application, except it's different! (That's a joke, by the way.) To create a simple NDK-enabled application, do the following:

1. **Use Android Studio to create a new project.**

As you create the new project, you can fill in the dialog boxes' fields any way you like, but if you want to follow along with the steps in my example, name the application `My NDK App` with the default `MainActivity`. For the package name, select `com.allmycode.myndkapp`. For the Project Location, use a subdirectory named `MyNDKApp`.

Books I and II have all the information you'd need to create an "ordinary" simple Android application.

Directory names

An IDE, such as Android Studio, shields you from having to remember where files are located on your computer. For example, you can compile code without remembering the name of the folder containing the Android SDK on your computer. Android Studio remembers that stuff for you.

In this chapter, life is a bit different. Many of the steps required to create an NDK app don't have simple point-and-click shortcuts in Android Studio. You can use Android Studio for some of your work, but for many steps, you have to type long (sometimes complicated) commands. When you type these commands, you often have to include the full pathnames of certain directories. So it helps to keep track of the locations on your hard drive where important files are stored. In particular, here's what you have to know:

✔ **The location of your project**

This is the directory on your hard drive where the project is housed. In this chapter, I call it the *PROJECT_HOME* directory. This directory's name is in the Project Location field of Android Studio's New Project dialog box. On my Mac, this directory is

```
/Users/Barry/AndroidStudioProjects/
    MyNDKApp
```

On my PC, this directory is

```
c:\Users\Barry\AndroidStudioProjects\
    MyNDKApp
```

On your computer, the *PROJECT_HOME* directory might be some other directory.

Remember that, in phrases such as "the location of your project," the word "location" is shorthand for the root of a collection of files and folders. For example, Android Studio says that your Project Location is `/Users/yourUserName/ MyNDKApp`. What this really means is that your `/Users/yourUserName/ MyNDKApp` folder has subfolders named `app` and `gradle`, and that the `app` folder has an `src` subfolder, which in turn has a `main` subfolder, which has `java` and `res` subfolders, and so on.

(Here's a well-kept secret: The Windows command line accepts forward slashes as well as backslashes for file separators.

You can even mix forward and backward slashes in a pathname. For example, in an MS-DOS command, you can write `c:/Users\yourUserName/MyNDKApp`.)

✔ The location of the Android SDK

This is the directory where the standard Android developer tools and API classes live. This directory has subdirectories named `tools`, `platform-tools`, `platforms`, `extras`, and others.

In Book I, Chapter 2, I dub this location your `ANDROID_HOME` directory. If the name of your `ANDROID_HOME` directory isn't on the tip of your tongue, you can enlist Android Studio's help in remembering it. In Android Studio's main menu, choose File ➪ Project Structure ➪ SDK Location. The full pathname of your `ANDROID_HOME` directory is in the dialog box's Android SDK Location field.

On my PC, the `ANDROID_HOME` directory is

```
C:\Users\Barry\AppData\Local\Android\
      Sdk
```

On my Mac, the `ANDROID_HOME` directory is

```
/Users/Barry/Development/sdk
```

Your own `ANDROID_HOME` directory's name might be something entirely different.

✔ The location of the Android NDK

In this chapter's "Getting the NDK" section, I call this the `NDK_HOME` directory. It has a name like `android-ndk-r10d` and contains files with names like `ndk-build`, `ndk-gdb`, and `GNUmakefile`.

---

2. **With the Designer tool, add a Plain Text item (also known as an EditText) to `activity_main.xml` (the main layout).**

The palette has two similarly named items — the Plain TextView in the Widgets category, and the Plain Text in the Text Fields category. The one you want here is the Plain Text item in the Text Fields category. (This information is true as of mid-2015. If your version of Android Studio is different, look for any `EditText` item.)

For details about adding a Plain Text view (and for some details about the next several steps) see Book II, Chapter 1, and Book III, Chapter 2.

3. **Using the Designer tool, add a button to `activity_main.xml` (the main layout).**

4. **Assign a name to the button's click event listener.**

If you're following along at home, I give the button's `onClick` property the name `onButtonClick`. (I use the Properties view to set this property.)

**Book IV
Chapter 6**

Going Native

5. **Add event listener code to your app's activity.**

I don't know about your activity, but my activity contains the following event listener code:

```
public void onButtonClick(View view) {
    Editable name = ((EditText)
                findViewById(R.id.editText)).getText();
    Toast.makeText(getApplication(),
        getString() + name, Toast.LENGTH_LONG).show();
}
```

Most of this event listener code is fairly harmless. But please remember that the names in the code must correspond to names in your project. For example, the method name (in my example, onButtonClick) must be the same as the name you assigned as the button's onClick listener in Step 4. Also, the ID editText must be same as the ID of the view that you created in Step 2.

The only unusual thing about the event listener code is the call to a method named getString. You don't declare getString the way you declare most Java methods.

6. **To your activity class (named** MainActivity **in Step 1) add the following code:**

```
public native String getString();

static {
    System.loadLibrary("my-jni-app");
}
```

With or without Android, the Java technology suite comes with *JNI* — the *Java Native Interface*. The purpose of JNI is to help Java programs communicate with code written in other programming languages. In this step's code, JNI tells your program to expect the getString method's body to be written in a language other than Java.

The first line

```
public native String getString();
```

tells Java to look for the body of getString somewhere else (outside the Java class in which the line appears). The rest of the code

```
static {
    System.loadLibrary("my-jni-app");
}
```

tells your program to look for method bodies in a place called my-jni-app. And whaddaya know? This section's example includes some C-language code in a file named my-jni-app.c.

Listing 6-1 pulls together all the code in your MainActivity.java file.

Listing 6-1:   Your Project's Main Activity

```
package com.allmycode.myndkapp;

import android.app.Activity;
import android.os.Bundle;
import android.text.Editable;
import android.view.View;
import android.widget.EditText;
import android.widget.Toast;


public class MainActivity extends Activity {

  @Override
  protected void onCreate(Bundle savedInstanceState) {
    super.onCreate(savedInstanceState);
    setContentView(R.layout.activity_main);
  }

  public native String getString();

  static {
    System.loadLibrary("my-jni-app");
  }

  public void onButtonClick(View view) {
    Editable name = ((EditText)
                findViewById(R.id.editText)).getText();
    Toast.makeText(getApplication(),
          getString() + name, Toast.LENGTH_LONG).show();
  }

}
```

7. **In Android Studio's main menu, choose File ⇨ New ⇨ Folder ⇨ JNI Folder.**

   Android displays a Customize the Activity dialog box.

8. **In the Customize the Activity dialog box, click Finish.**

   As a result, the Project tool window's tree has a new branch labeled c. (See Figure 6-1.) The folder's real name is `app/src/main/jni`, but the label in the Project tool window is c.

9. **In the Project tool window, right-click the new c branch and then choose New ⇨ File. (Mac users Ctrl-click instead of right-click.)**

   Android Studio opens its New File dialog box.

10. **In the Enter a New File Name field, type Android.mk and then click OK.**

    A `.mk` file is like a C-language `make` file, except it's shorter. For more information, see the "Android.mk files" sidebar.

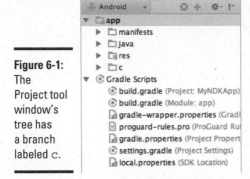

Figure 6-1:
The
Project tool
window's
tree has
a branch
labeled c.

The first time you create a .mk file, Android Studio may display a Register New File Type Association dialog box. If so, select the file type Text. (See Figure 6-2.)

Figure 6-2:
Registering
a new
file type
association.

11. Repeat Step 9 to create yet another file in the c branch.

12. In the Enter a New File Name field, type my-jni-app.c and then click OK.

This new file is destined to contain code written in C. You can give the file any name you want (but if you don't use the name my-jni-app, change my-jni-app to your alternate name everywhere else in these instructions). Of course, in this example, you're creating C code, so the filename should end with the .c extension.

13. Using Android Studio's editor, type the following code into the Android.mk file:

```
LOCAL_PATH := $(call my-dir)
include $(CLEAR_VARS)
LOCAL_MODULE := my-jni-app
LOCAL_SRC_FILES := my-jni-app.c
include $(BUILD_SHARED_LIBRARY)
```

Android.mk files

An `Android.mk` file tells your computer where your project's C program files are located. The computer uses this information to *build* your project (that is, to combine your files into a full-fledged Android application). An `.mk` file is like a `build.gradle` file, except that an `.mk` file applies specifically to C language code. (For a word or two about `build.gradle` files, refer to Chapter 4 in Book I.)

I copied the `Android.mk` file in Step 13 from Android's documentation pages (with only minor changes of my own). This `Android.mk` file provides five pieces of information:

✔ **The starting point for relative filenames inside this** `Android.mk` **file:** In this case, the starting point (the `LOCAL_PATH`) is the directory containing the `Android.mk` file (the `$(call my-dir)` directory).

✔ **That all instructions stored in the** `$(CLEAR_VARS)` **file must be included as part of the project:** These instructions initialize things like `LOCAL_MODULE`, `LOCAL_SRC_FILES`, `LOCAL_C_INCLUDES`, `LOCAL_CFLAGS`, and others. (By *initialize,* I mean "set as undefined.") Two of these variables become defined by subsequent lines in the `Android.mk` file.

✔ **The** `LOCAL_MODULE` **name:** In this case, the `LOCAL_MODULE` name is `my-jni-app`. This means that the library file

containing the compiled C code is stored in a file whose name has `my-jni-app` in the middle.

Android always puts `lib` before the middle and puts `.so` after the middle. So the full name of the library file is `libmy-jni-app.so`. (This `lib` and `.so` business comes from naming conventions in UNIX and Linux.) Sure enough, when you finish this chapter's instructions, you have a file (actually, many files) named `libmy-jni-app.so` in your Android Studio project.

✔ **The location for your stored C source code (that is,** `LOCAL_SRC_FILES`**):** Here, the C source code is stored in a file named `my-jni-app.c`. (You create a new, empty `my-jni-app.c` file in Step 12. You put a C program in that file in Step 14.)

✔ **That all instructions stored in the** `$(BUILD_SHARED_LIBRARY)` **file must be included as part of the project:** This file contains instructions to scoop up all the available information and then build an Android project from the Java code, the C code, the binary files, and all the other useful things in your project directories.

For more information, including a list of available variables and commands, see the file named `ANDROID-MK.html` in your `NDK_HOME` folder's `docs` subfolder.

This code tells the computer how to put the parts of your project together into an Android application. For more details, see the "Android.mk files" sidebar.

14. **Using Android Studio's editor, type the code from Listing 6-2 into the** `my-jni-app.c` **file.**

Listing 6-2:   Your C Program

```c
#include <string.h>
#include <jni.h>
jstring
Java_com_allmycode_myndkapp_MainActivity_getString
  (JNIEnv* env, jobject obj)
{
  return (*env)->NewStringUTF(env, "Hello, ");
}
```

In Listing 6-2, the name `Java_com_allmycode_myndkapp_Main Activity_getString` is *not* arbitrary. You must use your app's package name (in this example, `com.allmycode.myndkapp`) in your C code.

If you're not a seasoned C programmer, you may be wondering what the code in `my-jni-app.c` means. Well, you're in luck. There's a sidebar for that! (The sidebar's name is "C programming in 600 words or less.")

C programming in 600 words or less

You won't become a C programmer by reading this chapter, but you might want to know something about the C code in Listing 6-2.

First of all, C code doesn't normally run on a virtual machine. You compile your C program into a *native executable* file — a low-level binary file that runs only on an Intel x86 processor, an ARM processor, or some other kind of processor. This absence of a virtual machine makes C much more dependent on exotic binary file types. When you finish this chapter's steps, you have the `.c` file in Step 14, but you also have an `.o` object file, an `.o.d` file, and some `.so` library files.

I'll be criticized by the purists for trying to translate Listing 6-2 into Java. Even so, you can use my fake Java code to understand the C program:

```java
/*
 * Disclaimer:
 * This is a rough translation of the
 * C program in Listing 6-2. This code
 * illustrates the meaning of the
 * my-jni-app.c program. But this Java
 * code cannot replace the my-jni-app.c
 * program in Listing 6-2.
 */
package com.allmycode.myndkapp;

import java.lang.String;
import java.lang.Runtime;

public class MainActivity {

    public String getString() {
        return "Hello, ";
    }
}
```

The actual `my-jni-app.c` program in Listing 6-2 defines a single method — the method `Java_com_allmycode_myndkapp_MainActivity_getString`. The long method name follows JNI rules to implement the `getString` method in Listing 6-1. The

`MainActivity` class in Listing 6-1 declares a native method whose fully qualified name is `com.allmycode. myndkapp. MainActivity.getString`. To form the C-language JNI name in Listing 6-2, you replace the dots with underscores and preface the whole business with `Java_`.

The C programming language doesn't sweep pointers under the rug. In C, you use asterisks and arrows to refer explicitly to pointers, and you can use pointers to pass objects to functions. For example, the name `JNIEnv` refers to a class whose objects have about 200 fields. Each `JNIEnv` field is a pointer to a function. When you call the method in Listing 6-2, you pass a pointer to a `JNIEnv` object. (That is, you pass something of type `JNIEnv*`.) The parameter `env` stores that pointer to a `JNIEnv` object. (See the figure in this sidebar.)

In a C program, when you type ***env**, you're dereferencing the pointer stored in `env`. In other words, `*env` stands for whatever object env points to. So in Listing 6-2, `(*env)` stands for a `JNIEnv` object.

In C, an expression like `x->y` is shorthand for "the thing pointed to by the `y` field of the `x` object." In Listing 6-2, the text `(*env)->NewStringUTF` stands for the function that's pointed to by the `NewStringUTF` field of `*env`. In other words, `(*env)->NewStringUTF` stands for the current JNI environment's version of the `NewStringUTF` function.

The `return` statement in Listing 6-2 creates a new `java.lang.String` object (which is called a `jstring` object in a JNI C program). The new `String` object becomes part of the Java calling environment, and the Java calling environment gets the return value `"Hello, "`.

And if this isn't complicated enough, the whole thing works a bit differently when you shun plain old C and write your native code in C++ instead. Whew!

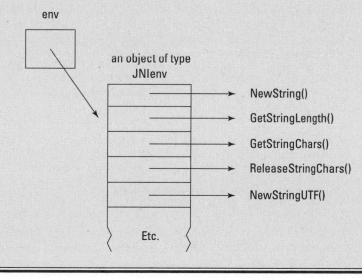

env

an object of type
JNIenv

→ NewString()

→ GetStringLength()

→ GetStringChars()

→ ReleaseStringChars()

→ NewStringUTF()

Etc.

15. **Click the Terminal button at the bottom of Android Studio's main window.**

A Terminal window opens in the lower portion of Android Studio's main window. (On Windows computers, this Terminal window is actually an MS-DOS command window.)

16. **In the Terminal window, type the command**

```
cd app/src/main
```

and then press Enter.

In this step, I assume that you've just opened the Terminal window, and that you haven't done any directory-changing in that window. If that's not the case, type `cd PROJECT_HOME/app/src/main`. In place of `PROJECT_HOME`, type the full pathname of the directory where your project is housed. (Refer to this chapter's "Directory names" sidebar.)

When you issue this command, you navigate to the directory containing your project's `AndroidManifest.xml` file.

Don't navigate away from your Android project's `app/src/main` directory. Or if you do navigate away, navigate back to the `app/src/main` directory before proceeding to the next step.

17. **In the Terminal window, type the following command and then press Enter:**

```
ANDROID_HOME/tools/android update project
--path . --subprojects --target android-21
```

In the command, where I have `ANDROID_HOME`, type the location of the Android SDK on your development computer. In place of `21`, type the `targetSdkVersion` number for this Android project (from the project's `build.gradle` file).

So for example, on my PC, I type the following:

```
C:\Users\Barry\AppData\Local\Android\sdk/tools/android
update project --path . --subprojects
--target android-21
```

If a pathname contains blank spaces (on a Mac or a PC), I enclose the entire pathname in quotation marks. For example, if my `ANDROID_HOME` is `c:\Program Files\Android\sdk`, I type

```
"C:\Program Files\Android\sdk/tools/android"
update project --path . --subprojects
--target android-21
```

In spite of the way things look on this printed page, I type the entire command on a single line (with a blank space before `update` and a blank space before `--target`).

I begged the people at John Wiley & Sons, Inc., to publish a book whose pages are two feet wide, but they didn't do it! When you type this step's command, you don't intentionally start a new line anywhere in the middle of the command. In this step, the command that I type looks like it's two or three lines long, but that's only because this book's page is too narrow. Normally you just keep typing along one line. (And if the Terminal window takes its own initiative to wrap your typing to a new line, you're okay.)

This step's `android update project` command creates a `build.xml` file. This `build.xml` file contains a set of instructions telling Java how to bundle your application. This project needs a `build.xml` file because of the special NDK stuff in the project.

If all goes well, the Terminal window responds to your command with text like

```
Updated local.properties
No project name specified, using Activity name
'MainActivity'.
If you wish to change it, edit the first line of
build.xml.
Added file ./build.xml
Added file ./proguard-project.txt
```

Don't navigate away from your Android project's `app/src/main` directory. Or if you do navigate away, navigate back to the `app/src/main` directory before proceeding to the next step.

18. **Type the following command and then press Enter:**

    ```
    NDK_HOME/ndk-build
    ```

    Where I have *NDK_HOME*, type the location of your Android NDK installation. (See this chapter's "Getting the NDK" section.)

    After issuing the `ndk-build` command, your computer responds with a message like this:

    ```
    Compile thumb  : my-jni-app <= my-jni-app.c
    SharedLibrary  : libmy-jni-app.so
    Install        : libmy-jni-app.so =>
                        libs/armeabi/libmy-jni-app.so
    ```

    Congratulations! The message indicates that your C code has been translated into a usable library for ARM processors.

19. **Add the following code to your project's `build.gradle` file.**

    ```
    ndk {
        moduleName "my-jni-app"
    }
    ```

ARM alphabet soup

A run of the `ndk-build` command creates a folder named `armeabi`. What's that all about?

The acronym *ARM* comes originally from the term *Advanced RISC Machines*, which in turn comes from *Advanced Reduced Instruction Set Computing Machines*. (I love these multilevel acronyms!) The company named ARM, Ltd., designs and licenses its ARM processors for use in mobile devices around the world. (ARM, Ltd., doesn't build processors. Instead, the company does all the thinking and sells ideas to processor manufacturers.)

The acronym *ABI* stands for *Application Binary Interface*. An ABI is like an API, except that an ABI describes the way one piece of software communicates with another on a binary level. For example, in an API you'd say, "To create a string that represents an object, call the object's `toString` method." In an ABI, you might say, "A signed double word consists of 8 bytes and has byte-alignment 8 [whatever that means]."

The ARM EABI is ARM's *Embedded Application Binary Interface*. *Embedded* refers to the tendency of ARM processors to appear in specialized devices — devices other than general-purpose computers. For example, the main processor inside your laptop isn't an embedded processor. Your laptop's main processor does general-purpose computing — word processing one minute and playing music the next. In contrast, an embedded processor sits quietly inside a device and processes bits according to the device's specialized needs. Your car is loaded with embedded processors.

You may argue that the processor inside your mobile device isn't a special-purpose processor. Thus, the *E* in *ARM EABI* doesn't apply to mobile development. Well, argue all you want. This terminology's usage can wobble in many directions, and regardless of what you think is inside your phone, many phones use ARM processors, and the `ndk-build` command creates code according to ARM EABI specifications.

Put this code inside the existing `defaultConfig` block:

```
defaultConfig {
    applicationId "com.allmycode.myndkapp"
    minSdkVersion 21
    targetSdkVersion 21
    versionCode 1
    versionName "1.0"

    ndk {
        moduleName "my-jni-app"
    }
}
```

20. **Add your** NDK_HOME **directory name to the end of one of your project's** `local.properties` **files.**

On my Mac, the project's `local.properties` file ends with these two lines:

```
sdk.dir=/Users/Barry/Development/sdk
ndk.dir=/Users/Barry/android-ndk-r10d
```

On a PC, the use of slashes is a bit strange, so the project's `local.properties` file ends with these two lines:

```
sdk.dir=C\:\\Users\\Barry\\AppData\\Local\\Android\\Sdk
ndk.dir=C\:\\android-ndk-r10d
```

One way or another, Android Studio knows where the Android NDK lives.

You can find two files named `local.properties` in your project. One such file lives inside your project's `app/src/main` directory. Don't add the `ndk.dir` line to the end of that `local.properties` file. Add the `ndk.dir` line to the end of the `local.properties` file that's in your project's root directory.

21. Run your Android project.

After some delay (and much anticipation), you see a screen like the one in Figure 6-3.

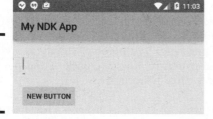

Figure 6-3:
Your app
starts
running.

22. Type your name in the EditText view and then click the button.

A toast notification appears on your emulator's screen. In Figure 6-4, the name *Barry* comes from the activity's EditText view. (It's no big deal.) But the word *Hello* in the notification comes from a C-language program — namely, the program in Listing 6-2.

Sure! Fetching a `"Hello"` string from a C program isn't the most useful app you've ever seen. But the ability to call C code to help with an Android app's work has lots of potential.

The most common hurdle for new NDK programmers involves correctly connecting a method call with its method. In Listing 6-1, for example, your Java program calls `getString()`, but with all the naming conventions and linking tricks, the system may not see the connection to the C-language method `Java_com_allmycode_examples_ndk_MyActivity_getString` in Listing 6-2. Your application crashes, and Android Studio's Logcat view displays an `UnsatisfiedLinkError`.

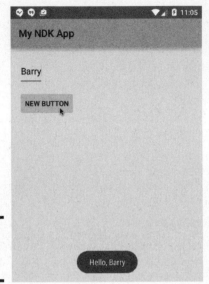

Figure 6-4:
You've
made toast!

If this happens to you, retrace your steps. The connection between a Java method and its corresponding C/C++ method can be very brittle. Check the spelling of names, check the messages you receive when you invoke ndk-build, and check your folder structure. If you're patient and persistent, you can get the stars and planets to align beautifully.

When you try to run this chapter's app, you might see a frightening *No rule to make target* error message. If you do, try changing NDK_HOME to a path with fewer characters and with no blank spaces. Check the Android.mk file for any stray blank spaces. And finally, on Windows, add an additional *whatever*.c file to your project's c branch. Then redo Steps 17 and 18. The new .c file doesn't have to contain any text. It simply has to exist. No doubt about it . . . the need for a second .c file is a bug, not a feature!

Book V

Apps for Tablets, Watches, and TV Sets

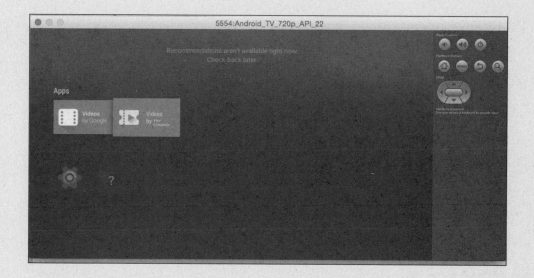

To see how you can put Google's Project Tango to good use, check out the online article at www.dummies.com/extras/androidappdevelopmentaio.

Contents at a Glance

Chapter 1: Apps for Tablets

In This Chapter

✐ **Adjusting for screen size and screen orientation**

✐ **Managing multipanel activities**

✐ **Writing apps that run on both phones and tablets**

Don't think about an elephant.

Okay, now that you're thinking about an elephant, think about an elephant's legs. The diameter of an elephant's leg is typically about 40 centimeters (more than four-tenths of a yard).

And think about spiders of the *Pholcidae* family (the "daddy longlegs") with their hair-like legs. And think about Gulliver with his Brobdingnagian friends. Each Brobdingnagian was about 72 feet tall, but a Brobdingnagian adult had the same physical proportions as Gulliver.

Gulliver's Travels is a work of fiction. An animal whose height is 12 times a human's height can't have bone sizes in human proportions. In other words, if you increase an object's size, you have to widen the object's supports. If you don't, the object will collapse.

This unintuitive truth about heights and widths comes from some geometric facts. An object's bulk increases as the cube of the object's height. But the ability to support that bulk increases only as the square of the object's height. That's because weight support depends on the cross-sectional area of the supporting legs, and a cross-sectional area is a square measurement, not a cubic measurement.

Anyway, the sizes of things make important qualitative differences. Take an activity designed for a touchscreen phone. Zoom that activity to a larger size without making any other changes. Then display the enlarged version on a ten-inch tablet screen. What you get on the tablet looks really bad. A tiny, crisp-looking icon turns into a big, blurry blob. An e-book page adapts in order to display longer line lengths. But, with lines that are 40 words long, the human eye suffers from terrible fatigue.

The same issue arises with Android activities. An activity contains enough information to fill a small phone screen. When the user needs more information, your app displays a different activity. The new activity replaces the old activity, resulting in a complete refresh of the screen.

If you slap this activity behavior onto a larger tablet screen, the user feels cheated. You've replaced everything on the screen even though there's room for both the old and new information. The transition from one activity to the next is jarring, and both the old and new activities look barren.

No doubt about it, tablet devices require a design that's different from phone designs. And to implement this design, Android has fragments.

What Fragments Can Do for You

A *fragment* is halfway between a view and an activity. Like a view, a fragment can be one of many elements on the device's screen. But unlike a view, a fragment has its own lifecycle. Table 1-1 lists the fragment lifecycle methods.

Table 1-1	Fragment Lifecycle Methods
Method Name	*When Android Calls This Method*
onAttach	Called when the fragment becomes part of a particular activity
onCreate	Called when the fragment is created (similar to an activity's onCreate method)
onCreateView	Called when Android creates the fragment's visible interface (comparable to an activity's setContentView method)
onViewCreated	Called after onCreateView has returned but before any saved state has been restored
onActivityCreated	Called when Android finishes executing the associated activity's onCreate method
onStart	Called when the fragment becomes visible to the user (typically, when Android executes the associated activity's onStart method)
onResume	Called when the fragment begins interacting with the user (typically, when Android executes the associated activity's onResume method)

Method Name	When Android Calls This Method
onPause	Called when the fragment no longer interacts with the user (similar to an activity's onPause method)
onStop	Called when the fragment is no longer visible to the user (similar to an activity's onStop method)
onDestroyView	Called when Android destroys the fragment's visible interface
onDestroy	Called when Android clobbers the fragment (similar to an activity's onDestroy method)
onDetach	Called when the fragment ceases to be part of a particular activity

A fragment has a lifecycle. Your first response to this news might be "Oh, no! More onSuchAndSuch methods to manage!" But the reality is, components' lifecycle methods are your friends. Lifecycle methods coordinate the comings and goings of individual components. Sure, it means you're going to have to manage your own app's interface. But without lifecycle methods, you'd have to micromanage your own app's interaction with other apps *and* with the Android operating system.

Programming with fragments

The user interface in this section's example has three panels — a list of items, a detail panel describing whichever item is selected in the list, and a details-in-more-depth panel. On a small smartphone screen, each panel might be a separate activity. But a tablet screen in landscape mode has room for more than one panel.

Figure 1-1 shows this section's app with two of the three panels. The panel on the left displays a list of Android SDK components. The panel on the right displays a description of whatever component is chosen in the list on the left. (The description is actually the first few sentences of the component's SDK documentation.) This details-on-the-right pattern is part of many user interfaces.

To create the display in Figure 1-1, you build one activity. The activity has two fragments — a fragment on the left and another on the right. The left panel displays the same fragment throughout the run of the app, so you can declare that fragment in the activity's layout file. The right panel displays one fragment at a time, but the fragment changes during the app's run. So you declare a frame layout in the right panel. Listing 1-1 has the code.

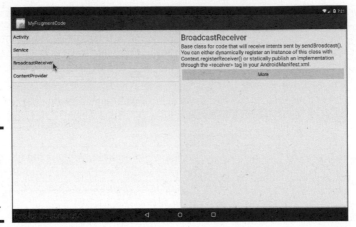

Figure 1-1:
Two
fragments
attached to
one activity.

Listing 1-1:   The Main Activity's Layout

```xml
<?xml version="1.0" encoding="utf-8"?>
<LinearLayout xmlns:android=
     "http://schemas.android.com/apk/res/android"
    android:orientation="horizontal"
    android:layout_width="match_parent"
    android:layout_height="match_parent">

    <fragment class=
         "com.allmycode.frag.ComponentNamesFragment"
        android:id="@+id/component_names"
        android:layout_height="match_parent"
        android:layout_width="0px"
        android:layout_weight="1" />

    <FrameLayout android:id="@+id/docs"
        android:layout_height="match_parent"
        android:layout_width="0px"
        android:layout_weight="1"
        android:background=
          "?android:attr/detailsElementBackground" />

</LinearLayout>
```

In Listing 1-1, the `android:layout_whatever` attributes divide the screen
into two halves — one half for the `fragment` element and the other half for
the `FrameLayout` element. The strategy with these attributes is to start by
assigning a minimum of zero pixels for each element. Of course, zero pixels
means no width at all (which is the same as being invisible). To keep the two
halves of the layout from being invisible, assign equal non-zero `layout_weight` values to the two halves. With non-zero weight values, each half
expands to fill the available space in the layout.

In Listing 1-1, the use of the fragment's fully qualified class name (com.allmycode.frag.ComponentNamesFragment) is intentional. An abbreviated name (such as .ComponentNamesFragment) won't cut the mustard.

In case you're wondering, Android's built-in detailsElementBackground (also in Listing 1-1) provides a uniform look for things like the right half of Figure 1-1 (things that display details about an item that the user has selected).

The app's main activity code is impressively uninteresting. (See Listing 1-2.)

Listing 1-2:   The Main Activity

```
package com.allmycode.frag;

import android.app.Activity;
import android.os.Bundle;

public class AllPurposeActivity extends Activity {

  @Override
  protected void onCreate(Bundle savedInstanceState) {
    super.onCreate(savedInstanceState);
    setContentView(R.layout.main);
  }
}
```

Listing 1-3 contains the ComponentNamesFragment class. By virtue of the layout in Listing 1-1, Android plants a ComponentNamesFragment on the left side of the device's screen (refer to Figure 1-1).

Listing 1-3:   A Fragment Containing a List of Items

```
package com.allmycode.frag;

import android.app.FragmentManager;
import android.app.FragmentTransaction;
import android.app.ListFragment;
import android.os.Bundle;
import android.view.View;
import android.widget.ArrayAdapter;
import android.widget.ListView;

public class ComponentNamesFragment extends ListFragment {

  final static String[] COMPONENTS = { "Activity",
      "Service", "BroadcastReceiver", "ContentProvider" };
```

(continued)

Listing 1-3 *(continued)*

```
@Override
public void onActivityCreated
                        (Bundle savedInstanceState) {
  super.onActivityCreated(savedInstanceState);
  setListAdapter(new ArrayAdapter<>(getActivity(),
      android.R.layout.simple_list_item_1, COMPONENTS));
}

@Override
public void onListItemClick(ListView l, View v,
                            int index, long id) {

  //Create fragment with index
  DocsFragment docsFragment = new DocsFragment();
  Bundle args = Helper.getBundleWithIndex(index);
  docsFragment.setArguments(args);

  //Clear the back stack
  FragmentManager fragmentManager =
                              getFragmentManager();
  int backStackEntryCount =
              fragmentManager.getBackStackEntryCount();
  for (int i = 0; i < backStackEntryCount; i++) {
    fragmentManager.popBackStackImmediate();
  }

  //Perform the transaction
  FragmentTransaction fragmentTransaction =
                  fragmentManager.beginTransaction();

  fragmentTransaction.replace(R.id.docs, docsFragment);
  fragmentTransaction.addToBackStack(null);

  fragmentTransaction.commit();
  }
}
```

The class in Listing 1-3 extends Android's ListFragment class. A ListFragment is a fragment that displays a list. Early on in the fragment's lifecycle, the code in Listing 1-3 sets a list adapter (more specifically, an ArrayAdapter) for the fragment. So how early is "early on"?

As in the examples from Chapter 2 of Book IV, the ArrayAdapter constructor's first parameter is a context. But wait! Unlike an activity, a fragment isn't a context. So you can't use the keyword this for the ArrayAdapter constructor's first parameter.

Fortunately, a fragment has a getActivity method. A call to getActivity grabs the activity to which the fragment is attached. So, for the Array Adapter constructor's first parameter, you can call getActivity. Of course, you can't call getActivity until the fragment is attached to an existing activity. That's why, in Listing 1-3, I override the fragment's onActivityCreated method. Android calls onActivityCreated *after* attaching the fragment and calling the activity's onCreate method. So everything works as planned.

The android.app.Activity class's great-grandparent class is android. content.Context. But the android.app.Fragment class's parent class is plain old java.lang.Object. Therefore, in an activity's code, the keyword this refers to a context. But in a fragment's code, the keyword this doesn't refer to a context.

A ListFragment is like a ListActivity — except that it's a fragment, not an activity. Many of the ListActivity class's concepts apply as well to the ListFragment class. To read about Android's ListActivity class, see Chapter 2 in Book IV.

In Listing 1-3, the constructor for the ArrayAdapter has three parameters.

✦ **The first parameter is the context — that nasty parameter that forces me to put the constructor inside the** onActivityCreated **method.**

✦ **The second parameter is** simple_list_item_1 — **a standard Android layout.**

The simple_list_item_1 layout creates the look that you see on the left side in Figure 1-1. Android has lots of these standard layouts. For a roundup of the available layouts, visit http://developer.android. com/reference/android/R.layout.html.

✦ **The third parameter is the collection of items that will appear in the list.**

In this example, those items come from the COMPONENTS array, which is declared in that same listing — Listing 1-3.

Like a ListActivity, a ListFragment has an onListItemClick method. In Listing 1-3, I respond to a click by working with a DocsFragment, a FragmentTransaction, and a FragmentManager:

✦ The DocsFragment instance in Listing 1-3 represents the right side of Figure 1-1.

✦ A *fragment transaction* is a bunch of things you do with fragments. For example, setting up to replace one fragment with another (as in Listing 1-3) is a transaction.

✦ A *fragment manager* does what its name suggests. It manages fragments' arrivals and departures.

The fragment

You don't get to see the `DocsFragment`'s code until Listing 1-4. For now, the actual fragment created when you construct a new `DocsFragment` is a black box. (I shouldn't build up the suspense this way. I just don't want you to get sidetracked.)

One way or another, the fragment on the right side in Figure 1-1 has to know which of the items the user clicks on the left side. In this chapter's code, I call this "which item" business the `index`. If the user clicks the topmost item on the left (the *Activity* item), the `index` has value 0. If the user clicks the second item on the left (the *Service* item), the `index` has value 1. And so on.

When you create a new fragment, you don't create an intent, so you can't use an intent's extras to pass an index to the fragment. To take the place of extras, you have *arguments*. In Listing 1-3, to pass the `index` value to the newly created `DocsFragment` instance, I put the `index` value into a `Bundle` and add the `Bundle`'s info to the new fragment's arguments.

To read about bundles, refer to Chapter 3 in Book III.

In this chapter's examples, I move a few frequently used (and frankly, uninteresting) pieces of code to methods outside of my mainstream listings. For example, instead of manufacturing a bundle in Listing 1-3, I call a `Helper` class's `getBundleWithIndex` method. If you can't wait to see the puny body of the `getBundleWithIndex` method, jump ahead to Listing 1-9 where I show you the entire `Helper` class.

The fragment transaction

The term *transaction* comes from the world of databases. A transaction is a bunch of operations. These operations live inside an all-or-nothing bubble. That is, either all the operations in the transaction take place, or none of the operations in the transaction takes place.

In Listing 1-3, you turn a bunch of statements into a transaction. In particular, you sandwich a bunch of statements between calls to `beginTransaction` and `commit`. One of these statements, `fragmentTransaction.replace` `(R.id.docs, docsFragment)`, prepares to replace whatever's currently in the `docs` frame layout (in Listing 1-1) with a new fragment. The replacement occurs when Android executes the `fragmentTransaction.commit` method call.

I recently had an unpleasant experience when I used the wrong value for the first parameter in the `replace` method call. The app crashed, but the stack trace in the Logcat panel didn't list any of my own app's classes. I couldn't figure out where, in my code, the error had occurred. Somewhere before the stack trace, I found an entry with the text *No view found for fragment,* and eventually, I located the bad method parameter. So my advice is, don't let this error get the best of you. Always double-check your `replace` method parameters.

The fragment manager

An instance of the `android.app.FragmentManager` class takes care of your app's fragments. For example, in Listing 1-3, the manager's `replace` method changes the fragment that's shown on the user's screen. The manager also helps you fiddle with your activity's back stack.

Book III, Chapter 1 describes the way activities pile up on top of one another with successive `startActivity` calls. When the user presses Back, Android pops an activity off the stack. The most recently added activity is the first to be popped. It's as if Android, the boss, has an agreement with members of the Activities Union. Android fires activities in reverse order of seniority.

With the introduction of fragments in Android 3.0, an activity can have its own private stack. You can display fragment A and then call `fragment-Transaction.replace` and `fragmentTransaction.addToBackStack`. The combination of method calls makes fragment B overwrite fragment A. When the user presses Back, fragment B goes away, and fragment A returns to its place on the activity's screen. Android doesn't destroy an entire activity until the activity has no fragments that it can jettison.

In the `Clear the back stack` part of Listing 1-3, the fragment manager does some quick housekeeping of the activity's fragment stack. To read more about this housekeeping, cast your eyes to the "Trimming the fragment stack" section.

When you call `addToBackStack`, you have the option of supplying a name for the entry that you're putting on the back stack. If you supply `null` as the argument to the `addToBackStack` call (as I do in Listing 1-3), then the entry is unnamed. If you supply a string at that time, later in the code, you can retrieve the entry by calling `FragmentManager.findFragmentByTag`.

Fragments, more fragments, and even more fragments

The right panel in Figure 1-1 has a More button. When the user presses this More button, the app displays a more verbose description of the selected component. To find out how this happens, stare thoughtfully (but joyfully) at the code in Listing 1-4.

Listing 1-4:   Code to Create the Fragment on the Right Side of Figure 1-1

```
package com.allmycode.frag;

import android.app.Fragment;
import android.app.FragmentTransaction;
import android.os.Bundle;
import android.view.LayoutInflater;
import android.view.View;
import android.view.View.OnClickListener;
import android.view.ViewGroup;
import android.widget.Button;
import android.widget.LinearLayout;
import android.widget.TextView;

public class DocsFragment extends Fragment
                          implements OnClickListener {
  TextView textView1;

  @Override
  public View onCreateView(LayoutInflater inflater,
                           ViewGroup container,
                           Bundle savedInstanceState) {

    return myLayout();
  }

  @Override
  public void onClick(View view) {
    int index = getArguments().getInt("index");


    //Create fragment with index
    DocsFragmentVerbose docsFragmentVerbose =
                        new DocsFragmentVerbose();
    Bundle args = Helper.getBundleWithIndex(index);
    docsFragmentVerbose.setArguments(args);

    //Perform the transaction
    FragmentTransaction fragmentTransaction =
            getFragmentManager().beginTransaction();
    fragmentTransaction.replace(R.id.docs,
                                docsFragmentVerbose);
    fragmentTransaction.addToBackStack(null);
    fragmentTransaction.commit();
  }
  final static int[] DOCS = {
      R.string.doc_activity,
      R.string.doc_service,
      R.string.doc_broadcast_receiver,
      R.string.content_provider
  };

  private LinearLayout myLayout() {
```

```
LinearLayout layout = new LinearLayout(getActivity());
layout.setOrientation(LinearLayout.VERTICAL);

int index = getArguments().getInt("index");

textView1 = new TextView(getActivity());
textView1.setTextSize(30);
textView1
    .setText(ComponentNamesFragment.COMPONENTS[index]);
layout.addView(textView1);
TextView textView2 = new TextView(getActivity());
textView2.setTextSize(20);
textView2.setText(DOCS[index]);
layout.addView(textView2);

Button button = new Button(getActivity());
button.setText(R.string.more);
button.setOnClickListener(this);
layout.addView(button);

return layout;
  }
}
```

In Listing 1-4, the onCreateView and myLayout methods use Java code to
compose a layout — the layout on the right side in Figure 1-1. The listing's
onCreateView method returns a linear layout, which is a view group, which
is a view. And that view becomes the fragment's visible presence on the
tablet screen.

In Listing 1-4, I define a fragment's layout using Java code instead of a
res/layout XML document. Book IV, Chapter 1 goes into more detail on
using Java code to define views and layouts.

The DOCS array near the bottom of Listing 1-4 is interesting. I use this array
in the middle of the listing to set the text in a text view. This array is an array
of int values — an array of code numbers for strings defined in the project's
res/values/strings.xml file. The lines in the file are very long, so I don't
paste the entire strings.xml file onto this page. But here's a chopped-off
version of the file:

```
<?xml version="1.0" encoding="utf-8"?>
<resources>
  <string name="app_name">MyFragmentCode</string>
  <string name="more">More</string>
  <string name="doc_activity">An activity is a single, focused thing that
    <string name="doc_service">A Service is an application component representing
  <string name="doc_broadcast_receiver">Base class for code that will receive
  <string name="content_provider">Content providers are one of the primary
</resources>
```

The text in each string is a few sentences copied from the Android SDK doc-umentation. (Just for fun, try turning this printed page so that you're reading it in landscape mode. Maybe then you'll see the chopped-off portion of the `strings.xml` file.)

In the description of a broadcast receiver, the documentation contains the phrase *the <receiver> tag*, with angle brackets and all. (Refer to Figure 1-1.) You can't just plop the text *the <receiver> tag* inside your `strings.xml` file because the angle brackets in

```
<string name="...">Base class...<receiver>...</string>
```

would confuse an XML parser. You have to tell the XML parser that the angle brackets surrounding the word *receiver* are plain old text — not official parts of the XML code. Fortunately, XML provides a standard way of doing this. You enclose the angle brackets in CDATA sections:

```
the <![CDATA[<]]>receiver<![CDATA[>]]> tag
```

Building the fragment stack

In Listing 1-4, the `onClick` method replaces the right side of Figure 1-1 with a brand-new fragment — an instance of my `DocsFragmentVerbose` class. And clever guy that I am, I programmed the `DocsFragmentVerbose` class to display a page from the official Android documentation website. Listing 1-5 contains the code.

Listing 1-5: A Fragment Containing a Web View

```
package com.allmycode.frag;

import android.app.Fragment;
import android.os.Bundle;
import android.view.LayoutInflater;
import android.view.View;
import android.view.ViewGroup;
import android.webkit.WebView;

public class DocsFragmentVerbose extends Fragment {

  @Override
  public View onCreateView(LayoutInflater inflater,
                           ViewGroup container,
                           Bundle savedInstanceState) {

    WebView webView = new WebView(getActivity());
    int index = getArguments().getInt("index");
```

```
webView.loadUrl(
    "http://developer.android.com/reference/android/"
        + ((index < 2) ? "app/" : "content/")
        + ComponentNamesFragment.COMPONENTS[index]
        + ".html");

    return webView;
}
}
```

At this point, I can describe the whole storyboard for this section's grand example:

✦ **The user sees a list — namely, the list of component names in the left fragment in Figure 1-1.**

✦ **The user selects an item in the list.**

In response, the app displays a brief description of the selected item. In Figure 1-1, the description is the first few sentences of Android's `BroadcastReceiver` documentation.

To display the description, the code in Listing 1-3 calls `replace(R.id. docs, docsFragment)`. That is, the code places a fragment into the `R.id.docs` view.

✦ **The newly displayed fragment contains a brief description and a button. (Refer to Figure 1-1.) If the user clicks the button, the app covers this fragment with an even newer fragment.**

In Figure 1-2, the new fragment displays the `BroadcastReceiver`'s online documentation page.

Figure 1-2:
A fragment contains a web view.

To load a page from the Internet, your app's `AndroidManifest.xml` document must have a `<uses-permission android:name="android.permission.INTERNET" />` element.

Trimming the fragment stack

When I created the first draft of the code in Listing 1-3, I didn't include anything about `getBackStackEntryCount` or `popBackStackImmediate`. "Whew! I'm done!" I said to myself. But then I tested the code. What I discovered in testing was that a user's attention shifts abruptly with the selection of a new list item.

Imagine selecting `BroadcastReceiver` and then clicking the More button. After a look at the `BroadcastReceiver`'s documentation page (refer to Figure 1-2), you turn your attention leftward to the list of components. As soon as you select a different component, you tend to forget all about broadcast receivers. If you click the Back button, you probably don't want to rummage back through your old selections. In other words, selecting an item in the list of components represents a fresh start. When you select an item in the list of components, the app should clear whatever fragment stack you created previously.

The `Clear the back stack` part of Listing 1-3 does the desired stack cleanup. The code calls the fragment manager's `getBackStackEntryCount` method to find out how many fragments you have on the stack. Then the `for` loop uses the entry count to decide how many fragments to pop off the stack. When the loop finishes its work, the stack of fragments is empty; now you can safely call the current transaction's `addToBackStack` method. The strategy works very nicely.

Getting the Best of Both Worlds

The previous sections in this chapter describe an app that uses fragments. The app works very nicely but has one tiny limitation. You must not let the user turn the tablet sideways. If the tablet device is in portrait mode, the app looks silly. (Yes, I'm being sarcastic if I call this problem a "tiny limitation.")

Figure 1-3 shows the app on a display that's taller than it is wide. You have lots of wasted space on the left side, and you have no room for the page heading (BroadcastReceiver) on the right side.

The problem isn't limited to portrait mode on tablets. The same nastiness happens if you run the app on a small screen device. Landscape or portrait — you can't run the previous section's code on any phone that has less-than-stunning resolution. If you do the app looks awful.

I'm the first to admit that this book's examples vary from plain-looking to ugly. But with other examples, the fault is with my lack of artistic flair. In this chapter's example, the fault is in the code. ("The fault, dear Brutus, is not in our arts, But in our code. . . .")

Figure 1-3:
Screen orientation matters a lot!

To remedy the visual faux pas in Figure 1-3, you can make four enhancements to your code:

✦ **You create an additional activity.**

 The new `DocsActivityVerbose` activity has only one view — namely, a view to display the web page fragment from Listing 1-5. Unlike the narrow fragment in Figure 1-3, the new activity consumes the entire screen. (See Figure 1-4.)

✦ **You tweak the code in Listing 1-4 to display either the `DocsFragment Verbose` or the new `DocsActivityVerbose`, depending on the screen's orientation.**

Figure 1-4:
The web page fragment takes up the entire screen.

✦ **You tweak the app's main activity in a similar fashion.**

✦ **You create an additional layout for portrait mode and for small screen densities.**

In the new layout, the `DocsFragment` doesn't appear beside the list of component names. Instead, the `DocsFragment` appears below the list of component names (instead of beside the list of names). See Figure 1-5.

In what follows, I call these enhancements Change 1, Change 2, Change 3, and Change 4.

Change 1: Create an additional activity

Listing 1-6 contains the new `DocsActivityVerbose` activity.

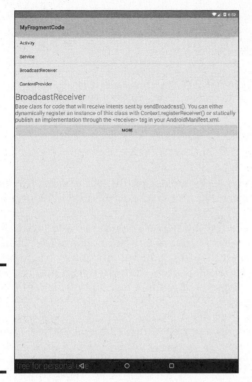

Figure 1-5:
A layout
for narrow
screens
and small
screens.

Listing 1-6:   An Activity That's a Wrapper for a Fragment

```
package com.allmycode.frag;

import android.app.Activity;
import android.app.FragmentManager;
import android.app.FragmentTransaction;
import android.os.Bundle;

public class DocsActivityVerbose extends Activity {

  @Override
  public void onCreate(Bundle bundle) {
    super.onCreate(bundle);
    setContentView(R.layout.docs_verbose);

    int index = getIntent().getIntExtra("index", 0);

    //Create fragment with index
    DocsFragmentVerbose docsFragmentVerbose =
                         new DocsFragmentVerbose();
    Bundle args = Helper.getBundleWithIndex(index);
    docsFragmentVerbose.setArguments(args);
```

(continued)

Listing 1-6 *(continued)*

```
//Perform the transaction
FragmentManager fragmentManager =
                            getFragmentManager();
FragmentTransaction fragmentTransaction =
                fragmentManager.beginTransaction();
fragmentTransaction.replace(R.id.docs_verbose_frame,
                        docsFragmentVerbose);

    fragmentTransaction.commit();
  }
}
```

The new `DocsActivityVerbose` class performs the same fragment transaction that's performed by the `onClick` method in Listing 1-4.

Notice that the code in Listing 1-6 doesn't call the `addToBackStack` method. If you were to call `addToBackStack` in Listing 1-6, Android would push the web page fragment on top of an initially empty fragment. Then, if the user were to press the Back button, Android would pop the web page fragment off the stack. The user would see an empty fragment that consumes the entire screen.

When you add an activity to a project (such as the activity in Listing 1-6), you must add an `<activity>` element to the project's `AndroidManifest.xml` document. For the code in Listing 1-6, the new `<activity>` element looks like this:

```
<activity android:name=
  "com.allmycode.frag.DocsActivityVerbose" />
```

If you create the new activity using Android Studio's tools, the `<activity>` element is added automatically. But if you create a new Java class and then turn the class into an activity, you must add the `<activity>` element manually.

Like many activity classes, the new `DocsActivityVerbose` class uses its own layout resource. And sure enough, the `onCreate` method in Listing 1-6 refers to an `R.layout.docs_verbose` resource. Listing 1-7 contains my `docs_verbose.xml` file.

Listing 1-7: A Layout for the New DocsActivityVerbose Class

```
<?xml version="1.0" encoding="utf-8"?>
<LinearLayout xmlns:android=
    "http://schemas.android.com/apk/res/android"
    android:layout_width="match_parent"
    android:layout_height="match_parent">
```

```
<FrameLayout android:id="@+id/docs_verbose_frame"
    android:layout_height="match_parent"
    android:layout_width="match_parent"
    android:layout_weight="1" />
</LinearLayout>
```

The layout for the `DocsActivityVerbose` class contains only one element — namely, the fragment that displays an Android documentation web page.

Change 2: Tweak the DocsFragment code

Having created the new `DocsActivityVerbose` class and its required layout resource, you're ready to integrate these files into the rest of the app's code. To do this, consider two situations:

✦ *When the user presses the More button,* you either replace the existing fragment or start your new `DocsActivityVerbose`, depending on the screen's orientation.

✦ *When the user turns the device sideways,* you check whether the new orientation will cause the awkward crunch shown back in Figure 1-3. If so, you need to back away from displaying the web page fragment.

To handle the first situation, replace the `DocsFragment` code's `onClick` method (see Listing 1-8).

Listing 1-8: Deciding What to Do When the User Clicks a Button

```
@Override
public void onClick(View view) {
  int index = getArguments().getInt("index");

  if (Helper.isDenseWideScreen(getActivity())) {

    //Create fragment with index
    DocsFragmentVerbose docsFragmentVerbose =
                    new DocsFragmentVerbose();
    Bundle args = Helper.getBundleWithIndex(index);
    docsFragmentVerbose.setArguments(args);

    //Perform the transaction
    FragmentTransaction fragmentTransaction =
          getFragmentManager().beginTransaction();
    fragmentTransaction.replace(R.id.docs,
                      docsFragmentVerbose);
    fragmentTransaction.addToBackStack(null);
    fragmentTransaction.commit();
```

(continued)

Listing 1-8 *(continued)*

```
   } else {

     Intent intent = new Intent();
     intent.setClass(getActivity(),
                     DocsActivityVerbose.class);
     intent.putExtra("index", index);
     startActivity(intent);

   }
}
```

The original `DocsFragment` class in Listing 1-4 doesn't check the screen's size or orientation. But the code in Listing 1-8 responds in different ways, depending on the result of the `isDenseWideScreen` method call. On a dense, wide screen, the code in Listing 1-8 mimics the code in Listing 1-4. But on a lesser screen, Listing 1-8 starts an instance of the new `DocsActivityVerbose` class.

The code for the `isDenseWideScreen` method is in Listing 1-9, along with the rest of this chapter's `Helper` class.

Listing 1-9:   The Helper Method

```
package com.allmycode.frag;

import android.app.Activity;
import android.content.res.Configuration;
import android.os.Bundle;
import android.util.DisplayMetrics;

public class Helper {

  static Bundle getBundleWithIndex(int index) {
    Bundle bundle = new Bundle();
    bundle.putInt("index", index);
    return bundle;
  }

  static boolean isDenseWideScreen(Activity activity) {
    DisplayMetrics metrics = new DisplayMetrics();
    activity.getWindowManager().
      getDefaultDisplay().getMetrics(metrics);
    boolean isDenseScreen =
      metrics.densityDpi >= DisplayMetrics.DENSITY_XHIGH;
    boolean isWideScreen =
      activity.getResources().
        getConfiguration().orientation ==
                  Configuration.ORIENTATION_LANDSCAPE;
    return isDenseScreen && isWideScreen;
  }

}
```

Change 3: Tweak the app's main activity

When the user turns the device sideways, Android destroys the current activity and creates the activity anew. If the turn is from landscape to portrait mode, you don't want a fragment that displays a web page to hang around awkwardly on the right side of the screen. So, when Android calls your main activity's `onCreate` method, you need to test for a dense, wide screen. If the user's screen doesn't pass this test, then remove any web pages from the fragment's back stack.

Listing 1-10 contains the enhanced `AllPurposeActivity` code.

Listing 1-10:   Your New, Improved Main Activity

```
package com.allmycode.frag;

import android.app.Activity;
import android.app.FragmentManager;
import android.os.Bundle;

public class AllPurposeActivity extends Activity {

  @Override
  protected void onCreate(Bundle savedInstanceState) {
    super.onCreate(savedInstanceState);
    setContentView(R.layout.main);

    //Clear the back stack if necessary
    if (!Helper.isDenseWideScreen(this)) {
      FragmentManager fragmentManager =
        getFragmentManager();
      if (fragmentManager.getBackStackEntryCount() > 1) {
        fragmentManager.popBackStackImmediate();
      }
    }
  }
}
```

The code in Listing 1-10 asks how many fragments are currently on the activity's stack of fragments. If the count is more than one, the most recently created fragment is the dreaded web page fragment. To eliminate the danger, the code pops the web page fragment off the stack.

Change 4: Create an additional layout

With or without a web page, you don't want any side-by-side fragments when the screen is small. In this section's example, a "small screen" means a screen whose width is less than 320 dp or (whatever the width) a screen in portrait mode. To make these requirements stick, I put the layout in Listing 1-11 in the app's `res/layout-w320dp-port` folder.

Using the dp measurement, 160 dp represents one inch. So 320 dp is two inches. Indeed, a screen whose width is less than two inches is a very small screen.

To read more about the dp measurement, refer to Chapter 1 in Book IV.

Listing 1-11:   A Layout for Small (or Narrow) Screens

```xml
<?xml version="1.0" encoding="utf-8"?>
<LinearLayout xmlns:android=
    "http://schemas.android.com/apk/res/android"
    android:orientation="vertical"
    android:layout_width="match_parent"
    android:layout_height="match_parent">

    <fragment class=
        "com.allmycode.frag.ComponentNamesFragment"
        android:id="@+id/component_names"
        android:layout_height="wrap_content"
        android:layout_width="match_parent"
        android:layout_weight="0" />

    <FrameLayout
        android:id="@+id/docs"
        android:layout_height="0px"
        android:layout_width="match_parent"
        android:layout_weight="1"
        android:background=
          "?android:attr/detailsElementBackground" />

</LinearLayout>
```

The file in Listing 1-11 must have the same name as the main activity's layout file. (If you're working directly with Listing 1-10, the file in Listing 1-11 is named `main.xml`.)

Listing 1-11 is very much like the code in Listing 1-1, but there are a few differences:

✦ **In Listing 1-1, the overall layout's orientation is** `horizontal`**; in Listing 1-11, the orientation is** `vertical`**.**

In Figure 1-1, the two fragments in the activity are side-by-side. But in Figure 1-5, one fragment is underneath the other.

✦ **In Listing 1-1, both fragments have** `layout_weight` **set to** 1**. But in Listing 1-11, the** `ComponentNamesFragment` **has the** `layout_weight` **value set to** 0**.**

In Figure 1-1, both fragments expand to fill the screen. But in Figure 1-5, the `ComponentNamesFragment` doesn't expand. (The lower fragment expands in Figure 1-5, but you don't see the expansion because most of that lower fragment is blank.)

✦ **After changing the** `layout_weight` **for the** `ComponentNamesFragment`, **you have to adjust the fragment's** `layout_height` **values.**

In Listing 1-1, the fragments' layout sizes are `match_parent` and `0px`. But in Listing 1-11, the `ComponentNamesFragment` has the `layout_weight` value set to `0`. Accordingly, the `ComponentNamesFragment` takes up no more space than it requires on the screen. If you don't describe this space requirement, the `ComponentNamesFragment` shrinks to nothing. To specify the space requirement, you make the `layout_height` of the `ComponentNamesFragment` be `wrap_content`.

With the changes that you make in this section's steps, the user can turn the device sideways, upside-down, or whatever. When the user wants to see a web page, the app displays the page in a fragment or in an entire activity, whichever is best.

Chapter 2: Developing for Android Wear

In This Chapter

✔ **Running Android apps on wearables**

✔ **Creating a basic wearable app**

✔ **Creating a watch face app**

*N*ot long ago, when I was writing an article for a technology website, I asked a Google staff member about the range of uses for the Android operating system. "Android runs phones, tablets, watches, automobiles, televisions, autos, and other things. What is it about Android that makes the platform so versatile?" The staff member sensed that I was a) feeding him an easy question and b) trying to sound "pro-Google," so he didn't answer the question. I should have known better. In any case, the applicability of Android to so many form factors is impressive.

Many of this book's concepts work on all kinds of devices. But when I describe a particular feature, I usually think "smartphone or tablet." In this chapter, I veer briefly from that path and deal exclusively with wristwatches (known formally as *Android Wear devices*, or *wearables* for short).

Setting Up Your Testing Environment

To run this chapter's example, the only thing you need is an Android Wear AVD. Here's how you get one:

1. **In Android Studio's main menu, choose Tools ➪ Android ➪ SDK Manager.**

2. **Make sure that your SDK Tools is Version 23.0.0 or higher.**

   If not, install an updated SDK Tools version.

3. **Make sure that your SDK is API Level 20 or higher.**

   If not, install an updated SDK level.

4. **Close the SDK Manager.**

   (You were probably planning to do that anyway.)

5. **In Android Studio's main menu, choose Tools ⇨ Android ⇨ AVD Manager.**

   The AVD Manager opens.

6. **In the AVD Manager window, click the Create Virtual Device button.**

   The Virtual Device Configuration dialog box appears. The left side of the dialog box contains a Category list, and the middle contains a list of hardware profiles.

7. **In the Category list, select Wear.**

   Doing so narrows the list of hardware profiles to the ones that are specifically for Android Wear.

8. **Select a hardware profile from the list and click Next.**

   The choices probably include square and round watches and different numbers of pixels on the faces. To run this chapter's example, any choice will do.

   It's true. To run this chapter's example, any Android wear choice will do. But to run the emulator on your development computer, some choices might be better than others. Some AVDs consume too much memory. Other choices (such as x86 or armeabi in the next step) might be wrong for your computer's configuration. If at first you don't succeed, try some different choices.

   When you click Next, another Virtual Device Configuration dialog box appears. The new dialog box lists system images. Each system image is a version of Android (5.0.2, for example) along with a target processor architecture (x86 or armeabi).

   For a reminder about what a system image is, refer to Chapter 2 in Book I.

9. **Select an item in the list and click Next.**

   At this point, yet another Virtual Device Configuration dialog box appears. The defaults in this dialog box are okay by me.

10. **Click Finish.**

After following these steps, you have an emulated device that does what an Android wearable does. You can test your Android Wear code on this emulated device.

Other testing configurations

In real life, an Android Wear device seldom runs on its own. Instead, the wearable runs in concert with a phone. The phone does all the heavy lifting (networking to the Internet, for example) while the wearable does things that tiny wrist devices should do (display the time, show notifications, count your steps, and so on).

In the previous paragraph, I write "phone" when I should really write "hand-held device." You can connect a tablet device to an Android watch. But for a watch to be useful, you should connect it to something that's with you all the time. And people are much more likely to carry phones than to haul around a tablet device.

For the full Android Wear experience, you probably want two devices — a wearable and a phone. The obvious question is, of the two devices, are one or both of them emulated? Are one or both of them real?

To help answer this question, the Android documentation provides a few scenarios:

✦ **Ignore the phone and use an emulated Android Wear device.**

That's the scenario that I recommend for this chapter's example.

✦ **Connect a real phone to your development computer and use an emulated Android Wear device.**

See my brief list of tips in this section.

✦ **Use a real phone and a real Android Wear device.**

Again, see my brief list of tips.

Notice one combination that's missing from this list. None of the scenarios involves an emulated phone. People have posted instructions for connecting two emulators — one for a phone and another for Android Wear. I've tried following the instructions, but I've never had time to reach the finish line. (I've been too busy writing *Android Application Development All-in-One For Dummies,* 2nd Edition.)

The Android developer training pages have detailed instructions on setting up phones for testing with Android Wear. So I don't dwell on the details in this chapter. Instead, I point out some of the highlights. These highlights might help you see the forest for the trees while you march step-by-step through the instructions on the Android developer site's pages.

The Android developer site's pages on testing with real devices are `http://developer.android.com/training/wearables/apps/creating.html` and `http://developer.android.com/training/wearables/apps/bt-debugging.html`.

When you set up a phone for testing with Android Wear, you perform some or all of the following steps:

✦ Install the Android Wear app from the Google Play Store on your phone.

✦ Use the Developer options in the phone's Settings screen to enable USB debugging on the phone.

✦ (With an Android Wear emulator) Type the following command in your development computer's command prompt window or Terminal app:

```
adb -d forward tcp:5601 tcp:5601
```

This command forwards your emulator's communications to the connected phone.

✦ (On a real wearable device) Use the Developer options in the device's Settings screen to enable ADB debugging on the Wear device.

✦ In the Android Wear app on the phone, pair the phone with the emulator (or with the real wearable device).

For connecting a real wearable device, you have two options:

✦ **Connect the device to your development computer using a USB cable.**

Alas! Some Android wearables don't have USB ports.

✦ **Create a Bluetooth connection between the phone and the wearable.**

For this option, you have to enable the Debugging over Bluetooth option on the wearable. You also have to set up Debugging over Bluetooth in the Android Wear app on the phone, and type the commands

```
adb forward tcp:4444 localabstract:/adb-hub
adb connect localhost:4444
```

on your development computer.

A "Hello" example

Most of the classes and methods that you use to write phone apps work on Android Wear apps as well. For evidence of this fact (but not proof of this fact), follow these steps:

1. **In Android Studio, start a new project.**

2. **In the Target Android Devices dialog box, select two form factors: the Phone and Tablet form factor, and the Wear form factor.**

   The real story about form factors depends on your stage of development. To publish a wearable app, you must package your app as part of a phone or tablet app. Consumers have no way of pushing apps directly to their wearables, so they must install an app on their phones and have the phone push the app onto the paired wearable. Therefore, you develop your app for both form factors.

Strangely enough, when you're in the testing stage, the opposite is true. Yes, you choose two form factors when you create the new project. But for testing, when you push your app onto a device or an emulator, you push only the wearable part of the app.

Why is there such a big difference between testing and publishing a wearable app? When you do testing, you don't sign your app. That is, you don't add an electronic certificate ensuring that your app comes from a valid source. For more information about signing apps, see Chapter 1 in Book VI.

3. **In the usual Add an Activity dialog box, select Add No Activity.**

   In this section's example, you don't need an activity for a phone or a tablet. But after selecting Add No Activity and clicking Next, you see a new Add an Activity to Wear dialog box.

4. **In the Add an Activity to Wear dialog box, select Blank Wear Activity.**

   The blank wear activity will appear on your wearable device.

5. **Click Next and Finish as often as it takes to get back to the main Android Studio window.**

   Your new project has two modules — one named `mobile` and another named `app`. (See Figure 2-1.)

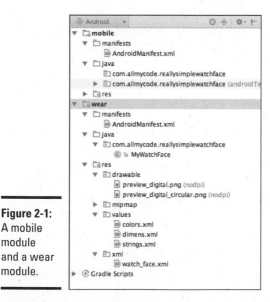

Figure 2-1:
A mobile
module
and a wear
module.

- The `mobile` module contains code for a phone or a tablet device.

- The `wear` module contains code for the wearable.

Both modules have manifests, Java files, `res` folders, and all that other stuff.

In this example, you work exclusively inside the `wear` module.

6. **Expand the `wear/res/layout` branch in the Project tool window.**

    You probably see three layout files — `activity_main.xml`, `rect_activity_main.xml`, and `round_activity_main.xml`.

7. **Double-click the layout file for your favorite Android Wear emulator.**

    If your emulator has a rectangular watch face, double-click the `rect_activity_main.xml` branch. If your emulator has a round watch face, double-click the `round_activity_main.xml` branch.

8. **Go to the Text view in the Designer tool.**

9. **In the layout file, add the following `Button` element:**

    ```
    <Button android:layout_width="wrap_content"
      android:layout_height="wrap_content"
      android:text="Click me"
      android:onClick="onButtonClick"/>
    ```

    It's nothing special! That's the whole point.

10. **In the `MainActivity` Java file for the `wear` part of the app, add the following code:**

    ```
    public void onButtonClick(View view) {
      mTextView.setText("You clicked!");
    }
    ```

    I'm assuming that Android Studio has already placed a text view in the layout and added the following lines somewhere in the `MainActivity` file:

    ```
    TextView mTextView;

    mTextView = (TextView) stub.findViewById(R.id.text);
    ```

    If my assumption is incorrect, add the appropriate stuff to your project.

11. **With the Android Wear emulator running, choose Run ➪ Run 'wear' in Android Studio's main menu.**

    When you do, this example's main activity (with a text field and a button) appears on the wearable emulator's screen. If you click the button, the text inside the text view changes. It's the same as an ordinary phone app. (See Figure 2-2.)

Figure 2-2:
A Wear app
displays
an Android
activity.

Wearable Apps: What's the Big Deal?

In the previous section, I spend considerable effort to convince you that Wearable apps are very much like phone apps. But if things are so similar, why have a separate Android Wear chapter? Why not just write "Follow the steps you followed in all the other chapters" and be done with it?

The answer is, some aspects of wearable app development are different from their phone and tablet counterparts. The most obvious difference is screen size. You can't display very much on a one-inch screen, so you have to design your app accordingly. A wearable app typically comes in two parts — one part that runs on the wearable device, and another part that runs on the user's phone. The phone part can make use of the larger screen size, so the phone part can contain menus, setup screens, and other features. (Imagine that! I refer to a phone, and I write "larger screen size!")

Another limitation for wearables is the number of classes in the API. The following packages don't work with wearables:

✦ `android.webkit`

✦ `android.print`

✦ `android.app.backup`

✦ `android.appwidget`

✦ `android.hardware.usb`

Like their phone counterparts, each make and model of wearable supports its own set of features. For example, some models have built-in heart rate monitors; others don't. You can test for the presence of a heart rate monitor with the following code:

```
import android.content.pm.PackageManager;
...
PackageManager = context.getPackageManager();
if (packageManager.hasSystemFeature
            (PackageManager.FEATURE_SENSOR_HEART_RATE)) {
   // Etc.
```

The `PackageManager` class has dozens of constants like `FEATURE_SENSOR_HEART_RATE` for the many features that a device may or may not have.

Another important aspect of wearable development is the device's timeout behavior. When you wake up a phone, you see a lock screen. And when you unlock the screen, you see whatever activity was running when the phone went to sleep. But wearables are different. When you wake up a wearable, there's no lock screen. Instead, you see either the watch face (typically, the current time) or a new notification. One way or another, activities on wearables don't automatically stick around the way they do on phones and tablets. So if you want something that stays on the screen, you need an *always-on app*.

For information about always-on apps, visit `developer.android.com/training/wearables/apps/always-on.html`.

Case Study: A Watch Face

In any language, the meanings of words change over time. Eventually, the original meanings fade into obscurity. Only linguists and lexicographers know how words' meanings have evolved.

Take, for example, the word "telephone." In the late 1800s, this word came from "tele" (meaning "across") and "phone" (meaning "sound"). In the 1900s, when these devices became widely available, people shortened the word from "telephone" to "phone."

In the 2000s, phones expanded their functionality to include texting, web surfing, game playing, and other activities not directly related to sound or to sending sound across regions of space. Way back when our grandparents were young (as early as the year 2015) phones were replacing credit cards as a primary method of making point-of-sale payments. Now, in the year

2065, we use phones to wash our clothes, mow our lawns, build our cities, and raise our children. Who among us remembers even remotely that the word "phone" came from a root word related to "sound?"

The same kind of thing is true about "watches" and "wearables." Nowadays, people wear watches to look good and to make positive impressions on other people. But in the old days, watches were about telling time. The word "watch" originates from workers being on watch duty carrying devices to help them mark time. Even in the early 2000s, some fashion-challenged people wore watches to keep track of the current time. In fact, one author (Barry Burd, ca. 2015) included a time-display watch face program in this Android book. In addition to displaying time, the example illustrated some interesting wearable app features. For purely historical reasons, I reproduce his instructions (verbatim and in their entirety) here:

1. **Start a new Android project.**

2. **When you get to the Target Android Devices dialog box, select two form factors: the Phone and Tablet form factor, and the Wear form factor.**

3. **When you get to the Add an Activity to Mobile dialog box, select Add No Activity and press Next.**

   The Add an Activity to Wear dialog box appears.

4. **In this dialog box, select Watch Face.**

   The title of this dialog box is misleading. A Watch Face isn't an activity. But the creators of Android Studio can't worry about every little detail.

   When you select Watch Face in this step, you're telling Android Studio to write a lot of code for you. I explore some of this code in the next section. For now, just keep clicking.

5. **Click Next.**

   This takes you to a Customize the Activity dialog box. In this dialog box, you specify a Service Name and a Style.

   - **The Service Name is the name of the main class in your app.**

     The main class isn't an Android activity. It's an Android service.

     In this example, I accept the default `MyWatchFace` name.

   - **The Style is Analog or Digital.**

     Android Studio adds code to your app based on your Style choice.

     In this example, I choose Digital.

6. Click Finish.

The dialog box disappears and you return to Android Studio's main window. The main window contains a skeletal Android Wear app with a very basic digital watch face.

You can run the app that Android Studio has created.

7. In Android Studio's main window, choose Run ⇨ Run 'wear'.

When you do, the wheels start churning. Eventually, the Choose Device dialog box appears.

8. Select a real wearable or an AVD that emulates a wearable device.

For help with AVDs, refer to this chapter's "Setting Up Your Testing Environment" section.

9. Click OK.

After a brief wait, you look at your emulator (or device) screen and . . . nothing! The emulator responds the way all Android Wear devices respond when you load a new watch face. Nothing changes. To see the fruits of your labor, you must switch to the new watch face on your wearable or emulator. Here's how:

10. In the `wear` part of the project, look for a `service` element in the `AndroidManifest.xml` file.

11. Find the value of the `service` element's `android:label` attribute.

In the early 2015 version of Android Studio, this attribute's value is `My Digital`.

Both the `service` and the `application` elements can have `android:label` attributes. The attribute that you want belongs to the `service` element.

12. Tap the wearable's (or emulator's) screen.

A menu item appears.

13. If necessary, scroll the screen until you see the Settings menu item.

14. Tap the Settings menu item.

Lo and behold! Another list of menu items appears.

15. Scroll the list until the Change Watch Face item is highlighted in the center of the screen.

16. Tap the Change Watch Face menu item.

You see a preview of a watch face. The preview is an image and a name.

17. **Scroll leftward until you see a preview with the name that you found in Step 11 (the value of the** `service` **element's** `android:label` **attribute).**

18. **Tap the preview.**

As a result, the preview goes away. The device displays its new watch face screen with numbers ticking the time in hours, minutes, and seconds. To see the watch face that Android Studio version 1.2 creates, look at Figure 2-3.

Figure 2-3:
A simple
digital
watch face.

As you develop an app, it's common to run the app many times, making slight changes in the app's code each time. If your device or emulator displays a particular watch face, and you make changes in that watch face's code, you don't have to perform Steps 10 to 18 every time you run the app. Any changes that you make to the project's watch face take effect as soon as you rerun the project.

Dissecting the skeletal watch face project

Many interesting things lurk inside a typical watch face project's code. This section describes a few of them. As you read this section, you can follow along by examining the code that Android Studio created in the previous set of steps.

The manifest file

When Android Studio creates a skeletal app, you get an `AndroidManifest.xml` file. The `AndroidManifest.xml` file for the skeletal watch face app contains elements that don't appear in skeletal phone apps.

✦ **The** `<uses-feature>` **element**

The code

```
<uses-feature
    android:name="android.hardware.type.watch" />
```

tells the Google Play Store that your app is for wearable devices. The Play Store won't offer to load your app on phones, tablets, or other non-wearable gizmos.

The Google Play Store consults a manifest file's `<uses-feature>` element, but an Android device does *not* consult that element. In other words, having a `uses-feature . . . type.watch` element in your app's manifest file does *not* prevent an ordinary phone from installing your app. Using Android Studio's Run ➪ Run 'wear' command, you can bypass the Play Store and run a wearable app on a phone, a tablet, or an Android-enabled toaster oven. If you don't have an entire project (but have only a project's `.apk` file), you can use Android's `adb` command to side load the `.apk` file onto a non-wearable device. I don't promise that your wearable app will run smoothly (or run at all) on a non-wearable device, but the `<uses-feature>` element won't prevent you from trying.

✦ **The references to preview images**

Android Studio's skeletal watch face app has a `wear/res/drawable` folder. And within that folder, you'll find a few preview images such as `preview_digital.png` and `preview_digital_circular.png`. Unlike most of the items in the Project tool window's `drawable` branch, you don't display these images within the app itself. Instead, Android displays these images when the user scans the list of installed watch faces.

To tell Android about these images, you put references to the images in the manifest file's `<meta-data>` elements:

```
<meta-data
  android:name=
    "com.google.android.wearable.watchface.preview"
  android:resource="@drawable/preview_digital" />
<meta-data
  android:name="com.google.android.wearable.
                     watchface.preview_circular"
  android:resource=
              "@drawable/preview_digital_circular" />
```

✦ **The references to wallpaper**

When you create this chapter's watch face app, you don't create an activity. That's fine, but if your watch face isn't an activity, what is it? The answer: Your watch face is a service. More specifically, your watch face is a *live wallpaper* service.

The live wallpaper feature appeared in Android version 2.1 to provide animated, interactive backgrounds for users. To establish your watch face as a live wallpaper, you put several elements in the `AndroidManifest.xml` file. These include the following:

- A `<meta-data>` element pointing to your app's `res/xml` folder

- The `android.service.wallpaper.WallpaperService` action in an intent filter

- A `<uses-permission>` element with the name `com.google.android.permission.PROVIDE_BACKGROUND`

All these elements turn your watch face into a kind of background for the display on a wearable device.

The Java code

Your app's main Java file extends `CanvasWatchFaceService` (a class in the `android.support.wearable.watchface` package). A full tour of the file is much more than you need for this first watch face app, but I want to point out a few highlights.

The heart of the code is the `onDraw` method. That's not surprising because the name `onDraw` means "here's what you do when you want to draw my watch face." In Android Studio's skeletal app, the `onDraw` method contains the code in Listing 2-1.

Listing 2-1: The onDraw Method

```
@Override
public void onDraw(Canvas canvas, Rect bounds) {

  canvas.drawRect(0, 0, bounds.width(),
                  bounds.height(), mBackgroundPaint);
  mTime.setToNow();
  String text = mAmbient
      ? String.format("%d:%02d", mTime.hour, mTime.minute)
      : String.format("%d:%02d:%02d", mTime.hour,
                      mTime.minute, mTime.second);
  canvas.drawText(text, mXOffset, mYOffset, mTextPaint);
}
```

A *canvas* is where the things that you draw will eventually appear. You draw on a canvas with methods such as `drawLine`, `drawArc`, `drawBitmap`, `drawRect`, and `drawText`. The `drawText` method takes four parameters:

✦ **The first parameter (`text`) is the string of characters to be drawn on the screen.**

In Listing 2-1, this string is either

```
String.format("%d:%02d", mTime.hour, mTime.minute)
```

or

```
String.format("%d:%02d:%02d", mTime.hour,
              mTime.minute, mTime.second)
```

depending on whether the device is in ambient mode or not. *Ambient mode* is the sleepy state in which a device curtails its behavior in order to conserve battery power. Several changes take place automatically when a device switches from interactive to ambient mode. One of them is that, in ambient mode, the screen doesn't get second-by-second updates. Updates take place only minute by minute.

So, with the device in ambient mode, you don't want to display the time in seconds. (If you do, the user sees a seconds counter that updates only once per minute. That's not good.)

✦ **The second and third parameters (**mXOffset and mYOffset**) are float values.**

These values store measurements. One value (mXOffset) is the number of pixels from the left of the device's screen to the leftmost edge of the text. The other value (mYOffset) is the number of pixels from the top of the screen to the top of the text.

The values of mXOffset and mYOffset come from calculations done elsewhere in the same .java file. These calculations involve numbers in your app's res/values/dimens.xml (dimensions) file.

✦ **The fourth parameter (**mTextPaint**) is a value of type** Paint.

Some of the code to create mTextPaint looks like this:

```
Paint mTextPaint;

mTextPaint = new Paint();
mTextPaint = createTextPaint
  (resources.getColor(R.color.digital_text));

float textSize = resources.getDimension(isRound
  ? R.dimen.digital_text_size_round
  : R.dimen.digital_text_size);

mTextPaint.setTextSize(textSize);
```

The value of R.color.digital_text is defined in the project's res/values/colors.xml file:

```
<?xml version="1.0" encoding="utf-8"?>
<resources>
    <color name="digital_background">#000000</color>
    <color name="digital_text">#ffffff</color>
</resources>
```

The color #ffffff represents the color white (the maximum amount of red, the maximum amount of green, and the maximum amount of blue). For more info, refer to Book IV, Chapter 1.

In the Android world, what's already been drawn is either valid or invalid, with "invalid" meaning "the drawing is obsolete." Android calls the onDraw method whenever the current drawing becomes invalid. And to make the drawing obsolete, your app's code calls the invalidate method.

When the device is in ambient mode, your code's onTimeTick method calls invalidate:

```
@Override
public void onTimeTick() {
  super.onTimeTick();
  invalidate();
}
```

When the device is in interactive mode, your code sends itself a MSG_UPDATE_TIME message at regular intervals, and the receipt of that message triggers an invalidate call:

```
final Handler mUpdateTimeHandler = new Handler() {
  @Override
  public void handleMessage(Message message) {
    switch (message.what) {
      case MSG_UPDATE_TIME:
        invalidate();
        if (shouldTimerBeRunning()) {
          long timeMs = System.currentTimeMillis();
          long delayMs = INTERACTIVE_UPDATE_RATE_MS
              - (timeMs % INTERACTIVE_UPDATE_RATE_MS);
          mUpdateTimeHandler.sendEmptyMessageDelayed
                        (MSG_UPDATE_TIME, delayMs);
        }
        break;
    }
  }
};
```

Enhancing the skeletal watch face project

Android Studio creates the skeletal app that's described in the previous section. You get the skeletal app for free simply by clicking buttons when you create a new project. Of course, freebies have disadvantages. For one thing, they seldom do exactly what you want your app to do. For another, looking at canned code isn't as satisfying as writing your own code.

I can't wave a magic wand and have you write your own code. But I can give you instructions for adding some of my code to the skeletal watch face app. My code displays the date (in addition to the current time) in Android Studio's skeletal watch face app.

1. **Add the code in the upcoming Listing 2-2 to the end of the** onDraw **method.**

   When you add this code, Android Studio complains about your new mDatePaint variable. You haven't declared that variable yet. Declaring mDatePaint is your job in the next few steps.

2. **Look for the start of an inner class named** Engine.

   Every Android wallpaper class needs an engine. In this chapter's example, the inner Engine class is a subclass of the CanvasWatchFace Service.Engine class. In fact, this inner class makes up most of the app's Java code.

3. **Add the following declaration near the start of the** Engine **class:**

   ```
   Paint mDatePaint;
   ```

   Next, you have to set the mDatePaint field's properties. You do this by copying the properties that are used for displaying the time of day and then shrinking the size of the text. Here goes:

4. **Add the following statement inside the** onCreate **method:**

   ```
   mDatePaint = new Paint(mTextPaint);
   ```

5. **Add the following statement inside the** onApplyWindowInsets **method:**

   ```
   mDatePaint.setTextSize(textSize / 2);
   ```

   The characters in the date display are half the size of the characters in the time-of-day display. Notice that the size of the text is a property of your paint. Unlike your standard house paint, Android canvas paint determines the size of the characters in your text.

Listing 2-2:   Displaying the Date

```
String dateString = mTime.format("%m/%d/%Y");
Resources resources = MyWatchFace.this.getResources();
float textSize =
    resources.getDimension(R.dimen.digital_text_size);
int width = bounds.width();
double centerX = width / 2;
int startX =
    (int) (centerX - mDatePaint.measureText(dateString) / 2);
canvas.drawText(dateString, startX,
            mYOffset + textSize + 10, mDatePaint);
```

That it! You're done! When you run the app, you see a display like the one in Figure 2-4.

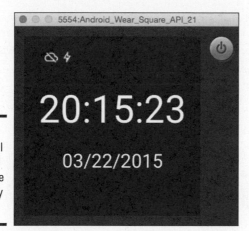

Figure 2-4:
The skeletal
watch face
app with the
date display
added.

The code in Listing 2-2 does almost all the work. First, a `format` call creates a `String` using the current time. Instead of having hours, minutes, and seconds, this string has the month (`%m`), the day of the month (`%d`), and the year (`%y`).

The string `"%m/%d/%Y"` is called a *pattern string*, and the letters in the string (m, d, and Y) are called *pattern characters*. To find out what other pattern characters you can use, visit `http://developer.android.com/reference/java/text/SimpleDateFormat.html`.

In the skeletal app, the variable `mTime` belongs to the `android.text.format.Time` class. As I write this chapter, the `Time` class has been deprecated. In Java-land, the word *deprecated* means "made obsolete." So, starting with Android API Level 22, Android developers aren't supposed to use the `Time` class. (Instead, we're supposed to use the `java.util.GregorianCalendar` class.) The trouble is, early in 2015, the skeletal code that Android Studio writes still uses the old `Time` class. I see a line through the call to the `Time` class's constructor in Android Studio's editor. (A line through a name means that the name has been deprecated.) By the time you follow this chapter's instructions, the skeletal app might use the newer `GregorianCalendar` class. If so, the following code will create a date string:

```
SimpleDateFormat dateFormat =
                new SimpleDateFormat("MM/dd/yyyy");
dateFormat.setCalendar(calendar);
String dateString =
                dateFormat.format(calendar.getTime());
```

In Listing 2-2, after creating `dateString`, I do some math to figure out where to draw the `dateString` string on the screen. I want to center the date string horizontally, so I make `centerX` be half the width of the screen.

Then I call the paint's `measureText` method to find out how many pixels wide the `dateString` is. Finally, I put the left edge of the date string (the `startX` value) at `centerX` minus half the width of the date string. (See Figure 2-5.)

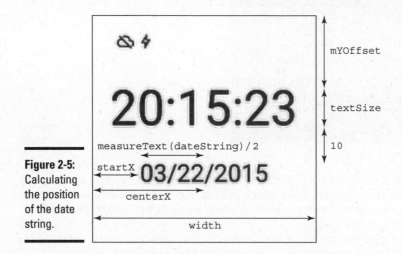

Figure 2-5: Calculating the position of the date string.

The `drawText` method's third parameter is the distance (in pixels) from the top of the screen to the top of the date string. I confess. In Listing 2-2, I guess at this measurement. I start with the top of the big time of day string (`mYOffset`), I add the height of the time of day string (`textSize`), and then I add 10 pixels for good measure. (Again, refer to Figure 2-5.) You can do better than simply guessing the way I do. But there's not much news in the more accurate code. The calculations for the date string's height are similar to the ones I do for the horizontal position.

Chapter 3: Developing for Android TV

In This Chapter

✔ **Running Android apps for television sets**

✔ **Running Android Studio's TV app**

✔ **Creating an Android TV app**

D o you remember the first time you heard about "the cloud"? I'm not referring to condensed water vapor. I'm referring to that collection of hardware and software that feeds us our contacts, our calendars, and our bookmarks wherever we go. Some buzzwords like the word "cloud" enter our psyches without fuss or fanfare. Other buzzwords knock us on the head and say "Pay attention to me. I will become important."

I had an interesting response when I first heard about the *ten-foot experience*. I was at a seminar on Amazon Fire TV, and I was wondering why anyone needed a ten-foot TV screen. I had seen 70-inch TV screens in stores and wanted to know how a ten-foot device would fit into the average consumer's living room.

Of course, I was getting the story all wrong. In the phrase *ten-foot experience*, "ten feet" doesn't refer to the screen size. It refers to the user's distance from the device. The basic idea is, when a user isn't right up against a screen (the way we are with computer monitors and cellphone screens), the user interface must be designed accordingly. You can't have lots of detail on a television screen because the user can't see very much detail. In addition, most TVs don't have the kinds of input facilities that computers (or even smartphones) have. A remote control or a game controller is a crude instrument compared with a keyboard, a mouse, or even a virtual keypad on a smartphone screen. So when you design an app for Android TV, you can't expect the user to do much scrolling or typing.

The ten-foot experience plays an important role in the creation of good Android TV apps. For many apps, the user doesn't do any continuous (smooth) scrolling. Instead, scrolling jumps from one item to the next. Of course, when the user searches for his or her favorite program, you need text or speech input. For text input, a keyboard appears on the screen, and the user scrolls from key to key (a slow and tedious process). For speech input, the user says a phrase out loud. When the device's voice recognizer gets the phrase all wrong, the user says the phrase a second time (much louder this time). Yelling titles into a remote control device can be embarrassing if you're living in a house with other people.

Anyway, in this chapter, I provide a brief introduction to Android's TV app development environment.

Getting Started

To get started with Android TV development, plug an Android TV device into your development computer. If you don't have such a device (or you don't want to move the device from your living room to your office), create an Android TV AVD on your development computer. To do so, follow the steps that you follow in Chapter 2 of this minibook for creating an Android Wear AVD. (The only change is to select TV instead of Wear when you pick a device category.)

After creating an AVD, you're ready to start a TV project. Follow the same steps that you follow for creating a Phone and Tablet project, but make the following changes:

✦ In the Target Android Devices dialog box, remove the Phone and Tablet check mark, and put a check mark in the TV box.

✦ When you reach the Add an Activity dialog box, select Android TV Activity.

You probably would have done these things without reading about them in this chapter. One way or another, you get a skeletal app with an enormous amount of meat on its bones. (The word "skeletal" doesn't do justice to this newly created app.) The Project tool window's tree is shown in Figure 3-1.

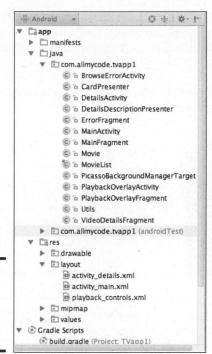

Figure 3-1:
Android
Studio's
skeletal TV
app.

Running the Skeletal App

Television sets don't have touch screens. So when you start up the emulator
and click your mouse on the TV screen's icons, you find the emulator to be
particularly unresponsive. Look for a small panel of buttons on the edge of
the emulator window. Figure 3-2 has an example.

Figure 3-2:
An
Android TV
emulator's
buttons.

In Figure 3-2, the capsule-shaped button and the left/right/up/down buttons surrounding that capsule do most of the work. Use these directional buttons to scroll from one screen item to another. Use the capsule-shaped button as a kind of Enter key.

If you look at the emulator's Home screen, you might see an icon displaying the words Videos by Your Company. (See Figure 3-3.)

Figure 3-3:
The skeletal app's icon.

When you click the Videos by Your Company icon, the emulator fires up the activity shown in Figure 3-4.

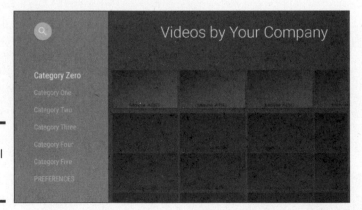

Figure 3-4:
The skeletal app's main activity.

The app's layout has several rows. In Figure 3-4, the top row has the heading Category Zero and has several Movie ABC entries. The next several rows don't look like real rows. In fact, only one of the headings (Category Zero) appears immediately to the left of its corresponding items. The Category Two row heading appears roughly midway between the top and bottom of the screen, but the movie items in the Category Two row appear near the bottom of the screen. This happens because the items are taller than the headings, and the layout tries to keep as many headings on the screen as possible.

When the user scrolls from one heading to another (say, from Category Zero to Category Two), the rows of items scroll proportionately so that the Category Two heading is immediately to the left of its Category Two items.

In Figure 3-4, Category Zero is highlighted. If you scroll rightward from Category Zero, you see a highlighted version of a video (the leftmost video in the Category Zero row). See Figure 3-5.

Figure 3-5:
You've
scrolled to
one of the
videos.

If you press Enter with a video selected, you see a detail screen for that particular video. (See Figure 3-6.)

Figure 3-6:
A detail
screen.

None of the videos in the fictional app really exist, so the detailed description of each video is mumbo-jumbo. (According to Google Translate, the first few sentences in Figure 3-6 are Latin for "Clinical this traffic. This cartoon always drink. Unfortunately, sad, clinical, but always the latest and the mass of Zen as it has been, it is not the earth, who Planning relax." Does this sound like a movie that you'd want to rent or buy?)

The emulator's Back button returns you to the grid full of videos. If you scroll downward, you eventually reach a list of preferences. (See Figure 3-7.)

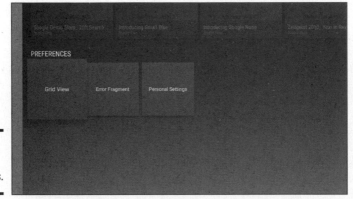

Figure 3-7:
Some
preferences.

The richness of Android Studio's skeletal TV app might seem strange. But (I think) there's method to this madness. It's all about the ten-foot experience, also known as the *lean-back experience*.

When you use a computer, you're in work mode. You lean forward and try to accomplish something. (It might be something frivolous, but it's an accomplishment nevertheless.) When you watch television, you're not in work mode. You want to minimize any accomplishment phase. Your primary purpose is to lean back and enjoy the show. You want to relax. So, with Android TV, it's especially important that the user interface is unobtrusive. You want every interface to look like every other interface. That way, you can use simple reflexes to navigate from category to category, from movie to movie, and from a highlighted movie to details about the movie. If the skeletal app has so much pre-built scaffolding, it's to make that scaffolding be the same for every app's interface. With such a familiar interface, users can ignore the app's interface and relax with their favorite movies.

Creating a TV App

The skeletal TV app that Android Studio creates contains too much code for leisurely bedside reading. In this section, I present an app that's scaled down from Android Studio's skeletal app. My app illustrates the backbone features in the skeletal app. Figures 3-8 and 3-9 illustrate my simple app's behavior.

Figure 3-8:
A super
simple
sample.

Figure 3-9:
The user
moves to a
movie item.

You can download my simple app from this book's web site (`allmycode.com/android`). What the heck? You can download all the apps in this book from the book's web site!

My app starts with the layout shown in Listing 3-1.

Listing 3-1:   The Layout for This Section's App

```
<LinearLayout xmlns:android=
    "http://schemas.android.com/apk/res/android"
   android:layout_width="match_parent"
   android:layout_height="match_parent"
   android:orientation="vertical">

   <fragment android:name=
       "android.support.v17.leanback.app.BrowseFragment"
      android:id="@+id/browse_fragment"
      android:layout_width="match_parent"
      android:layout_height="match_parent" />
</LinearLayout>
```

The layout contains only one element — an instance of Android's pre-declared `BrowseFragment` class. A `BrowseFragment` is an elaborate layout element consisting of one or more rows. Each row has a header and several "movie" items. (Refer to Figure 3-8.)

The app's main activity grabs the layout's `BrowseFragment` and populates it with data. The main activity is in Listing 3-2.

Listing 3-2: The Main Activity

```
package com.allmycode.catalogbrowser;

import android.app.Activity;
import android.app.FragmentManager;
import android.os.Bundle;
import android.support.v17.leanback.app.BrowseFragment;
import
    android.support.v17.leanback.widget.ArrayObjectAdapter;
import android.support.v17.leanback.widget.HeaderItem;
import android.support.v17.leanback.widget.ListRow;
import android.support.v17.leanback.widget.ListRowPresenter;

public class BrowseMediaActivity extends Activity {

  protected BrowseFragment mBrowseFragment;

  @Override
  protected void onCreate(Bundle savedInstanceState) {
    super.onCreate(savedInstanceState);
    setContentView(R.layout.browse_fragment);

    final FragmentManager fragmentManager =
                                  getFragmentManager();
    mBrowseFragment = (BrowseFragment) fragmentManager.
              findFragmentById(R.id.browse_fragment);

    mBrowseFragment.
        setHeadersState(BrowseFragment.HEADERS_ENABLED);
    mBrowseFragment.
        setTitle(getString(R.string.app_name));
    mBrowseFragment.setBadgeDrawable(getResources().
        getDrawable(R.drawable.ic_launcher, null));

    buildRowsAdapter();
  }

  private ArrayObjectAdapter mRowsAdapter;
  private static final int NUM_ROWS = 4;

  private void buildRowsAdapter() {
    mRowsAdapter =
          new ArrayObjectAdapter(new ListRowPresenter());
```

```
for (int i = 0; i < NUM_ROWS; ++i) {
  ArrayObjectAdapter listRowAdapter =
      new ArrayObjectAdapter(new CardPresenter());
  listRowAdapter.add("Media Item " + i + ".1");
  listRowAdapter.add("Media Item " + i + ".2");
  listRowAdapter.add("Media Item " + i + ".3");
  HeaderItem header =
                new HeaderItem(i, "Category " + i);
  mRowsAdapter.add
                (new ListRow(header, listRowAdapter));
}

mBrowseFragment.setAdapter(mRowsAdapter);
  }
}
```

Each row consists of a heading and a bunch of individual items. For example, in Figure 3-8, shown earlier, the selected row's heading contains the text *Category 1*, and the row's items (like all other items) display the slanted *Movie!* graphic. The code in Listing 3-2 puts these things onto the screen.

In Listing 3-2, the body of the `buildRowsAdapter` method contains a `for` loop. The loop performs an iteration for each row. During one loop iteration, three calls to `listRowAdapter.add` create the movies in a row, and a call to the `HeaderItem` constructor creates a category heading (such as the *Category 1* heading in Figure 3-8). At the end of a loop iteration, the call to `mRowsAdapter.add` puts the entire row onto the user's screen.

The Adapter and the Presenter

Central to the mission of the code in Listing 3-2 are the notions of an `Adapter` and a `Presenter`. An `Adapter` stores data, and a `Presenter` displays the data that an `Adapter` stores. That's the way Android's TV classes separate data from presentation.

It's a classic principle of app development:

> *Data and presentation don't belong in the same parts of your code.*

If you interleave your data code with your presentation code, it's difficult to modify the presentation without messing up the data. Data is data, whether it's displayed on a 70-inch TV or a one-inch watch screen.

Imagine dealing with data about a movie as in Figure 3-6, shown earlier. In a more realistic app, the data might include the title, the release date, a synopsis, the actors' names, a link to a trailer, and other information. A user might view the data on an Android TV. But in another setting, the same user might view the same data on a computer, a smartphone, or whatever other device is available. With the presentation code separated from the data code, you can provide several alternatives for displaying the same data. With one class to store the data, you can plug in a big TV display one time, a smartphone display another time, and a 10-inch laptop display the next time. You can offer the user a choice of interfaces — one for daytime browsing and another for nighttime perusal. You're ready for any kind of display because the code to control the data doesn't care what display logic is behind it.

Imagine changing the way you store each movie's release date. Instead of storing an ordinary Gregorian calendar date, you decide to store each movie's Star Trek star date. (According to one online calculator, the first *Matrix* movie was released in the United States on star date –323754.8.) With the data decoupled from the display, you don't have to inform your display code about this data storage change. The data code already has a method named `getReleaseDate`, and the presentation code calls this method during the app's run. While you're setting up the data code to handle star dates, you modify the `getReleaseDate` method to convert between star dates and Gregorian dates. The display code doesn't know about this change, and what the display code doesn't know won't hurt it.

Using the Adapter class

Figure 3-10 illustrates the relationships among classes used in Listing 3-2.

For an adapter, TV apps normally use the `ArrayObjectAdapter` class (a member of the `android.support.v17.leanback.widget` package). When you construct a new `ArrayObjectAdapter`, you supply a `Presenter` in the constructor call.

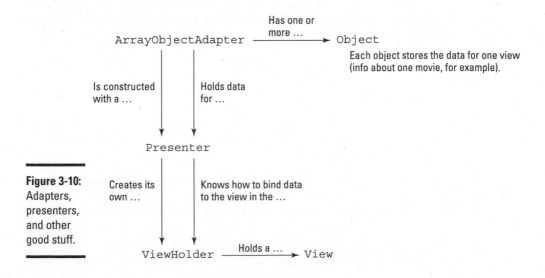

Figure 3-10: Adapters, presenters, and other good stuff.

```
private ArrayObjectAdapter mRowsAdapter;
...
mRowsAdapter =
      new ArrayObjectAdapter(new ListRowPresenter());
...
ArrayObjectAdapter listRowAdapter =
      new ArrayObjectAdapter(new CardPresenter());
```

Thus, each `ArrayObjectAdapter` has its own `Presenter`.

But that's not all. Each `Presenter` constructs its own `ViewHolder`. (The `ViewHolder` class is an inner class of the `Presenter` class. Each `Presenter` actually constructs its own `Presenter.ViewHolder`.)

A `ViewHolder` holds a view. (Don't look so surprised!) An instance of the `ViewHolder` class has no methods of its own and has only one public field. The public field is the `view` field. A `ViewHolder` instance's `view` field refers to whatever view the `ViewHolder` is holding. A presenter displays views, and a presenter gets its views from the `ViewHolder`. You can think of the `ViewHolder` as a cache for views. The `ViewHolder` stores views so that you don't have to call `findViewById` to get a view.

But wait! Why would you avoid calling `findViewById`?

Calling `findViewById` means digging into the hierarchy of elements in an XML file, and this hierarchy might be fairly deep. So calling `findViewById` can be computationally expensive. You don't mind calling `findViewById` once or twice in an `onCreate` method, but you don't want to call `findViewById` repeatedly as movie items (views) scroll on and off of a screen. What's more, there's room on the screen for only a certain number of movie items. As one item scrolls onto one side of the screen, another item scrolls off the other side of the screen. This means that views can be recycled and reused. The view that you see leaving the left edge of the screen might be the same view that you eventually see entering on the right side. (The view has been recycled, so the movie on that view isn't the same from one appearance of that view to the next.) The `ViewHolder` manages this recycling behavior so that precious views don't go to waste, and calls to `findViewById` are unnecessary.

In Listing 3-2, a call to an adapter's `add` method adds an object to the adapter. This adding process happens in two ways.

✦ In my not-so-realistic code, adding a movie to a row means adding a string.

```
listRowAdapter.add("Media Item " + i + ".1");
```

✦ After adding movies to a row, you add the row to the grid.

```
mRowsAdapter.add
            (new ListRow(header, listRowAdapter));
```

The mRowsAdapter variable refers to the entire grid. In addition to several movies, each row of the grid has a header. In the previously shown Figure 3-8, the highlighted row's header is the text *Category 1*.

When you're done calling the add methods in Listing 3-2, you have the adapters shown in Figure 3-11.

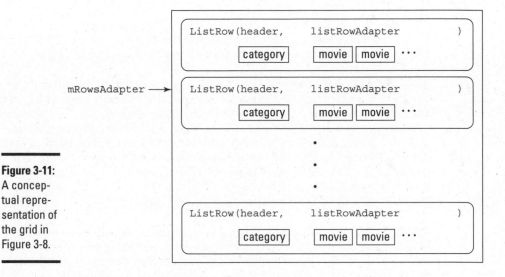

Figure 3-11:
A conceptual representation of the grid in Figure 3-8.

Using the Presenter class

When you construct a new ArrayObjectAdapter, you supply a presenter in the constructor call. Thus, an ArrayObjectAdapter has its own presenter. Keep that idea in mind while you read the following facts:

✦ The presenter belonging to a row of items handles the presenting of an individual item (a movie, for example).

✦ The presenter belonging to an entire grid handles the presenting of an individual row in the grid.

I illustrate these facts in Figure 3-12. In the figure, each listRowAdapter stores an entire row of movies. But each listRowAdapter has one CardPresenter instance. At any given time, that CardPresenter instance handles the display of a single movie item.

A *card* is a rectangular area in which an object's data are displayed. In Figure 3-5, the highlighted card's title is *Zeitgeist 2010_ Year in Review*.

In Figure 3-12, the mRowsAdapter stores several rows. But the mRows-Adapter has one ListRowPresenter instance. At any given time, that ListRowPresenter instance handles the display of a single row.

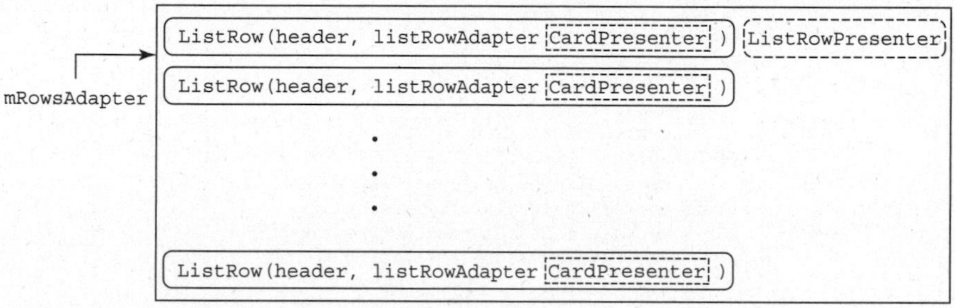

Figure 3-12:
The
relationship
between
adapters
and
presenters.

You don't have to define the ListRowPresenter class. That class is declared in Android's own android.support.v17.leanback.widget package. But you do have to define a CardPresenter class. Listing 3-3 contains my simple app's CardPresenter class.

Listing 3-3:   The Presenter

```
package com.allmycode.catalogbrowser;

import android.content.Context;
import android.support.v17.leanback.widget.ImageCardView;
import android.support.v17.leanback.widget.Presenter;
import android.view.View;
import android.view.ViewGroup;

public class CardPresenter extends Presenter {

  private static Context mContext;
  private static int CARD_WIDTH = 313;
  private static int CARD_HEIGHT = 176;

  static class ViewHolder extends Presenter.ViewHolder {
    private ImageCardView mCardView;

    public ViewHolder(View view) {
      super(view);
      mCardView = (ImageCardView) view;
    }
  }

  @Override
  public ViewHolder onCreateViewHolder(ViewGroup parent) {
    mContext = parent.getContext();
    ImageCardView cardView = new ImageCardView(mContext);
```

(continued)

Listing 3-3 *(continued)*

```
    cardView.setFocusable(true);
    cardView.setFocusableInTouchMode(true);
    return new ViewHolder(cardView);
}

@Override
public void onBindViewHolder
        (Presenter.ViewHolder viewHolder, Object item) {
    ((ViewHolder) viewHolder).mCardView.
        setTitleText((String) item);
    ((ViewHolder) viewHolder).mCardView.
        setMainImageDimensions(CARD_WIDTH, CARD_HEIGHT);
    ((ViewHolder) viewHolder).mCardView.
        setMainImage(mContext.getResources().
        getDrawable(R.drawable.movie_poster, null));
}

@Override
public void onUnbindViewHolder
                    (Presenter.ViewHolder viewHolder) {
    //No unbinding code needed in this simple example
}
}
```

The presenter in Listing 3-3 has three required methods:

✦ **The** `onCreateViewHolder` **method does what its name suggests. It creates a** `ViewHolder` **instance.**

The `ViewHolder` instance has a view. How nice!

✦ **The** `onBindViewHolder` **method binds data to a** `ViewHolder` **instance.**

In Listing 3-3, the view in the `ViewHolder` gets the properties that you see in Figure 3-9. In particular, the card's title becomes `Movie Item 1.1` (or whatever other string you pass in Listing 3-2). The card's background becomes `R.drawable.movie_poster` (my own image — the diagonal word *Movie!* on a white background).

✦ **The** `onUnbindViewHolder` **method can do some cleanup when the data in a view becomes obsolete.**

In Listing 3-3, the `onUnbindViewHolder` method does nothing. But in a more complicated example, the `onUnbindViewHolder` method sets fields to `null` and releases resources that were being hogged by the view. For example, if your movie item plays music, you probably call `MediaPlayer.create` in the `onBindViewHolder` method. So, in the `onUnbindViewHolder` method, you call the `MediaPlayer` class's `release` method.

Book VI

The Job Isn't Done Until . . .

Contents at a Glance

Chapter 1: Publishing Your App to the Google Play Store

In This Chapter

✔ **Creating a developer account**

✔ **Prepping your code**

✔ **Uploading your app**

First-time app publishing is both exciting and scary. It's exciting because, after months of development work, you're finally doing something "real" with your app. It's scary because you're exposing your app to the public. You're afraid of pressing the wrong button on the Google Play developer page, and accidentally telling the world that your app kills kittens.

Well, you can relax about killing kittens. The Google Play developer page helps you get things right. And if you get something wrong, you can correct it pretty quickly. As for the excitement of publishing, there's nothing quite like it.

In this chapter, you take those courageous steps. You create a developer account and publish your first app. When you've stopped glowing from the overall experience, you can send me an email telling me what you've done. (That way, I can glow a little bit, too.)

Creating a Google Play Developer Account

Choosing Android for your app platform has some distinct advantages. To develop for the iPhone, you pay an annual $99 fee. I've been developing mobile apps for over five years. So, as an iPhone developer, I would have paid $495 by now. (I would have incurred this fee even if I wanted to test my apps on my own physical devices, without actually publishing any apps.) As an Android developer, working over the same five-year period, I've paid $25. That's all.

To create a Google Play developer account, visit `https://play.google.com/apps/publish/signup`. On this page, you do the following:

✦ **Agree to the Google Play developer distribution rules.**

✦ **Pay the $25 fee.**

✦ **Provide your account details.**

These details include your name, email, phone, and (optionally) your website URL.

If you're working with a team, you can provide your coworkers' email addresses and set up each coworker's permissions on your account.

If you plan to collect money through your app, you can set up a merchant account. When you do so, you provide your business name, contact name, address, phone, website URL, customer service email, and credit card statement name. There's also a What Do You Sell drop-down list. There are so many choices in this drop-down list that my mind starts to wander. Can I sell Automotive and Marine supplies? Nutrients and Supplements? Timeshares? And what about Other? Can I also sell Other?

None of the information that you provide when you first sign up is cast in stone. You can change this information later using the Google Play's Settings page.

Preparing Your Code

At this point, you're probably tired of looking at your own app. You've written the basic app, tested the app, fixed the bugs, tested again, added features, done more testing, stayed up late at night, and done even more testing. But if you plan to publish you're app, I have one piece of advice: After you've finished testing, test some more.

Ask yourself what sequences of buttons you avoided clicking when you did your "thorough" testing. Then muster the courage to click the buttons and use the widgets in those strange sequences. And while you're at it, tilt the device sideways, turn the device upside down, hold the device above your head, and try using the app. If your device is a phone, interrupt the app with an incoming call.

Are you finished testing? Not yet. Have your friends test the app on their devices. Whatever you do, don't give them any instructions other than the instructions you intend to publish. Better yet, don't even give them the instructions that you intend to publish. (Some users won't read those instructions anyway.) Ask your friends about their experiences running your app. If you sense that your friends are being too polite, press them for more details.

You can "publish" your app on Google Play so that only your designated friends can install the app. For more information, skip ahead to the "More Testing" section.

Can I overemphasize the need for testing? I don't think so. When you test your app, be your app's worst enemy. Try as hard as you can to break your app. Be overly critical. Be relentless. If your app has a bug and you don't find it, your users will.

Un-testing the app

When you test an app, you find features that don't quite work. You check the logs, and you probably add code to help you diagnose problems. As you prepare to publish your app, remove any unnecessary diagnostic code, remove extra logging statements, and remove any other code whose purpose is to benefit the developer rather than the user.

In developing your app, you might have created some test data. (Is there a duck named "Donald" in your app's contact list?) If you've created test data, delete the data from your app.

Check your project's `AndroidManifest.xml` file. If the `<application>` element has an `android:debuggable="true"` attribute, remove that attribute. (The attribute's default value is `false`.)

**Book VI
Chapter 1**

Publishing Your App
to the Google Play
Store

Choosing Android versions

When you create a new project, Android Studio asks you for a Minimum SDK version. Your project's `build.gradle` file keeps a record of your choice in its `minSdkVersion` field. You can change this number by editing the `build.gradle` file.

This `minSdkVersion` number is important because it shouldn't be too low or too high.

✦ **If the** `minSdkVersion` **number is too low, your app isn't using features from newer Android versions.**

If your app is very simple, this is okay. But if your app does anything that looks different in newer Android versions, your app's vintage look might turn users off.

✦ **If the** `minSdkVersion` **number is too high, the Play Store won't offer your app to users with older devices.**

In fact, if your app's `minSdkVersion` is 21, a user who visits the Play Store on a KitKat device doesn't even see your app. (You might have already encountered the `INSTALL_FAILED_OLDER_SDK` error message. Android Studio can't install an app on the emulator that you selected because the emulator's SDK version is lower than the app's `minSdk Version`.)

You don't want to eliminate users simply because they don't have the latest and greatest Android devices. So to reach more users, keep the `minSdkVersion` from being too high. If your app doesn't use any features that were introduced after API Level 11, set your `minSdkLevel` to 11.

Try running your app on emulators with many API levels. When you run into trouble (say, on an emulator with API level 10) set your project's `minSdk Level` to something higher than that troublesome level.

When you create a new project, the Target Android Devices dialog box contains a Help Me Choose link. When you click this link, you see a chart showing the percentage of devices running Lollipop, KitKat, Jelly Bean, and other Android versions. This clickable chart describes the features in each Android version and (most importantly) shows the percentage of devices that are running each version. With information from this chart, you can choose the best compromise between the latest features and the widest user audience.

Android's *support libraries* allow devices with older Android versions to take advantage of newer Android features. For info, visit `http://developer. android.com/tools/support-library`.

For information about minimum SDK versions, compile SDK versions, and target SDK versions, see Book I, Chapter 4.

Setting your app's own version code and version name

When you create a new project, Android Studio puts some default attributes in your `build.gradle` file. These attributes include the `versionCode` and `versionName` fields:

```
defaultConfig {
  ...
  versionCode 1
  versionName "1.0"
}
```

The version code must be an integer, and your app's code numbers must increase over time. For example, if your first published version has version code 42, your second published version must have a version code higher than 42.

Users never see the version code. Instead, users see your app's version name. You can use any string for your app's version name. Many developers use the `major-release.minor-release.point` system. For example, a typical version name might be 1 . 2 . 2. But there are no restrictions. Android has all the dessert names, and Apple used to use jungle-cat names, so I add something like

```
versionName "sea squirt"
```

to my build.gradle file. (Look it up!)

If you intend to publish on the Amazon Appstore, don't use phrases like sea squirt for your versionName. The Amazon Appstore insists on a version Name of up to five integers separated from one another by dots. For example, versionName values such as 2.30 and 1.2.0.325.0 work just fine.

Choosing a package name

Every Android app has its own package name. So, if your first published app is in the com.example.earnmeamillion package, put your second app in a com.example.secondtimeisacharm package.

Your package name should help to identify you or your company. If you have a domain name, start the package name with the domain name's parts reversed. For example, I'm the proud owner of the domain name allmy code.com, so I publish an app with the package name com.allmycode. clicks. (If *you* publish an app with package name com.allmycode. clicks, you'll hear from my lawyer!)

Preparing Graphic Assets for the Play Store

When you publish an app to the Play Store, you interact with Google Play's *Developer Console*. The essential step in this interaction is the step in which you upload your app's APK file. It's the essential step, but it's by no means the only step. You must also use the Play Store's Developer Console to describe your app in detail. In the Developer Console, you answer many questions about the app, and you provide some important graphic assets. This section describes those graphic assets.

Creating an icon

When you create a new project, Android Studio puts some default attributes in your AndroidManifest.xml file. One of them is the android:icon attribute:

```
<application android:icon="@mipmap/ic-launcher"
    ...                                           >
```

Before publishing your app, replace this default icon name with your own icon's name. Create nice-looking icons by visiting `http://romannurik.github.io/AndroidAssetStudio/icons-launcher.html`. Also check Android's Icon Design Guidelines at `http://developer.android.com/design/style/iconography.html`.

Creating screenshots

Along with every app that you submit to the Play Store, you must submit screenshots. As of early 2015, you must submit at least two screenshots. The Developer Console has slots for phone screenshots, 7-inch tablet screenshots, 10-inch tablet screenshots, and TV screenshots. (From where I sit, early in 2015, there's no special place for an Android Wear screenshot: You just upload that screenshot anywhere you can.) Each screenshot must be JPEG or 24-bit PNG with no alpha transparency. The minimum length for any side is 320 pixels, and the maximum length for any side is 3840 pixels.

There are many ways to take screenshots of your running app. The easiest way is to use Android Studio's built-in Screen Capture facility. Here's what you do:

1. **Use Android Studio to run your app on an emulator or a real device.**

2. **At the far left edge of the Android tool window, look for a little camera icon.**

   When you hover over this icon, you see the words Screen Capture. That's a good sign!

3. **Click the Screen Capture icon.**

   A new window appears. The window shows a screen capture of your device or emulator. You can click the Save button immediately. But you can also click Reload, Rotate, or make several other adjustments.

If Android Studio's Screen Capture facility isn't your thing, you have several alternatives. For example, you can use your operating system's screen capture facility to take a screenshot of a running emulator.

In Windows

1. **Launch your app in the emulator.**

2. **Click the emulator window (so that the emulator window is the active window).**

3. **While you hold down the Alt key, press the Print Screen key in the upper-right corner of the keyboard.**

   Depending on your keyboard's make and model, the key might be labeled PrintScr, PrtSc, or some other variant of Print Screen.

4. **Open an image-editing program.**

   My favorite image-editing program for Windows is IrfanView (www. irfanview.com). I wish I could get a free copy by plugging the software this way. But, alas, the program is completely free.

5. **Press Ctrl-V to paste your new screenshot into the image-editing program.**

On a Mac

1. **Launch your app in the emulator.**

2. **Press Cmd+Shift+4.**

   This tells the Mac that you intend to take a screenshot.

3. **Press the spacebar.**

   This tells the Mac that the screenshot will capture a single window.

4. **Click anywhere inside the emulator window.**

   Your computer creates the screenshot and places it on the desktop.

You can use your development computer's screen capture facility to take a screenshot from a physical device. On your development computer, download a program named Android Screen Monitor (https://code.google. com/p/android-screen-monitor). Connect the physical device via USB to your development computer. When you run Android Screen Monitor, the program displays the physical device's screen in a window on your computer screen.

In theory, on devices running Android 4.0 or later, you can press the Volume Down and Power buttons simultaneously to take a screenshot. The trouble is, the exact sequence of presses and button holds varies from one make and model to another. Check your device's documentation (and other sources) for more info.

Your options for creating screenshots are endless. The paid versions of the Genymotion emulator have their own screen capture facilities. If all else fails (and, in fact, all else seldom fails), you can get screenshots from running emulators and devices using Android Studio's Terminal window. Search the web for adb shell/system/bin/screencap.

Creating a feature graphic and a promo video

If your app is featured on the Play Store (or maybe I should say "*when your app is featured*"), a *feature graphic* appears on your store listing page. Your feature graphic must be a JPEG or 24-bit PNG file with no alpha transparency. Its dimensions must be 1024 by 500 pixels. You can also put a promotional video on the store listing page. To do so, type the promotional video's URL in the Developer Console's Promo Video field.

The blog page `http://android-developers.blogspot.com/2011/10/android-market-featured-image.html` has lots of advice on creating feature graphics. The key is to create an eye-catching image that promotes your app without replicating your app's screen. You should also make sure that the image looks good no matter what size screen displays it.

Creating a Publishable APK File

When you create an app that runs on an emulator or a device, Android Studio packages your app in an APK file — one file specially formatted to contain all your app's code and all your app's data. While you're still developing and testing your app, this APK file is fairly primitive. It doesn't have any of the bells and whistles that the Play Store requires for real, distributable apps.

An app that's ready for release requires a much more solid APK file. Here are some details:

✦ **The APK file must contain your own digital signature.**

A *digital signature* is a sequence of bits that only you (and no one else) can provide. If your APK file contains your digital signature, then no one can pretend to be you. (No one can write a malicious version of your app and publish it on the Play Store site.)

When you follow this section's instructions, you use Android Studio to create your own digital signature. This signature lives in a directory on your computer's hard drive. You can't examine this signature with an ordinary text editor (with Notepad or with TextEdit, for example), but you should treat that directory the way you treat any other confidential information. Do whatever you normally do with data to prevent the loss of the data and to keep others from using it.

You can read more about digital signatures in this chapter's "Understanding digital signatures" sidebar.

✦ **The code must be obfuscated.**

Obfuscated code is confusing code. And, when it comes to foiling malicious hackers, confusing code is good code. If other people can make sense of your Java code, they can steal it. They can make money off of your ideas, or they can add snippets to your code to rob users' credit card accounts.

Understanding digital signatures

When you digitally sign an APK file, you add a sequence of bits that only you can add. You use sophisticated software to create the sequence and to embed the sequence in your APK file. The software to create this sequence uses techniques from number theory. (Sometime between 1777 and 1855, Carl Friedrich Gauss called number theory "the queen of mathematics," and he wasn't kidding!)

Digital signing actually involves two sequences of bits:

✔ **A private key:** A sequence that you don't share with others.

✔ **A public key:** A sequence that you do share with others.

The private key never leaves your office, but you can display the public key on a neon sign in Times Square. If you tell someone your private key, you'd have to . . . (well, you know). But you can hire a pilot to write your public key with white smoke in the sky over the Golden Gate Bridge.

To sign an app, you run software that adds a certificate to your app. A *certificate* is a bunch of information that includes your private key, your public key, some information to identify you, and some other information. Like your signature on a contract, a certificate's private key is difficult to fake. But with the certificate's public key, a program on the user's device verifies that your app is authentic.

A user gets keys from your app's certificate. But as a developer, you store keys apart from any certificate. You keep public and private keys in a place where your software can retrieve them — a *key store* file. When you digitally sign an app, software grabs keys from a key store file, uses the keys to create a certificate, and melds the certificate into your APK file. If you visit your user home directory, and drill down to an .android subdirectory (starting with a dot), you probably find the debug.keystore file. When you test an app on an emulator or on your own device, Android Studio quietly signs your app with a simple key from this debug.keystore file. (For help finding your user home directory, see Book I, Chapter 2.)

A key store file contains sensitive information, so every key store file is password-protected. Android's debug.keystore file is password-protected. But unlike most key store files, the debug.keystore file's password is freely available. The password is android. Anyone can sign any app using keys from the debug.keystore file. That's okay because the debug.keystore file's keys don't work for apps that you publish on the Play Store (or anywhere else, for that matter). So before publishing your app, Android Studio adds your own keys to the app.

After downloading your app, a user's software applies a public key to verify that your app is signed properly. And what does that prove? Well, if a hacker tampers with your app somewhere between publication and the user's downloading, the test for proper signing detects the tampering. "Sorry," says Android, "I refuse to install this app."

But what about a malicious hacker who creates a damaging app and uses Android's freely available tools to sign it? To the world in general, the app looks fine. Signing doesn't verify that an app's developer has good intentions.

The weak link in the chain is the fact that Android apps are *self-signed*. When you add a digital signature to your app, no one else signs with you.

(continued)

(continued)

For scenarios that require more security (scenarios not normally associated with mobile devices), a developer can get help from a certificate authority. A *certificate authority* is an organization that issues special digital signatures — signatures that the world recognizes as very trustworthy. To get such a signature, you convince a certificate authority that you're a good person, and you pay some money to the certificate authority. Some certificate authorities issue signatures for free. These free signatures are okay, but they aren't as trusted as the paid signatures, and they don't have the same clout as the paid signatures.

For more information about Android app signing, visit `http://developer.android.com/tools/publishing/app-signing.html`.

You want developers on your team to read and understand your code with ease, but you don't want some outsider (like my friend, Joe S. Uptonogood) to understand your code. That's why, when you follow this chapter's instructions, Android Studio creates an APK file with obfuscated code.

You can read more about obfuscated code in this chapter's "Don't wait! Obfuscate!" sidebar.

Don't wait! Obfuscate!

Nestled quietly inside your project's directory is a `proguard-rules.pro` file, and sitting humbly on your computer's hard drive is a `proguard-android.txt` file. These two files contain configuration information for the ProGuard program. The ProGuard program minifies, preverifies, and obfuscates your code.

To *minify* code is to make the code smaller by removing unnecessary classes, fields, and methods. This includes classes belonging to the Java and Android libraries.

Preverifying code means performing a certain kind of safety check on the code. This safety check looks for places where the code can escape from its virtual machine and start running wild on the rest of the device's operating system. Code that doesn't pass this check gets a failing grade from ProGuard.

When you *obfuscate* something, you make it difficult to read. You scramble stuff and generally do the opposite of what you're supposed to do when you write clear, maintainable code.

Why do this? An obfuscated program can be executed without modification by an appropriate device. The device doesn't need a password and doesn't have to decrypt anything in order to run the code. In fact, an obfuscated program contains nothing unusual as far as the Android runtime (ART) is concerned. But for a person trying to reverse-engineer your code, the obfuscation is a nightmare. That's because the human mind doesn't process code mechanically. Instead, humans get the big picture; humans have to understand things in order to work with them; humans feel stress when they work with things that are terse, circuitous, and highly compressed.

So with obfuscated code, evil people can't easily figure out how your code works. They have trouble stealing your tricks, and (more important) they can't easily add viruses to your published code.

Before publishing on the Play Store, you must obfuscate your app's code. Fortunately, the steps in this chapter's "Creating a Publishable APK File" section do the obfuscation for you. Android Studio applies ProGuard tools to your code, turning your code into a dizzying mess for anyone trying to tinker with it.

ProGuard is an open-source project; its website lives at `http://proguard.sourceforge.net`.

✦ **The code must be zipaligned.**

Zipaligned code is easier to execute than code that's not zipaligned. Fortunately, when you follow this chapter's steps, Android Studio zipaligns your code (and does so behind your back, without any intervention on your part).

You can read more about zipalignment in this chapter's "Byte off more than you can view" sidebar.

Byte off more than you can view

The Android operating system (along with all other UNIX-like systems) has a mmap program. The letters mm in mmap stand for *memory-mapped* input and output. The mmap program grabs data from a file and makes the data available to applications. The mmap program is a real workhorse, providing quick and efficient data access for many apps at once.

The nimbleness of mmap doesn't come entirely for free. For mmap to do its work,

certain values must be stored so they start at four-byte boundaries. To understand four-byte boundaries, think about a chunk of data in your application's APK file. A *byte* is eight bits of data (each bit being a 0 or a 1). So four bytes is 32 bits. Now imagine two values (Value A and Value B) stored one after the other in your APK file. (See the figure in this sidebar.) Value A consumes three bytes, and Value B consumes four bytes.

(continued)

(continued)

Without four-byte alignment, the computer might store the first byte of Value B immediately after the last byte of Value A. If so, Value B starts on the last byte of a four-byte group. But mmap works only when each value starts at the beginning of a four-byte group. So Android's zipalign program moves data, as shown in the lower half of the figure below. Instead of using every available byte, zipalign wastes a byte in order to make Value B easy to locate.

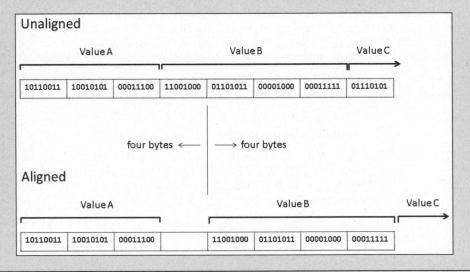

This section starts with my lengthy description of the ways publishable APK files differ from other APK files. With all that chatter about publishable APK files, you'll be surprised to find out that creating a publishable APK file isn't very complicated. Just follow these instructions:

1. **Make the changes described in this chapter's "Preparing Your Code" section.**

2. **In Android Studio's main menu, choose Build ⇨ Generate Signed APK.**

   The Generate Signed APK dialog box appears. (See Figure 1-1.) This dialog box has a drop-down list in which you select one of your project's modules. Most of this book's examples have only one module — namely, the app module.

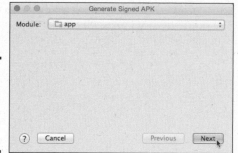

Figure 1-1:
The first
Generate
Signed APK
dialog box.

3. **Click Next.**

   As a result, another Generate Signed APK dialog box appears. (See Figure 1-2.) This box contains a Key Store Path field.

Figure 1-2:
Android
Studio asks
for a Key
Store Path.

For some good bedtime reading about key stores, see the "Understanding digital signatures" sidebar.

In what follows, I assume that you haven't yet created a key store. (If you've created one, you'll know that you did.)

4. **Click the Create New button.**

   As a result, a New Key Store dialog box opens.

5. **Choose a name and a location for your key store. Put the full path name (the location and filename) of the new key store in the dialog box's Key Store Path field.**

   See the first field in Figure 1-3. I create a key store file named `android.jks`, and I put the new file in a directory named `/Users/barryburd/keystores`. (In the filename `android.jks`, the extension `.jks` stands for *Java key store*.) Notice that I don't put the new key store in my project's directory. As I publish more apps, I'll probably use this key store to sign other projects' APK files.

Figure 1-3:
The New
Key Store
dialog box.

Signing all your Android projects with the same key is a very good idea. Android treats the key as a kind of fingerprint, and two apps with the same fingerprint can be trusted to communicate with one another. When two apps have the same key, you can easily get these apps to help one another out.

Android Studio's New Key Store dialog box won't create a directory for you. If you type `/Users/myUserName/keystores/something.jks` in the Key Store Path field, you must have a `/Users/myUserName/keystores` directory before you click OK.

At this point, it helps to understand the difference between a key store file and a single key. A *key* is what you use to digitally sign your Android app. A *key store file* is a place to store one or more keys. That's why, in Figure 1-3, you supply two passwords — one for the new key store file, and another for the key that you'll be putting in the key store file.

6. **Enter passwords in the Password and Confirm fields.**

   Do yourself and favor and make 'em strong passwords.

(In the lingo of *For Dummies* books, this is a Remember icon.) Please remember to remember the passwords that you create when you fill in the Password and Confirm fields. You'll need to enter these passwords when you use this key to sign another app.

In a key store file, each key has a name (an *alias*, that is).

7. **Type a name in the Alias field.**

   The alias can be any string of characters, but I recommend against being creative when you make up an alias. Avoid blank spaces and punctuation. If you ever create a second key with a second alias, make sure that the second alias's spelling (and not only its capitalization) is different from the first alias's spelling.

8. **Accept the default validity period (25 years).**

   If you create a key on New Year's Day in 2016, the key will expire on New Year's Day in 2041. Happy New Year, everybody! According to the Play Store's rules, your key must not expire until sometime after October 22, 2033, so 25 years from 2016 is okay. (I can't imagine how the creators of Android came up with the date October 22, 2033. I'm wondering what kind of party I should throw when this day finally rolls around.)

9. **In the Certificate section, fill in at least one of the six fields. (Refer to Figure 1-3.)**

   The items *First and Last Name, Organizational Unit,* and so on are part of the *X.500 Distinguished Name* standard. The probability of two people having the same name and working in the same unit of the same organization in the same locality is close to zero.

   When you finish, your dialog box resembles Figure 1-3.

10. **Click OK.**

    As a result, the Generate Signed APK dialog box from Figure 1-2 reappears. This time, many of the box's fields are filled in for you. (See Figure 1-4.)

11. **Click Next.**

    When you do, one last Generate Signed APK dialog box appears. (See Figure 1-5.)

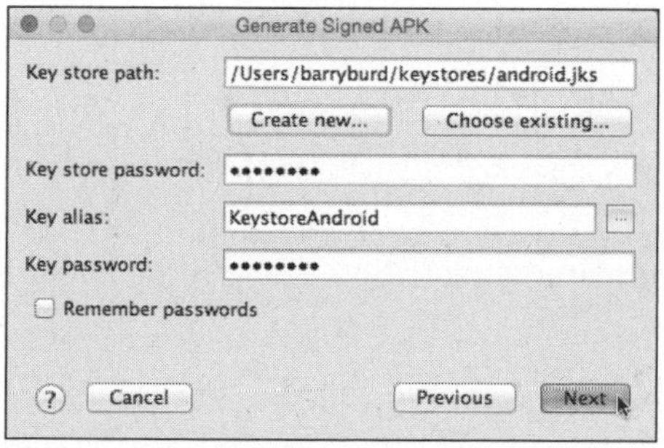

Book VI
Chapter 1

Publishing Your App
to the Google Play
Store

Figure 1-4:
On your way
to an APK.

● ● ●	Generate Signed APK
Key store path:	/Users/barryburd/keystores/android.jks
	Create new... Choose existing...
Key store password:	••••••••
Key alias:	KeystoreAndroid
Key password:	••••••••
☐ Remember passwords	
⑦ Cancel	Previous Next

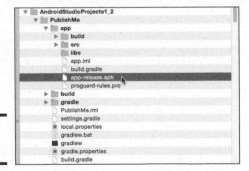

Figure 1-5:
Don't delay.
Make an
APK!

In this final Generate Signed APK box, take note of the APK Destination Folder. Also, be sure to select Release in the Build Type drop-down list.

And finally . . .

12. **Click Finish.**

Android Studio offers to open the folder containing your shiny, new APK file. That's great! Open the folder, and stare proudly at your work. (See Figure 1-6.)

If Android Studio opens a folder, and you don't see an APK file in the folder, your operating system might be hiding things such as the letters apk at the ends of filenames. For a solution to this problem, see the sidebar titled "Those pesky filename extensions" in Book I, Chapter 2.

Figure 1-6:
Very nice!

Congratulations! You've created a distributable APK file and a reusable key store for future updates.

Sometimes I become nervous. I want to double-check to make sure that my APK file has been signed. To do so, I type JAVA_HOME/bin/jarsigner -verify -verbose -certs APKfileName.apk in Android Studio's Terminal window. If the output includes the words jar verified, and it doesn't include CN="android debug", then all is well.

More Testing

When testing your app with friends and relatives, you don't always get reliable results. Sure, they're polite, but they might also know something about your app — something that other users won't already know. So your casual acquaintances living on other continents should test your app, too. In fact, you should test so much that you'd have trouble mailing your APK file to all your testers.

That's why the Play Store allows you to publish an app with invitation-only access. Look for Alpha and Beta Testing sections in the Developer Console. When you enter one of these sections, you upload an APK file. The Developer Console tells you how many kinds of Android devices can run your app and provides other useful information about your APK file.

After uploading the APK file, you can provide a list of beta testers — a relatively small number of people who can download the file from the Play Store. When these people use your app, the Play Store keeps track of crashes, application not responding (ANR) occurrences, and other unwanted events. The Developer Console can filter its reporting of these events by Android version and by device type.

I highly recommend the Play Store's beta testing. And if you want more testing, you can download a testing framework. *A testing framework* is an API with classes and method calls for testing your app. You add the framework's method calls to your existing code. Google's own *Android Testing Support Library* has several testing frameworks, and another (independently developed) framework named *Robotium* is very popular.

And, if you want even more testing, you can enroll your app with a company that automates the testing and tests your app on many different devices at once. Testdroid and AppThwack are examples of such companies.

For info about the Android Testing Support Library, visit `http://developer.android.com/tools/testing-support-library`. For straight talk on Robotium, visit `https://code.google.com/p/robotium`. The Testdroid and AppThwack sites are `http://testdroid.com` and `https://appthwack.com`.

Publishing Your App

To start this section's adventure, visit `https://play.google.com/apps/publish`. Look for a button or a link with words like Add New Application. Click that button or link, and get ready to roll.

Nothing permanent happens until you click the Publish App button. If the Publish App button makes you nervous, there's also a friendly Save Draft button. So you can pause your work, think about things for a while, and log on again later. For more extreme situations (severe cases of Developer's Remorse), there's an Unpublish App link. Neither the Publish nor the Unpublish requests take effect immediately. So don't be upset if you have to wait a few hours.

During your visit to `https://play.google.com/apps/publish`, the most important step is the uploading of the APK file. When you followed the steps in the "Creating a Publishable APK File section," Android Studio named this file `app-release.apk` and put the file in your project's `app` subdirectory. So, when the big upload moment comes (when you've clicked an Upload APK button), drop that `app-release.apk` file in the Drop Your File Here box, or click the Browse button and use your File Explorer or Finder to navigate to this `app-release.apk` file.

Aside from the momentous APK upload, you have many questions to answer, many fields to fill in, many files to upload, and many terms to agree to. In the remainder of this section, I describe several of these items.

✦ **Title of your app**

In my experience, a great title can jump-start an app's popularity. So make your title something snappy.

✦ **Short description**

You may enter up to 80 characters.

✦ **Full description**

You may enter up to 4,000 characters.

✦ **If this isn't the first version of your app, what's new in this version?**

You may enter up to 500 characters.

✦ **Graphic assets**

This includes all the images that I describe in the "Preparing Graphic Assets for the Play Store" section. (You don't want me to repeat all that information in this section, do you?)

✦ **Your app's category**

Is it a game? If so, what type of game? (Choose from Action, Adventure, Card, Puzzle, Racing, Role Playing, and many other types.) If it's not a game, what type of app is it? (Choose from Business, Communication, Education, Finance, Health, and a bunch of other types.)

✦ **Content rating**

Complete a questionnaire to determine your app's content rating under several standards (international and otherwise). Does your app involve violence, sexuality, potentially offensive language, or references to illegal drugs? Does your app involve the exchange of any personal information?

✦ **Your contact details**

You must supply an email address, and users have access to this address. Optionally, you can supply a website and a phone number.

✦ **Language**

You specify the default language for your listing on the Play Store. You can provide translations in other languages, or have Google Translate furnish its own guesses. (This can a0ccidentally lead to some fairly amusing results.) You can also purchase translations straight from the Developer Console. For a very simple app, translation costs between $7 and $15 per target language.

✦ **Countries for distribution**

Pick and choose from more than 190 countries.

✦ **Target devices**

Android Wear? Android TV? Android Auto?

✦ **Free or paid?**

For many people, this involves some serious thinking. So I delve deeply into this topic in the next chapter. For now, the only thing you have to know is that changing your mind is a one-way street. You can change an app from being paid to free, but you can't change an app from being free to being paid. Of course, you can publish a new app that's very much like the original free app, except that the new app is a paid app.

In addition to the required items, you can specify many additional features for your app. Here are a few of them:

✦ **Do you want additional alpha or beta testing for your app?**

✦ **Will you point to a URL containing your app's privacy policy?**

✦ **Will you bill users for goods or services through your app?**

For a discussion about this possibility, see the next chapter.

✦ **Will you use app licensing?**

Licensing protects your app from illegal use. For more info, see the following "About app licensing" sidebar.

About app licensing

If you license your app, no device can run your app unless the device checks in with a server. The server ensures that the device has permission to run your app. Here are some scenarios for an app (free or paid), with and without licensing:

✔ **Best case scenario with licensing:** A user buys your app and copies the .apk file to another user's device. The other user hasn't paid for your app. The other user tries to run the app, but can't run it because of the licensing restrictions.

✔ **Worst case scenario without licensing:** A user buys your app and copies the .apk file to a file-sharing website. People download and install your .apk file and run the code for free. (Ooo! That's bad!)

✔ **Worst case scenario with licensing:** A user buys your app, cracks the licensing, and copies the .apk file to a file-sharing website. People download and install the cracked version of your .apk file and run the code for free. (That's bad, too.)

✔ **Best case scenario without licensing:** No one ever tries to steal your app. Or, if someone steals your app, the additional distribution of your app works to your advantage.

All things considered, I'd prefer to do licensing with any paid app. Licensing is also a good precaution with a free app (to help you maintain ownership of the app's concept).

To enable licensing in your app, you must install the *Google Play Licensing Library* (also known as *LVL* — the *Licensing Verification Library*) using the Android SDK Manager. You must add that library to your app's project. You must obtain the app's licensing key (a sequence of about 400 gibberish characters) from the Developer Console and add the key to your main activity. You must add additional code in your app to check a device's license and to respond (based on the result of the check). The additional code implements one of three possible policies:

✔ **Strict policy:** Whenever the user tries to launch your app, the device asks the Google Play server for approval to run the app. If the user tries to launch your app when the device has no connectivity, the user is out of luck. Life's tough.

✔ **Server-managed policy:** The user's device stores a copy of the user's license. The device uses the copy when network connectivity is unavailable. The license is obfuscated (so it's tamper-resistant), and the license keeps track of trial periods, expiration dates, and other stuff. This is the default policy, and it's the policy that Google highly recommends.

✔ **Custom policy:** Create your own policy with Java code in your app. As a developer, this choice would make me nervous. But for very sensitive situations, this choice might be the best.

In this chapter's "More Testing" section, I mention using the Developer Console to create beta testers for your soon-to-be-published app. You can also name some special beta testers for your app's licensing scheme. Your testers attempt to run the app when (as they know darn well) they shouldn't get permission. The Developer Console keeps track of successes and failures so you can find out if your licensing scheme works correctly.

For all the details about the licensing of apps, visit `http://developer.android.com/google/play/licensing/index.html`.

✦ **Will you use any of Google's back-end services?**

A *back-end service* is computing done on the cloud. And why would your app need to deal with the cloud? Maybe your game has a leaderboard, and you want to compare the scores of users around the world. Maybe you want to send data to your users using Google Cloud Messaging. Maybe you want Google's search engine to look for content within your app. All these things involve back-end services.

Publishing Elsewhere

Google's Play Store isn't the only game in town. (It's a very important game, but it's not the only game.) You can also publish on the Amazon Appstore, on several independent websites, or on your own website.

The Amazon Appstore

In this section, I describe a few things you should know about publishing on Amazon Appstore for Android. I don't cover these things in great detail for three reasons:

✦ The steps for publishing with Amazon resemble the steps for publishing with Google. You might not mind my copying and pasting text from previous sections of this chapter, but to me, copying and pasting wouldn't seem right.

✦ I'd go crazy if I had to reword ideas from previous sections to make them sound fresh and new in this section.

✦ (This one is a secret. It's just between you and me. Okay?) The editors at Wiley will go ballistic (and rightfully so) if I delay this book's publication by writing too much more material in this chapter.

So with all those excuses in mind, please read on about the Amazon Appstore.

Publishing on Amazon's Appstore is less expensive than publishing on Google's Play Store (if you call not paying a one-time $25 developer fee "less expensive"). The Amazon Developer Portal pages look a bit different from the Google Play Developer Console pages, but the basic ideas are almost all the same. The only major difference is Amazon's approval process.

Apps submitted to Amazon's Appstore go through an approval process before they can be published. (This differs from Google's Play Store, where even my Do Nothing Except Get Published app was briefly listed.) To qualify for publication, an app must meet Amazon's technical specifications. (Visit `https://developer.amazon.com/appsandservices/support/faq` for more info.)

In addition, an app must meet Amazon's nontechnical specifications. These include things like the clarity of images, your right to use the images, the presence or absence of in-app advertising, the app's appropriateness for various audiences, and other things. (Again, visit `https://developer.amazon.com/appsandservices/support/faq`.)

When you submit an app for approval, you can include testing instructions. Now imagine, for a moment, that you work for Amazon. You normally enjoy testing apps that developers submit, but today you're a little grumpy. All the apps that you evaluate are beginning to look alike. And besides, the office's coffee machine isn't working!

Along comes an app that a developer has submitted. The app looks good, but you get stuck trying out some of the app's features. You read the testing instructions, but these instructions aren't informative. The instructions were hastily written. (Who, aside from a *For Dummies* author, wants to spend time writing instructions?) The instructions assume that you already know almost everything about the app. They assume that you're only trying to get around some quirk that interests the developer. You think about pressing forward with your testing, but you're not sure what the app wants you to do next, and the testing instructions aren't crystal clear. To top it all off, someone stole your sandwich from the fridge in the break room. That settles it. You reject this app.

As an app's developer, you're intensely aware of the app's requirements and of all your presuppositions in creating the app. But the person who tests your app knows none of this. If the lack of a simple testing prerequisite can turn your app from a lifesaving utility into a useless waste of kilobytes, you must describe the prerequisite clearly in the Appstore's Testing Instructions field.

Extra advertising, good marketing, and useful features make the difference between 1,000,000 downloads and 1,000 downloads. But presenting road-blocks or inconveniences in the approval process makes the difference between downloads and no downloads.

Digital rights management

When you publish an app, you have the option of applying Amazon's *digital rights management (DRM)* to your app. This is the Amazon equivalent of Google's Licensing Verification Library. Like the DRM for Amazon Kindle books, the Appstore's DRM electronically grants permission to run each app on a device-by-device basis. And like any other scheme for managing users' privileges, the Appstore's DRM inspires vast waves of controversy in blogs and online forums.

Amazon doesn't publish gobs of information about the workings of its DRM scheme. But one thing is clear: Without digital rights management, any user can run your application. With DRM, a user can replace his or her device and, by logging onto the new device as the same Amazon user, have access to his or her rightfully purchased apps. Users can run paid apps without having an Internet connection because, when a user buys an app, the user receives an offline token for that app. There's no doubt about it: When you publish a paid app, DRM is the way to go.

Amazon answers some questions about DRM in a blog post with the following unwieldy URL: `https://developer.amazon.com/public/community/post/Tx16GPJPAW8IKLC/Amazon-Appstore-Digital-Rights-Management-simplifies-life-for-developers-and-cus`.

A few other differences

Amazon's graphic assets requirements are different from Google's. The image sizes are different, and the number of images that you must submit are different. (By the time you read this book, Google's own requirements might be different from the ones that I describe in this chapter.) Fortunately, when you're submitting your app and you encounter these differences, you can save your Developer Portal work, set the Developer Portal aside, and create more images.

Amazon's app-signing procedure is a bit different from Google's. By default, Amazon applies its own certificate to each app published on the Amazon Appstore. The certificate is unique to your account. But, otherwise, it's a boilerplate certificate.

Then there's the SKU. When you submit an app, Amazon's Developer Portal lets you supply a SKU. The acronym *SKU* stands for *Stock Keeping Unit*. It's a way that you, the seller, keep track of each kind of thing that you sell. For example, imagine that you sell only two kinds of shirts — green shirts and blue shirts. When the customer buys a shirt, the only thing the customer decides is whether to buy a green shirt or a blue shirt. Then you might assign SKU number 000001 to your green shirts and 000002 to your blue shirts. It's up to you. Instead of 000001 and 000002, you might assign 23987823 to your green shirts and 9272 to your blue shirts. Anyway, when you submit an app, you can create your own SKU number for that app.

The only interesting thing about the Developer Portal's SKU number field is figuring out why I care about this field. If I'm not mistaken, the field was required way back when I first submitted an app, and the explanation surrounding this field wasn't very helpful. Since then, I've had SKU numbers on my mind.

Waiting anxiously for approval

After you've submitted your app for approval, the ball is in Amazon's court. You can check the status of your app's approval by visiting the Developer Portal and checking the portal's Dashboard. (Visit `https://developer.amazon.com/home.html`.) Amazon sends you an email if any questions arise during the testing process. You also receive an email when your app is approved.

Other venues

Some of the lesser known Android app websites offer apps that consumers can't get through Google Play or Amazon Appstore. In addition, many sites offer reviews, ratings, and links to the Google and Amazon stores. You can search for these sites yourself, or you can find lists of such sites. To get started, visit Digital Trends (`www.digitaltrends.com/mobile/android-app-stores`) and Joy of Android (`http://joyofandroid.com/android-app-store-alternatives`).

Sites differ from one another in several ways. Does the site specialize in any particular kind of app? Is the site linked to a particular brand of phone? Are the site's reviews more informative than those of other sites? Does the site vet its apps? Is the site's interface easy to use? And here's a big one — how does a user install one of the site's apps?

Before there were app stores, there were websites with files that you could download and install. Installing meant clicking an icon, issuing some commands, or doing other things. That model is still alive in the desktop/laptop world. But for mobile devices, where installation procedures can be cumbersome, the one-stop app store model dominates.

Some Android app sites still use the download-and-install-yourself model. For a patient (or a truly determined) consumer, the install-yourself model is okay. But most mobile-device owners are accustomed to the one-step app store installation process. Besides, some mobile service providers put up roadblocks to keep users from installing unrecognized apps. On many phones, the user has to dig into the Settings screen to enable installation of apps from unknown sources. On some phones, that Settings option is either hidden or unavailable.

For users who know and trust your work, there's always one oft-forgotten alternative. Post a link to your app's APK file on your own website. Invite users to visit the page with their mobile phones' browsers and download the APK file. After downloading the file, the user can click the download notification to have Android install your app.

Here's one thing to consider. In order to pre-load the Google Play Store on a device, the device manufacturer must obtain Google's approval. The approval comes in the form of a certification, which asserts that the device and its software meet certain compatibility standards. Because of the expense in meeting the standards or in obtaining certification, some device manufacturers don't bother to apply. Their devices don't have the Play Store pre-loaded. Many of these devices have alternative app stores pre-loaded on their home screens but the Play Store app is conspicuously absent. Some users find workarounds and manage to install the Play Store app, but many users rely on apps from other sources. To reach these users, you have to find alternate publishing routes. (I admit it. I don't know the percentage of users who live in this uncertified world. It could be very small, or it could be larger than I imagine. One way or another, these people deserve to have access to your app.)

Chapter 2: Monetizing and Marketing Your App

In This Chapter

✔ **Charging money for your app**

✔ **Not charging for your app (if that's your thing)**

✔ **Increasing your app's downloads**

*T*he *Honeymooners* aired from 1955 to 1956 on the CBS television network in the United States. Comedian Jackie Gleason played Ralph Kramden, a bus driver living in a small Brooklyn, New York, apartment with his wife, Alice. (In earlier sketches, actress Pert Kelton had played the role of Alice. But Kelton was blacklisted by McCarthy's House Committee on Un-American Activities, so actress Audrey Meadows assumed the role of Alice.)

One of Ralph Kramden's fatal flaws was his affinity for get-rich-quick schemes. In a hilarious *Honeymooners* episode, Ralph and his buddy Ed Norton (played by Art Carney) did a live television infomercial for their Handy Housewife Helper gadgets. (Visit `https://www.youtube.com/watch?v=xPq_lgtidbQ` to check it out.) Ralph's sudden stage fright made him stumble and shake instead of effectively showing off his product.

While I'm on the subject of getting rich quickly, I can segue seamlessly to the subject of making money from your Android app.

Choosing a Revenue Model

In the old days (whenever they were), making money was simple. You provided either a product or a service. You charged a certain amount per unit for the product (more than it cost you to acquire that unit), or you charged a certain amount per hour for the service. If you charged $10 for one widget, then you charged $20 for two widgets. You didn't overthink the process because information didn't spread very quickly or very far. If you had an interesting twist on the sales of your goods or services, very few people would know about it.

Along came the phenomenon known as advertising. The more effectively you advertised, the more products or services you sold. (I know it's difficult to believe, but some advertisements made false claims about the things they were selling!) There were also sales promotions. An article entitled "History of Sales Promotion" (`www.englisharticles.info/2011/07/05/ history-of-sales-promotion`) identifies the first such promotion as a penny-off coupon. The C. W. Post Company issued the coupon for Grape Nuts cereal in 1895. No longer was the amount of money you earned strictly proportional to the number of units people wanted to buy. The amount depended on psychological factors (which you, the seller, could influence) and on variations in pricing (which you could determine).

The information age has companies whose revenue streams resemble labyrinths. One company spends millions to create software, and then gives away the software so that other companies will buy its consulting services. Another company gives away all of its services but collects data on the use of those services and sells the data to other companies. Company A makes money by advertising Company B which, in turn, makes money by advertising Company A.

When you first think about profiting from your app, you might think "Either I sell the app and make money or I give the app way for free and make no money at all." That's not the way it works. Not at all.

This section describes the many ways that you can profit from the distribution of your Android app. Unfortunately, the section doesn't contain any "here's-exactly-what's-right-for-you" advice. There's no single, one-size-fits-all revenue model. Many models are better for some kinds of apps and worse for other kinds of apps. Some models are best for the country you live in, but not for other countries. I can try to classify apps into certain categories based on their ideal revenue models, but the boundaries between categories are thin, and the criteria for placing apps' categories are subtle. You have to think about your own app and decide which model (or which combination of models) is best for you.

Charging for your app

You can set a price for your app. If you publish on Google's Play Store or Amazon's Appstore, you pay a 30 percent commission. That's not bad considering that Google paid seven billion dollars to app developers between February 2014 and February 2015. (See `www.theverge.com/ google/2015/2/26/8112475/google-play-android-app-store- ads-sponsored-search`.)

If you decide to charge for your app, what price should you set?* The following sections offer you some advice.

*When I was a very young fellow, my parents gave me a chemistry set. I mixed together a few chemicals and declared the concoction to be a new kind of soap. (I had no good reason for believing that these chemicals had any cleansing properties. I made it all up in my head.) I decided to sell my new product, so I needed to figure out how much to charge for it. I put a vial of the stuff on one side of my father's pharmacy scale, and put a wad of coins on the other side. When the two sides balanced, I knew how much to charge.

Consider the competition, including the free competition

Check other apps with functionality that's similar to your app. Look at the prices for those apps. Ask yourself where your app fits in. Does your app have more features? Does your app present a smoother user experience? If so, you can charge a bit more. If not, you better lower your asking price. If you find free apps that do what your app does, ask yourself why a user would choose your paid alternative.

Use psychological pricing

Studies have shown that, as far as consumers are concerned, whole numbers aren't equidistant from one another. In a consumer's mind, the price $0.99 is much less than the price $1.00. Here in the United States, I can't remember ever seeing a gasoline price that didn't end in nine-tenths of a cent per gallon. This phenomenon, where prices are best set a bit less than a round number, is known as *odd pricing*.

Odd pricing is just one form of *psychological pricing*. Another psychological pricing principle is that users don't like spending amounts that seem to be strange or arbitrary. What do you think if you're asked to pay $1.04 for something? Why are you being asked to pay four extra cents?

Vary your price

On Google Play Store, you can't turn a free app into a paid app. But there's no rule about increasing or decreasing the price of a paid app.

There are two competing strategies for evolving your pricing, and you might want to use a combination of these strategies.

✦ **Start high; eventually go lower.**

   If your app has little or no competition, you can start high. Attract users who think of themselves as high rollers, and get the highest price from these users that you can get.

   As a variation on this strategy, consider premium pricing. With *premium pricing*, you intentionally set a high price in order to convince users that you have a high-quality app. (Of course, if you try this trick, you better not disappoint your users. You must maintain the perception of high quality. If your app is truly a high-quality app, you have a leg up.)

   If you start with a high price, your sales eventually slow down. This can happen because you've found all the people who are willing to pay the higher price, or because other developers have started undercutting your price. One way or another, you can lower your price.

   And then, there's the competing strategy . . .

✦ **Start low; eventually go higher.**

> Start by undercutting the competition. Then, when you've developed a good reputation, raise the price of your app.

If your app is popular (so popular that people might notice a change in price), you should consider the timing of your change. Decrease the price when the change will be noticed. (For example, if your app has a seasonal aspect, lower the price very conspicuously as that season's purchases rev up.) Increase the price in small increments when users are least likely to notice. Alternatively, you can coordinate price changes with other changes. You can increase the price when you release a new version with new features. Or, when you increase the price of one of your apps, you can announce loudly that you're decreasing the price of another app.

Look for statistics and other hard data

> "... if you torture the data enough, nature will always confess ..."
>
> *(from "How Should Economists Choose?" by Ronald H. Coase)*

A chart posted at www.appbrain.com/stats/free-and-paid-android-applications indicates that, on Google Play Store, about half of all free apps have fewer than 500 downloads. Compare this with the paid apps where between 80 percent and 90 percent of all apps have fewer than 500 downloads. Interestingly, for paid apps, these percentages don't vary directly in proportion to price.

✦ For apps priced less than one dollar *and* for apps priced more than ten dollars, about 90 percent have fewer than 500 downloads.

✦ For apps in the middle (apps priced between $2.50 and $5.00), the percentage of apps with fewer than 500 downloads drops to a more comfortable 80 percent.

There's some aspect of psychological pricing that's operating favorably in the $2.50 to $5.00 range. You might not understand why this happens (and in fact, I don't know why it happens). Even so, the fact that there's a sweet spot between $2.50 and $5.00 is worth noting.

One way or another, it never hurts to search for statistics. Trends change, so look for pages that are updated frequently. Be skeptical of facts and figures from years gone by.

When you look for hard data, lots of good things happen. At best, you learn that your preconceived notions about app pricing are wrong and that you should modify your pricing strategy. At the very least, you become aware that what you intend to do isn't backed up by the facts. So you keep doing what you intend to do, but you do it with your eyes wide open.

Promotional pricing

Every day, Amazon's Appstore takes a paid app and offers that app for free. When you first publish your app, you opt in or out of that Free App of the Day program. Of course, opting in doesn't mean that your app will be featured in this way. It means only that you'd like your app to be considered.

Amazon's Free App of the Day program is an extreme example of promotional pricing. More generally, *promotional pricing* means temporarily lowering your price in order to attract more users. You'd like users to pay the higher price. But if they don't buy at the higher price, they might buy at the lower price. What's more, a temporary drop in price might be enough to attract lots of new users, even if it's a drop from an unreasonably high price to a slightly less unreasonable price.

The trick with promotional pricing is to do it at the right time and with the right price. If you lower your price too frequently or for a long period of time, users start thinking of the promotional price as the "real" price. They lose all interest in the regularly posted price. If the discounted price is too close to the regular price,

users don't see much of an advantage in rushing to buy. (Think of the penny-off coupon in the 1895 Grape Nuts cereal promotion. Would you get in your time machine to take advantage of that one?)

If the discounted price is too low, you might earn less during the promotion than you spend to maintain your app. On a temporary basis, this might be okay. But if the promotion doesn't help to attract buyers at the regular price, it's not okay.

When you offer a promotion, avoid any taunting of users who purchased the app at the regular price. If you can avoid advertising the promotion to those users, do so. Consider offering something extra to your existing paid users (especially the ones who purchased your app very recently).

Note: Some countries have laws governing the use of promotional pricing. Your app will probably be offered for sale in these countries. So check the laws before you go crazy with promotional pricing.

Book VI
Chapter 2

Monetizing and Marketing Your App

Search the web for information about *pricing strategies*. You'll find a lot of good reading there. If you want a one-stop shopping stats page, pay a visit to `http://mobiforge.com/research-analysis/global-mobile-statistics-2014-home-all-latest-stats-mobile-web-apps-marketing-advertising-subscriber`.

Offering an extended free trial

Google Play buyers can return an app within two hours for a full refund. If you want the trial period to last longer, you have to outfit your app. One way to do it is to have the app record the time when it was first launched and compare this to the current system time. Of course, saving this information in `SharedPreferences` isn't foolproof. A user with some programming skill can hack the scheme and can share this hack with others. (Once your app has been hacked, there's no going back. You can't track down all sources of illicit information and stop them in their tracks. Bad information spreads very quickly. No matter what you do, a tip about hacking your app will be available online forever.)

Instead of storing times and dates on the user's device, you can send this information to a server along with the device's identification number. Have the app check that server regularly. Like the `SharedPreferences` scheme, this server-based scheme isn't foolproof. But storing times and dates on a server is harder to crack than storing information on the user's device.

On a phone, you get the device's identification number by calling the `TelephonyManager` class's `getDeviceId` method. For a device that's not a phone, you can ask for the `Settings.Secure.ANDROID_ID` field.

Another way to implement a many-day trial period is to create two apps with two different licensing arrangements. The free trial app's license expires in 30 days. But as the trial app breathes its dying breath, it reminds the user to visit the Play Store and purchase the paid app.

If you don't like maintaining two separate apps, you can cut the cake in a different place. Create one app that implements both the trial version and the full version. Distribute this app freely. But as part of this dual-version app's logic, have the app check the user's device for the presence of a second, paid app. The second app does nothing except either exist or not exist on a user's device. If the second app exists, the dual-version app behaves like the full version. But if the second app doesn't exist, the dual-version app behaves like the trial version.

One way or another, the Play Store's app licensing tools are more reliable than most home-grown date-checking techniques. Using licensing to police the trial period is a good idea.

For a few words on the Play Store's app licensing tricks, see Chapter 1 in this minibook.

Freemium apps

A mobile app with a paid-only revenue model is rare indeed. By one count, there were ten times as many free apps as paid apps in 2013. (See and www. statista.com/statistics/241587/number-of-free-mobile-app-downloads-worldwide and www.statista.com/statistics/241589/number-of-paid-mobile-app-downloads-worldwide.)

In the freemium revenue model, one useful version of your app serves as advertising for an even more useful version. This form of advertising has several advantages over more traditional advertising modes.

✦ **The advertising is well-targeted.**

People who install your free version are potential buyers for your paid version.

✦ **It directly demonstrates your app's benefits.**

Instead of reading about your app, or hearing about your app, users experience your app.

✦ **It's repetitive without being annoying.**

A potential customer probably uses the free version on a regular basis.

✦ **It can be inexpensive.**

You incur an expense when you create the app, and you have to create the app anyway. But after you've published the app, the marginal cost of each free download is almost nothing. (This assumes that you don't offer services for each active user. Yes, the free users might find bugs, and fixing the bugs takes your time and effort. But the effort you spend fixing these bugs doesn't count as an advertising expense. You'd be fixing these bugs no matter who found them.)

✦ **It enhances your reputation.**

This one is a "biggie." With conventional advertising, you can come off as a snake oil salesman. But with a free version of your app, you're a benevolent developer (a benevolent developer who might occasionally ask for well-deserved remuneration). Think back to the last few times you upgraded from free to premium. For me, it wasn't because I needed the enhanced features. Instead it was because, through repeated use of the app, I had formed a certain respect for the originator.

As with several other revenue models, the main question is "how much?" In the freemium model, which parts of your app do you give away for free? Which parts do you keep for the paid version? As usual, there's no prepackaged answer. But there are some general strategies:

✦ **Divide your users into two categories — the high-rollers and the not-so-high-rollers.**

The high-rollers might be the corporate users; the others are individuals. The high-rollers need premium features and have the resources to pay for those features. The others don't. Which features of your app appeal primarily to the high-rollers? Put those features in the premium version.

✦ **If you don't incur a cost each time someone uses a particular feature, give that feature away for free. If you incur an ongoing cost, charge for that feature.**

An app on a phone or a tablet can do only so much work. Maybe, to implement certain features, your app ships work out to a server. Access to the server costs money, and the amount of money depends on the workload. The more people use these costly features, the more revenue you must have. (Otherwise, you'll go broke.) So tie the price of the app to the use of these features. The app's premium version includes these costly features; the app's free version doesn't.

✦ **If volume usage is relevant for your app, create a soft paywall.**

A *hard paywall* is an all-or-nothing restriction on the use of a resource. But with a *soft paywall*, users get 500 wha'cha'ma'call'its for free each month. Users who need more than 500 wha'cha'ma'call'its each month buy a recurring subscription. You can change the number when you see the need. But when you do, be aware of the impression you make on your existing users (both the free users and the paid users).

For some good reading about recurring subscriptions, see this chapter's "Subscription pricing" section.

✦ **Advertise or nag in the free version.**

If the previous approaches are like carrots, this approach is like a stick. With this approach, you entice users to pay for your app by putting something undesirable in the free version. Unfortunately, Android has no `emitUnpleasantOdor` method. So, for the undesirable feature, most developers advertise or nag.

Nagging involves displaying a pop-up alert box reminding the user to buy the retail version. You decide how often you want the pop-up to appear, and what the user must do in order to dismiss it.

The advertising option has a few advantages over the nagging option. For one thing, advertising can be unobtrusive. (Who ever heard of unobtrusive nagging?) When advertising is unobtrusive, users tend not to associate it with the app or with the developer. So, with advertising, your image remains largely untarnished. And let's not forget — advertising can bring you some revenue while you wait for users to purchase your app's full version.

✦ **(Not recommended) In the free app, include only enough functionality to demonstrate the paid app's usefulness.**

Apps that involve saving data tend to use this strategy. With the free version, you put the app through its paces. You examine the results to see the how effectively the app does its job, but you can't save the results. The user is disappointed because, in the final analysis, the free app is nothing but a tease.

With this approach, you undermine some of the freemium model's advantages. For one thing, you lose the repetition advantage. A potential user tries your app once to find out if it's worth buying. Months later, when the need for your app arises in a more serious context, the user has forgotten about your app and finds another app in its place.

More importantly, this approach ignores the benefits of customer loyalty. Instead of impressing users with your generosity, you annoy users with your stinginess. You lead a user to the brink of success. But then, at the last minute, you confront the user with a mean-spirited roadblock. Whether you think of your app this way or not isn't relevant. What's relevant is that users feel this way.

If you have a killer app, and all you need to do is assure users that your app can perform its supposedly herculean tasks, then this approach is for you. Otherwise, you should avoid using it.

For most apps, the percentage of free-version users who become paid-version users is in the single digits. But that's okay, because free users aren't "deadbeat" users. Free users form an important part of your marketing ecosystem. They help spread the word about your app. If your app has any social aspects, the more users you have (free or paid), the better. And if anyone checks your app's usage statistics, free users count. So, by all means, give the free users access to your app's essential features.

Selling things with your app

Google's Play Store and Amazon's Appstore differ on the kinds of things you can sell. With Amazon's Appstore, you can sell physical goods. (Amazon has never been squeamish about shipping physical items.) On Google Play, you can sell only digital content. So, if you publish a game, and you want to sell action figures of the game's characters, you have to use Amazon's Appstore. (You can sell action figures for a game on Google's Play Store. You just can't embed the purchase as a feature of the game.)

To set up in-app billing, you make additions to your app's code. You create a service, a broadcast receiver, an AIDL file, and some other stuff. You add a permission in the app's `AndroidManifest.xml` file:

```
<uses-permission
        android:name="com.android.vending.BILLING" />
```

On Google's Developer Console, you visit the in-app billing pages. You select the kind of billing you want for your app.

For help getting to the Play Store's Developer Console, refer to Chapter 1 in this minibook.

✦ **Managed product:** The Play Store manages this one-time sale.

✦ **Unmanaged product:** You manage this sale.

✦ **Subscription:** The Play Store manages this recurring sale. (See the next section.)

In the Developer Console, you give the product a name (a *title*). You enter a description and you specify the price. You can accept the default conversions into other countries' prices, or you can name your own local prices.

The Play Store can manage the billing for your product, but the Play Store doesn't deliver content. Delivery of the purchased content is up to you.

For some of the gory details about in-app billing, visit `http://developer.android.com/guide/market/billing/billing_integrate.html`.

Go Global

While you're developing an app, you're worried about the user interface, the layout, and the code logic. Translating the app into other languages might not be foremost in your thoughts. But research shows that attention to international markets pays off. Google tallied the earnings for two categories of U.S. developers — those whose sales are primarily U.S.-based, and those whose sales are primarily international. Earnings for the second group were 2.5 times the earnings for the first group. (Don't take my word for it. Watch the video at `https://www.google.com/events/io/schedule/session/5b7836c8-82bf-e311-b297-00155d5066d7`. Many of the facts in this sidebar come from that video.)

When you *localize* an app, you translate the app's text into the user's native language. Localization is important, but in today's market, users expect more. An app's characters should look and dress like regional characters. Characters should act in a way that matches local customs. The game's actions should even be tailored to regional styles of play. For example, while users in the United States tend to play for long periods of time, users in Asia play in short bursts, taking time out to do other things between intervals of play. These and other subtle considerations go beyond localization and involve the broader issue of *culturalization*.

When you publish an app, you provide the app's title, a short description of the app, and a long description. You can purchase translations for these entries, you can add your own translations, or you can ignore the translations problem. Research shows that the third alternative — ignoring the issue — is a bad idea. The sales for apps with localized Play Store listings are six times those of apps without localized listings.

When you reach the pricing page, you name your price. Imagine entering USD 0.99 (almost one U.S. dollar). You do this because you remember my advice about odd pricing. (Refer to the "Use psychological pricing" section.) You also click the Play Store's Auto-Convert Prices Now button. The Play Store converts your price in local currencies for the 130+ countries where your app will be sold. The price in Japan is set to JPY 118. For Columbia, the price is COP 2,428. These numbers violate the rule about avoiding prices that seem strange or arbitrary.

In the United States, users don't stop to think about spending $0.99 for an app. In the consumer's mind, $0.99 is an easy "throw away" amount. Every country has its own throw away price, but that price might not be the result of mechanically converting $0.99 in the country's local currency. The folks at Google tested the throw-away theory when they varied apps' prices by only a few Yen in the Japan market. They found that, at a certain threshold amount, lowering the price by one or two Yen caused a doubling in sales. The moral of this story is, pay careful attention to local pricing. In the Play Store's Developer Console, you can click Auto-Convert Prices Now and be done with it. But you can set the price manually for at least 65 countries, and doing so might pay off nicely.

Customization for the global market doesn't end with app pricing. You might even modify your business model from country to country. In-app purchases and subscriptions work better in some countries than in others. And the use of certain payment methods varies from one country to another. For example, in the United States, the credit card is king. But India has only a nine-percent credit card penetration. Japan's users like direct carrier billing, and Germany is big on using PayPal. In some countries, gift cards are the best way to go.

When you market your app, think carefully about the international market. Think about it at every step in the development, publishing, and marketing process.

Subscription pricing

Some apps require care and feeding when they run. They consume data that needs to be updated periodically, or they consume services that you must provide. For apps of this kind, subscriptions might be appropriate.

A subscription charges the user repeatedly. As an app's developer, you get to choose what "repeatedly" means. The options are monthly, yearly, and seasonal. (The seasonal option is like the yearly option, except that renewal occurs only during a certain part of the year — a part that you specify with start and end dates.)

If your app's content requires regular refreshing, the subscription model is worth your consideration. You can build up a steady income flow, and that's worth a lot.

Subscription pricing works only if your content requires it. I've seen apps with artificially imposed subscription policies (having the app self-destruct after a certain period of time). Apps of this kind work well for big business clients, but they have little appeal for individual users.

For more information on subscription billing through the Play Store, visit `https://developer.android.com/google/play/billing/billing_subscriptions.html`.

Earning revenue from advertising

There was probably a time when you had to jump through hoops before you could display ads inside your app. You'd find people who wanted to advertise their goods or services, write code to display their ads, strike up an agreement on the price for your advertising, and so on. Nowadays, it's not difficult at all. It's a smooth-running assembly line.

In this section, I outline the steps you need to take in order to display ads in your app. I don't provide much detail because the details change frequently. Instead, this section's outline describes what you can expect to do when you dive into the advertising game. Google's AdMob facility handles all the nitty-gritty details, and the AdMob web pages guide you through every step of the process.

Here's the outline:

1. **Visit `https://apps.admob.com/admob/signup`.**

2. **Sign in with a Google account.**

   You can use the same account that you use when you sign in to the Play Store's Developer Console.

3. **Enter the required information about yourself.**

   Don't worry. It's not too much information.

4. **Click a Monetize New App button, or something like that.**

   When you do, you see a page where you enter the name of your app. AdMob finds your app on the Play Store.

5. **Enter some information about the ads that you want to display.**

   How do you want the ads to appear? The choices are banner or interstitial.

   - **A *banner* ad appears as a small band somewhere on the app's screen.**

     A banner ad can appear or disappear any time during the run of your app.

- **An *interstitial* ad takes up a large part of the device's screen.**

    An interstitial ad shows up only when the user won't be terribly annoyed by the ad's appearance. For example, if your app is a game, you might code your app so that an interstitial ad appears only between rounds.

    If you're familiar with time/space tradeoffs, you'll recognize where the two types of ads fit in. A banner ad consumes very little space but can appear almost anytime. An interstitial ad consumes less time in order to gain some space.

    In this step, you also specify the refresh rate for ads, and some other things.

    The *refresh rate* is the amount of time that each ad remains on the user's screen (before being replaced by another ad). Research shows that a rate of 60 seconds or longer works best.

    At some point, the web page displays an *ad unit ID*. This ad unit ID number goes into your app's code. When a user runs your app, the app sends this ID number to the AdMob servers. The more the AdMob servers receive your ID, the more money you earn.

6. **Make a note of your ad unit ID.**

    Meanwhile, back on your development computer . . .

7. **Use the Android SDK Manager to install the Google Repository.**

    You'll find the Google Repository entry in the Android SDK Manager's Extras category.

8. **Add stuff to your project's files.**

    Here are a few of the things you do:

    - **You put your ad unit ID in the** `strings.xml` **file.**

        This identifies your app so you can earn money for displaying ads.

    - **You put a** `com.google.android.gms.ads.AdView` **element in your activity's layout.**

        This element can display ads.

    - **You add code to your app's activity.**

        The code loads ads into your layout's `AdView` widget. For a banner ad with AdMob, the code is pretty simple:

        ```
        AdView adView = (AdView) findViewById(R.id.adView);
        AdRequest = new AdRequest.Builder().build();
        adView.loadAd(adRequest);
        ```

TIP

Visit `https://developers.google.com/mobile-ads-sdk/docs/admob/android/quick-start` for all the details.

When your app goes live, the amount that you earn varies from one advertiser to the next. In most cases, the amount hangs on a "cost per something or other" measure. Here are a few possibilities:

✦ **CPC: Cost per click**

Your payment depends on the number of users who click on the ad in your app.

✦ **CPM: Cost per thousand impressions**

An *impression* is the appearance of an ad on a user's screen. A single impression isn't very impressive. So for every thousand ads that appear, you get paid.

✦ **CPA: Cost per action**

You earn money whenever a user performs a certain action. What constitutes an action depends on the advertiser. Examples of actions are clicks, sales, and registrations.

One way or another, advertising is a relatively low-maintenance way to earn some money for publishing your app.

Variations on in-app advertising

Your app is a place where others can advertise. Given that fact, there are dozens of ways you can tweak the advertising model. If your app complements an existing company's business, get the company to sponsor your app. You can meld references to the company's products and services into your app's interface. If you do it tastefully, users don't feel that they're being pressured. (This isn't a new idea. In the earliest days of U.S. television, shows integrated ads into their regular scripts. George and Gracie would move seamlessly from a kitchen comedy routine to a minute-long discussion of Carnation Evaporated Milk.)

Incentivized advertising is another option. With this option, advertisers reward users who perform certain actions within your app. For example, your app stores and displays recipes. For every ten recipes that the user completes, the app rewards the user with a coupon for cooking utensils. The advertiser gets the business, the user gets the goods, you get the revenue, and your app gets used. Everyone wins.

Both sponsorship and incentivized advertising are very well targeted. You're not promoting automobiles for ten year olds or weight-lifting equipment for me and my fellow college professors. Instead, you're riding a wave. It's a synergy wave between your app's theme and a company's wares.

Donationware

If you're not trying to earn a fortune, but you'd like some spare change from your most loyal users, try this strategy. Use in-app billing as in the "Selling things with your app" section. But instead of delivering a product, deliver a "thank you."

The rate of return will be very small. But I've done some donating for my favorite apps. So for all the apps that have ever been published, the return rate isn't zero.

Offering your app for free

You might argue against my decision to put this "absolutely free" subsection inside the "Choosing a Revenue Model" section. But let's face it — for a novice developer, "absolutely free" is a choice worth considering. For one thing, a free app attracts more users than a paid app. With your free app, you can start building your reputation among users. This reputation might be for you as a developer, or for the apps in your ongoing development plans. Besides, when you publish your first app, you learn a lot about the process. That's worth something even if it's not monetary.

Revenue or no revenue, an unmeasurable benefit is derived from giving freely to the community. When you think about publishing apps, don't forget about giving.

Getting paid to develop apps for others

Don't forget about this option. Find a local business or a big company. Write code or design user interfaces. Create the artwork for apps. Do what you do best and leave the rest to the business moguls.

Marketing Your Application

Imagine trying to find your friend at a gathering that has one million attendees. It's not easy, is it? Take the scenario one step further. The other person isn't your friend. You're looking for anyone with gray hair, blue eyes, and who weighs less than 150 pounds. What are your chances of finding my Uncle Eric?

Now imagine that you're not at a social gathering. You're surfing on Google's Play Store, and the Play Store has more than a million apps. You narrow your search to find a trivia quiz game. At first, the Play Store displays the top dozen trivia quiz games, so newly posted games aren't included. You widen the search by clicking the page's See More button. After the Play Store displays its first 300 trivia quiz apps, you stop clicking the See More button. What are the chances that you'll land on Jane Q. Novice's new app?

These stories aren't meant to discourage you. They're meant to remind you that your app doesn't market itself. Here are some ways for you to market your app:

✦ **Create a website.**

Use search engine optimization (SEO) techniques to get your site noticed.

✦ **Contact the press.**

This includes traditional journalists, but it also includes reviewers and bloggers. The worst they can say is "I'm not interested in writing about this." If they offer to write about your app for a fee, you can always say "no."

✦ **Use social media.**

You know the sites: Facebook, Twitter, Pinterest, Instagram. Post regularly to build up a following.

✦ **Add social features to your app.**

Nothing says "Try this app" like a post made directly from the app. You can also build loyalty by having users post to one another within the app.

✦ **Create your own blog or podcast.**

This requires work, but it can pay off bigtime.

✦ **Pay for advertising.**

Through AdMob, you can have other apps display ads for your app. If you don't mind spending some money, you can set up a regular paid ad campaign. But you can advertise for free in a house ad campaign.

When you allocate advertising space to promote your own wares, you're creating a *house ad*. AdMob doesn't charge for this kind of advertising. You create a house ad to promote one of your apps within another of your apps. Alternatively, by agreement with another developer, you can advertise your app in the other developer's app (and vice versa).

✦ **Update your app regularly (as a marketing strategy).**

An update can call attention to your app. A study by BI Intelligence (`www.businessinsider.com/app-update-strategy-and-statistics-2015-1`) found a positive correlation between the frequency of updates and user's ratings. That's good news.

✦ **Get help from Google's Play Store.**

The Play Store has a page with the title "Optimization Tips." This page analyzes your app and lists things that you've done (and haven't done) to enhance your app's visibility. For example, with one of my apps, the page reminds me to design for tablets. I should add custom drawables for tablet screen densities, and upload at least one screenshot for 7-inch and 10-inch tablets. Google's research shows that apps customized for tablets monetize ten times as much as apps designed with only phones in mind.

Brick Breaker Master: An app marketing case study

The epistolary novel has a long and noble history. In Rousseau's *Julie,* or *The New Heloise*, two lovers pass letters back and forth. Goethe's *The Sorrows of Young Werther* is a collection of letters from Werther to his friend William. Shelly's *Frankenstein* includes a sea captain's letters. More recently, such notables as Stephen King, Gary Shteyngart, and Daniel Handler (writing as Lemony Snicket) have featured diaries, news articles, and letters written by their novels' characters.

As far as I know, this section is the first use of the epistolary style in a *For Dummies* book.

I can't claim full credit for this accomplishment. The interchange that's documented here is mostly real. It's a bunch of excerpts from an email conversation between me and a reader. In these email messages, the reader (Daniel Levesque) does most of the heavy lifting. All I do is ask the right questions. I've trimmed some paragraphs to keep it relevant, and this book's copy editor will probably make some useful changes. Otherwise, the words that you see here are true and unadorned.

From: Daniel Levesque

To: Barry Burd

February 25, 2013

Good morning Barry.

I'm about to finish the book *Beginning Programming with Java For Dummies.* Then I will start later this week *Java For Dummies* . . .

From: Barry Burd

To: Daniel Levesque

February 25, 2013

Daniel,

I'm glad that you're enjoying my books. Have you noticed the last name of the project editor? (When your email arrived, I thought he was contacting me.) . . .

From: Daniel Levesque

To: Barry Burd

February 25, 2013

Yes I saw his name when I bought the book . . .

Many emails later . . .

From: Daniel Levesque

To: Barry Burd

August 14, 2013

Hi Barry,

A while ago you helped me with a couple of questions when I was reading your Java and Android books *For Dummies.* After all this "study," I finally published my first game!

Many emails later . . .

From: Daniel Levesque

To: Barry Burd

June 12, 2014

Hello Barry,

I just published my second Android game of 2014: "Space Garbage!" The goal of the game is very simple: survive in space while avoiding the floating objects! . . .

Many emails later . . .

From: Daniel Levesque

To: Barry Burd

February 1, 2015

Hi Barry,

I thought I would let you know that I just released my first game of 2015. It is my very first game using a game engine, and I am quite happy with the result. The game is currently number 20 in the Google Play "Top New Paid" category!!!

Check it out when you have a minute: `http://play.google.com/store/apps/details?id=com.d14studios.brickbreakermaster`

Best regards,

Daniel Levesque

From: Barry Burd

To: Daniel Levesque

February 3, 2015

Daniel,

I'd love for you to send me some tips on your getting to the number 20 spot. I'm revising my Android All-in-One book, and I'd like to quote you in the chapter on publishing apps. Do you have any advice for up-and-coming developers?

Barry

From: Daniel Levesque

To: Barry Burd

February 4, 2015

Hi Barry,

It's very difficult to do any marketing when you have a very small team or if you work on your own. Here's what I did with Brick Breaker Master to promote installs:

I figured out that Google uses some kind of algorithm to rank "new paid apps" and "new free apps," so I tried to generate several installs EVERY day for the first month.

I sent a message to my 200+ LinkedIn contacts asking them to install the game and give me a good rating (not sure how many actually did it).

I built a new App page on Facebook and asked all my family members and friends to "share" the page with their contacts (I figure that I probably got 50 shares through this, although the potential was more like 500).

I sent messages to my followers on Twitter every three days with a screenshot of one of the game levels (I didn't tweet too often — didn't want my followers to get upset and then unfollow me).

I updated my website as soon as I published the game on Google Play and on the Amazon Marketplace.

I submitted a summary of the game to the top ten Android review sites with the hope that they would publish a free review (most of them have an automated reply saying that they receive too many requests to guarantee a review but that for $100 they will . . . you get the picture). I didn't want to spend $1,000 for ten reviews without knowing in advance what rating they would give my game! Unless you know for sure that you have a knock-out app, this approach is very risky.

I hope this will help with your chapter in the book.

Best regards,

Daniel

From: Barry Burd

To: Daniel Levesque

February 4, 2015

Thank you, Daniel

Barry

Index

H

O

Q

R

T

X

Notes

Notes

Notes

About the Author

Barry Burd received an M.S. degree in Computer Science at Rutgers University and a Ph.D. in Mathematics at the University of Illinois. As a teaching assistant in Champaign-Urbana, Illinois, he was elected five times to the university-wide List of Teachers Ranked as Excellent by their Students.

Since 1980, Dr. Burd has been a professor in the Department of Mathematics and Computer Science at Drew University in Madison, New Jersey. When he's not lecturing at Drew University, Dr. Burd leads training courses for professional programmers in business and industry. He has lectured at conferences in the United States, Europe, Australia, and Asia. He is the author of several articles and books, including *Java For Dummies, Beginning Programming with Java For Dummies,* and *Java Programming for Android Developers For Dummies,* all from John Wiley & Sons, Inc.

Dr. Burd lives in Madison, New Jersey with his wife and two kids (both in their twenties, and mostly on their own). In his spare time, Dr. Burd enjoys being a workaholic.

Dedication

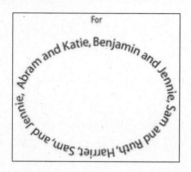

For

Jennie, Abram and Katie, Benjamin and Jennie, Sam and Ruth, Harriet, Sam, and

Authors' Acknowledgments

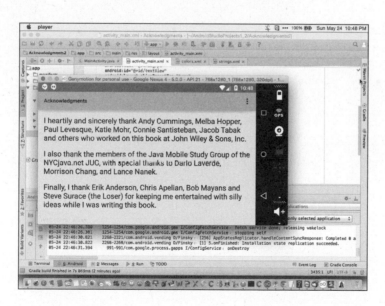

Publisher's Acknowledgments

Acquisitions Editor: Andy Cummings, Katie Mohr

Senior Project Editor: Paul Levesque

Copy Editor: Melba Hopper

Technical Editor: Jacob Tabak

Editorial Assistant: Claire Brock

Sr. Editorial Assistant: Cherie Case

Production Editor: Vinitha Vikraman

Cover Image: ©iStock.com/kirstypargeter

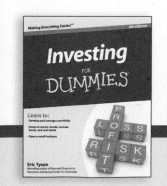

Math & Science

Algebra I For Dummies,
2nd Edition
978-0-470-55964-2

Anatomy and Physiology
For Dummies, 2nd Edition
978-0-470-92326-9

Astronomy For Dummies,
3rd Edition
978-1-118-37697-3

Biology For Dummies,
2nd Edition
978-0-470-59875-7

Chemistry For Dummies,
2nd Edition
978-1-118-00730-3

1001 Algebra II Practice
Problems For Dummies
978-1-118-44662-1

Microsoft Office

Excel 2013 For Dummies
978-1-118-51012-4

Office 2013 All-in-One
For Dummies
978-1-118-51636-2

PowerPoint 2013
For Dummies
978-1-118-50253-2

Word 2013 For Dummies
978-1-118-49123-2

Music

Blues Harmonica
For Dummies
978-1-118-25269-7

Guitar For Dummies,
3rd Edition
978-1-118-11554-1

iPod & iTunes
For Dummies, 10th Edition
978-1-118-50864-0

Programming

Beginning Programming
with C For Dummies
978-1-118-73763-7

Excel VBA Programming
For Dummies, 3rd Edition
978-1-118-49037-2

Java For Dummies,
6th Edition
978-1-118-40780-6

Religion & Inspiration

The Bible For Dummies
978-0-7645-5296-0

Buddhism For Dummies,
2nd Edition
978-1-118-02379-2

Catholicism For Dummies,
2nd Edition
978-1-118-07778-8

Self-Help & Relationships

Beating Sugar Addiction
For Dummies
978-1-118-54645-1

Meditation For Dummies,
3rd Edition
978-1-118-29144-3

Seniors

Laptops For Seniors
For Dummies, 3rd Edition
978-1-118-71105-7

Computers For Seniors
For Dummies, 3rd Edition
978-1-118-11553-4

iPad For Seniors
For Dummies, 6th Edition
978-1-118-72826-0

Social Security
For Dummies
978-1-118-20573-0

Smartphones & Tablets

Android Phones
For Dummies, 2nd Edition
978-1-118-72030-1

Nexus Tablets
For Dummies
978-1-118-77243-0

Samsung Galaxy S 4
For Dummies
978-1-118-64222-1

Samsung Galaxy Tabs
For Dummies
978-1-118-77294-2

Test Prep

ACT For Dummies,
5th Edition
978-1-118-01259-8

ASVAB For Dummies,
3rd Edition
978-0-470-63760-9

GRE For Dummies,
7th Edition
978-0-470-88921-3

Officer Candidate Tests
For Dummies
978-0-470-59876-4

Physician's Assistant Exam
For Dummies
978-1-118-11556-5

Series 7 Exam For Dumm
978-0-470-09932-2

Windows 8

Windows 8.1 All-in-One
For Dummies
978-1-118-82087-2

Windows 8.1 For Dummie
978-1-118-82121-3

Windows 8.1 For Dummie
Book + DVD Bundle
978-1-118-82107-7

Available in print and e-book formats.

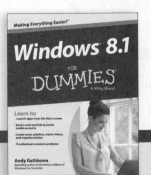

Available wherever books are sold. **For more information or to order direct visit www.dummies.com**

Take Dummies with you everywhere you go!

Whether you are excited about e-books, want more from the web, must have your mobile apps, or are swept up in social media, Dummies makes everything easier.

Leverage the Power

For Dummies is the global leader in the reference category and one of the most trusted and highly regarded brands in the world. No longer just focused on books, customers now have access to the For Dummies content they need in the format they want. Let us help you develop a solution that will fit your brand and help you connect with your customers.

Advertising & Sponsorships

Connect with an engaged audience on a powerful multimedia site, and position your message alongside expert how-to content.

Targeted ads • Video • Email marketing • Microsites • Sweepstakes sponsorship

21 Million Monthly Page Views & 13 Million Unique Visitors

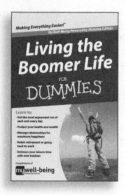

Dummies products make life easier!

- DIY
- Consumer Electronics
- Crafts
- Software
- Cookware
- Hobbies
- Videos
- Music
- Games
- and More!

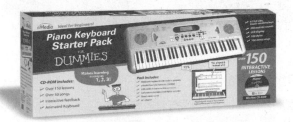

For more information, go to **Dummies.com** and search the store by category.

FOR
DUMMIE
A Wiley Bra